LIQUID CiTY

VOLUME THREE

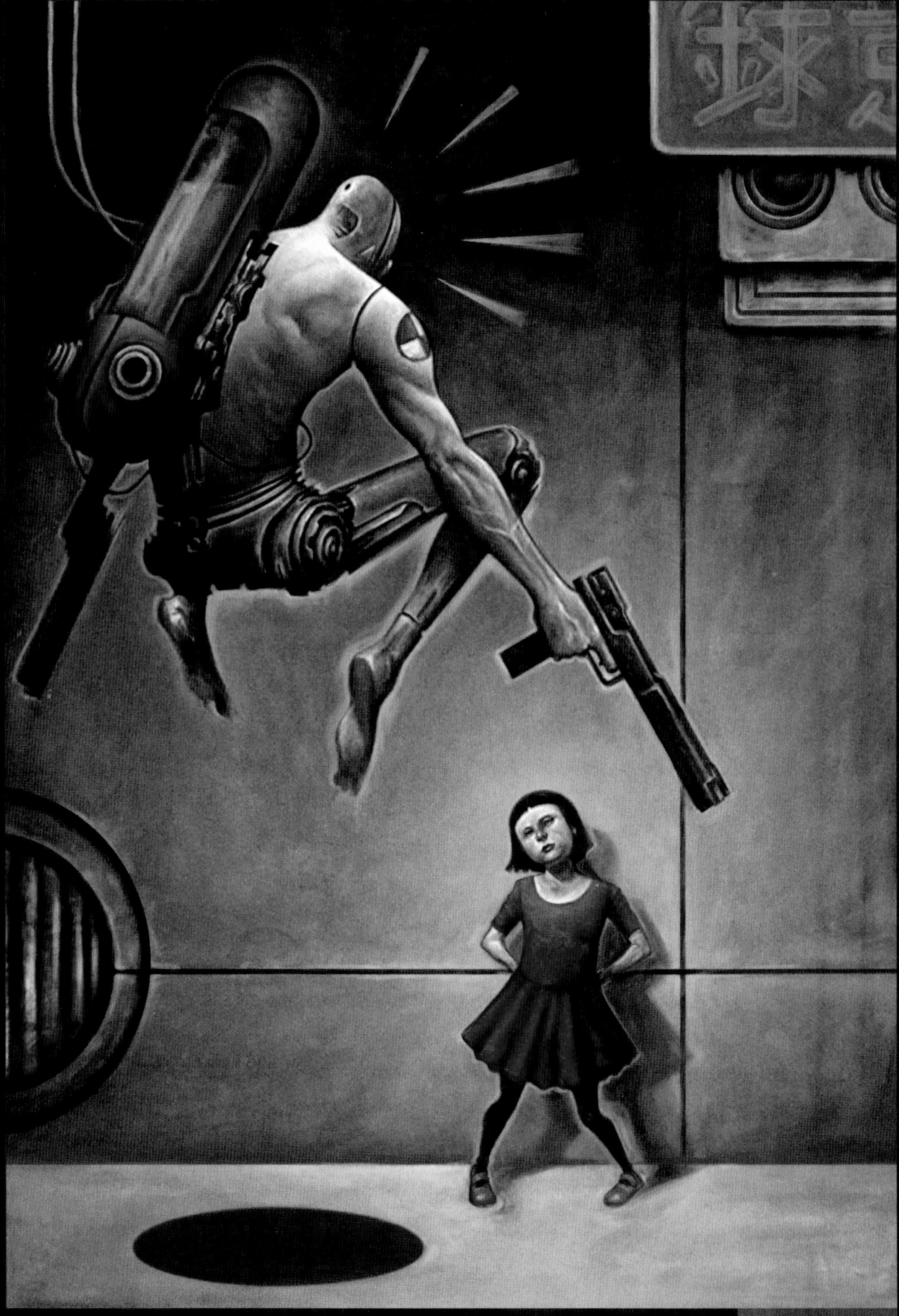

Jump (2003)
SONNY LIEW

PREFACE

What would you do if you knew that there was just one month, week or day left of life as you know it on this Earth?

The painting of the gun-toting robot and the little girl on the left was initially done as part of a story pitch for an idea that had been conceived together with a friend. Somehow or another, it never really got going, and this image is now all that remains of that world.

These half-formed universes — stories and characters that exist only in outlines, treatments and sketches — pepper most creators' lives and daydreams. The majority of these unrealized projects inevitably fall by the wayside and get forgotten, but some we hold closely on to, waiting for the day when they can finally find their way into the wider world.

When speculation about the Mayan end-of-the-world scenarios began intensifying around late 2011 and early 2012, it got us thinking about an 'apocalyptic' project of sorts, which would gather together some of these untold stories. What would a collection of such unrealized universes be like? The theme of this volume quickly coalesced. We asked our contributors:

If you knew the world was ending, what would be the story you would most want to tell?

Of course, as with the Y2K and occasional wild-haired predictions by UFO cults, the end of the Mayan calendar didn't bring about the end of the world as we know it. For the most part, our lives carried on as before, and we're glad to be able to share these wonderful works with you.

While some of the stories and art work collected in this third volume deal with apocalyptic themes, others offer more personal glimpses into cherished memories and poignant reflections. Above all, they provide a snapshot of the lives of Southeast Asian creators and their ultimate hopes, dreams and fears at world's end, capturing that one moment in their lives, when they dared to play a game of make-belief.

Sonny Liew

Contents

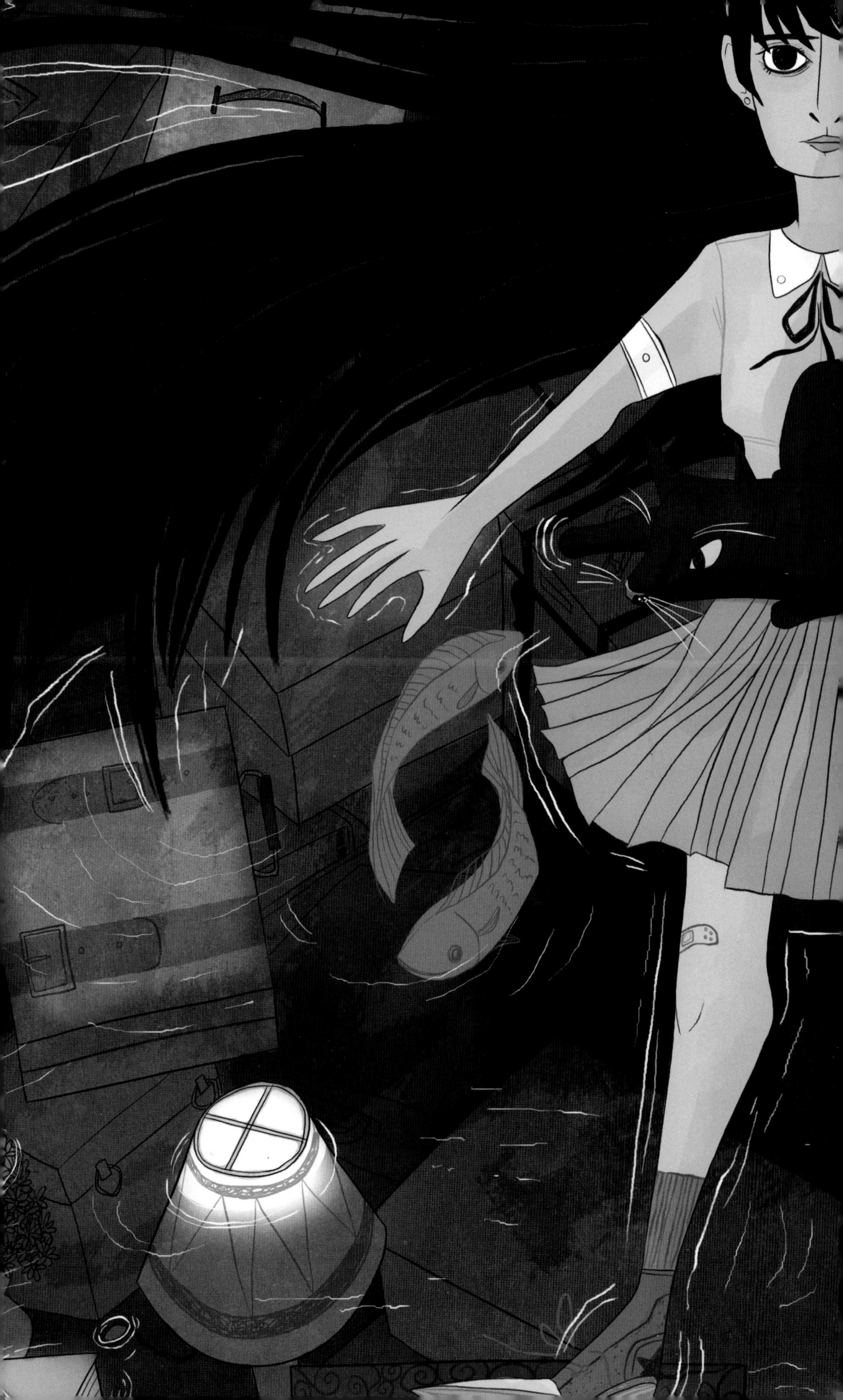

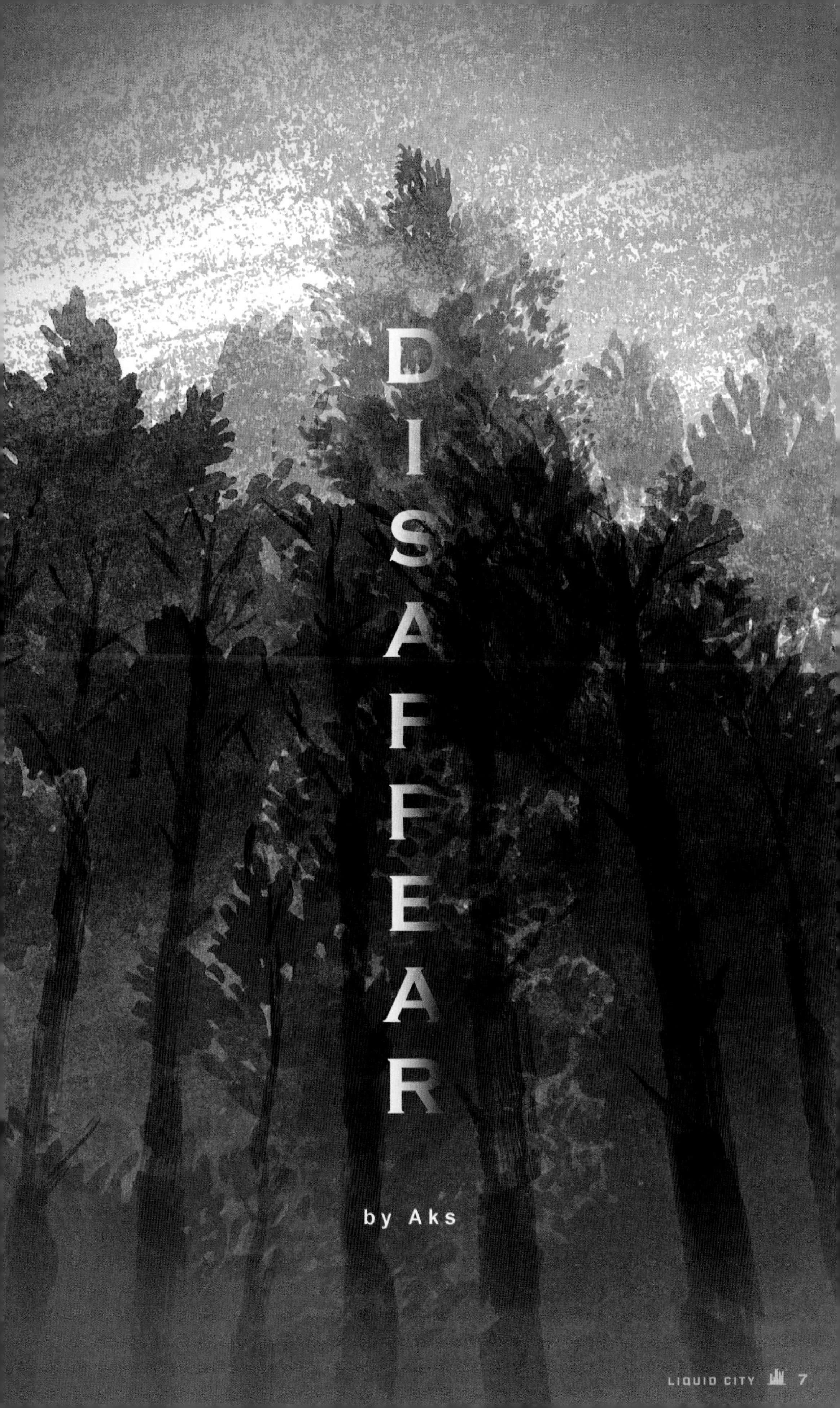

DISAFFEAR

by Aks

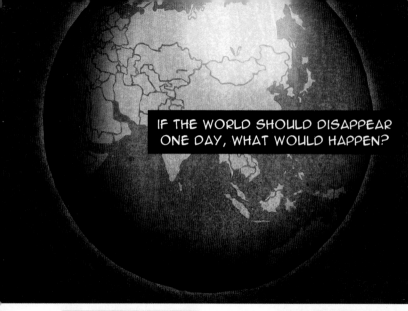

IF THE WORLD SHOULD DISAPPEAR ONE DAY, WHAT WOULD HAPPEN?

WOULD THERE BE AN EARTHQUAKE?

A TSUNAMI? WAR?

OR A VIRUS OUTBREAK?

WHAT WOULD IT BE LIKE AT THE END OF THE WORLD?

FOR MANY, IT MIGHT BE A WORLD WITH NO MORE COMPUTERS AND GADGETS...

...A WORLD WITHOUT ACCESS TO THE INTERNET AND VIDEO GAMES.

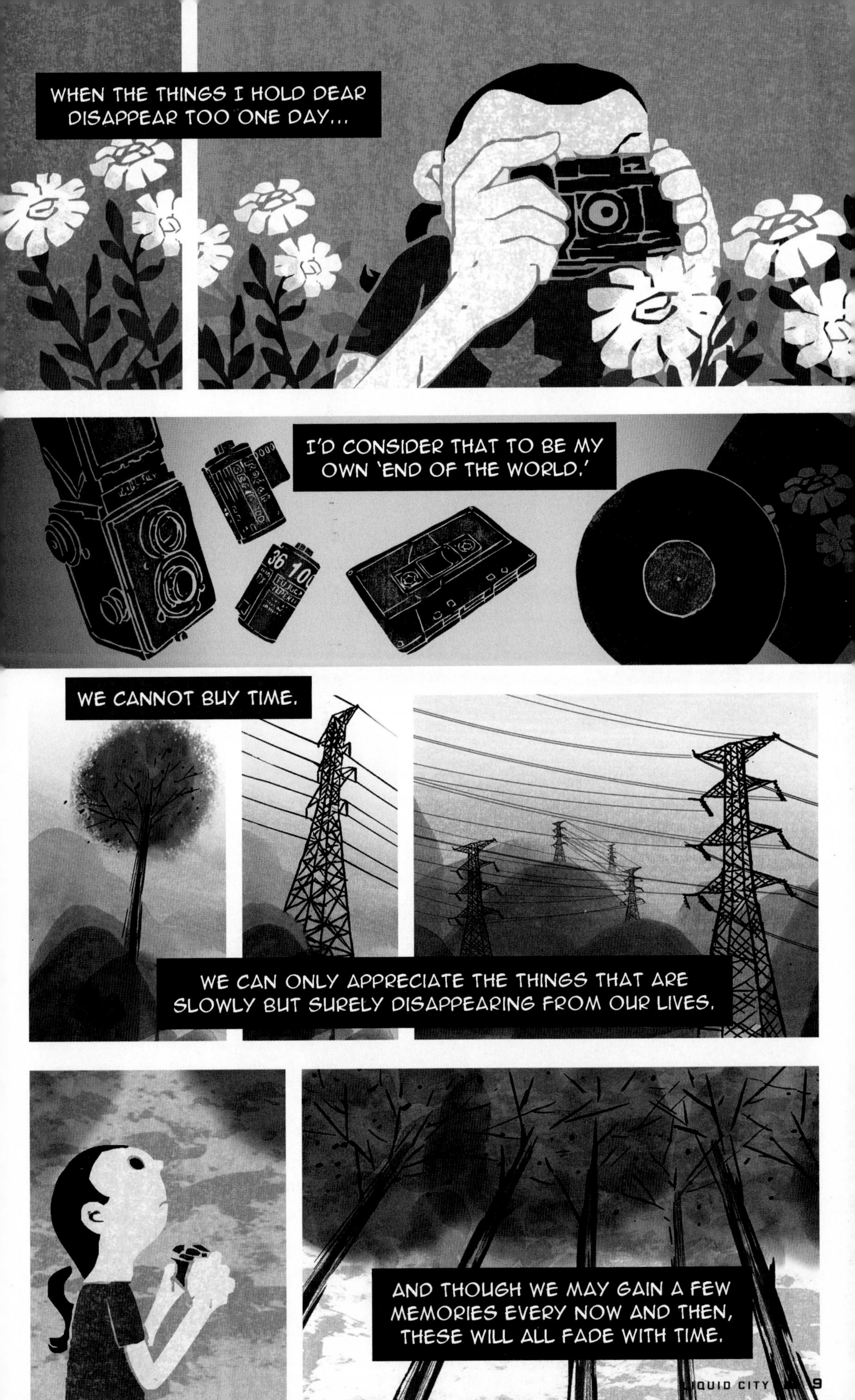
WHEN THE THINGS I HOLD DEAR DISAPPEAR TOO ONE DAY...
I'D CONSIDER THAT TO BE MY OWN 'END OF THE WORLD.'
WE CANNOT BUY TIME.
WE CAN ONLY APPRECIATE THE THINGS THAT ARE SLOWLY BUT SURELY DISAPPEARING FROM OUR LIVES.
AND THOUGH WE MAY GAIN A FEW MEMORIES EVERY NOW AND THEN, THESE WILL ALL FADE WITH TIME.

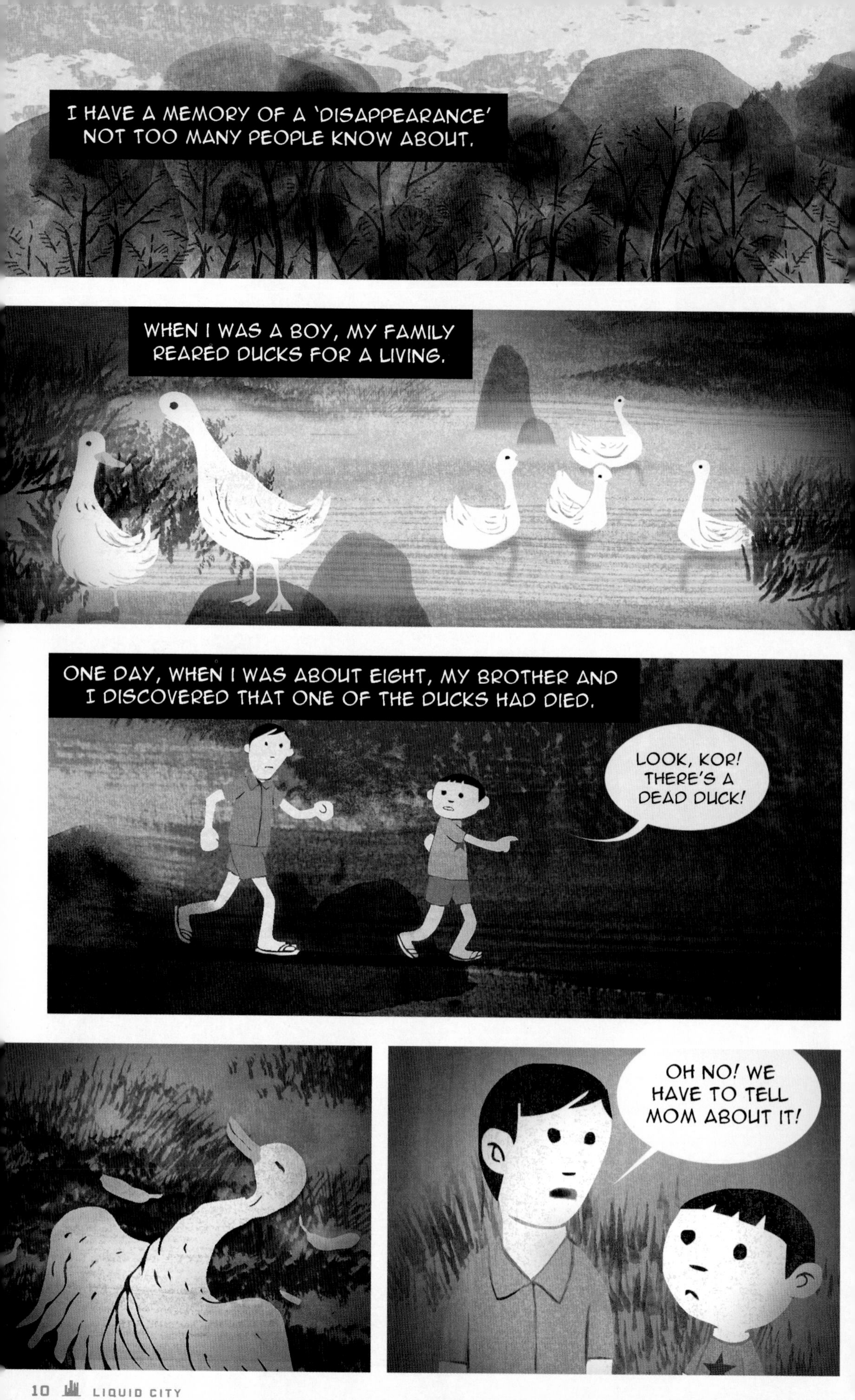
I HAVE A MEMORY OF A 'DISAPPEARANCE' NOT TOO MANY PEOPLE KNOW ABOUT.
WHEN I WAS A BOY, MY FAMILY REARED DUCKS FOR A LIVING.
ONE DAY, WHEN I WAS ABOUT EIGHT, MY BROTHER AND I DISCOVERED THAT ONE OF THE DUCKS HAD DIED.
LOOK, KOR! THERE'S A DEAD DUCK!
OH NO! WE HAVE TO TELL MOM ABOUT IT!

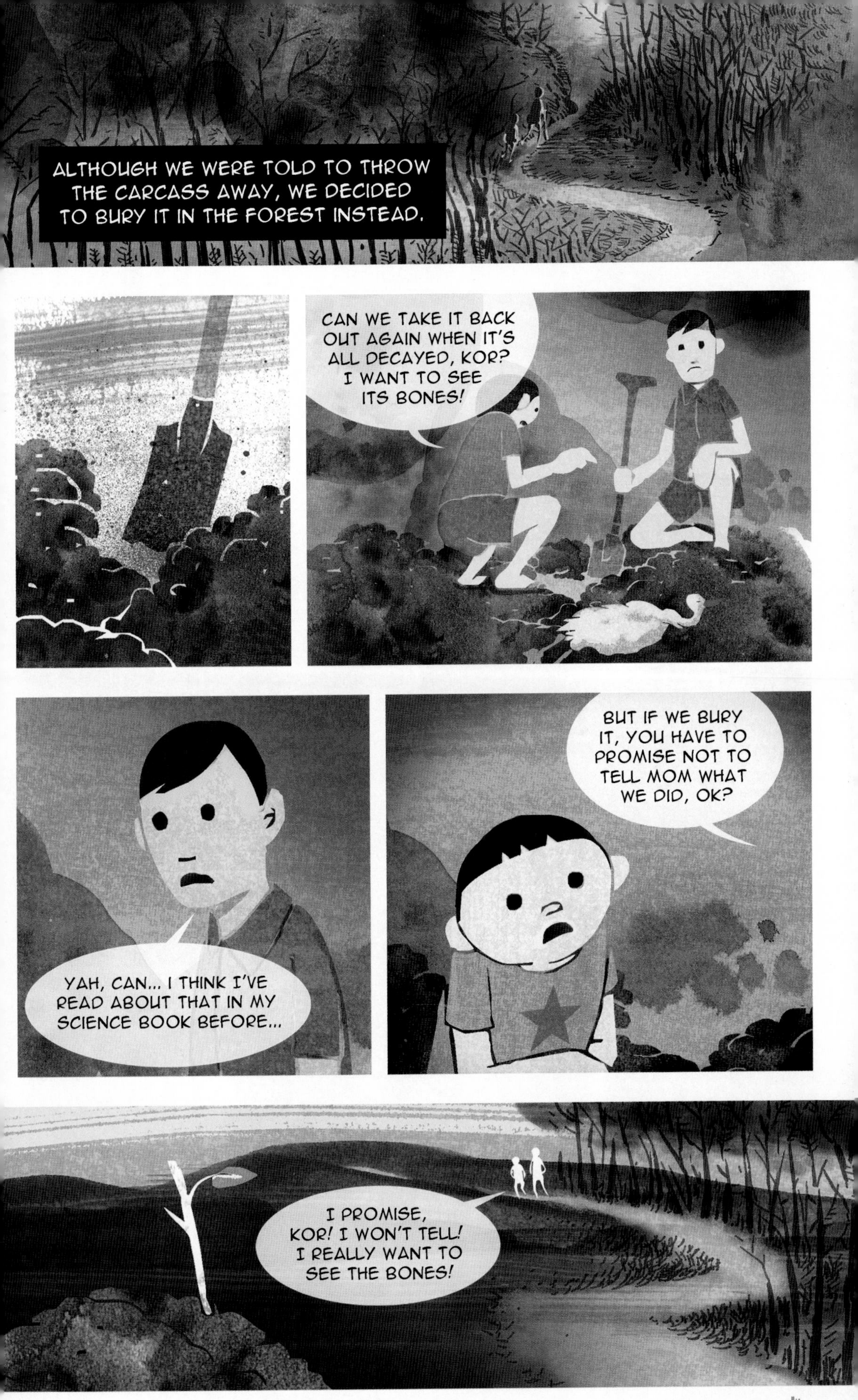
ALTHOUGH WE WERE TOLD TO THROW THE CARCASS AWAY, WE DECIDED TO BURY IT IN THE FOREST INSTEAD.
CAN WE TAKE IT BACK OUT AGAIN WHEN IT'S ALL DECAYED, KOR? I WANT TO SEE ITS BONES!
YAH, CAN... I THINK I'VE READ ABOUT THAT IN MY SCIENCE BOOK BEFORE...
BUT IF WE BURY IT, YOU HAVE TO PROMISE NOT TO TELL MOM WHAT WE DID, OK?
I PROMISE, KOR! I WON'T TELL! I REALLY WANT TO SEE THE BONES!

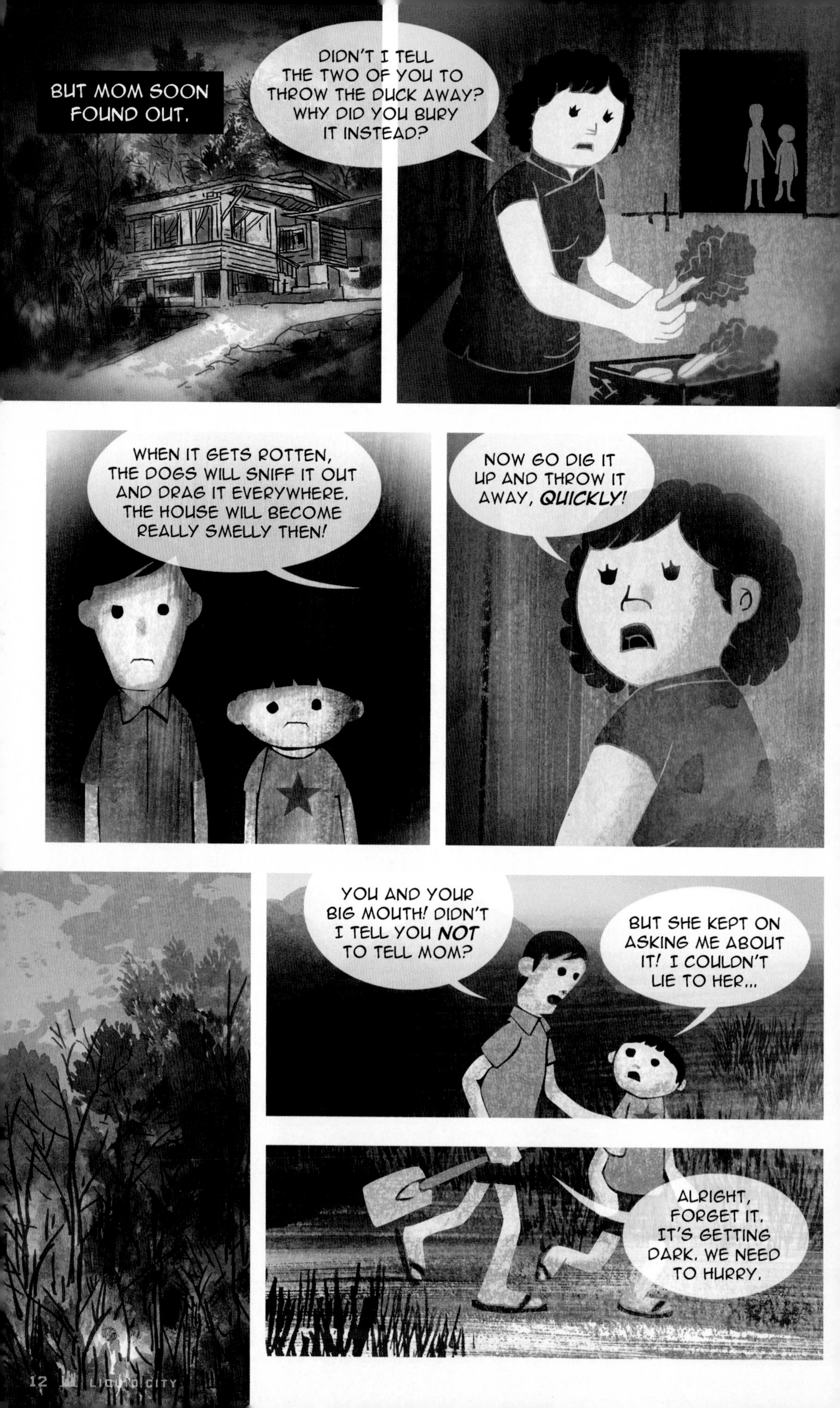
BUT MOM SOON FOUND OUT.
DIDN'T I TELL THE TWO OF YOU TO THROW THE DUCK AWAY? WHY DID YOU BURY IT INSTEAD?
WHEN IT GETS ROTTEN, THE DOGS WILL SNIFF IT OUT AND DRAG IT EVERYWHERE. THE HOUSE WILL BECOME REALLY SMELLY THEN!
NOW GO DIG IT UP AND THROW IT AWAY, ***QUICKLY***!
YOU AND YOUR BIG MOUTH! DIDN'T I TELL YOU ***NOT*** TO TELL MOM?
BUT SHE KEPT ON ASKING ME ABOUT IT! I COULDN'T LIE TO HER...
ALRIGHT, FORGET IT. IT'S GETTING DARK. WE NEED TO HURRY.

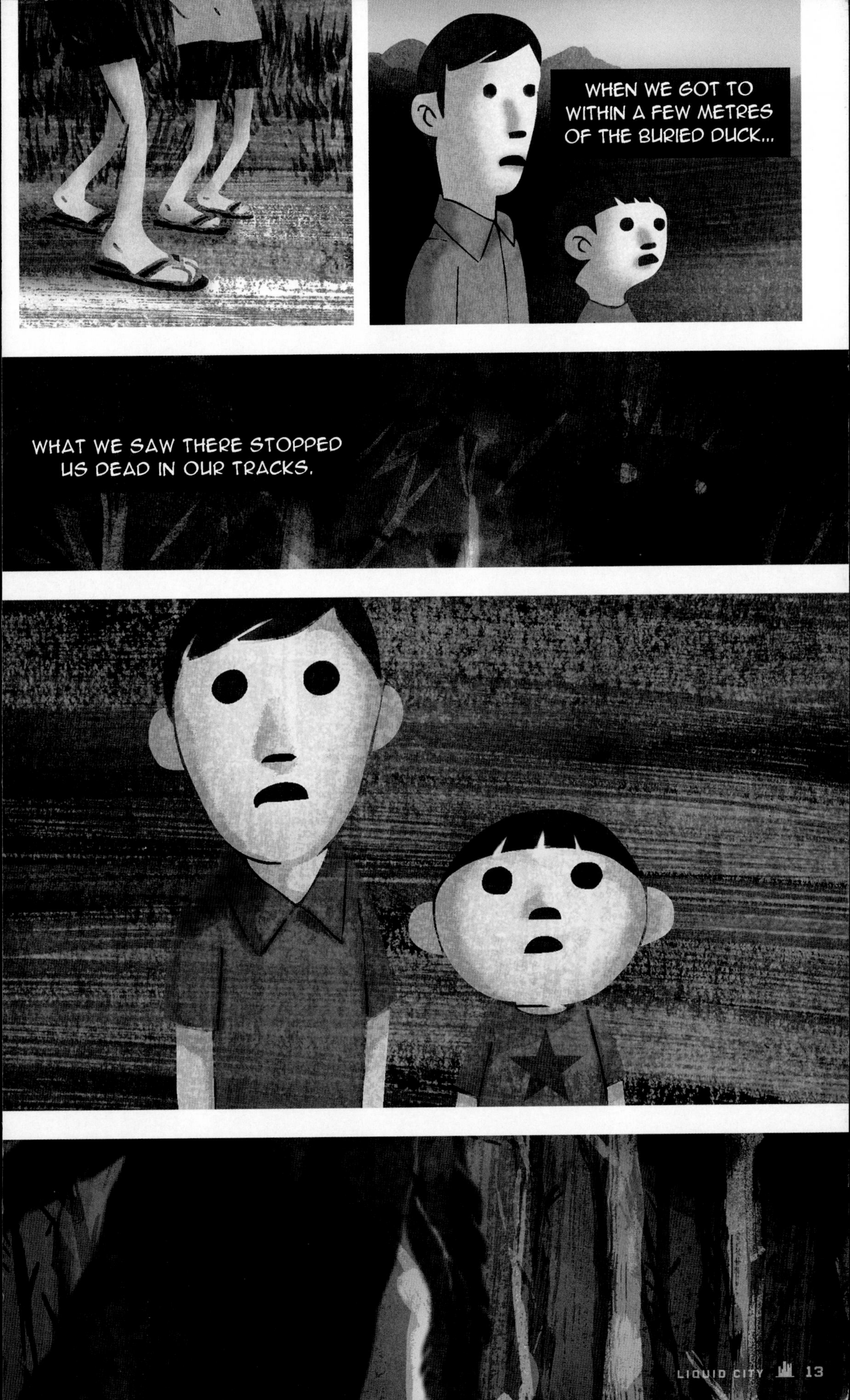
WHEN WE GOT TO WITHIN A FEW METRES OF THE BURIED DUCK...
WHAT WE SAW THERE STOPPED US DEAD IN OUR TRACKS.

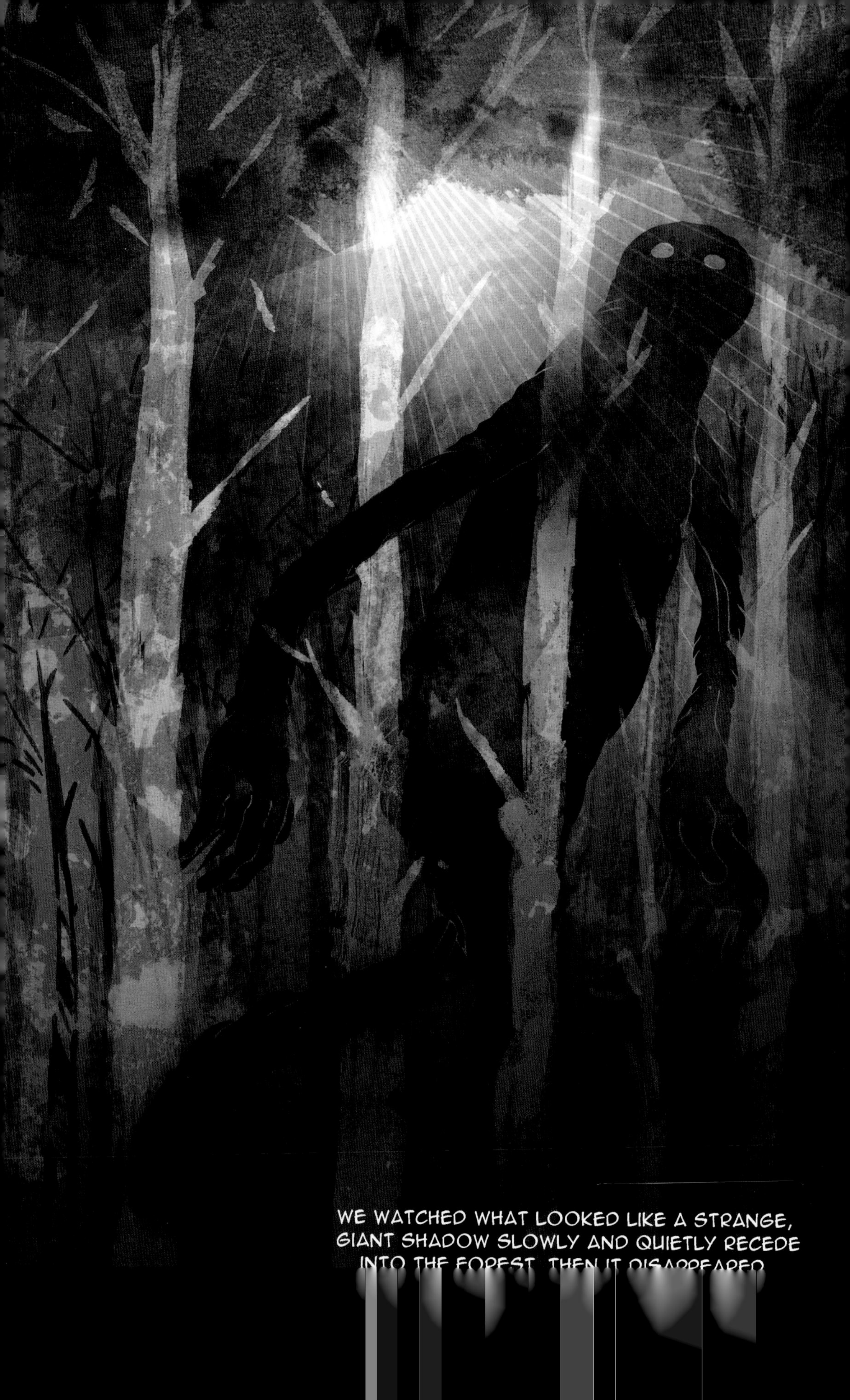
WE WATCHED WHAT LOOKED LIKE A STRANGE, GIANT SHADOW SLOWLY AND QUIETLY RECEDE INTO THE FOREST. THEN IT DISAPPEARED

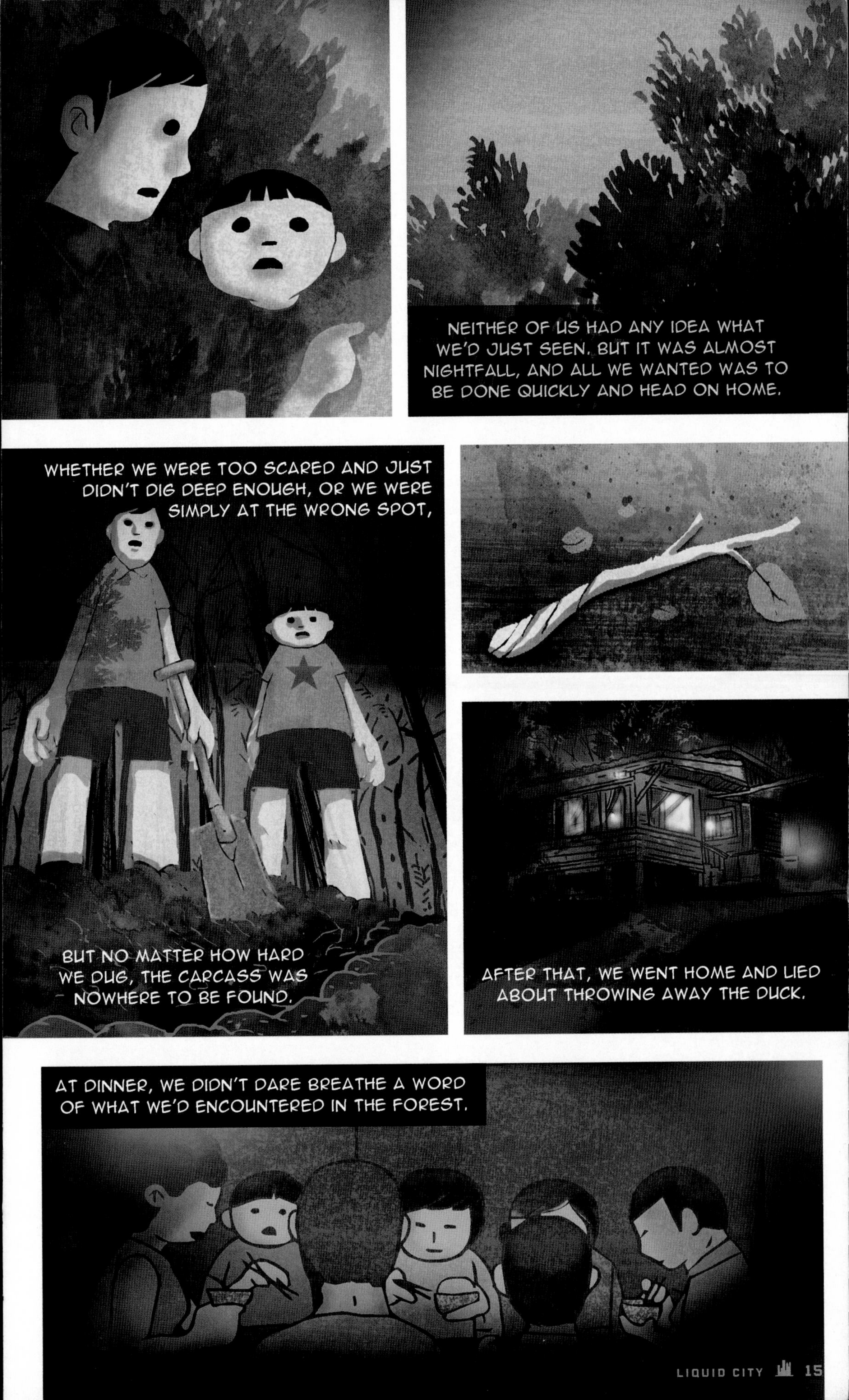
NEITHER OF US HAD ANY IDEA WHAT WE'D JUST SEEN. BUT IT WAS ALMOST NIGHTFALL, AND ALL WE WANTED WAS TO BE DONE QUICKLY AND HEAD ON HOME.
WHETHER WE WERE TOO SCARED AND JUST DIDN'T DIG DEEP ENOUGH, OR WE WERE SIMPLY AT THE WRONG SPOT,
BUT NO MATTER HOW HARD WE DUG, THE CARCASS WAS NOWHERE TO BE FOUND.
AFTER THAT, WE WENT HOME AND LIED ABOUT THROWING AWAY THE DUCK.
AT DINNER, WE DIDN'T DARE BREATHE A WORD OF WHAT WE'D ENCOUNTERED IN THE FOREST.

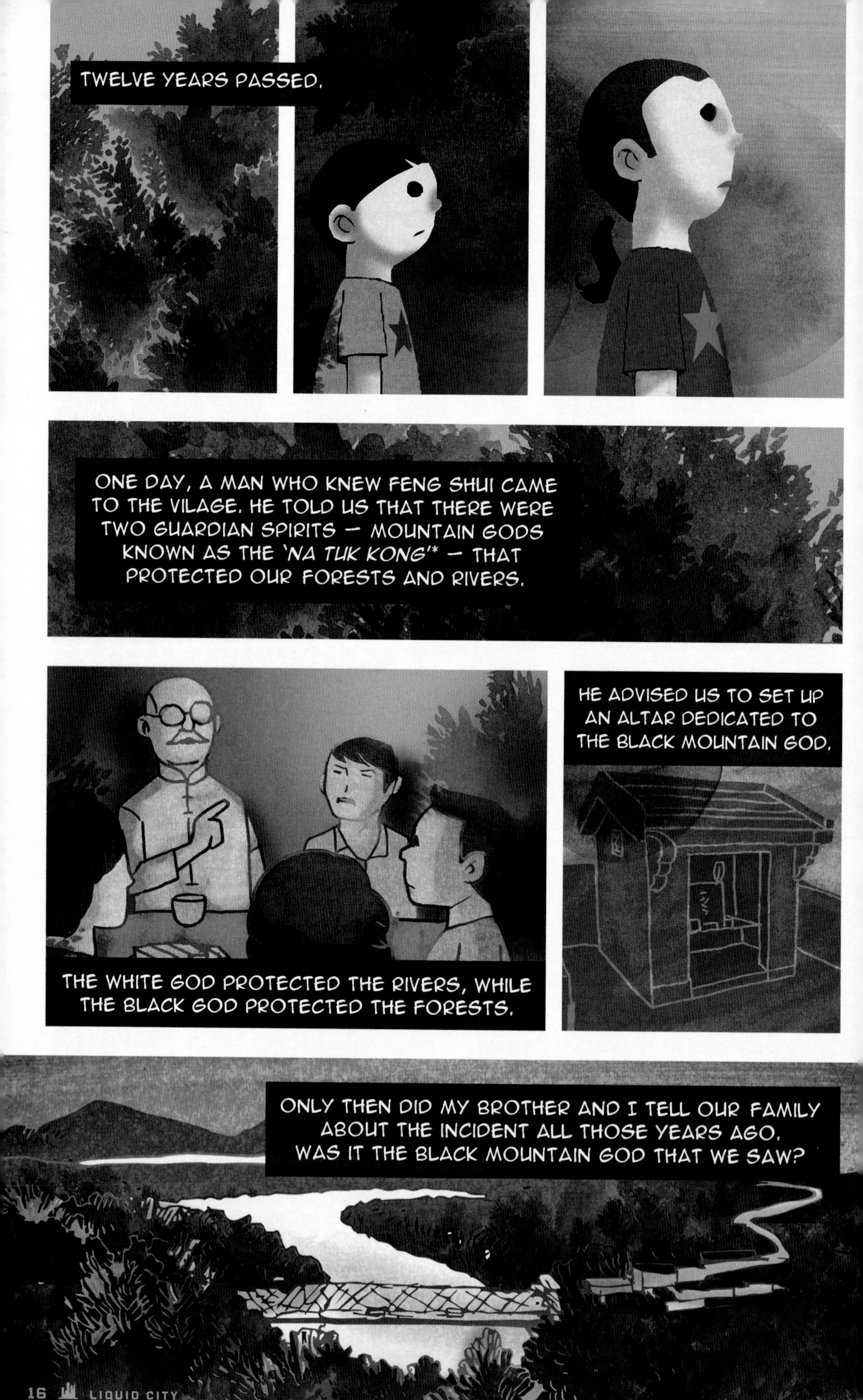
TWELVE YEARS PASSED.
ONE DAY, A MAN WHO KNEW FENG SHUI CAME TO THE VILAGE. HE TOLD US THAT THERE WERE TWO GUARDIAN SPIRITS — MOUNTAIN GODS KNOWN AS THE '*NA TUK KONG*'* — THAT PROTECTED OUR FORESTS AND RIVERS.
THE WHITE GOD PROTECTED THE RIVERS, WHILE THE BLACK GOD PROTECTED THE FORESTS.
HE ADVISED US TO SET UP AN ALTAR DEDICATED TO THE BLACK MOUNTAIN GOD.
ONLY THEN DID MY BROTHER AND I TELL OUR FAMILY ABOUT THE INCIDENT ALL THOSE YEARS AGO. WAS IT THE BLACK MOUNTAIN GOD THAT WE SAW?

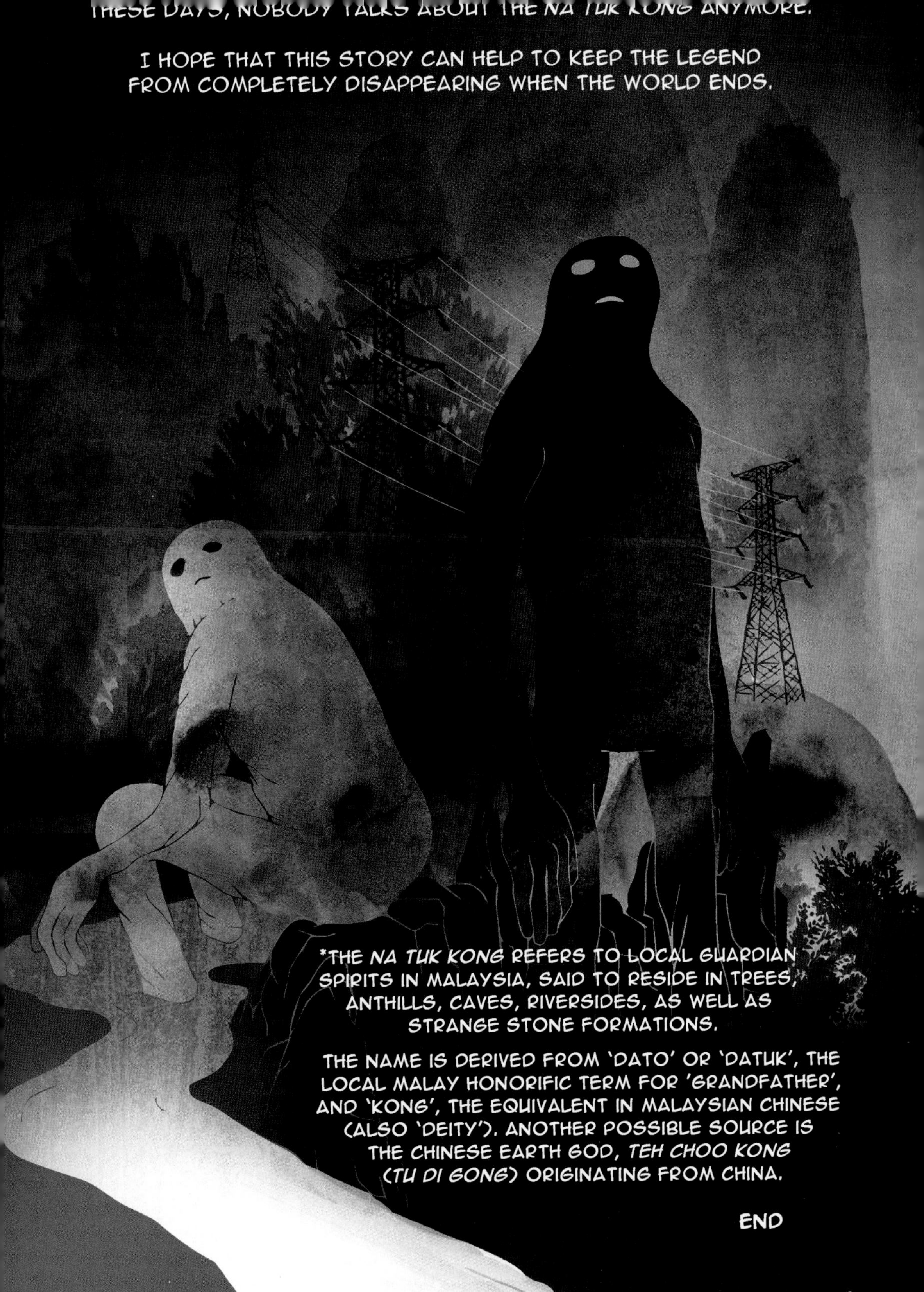
THESE DAYS, NOBODY TALKS ABOUT THE *NA TUK KONG* ANYMORE.
I HOPE THAT THIS STORY CAN HELP TO KEEP THE LEGEND FROM COMPLETELY DISAPPEARING WHEN THE WORLD ENDS.
*THE *NA TUK KONG* REFERS TO LOCAL GUARDIAN SPIRITS IN MALAYSIA, SAID TO RESIDE IN TREES, ANTHILLS, CAVES, RIVERSIDES, AS WELL AS STRANGE STONE FORMATIONS.
THE NAME IS DERIVED FROM 'DATO' OR 'DATUK', THE LOCAL MALAY HONORIFIC TERM FOR 'GRANDFATHER', AND 'KONG', THE EQUIVALENT IN MALAYSIAN CHINESE (ALSO 'DEITY'). ANOTHER POSSIBLE SOURCE IS THE CHINESE EARTH GOD, *TEH CHOO KONG* (*TU DI GONG*) ORIGINATING FROM CHINA.
END

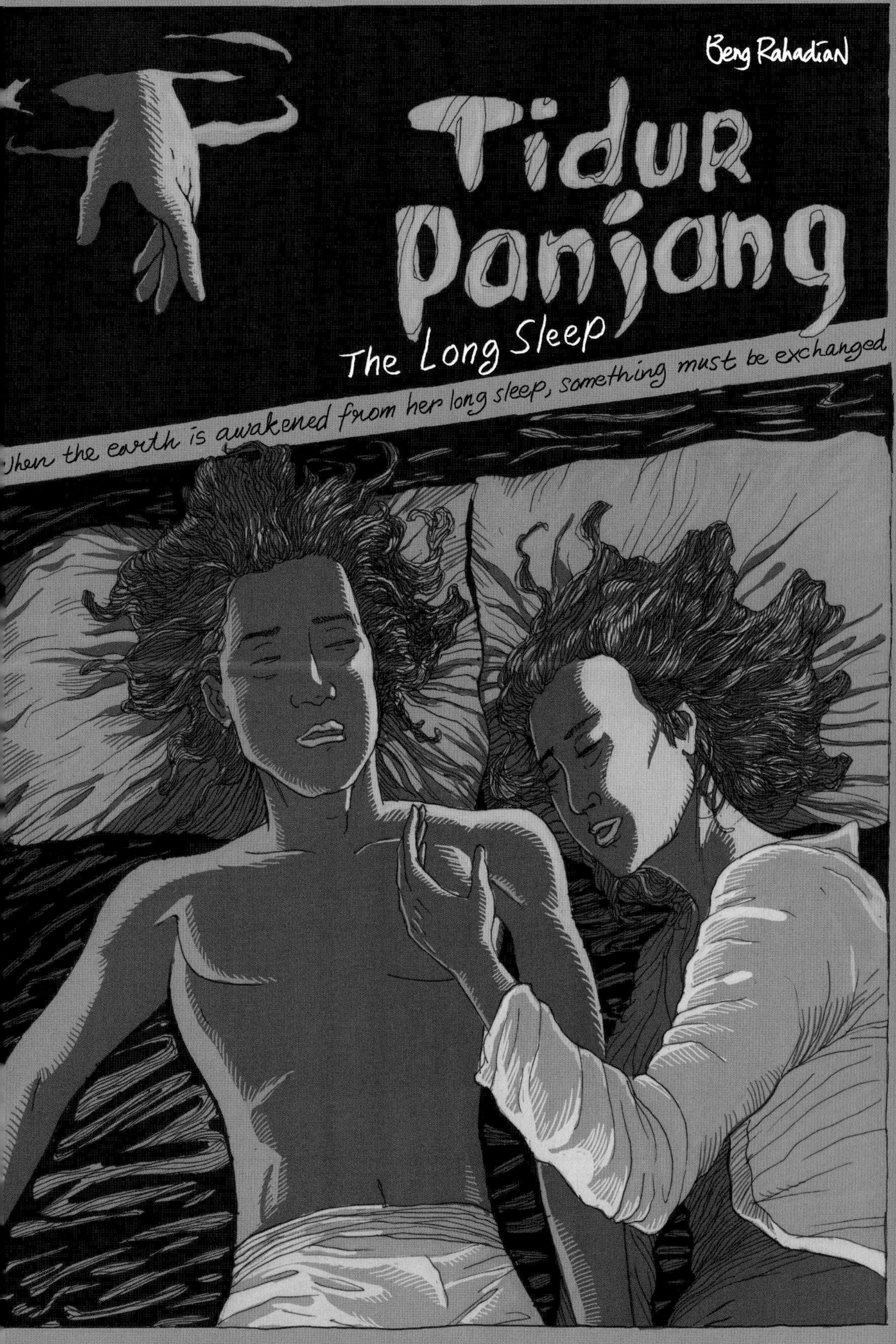
Beng Rahadian
Tidur Panjang
The Long Sleep
When the earth is awakened from her long sleep, something must be exchanged

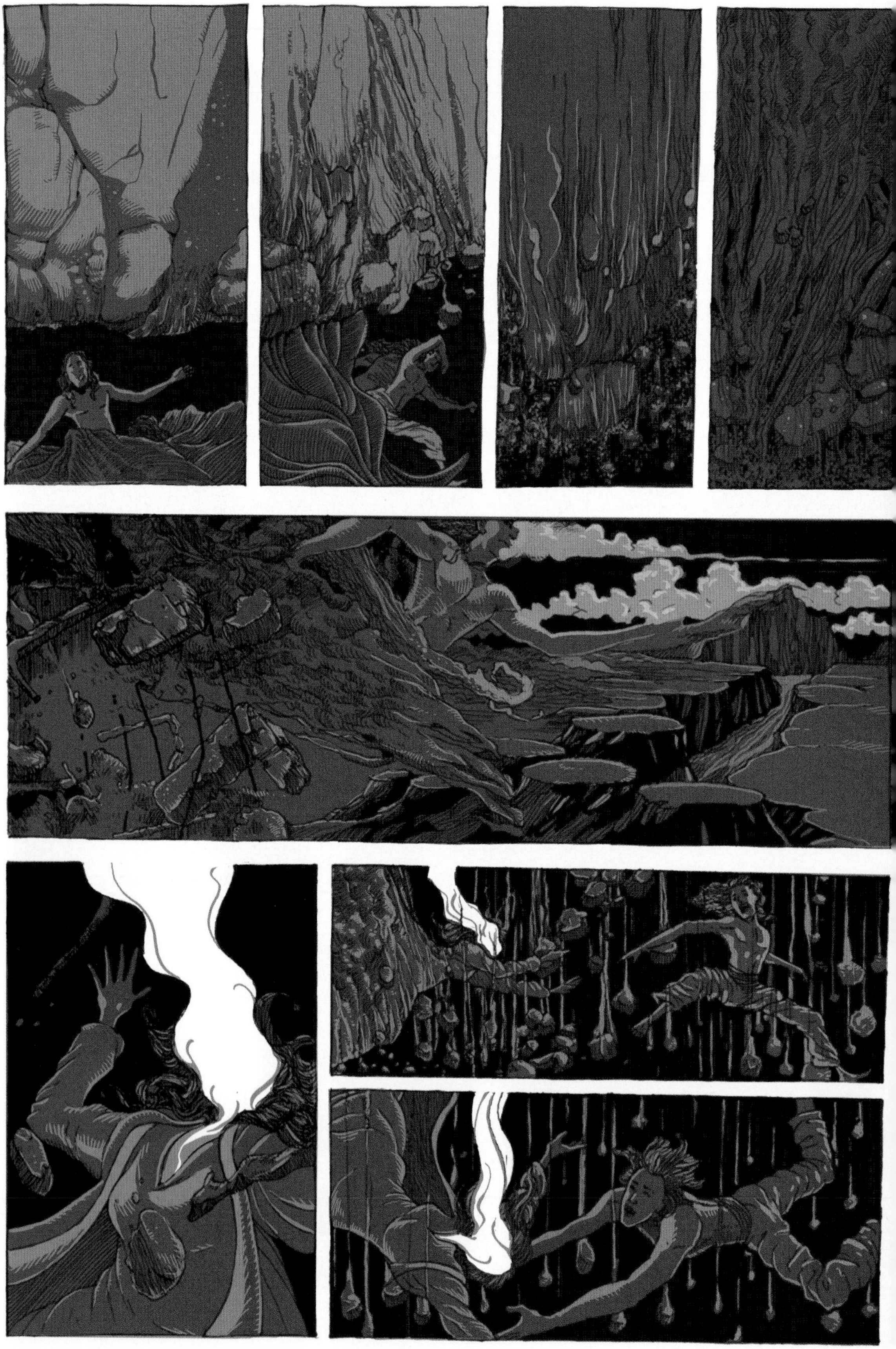

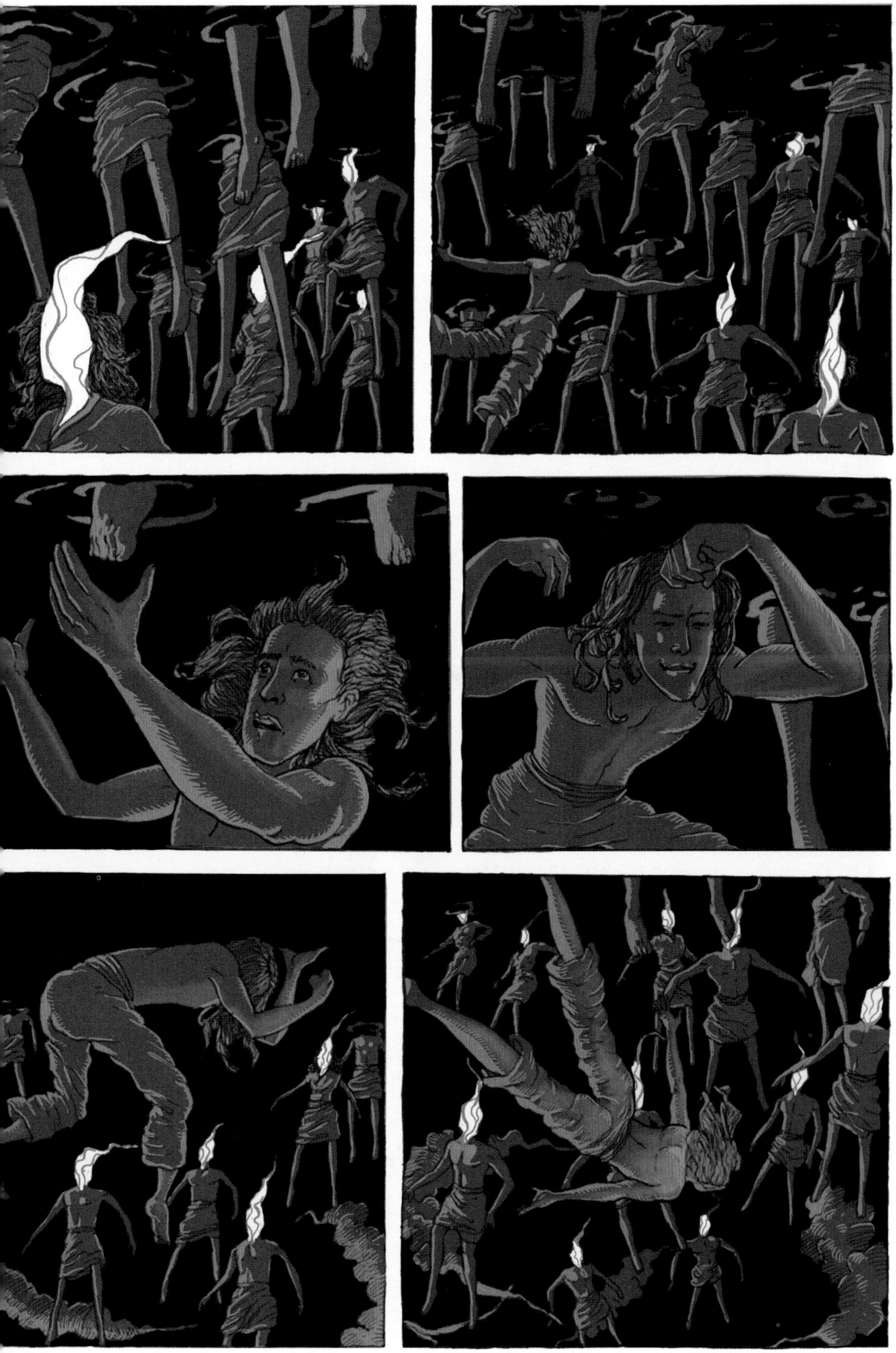

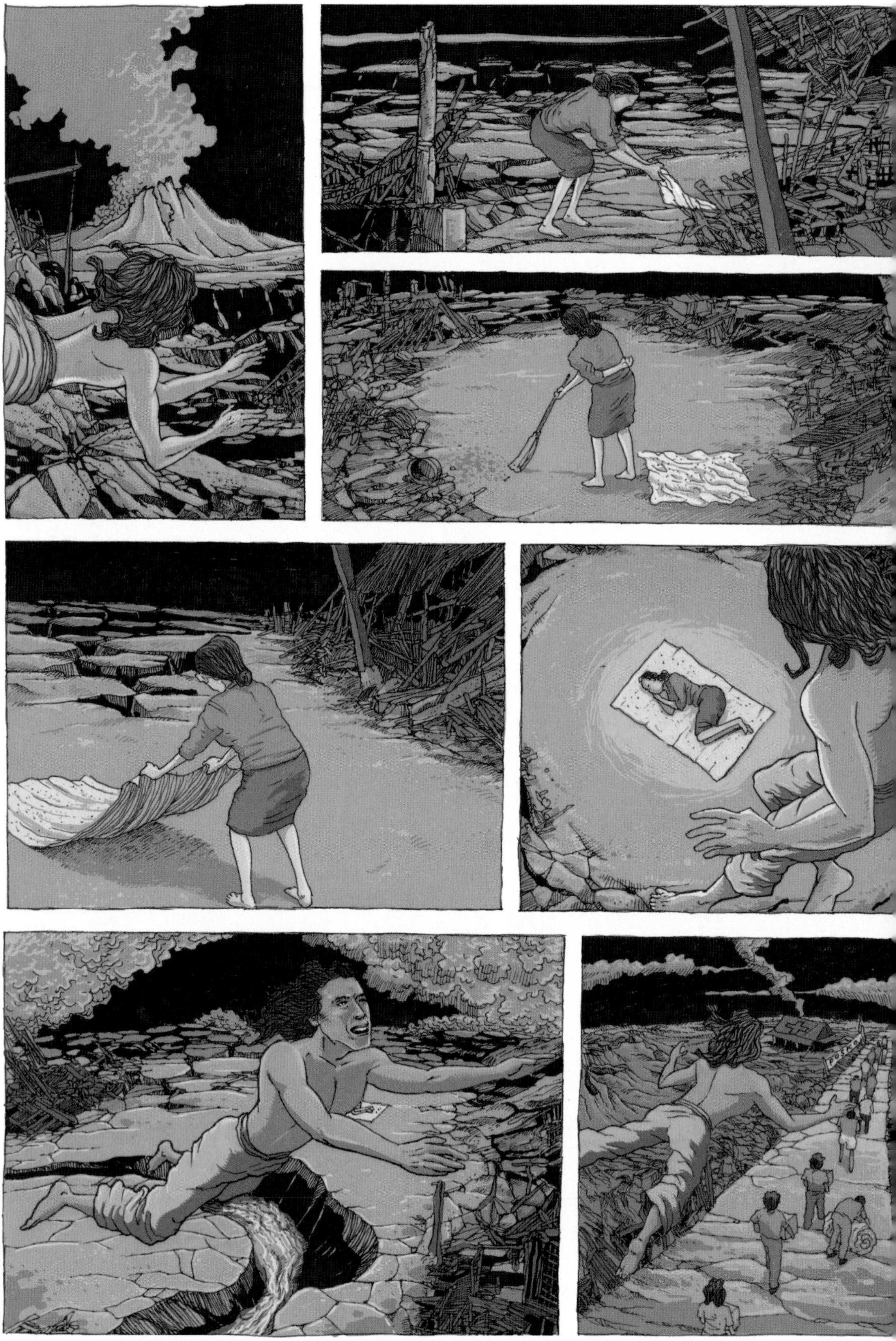
POSKO

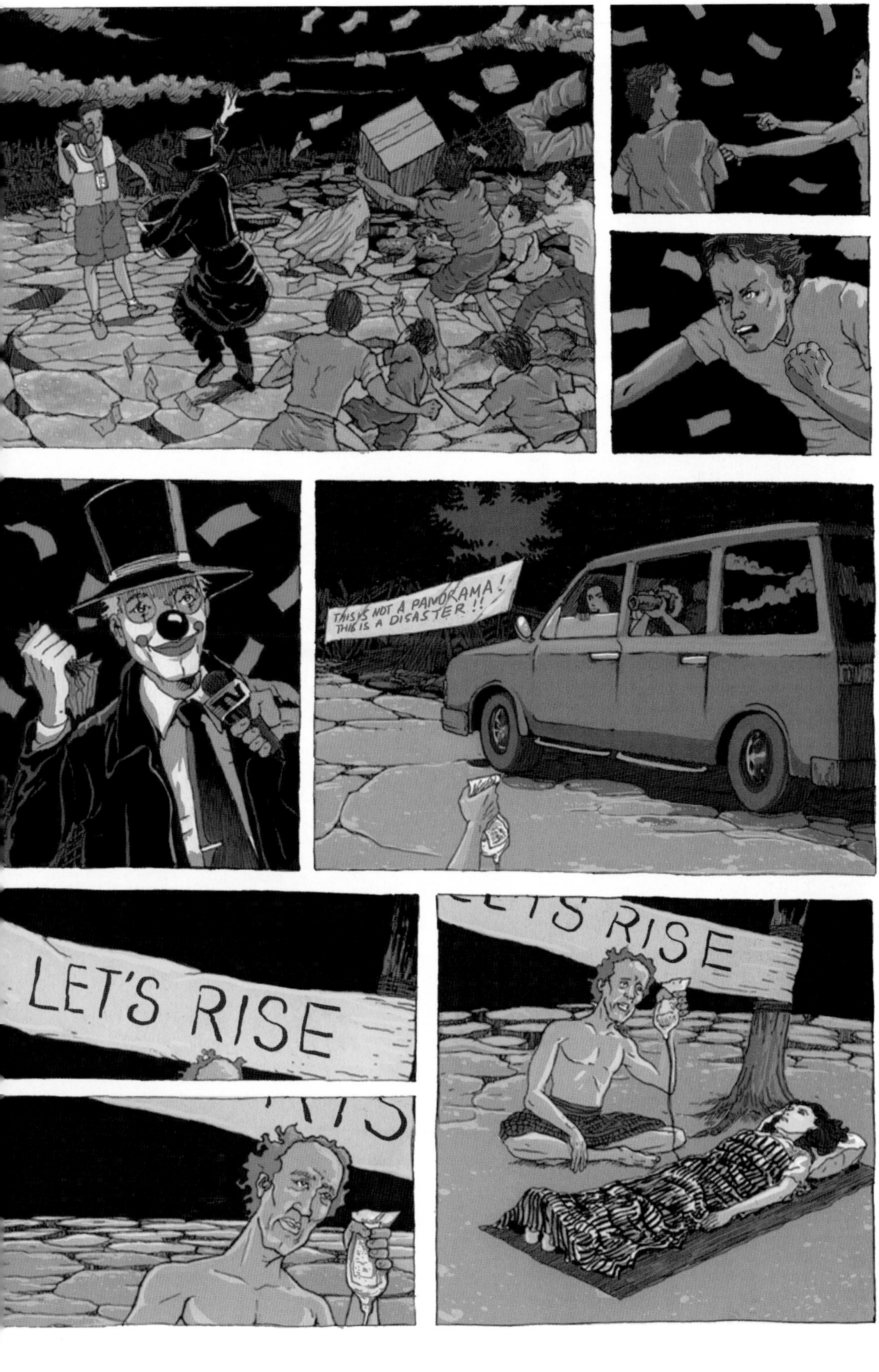
THIS IS NOT A PANORAMA!
THIS IS A DISASTER!!
LET'S RISE

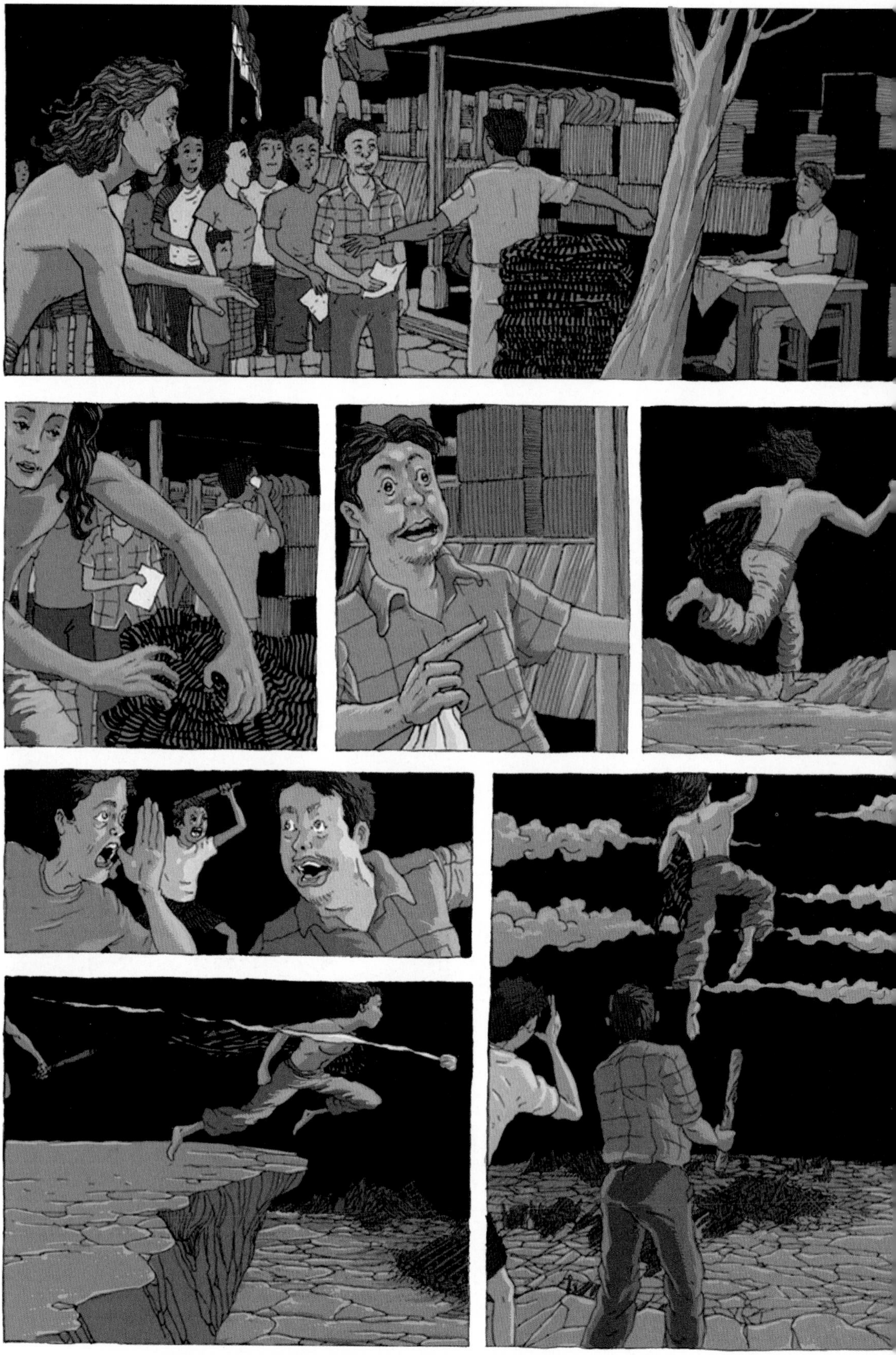

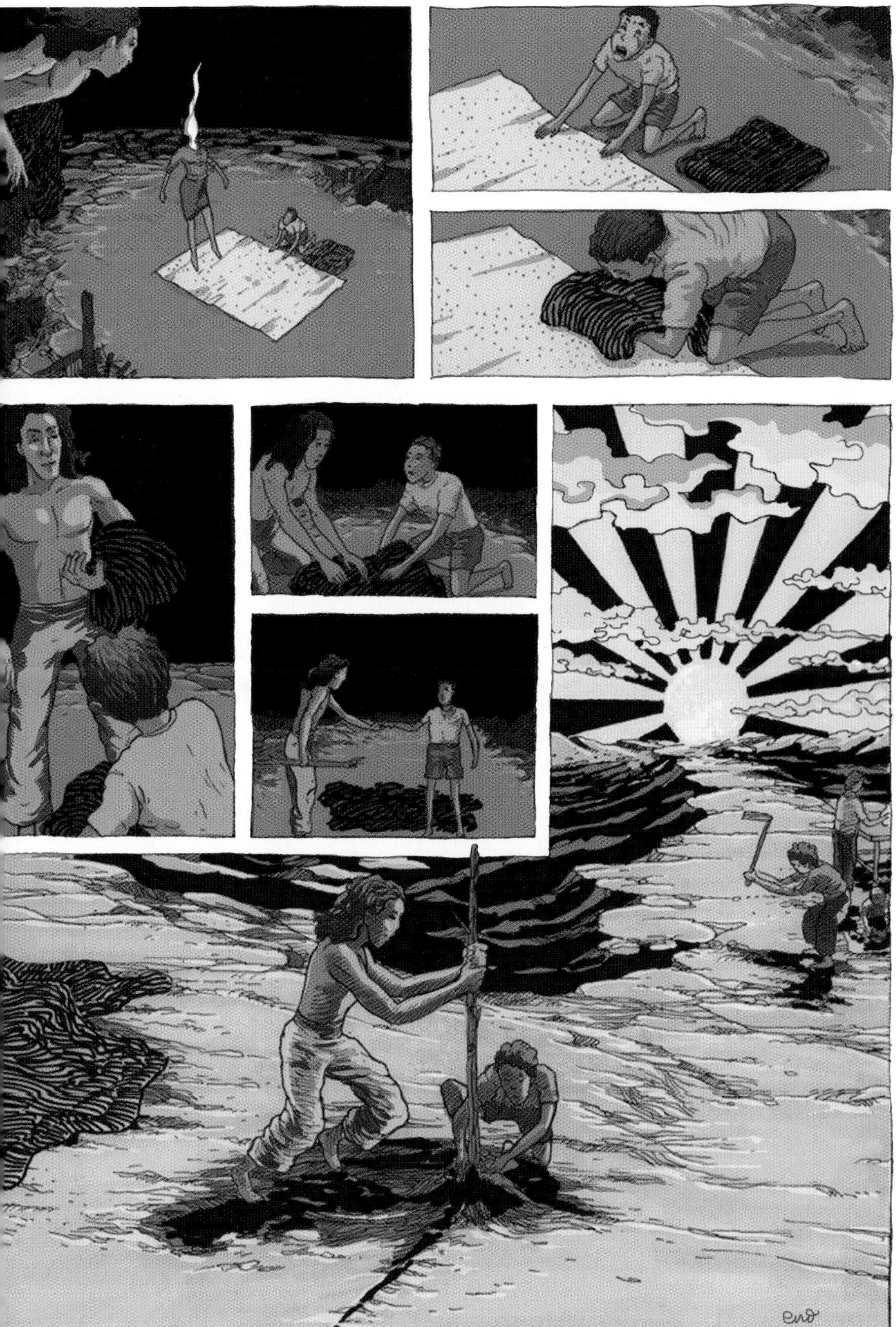
end

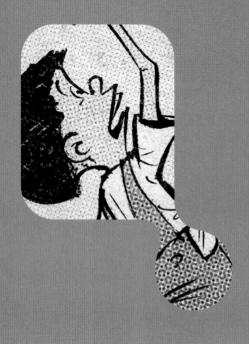

GEYLANG HILL 芽籠山

BY CHAN HOCK CHYE

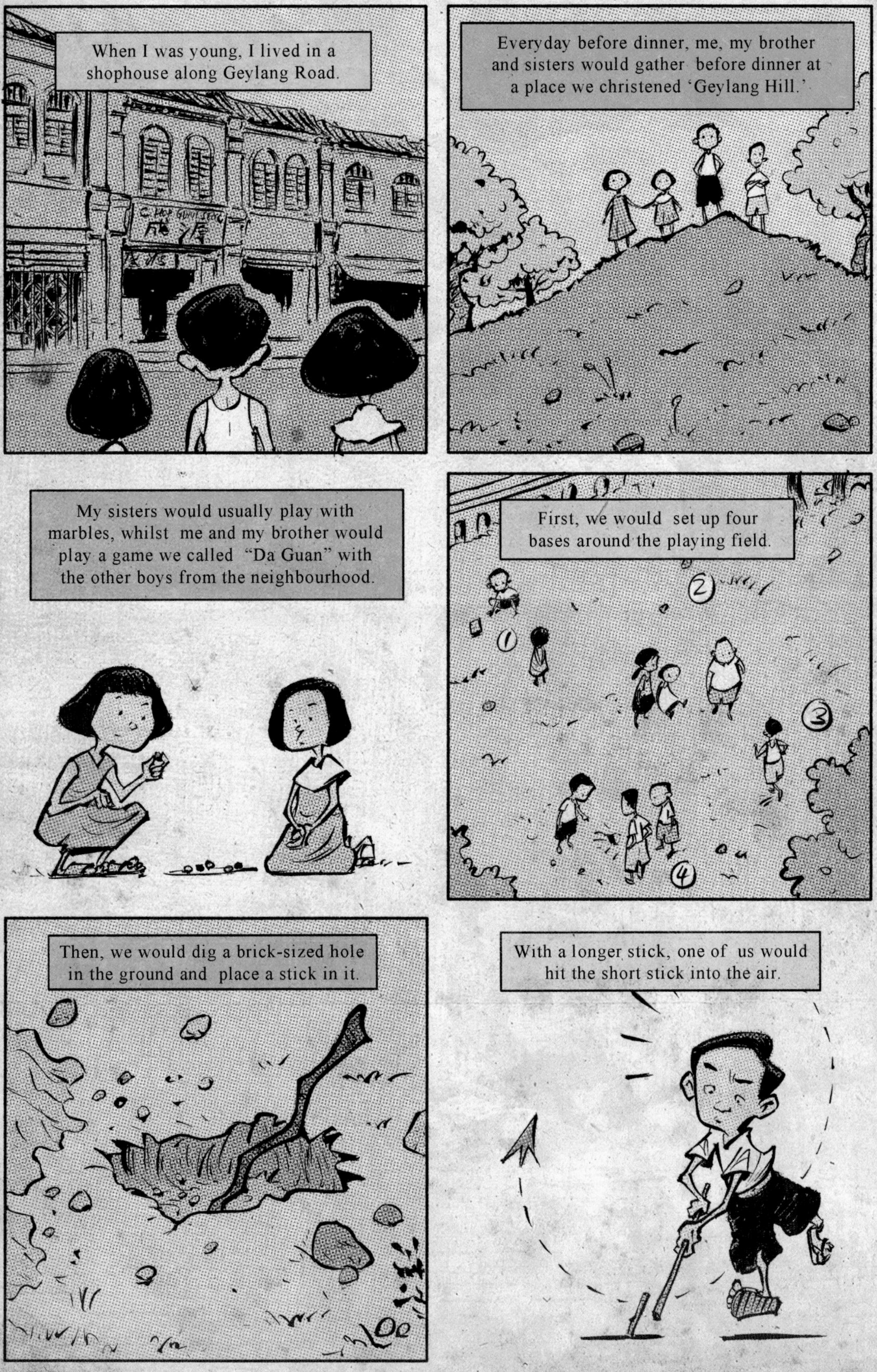
When I was young, I lived in a shophouse along Geylang Road.
Everyday before dinner, me, my brother and sisters would gather before dinner at a place we christened 'Geylang Hill.'
My sisters would usually play with marbles, whilst me and my brother would play a game we called "Da Guan" with the other boys from the neighbourhood.
First, we would set up four bases around the playing field.
Then, we would dig a brick-sized hole in the ground and place a stick in it.
With a longer stick, one of us would hit the short stick into the air.

Note: "Da Guan" - Cantonese, literally meaning "Hitting Stick"

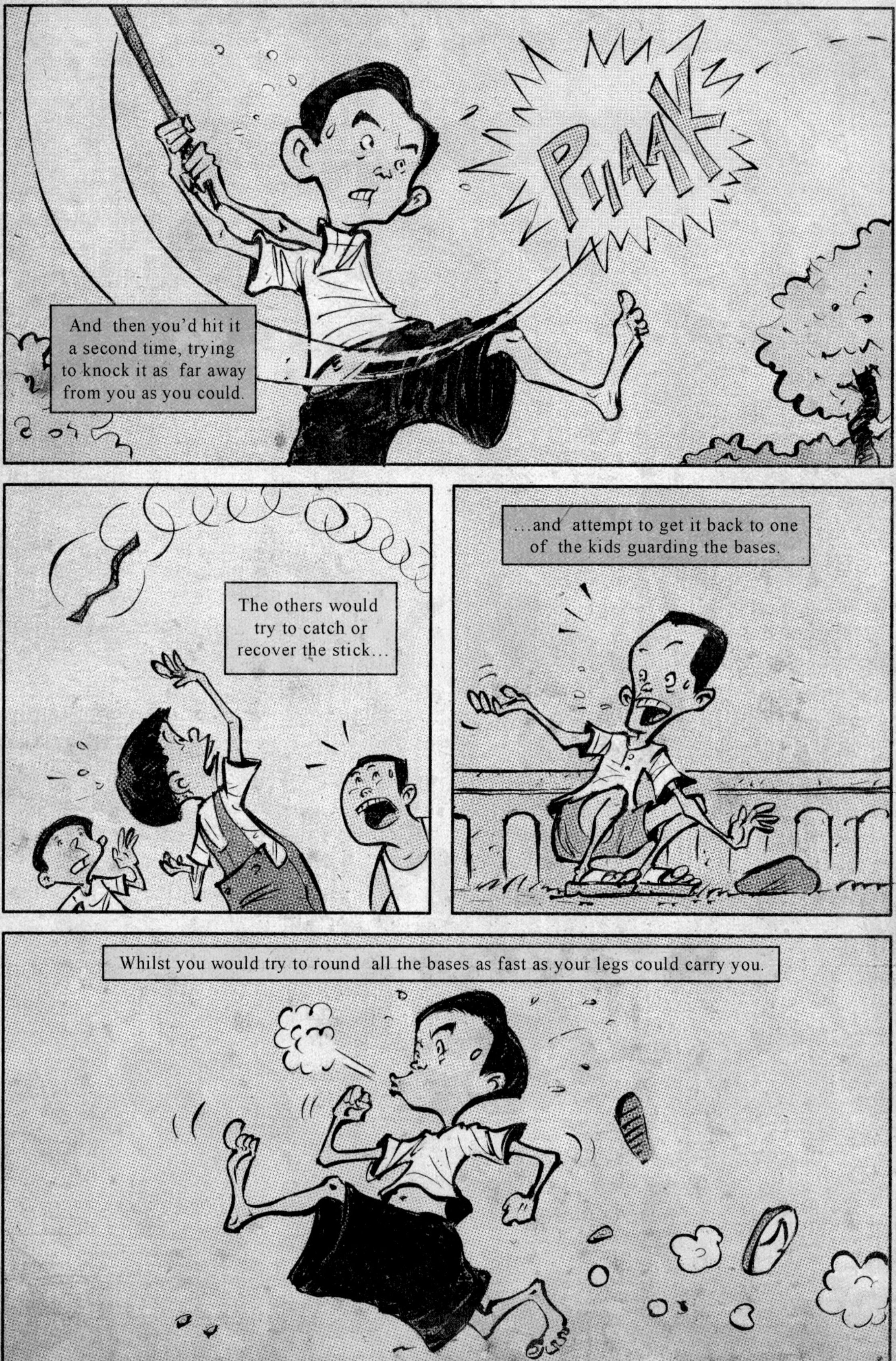
PHAAK
And then you'd hit it a second time, trying to knock it as far away from you as you could.
The others would try to catch or recover the stick...
...and attempt to get it back to one of the kids guarding the bases.
Whilst you would try to round all the bases as fast as your legs could carry you.

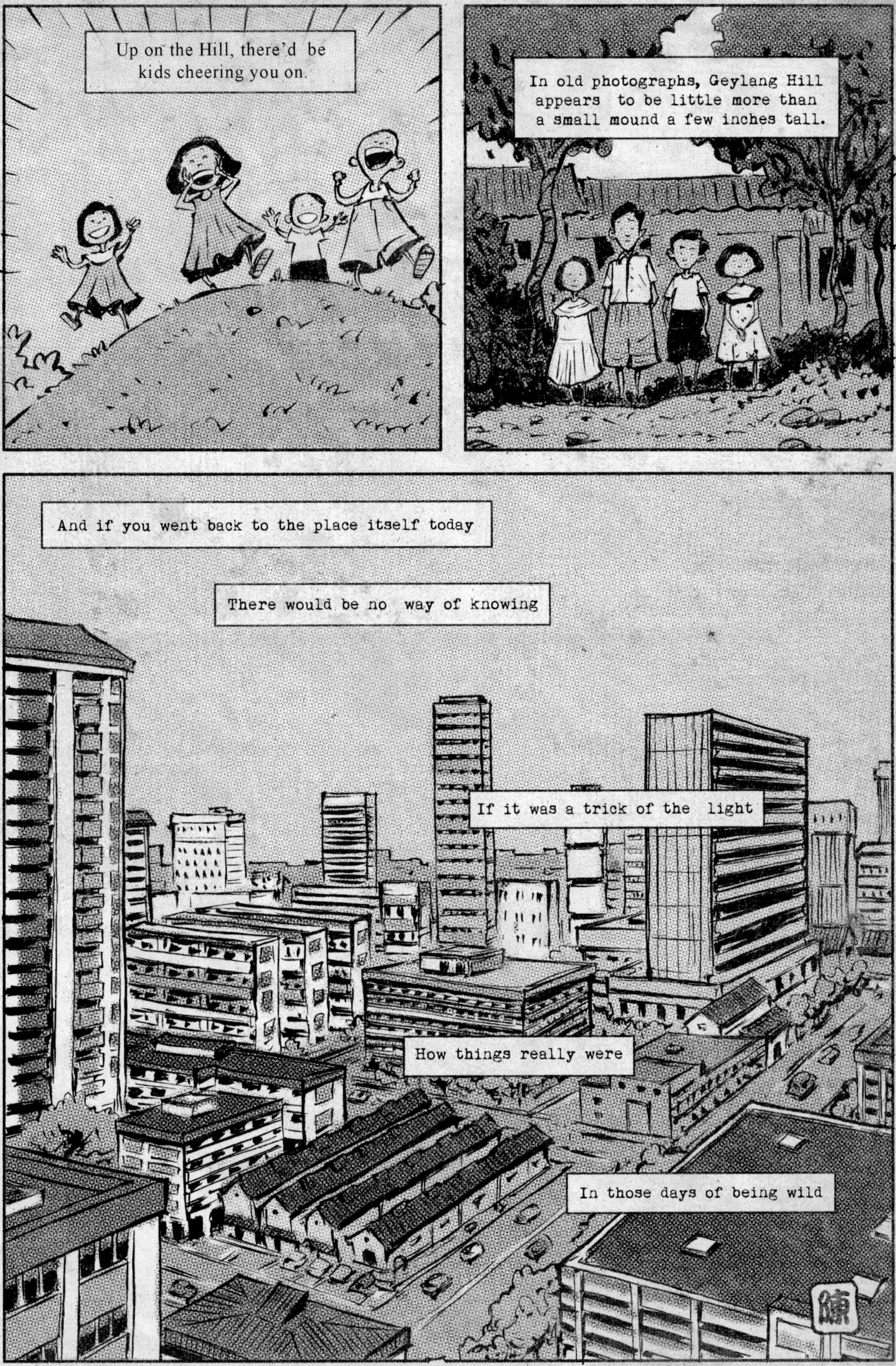

Up on the Hill, there'd be kids cheering you on.
In old photographs, Geylang Hill appears to be little more than a small mound a few inches tall.
And if you went back to the place itself today
There would be no way of knowing
If it was a trick of the light
How things really were
In those days of being wild

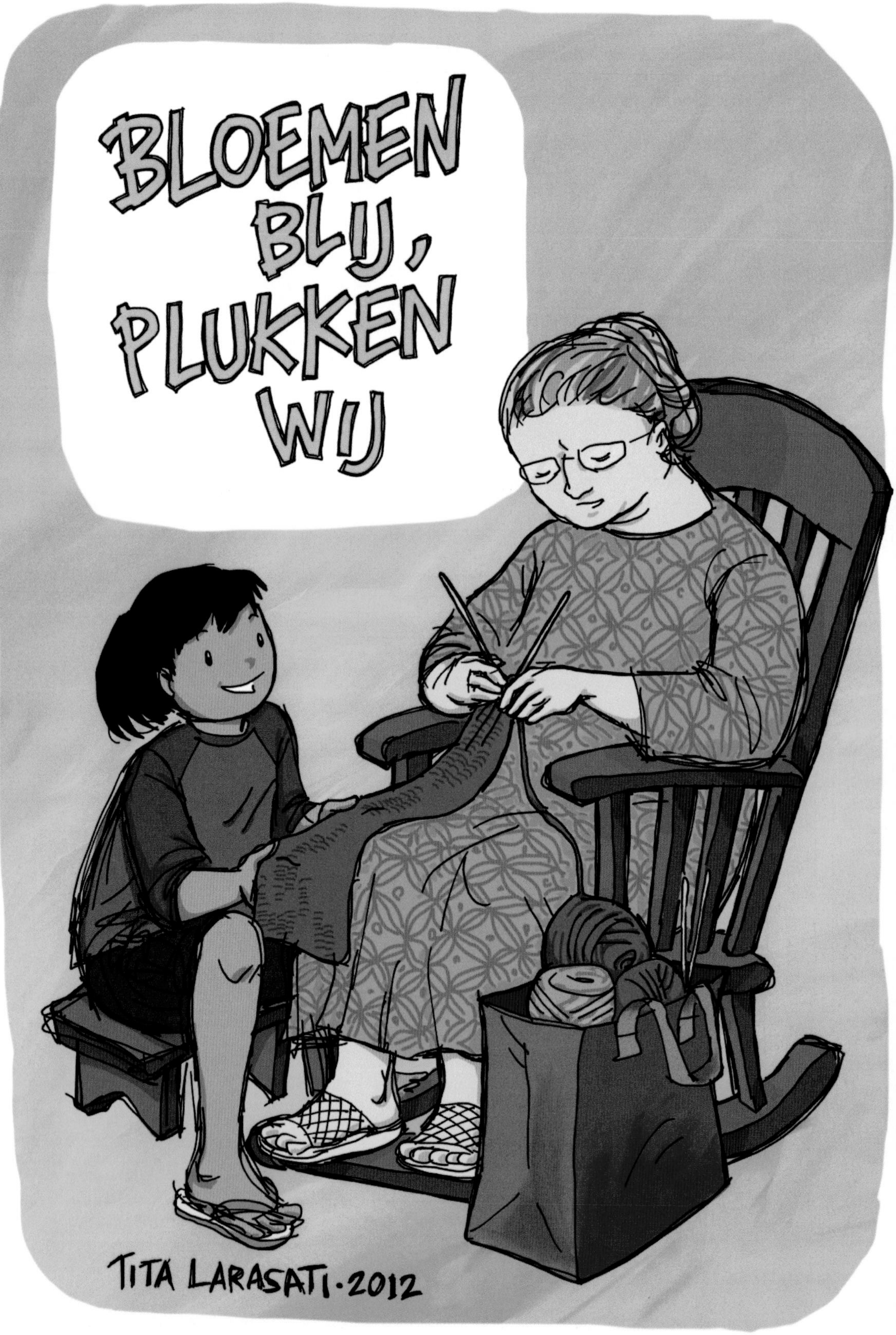
BLOEMEN BLIJ, PLUKKEN WIJ
TITA LARASATI · 2012

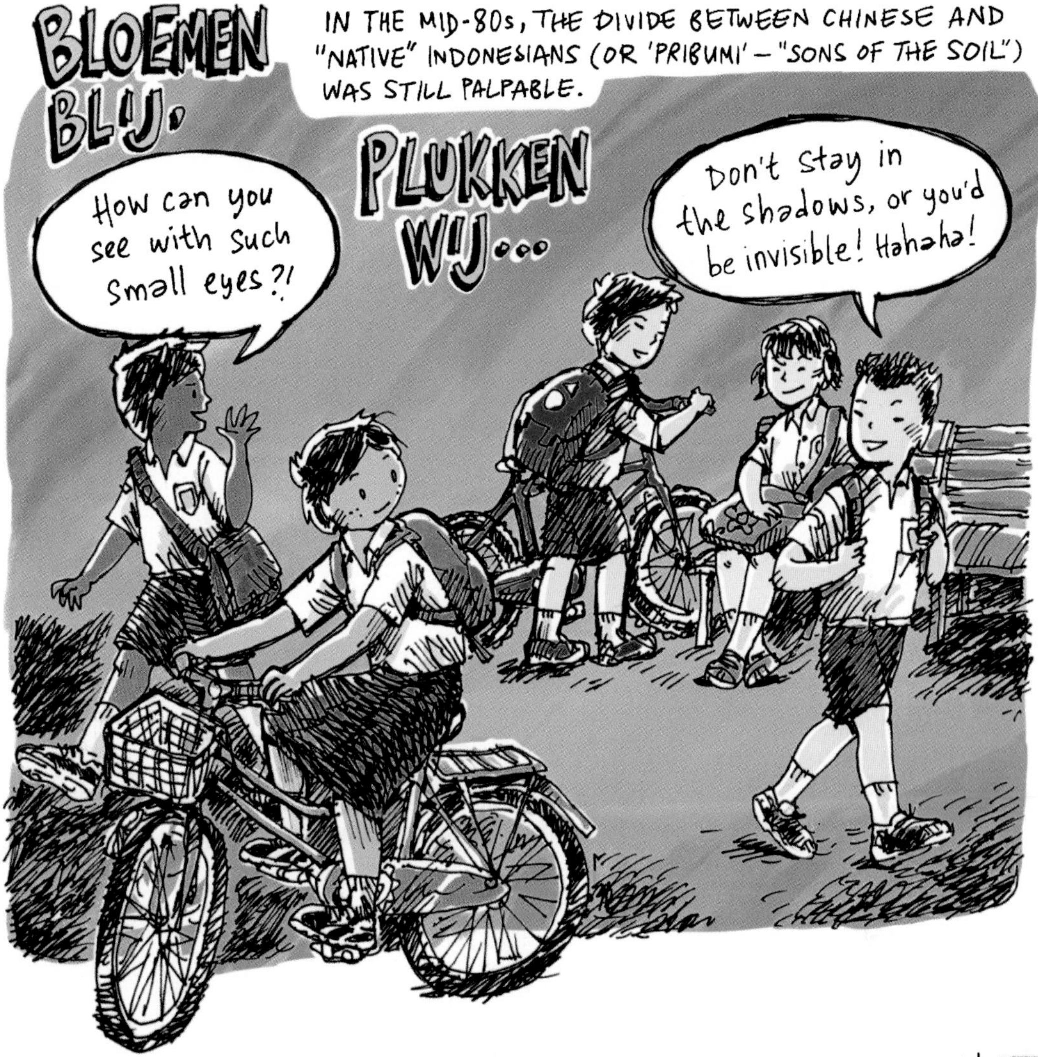
IN THE MID-80s, THE DIVIDE BETWEEN CHINESE AND "NATIVE" INDONESIANS (OR 'PRIBUMI' – "SONS OF THE SOIL") WAS STILL PALPABLE.
BLOEMEN BLIJ.
PLUKKEN WIJ...
How can you see with such small eyes?!
Don't stay in the shadows, or you'd be invisible! Hahaha!

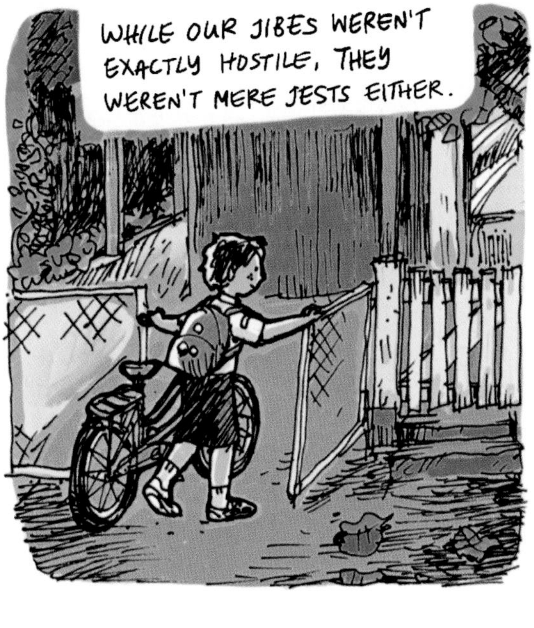
WHILE OUR JIBES WEREN'T EXACTLY HOSTILE, THEY WEREN'T MERE JESTS EITHER.

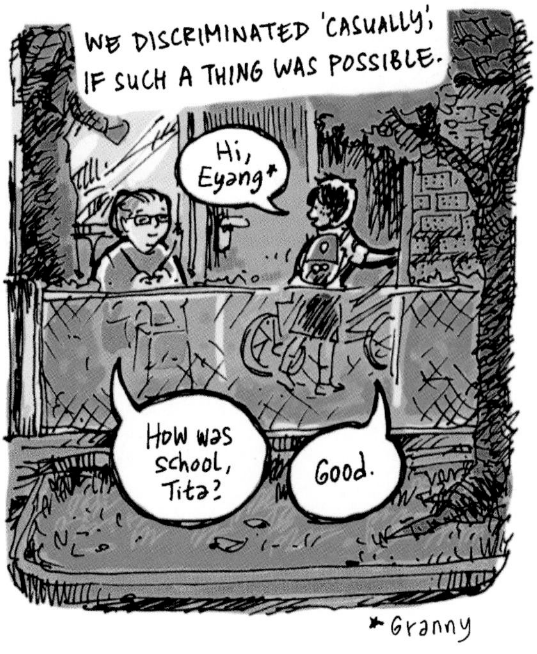
WE DISCRIMINATED 'CASUALLY', IF SUCH A THING WAS POSSIBLE.
Hi, Eyang*
How was school, Tita?
Good.

*Granny

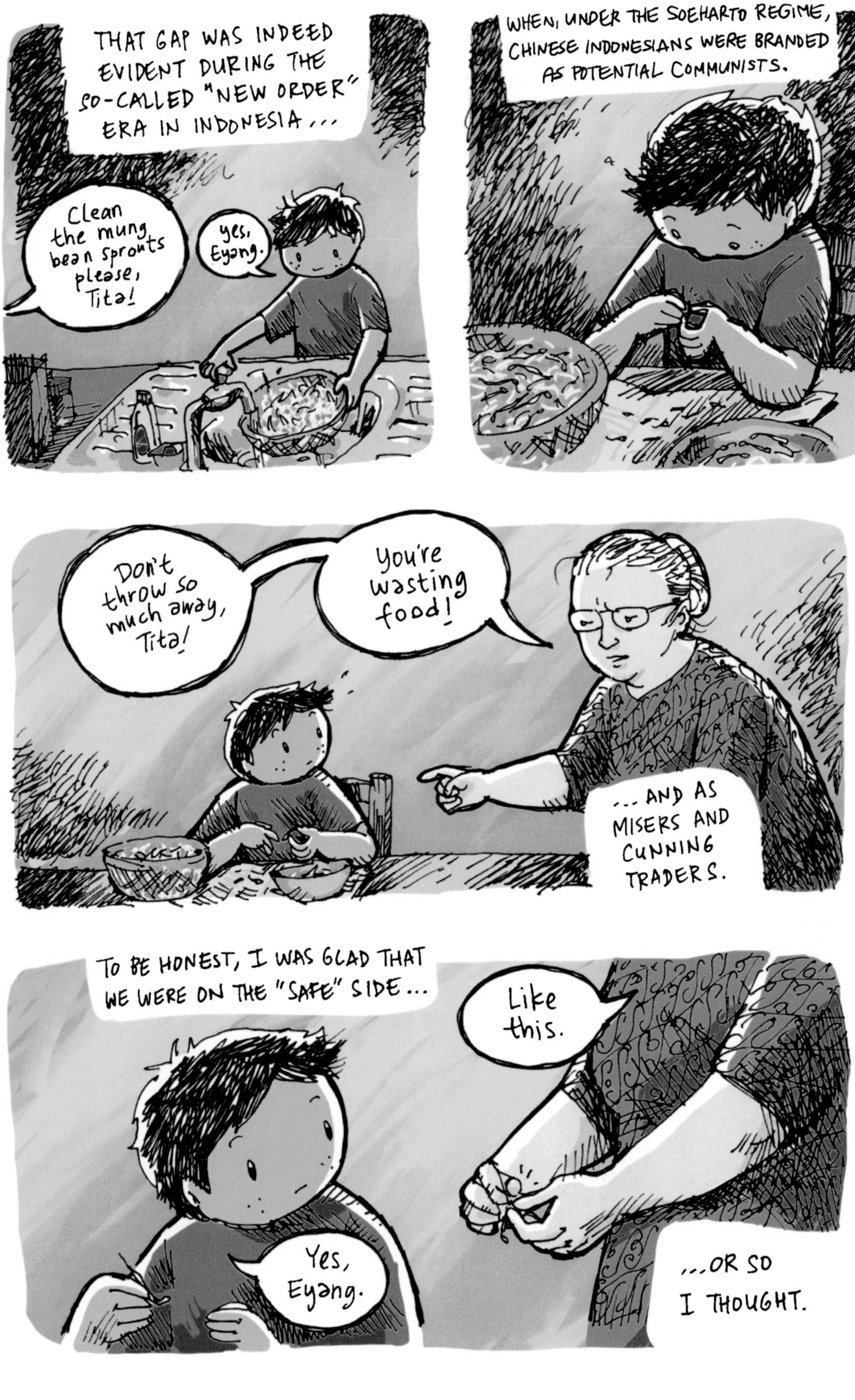
THAT GAP WAS INDEED EVIDENT DURING THE SO-CALLED "NEW ORDER" ERA IN INDONESIA...
Clean the mung bean sprouts please, Tita!
Yes, Eyang.
WHEN, UNDER THE SOEHARTO REGIME, CHINESE INDONESIANS WERE BRANDED AS POTENTIAL COMMUNISTS.
Don't throw so much away, Tita!
You're wasting food!
...AND AS MISERS AND CUNNING TRADERS.
TO BE HONEST, I WAS GLAD THAT WE WERE ON THE "SAFE" SIDE...
Like this.
Yes, Eyang.
...OR SO I THOUGHT.

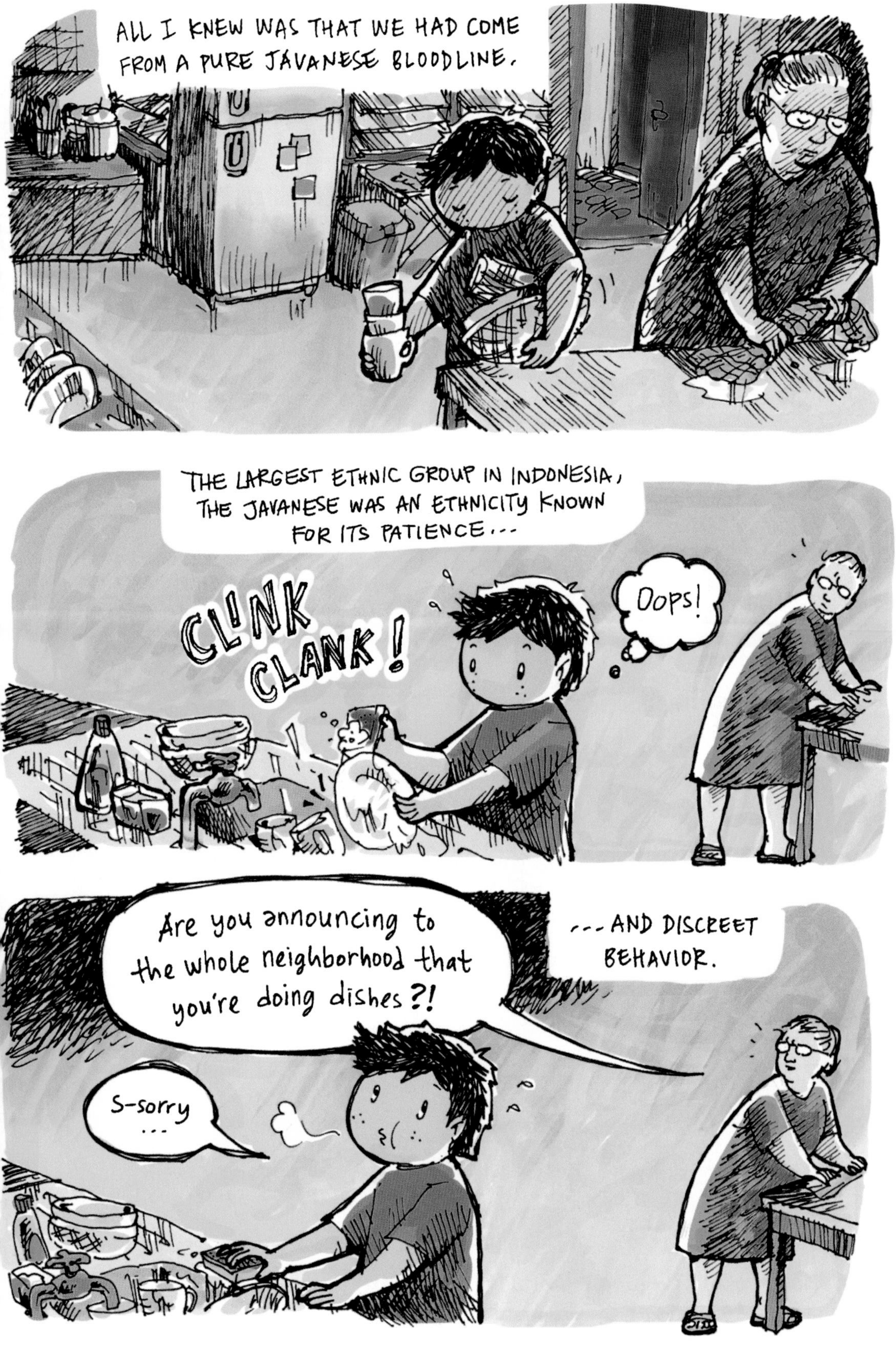
ALL I KNEW WAS THAT WE HAD COME FROM A PURE JAVANESE BLOODLINE.
THE LARGEST ETHNIC GROUP IN INDONESIA, THE JAVANESE WAS AN ETHNICITY KNOWN FOR ITS PATIENCE...
CLINK CLANK!
Oops!
Are you announcing to the whole neighborhood that you're doing dishes?!
...AND DISCREET BEHAVIOR.
S-sorry ...

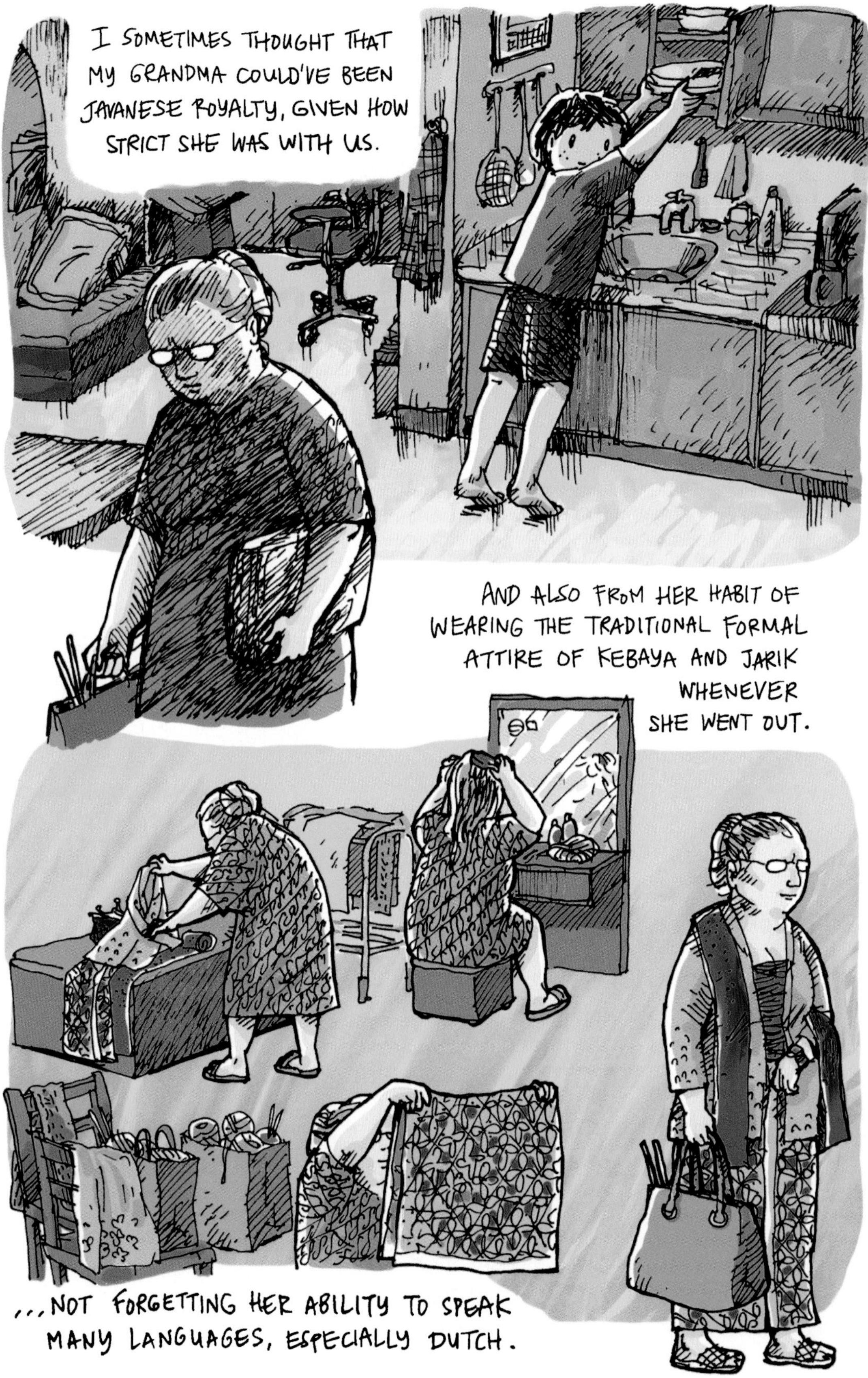
I SOMETIMES THOUGHT THAT MY GRANDMA COULD'VE BEEN JAVANESE ROYALTY, GIVEN HOW STRICT SHE WAS WITH US.
AND ALSO FROM HER HABIT OF WEARING THE TRADITIONAL FORMAL ATTIRE OF KEBAYA AND JARIK WHENEVER SHE WENT OUT.
...NOT FORGETTING HER ABILITY TO SPEAK MANY LANGUAGES, ESPECIALLY DUTCH.

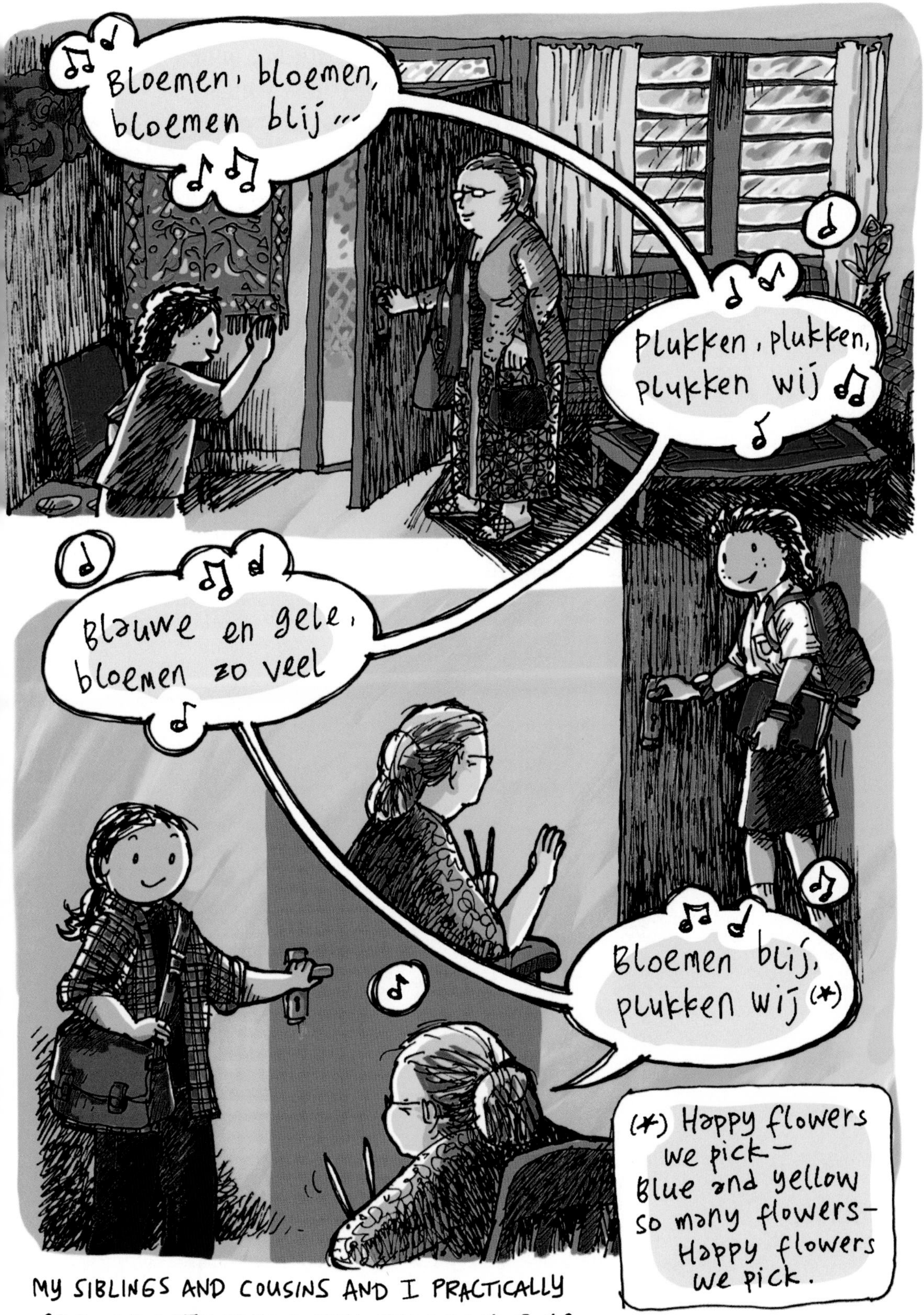

Bloemen, bloemen, bloemen blij...
plukken, plukken, plukken wij
Blauwe en gele, bloemen zo veel
Bloemen blij, plukken wij (*)
(*) Happy flowers we pick— Blue and yellow so many flowers— Happy flowers we pick.

MY SIBLINGS AND COUSINS AND I PRACTICALLY GREW UP WITH THIS DUTCH CHILDREN'S SONG.

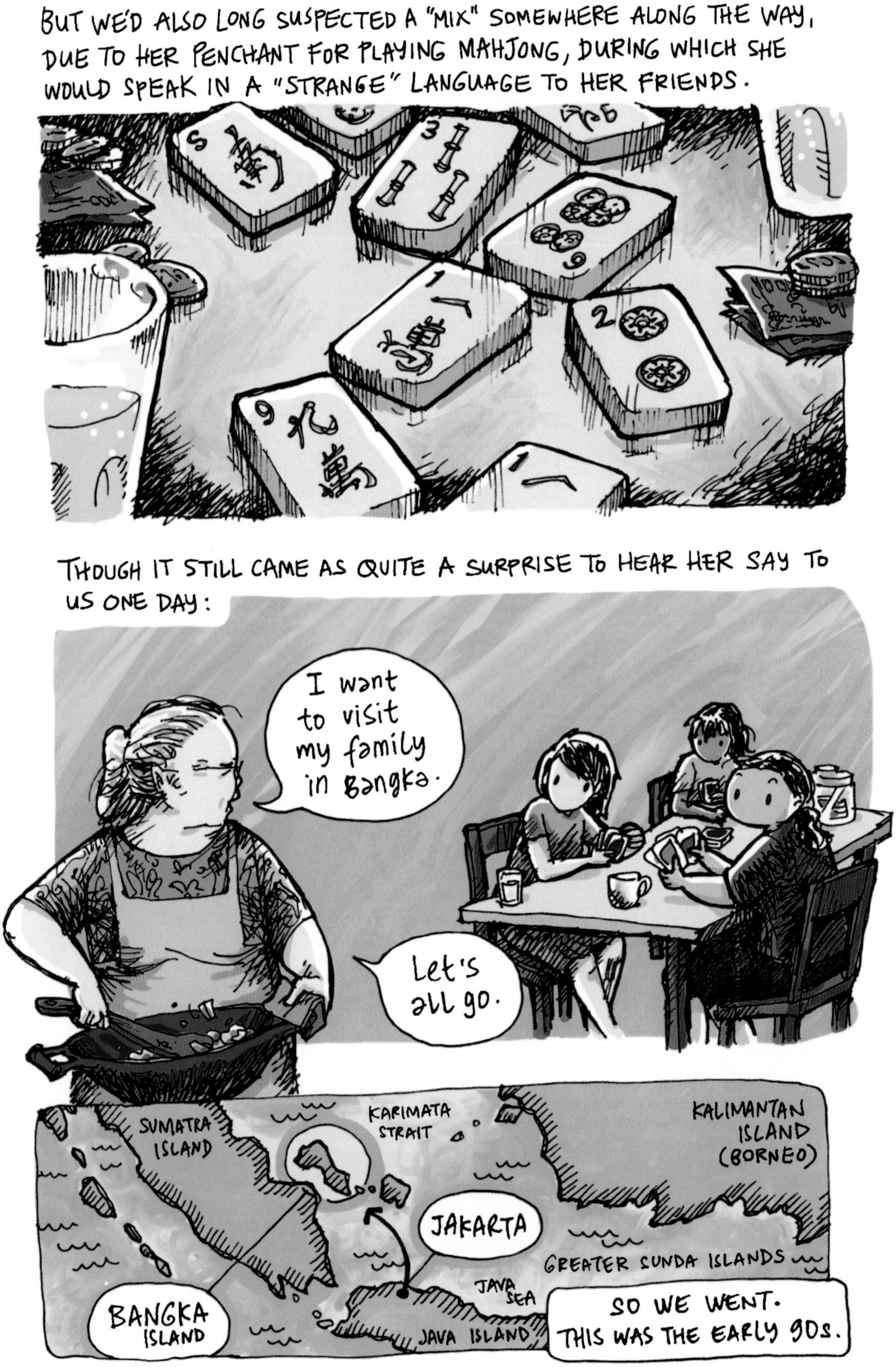
BUT WE'D ALSO LONG SUSPECTED A "MIX" SOMEWHERE ALONG THE WAY, DUE TO HER PENCHANT FOR PLAYING MAHJONG, DURING WHICH SHE WOULD SPEAK IN A "STRANGE" LANGUAGE TO HER FRIENDS.
THOUGH IT STILL CAME AS QUITE A SURPRISE TO HEAR HER SAY TO US ONE DAY:
I want to visit my family in Bangka.
Let's all go.
SUMATRA ISLAND
KARIMATA STRAIT
KALIMANTAN ISLAND (BORNEO)
JAKARTA
GREATER SUNDA ISLANDS
JAVA SEA
BANGKA ISLAND
JAVA ISLAND
SO WE WENT. THIS WAS THE EARLY 90s.

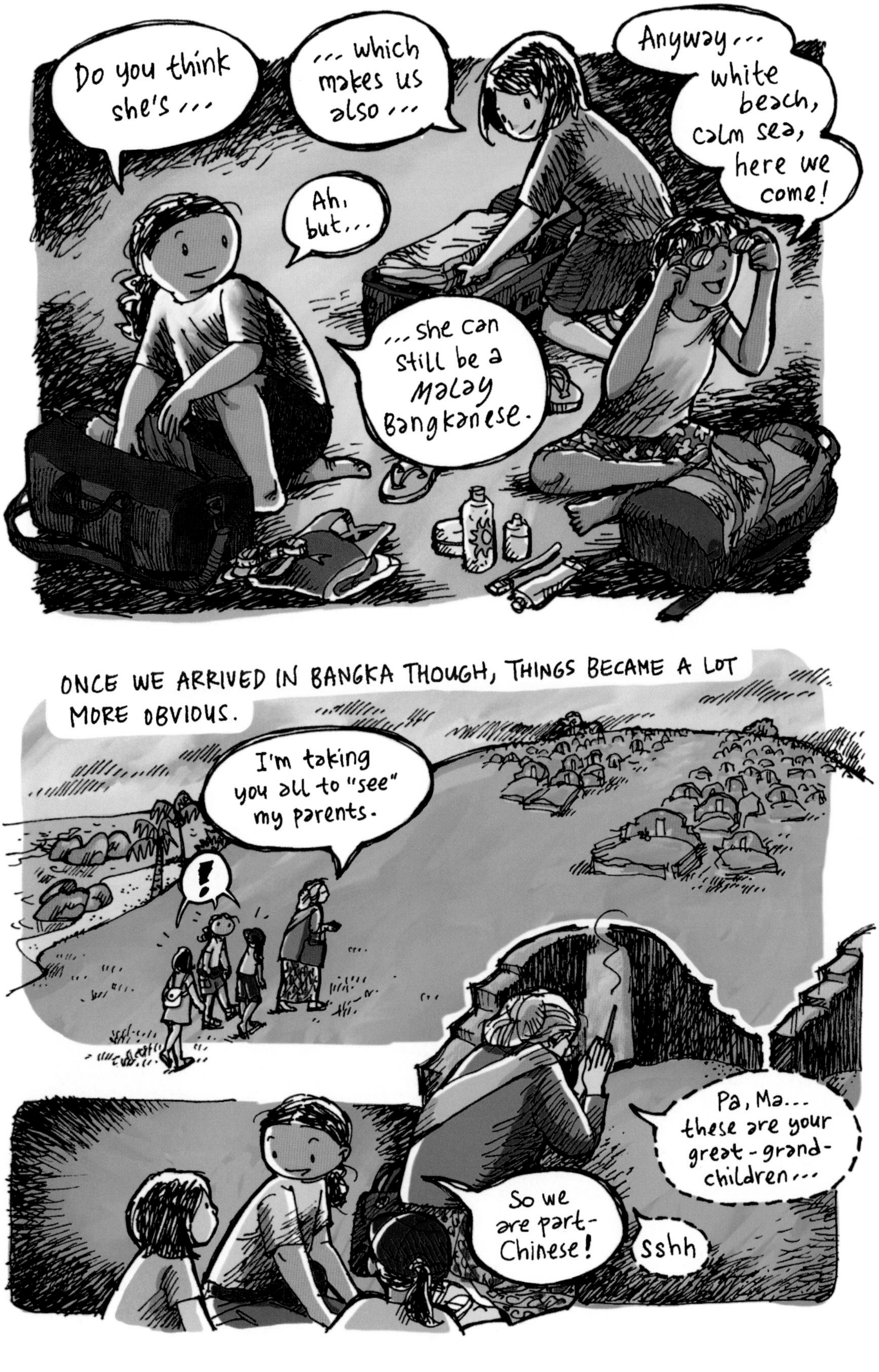
Do you think she's ...
... which makes us also ...
Anyway ... white beach, calm sea, here we come!
Ah, but ...
... she can still be a Malay Bangkanese.
ONCE WE ARRIVED IN BANGKA THOUGH, THINGS BECAME A LOT MORE OBVIOUS.
I'm taking you all to "see" my parents.
!
Pa, Ma... these are your great-grand-children...
So we are part-Chinese!
sshh

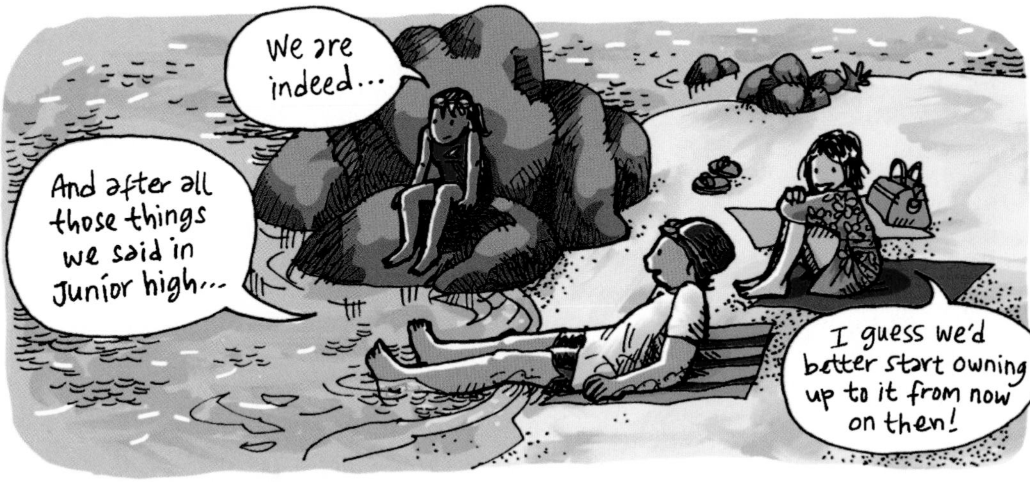
We are indeed...
And after all those things we said in Junior high...
I guess we'd better start owning up to it from now on then!

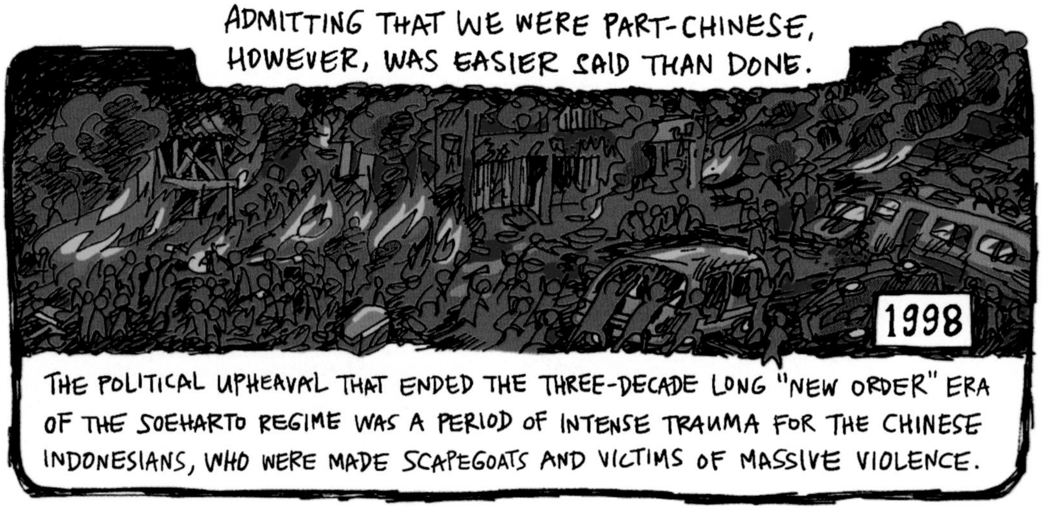
ADMITTING THAT WE WERE PART-CHINESE, HOWEVER, WAS EASIER SAID THAN DONE.
1998
THE POLITICAL UPHEAVAL THAT ENDED THE THREE-DECADE LONG "NEW ORDER" ERA OF THE SOEHARTO REGIME WAS A PERIOD OF INTENSE TRAUMA FOR THE CHINESE INDONESIANS, WHO WERE MADE SCAPEGOATS AND VICTIMS OF MASSIVE VIOLENCE.

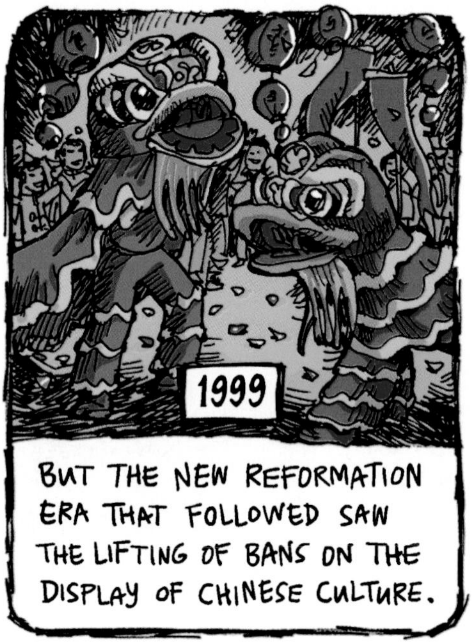
1999
BUT THE NEW REFORMATION ERA THAT FOLLOWED SAW THE LIFTING OF BANS ON THE DISPLAY OF CHINESE CULTURE.

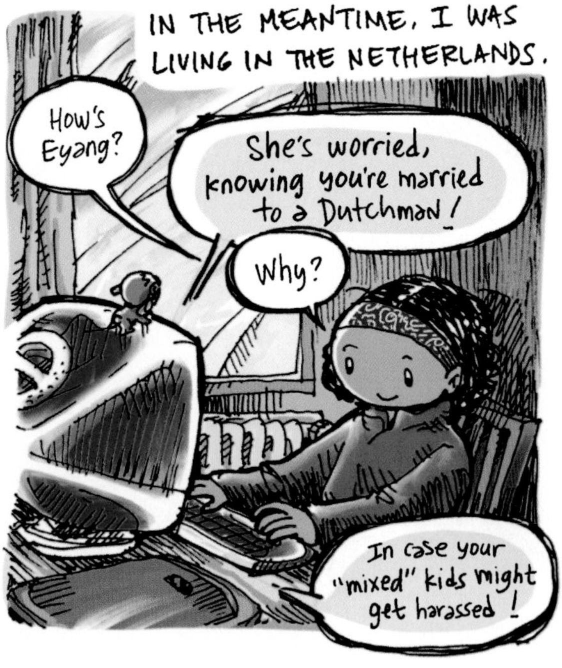
IN THE MEANTIME, I WAS LIVING IN THE NETHERLANDS.
How's Eyang?
She's worried, knowing you're married to a Dutchman!
Why?
In case your "mixed" kids might get harassed!

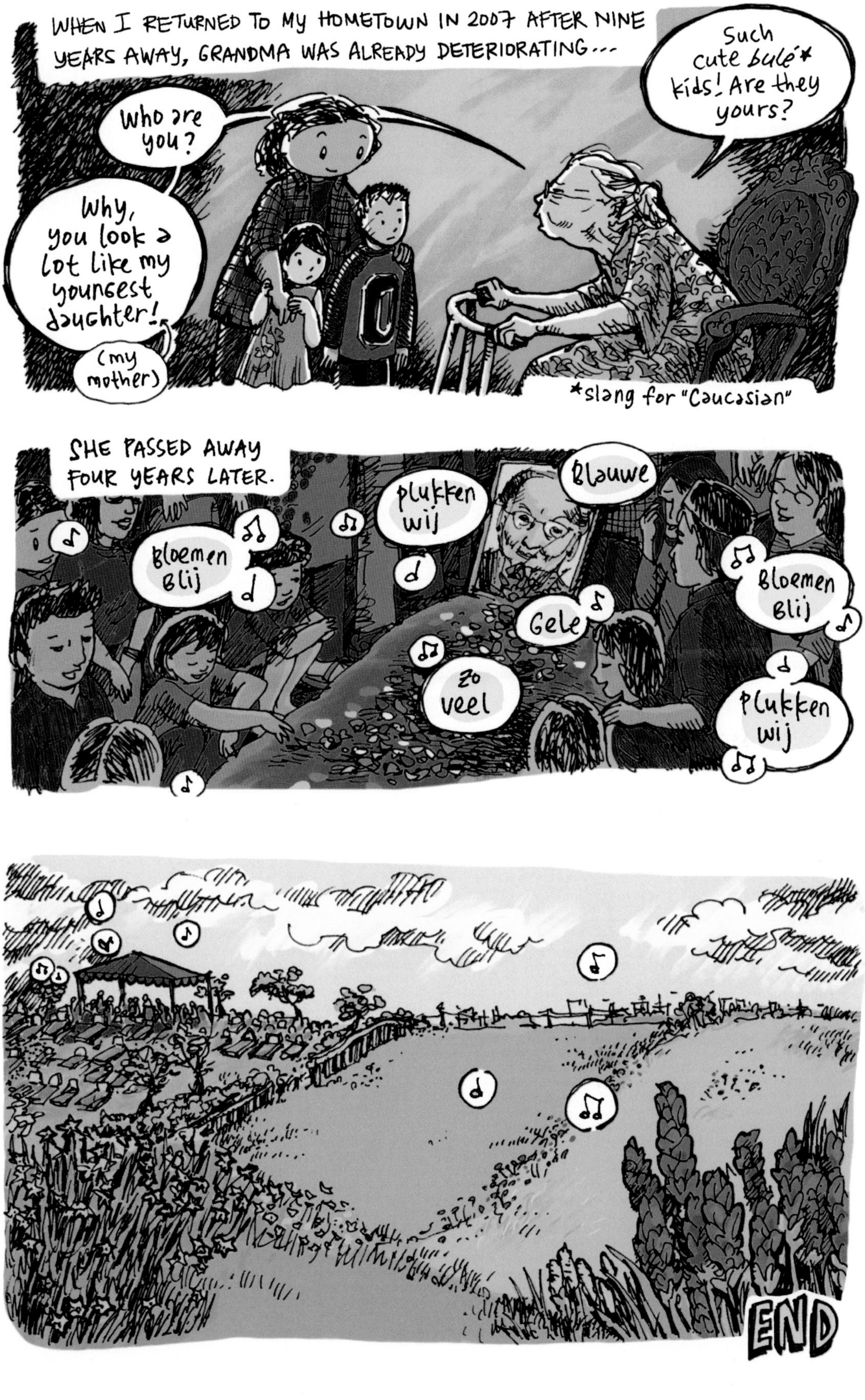
WHEN I RETURNED TO MY HOMETOWN IN 2007 AFTER NINE YEARS AWAY, GRANDMA WAS ALREADY DETERIORATING...
Who are you?
Why, you look a lot like my youngest daughter!
(my mother)
Such cute bulé* kids! Are they yours?
*slang for "Caucasian"
SHE PASSED AWAY FOUR YEARS LATER.
Bloemen Blij
plukken wij
Blauwe
Gele
zo veel
Bloemen Blij
plukken wij
END

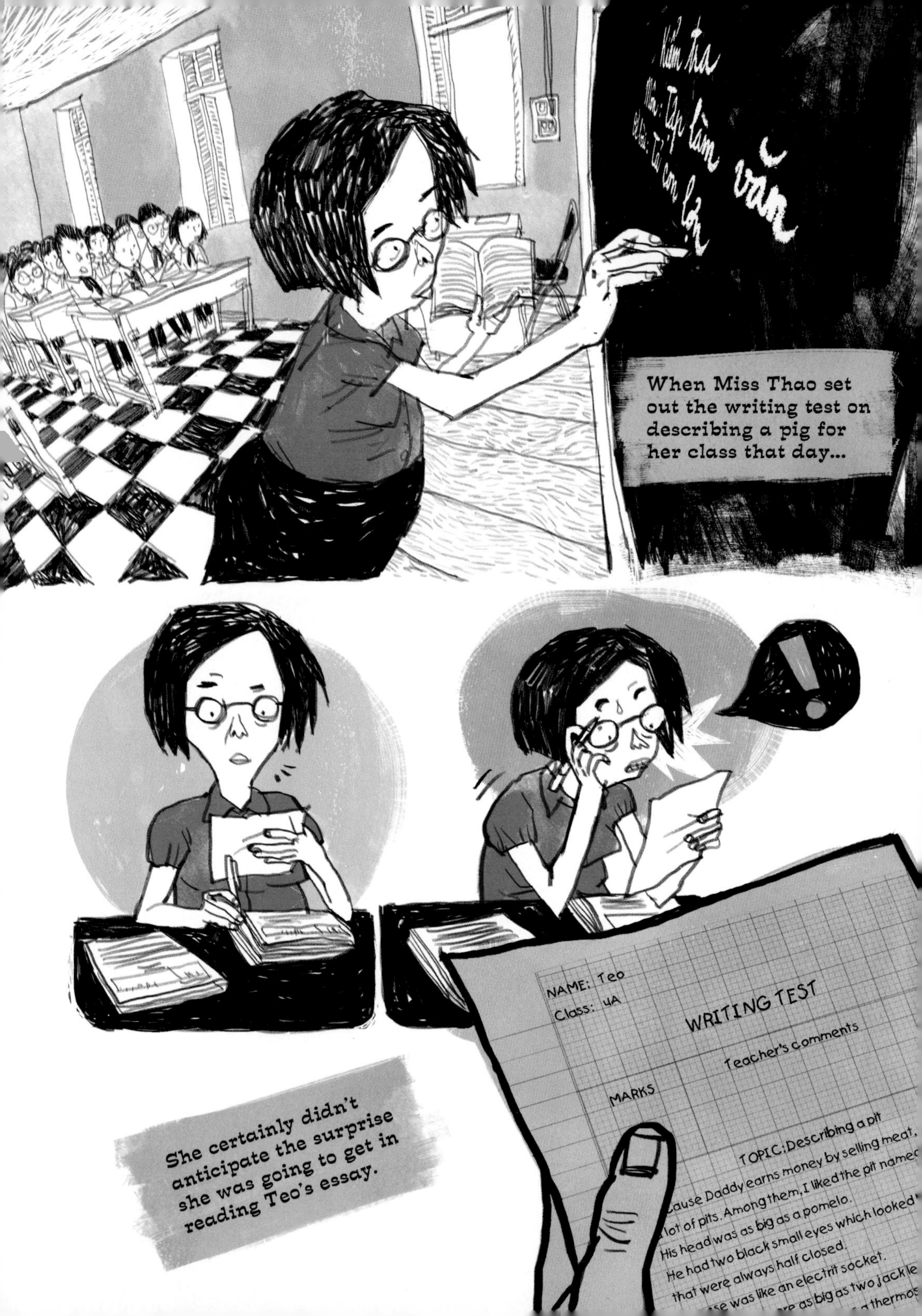

Kiểm tra
Tập làm văn
Tả con lợn
When Miss Thao set out the writing test on describing a pig for her class that day...
!
NAME: Teo
Class: 4A
WRITING TEST
Teacher's comments
MARKS
TOPIC: Describing a pit
earns money by selling meat,
lot of pits. Among them, I liked the pit named
His head was as big as a pomelo.
He had two black small eyes which looked
that were always half closed.
was like an electrit socket.
She certainly didn't anticipate the surprise she was going to get in reading Teo's essay.

Thành Phong + Gà ri

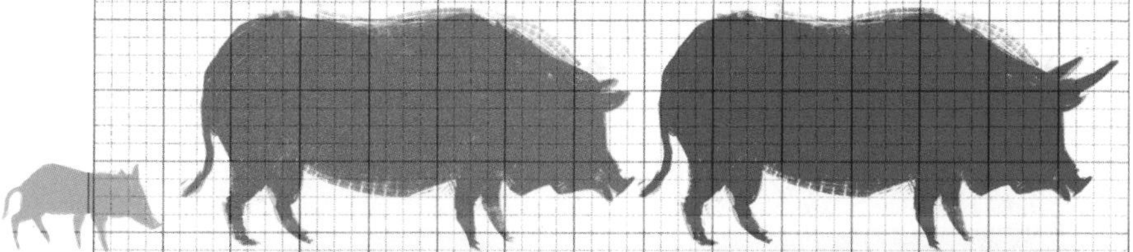

PIG WHEN SMALL - COW WHEN BIG

fong 2012

http://www.behance.net/fong210

Because Daddy earns money by selling meat, my family raises

a lot of pits. Among them, I liked the pit named 102 best.

pigs

pig

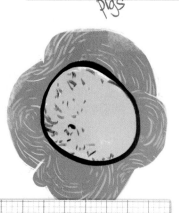

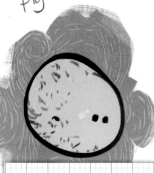

His head was as big as a pomelo.

He had two black small eyes
which looked like two marbles
that were always half-closed.

electric

His nose was like an electrit socket.

ears

His two years were as big
as two jack leaves.

His body was just as small as a thermos flask,

months

because he was only two month old.

hair

His air was as hard
as a brush.

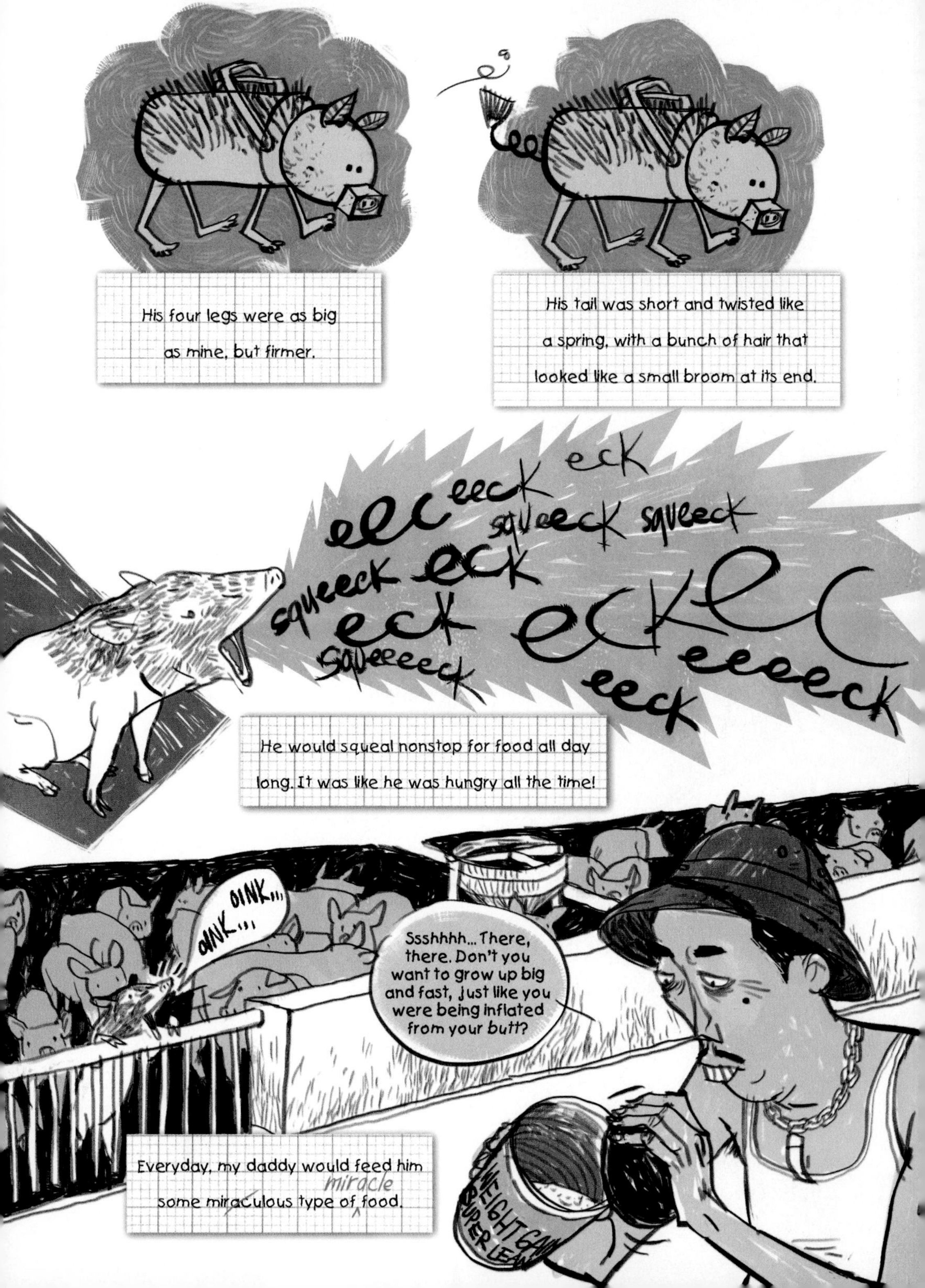
His four legs were as big as mine, but firmer.
His tail was short and twisted like a spring, with a bunch of hair that looked like a small broom at its end.
eck
eeck
squeeck squeeck
squeeck eck
eck
squeeeeck
eck
eeeeeck
eeck
He would squeal nonstop for food all day long. It was like he was hungry all the time!
OINK,,, OINK,,,
Ssshhhh... There, there. Don't you want to grow up big and fast, just like you were being inflated from your butt?
Everyday, my daddy would feed him some miraculous type of food.
miracle
WEIGHTGAIN
SUPER LEAN

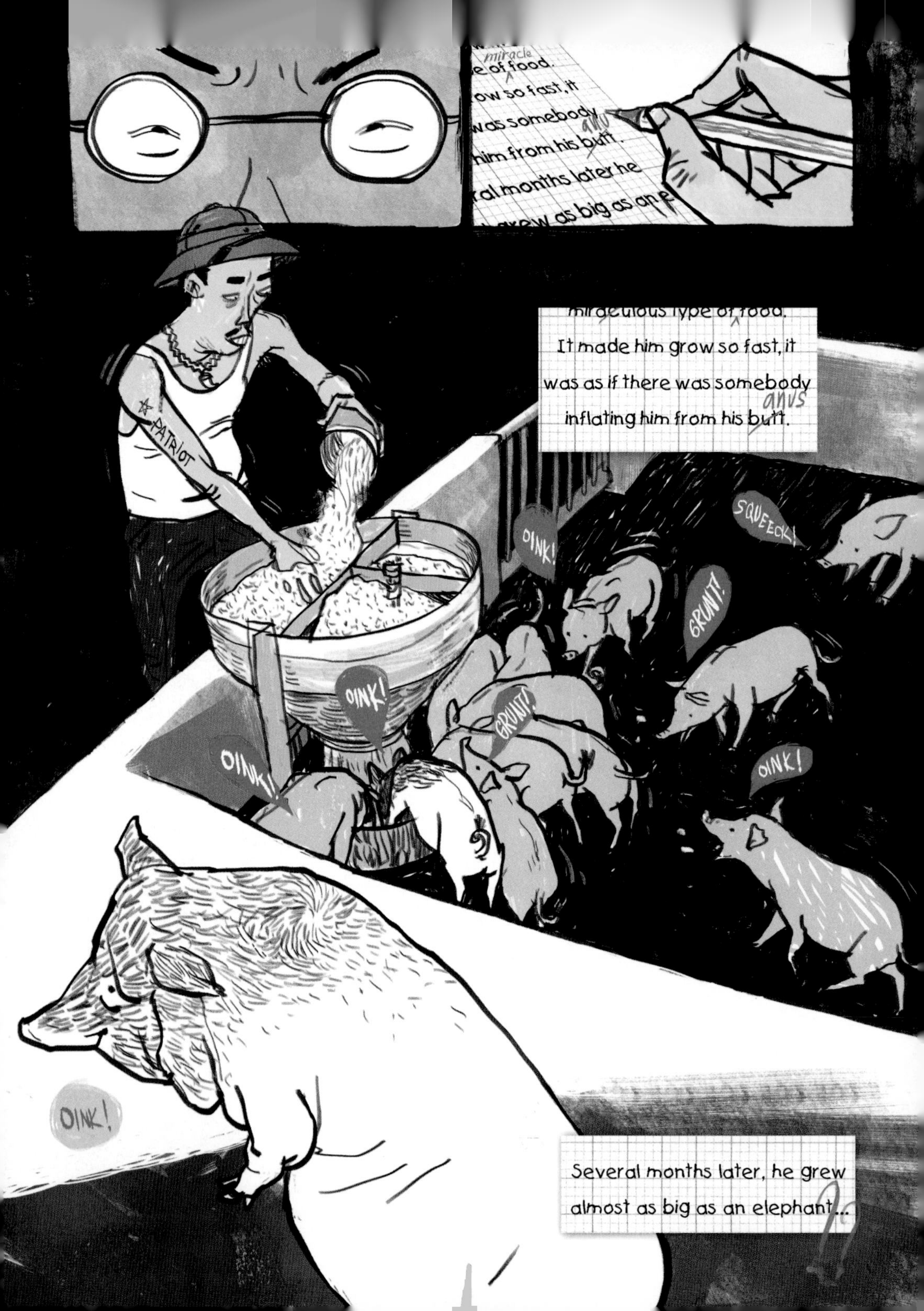

e of miracle food.
ow so fast, it
was somebody
him from his anus butt.
al months later he
grew as big as an e
PATRIOT
It made him grow so fast, it
was as if there was somebody
inflating him from his anus butt.
SQUEEECK!
OINK!
GRUNT!
OINK!
GRUNT!
OINK!
OINK!
OINK!
Several months later, he grew
almost as big as an elephant...

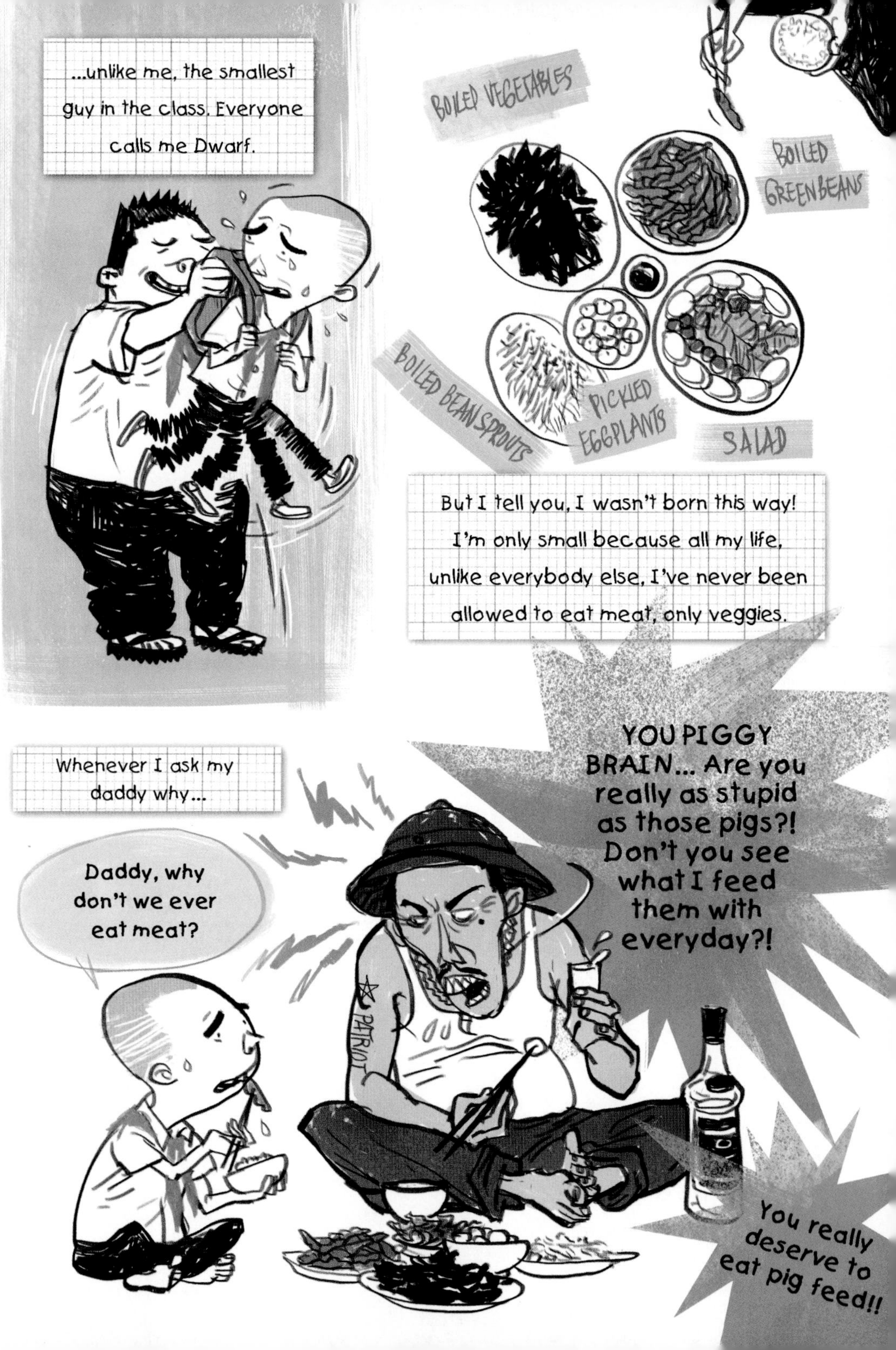

...unlike me, the smallest guy in the class. Everyone calls me Dwarf.
BOILED VEGETABLES
BOILED GREENBEANS
BOILED BEAN SPROUTS
PICKLED EGGPLANTS
SALAD
But I tell you, I wasn't born this way! I'm only small because all my life, unlike everybody else, I've never been allowed to eat meat, only veggies.
Whenever I ask my daddy why...
Daddy, why don't we ever eat meat?
YOU PIGGY BRAIN... Are you really as stupid as those pigs?! Don't you see what I feed them with everyday?!
You really deserve to eat pig feed!!
PATRIOT

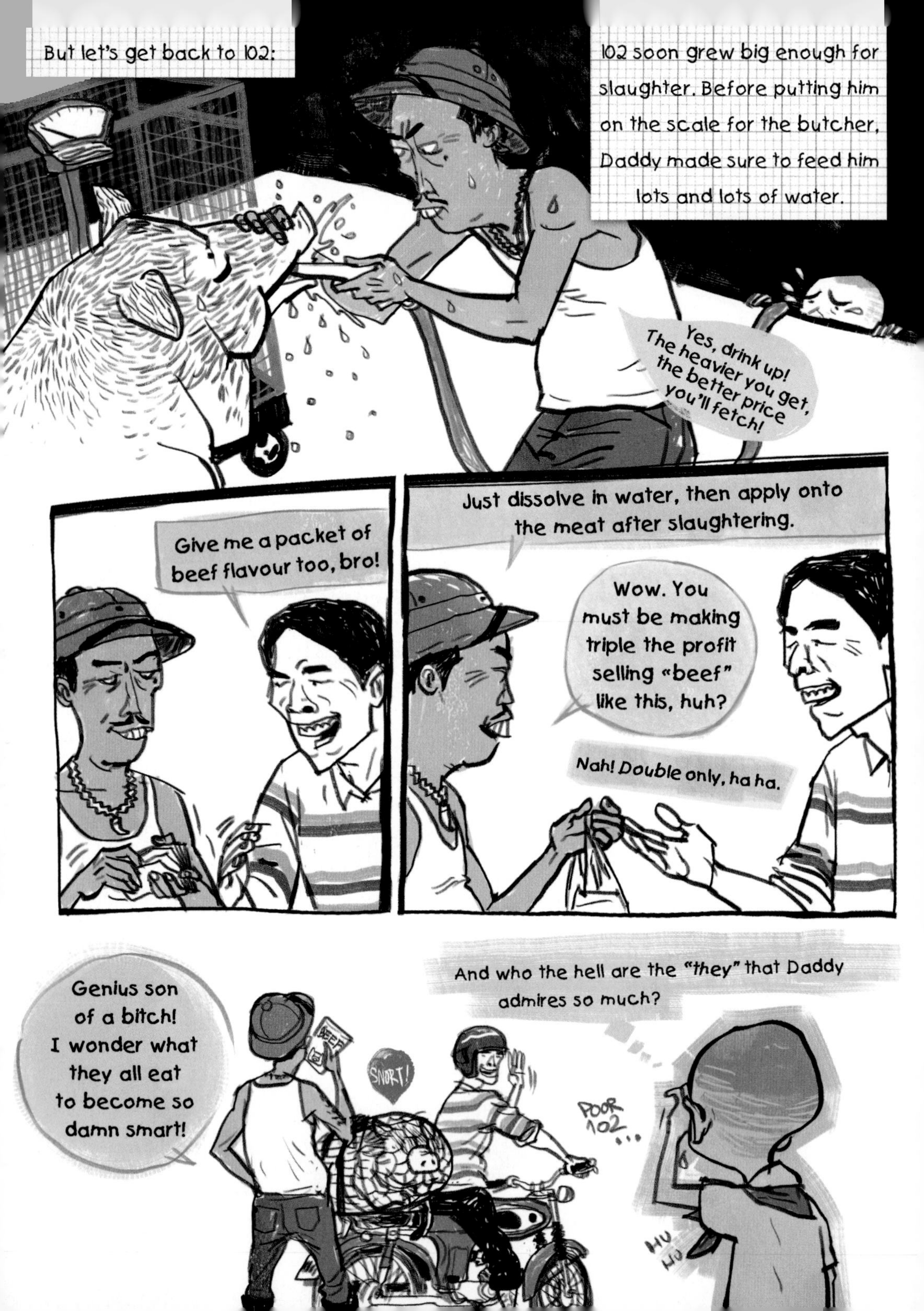

But let's get back to 102:
102 soon grew big enough for slaughter. Before putting him on the scale for the butcher, Daddy made sure to feed him lots and lots of water.
Yes, drink up! The heavier you get, the better price you'll fetch!
Give me a packet of beef flavour too, bro!
Just dissolve in water, then apply onto the meat after slaughtering.
Wow. You must be making triple the profit selling "beef" like this, huh?
Nah! Double only, ha ha.
Genius son of a bitch! I wonder what they all eat to become so damn smart!
BEEF
SNORT!
And who the hell are the "they" that Daddy admires so much?
POOR 102...
HU HU

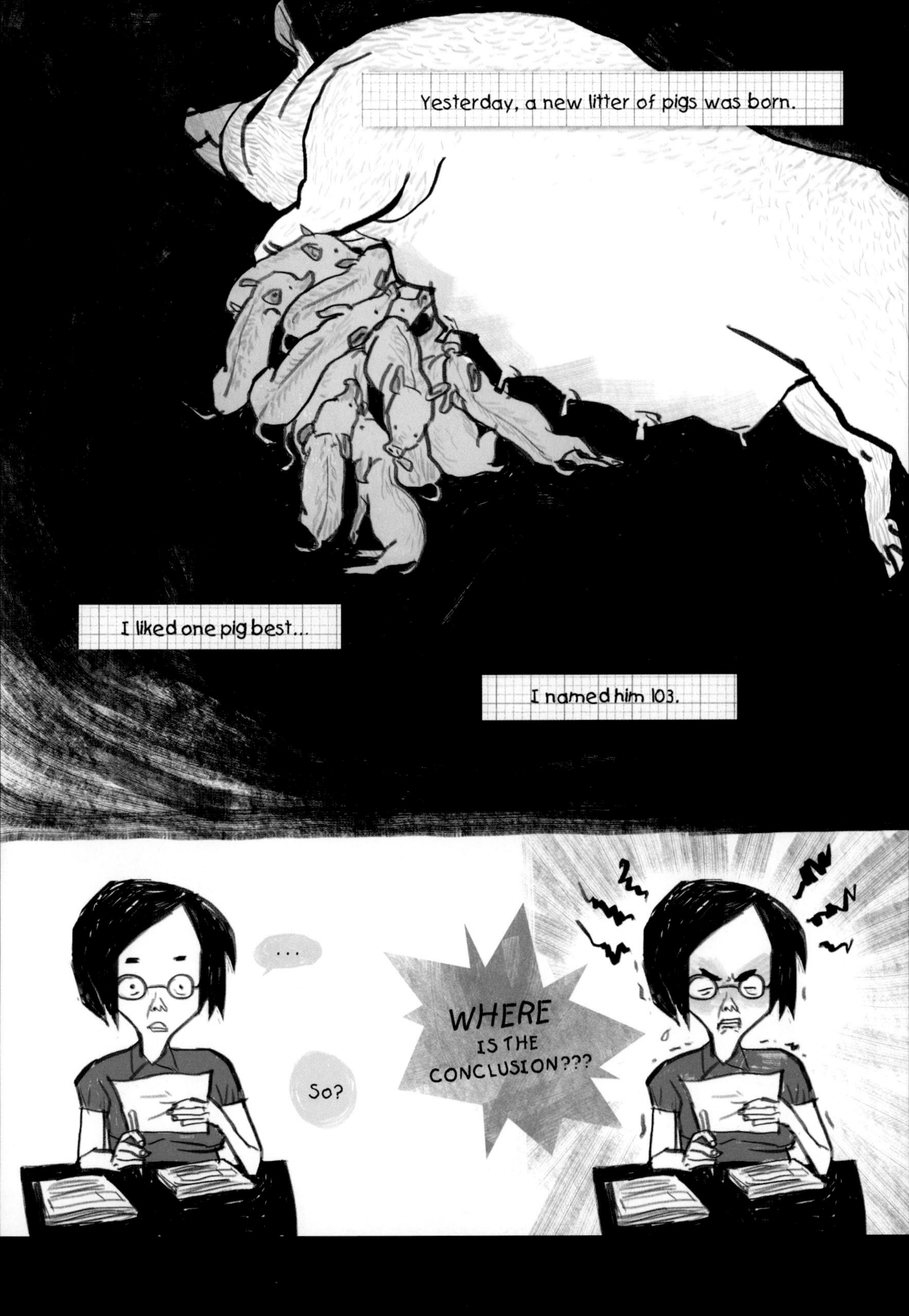
Yesterday, a new litter of pigs was born.
I liked one pig best...
I named him 103.
...
So?
WHERE IS THE CONCLUSION???

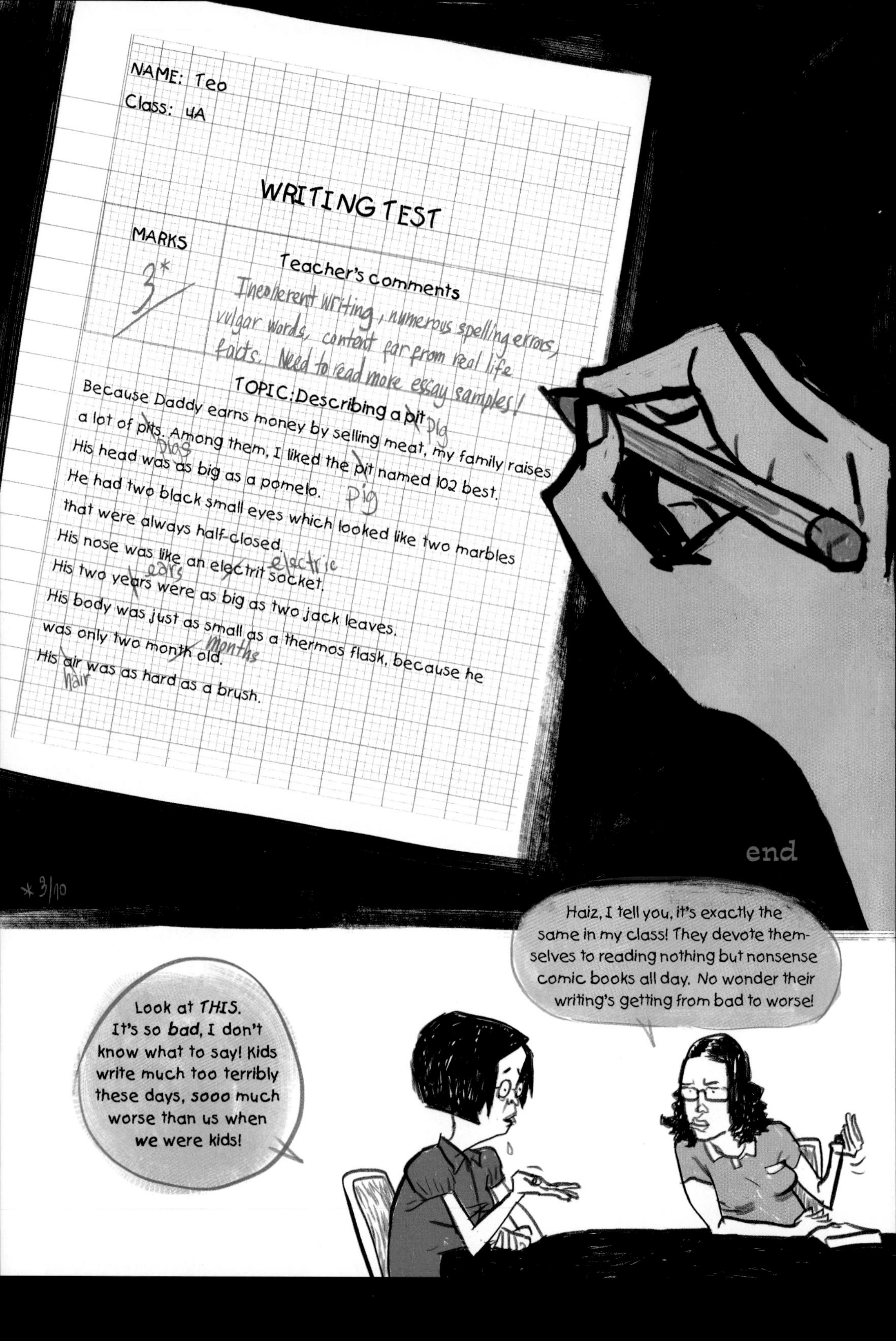
NAME: Teo
Class: 4A
WRITING TEST
MARKS
3*
Teacher's comments
Incoherent writing, numerous spelling errors, vulgar words, content far from real life facts. Need to read more essay samples!
TOPIC: Describing a pit pig
Because Daddy earns money by selling meat, my family raises a lot of pits. Among them, I liked the pit named 102 best.
pigs
pig
His head was as big as a pomelo.
He had two black small eyes which looked like two marbles that were always half-closed.
His nose was like an electrit socket.
electric
His two years were as big as two jack leaves.
ears
His body was just as small as a thermos flask, because he was only two month old.
months
His air was as hard as a brush.
hair
end
* 3/10
Look at THIS. It's so bad, I don't know what to say! Kids write much too terribly these days, sooo much worse than us when we were kids!
Haiz, I tell you, it's exactly the same in my class! They devote themselves to reading nothing but nonsense comic books all day. No wonder their writing's getting from bad to worse!

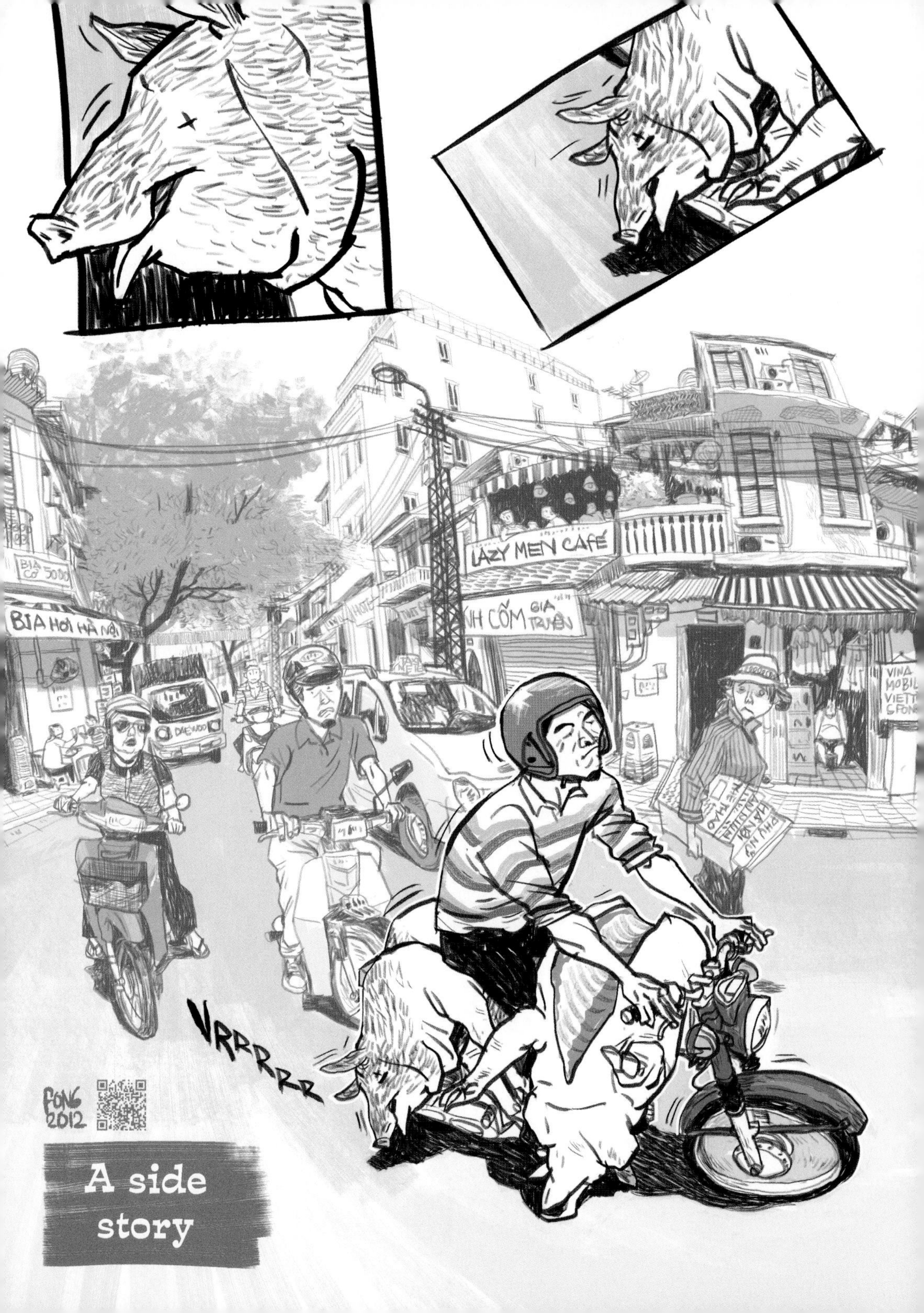
LAZY MEN CAFÉ
BIA HƠI HÀ NỘI
VRRRRRR
FONG 2012
A side story

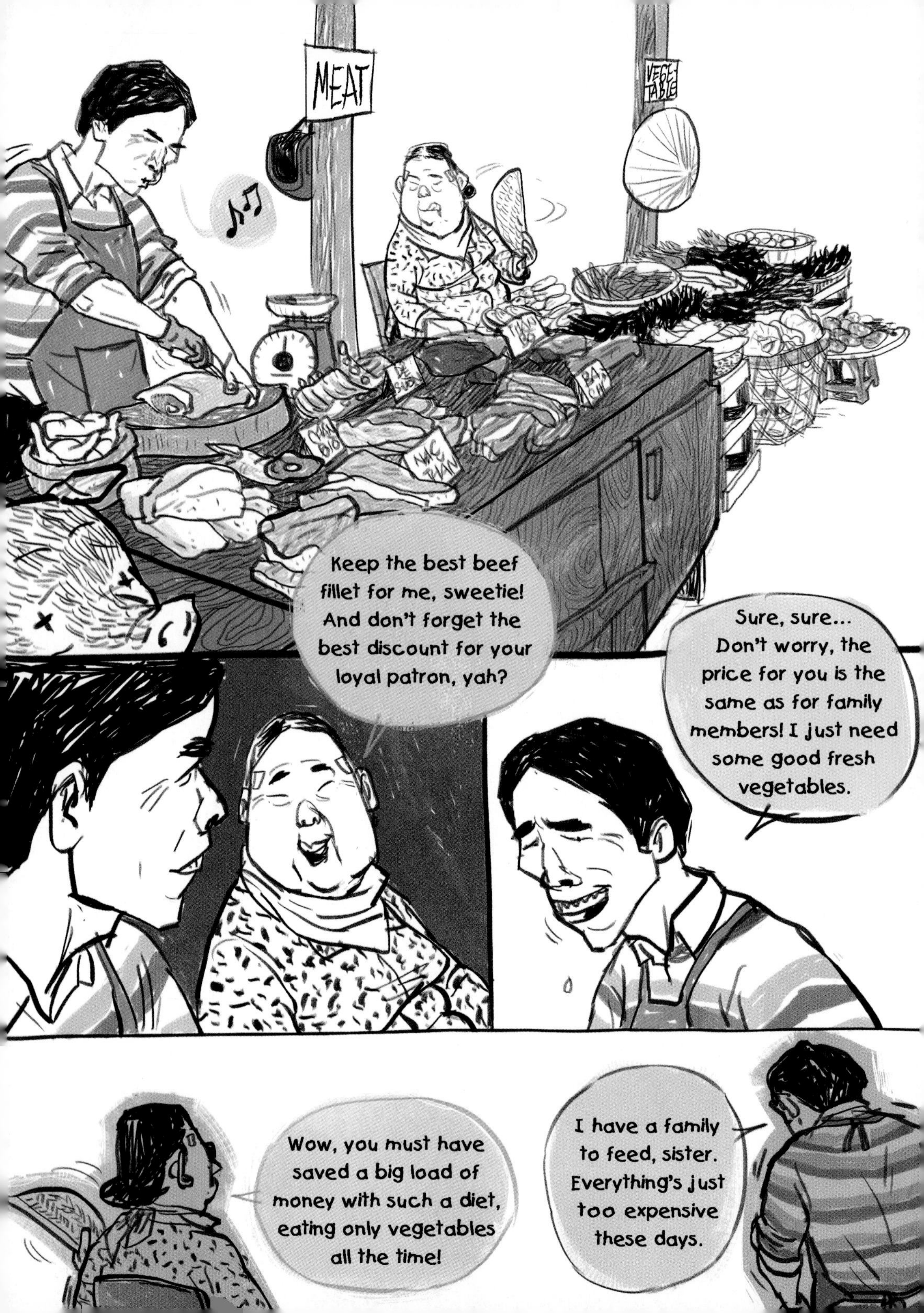
MEAT
VEGE-TABLE
Keep the best beef fillet for me, sweetie! And don't forget the best discount for your loyal patron, yah?
Sure, sure... Don't worry, the price for you is the same as for family members! I just need some good fresh vegetables.
Wow, you must have saved a big load of money with such a diet, eating only vegetables all the time!
I have a family to feed, sister. Everything's just too expensive these days.

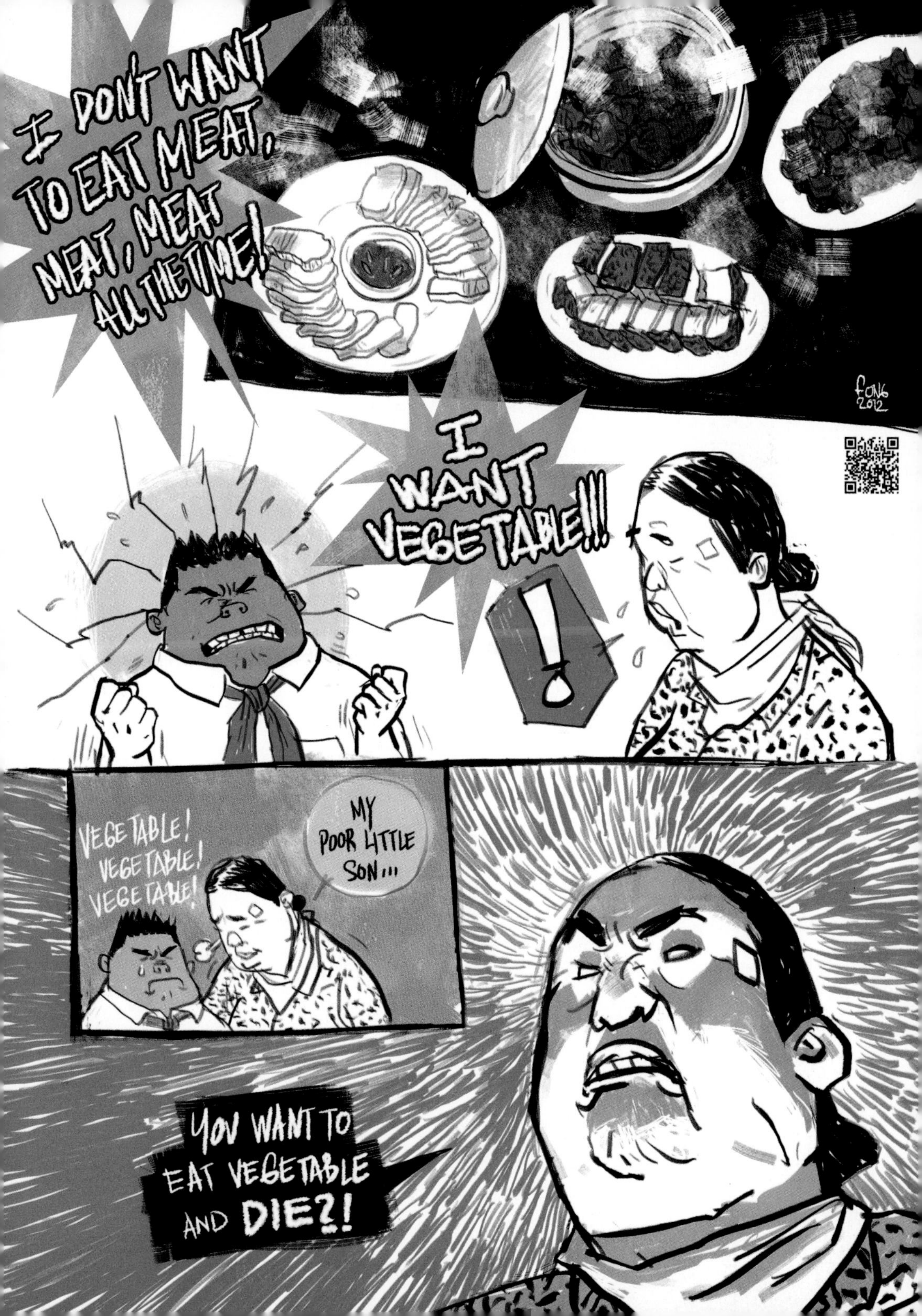

I DON'T WANT TO EAT MEAT, MEAT, MEAT ALL THE TIME!
FONG 2012
I WANT VEGETABLE!!!
!
VEGETABLE! VEGETABLE! VEGETABLE!
MY POOR LITTLE SON...
YOU WANT TO EAT VEGETABLE AND DIE?!

BEAST WARS
CARTOON NETWORK
HBO
JURASSIC PARK
Captain N
BILL NYE
ATCHING A RER
K OVER THE S

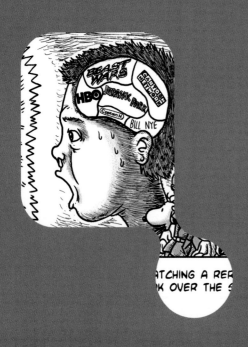

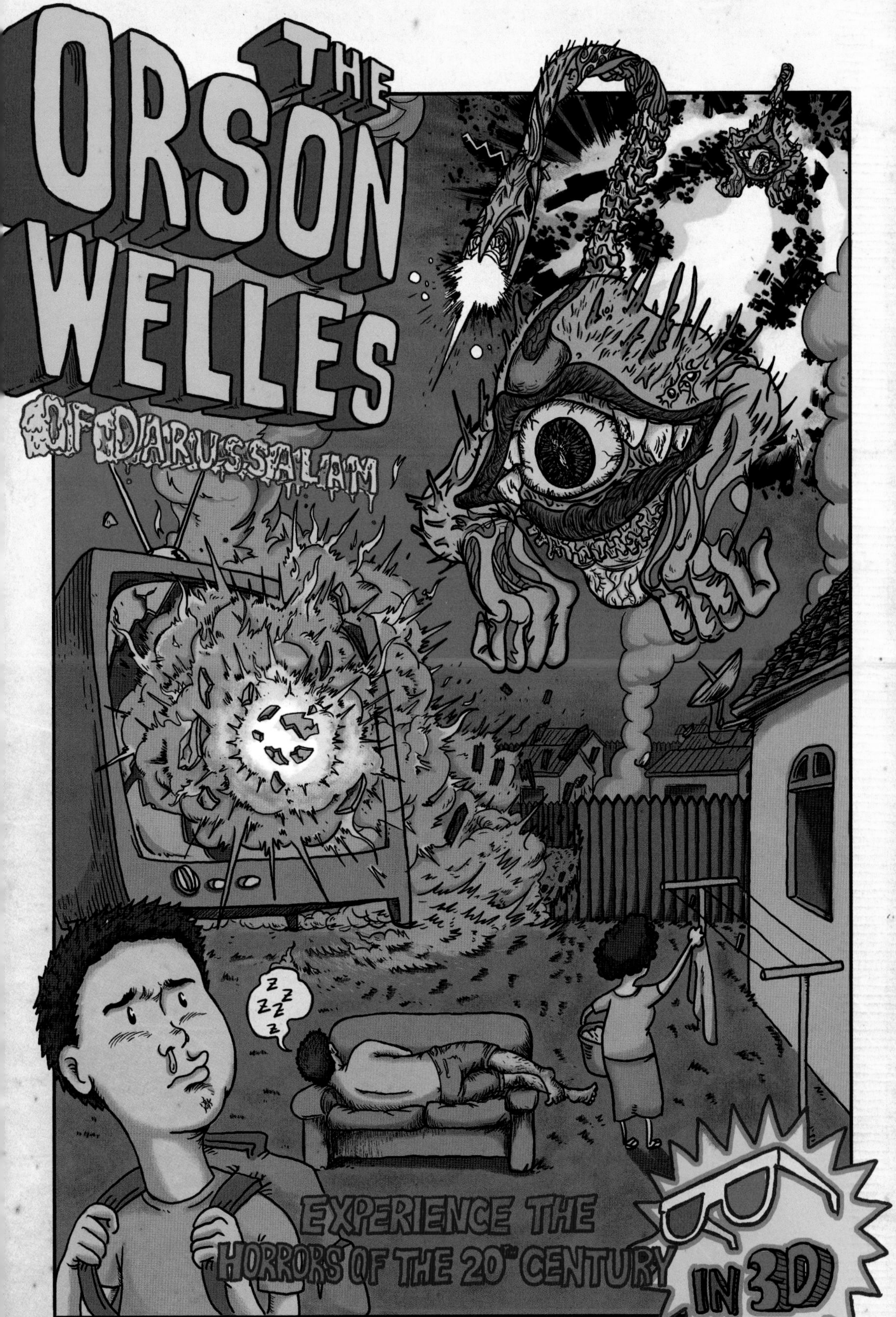
THE ORSON WELLES
OF DARUSSALAM
Z Z Z Z Z Z
EXPERIENCE THE HORRORS OF THE 20TH CENTURY
IN 3D
PRESENTED IN SPECTACULAR TECHNICOLOR
A COMIC BY: JIN HIEN LAU

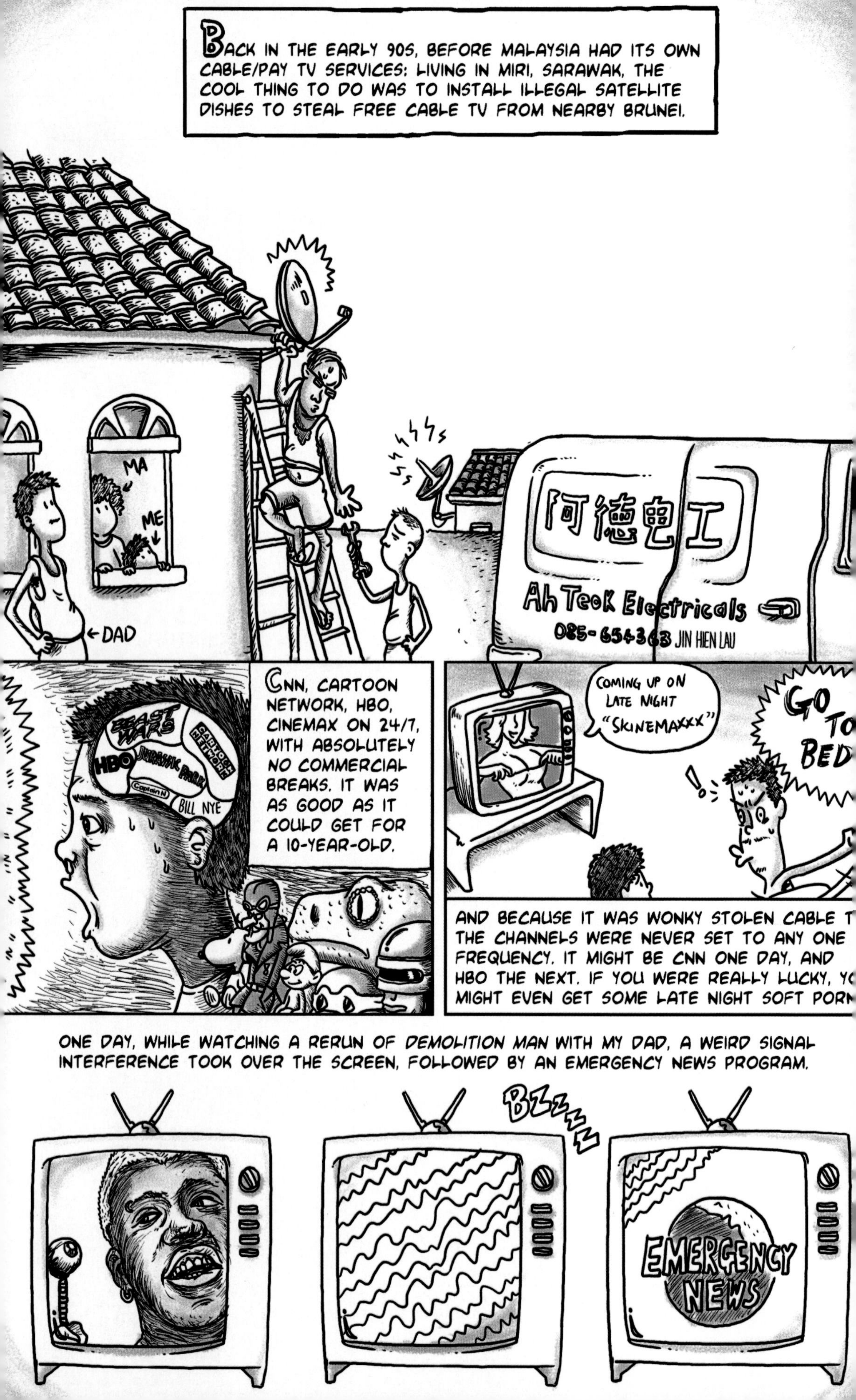

BACK IN THE EARLY 90S, BEFORE MALAYSIA HAD ITS OWN CABLE/PAY TV SERVICES: LIVING IN MIRI, SARAWAK, THE COOL THING TO DO WAS TO INSTALL ILLEGAL SATELLITE DISHES TO STEAL FREE CABLE TV FROM NEARBY BRUNEI.
MA
ME
← DAD
阿德电工
Ah Teok Electricals
085-654363
JIN HIEN LAU
BEAST WARS
CARTOON NETWORK
HBO
JURASSIC PARK
Captain N
BILL NYE
CNN, CARTOON NETWORK, HBO, CINEMAX ON 24/7, WITH ABSOLUTELY NO COMMERCIAL BREAKS. IT WAS AS GOOD AS IT COULD GET FOR A 10-YEAR-OLD.
COMING UP ON LATE NIGHT "SKINEMAXXX"
GO TO BED
!
AND BECAUSE IT WAS WONKY STOLEN CABLE T
THE CHANNELS WERE NEVER SET TO ANY ONE
FREQUENCY. IT MIGHT BE CNN ONE DAY, AND
HBO THE NEXT. IF YOU WERE REALLY LUCKY, YO
MIGHT EVEN GET SOME LATE NIGHT SOFT PORN
ONE DAY, WHILE WATCHING A RERUN OF DEMOLITION MAN WITH MY DAD, A WEIRD SIGNAL INTERFERENCE TOOK OVER THE SCREEN, FOLLOWED BY AN EMERGENCY NEWS PROGRAM.
BZZZZ
EMERGENCY NEWS

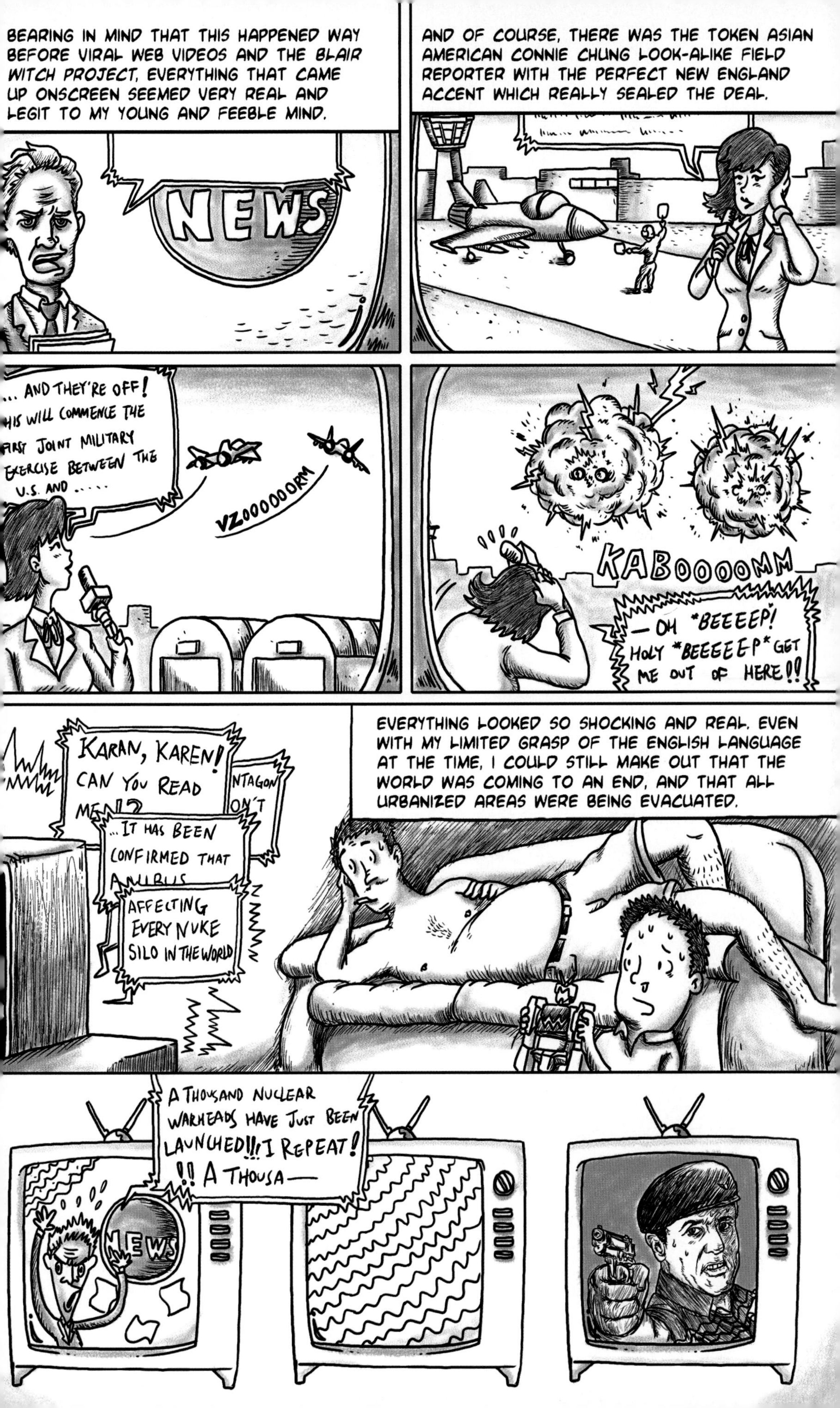

BEARING IN MIND THAT THIS HAPPENED WAY BEFORE VIRAL WEB VIDEOS AND THE BLAIR WITCH PROJECT, EVERYTHING THAT CAME UP ONSCREEN SEEMED VERY REAL AND LEGIT TO MY YOUNG AND FEEBLE MIND.
AND OF COURSE, THERE WAS THE TOKEN ASIAN AMERICAN CONNIE CHUNG LOOK-ALIKE FIELD REPORTER WITH THE PERFECT NEW ENGLAND ACCENT WHICH REALLY SEALED THE DEAL.
NEWS
... AND THEY'RE OFF! HIS WILL COMMENCE THE FIRST JOINT MILITARY EXERCISE BETWEEN THE U.S. AND .....
VZOOOOOORM
KABOOOOMM
— OH *BEEEEP! HOLY *BEEEEEP* GET ME OUT OF HERE!!
KARAN, KAREN! CAN YOU READ ME!?
NTAGON
ON'T
... IT HAS BEEN CONFIRMED THAT
AFFECTING EVERY NUKE SILO IN THE WORLD
EVERYTHING LOOKED SO SHOCKING AND REAL. EVEN WITH MY LIMITED GRASP OF THE ENGLISH LANGUAGE AT THE TIME, I COULD STILL MAKE OUT THAT THE WORLD WAS COMING TO AN END, AND THAT ALL URBANIZED AREAS WERE BEING EVACUATED.
A THOUSAND NUCLEAR WARHEADS HAVE JUST BEEN LAUNCHED!!! I REPEAT! !! A THOUSA—
NEWS

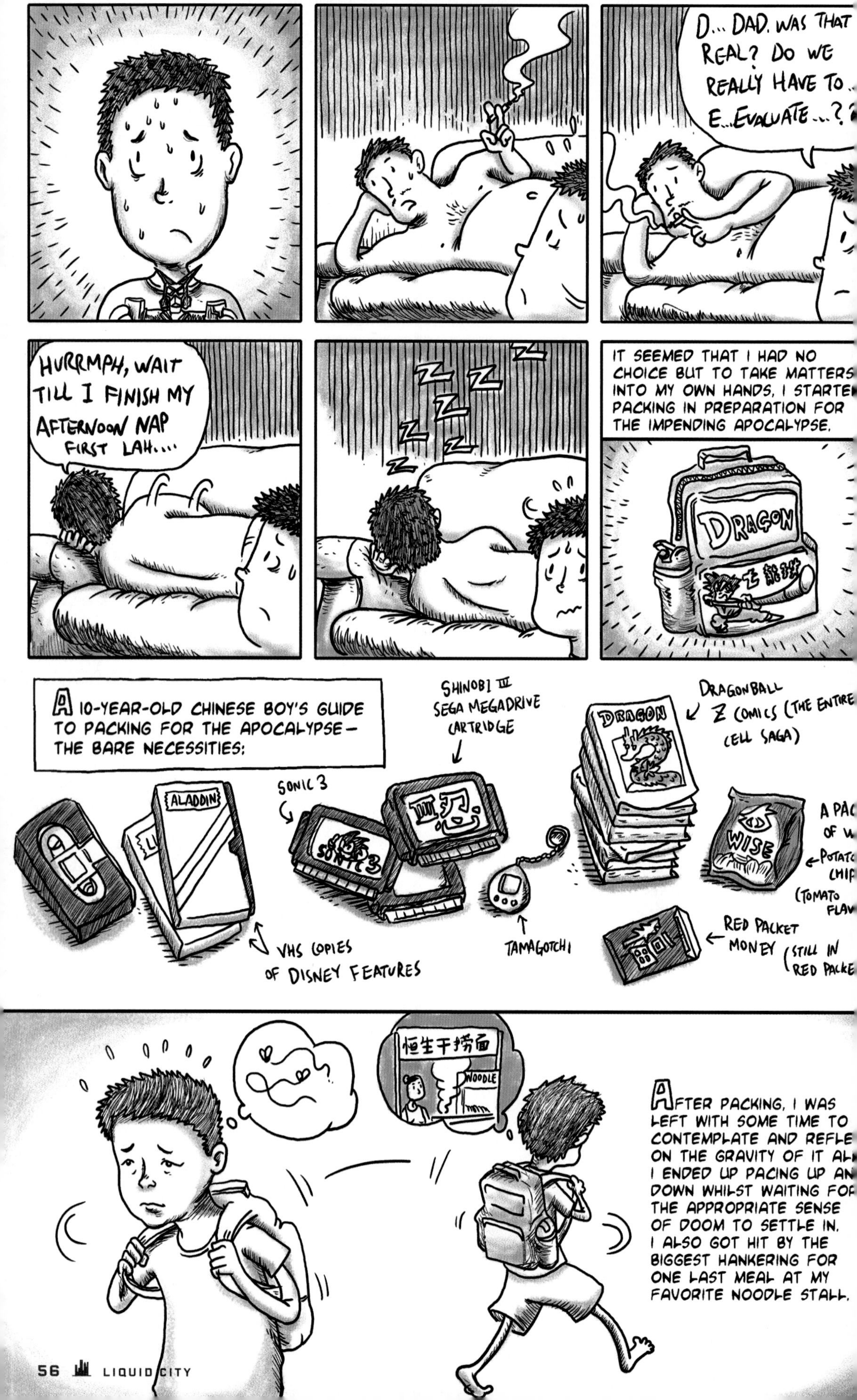
D... DAD. WAS THAT REAL? DO WE REALLY HAVE TO... E...EVACUATE...?
HURRMPH, WAIT TILL I FINISH MY AFTERNOON NAP FIRST LAH....
Z Z Z Z Z Z Z
IT SEEMED THAT I HAD NO CHOICE BUT TO TAKE MATTERS INTO MY OWN HANDS, I STARTE PACKING IN PREPARATION FOR THE IMPENDING APOCALYPSE.
DRAGON
A 10-YEAR-OLD CHINESE BOY'S GUIDE TO PACKING FOR THE APOCALYPSE – THE BARE NECESSITIES:
SHINOBI III SEGA MEGADRIVE CARTRIDGE
DRAGONBALL Z COMICS (THE ENTIRE CELL SAGA)
SONIC 3
ALADDIN
VHS COPIES OF DISNEY FEATURES
TAMAGOTCHI
DRAGON
WISE
POTATO CHIP
(TOMATO FLAV
RED PACKET MONEY (STILL IN RED PACKE
恒生干捞面
NOODLE
AFTER PACKING, I WAS LEFT WITH SOME TIME TO CONTEMPLATE AND REFLE ON THE GRAVITY OF IT AL I ENDED UP PACING UP AN DOWN WHILST WAITING FOR THE APPROPRIATE SENSE OF DOOM TO SETTLE IN. I ALSO GOT HIT BY THE BIGGEST HANKERING FOR ONE LAST MEAL AT MY FAVORITE NOODLE STALL.

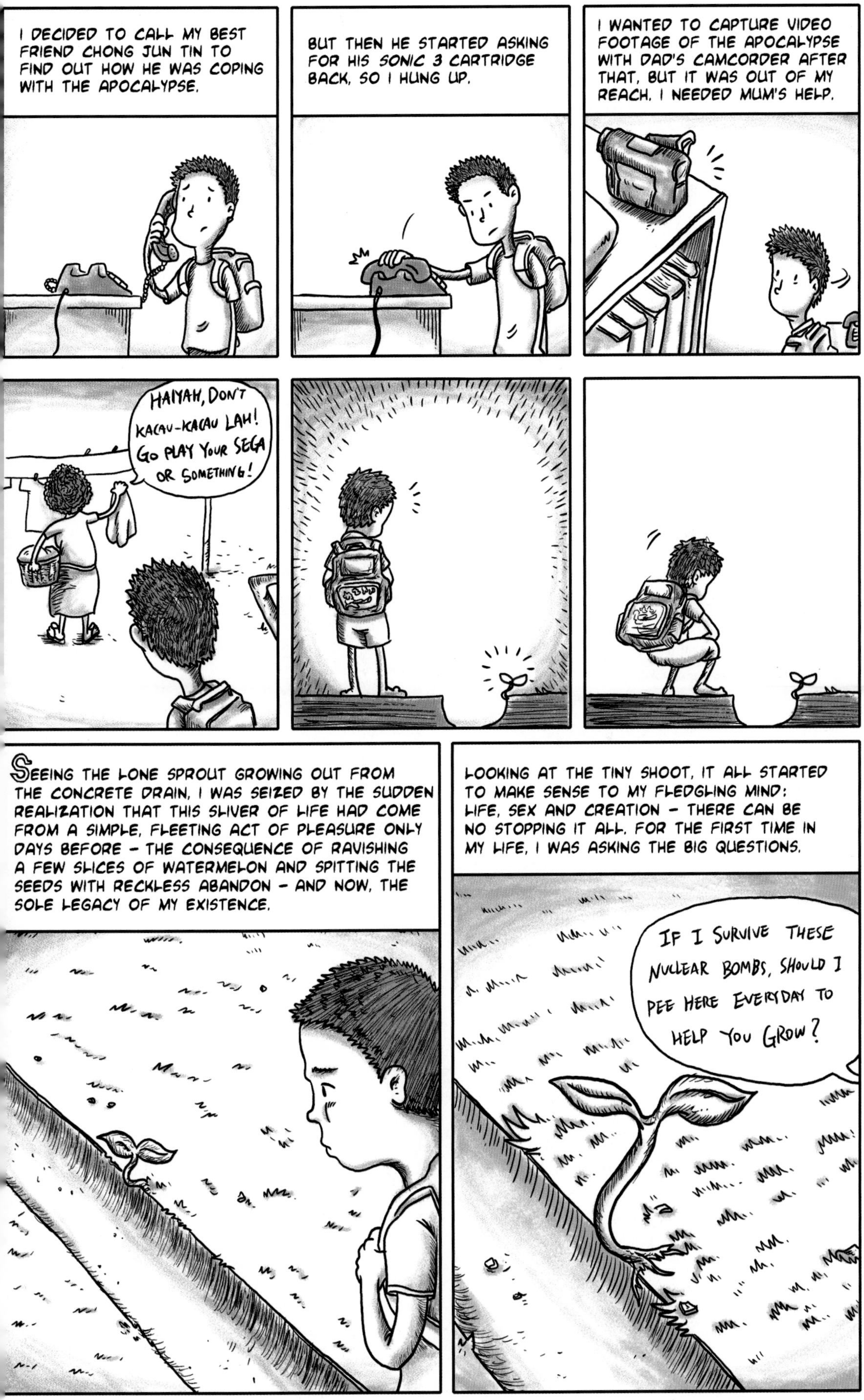
I DECIDED TO CALL MY BEST FRIEND CHONG JUN TIN TO FIND OUT HOW HE WAS COPING WITH THE APOCALYPSE.
BUT THEN HE STARTED ASKING FOR HIS SONIC 3 CARTRIDGE BACK, SO I HUNG UP.
I WANTED TO CAPTURE VIDEO FOOTAGE OF THE APOCALYPSE WITH DAD'S CAMCORDER AFTER THAT, BUT IT WAS OUT OF MY REACH. I NEEDED MUM'S HELP.
HAIYAH, DON'T KACAU-KACAU LAH! GO PLAY YOUR SEGA OR SOMETHING!
SEEING THE LONE SPROUT GROWING OUT FROM THE CONCRETE DRAIN, I WAS SEIZED BY THE SUDDEN REALIZATION THAT THIS SLIVER OF LIFE HAD COME FROM A SIMPLE, FLEETING ACT OF PLEASURE ONLY DAYS BEFORE – THE CONSEQUENCE OF RAVISHING A FEW SLICES OF WATERMELON AND SPITTING THE SEEDS WITH RECKLESS ABANDON – AND NOW, THE SOLE LEGACY OF MY EXISTENCE.
LOOKING AT THE TINY SHOOT, IT ALL STARTED TO MAKE SENSE TO MY FLEDGLING MIND: LIFE, SEX AND CREATION – THERE CAN BE NO STOPPING IT ALL. FOR THE FIRST TIME IN MY LIFE, I WAS ASKING THE BIG QUESTIONS.
IF I SURVIVE THESE NUCLEAR BOMBS, SHOULD I PEE HERE EVERYDAY TO HELP YOU GROW?

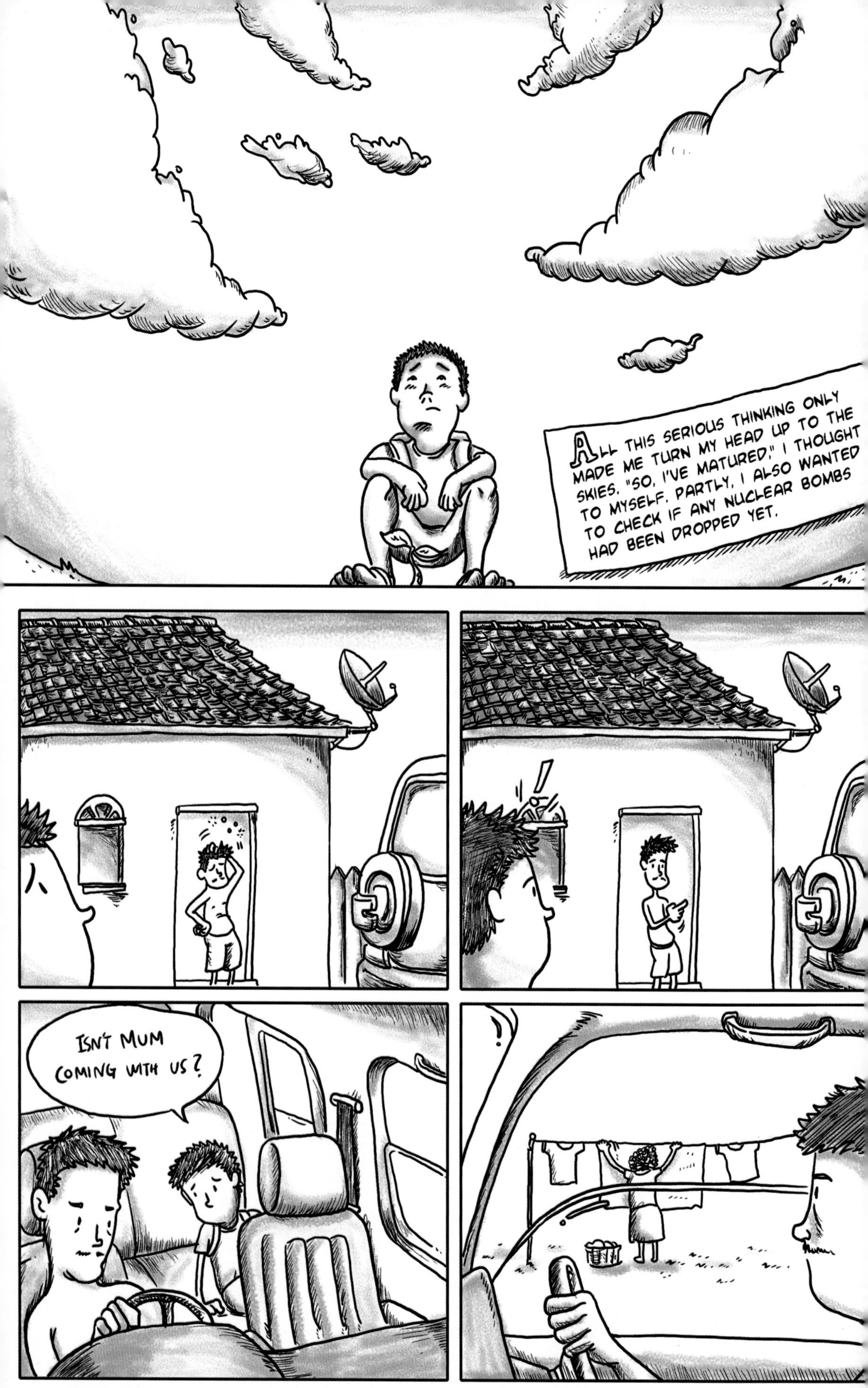
ALL THIS SERIOUS THINKING ONLY MADE ME TURN MY HEAD UP TO THE SKIES. "SO, I'VE MATURED," I THOUGHT TO MYSELF. PARTLY, I ALSO WANTED TO CHECK IF ANY NUCLEAR BOMBS HAD BEEN DROPPED YET.
!
ISN'T MUM COMING WITH US?
!

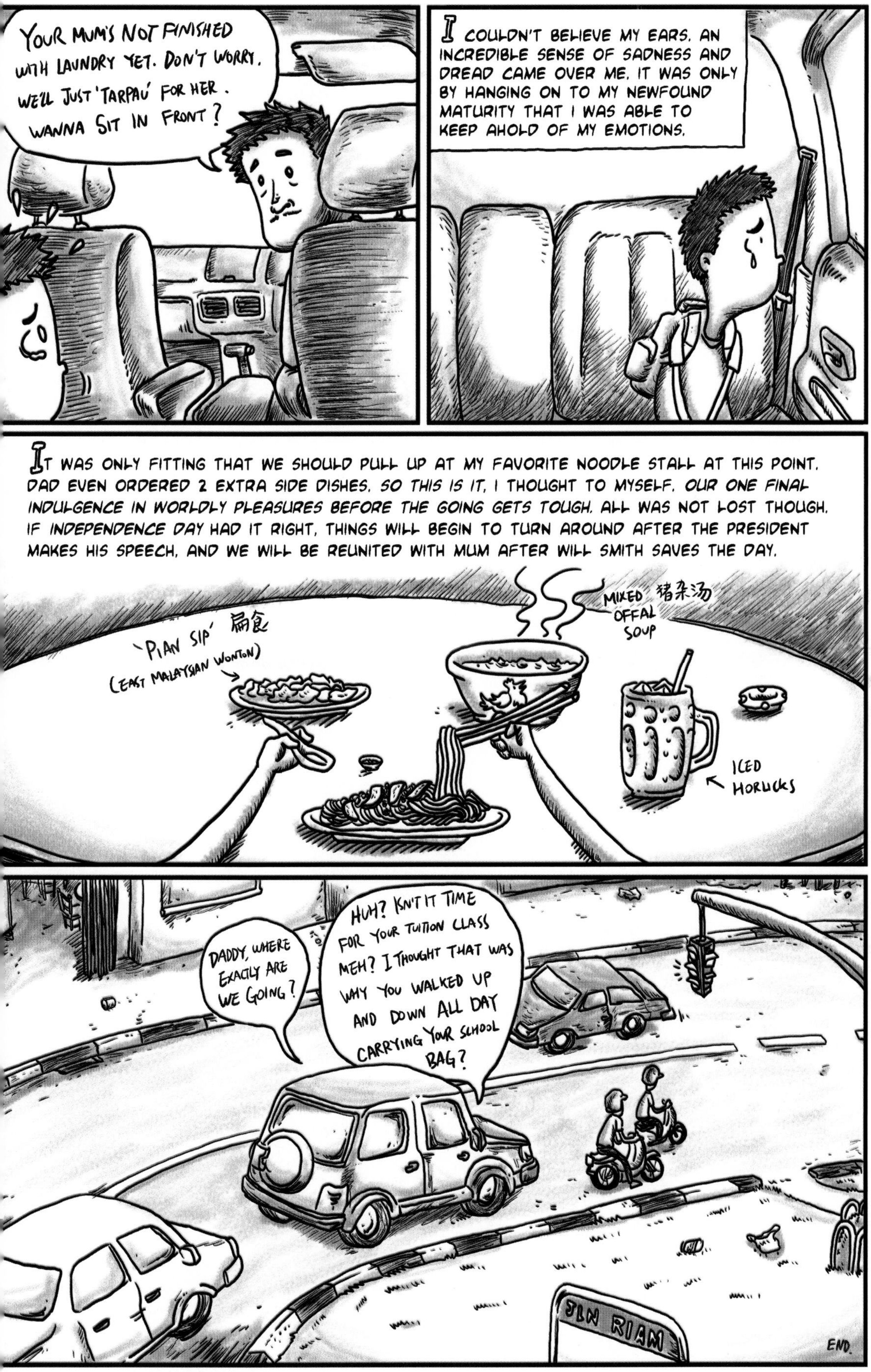
YOUR MUM'S NOT FINISHED WITH LAUNDRY YET. DON'T WORRY. WE'LL JUST 'TARPAU' FOR HER. WANNA SIT IN FRONT?
I COULDN'T BELIEVE MY EARS. AN INCREDIBLE SENSE OF SADNESS AND DREAD CAME OVER ME. IT WAS ONLY BY HANGING ON TO MY NEWFOUND MATURITY THAT I WAS ABLE TO KEEP AHOLD OF MY EMOTIONS.
IT WAS ONLY FITTING THAT WE SHOULD PULL UP AT MY FAVORITE NOODLE STALL AT THIS POINT. DAD EVEN ORDERED 2 EXTRA SIDE DISHES. SO THIS IS IT, I THOUGHT TO MYSELF. OUR ONE FINAL INDULGENCE IN WORLDLY PLEASURES BEFORE THE GOING GETS TOUGH. ALL WAS NOT LOST THOUGH. IF INDEPENDENCE DAY HAD IT RIGHT, THINGS WILL BEGIN TO TURN AROUND AFTER THE PRESIDENT MAKES HIS SPEECH, AND WE WILL BE REUNITED WITH MUM AFTER WILL SMITH SAVES THE DAY.
'PIAN SIP' 扁食
(EAST MALAYSIAN WONTON)
MIXED 猪杂汤 OFFAL SOUP
ICED HORLICKS
DADDY, WHERE EXACTLY ARE WE GOING?
HUH? ISN'T IT TIME FOR YOUR TUITION CLASS MEH? I THOUGHT THAT WAS WHY YOU WALKED UP AND DOWN ALL DAY CARRYING YOUR SCHOOL BAG?
JLN RIAM
END.

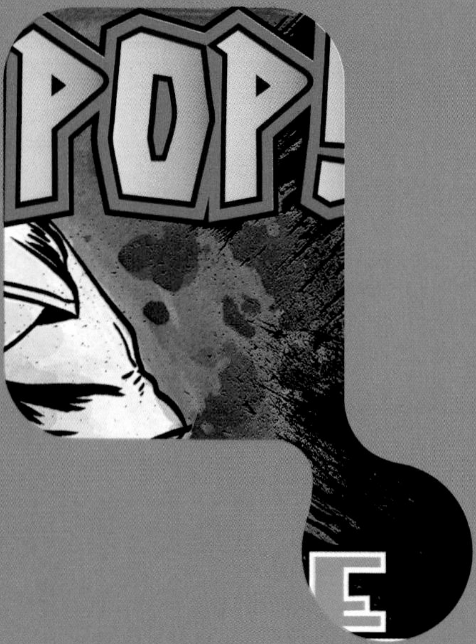
POP!

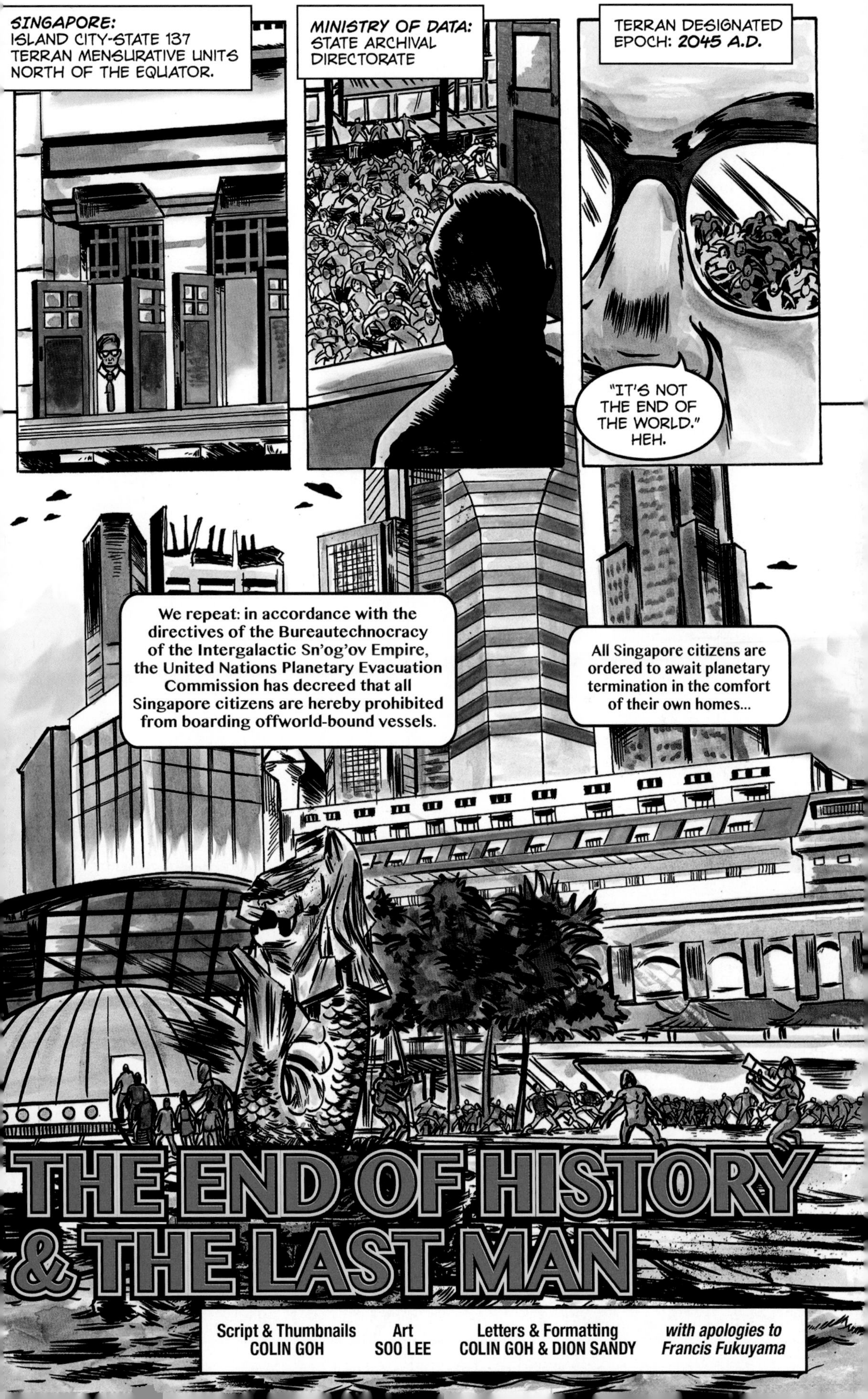
SINGAPORE:
ISLAND CITY-STATE 137 TERRAN MENSURATIVE UNITS NORTH OF THE EQUATOR.
MINISTRY OF DATA:
STATE ARCHIVAL DIRECTORATE
TERRAN DESIGNATED EPOCH: 2045 A.D.
"IT'S NOT THE END OF THE WORLD." HEH.
We repeat: in accordance with the directives of the Bureautechnocracy of the Intergalactic Sn'og'ov Empire, the United Nations Planetary Evacuation Commission has decreed that all Singapore citizens are hereby prohibited from boarding offworld-bound vessels.
All Singapore citizens are ordered to await planetary termination in the comfort of their own homes...
THE END OF HISTORY & THE LAST MAN
Script & Thumbnails COLIN GOH
Art SOO LEE
Letters & Formatting COLIN GOH & DION SANDY
with apologies to Francis Fukuyama

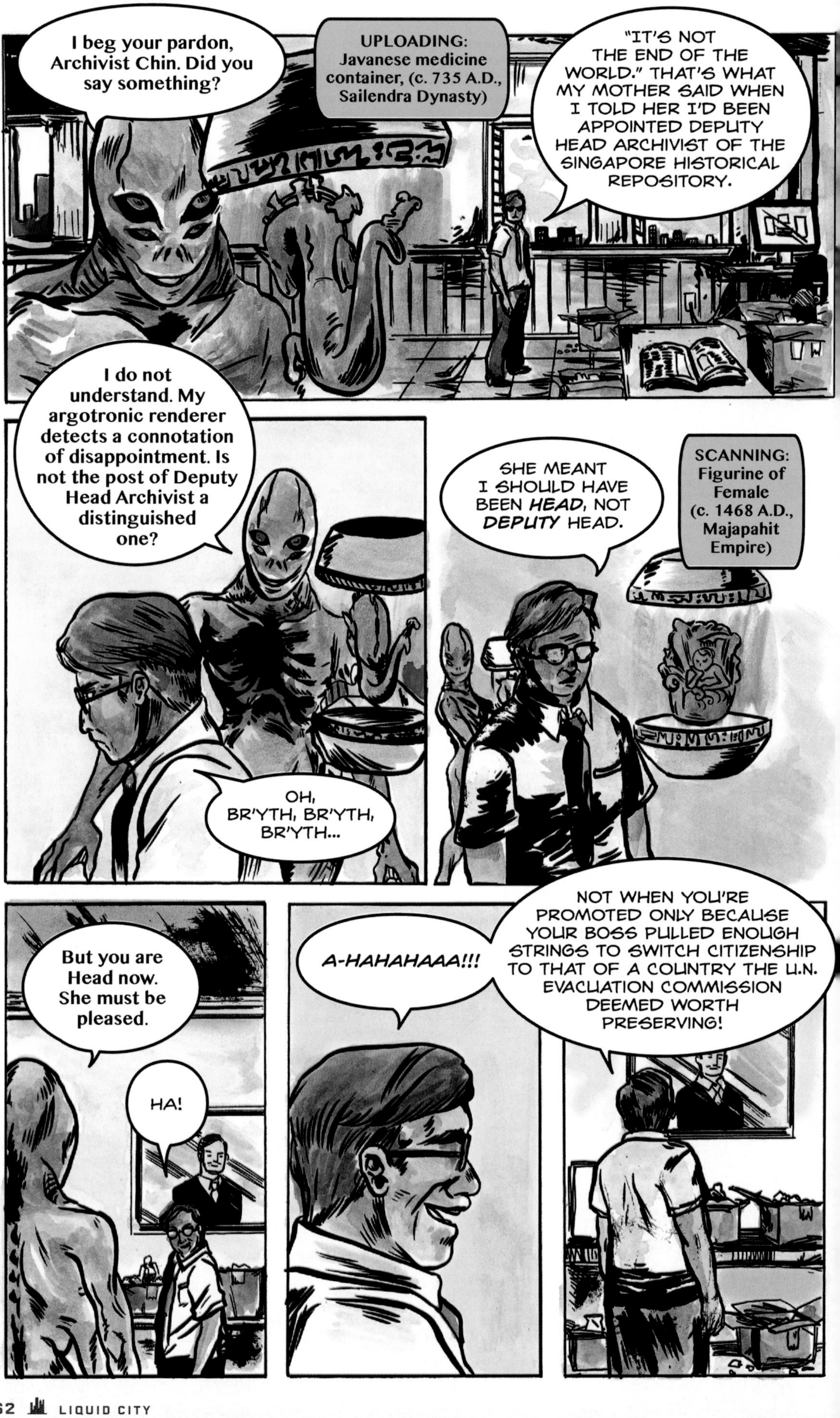
I beg your pardon, Archivist Chin. Did you say something?
UPLOADING: Javanese medicine container, (c. 735 A.D., Sailendra Dynasty)
"IT'S NOT THE END OF THE WORLD." THAT'S WHAT MY MOTHER SAID WHEN I TOLD HER I'D BEEN APPOINTED DEPUTY HEAD ARCHIVIST OF THE SINGAPORE HISTORICAL REPOSITORY.
I do not understand. My argotronic renderer detects a connotation of disappointment. Is not the post of Deputy Head Archivist a distinguished one?
OH, BR'YTH, BR'YTH, BR'YTH...
SHE MEANT I SHOULD HAVE BEEN *HEAD*, NOT *DEPUTY* HEAD.
SCANNING: Figurine of Female (c. 1468 A.D., Majapahit Empire)
But you are Head now. She must be pleased.
HA!
A-HAHAHAAA!!!
NOT WHEN YOU'RE PROMOTED ONLY BECAUSE YOUR BOSS PULLED ENOUGH STRINGS TO SWITCH CITIZENSHIP TO THAT OF A COUNTRY THE U.N. EVACUATION COMMISSION DEEMED WORTH PRESERVING!

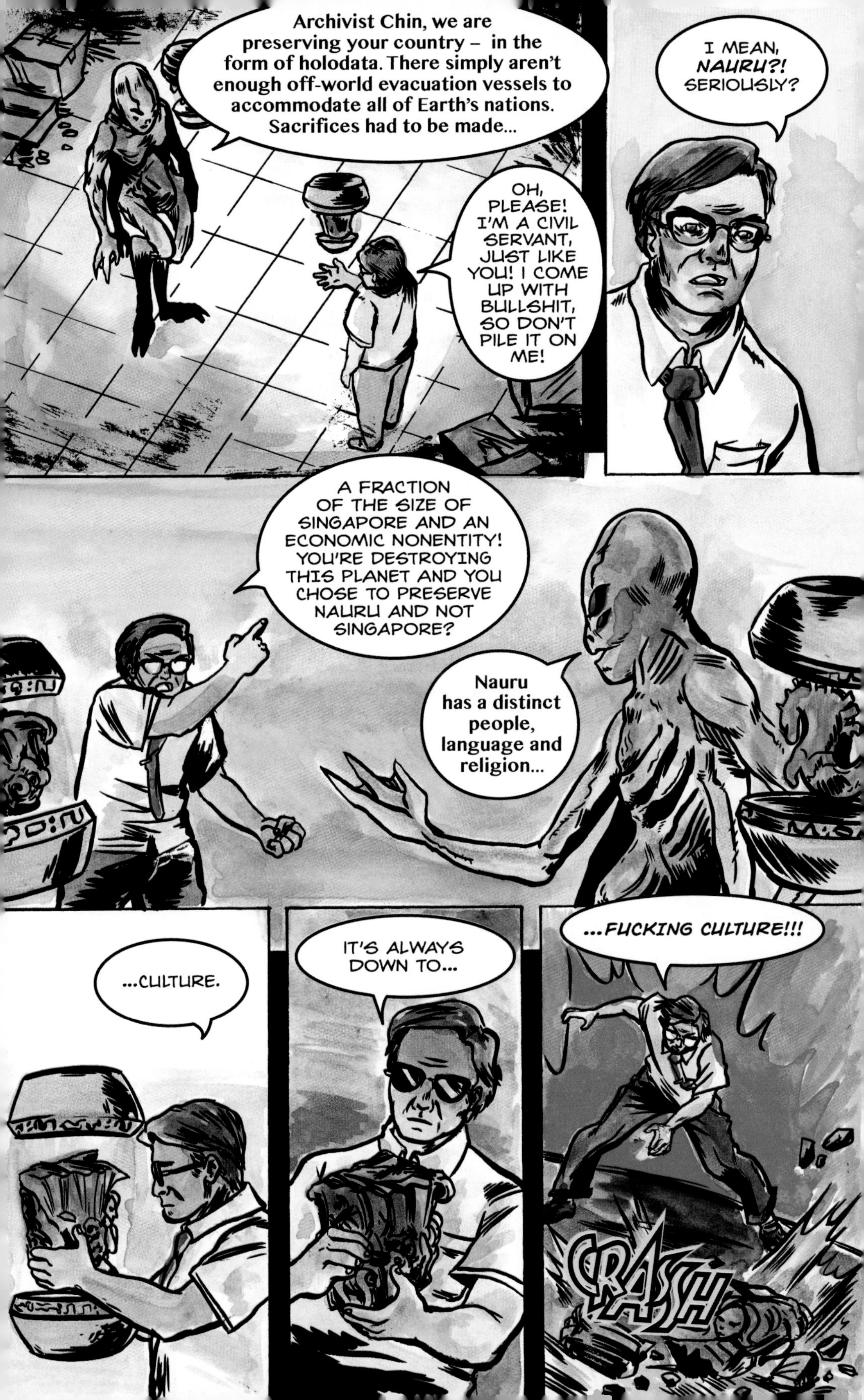
Archivist Chin, we are preserving your country – in the form of holodata. There simply aren't enough off-world evacuation vessels to accommodate all of Earth's nations. Sacrifices had to be made...
OH, PLEASE! I'M A CIVIL SERVANT, JUST LIKE YOU! I COME UP WITH BULLSHIT, SO DON'T PILE IT ON ME!
I MEAN, NAURU?! SERIOUSLY?
A FRACTION OF THE SIZE OF SINGAPORE AND AN ECONOMIC NONENTITY! YOU'RE DESTROYING THIS PLANET AND YOU CHOSE TO PRESERVE NAURU AND NOT SINGAPORE?
Nauru has a distinct people, language and religion...
...CULTURE.
IT'S ALWAYS DOWN TO...
...FUCKING CULTURE!!!
CRASH

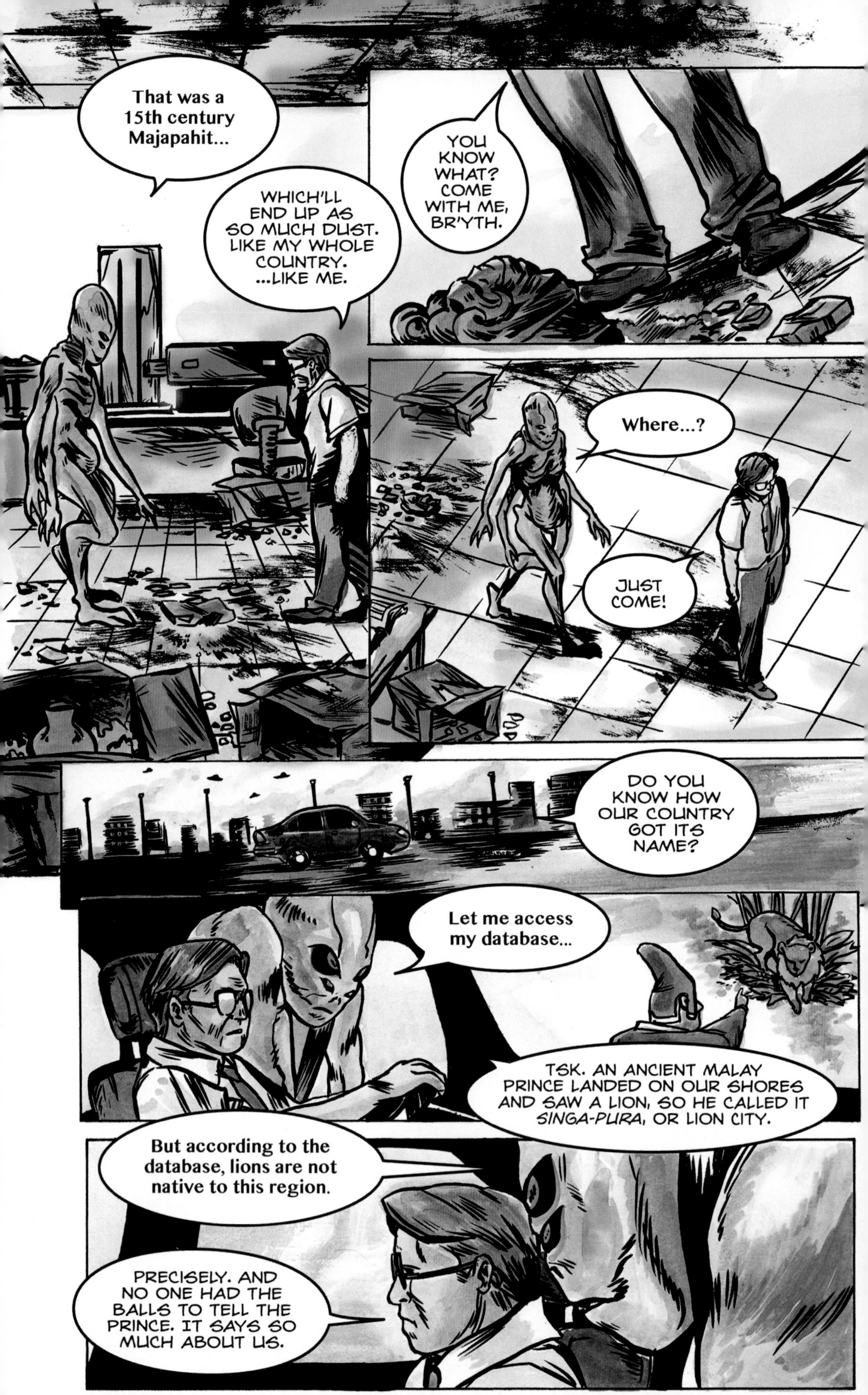
That was a 15th century Majapahit...
WHICH'LL END UP AS SO MUCH DUST. LIKE MY WHOLE COUNTRY. ...LIKE ME.
YOU KNOW WHAT? COME WITH ME, BR'YTH.
Where...?
JUST COME!
DO YOU KNOW HOW OUR COUNTRY GOT ITS NAME?
Let me access my database...
TSK. AN ANCIENT MALAY PRINCE LANDED ON OUR SHORES AND SAW A LION, SO HE CALLED IT *SINGA-PURA*, OR LION CITY.
But according to the database, lions are not native to this region.
PRECISELY. AND NO ONE HAD THE BALLS TO TELL THE PRINCE. IT SAYS SO MUCH ABOUT US.

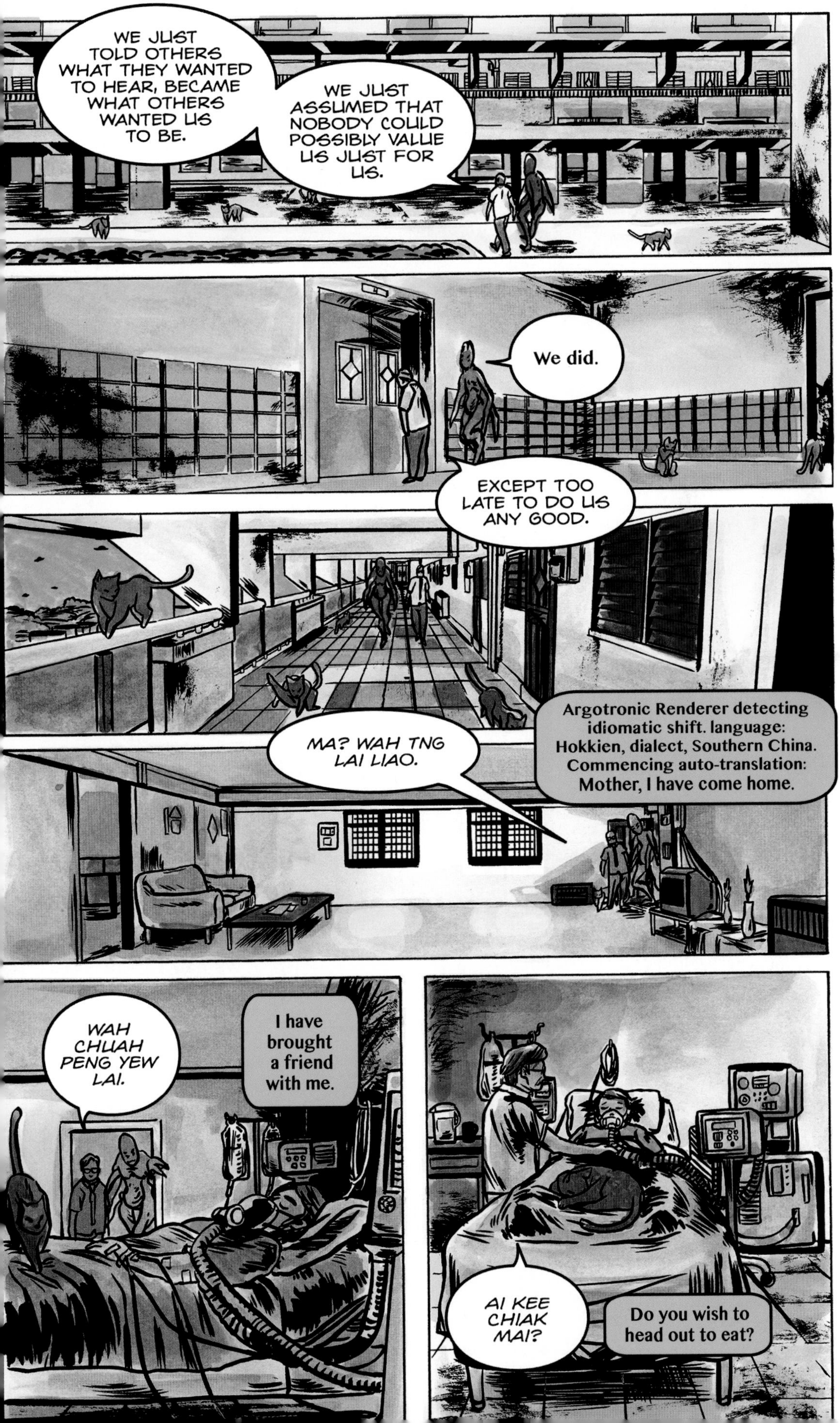
WE JUST TOLD OTHERS WHAT THEY WANTED TO HEAR, BECAME WHAT OTHERS WANTED US TO BE.
WE JUST ASSUMED THAT NOBODY COULD POSSIBLY VALUE US JUST FOR US.
We did.
EXCEPT TOO LATE TO DO US ANY GOOD.
MA? WAH TNG LAI LIAO.
Argotronic Renderer detecting idiomatic shift. language: Hokkien, dialect, Southern China. Commencing auto-translation: Mother, I have come home.
WAH CHUAH PENG YEW LAI.
I have brought a friend with me.
AI KEE CHIAK MAI?
Do you wish to head out to eat?

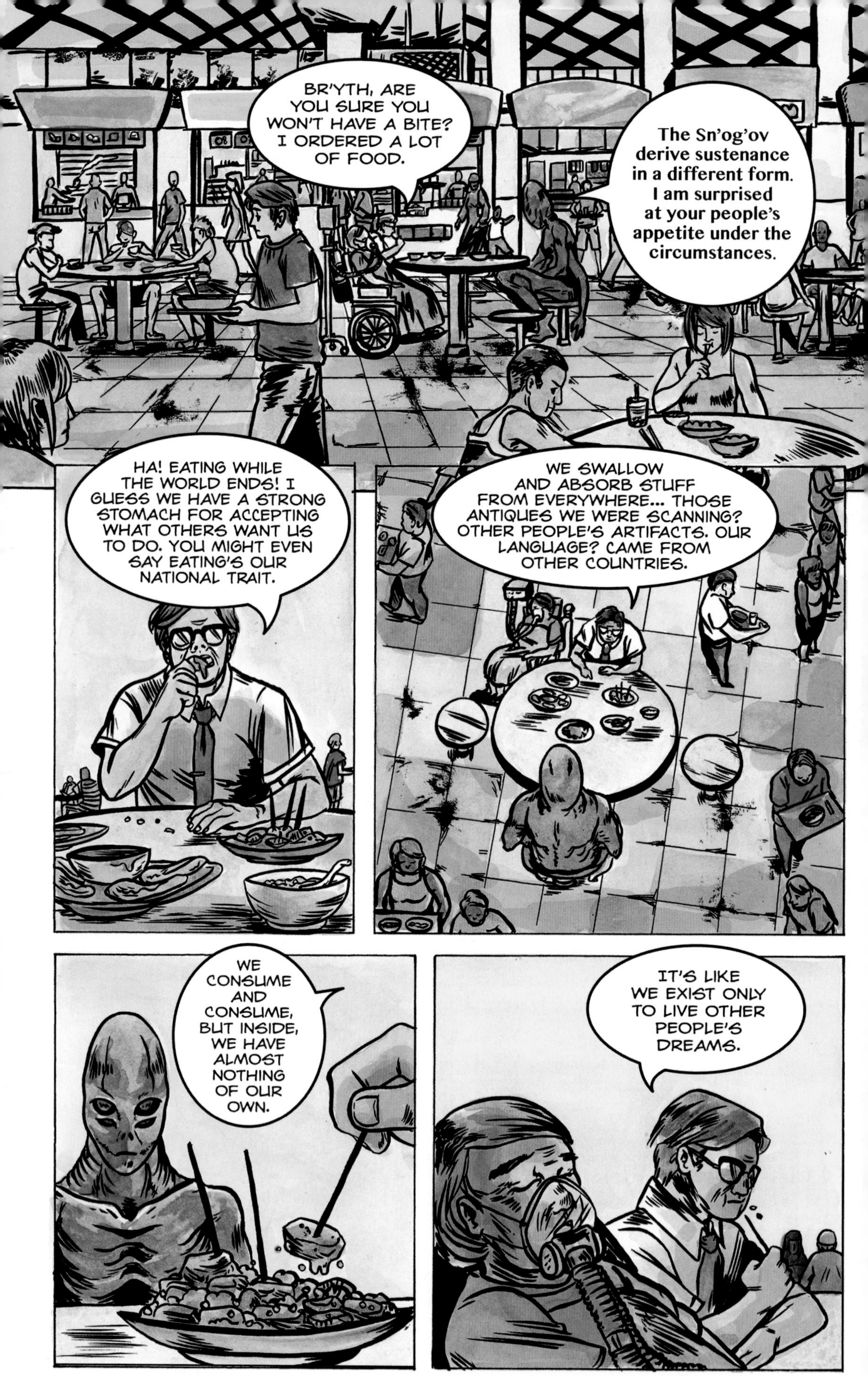
BR'YTH, ARE YOU SURE YOU WON'T HAVE A BITE? I ORDERED A LOT OF FOOD.
The Sn'og'ov derive sustenance in a different form. I am surprised at your people's appetite under the circumstances.
HA! EATING WHILE THE WORLD ENDS! I GUESS WE HAVE A STRONG STOMACH FOR ACCEPTING WHAT OTHERS WANT US TO DO. YOU MIGHT EVEN SAY EATING'S OUR NATIONAL TRAIT.
WE SWALLOW AND ABSORB STUFF FROM EVERYWHERE... THOSE ANTIQUES WE WERE SCANNING? OTHER PEOPLE'S ARTIFACTS. OUR LANGUAGE? CAME FROM OTHER COUNTRIES.
WE CONSUME AND CONSUME, BUT INSIDE, WE HAVE ALMOST NOTHING OF OUR OWN.
IT'S LIKE WE EXIST ONLY TO LIVE OTHER PEOPLE'S DREAMS.

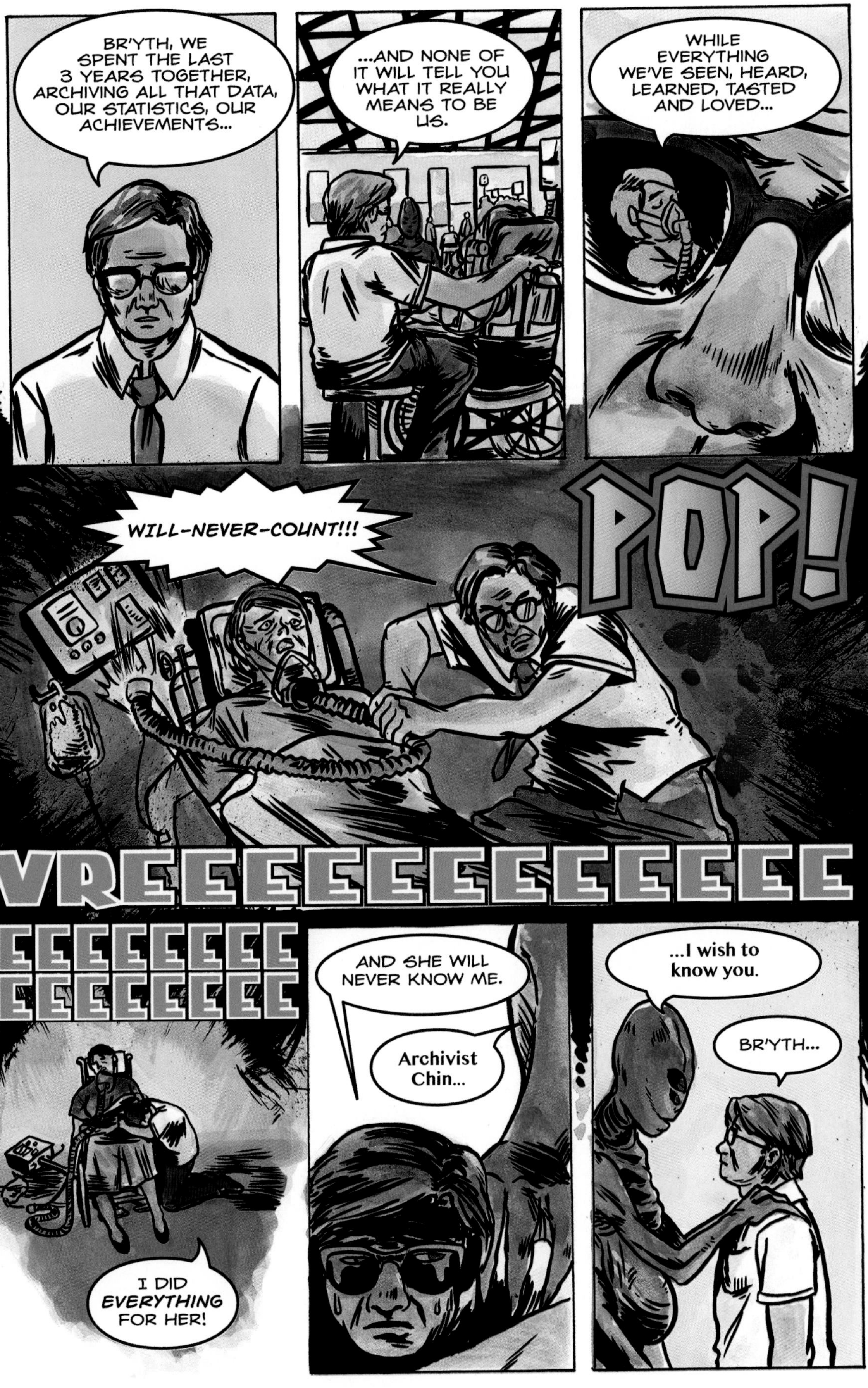
BR'YTH, WE SPENT THE LAST 3 YEARS TOGETHER, ARCHIVING ALL THAT DATA, OUR STATISTICS, OUR ACHIEVEMENTS...
...AND NONE OF IT WILL TELL YOU WHAT IT REALLY MEANS TO BE US.
WHILE EVERYTHING WE'VE SEEN, HEARD, LEARNED, TASTED AND LOVED...
WILL-NEVER-COUNT!!!
POP!
VREEEEEEEEEEEEEEEEEEEEEEEEEEE
I DID *EVERYTHING* FOR HER!
AND SHE WILL NEVER KNOW ME.
Archivist Chin...
...I wish to know you.
BR'YTH...

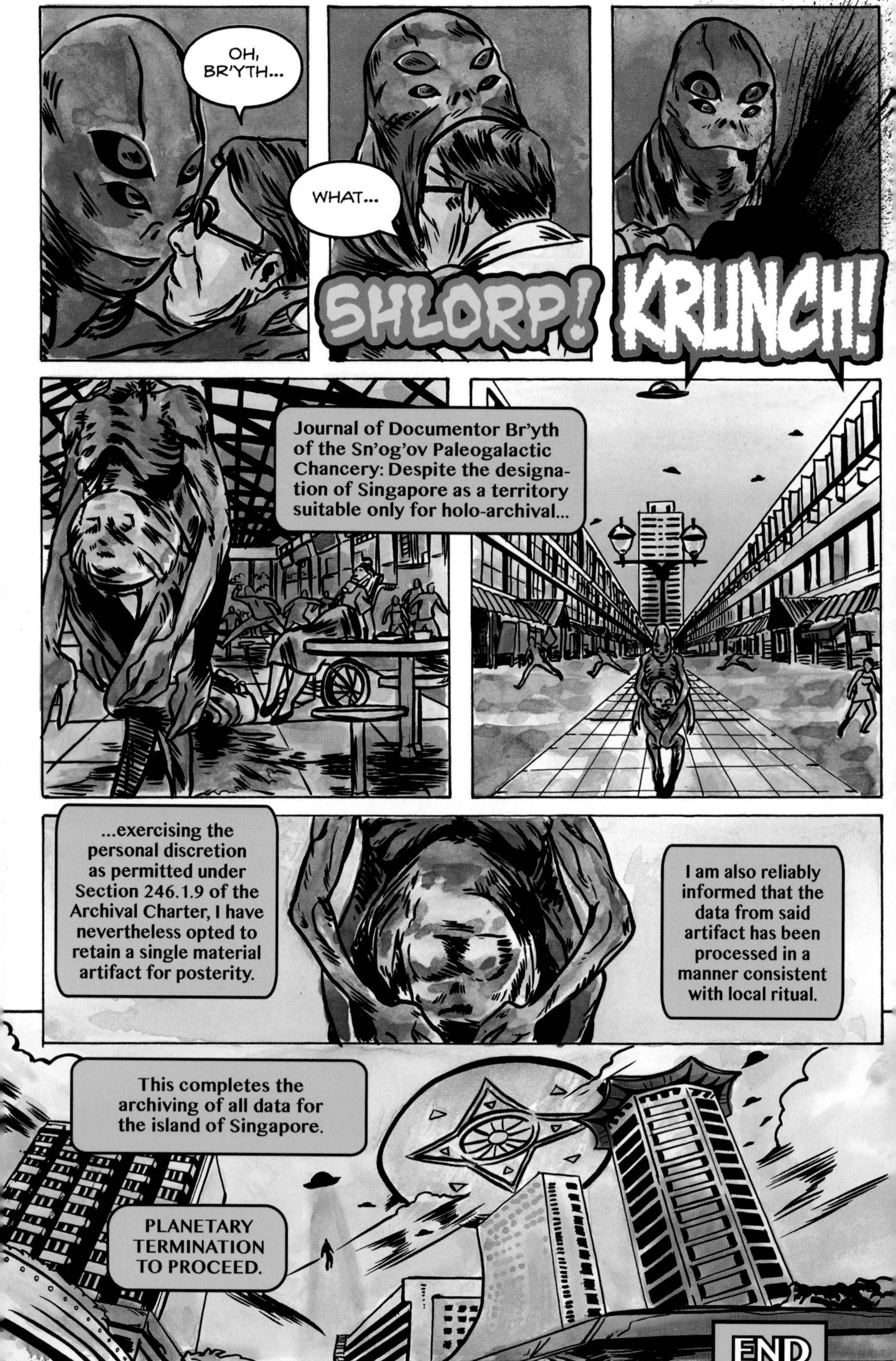

OH, BR'YTH...
WHAT...
SHLORP!
KRUNCH!
Journal of Documentor Br'yth of the Sn'og'ov Paleogalactic Chancery: Despite the designation of Singapore as a territory suitable only for holo-archival...
...exercising the personal discretion as permitted under Section 246.1.9 of the Archival Charter, I have nevertheless opted to retain a single material artifact for posterity.
I am also reliably informed that the data from said artifact has been processed in a manner consistent with local ritual.
This completes the archiving of all data for the island of Singapore.
PLANETARY TERMINATION TO PROCEED.
END

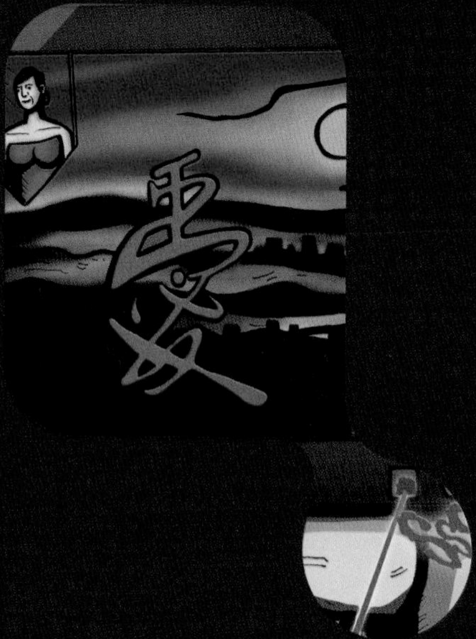
西安

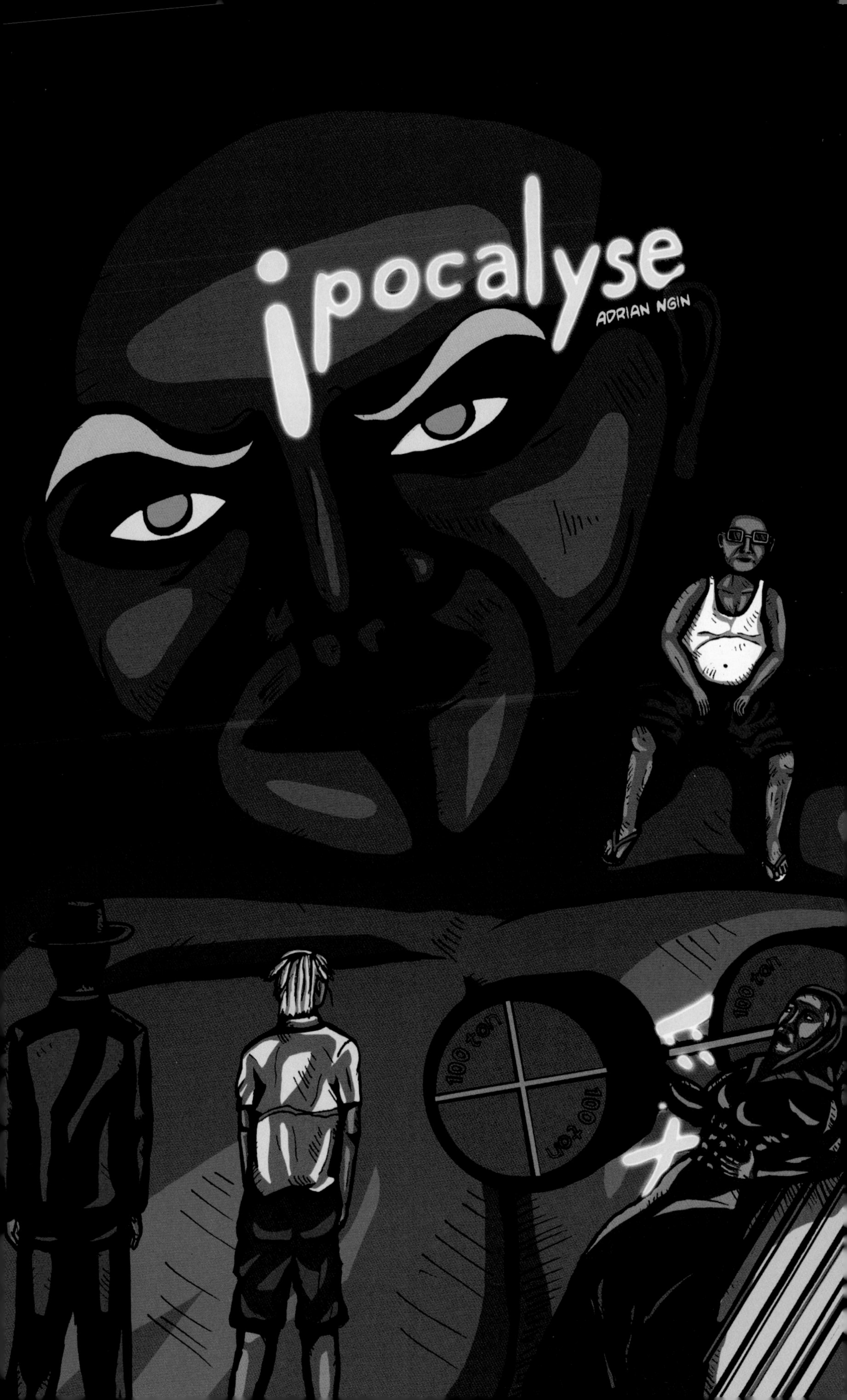
ipocalyse
ADRIAN NGIN
100 ton
100 ton
100 ton

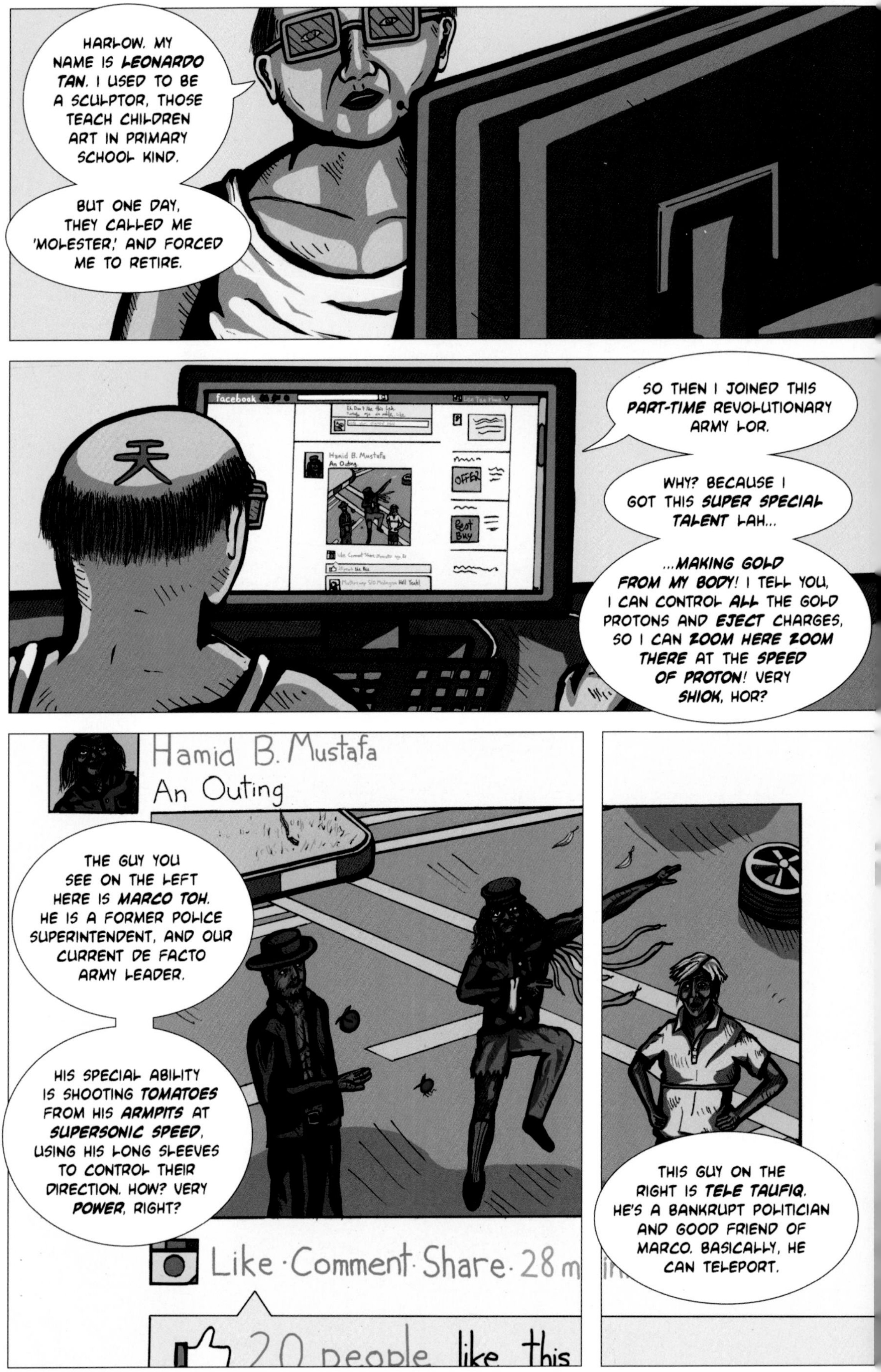
HARLOW. MY NAME IS LEONARDO TAN. I USED TO BE A SCULPTOR, THOSE TEACH CHILDREN ART IN PRIMARY SCHOOL KIND.
BUT ONE DAY, THEY CALLED ME 'MOLESTER,' AND FORCED ME TO RETIRE.
facebook
SO THEN I JOINED THIS PART-TIME REVOLUTIONARY ARMY LOR.
WHY? BECAUSE I GOT THIS SUPER SPECIAL TALENT LAH...
...MAKING GOLD FROM MY BODY! I TELL YOU, I CAN CONTROL ALL THE GOLD PROTONS AND EJECT CHARGES, SO I CAN ZOOM HERE ZOOM THERE AT THE SPEED OF PROTON! VERY SHIOK, HOR?
Hamid B. Mustafa
An Outing
THE GUY YOU SEE ON THE LEFT HERE IS MARCO TOH. HE IS A FORMER POLICE SUPERINTENDENT, AND OUR CURRENT DE FACTO ARMY LEADER.
HIS SPECIAL ABILITY IS SHOOTING TOMATOES FROM HIS ARMPITS AT SUPERSONIC SPEED, USING HIS LONG SLEEVES TO CONTROL THEIR DIRECTION. HOW? VERY POWER, RIGHT?
Like · Comment · Share · 28 m
20 people like this
THIS GUY ON THE RIGHT IS TELE TAUFIQ. HE'S A BANKRUPT POLITICIAN AND GOOD FRIEND OF MARCO. BASICALLY, HE CAN TELEPORT.

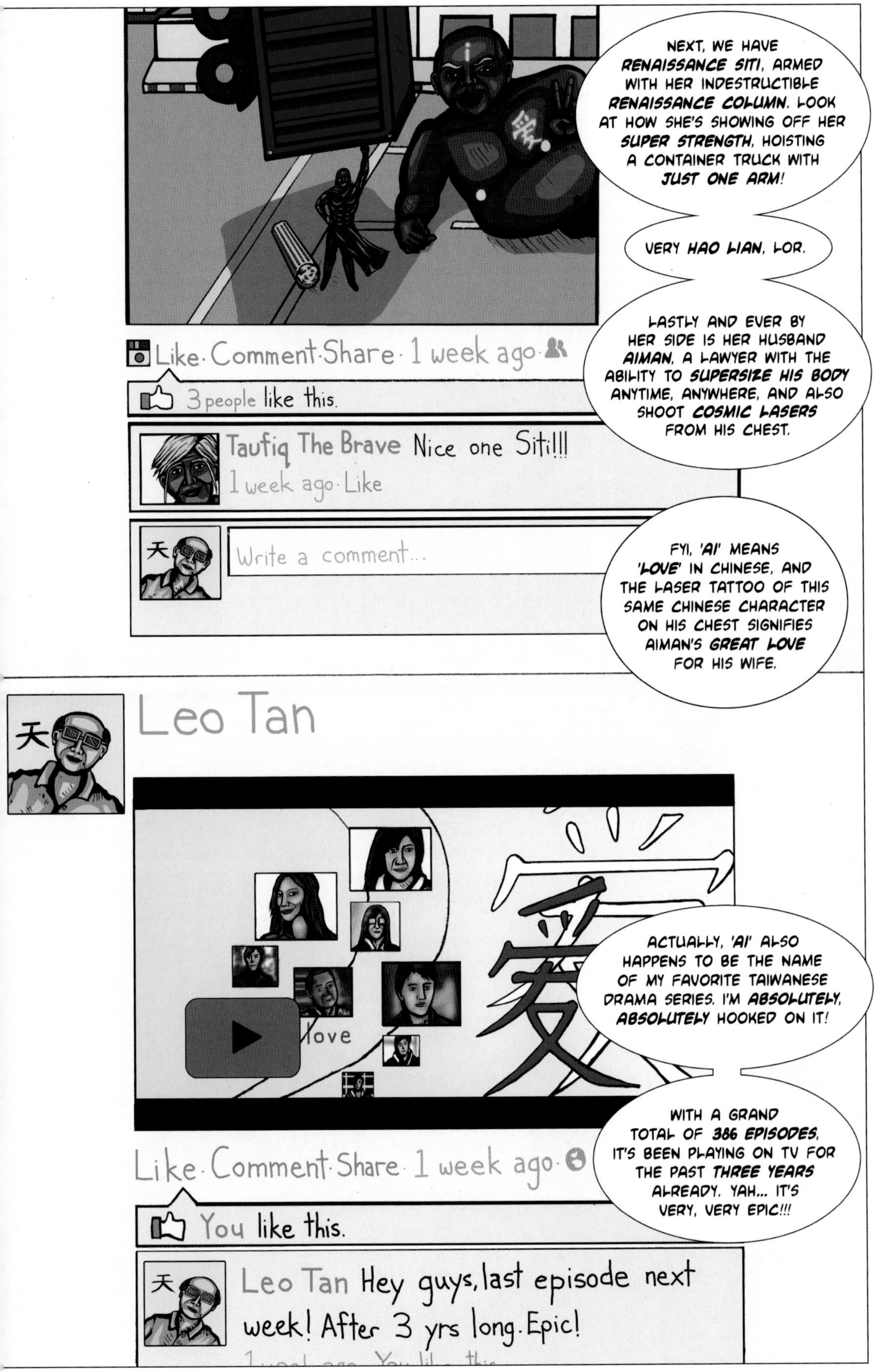
NEXT, WE HAVE RENAISSANCE SITI, ARMED WITH HER INDESTRUCTIBLE RENAISSANCE COLUMN. LOOK AT HOW SHE'S SHOWING OFF HER SUPER STRENGTH, HOISTING A CONTAINER TRUCK WITH JUST ONE ARM!
VERY HAO LIAN, LOR.
Like · Comment · Share · 1 week ago
3 people like this.
LASTLY AND EVER BY HER SIDE IS HER HUSBAND AIMAN, A LAWYER WITH THE ABILITY TO SUPERSIZE HIS BODY ANYTIME, ANYWHERE, AND ALSO SHOOT COSMIC LASERS FROM HIS CHEST.
Taufiq The Brave Nice one Siti!!!
1 week ago · Like
Write a comment...
FYI, 'AI' MEANS 'LOVE' IN CHINESE, AND THE LASER TATTOO OF THIS SAME CHINESE CHARACTER ON HIS CHEST SIGNIFIES AIMAN'S GREAT LOVE FOR HIS WIFE.
Leo Tan
love
爱
ACTUALLY, 'AI' ALSO HAPPENS TO BE THE NAME OF MY FAVORITE TAIWANESE DRAMA SERIES. I'M ABSOLUTELY, ABSOLUTELY HOOKED ON IT!
WITH A GRAND TOTAL OF 386 EPISODES, IT'S BEEN PLAYING ON TV FOR THE PAST THREE YEARS ALREADY. YAH... IT'S VERY, VERY EPIC!!!
Like · Comment · Share · 1 week ago
You like this.
Leo Tan Hey guys, last episode next week! After 3 yrs long. Epic!

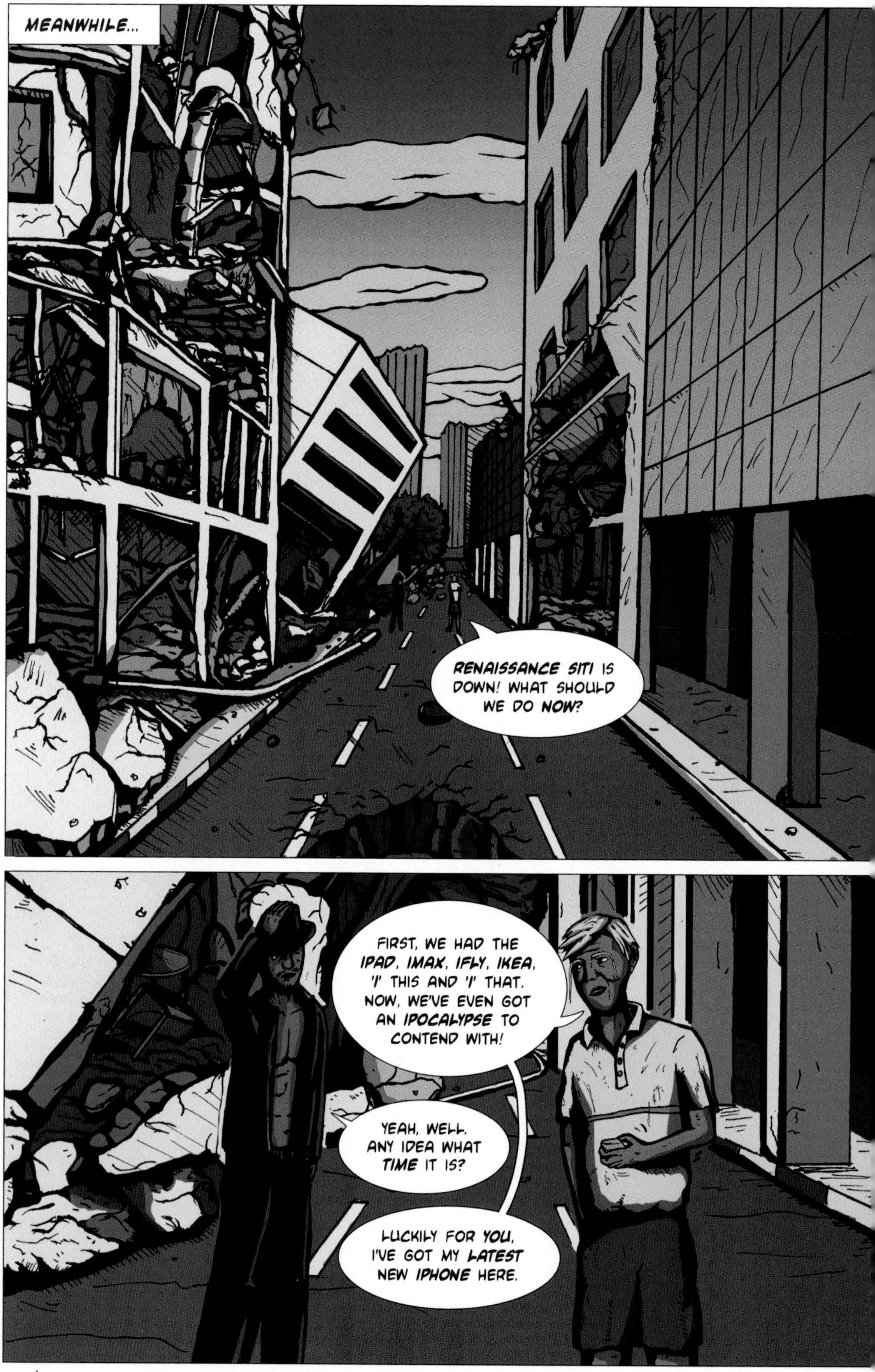
MEANWHILE...
RENAISSANCE SITI IS DOWN! WHAT SHOULD WE DO NOW?
FIRST, WE HAD THE IPAD, IMAX, IFLY, IKEA, 'I' THIS AND 'I' THAT. NOW, WE'VE EVEN GOT AN IPOCALYPSE TO CONTEND WITH!
YEAH, WELL. ANY IDEA WHAT TIME IT IS?
LUCKILY FOR YOU, I'VE GOT MY LATEST NEW IPHONE HERE.

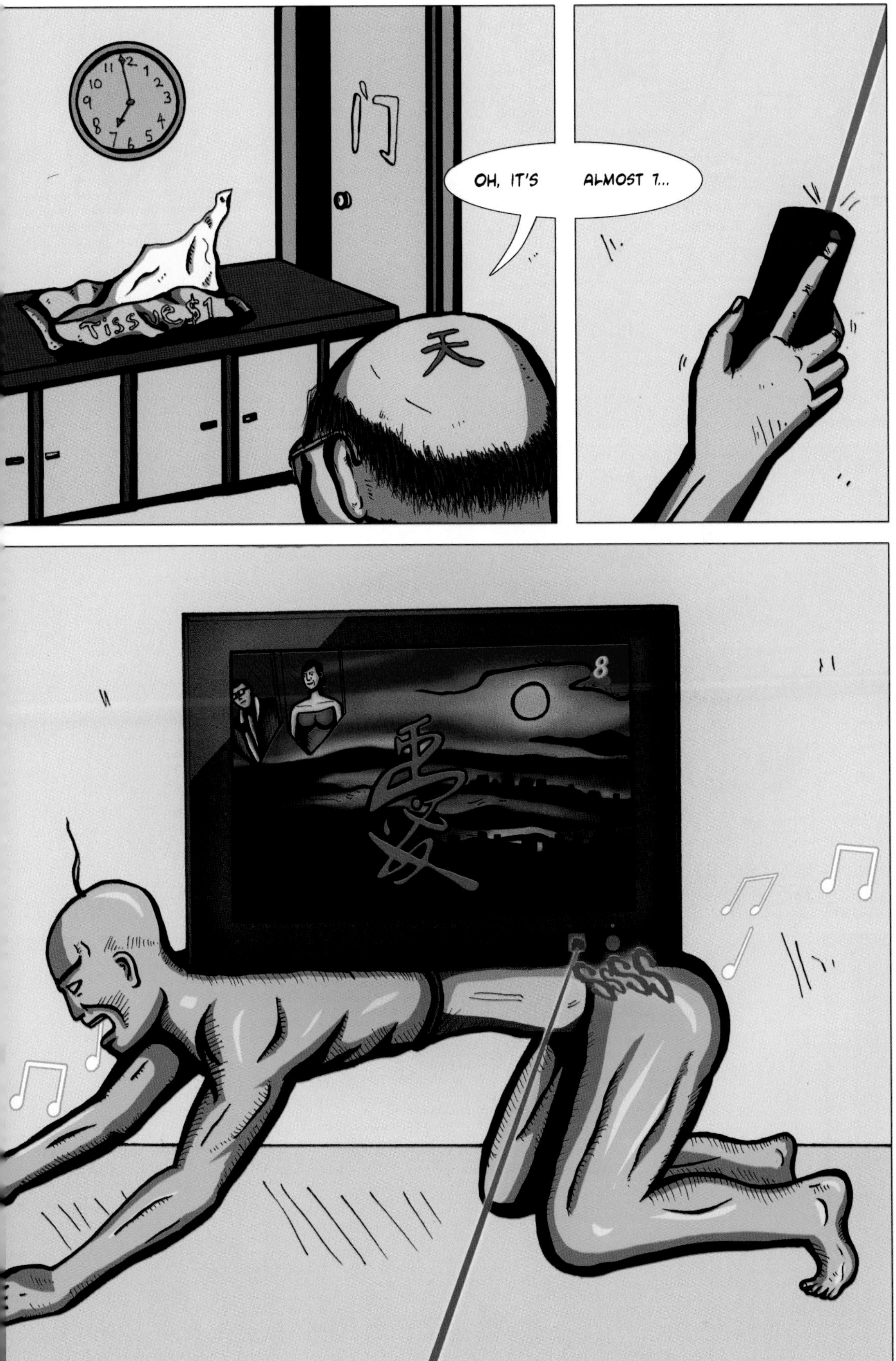
门
Tissue $1
天
OH, IT'S ALMOST 7...
8

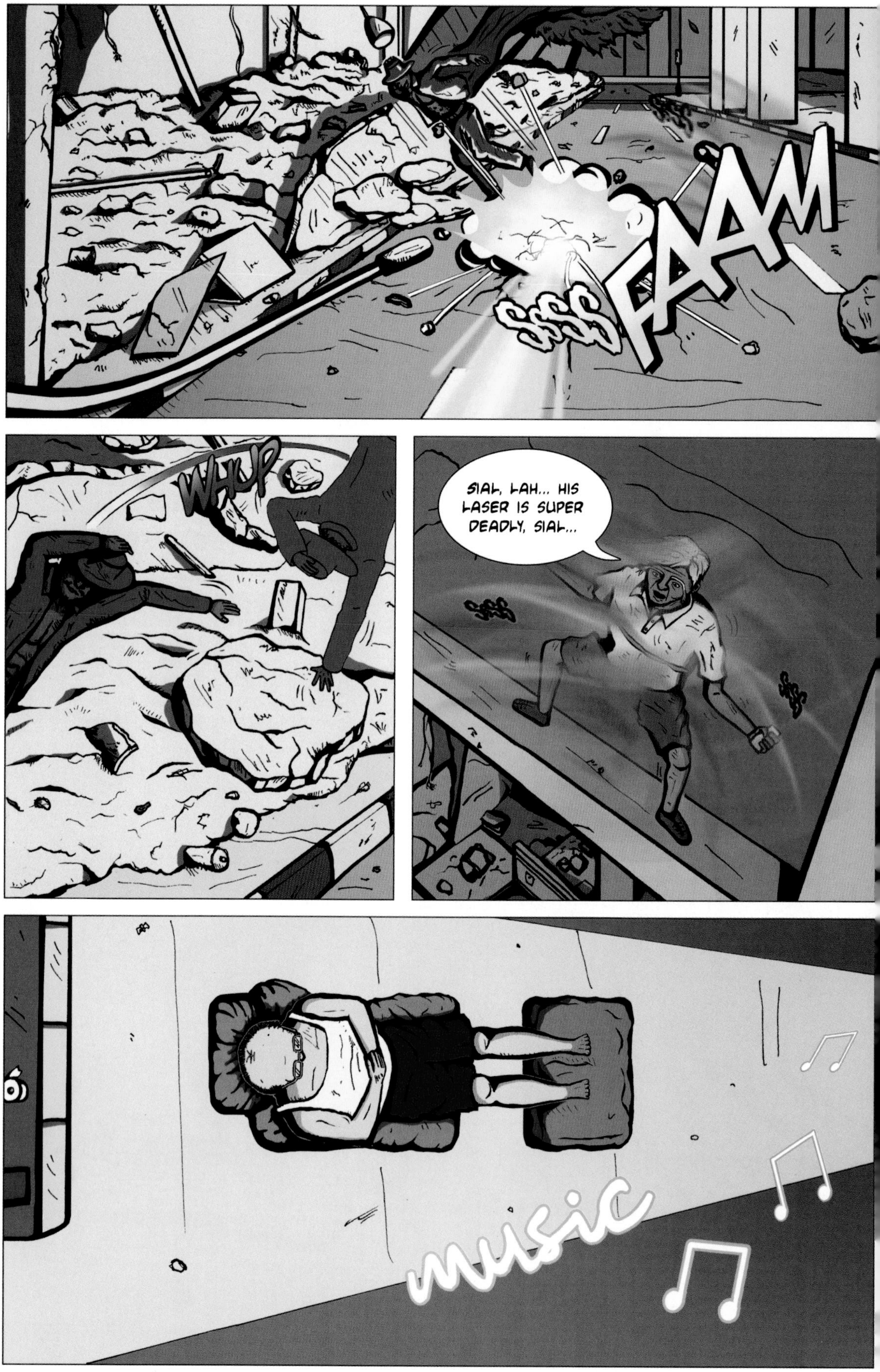
FAAM
SSS
WHUP
SIAL, LAH... HIS LASER IS SUPER DEADLY, SIAL...
music

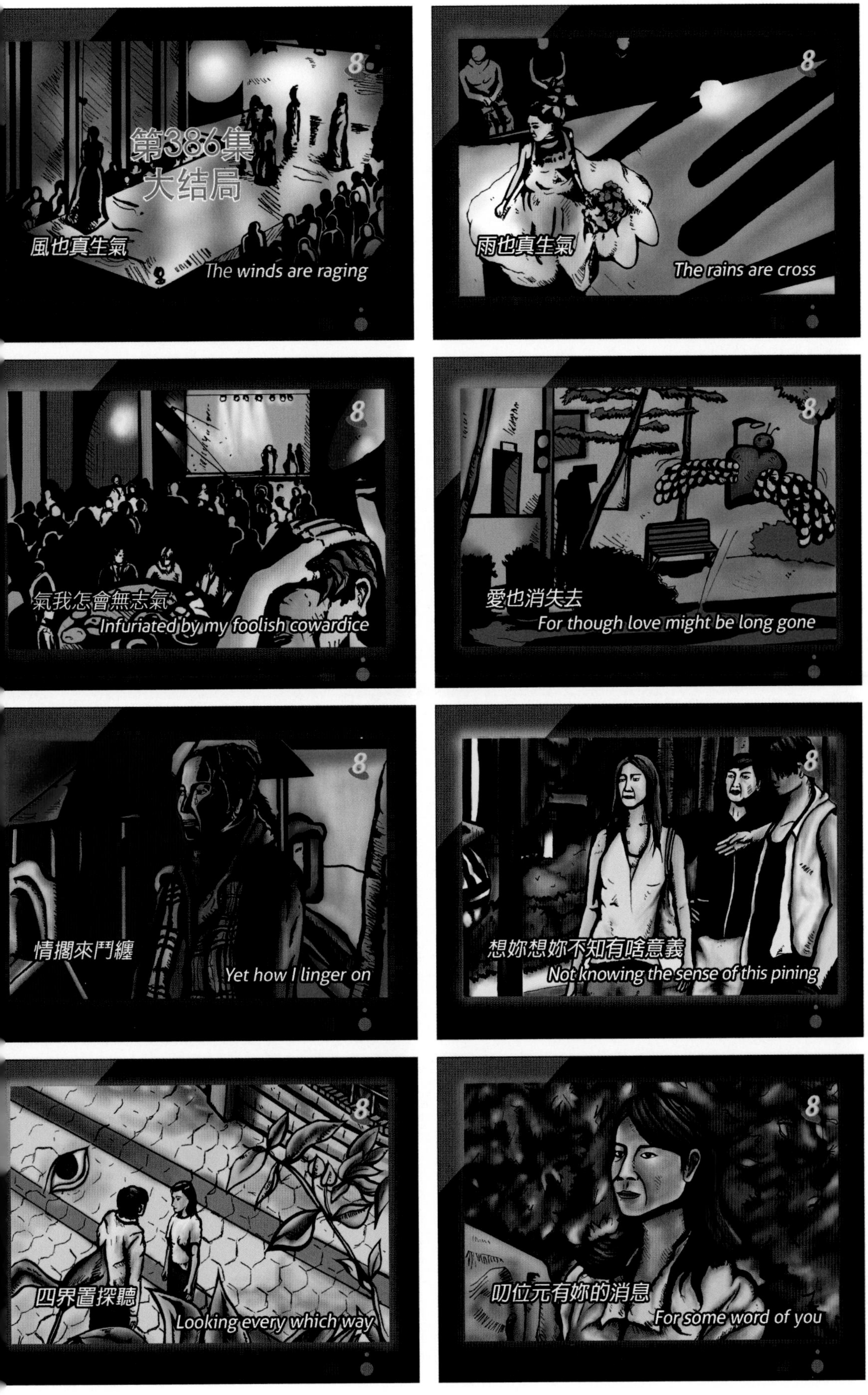
第386集
大结局
風也真生氣
The winds are raging
雨也真生氣
The rains are cross
氣我怎會無志氣
Infuriated by my foolish cowardice
愛也消失去
For though love might be long gone
情擱來鬥纏
Yet how I linger on
想妳想妳不知有啥意義
Not knowing the sense of this pining
四界置探聽
Looking every which way
叨位元有妳的消息
For some word of you

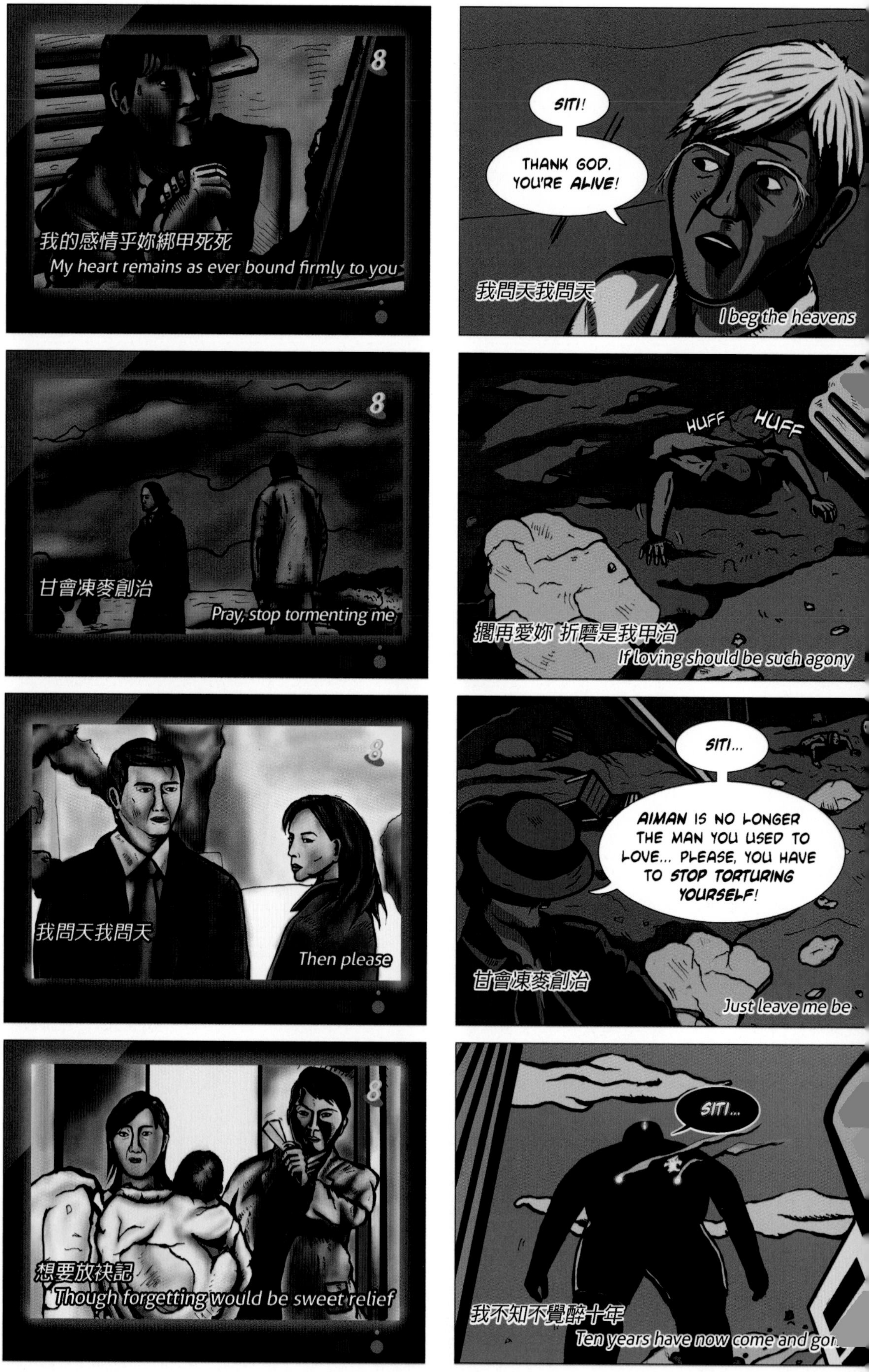
8
我的感情乎妳綁甲死死
My heart remains as ever bound firmly to you
SITI!
THANK GOD. YOU'RE ALIVE!
我問天我問天
I beg the heavens
8
甘會凍麥創治
Pray, stop tormenting me
HUFF
HUFF
擱再愛妳 折磨是我甲治
If loving should be such agony
8
我問天我問天
Then please
SITI...
AIMAN IS NO LONGER THE MAN YOU USED TO LOVE... PLEASE, YOU HAVE TO STOP TORTURING YOURSELF!
甘會凍麥創治
Just leave me be
8
想要放袂記
Though forgetting would be sweet relief
SITI...
我不知不覺醉十年
Ten years have now come and gon

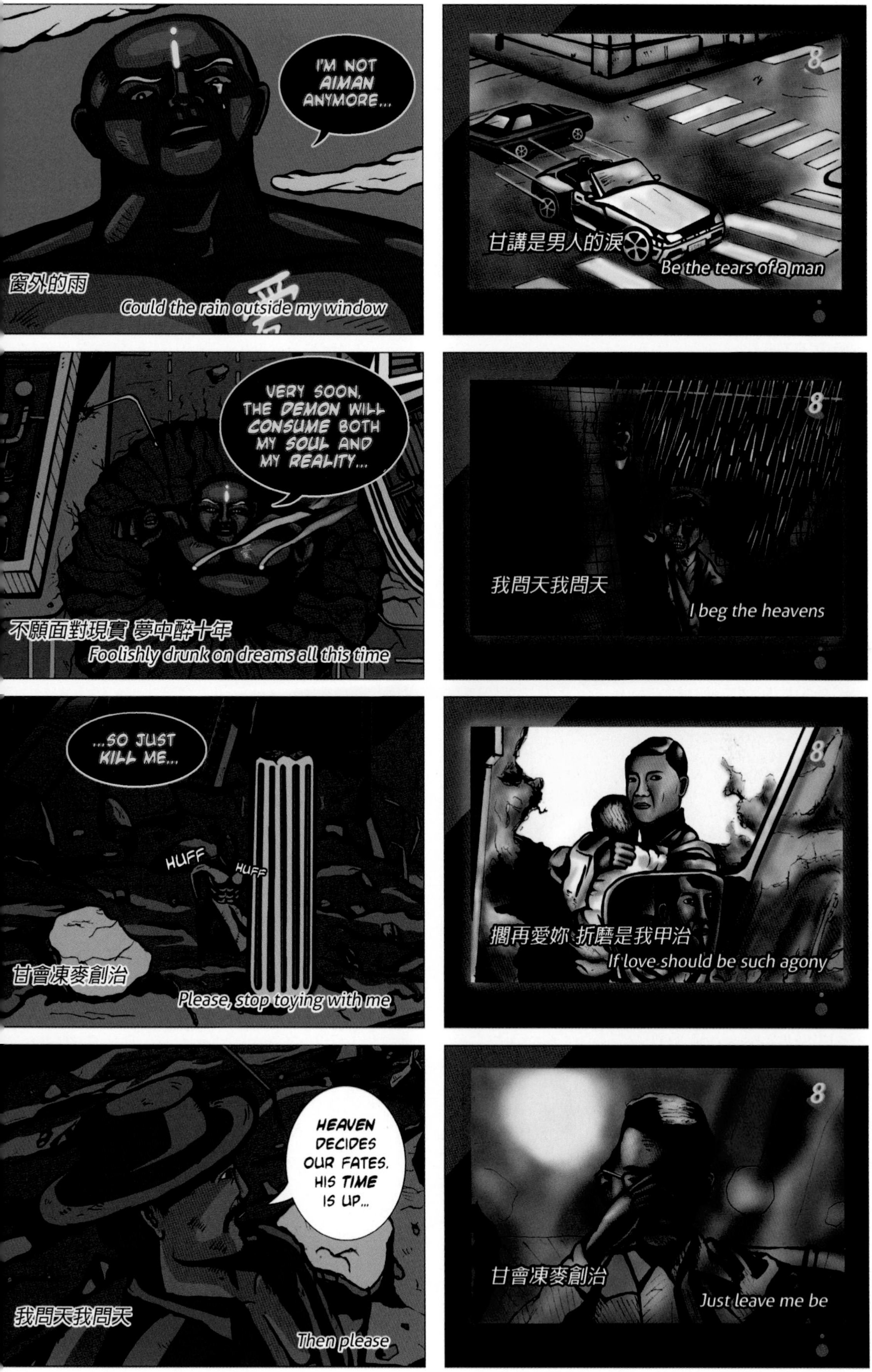
I'M NOT AIMAN ANYMORE...
窗外的雨
Could the rain outside my window
甘講是男人的淚
Be the tears of a man
VERY SOON, THE DEMON WILL CONSUME BOTH MY SOUL AND MY REALITY...
不願面對現實 夢中醉十年
Foolishly drunk on dreams all this time
我問天我問天
I beg the heavens
...SO JUST KILL ME...
HUFF
HUFF
甘會凍麥創治
Please, stop toying with me
擱再愛妳 折磨是我甲治
If love should be such agony
HEAVEN DECIDES OUR FATES. HIS TIME IS UP...
我問天我問天
Then please
甘會凍麥創治
Just leave me be

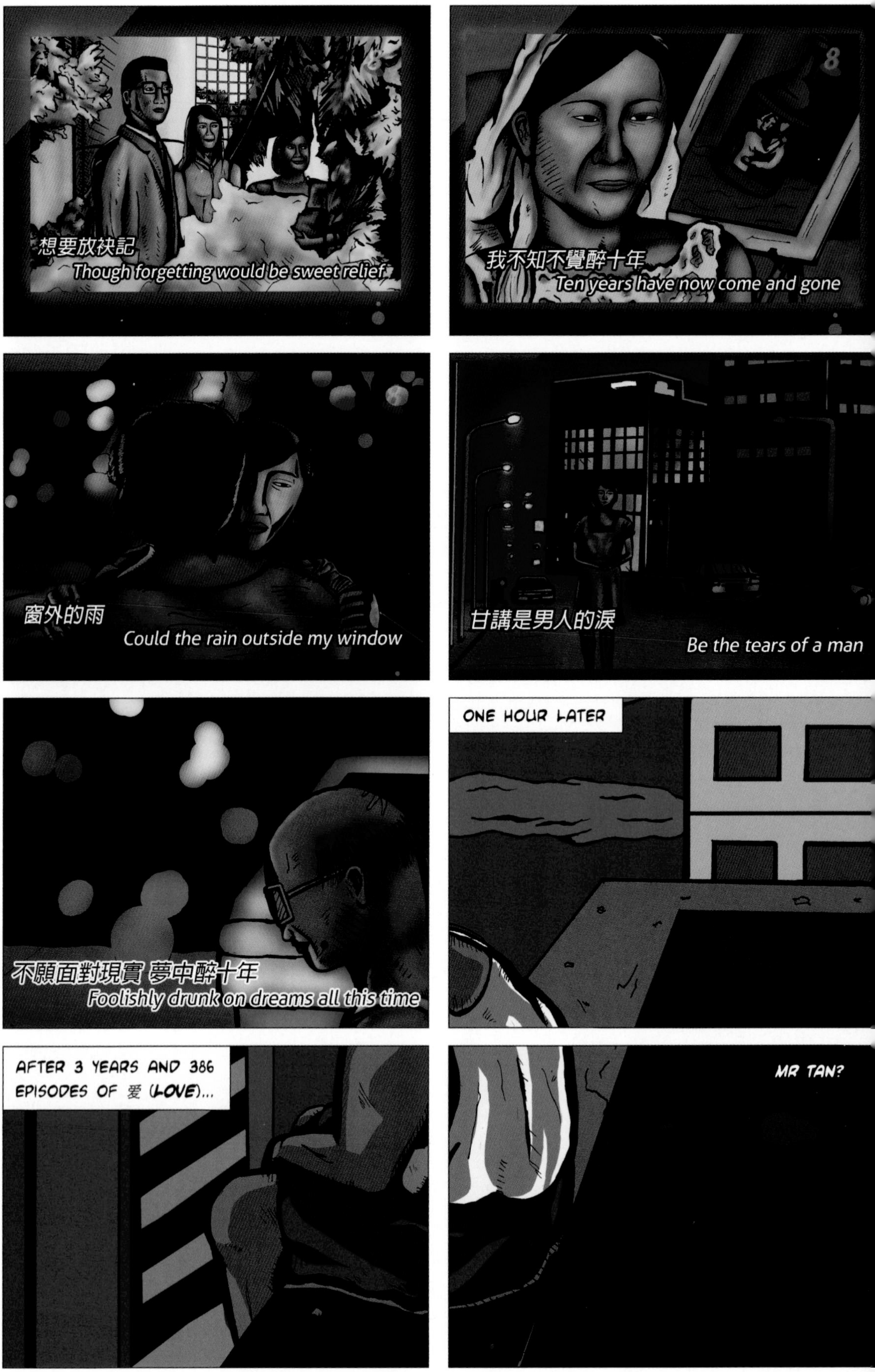

想要放袂記
Though forgetting would be sweet relief
我不知不覺醉十年
Ten years have now come and gone
窗外的雨
Could the rain outside my window
甘講是男人的淚
Be the tears of a man
不願面對現實 夢中醉十年
Foolishly drunk on dreams all this time
ONE HOUR LATER
AFTER 3 YEARS AND 386 EPISODES OF 爱 (LOVE)...
MR TAN?

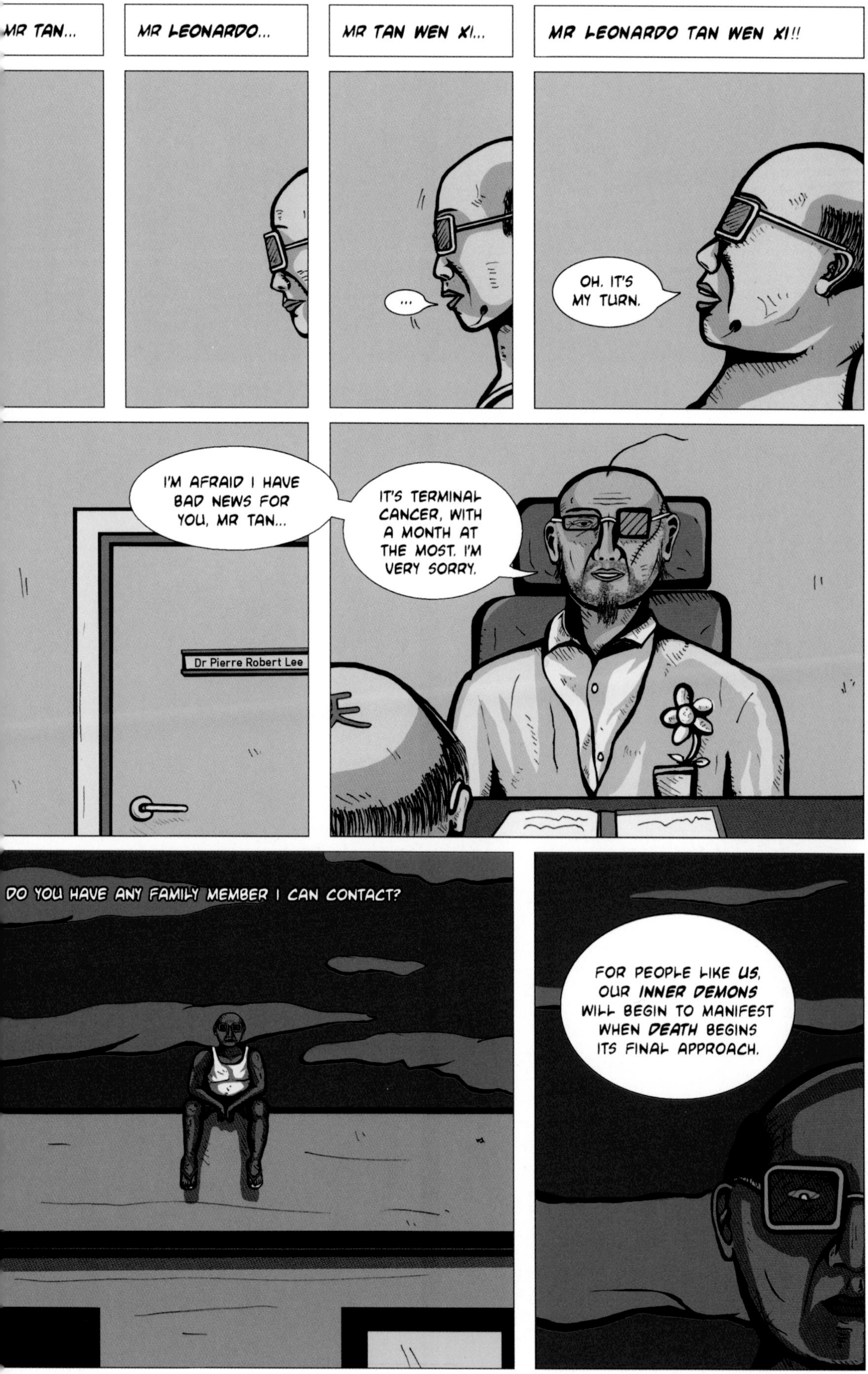
MR TAN...
MR LEONARDO...
MR TAN WEN XI...
MR LEONARDO TAN WEN XI!!
...
OH. IT'S MY TURN.
I'M AFRAID I HAVE BAD NEWS FOR YOU, MR TAN...
Dr Pierre Robert Lee
IT'S TERMINAL CANCER, WITH A MONTH AT THE MOST. I'M VERY SORRY.
DO YOU HAVE ANY FAMILY MEMBER I CAN CONTACT?
FOR PEOPLE LIKE US, OUR INNER DEMONS WILL BEGIN TO MANIFEST WHEN DEATH BEGINS ITS FINAL APPROACH.

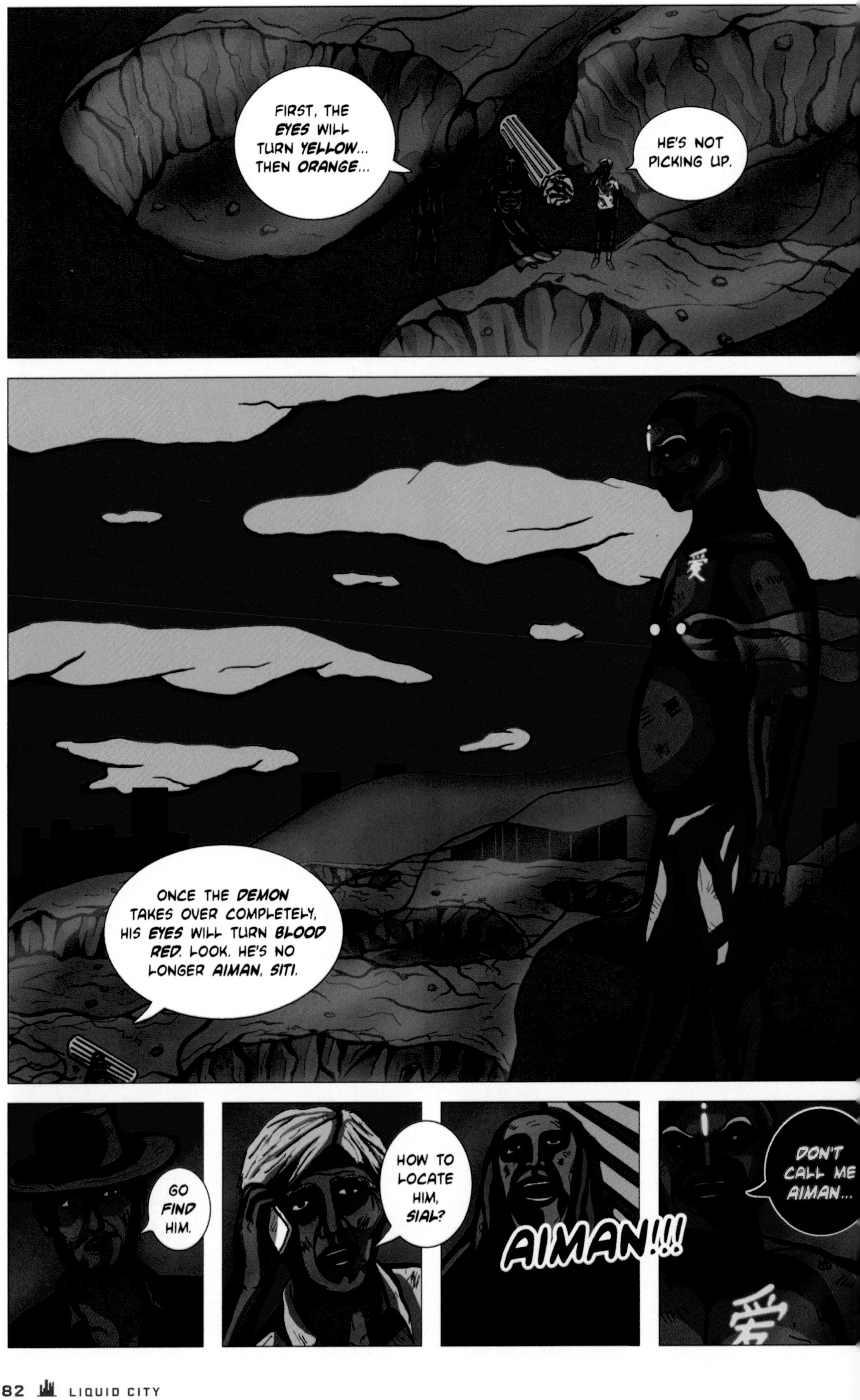

FIRST, THE EYES WILL TURN YELLOW... THEN ORANGE...
HE'S NOT PICKING UP.
ONCE THE DEMON TAKES OVER COMPLETELY, HIS EYES WILL TURN BLOOD RED. LOOK. HE'S NO LONGER AIMAN, SITI.
GO FIND HIM.
HOW TO LOCATE HIM, SIAL?
AIMAN!!!
DON'T CALL ME AIMAN...

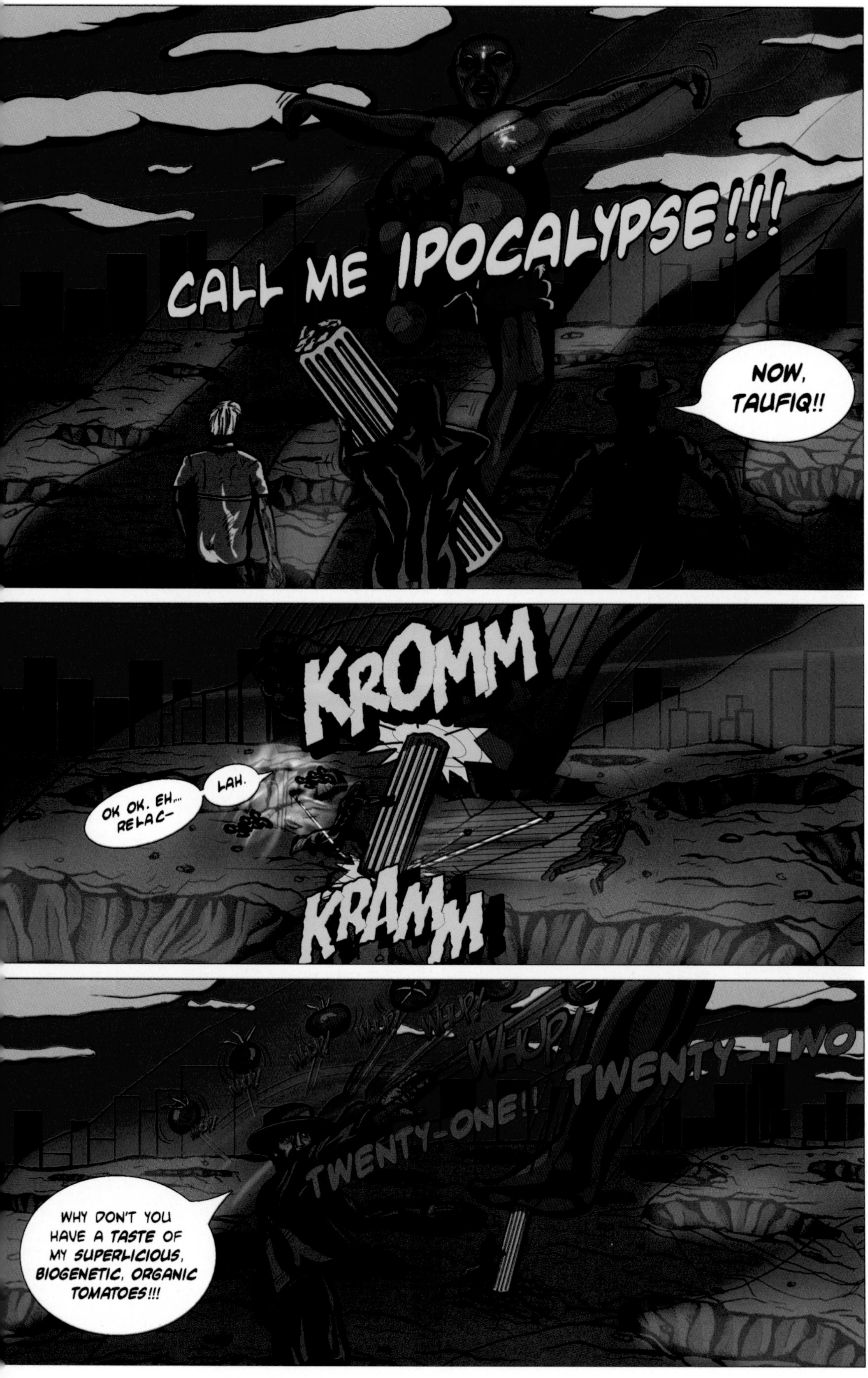

CALL ME IPOCALYPSE!!!
NOW, TAUFIQ!!
KROMM
OK OK. EH... RELAC-
LAH.
KRAMM
WHUP!
WHUP!
WHUP!!
TWENTY-ONE!!
TWENTY-TWO
WHY DON'T YOU HAVE A TASTE OF MY SUPERLICIOUS, BIOGENETIC, ORGANIC TOMATOES!!!

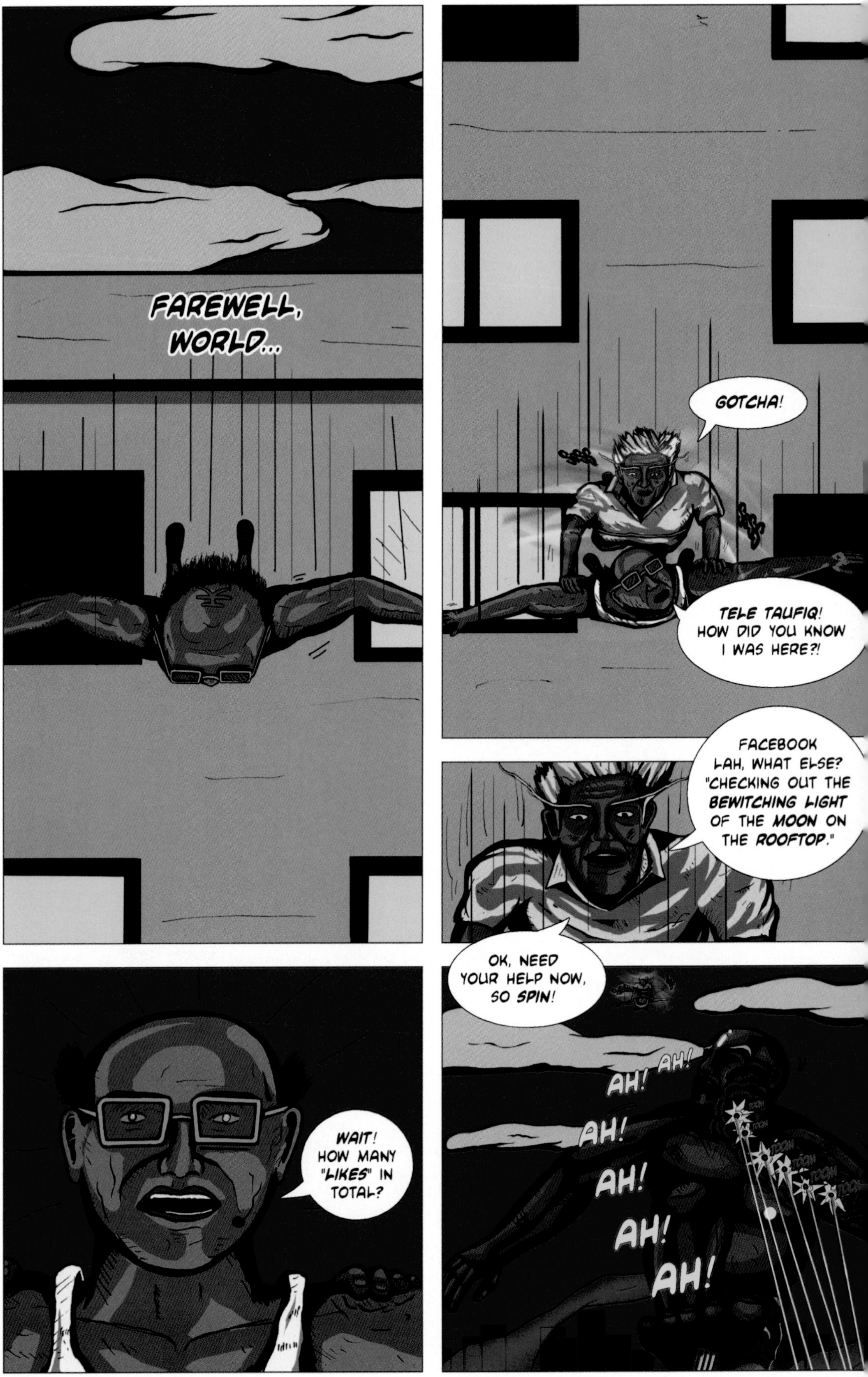
FAREWELL, WORLD...
GOTCHA!
TELE TAUFIQ! HOW DID YOU KNOW I WAS HERE?!
FACEBOOK LAH, WHAT ELSE? "CHECKING OUT THE BEWITCHING LIGHT OF THE MOON ON THE ROOFTOP."
WAIT! HOW MANY "LIKES" IN TOTAL?
OK, NEED YOUR HELP NOW, SO SPIN!
AH! AH!
AH!
AH!
AH!
AH!
TOOM
TOOM
TOOM
TOOM
TOOM
TOOM

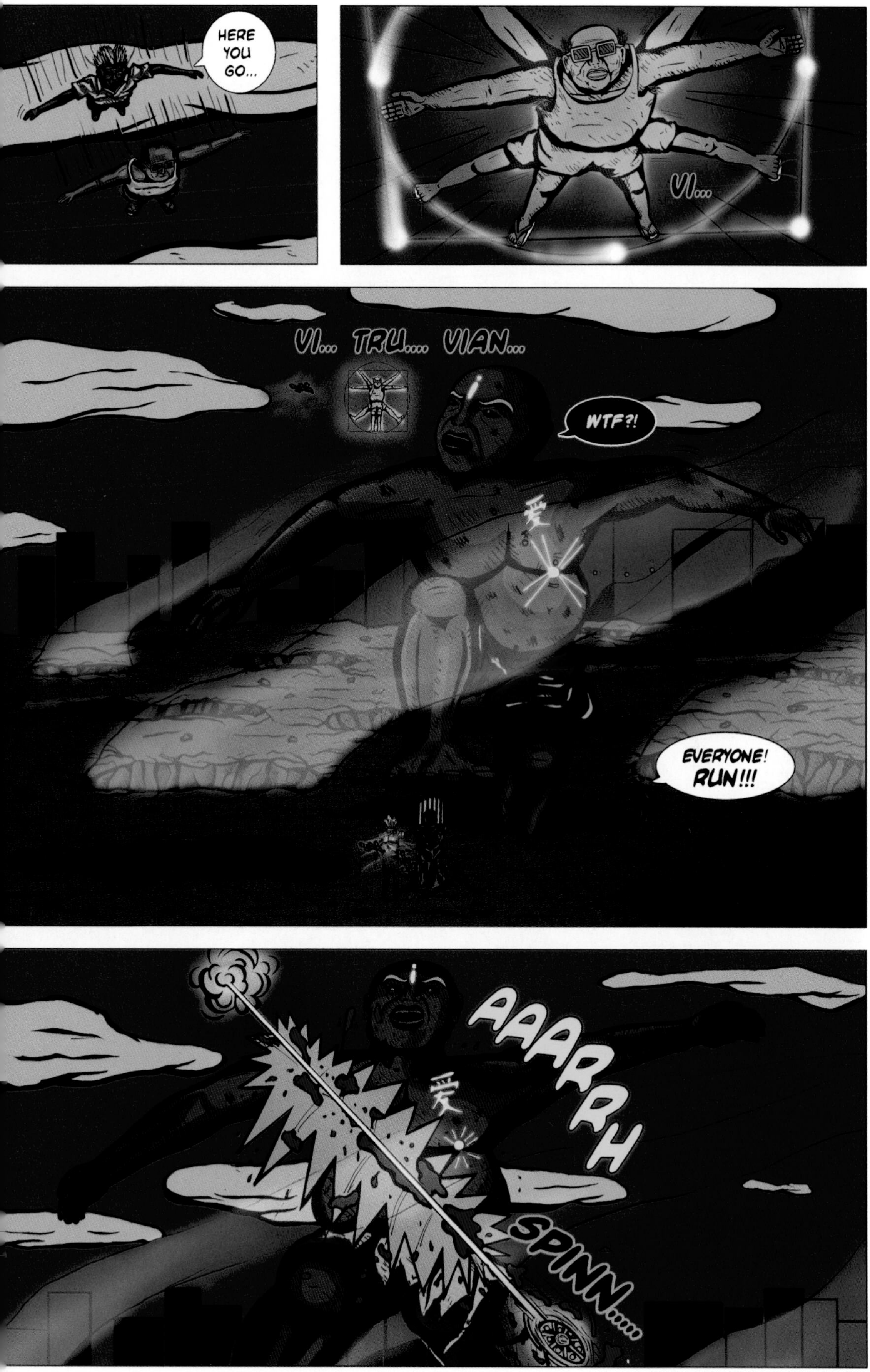
HERE YOU GO...
VI...
VI... TRU.... VIAN...
WTF?!
爱
EVERYONE! RUN!!!
AAARRH
爱
SPINN.....

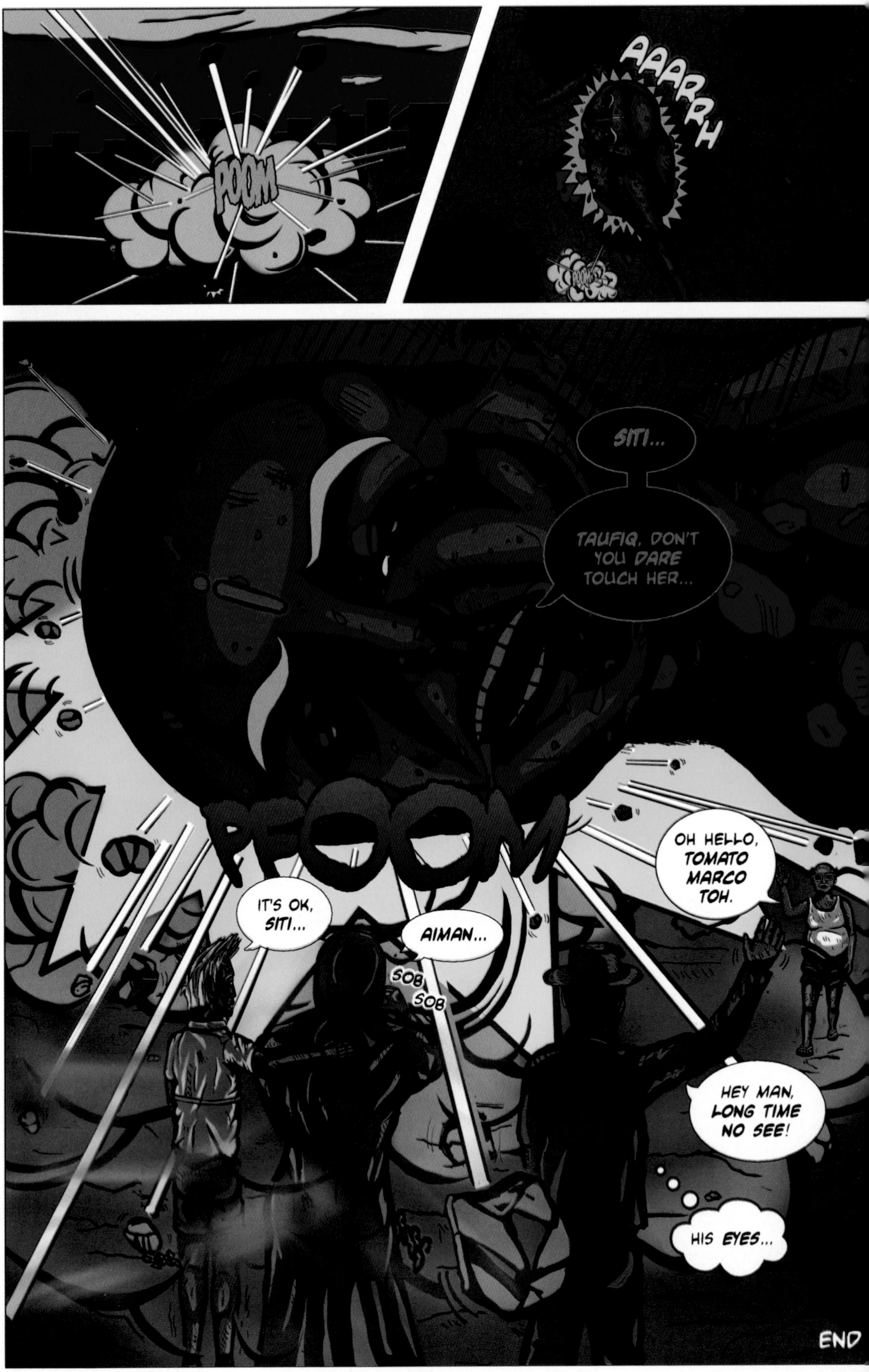
POOM
AAAARRH
SITI...
TAUFIQ, DON'T YOU DARE TOUCH HER...
PFOOM
IT'S OK, SITI...
AIMAN...
SOB SOB
OH HELLO, TOMATO MARCO TOH.
HEY MAN, LONG TIME NO SEE!
HIS EYES...
END

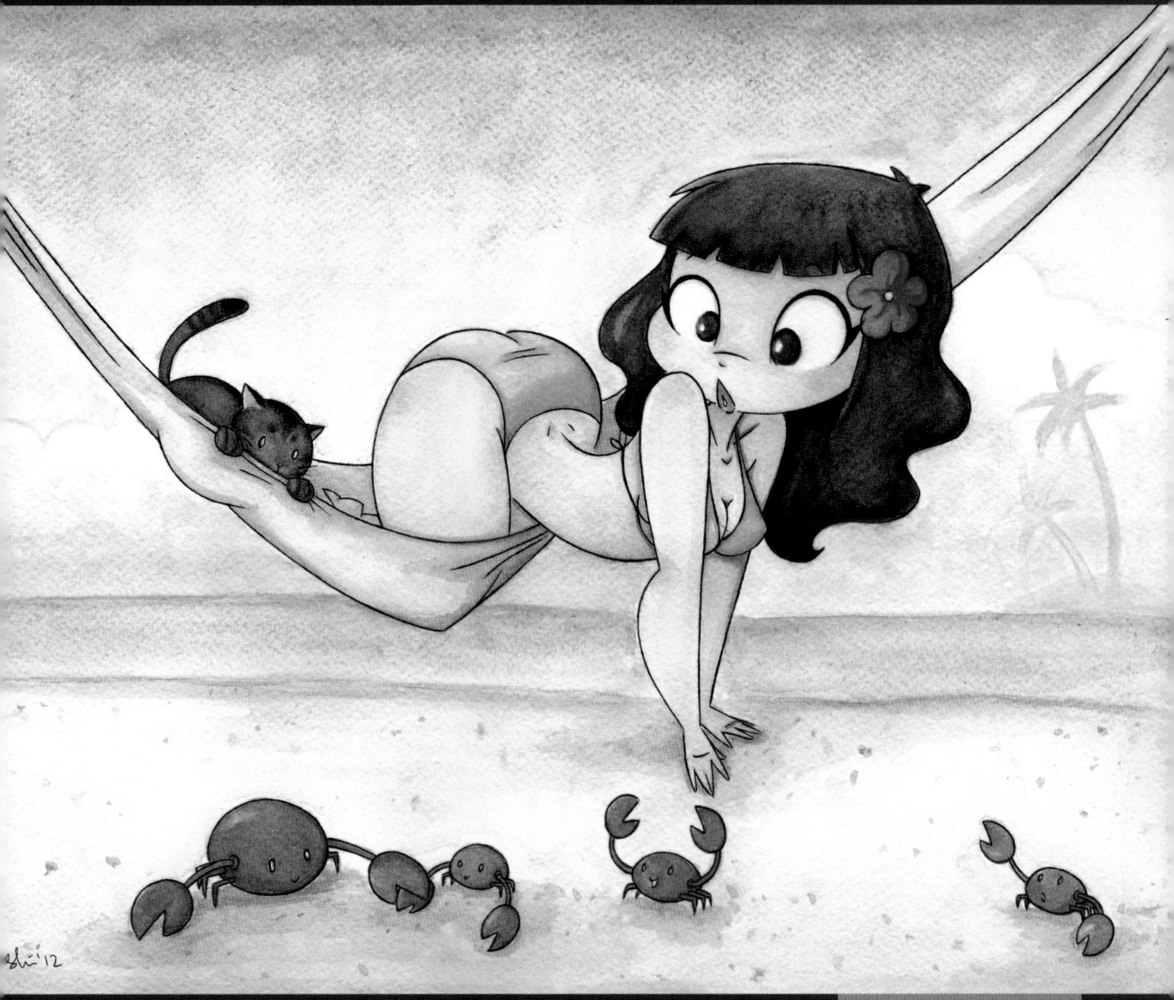

A Day at the Beach
WENDY CHEW

1.A.M

by Tidus Fair Supertramp

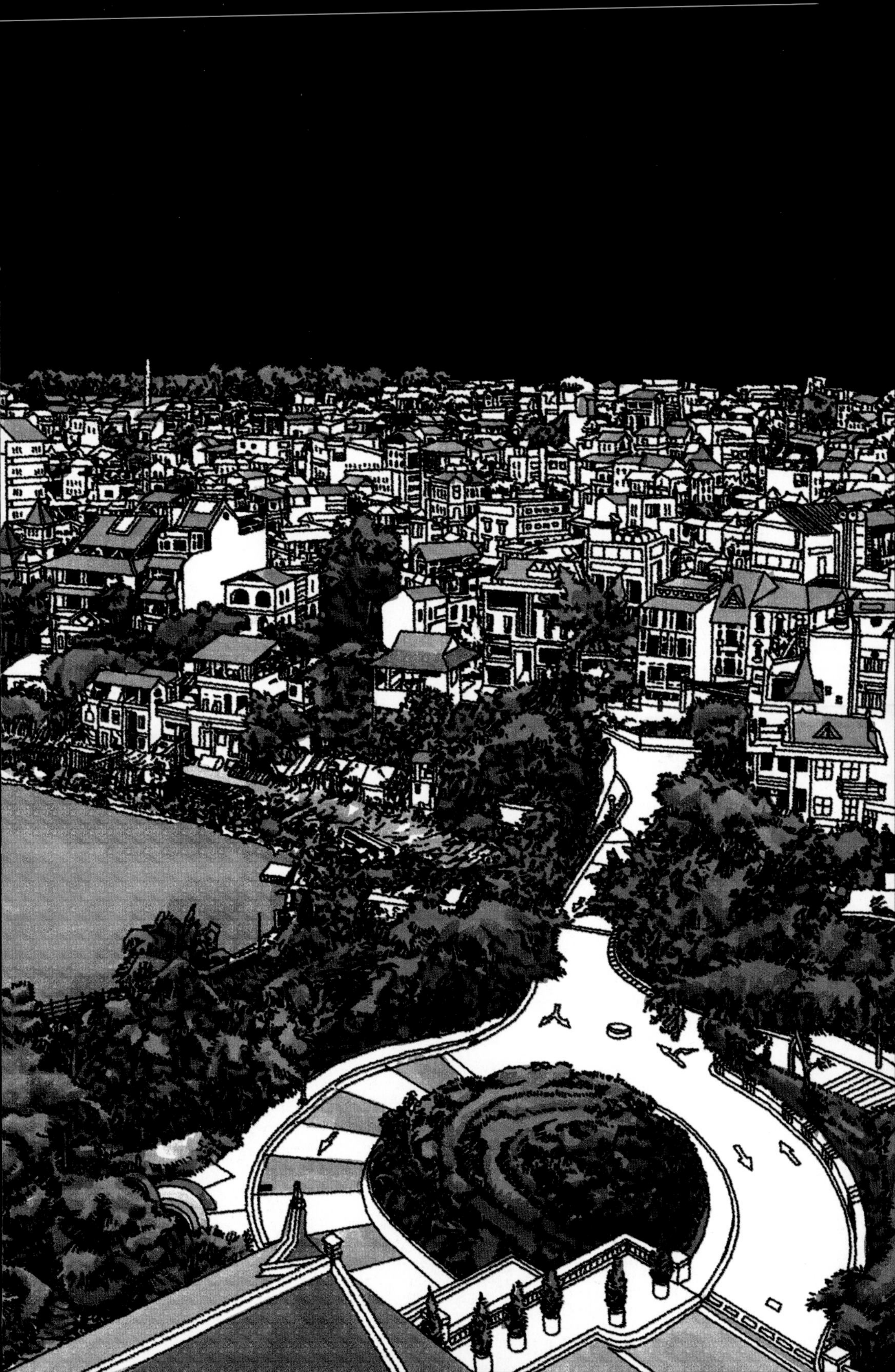

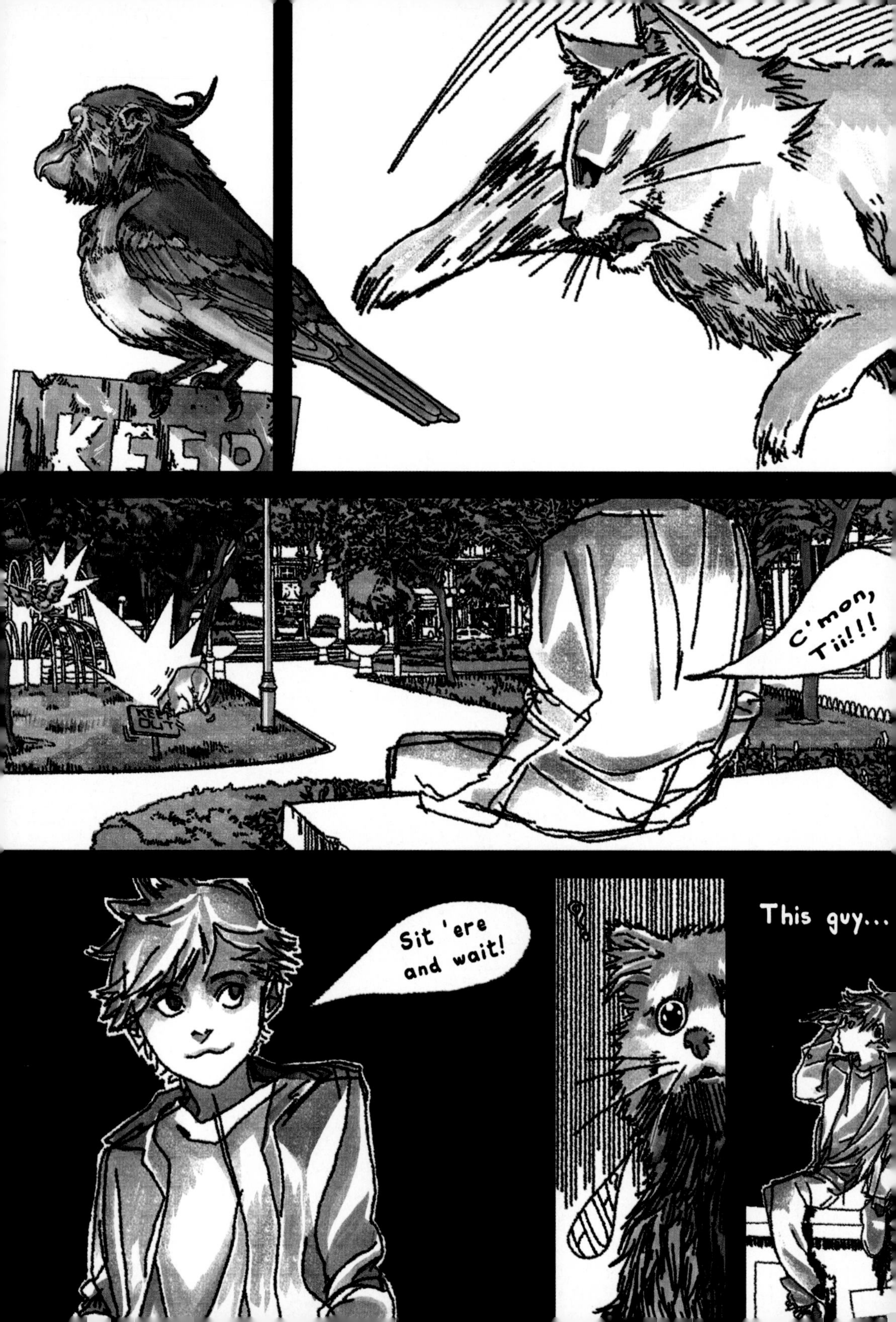
KEEP
KEEP OUT
C'mon, Tii!!!
Sit 'ere and wait!
This guy...

You know, even though I'm a cat, I usually go out with him late into the night. Why, you ask? It's quite simple, really. He's my real boss, after all.

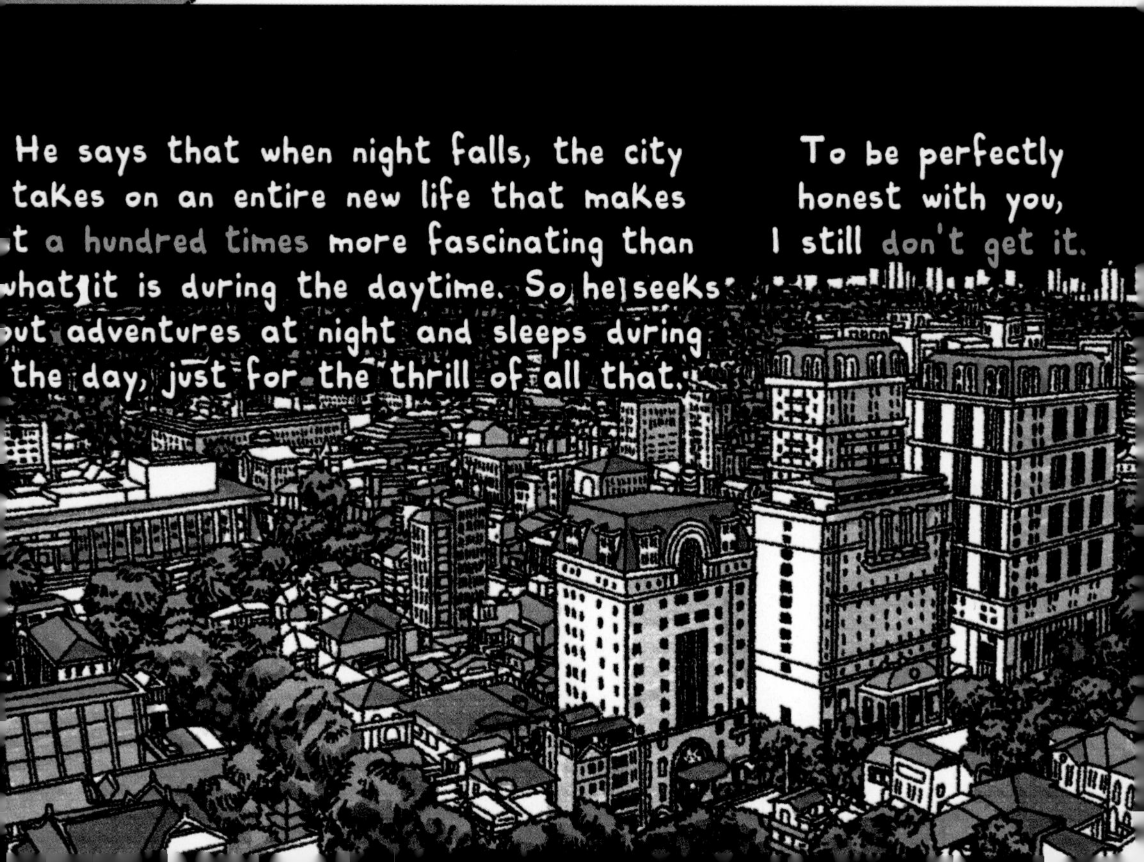

He says that when night falls, the city takes on an entire new life that makes it a hundred times more fascinating than what it is during the daytime. So he seeks out adventures at night and sleeps during the day, just for the thrill of all that.

To be perfectly honest with you, I still don't get it.

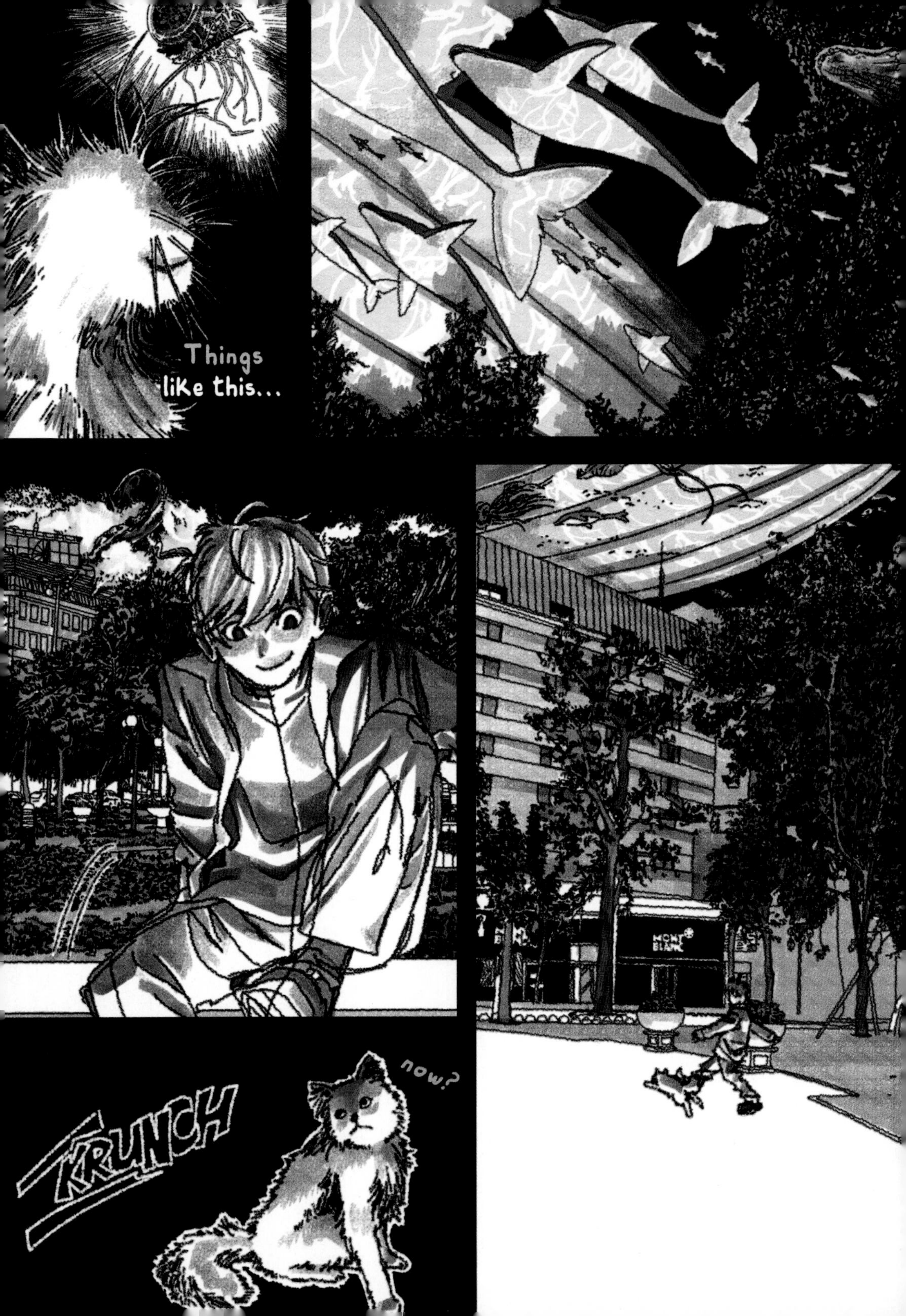
Things like this...
KRUNCH
now?
MONT BLANC

NHÀ HÁT LỚN HÀ NỘI

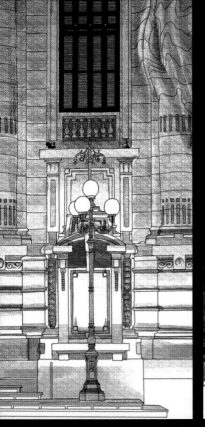

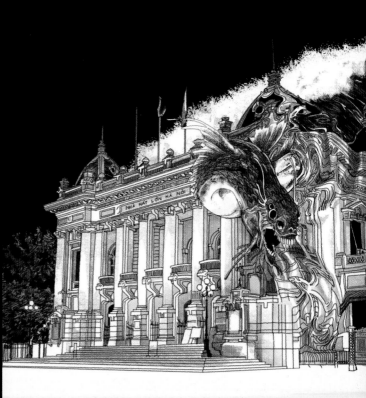

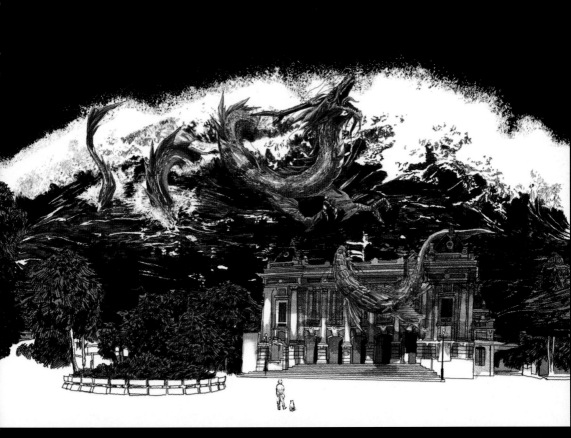

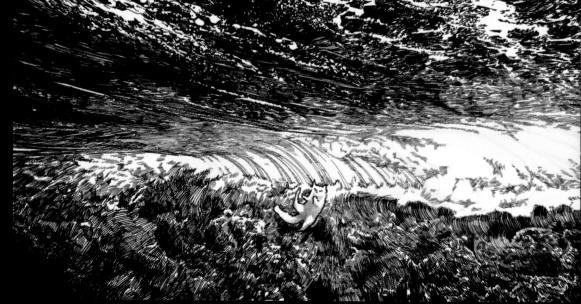

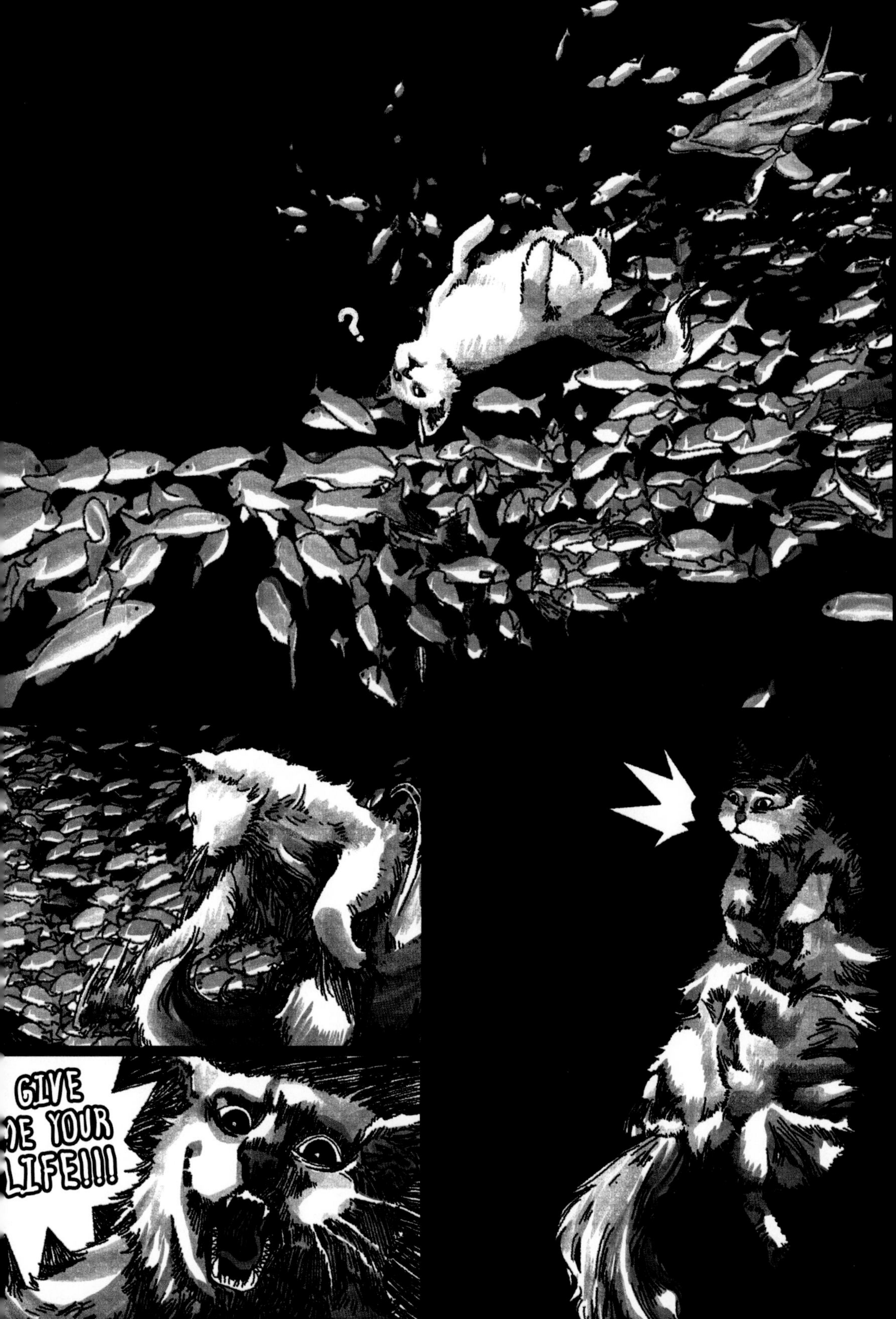
?
GIVE
E YOUR
LIFE!!!

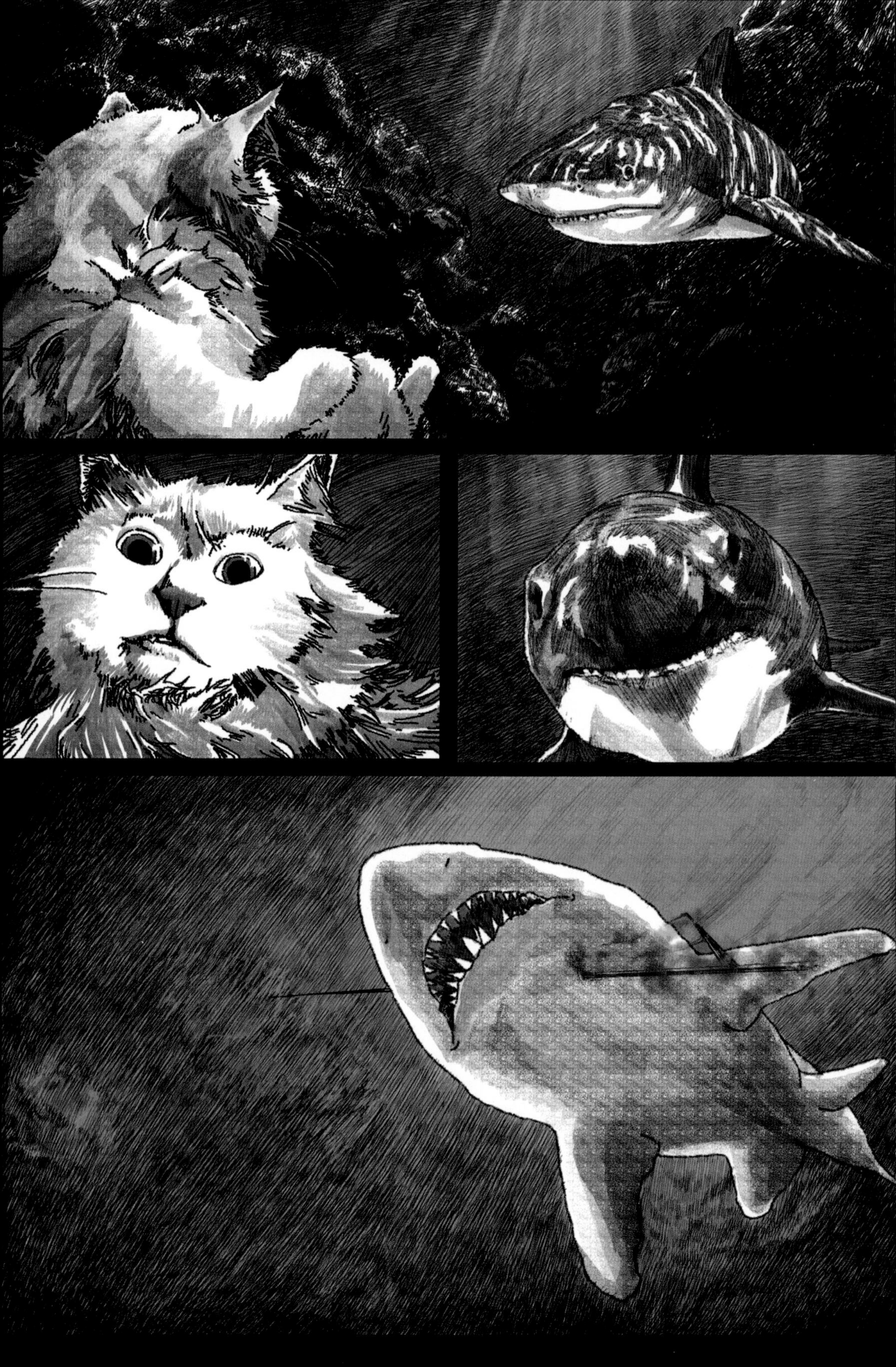

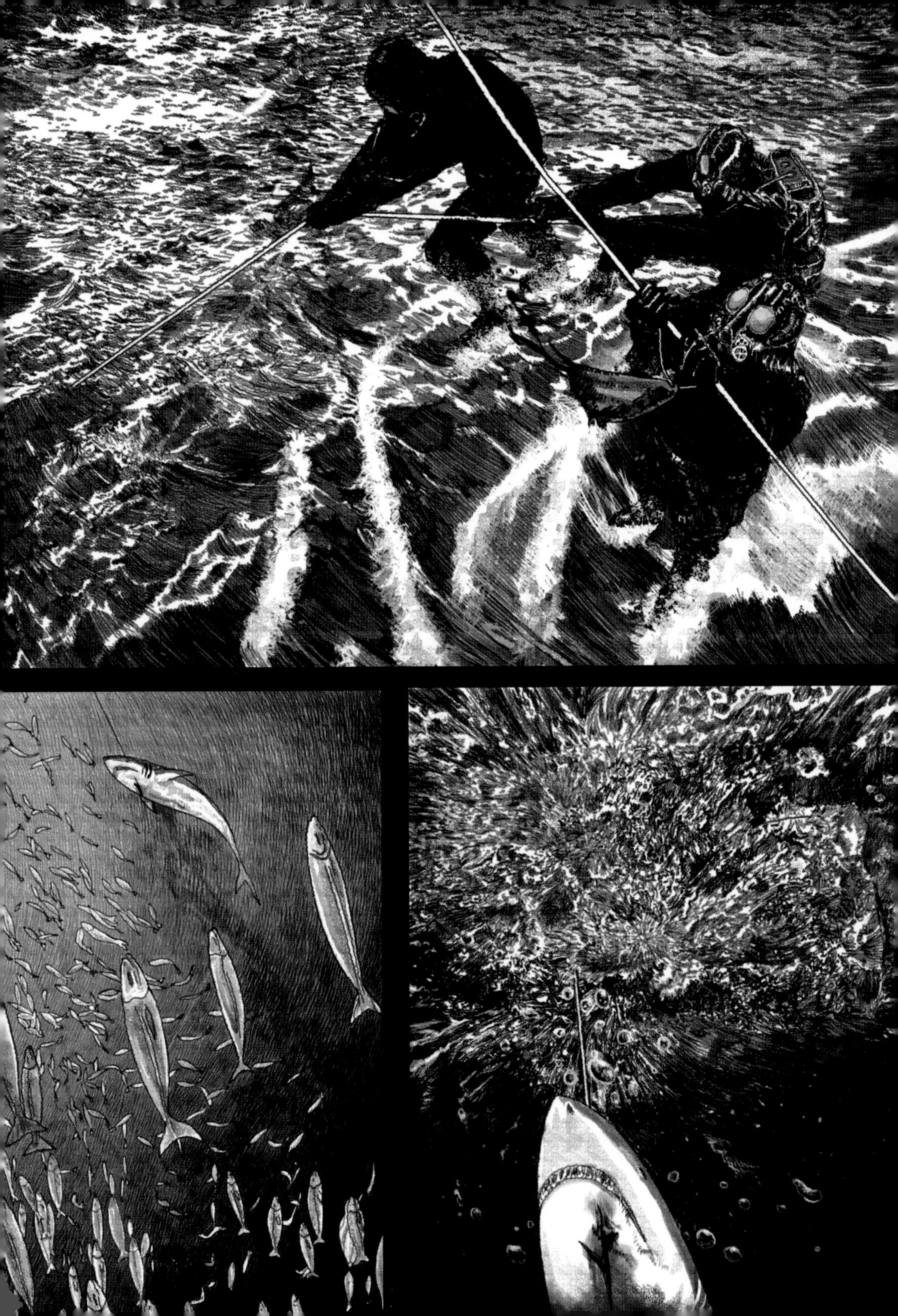

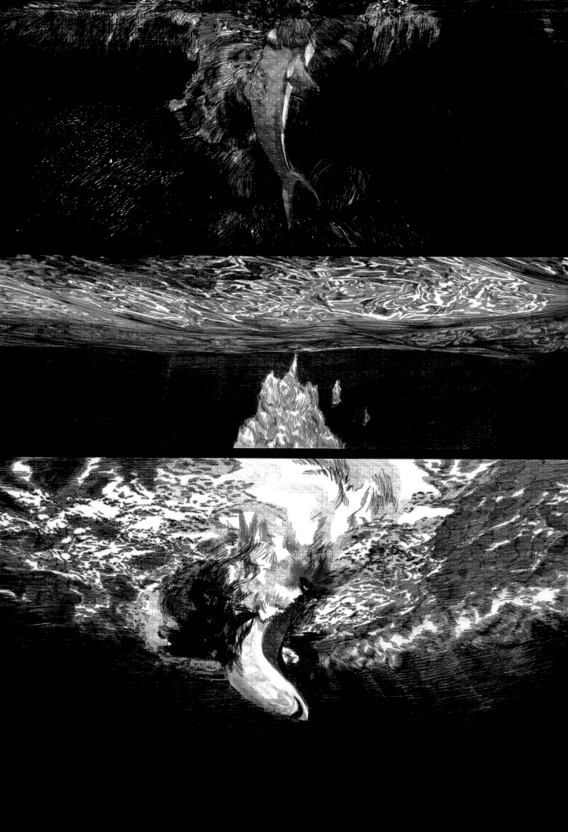

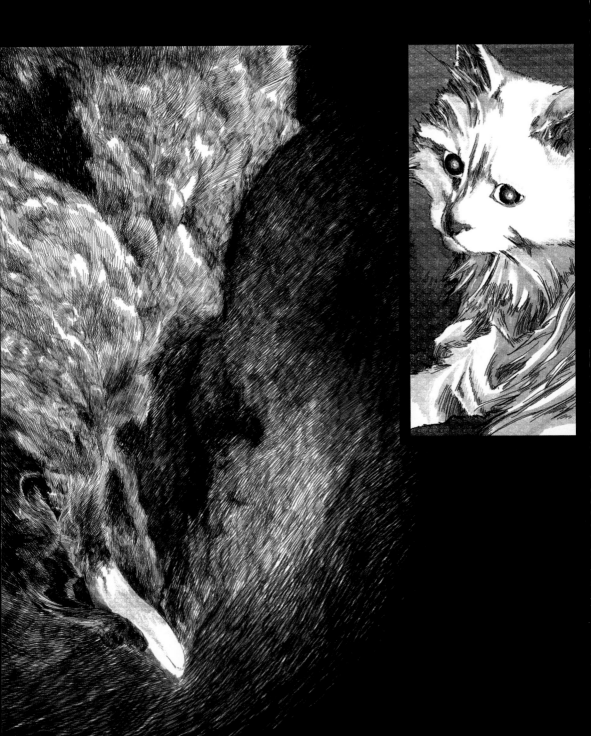

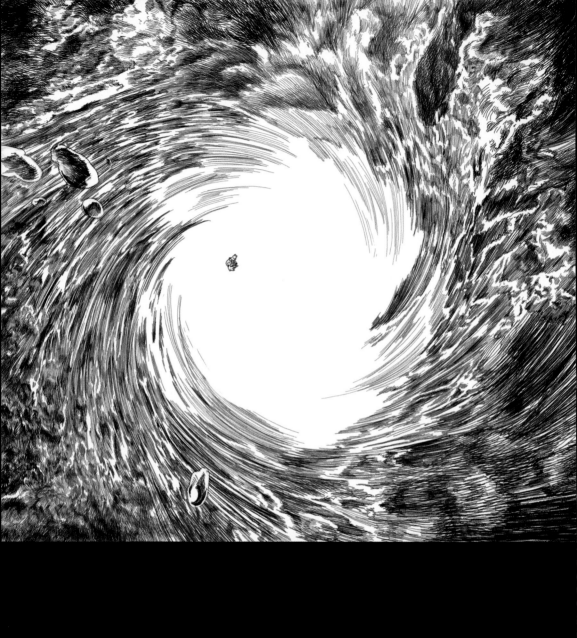

where is he?

hey, tii, tii!!

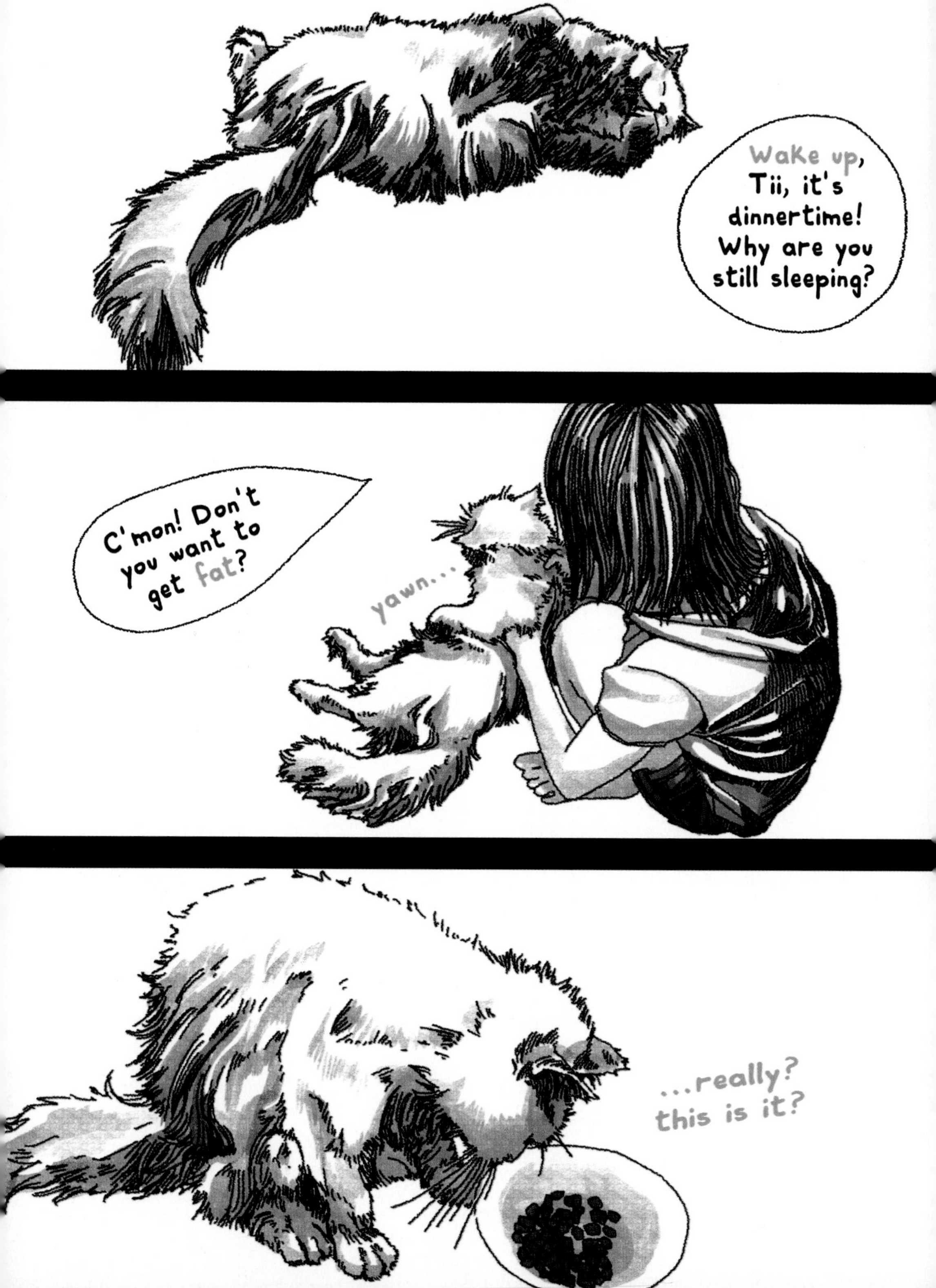
Wake up, Tii, it's dinnertime! Why are you still sleeping?
C'mon! Don't you want to get fat?
yawn...
...really? this is it?

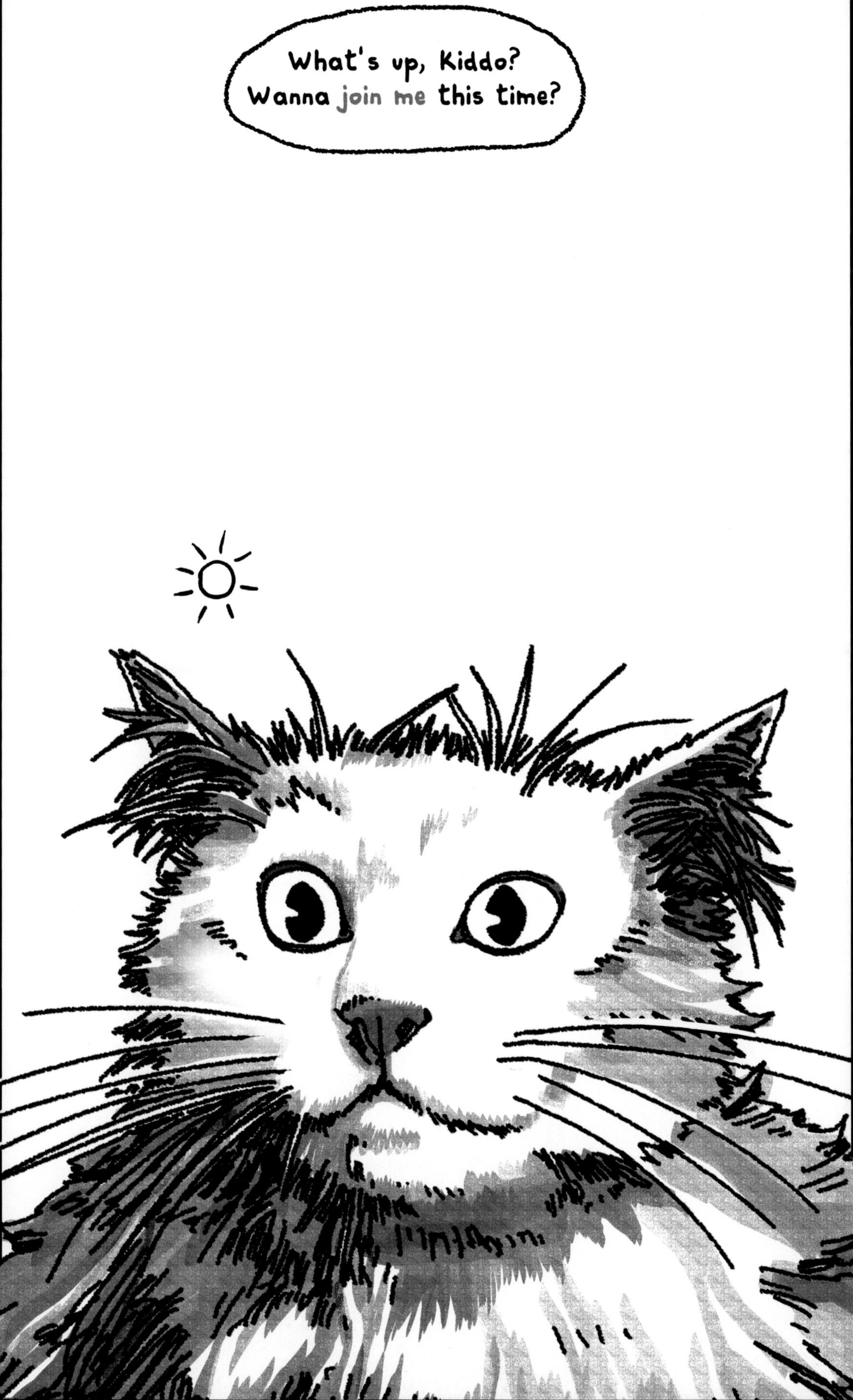
What's up, Kiddo? Wanna join me this time?

Life After the End of the World as We Know It

BABA CHUAH

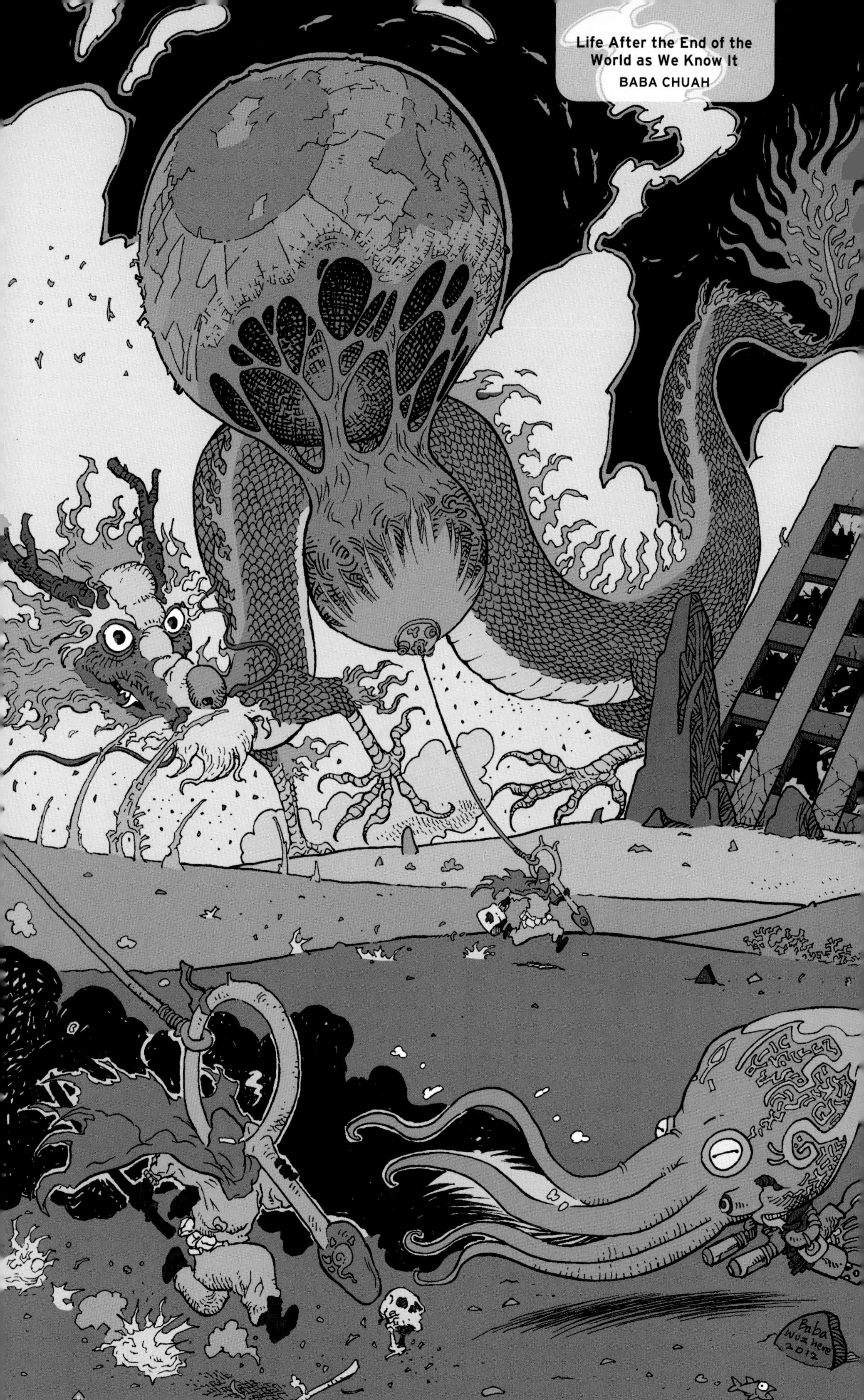
Baba wuz here 2012

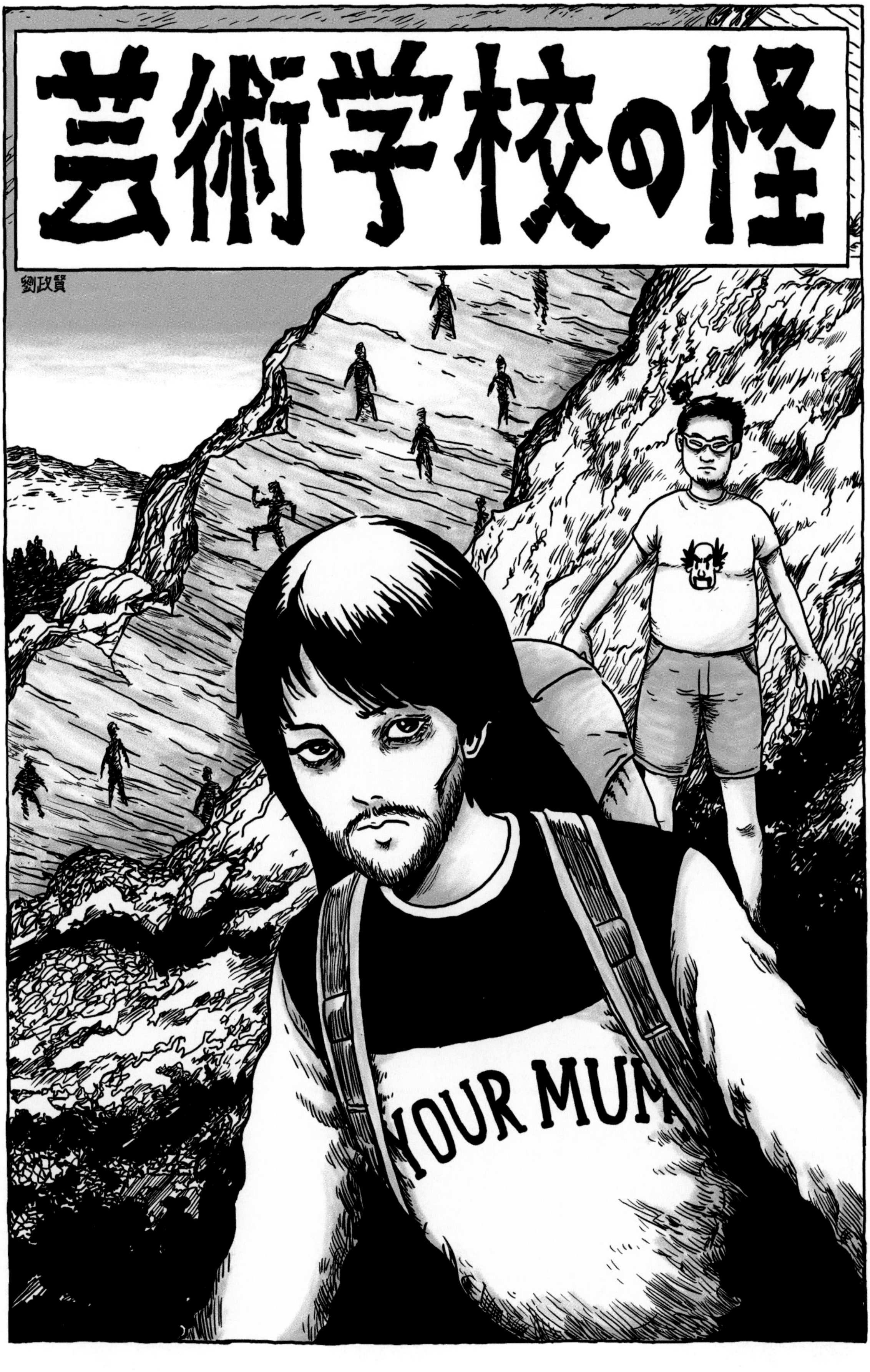
芸術学校の怪
劉政賢
YOUR MUM

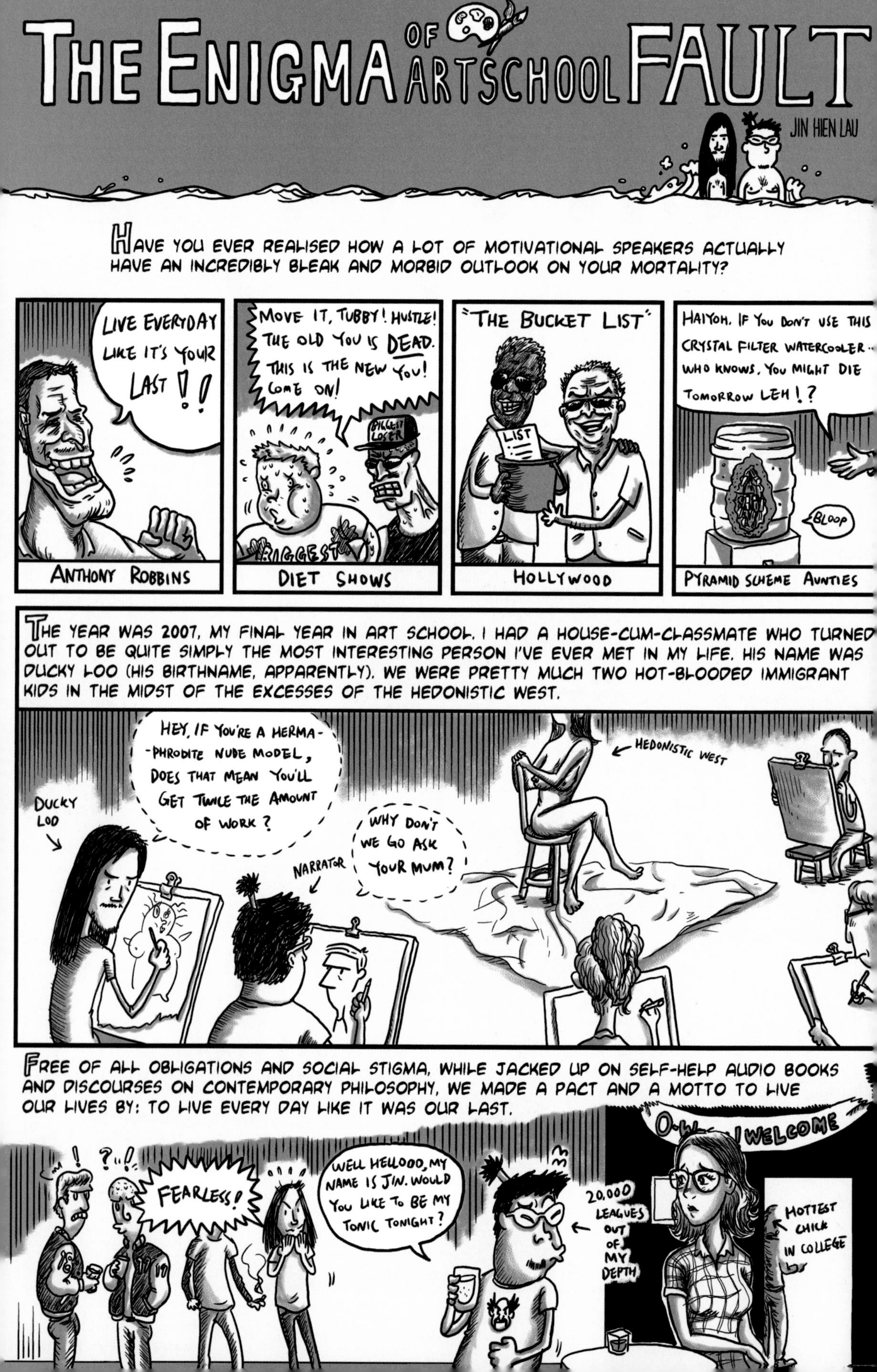
THE ENIGMA OF ARTSCHOOL FAULT
JIN HIEN LAU
HAVE YOU EVER REALISED HOW A LOT OF MOTIVATIONAL SPEAKERS ACTUALLY HAVE AN INCREDIBLY BLEAK AND MORBID OUTLOOK ON YOUR MORTALITY?
LIVE EVERYDAY LIKE IT'S YOUR LAST !!
ANTHONY ROBBINS
MOVE IT, TUBBY! HUSTLE! THE OLD YOU IS DEAD. THIS IS THE NEW YOU! COME ON!
BIGGEST LOSER
BIGGEST
DIET SHOWS
"THE BUCKET LIST"
LIST
HOLLYWOOD
HAIYOH, IF YOU DON'T USE THIS CRYSTAL FILTER WATERCOOLER... WHO KNOWS, YOU MIGHT DIE TOMORROW LEH!?
BLOOP
PYRAMID SCHEME AUNTIES
THE YEAR WAS 2007, MY FINAL YEAR IN ART SCHOOL. I HAD A HOUSE-CUM-CLASSMATE WHO TURNED OUT TO BE QUITE SIMPLY THE MOST INTERESTING PERSON I'VE EVER MET IN MY LIFE. HIS NAME WAS DUCKY LOO (HIS BIRTHNAME, APPARENTLY). WE WERE PRETTY MUCH TWO HOT-BLOODED IMMIGRANT KIDS IN THE MIDST OF THE EXCESSES OF THE HEDONISTIC WEST.
HEY, IF YOU'RE A HERMAPHRODITE NUDE MODEL, DOES THAT MEAN YOU'LL GET TWICE THE AMOUNT OF WORK?
DUCKY LOO
WHY DON'T WE GO ASK YOUR MUM?
NARRATOR
HEDONISTIC WEST
FREE OF ALL OBLIGATIONS AND SOCIAL STIGMA, WHILE JACKED UP ON SELF-HELP AUDIO BOOKS AND DISCOURSES ON CONTEMPORARY PHILOSOPHY, WE MADE A PACT AND A MOTTO TO LIVE OUR LIVES BY: TO LIVE EVERY DAY LIKE IT WAS OUR LAST.
WELCOME
FEARLESS!
WELL HELLOOO, MY NAME IS JIN. WOULD YOU LIKE TO BE MY TONIC TONIGHT?
20,000 LEAGUES OUT OF MY DEPTH
HOTTEST CHICK IN COLLEGE

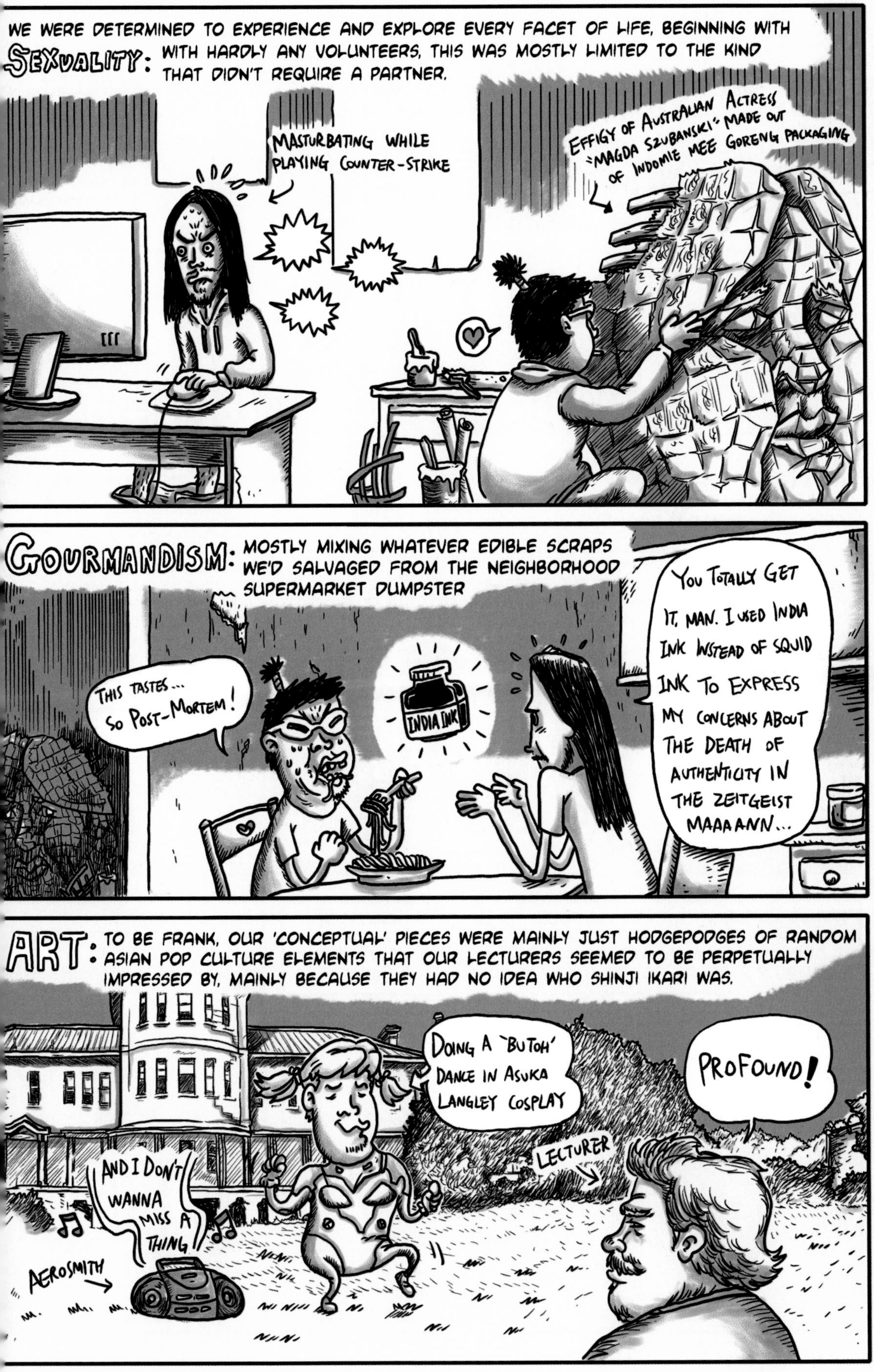

WE WERE DETERMINED TO EXPERIENCE AND EXPLORE EVERY FACET OF LIFE, BEGINNING WITH
SEXUALITY: WITH HARDLY ANY VOLUNTEERS, THIS WAS MOSTLY LIMITED TO THE KIND THAT DIDN'T REQUIRE A PARTNER.
MASTURBATING WHILE PLAYING COUNTER-STRIKE
EFFIGY OF AUSTRALIAN ACTRESS "MAGDA SZUBANSKI" MADE OUT OF INDOMIE MEE GORENG PACKAGING
GOURMANDISM: MOSTLY MIXING WHATEVER EDIBLE SCRAPS WE'D SALVAGED FROM THE NEIGHBORHOOD SUPERMARKET DUMPSTER
THIS TASTES... SO POST-MORTEM!
INDIA INK
YOU TOTALLY GET IT, MAN. I USED INDIA INK INSTEAD OF SQUID INK TO EXPRESS MY CONCERNS ABOUT THE DEATH OF AUTHENTICITY IN THE ZEITGEIST MAAAANN...
ART: TO BE FRANK, OUR 'CONCEPTUAL' PIECES WERE MAINLY JUST HODGEPODGES OF RANDOM ASIAN POP CULTURE ELEMENTS THAT OUR LECTURERS SEEMED TO BE PERPETUALLY IMPRESSED BY, MAINLY BECAUSE THEY HAD NO IDEA WHO SHINJI IKARI WAS.
DOING A 'BUTOH' DANCE IN ASUKA LANGLEY COSPLAY
PROFOUND!
LECTURER
AND I DON'T WANNA MISS A THING
AEROSMITH

GOING THROUGH FOUR FULL YEARS OF THE LAST DAY OF OUR LIVES MEANT THAT WE INEVITABLY HAD TO DISREGARD CERTAIN LESS PRESSING MATTERS, SUCH AS OUR DEGREE SHOW PROJECT.

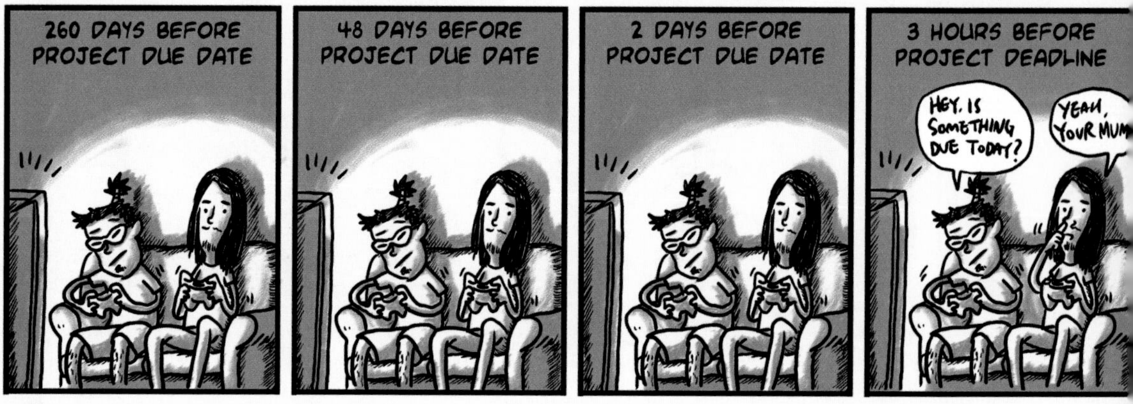
260 DAYS BEFORE PROJECT DUE DATE
48 DAYS BEFORE PROJECT DUE DATE
2 DAYS BEFORE PROJECT DUE DATE
3 HOURS BEFORE PROJECT DEADLINE
HEY, IS SOMETHING DUE TODAY?
YEAH, YOUR MUM

IN OUR DEFENCE, WE ADOPTED THIS WORK ETHIC IN ACCORDANCE TO OUR MOTTO. FOR WHAT COULD MAKE US MORE INSPIRED TO THRIVE AT OUR BEST, THAN THE ADRENALINE RUSH OF ABSOLUTE IMPENDING DOOM?

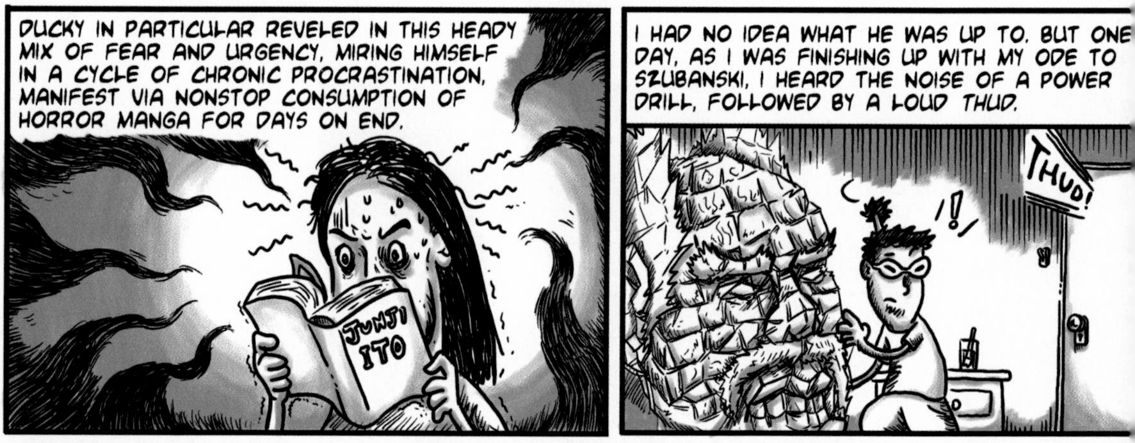
DUCKY IN PARTICULAR REVELED IN THIS HEADY MIX OF FEAR AND URGENCY, MIRING HIMSELF IN A CYCLE OF CHRONIC PROCRASTINATION, MANIFEST VIA NONSTOP CONSUMPTION OF HORROR MANGA FOR DAYS ON END.
JUNJI ITO
I HAD NO IDEA WHAT HE WAS UP TO, BUT ONE DAY, AS I WAS FINISHING UP WITH MY ODE TO SZUBANSKI, I HEARD THE NOISE OF A POWER DRILL, FOLLOWED BY A LOUD THUD.
THUD!
!

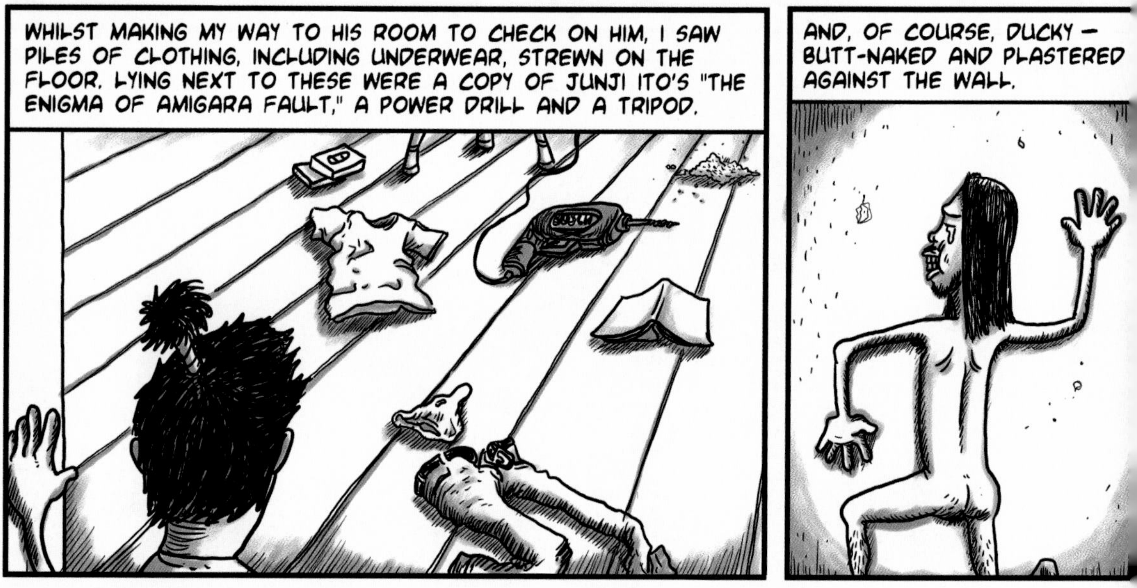
WHILST MAKING MY WAY TO HIS ROOM TO CHECK ON HIM, I SAW PILES OF CLOTHING, INCLUDING UNDERWEAR, STREWN ON THE FLOOR. LYING NEXT TO THESE WERE A COPY OF JUNJI ITO'S "THE ENIGMA OF AMIGARA FAULT," A POWER DRILL AND A TRIPOD.
AND, OF COURSE, DUCKY — BUTT-NAKED AND PLASTERED AGAINST THE WALL.

IT TURNED OUT THAT DUCKY HAD DRILLED A HOLE IN THE WALL, MEASURED TO THE HEIGHT OF HIS CROTCH. HE THEN RAN TOWARDS IT, SLAMMING HIS PENIS INTO THE HOLE AT FULL SPEED. THE VIDEO ENDED WITH AN INTIMATE CLOSE-UP OF A SINGULAR MAN-TEAR ROLLING DOWN HIS CHEEK.

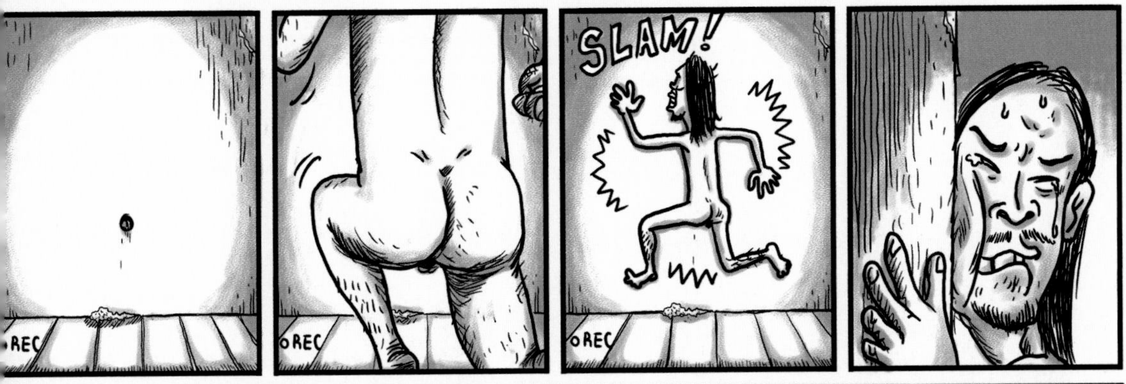
REC
REC
SLAM!
REC

HIS DARING PROJECT AND VIDEO NOT ONLY EARNED HIM A HIGH DISTINCTION, BUT ENDED UP BEING SHOWN IN QUITE A FEW PRESTIGIOUS GALLERIES AS WELL, GARNERING HIM INSTANT FAME WITHIN THE ART COMMUNITY.

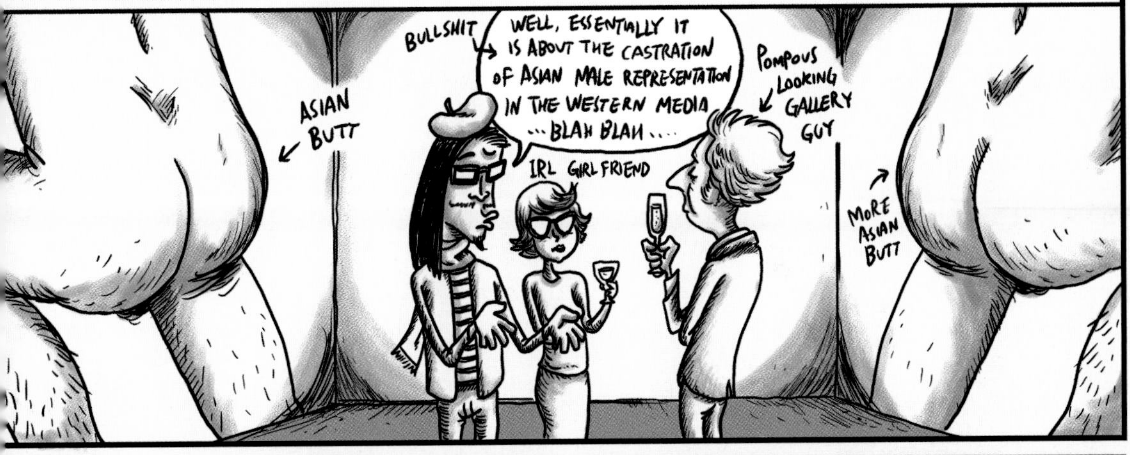
ASIAN BUTT
BULLSHIT
WELL, ESSENTIALLY IT IS ABOUT THE CASTRATION OF ASIAN MALE REPRESENTATION IN THE WESTERN MEDIA ...BLAH BLAH...
POMPOUS LOOKING GALLERY GUY
IRL GIRLFRIEND
MORE ASIAN BUTT

SOMEHOW, WE DIDN'T MANAGE TO STAY IN TOUCH AFTER GRADUATION. THEN BY TOTAL COIN-CIDENCE, I RAN INTO HIM IN SYDNEY A MONTH AGO. HE SEEMED TO BE DOING EXTREMELY WELL, RUNNING A SCAM BUSINESS THAT INVOLVED REPACKAGING DEFUNCT, BRANDED COMPUTERS FROM ALL ACROSS THE COUNTRY USING SOME KIND OF DECREPIT TECHNOLOGY, THEN SELLING THEM TO RURAL CHINESE SCHOOLS FOR A TIDY PROFIT. HE ALSO OFFERED ME LOTS OF ADVICE ON MISTRESS-KEEPING, EVEN THOUGH I'M STILL HAPPILY SINGLE. JUST LIKE THE GOOD OL' DAYS...

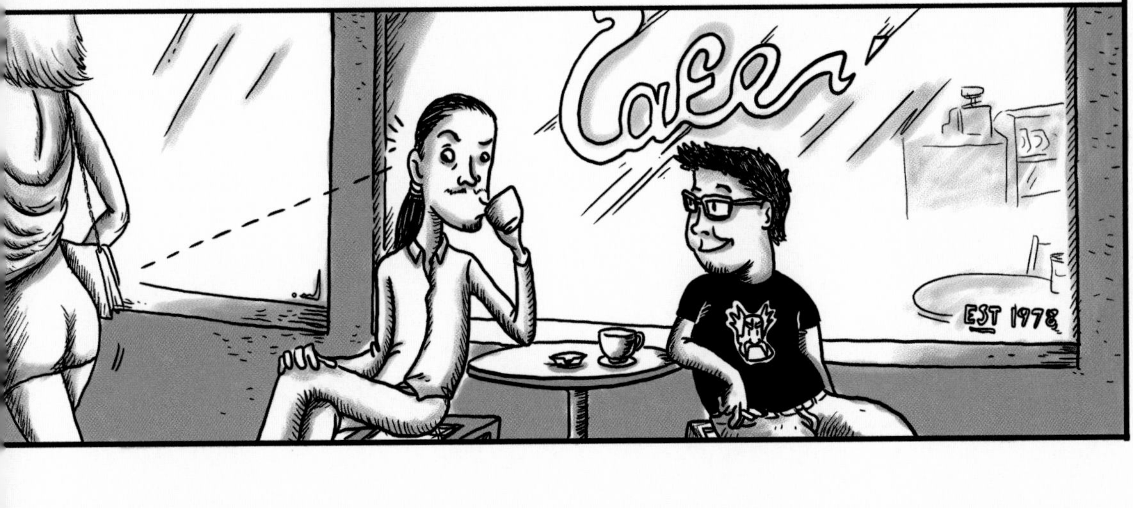
Cafe
EST 1978

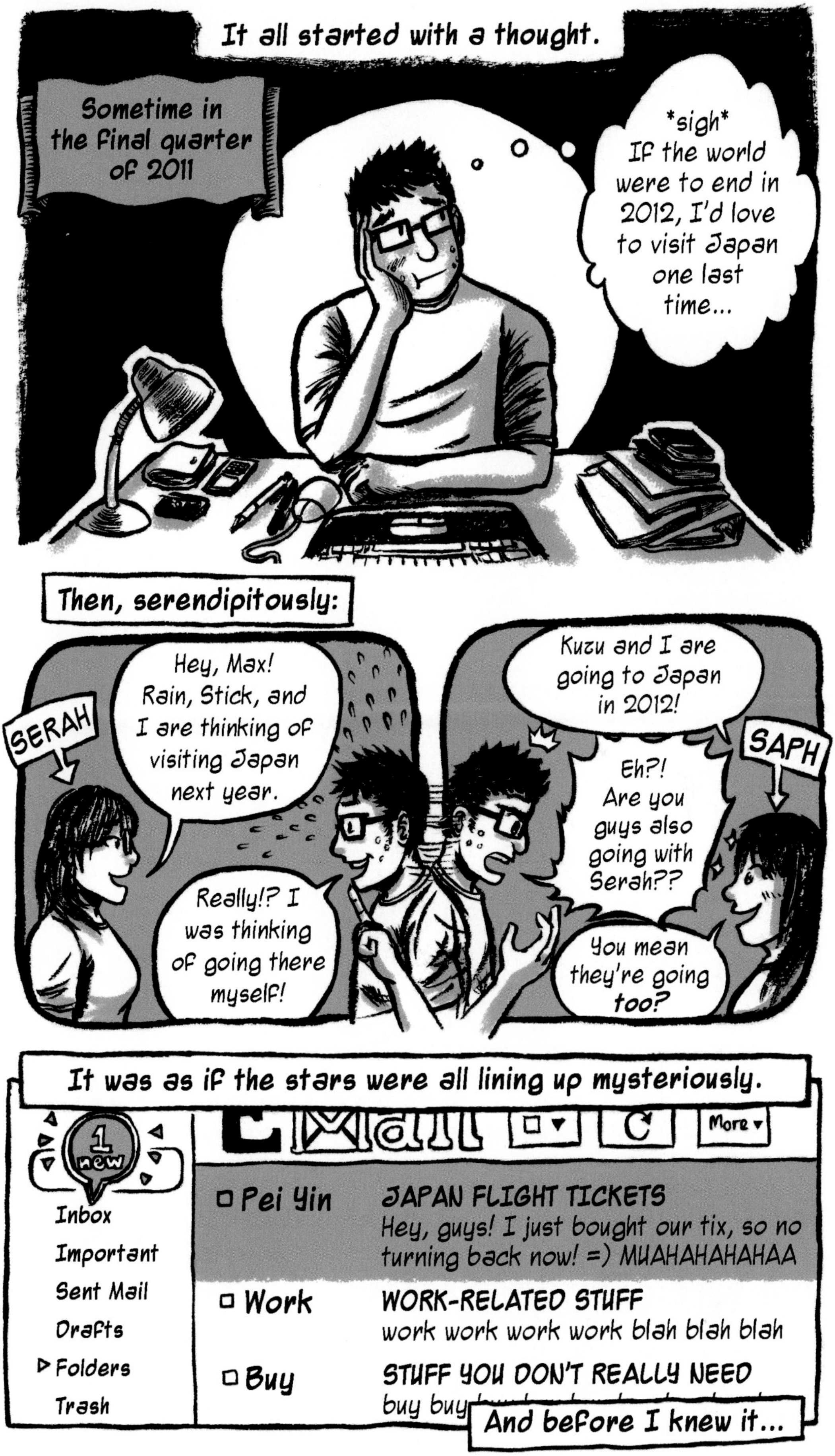
It all started with a thought.
Sometime in the final quarter of 2011
sigh If the world were to end in 2012, I'd love to visit Japan one last time...
Then, serendipitously:
SERAH
Hey, Max! Rain, Stick, and I are thinking of visiting Japan next year.
Really!? I was thinking of going there myself!
Kuzu and I are going to Japan in 2012!
SAPH
Eh?! Are you guys also going with Serah??
You mean they're going too?
It was as if the stars were all lining up mysteriously.
1 new
Inbox
Important
Sent Mail
Drafts
Folders
Trash
More
Pei Yin
JAPAN FLIGHT TICKETS
Hey, guys! I just bought our tix, so no turning back now! =) MUAHAHAHAHAA
Work
WORK-RELATED STUFF
work work work work blah blah blah
Buy
STUFF YOU DON'T REALLY NEED
And before I knew it...

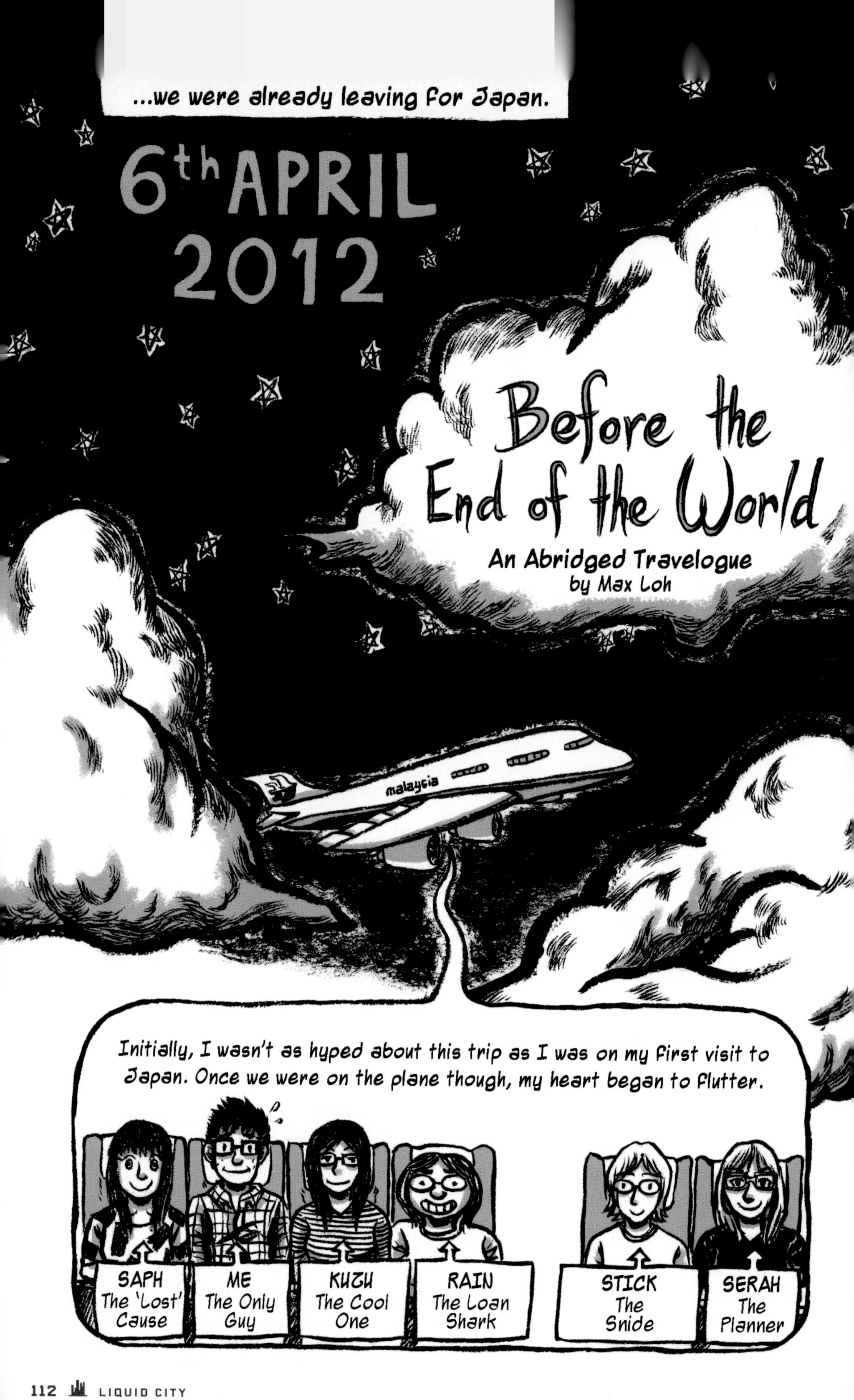
...we were already leaving for Japan.
6th APRIL 2012
Before the End of the World
An Abridged Travelogue
by Max Loh
malaysia
Initially, I wasn't as hyped about this trip as I was on my first visit to Japan. Once we were on the plane though, my heart began to flutter.
SAPH The 'Lost' Cause
ME The Only Guy
KUZU The Cool One
RAIN The Loan Shark
STICK The Snide
SERAH The Planner

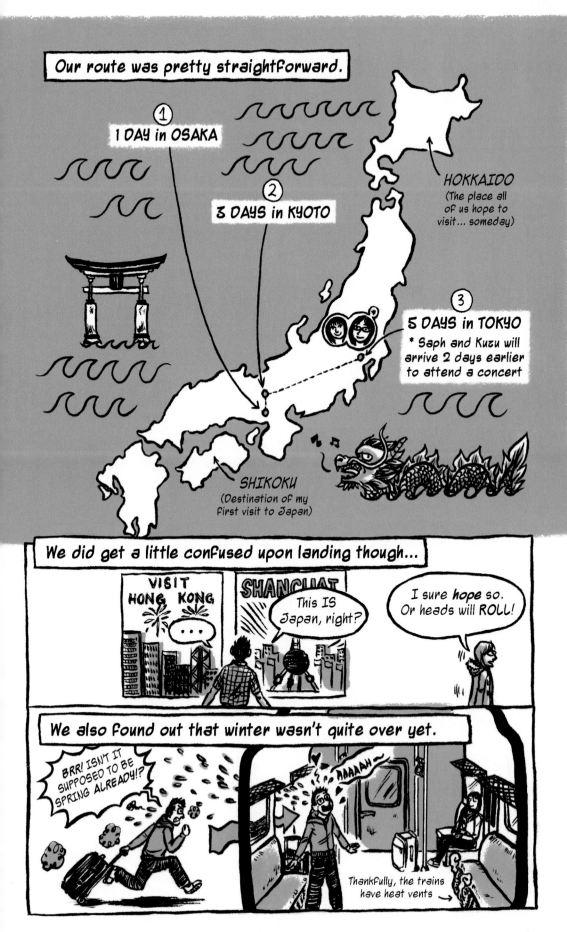

Our route was pretty straightforward.

① 1 DAY in OSAKA

② 3 DAYS in KYOTO

③ 5 DAYS in TOKYO
* Saph and Kuzu will arrive 2 days earlier to attend a concert

HOKKAIDO
(The place all of us hope to visit... someday)

SHIKOKU
(Destination of my first visit to Japan)

We did get a little confused upon landing though...

VISIT HONG KONG

SHANGHAI

This IS Japan, right?

I sure *hope* so. Or heads will ROLL!

We also found out that winter wasn't quite over yet.

BRR! ISN'T IT SUPPOSED TO BE SPRING ALREADY!?

AAAAH~

Thankfully, the trains have heat vents

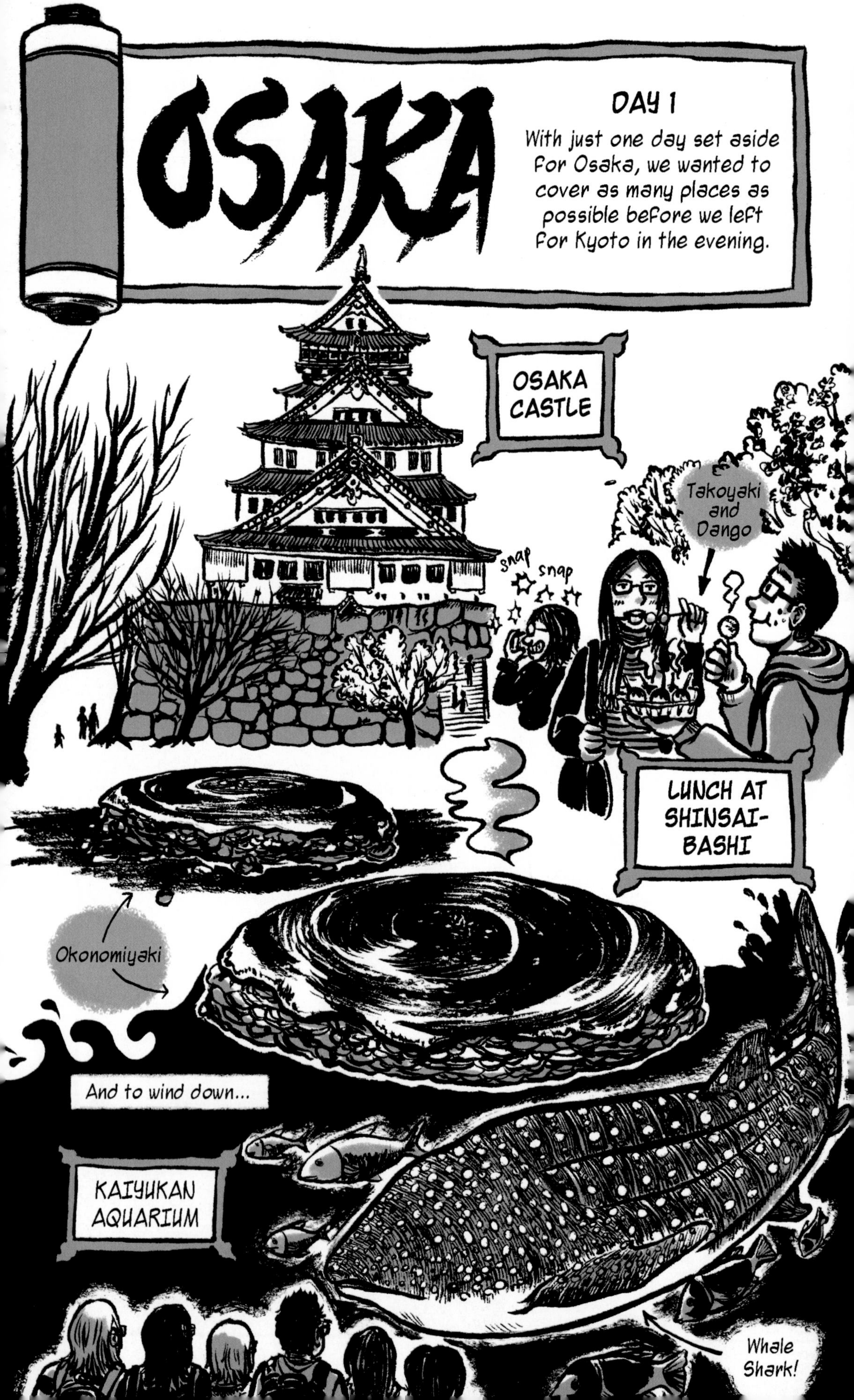
OSAKA
DAY 1
With just one day set aside for Osaka, we wanted to cover as many places as possible before we left for Kyoto in the evening.
OSAKA CASTLE
snap
snap
Takoyaki and Dango
LUNCH AT SHINSAI-BASHI
Okonomiyaki
And to wind down...
KAIYUKAN AQUARIUM
Whale Shark!

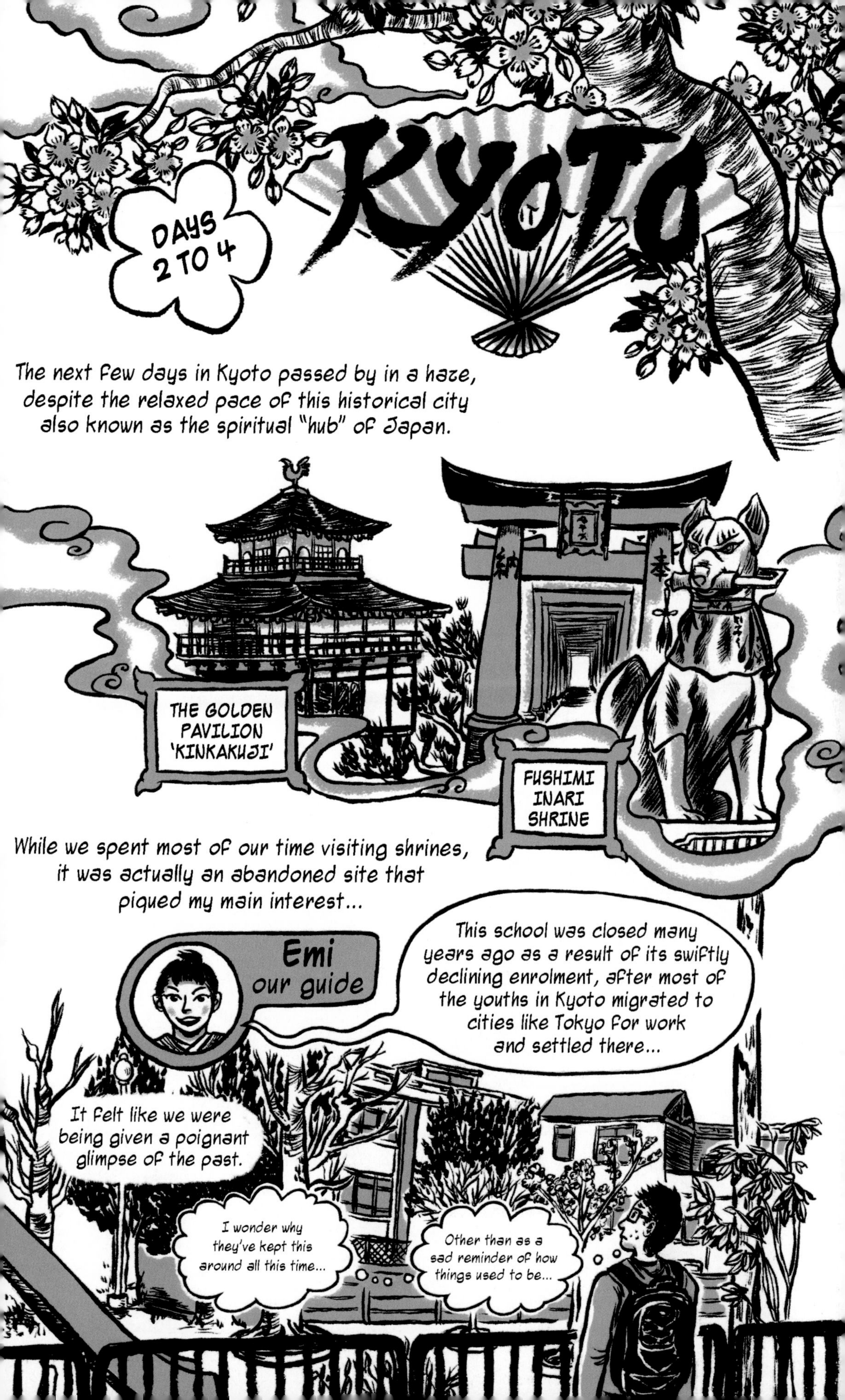
KYOTO
DAYS 2 TO 4
The next few days in Kyoto passed by in a haze, despite the relaxed pace of this historical city also known as the spiritual "hub" of Japan.
THE GOLDEN PAVILION 'KINKAKUJI'
FUSHIMI INARI SHRINE
While we spent most of our time visiting shrines, it was actually an abandoned site that piqued my main interest...
Emi our guide
This school was closed many years ago as a result of its swiftly declining enrolment, after most of the youths in Kyoto migrated to cities like Tokyo for work and settled there...
It felt like we were being given a poignant glimpse of the past.
I wonder why they've kept this around all this time...
Other than as a sad reminder of how things used to be...

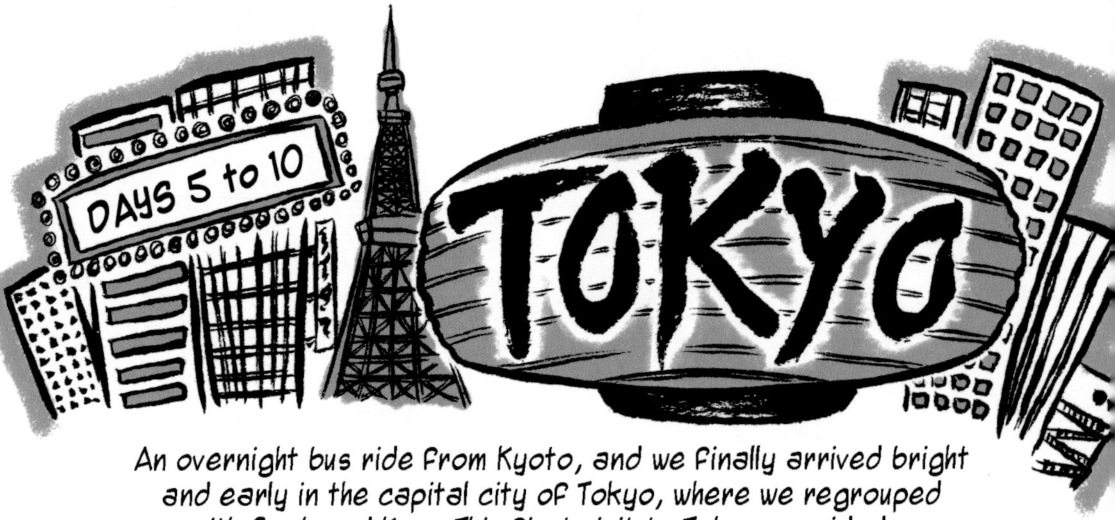
DAYS 5 to 10
TOKYO

An overnight bus ride from Kyoto, and we finally arrived bright and early in the capital city of Tokyo, where we regrouped with Saph and Kuzu. This first visit to Tokyo provided a real full-on assault for our senses — and our wallets.

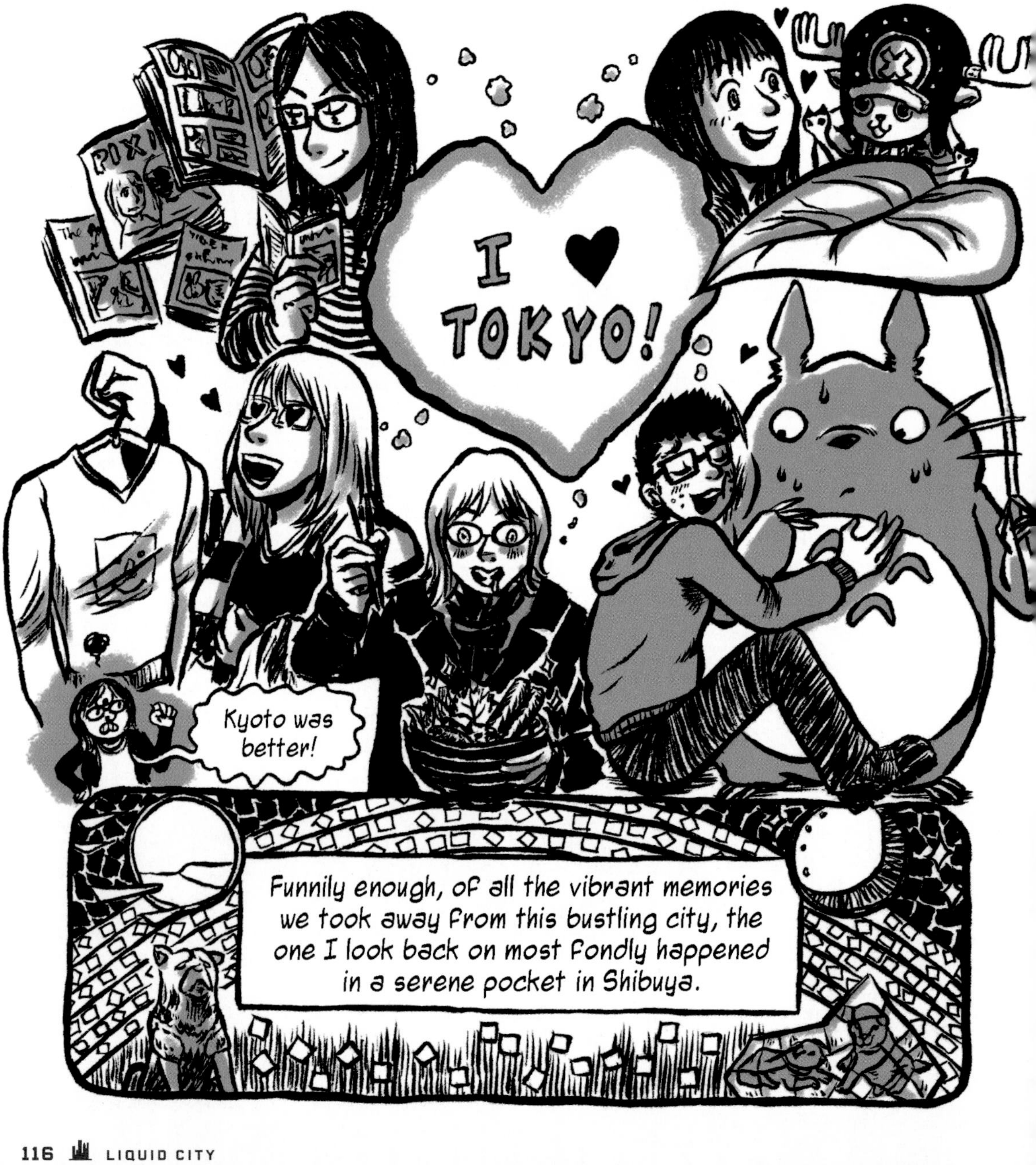
I ♥ TOKYO!
Kyoto was better!
Funnily enough, of all the vibrant memories we took away from this bustling city, the one I look back on most fondly happened in a serene pocket in Shibuya.

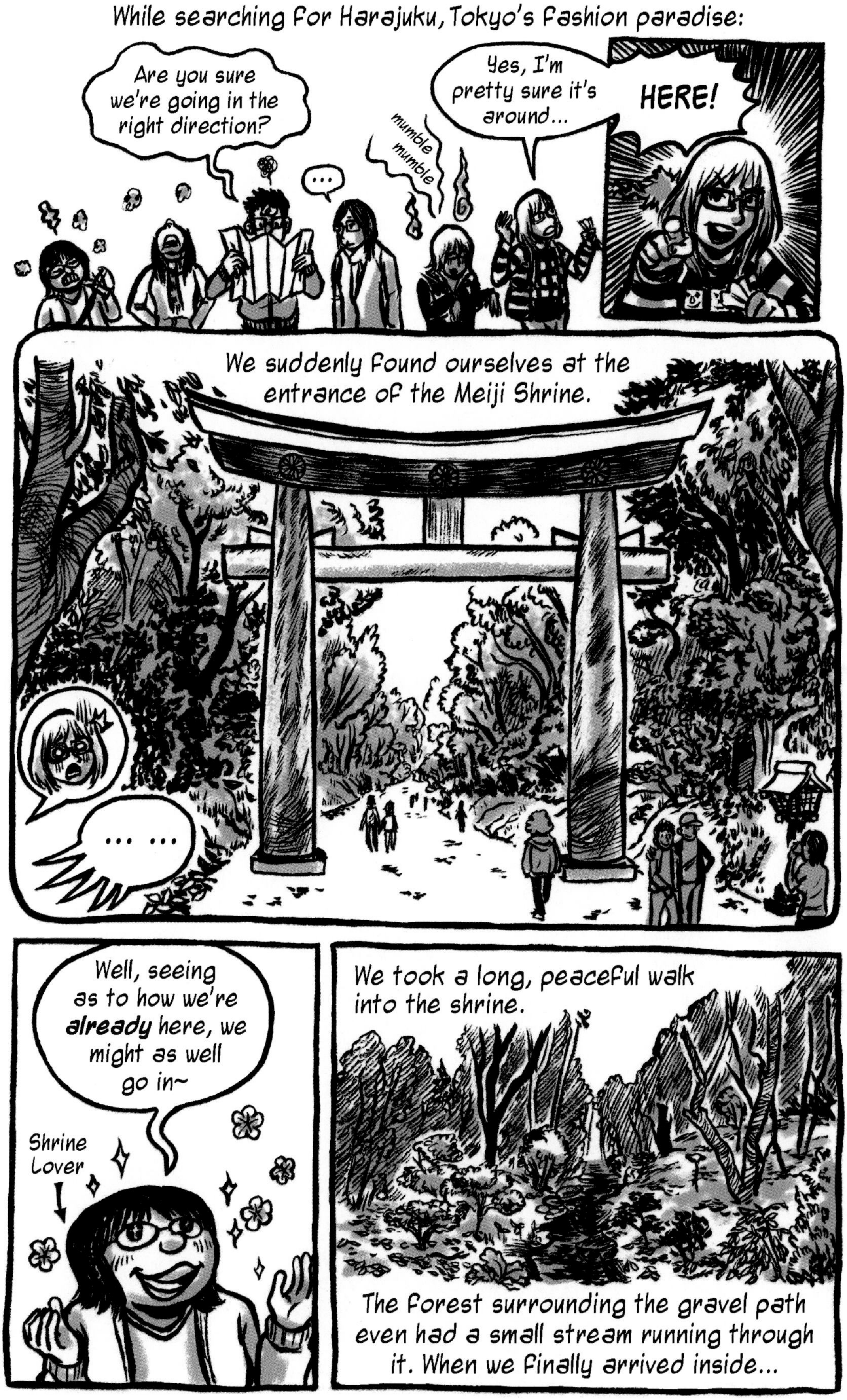

While searching for Harajuku, Tokyo's fashion paradise:
Are you sure we're going in the right direction?
...
mumble mumble mumble
Yes, I'm pretty sure it's around...
HERE!
We suddenly found ourselves at the entrance of the Meiji Shrine.
... ...
Well, seeing as to how we're ***already*** here, we might as well go in~
Shrine Lover
We took a long, peaceful walk into the shrine.
The forest surrounding the gravel path even had a small stream running through it. When we finally arrived inside...

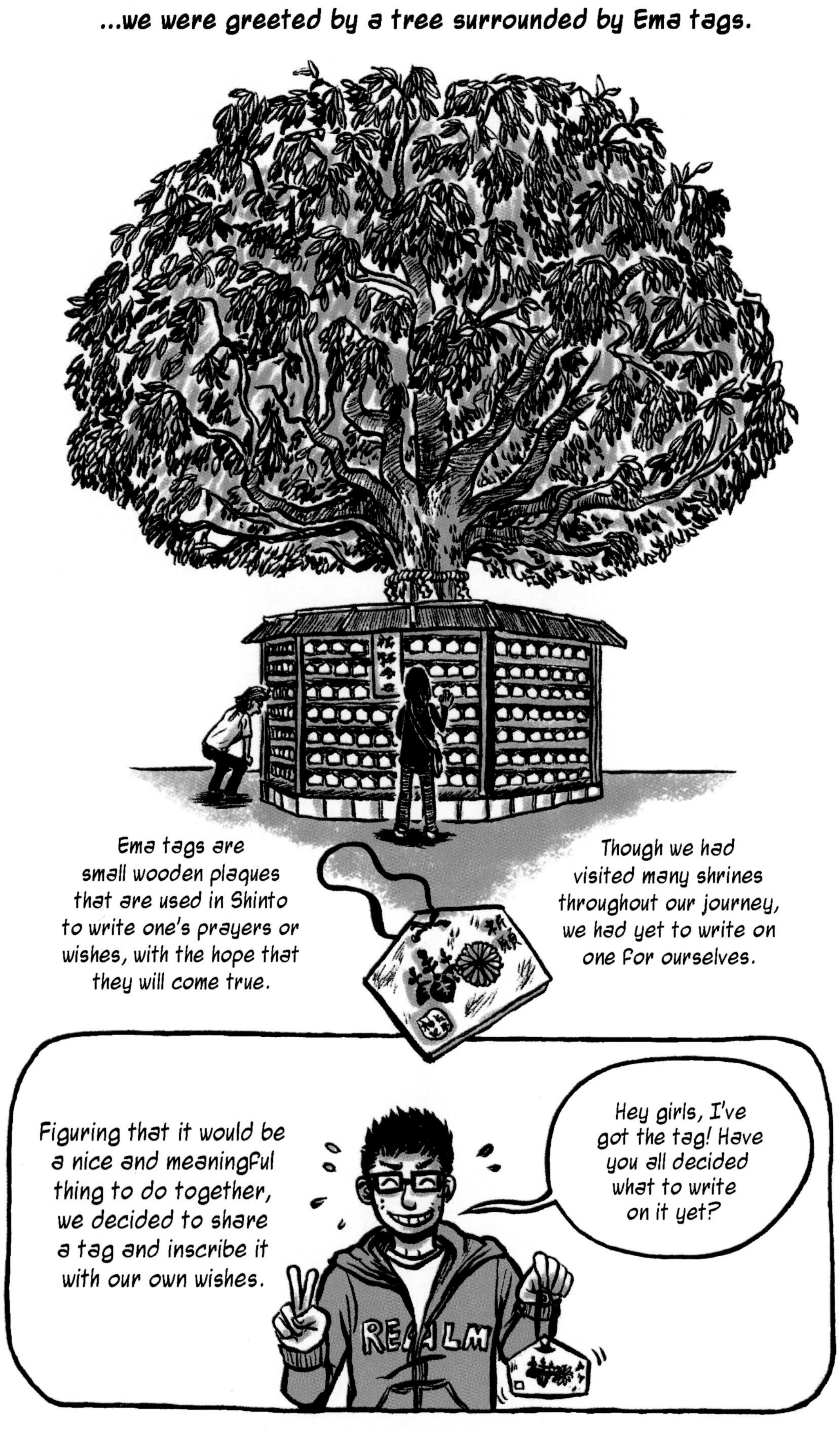
...we were greeted by a tree surrounded by Ema tags.
Ema tags are small wooden plaques that are used in Shinto to write one's prayers or wishes, with the hope that they will come true.
Though we had visited many shrines throughout our journey, we had yet to write on one for ourselves.
Figuring that it would be a nice and meaningful thing to do together, we decided to share a tag and inscribe it with our own wishes.
Hey girls, I've got the tag! Have you all decided what to write on it yet?
REALM

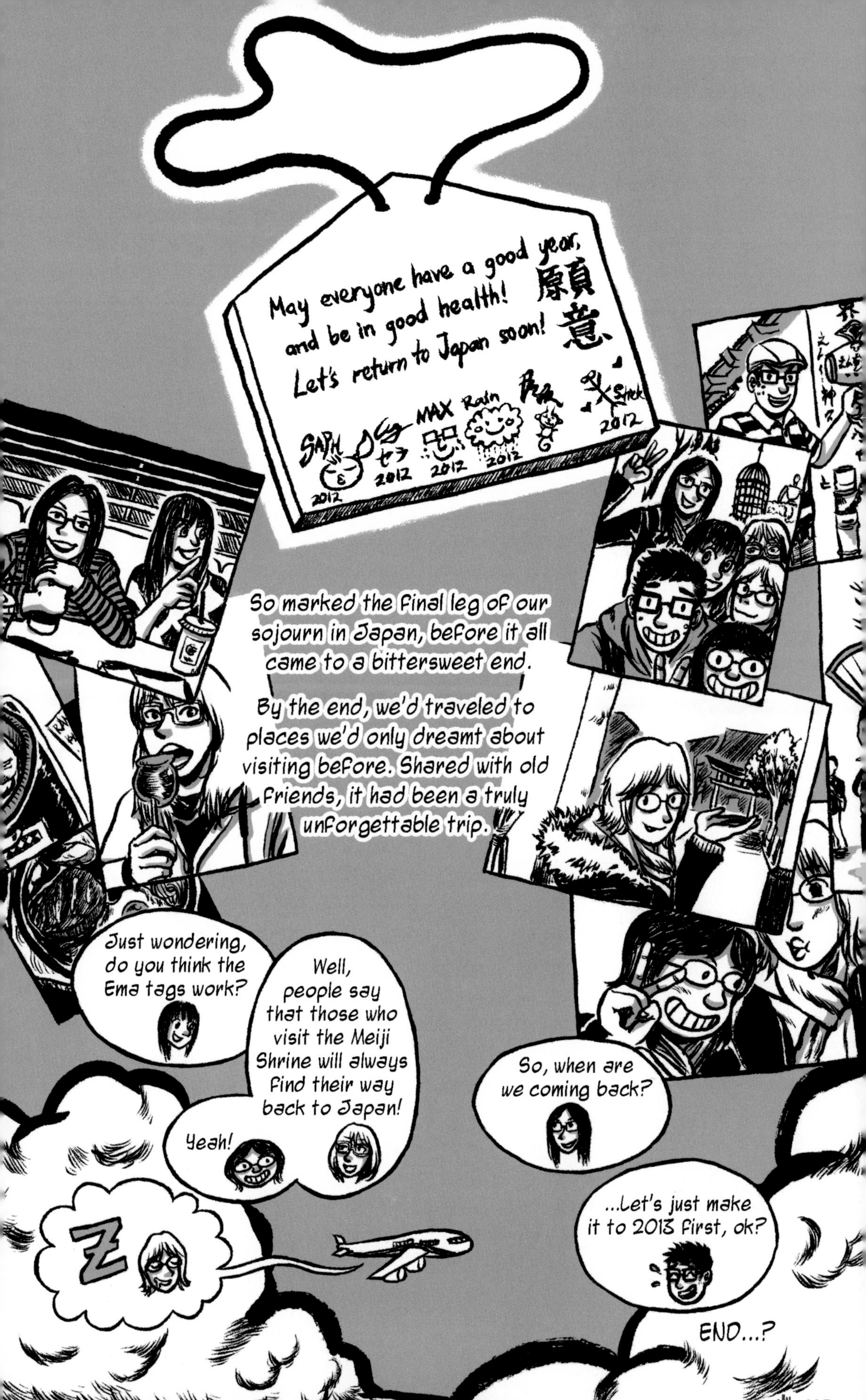
May everyone have a good year, and be in good health! Let's return to Japan soon! 願意
SAPH 2012
セラ 2012
MAX 2012
Rain 2012
Stick 2012
So marked the final leg of our sojourn in Japan, before it all came to a bittersweet end.
By the end, we'd traveled to places we'd only dreamt about visiting before. Shared with old friends, it had been a truly unforgettable trip.
Just wondering, do you think the Ema tags work?
Well, people say that those who visit the Meiji Shrine will always find their way back to Japan!
Yeah!
So, when are we coming back?
Z
...Let's just make it to 2013 first, ok?
END...?

Fantascene
CHONG FEI GIAP

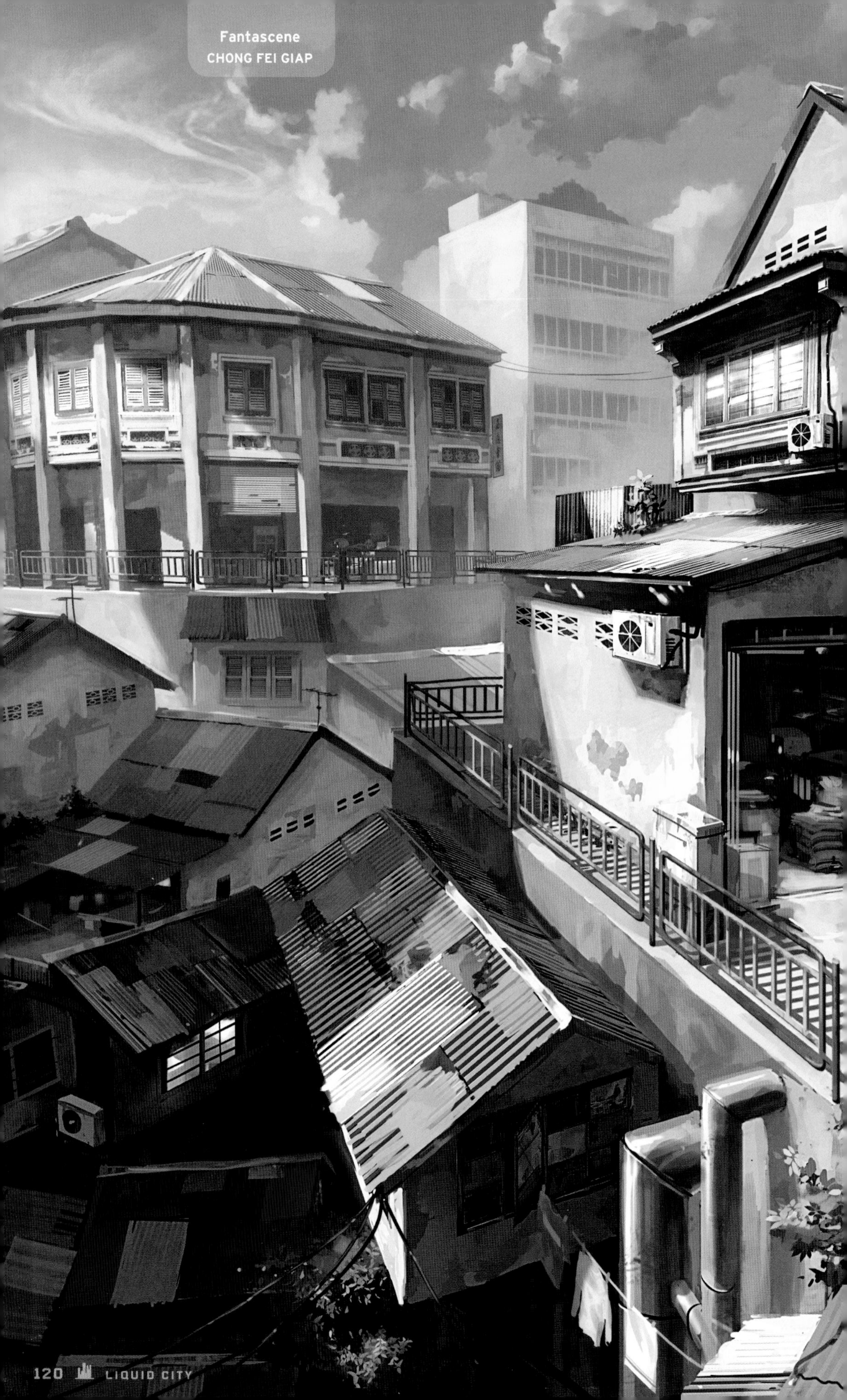

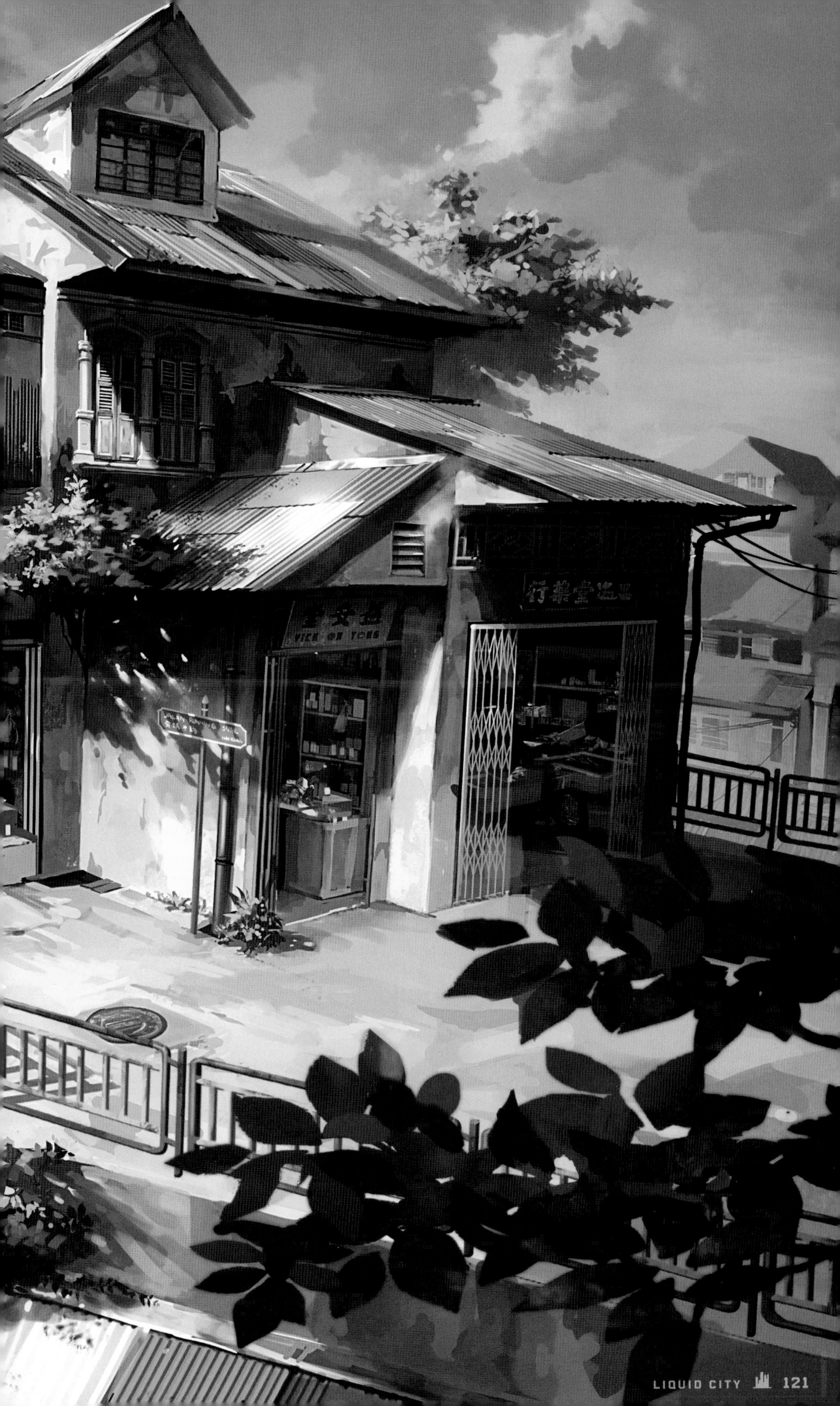

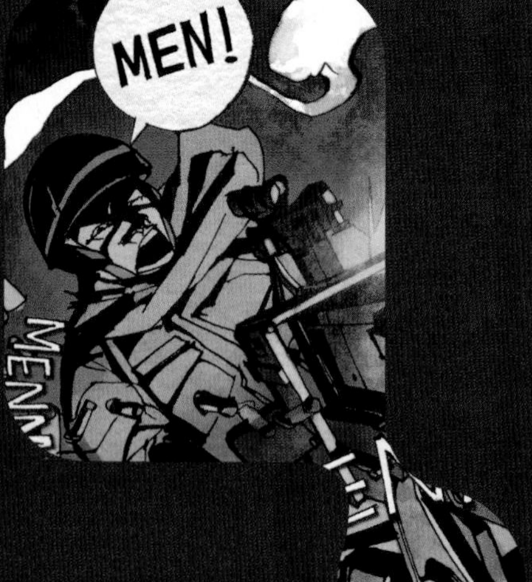
MEN!

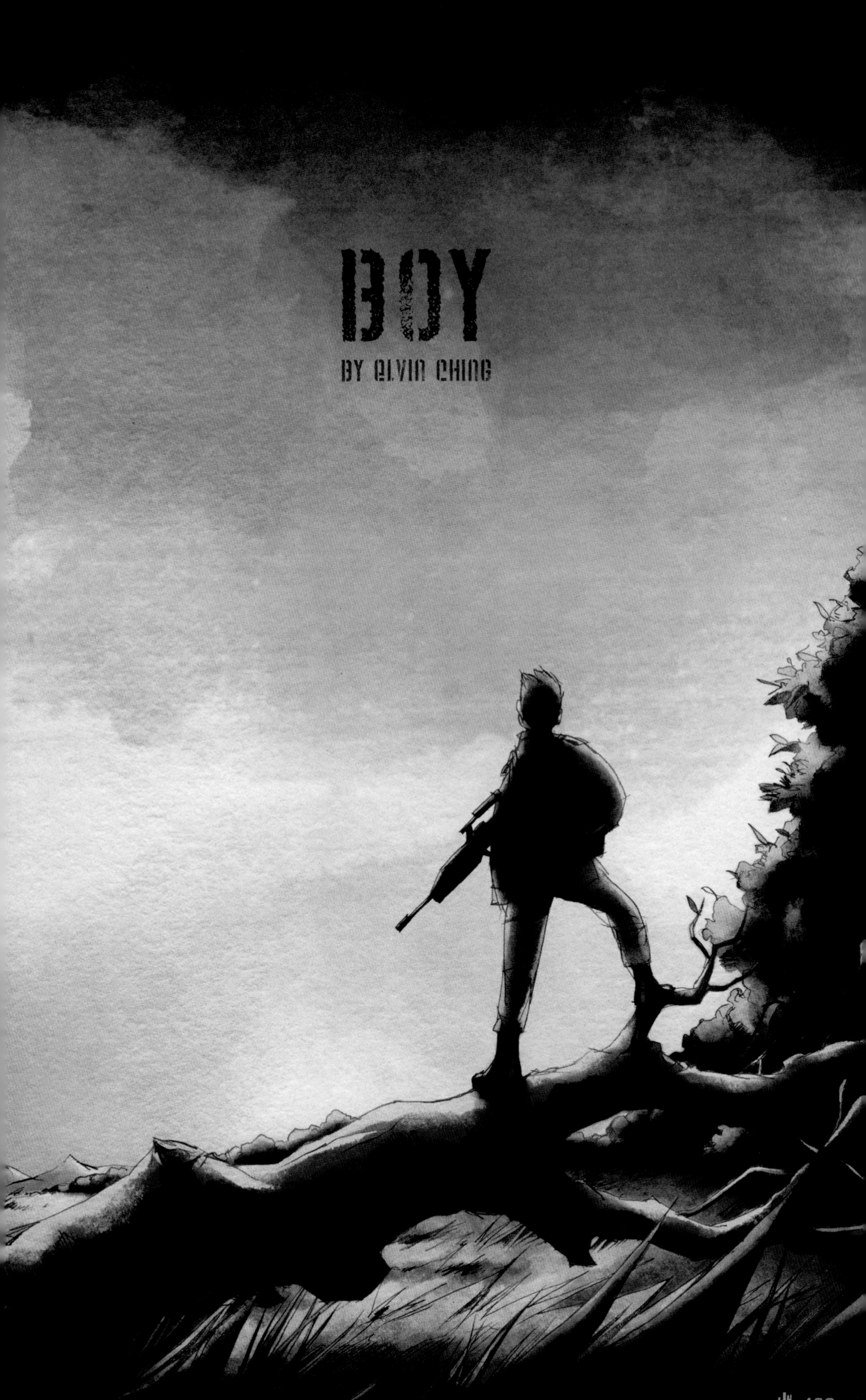
BOY
BY ELVIN CHING

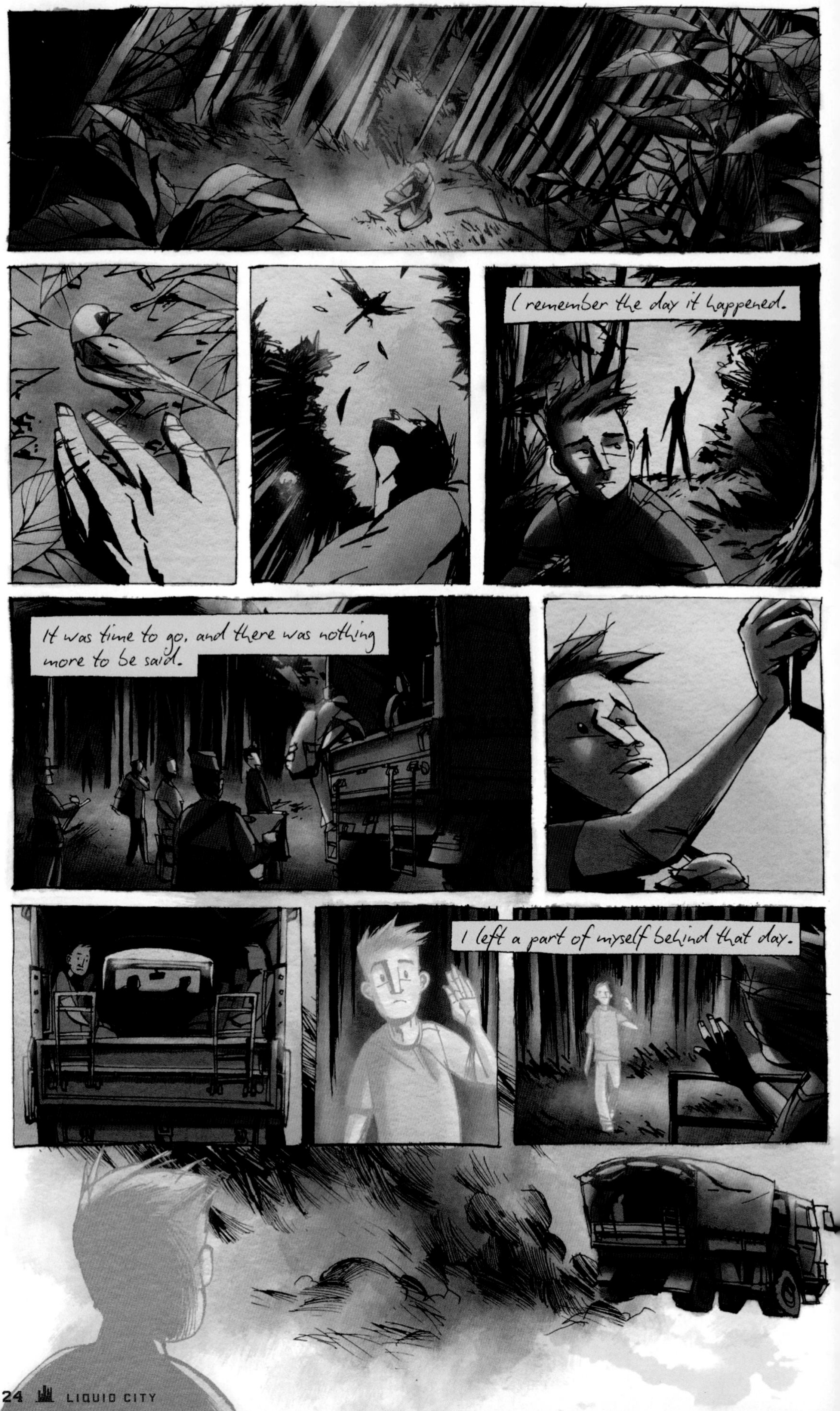
I remember the day it happened.
It was time to go, and there was nothing more to be said.
I left a part of myself behind that day.

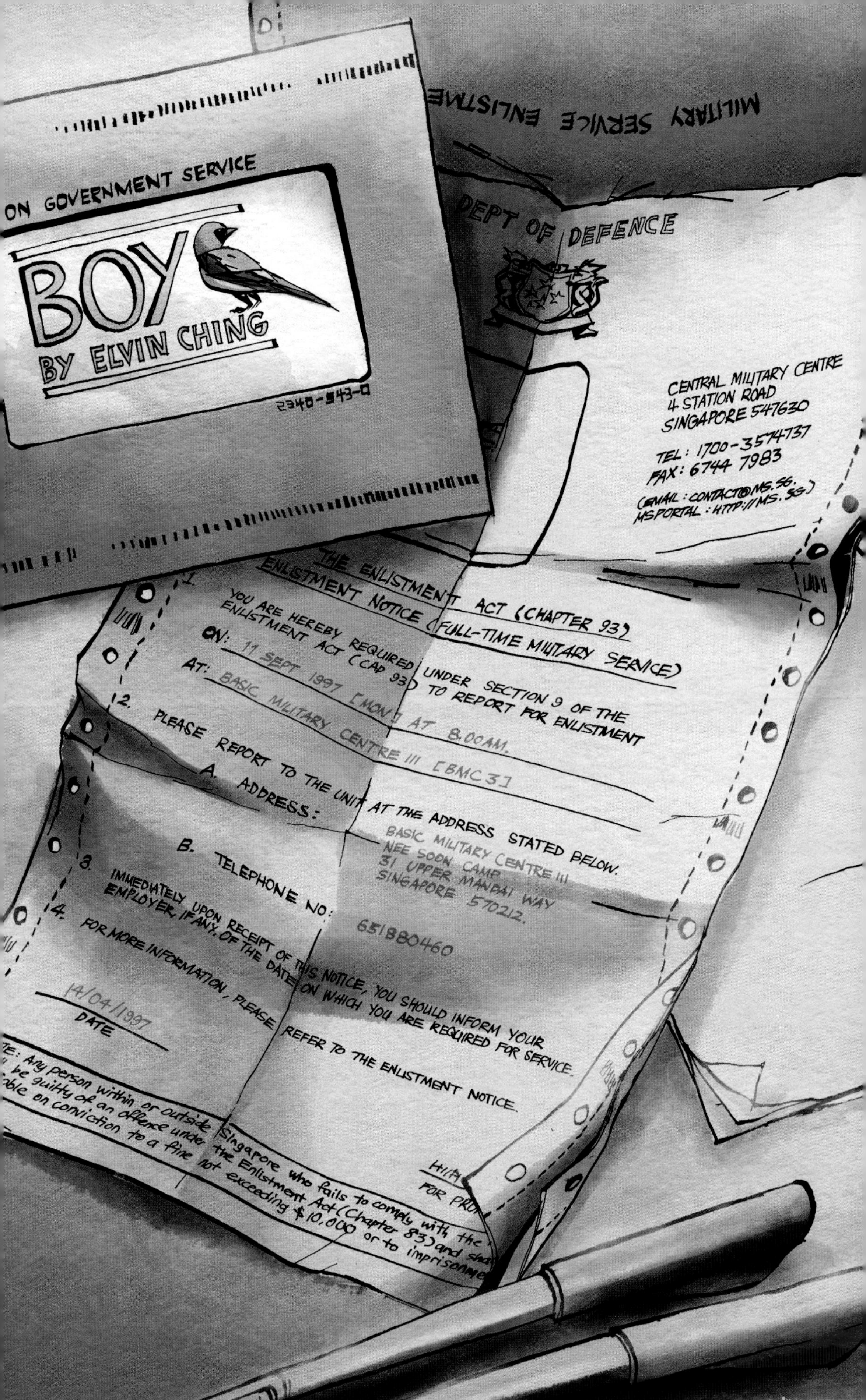
ON GOVERNMENT SERVICE
BOY
BY ELVIN CHING
2340-543-0
MILITARY SERVICE ENLISTME
DEPT OF DEFENCE
CENTRAL MILITARY CENTRE
4 STATION ROAD
SINGAPORE 547630
TEL: 1700-3574737
FAX: 6744 7983
(EMAIL: CONTACT@MS.SG.
MSPORTAL: HTTP://MS.SG)
THE ENLISTMENT ACT (CHAPTER 93)
ENLISTMENT NOTICE (FULL-TIME MILITARY SERVICE)
1. YOU ARE HEREBY REQUIRED UNDER SECTION 9 OF THE ENLISTMENT ACT (CAP 93) TO REPORT FOR ENLISTMENT
ON: 11 SEPT 1997 [MON] AT 8.00AM.
AT: BASIC MILITARY CENTRE III [BMC 3]
2. PLEASE REPORT TO THE UNIT AT THE ADDRESS STATED BELOW.
A. ADDRESS: BASIC MILITARY CENTRE III
NEE SOON CAMP
31 UPPER MANDAI WAY
SINGAPORE 570212.
B. TELEPHONE NO: 651880460
3. IMMEDIATELY UPON RECEIPT OF THIS NOTICE, YOU SHOULD INFORM YOUR EMPLOYER, IF ANY, OF THE DATE ON WHICH YOU ARE REQUIRED FOR SERVICE.
4. FOR MORE INFORMATION, PLEASE REFER TO THE ENLISTMENT NOTICE.
14/04/1997
DATE
Any person within or outside Singapore who fails to comply with the
be guilty of an offence under the Enlistment Act (Chapter 83) and sha
on conviction to a fine not exceeding $10,000 or to imprisonme
FOR PRO

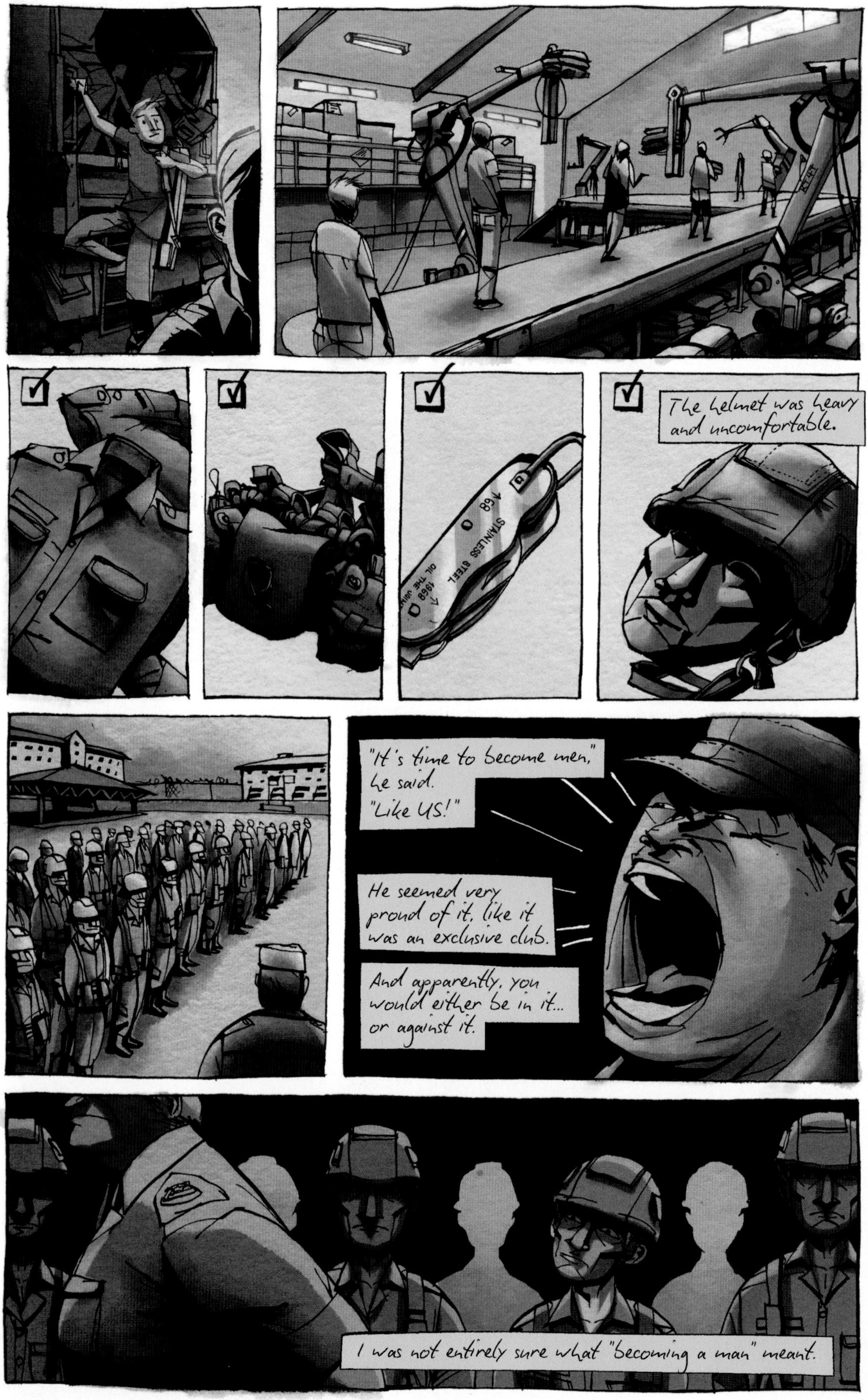
STAINLESS STEEL
1968
OIL THE JOINT
The helmet was heavy and uncomfortable.
"It's time to become men," he said.
"Like US!"
He seemed very proud of it, like it was an exclusive club.
And apparently, you would either be in it... or against it.
I was not entirely sure what "becoming a man" meant.

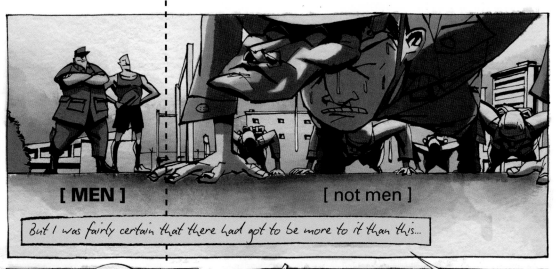

[MEN] [not men]

But I was fairly certain that there had got to be more to it than this...

MEN!

MEN MEN MEN MEN MEN MEN MENMENMENMENMENMEN

Or this...

Or this.

Then again, what did I know, right?

MEN

- Going Out Of Control -

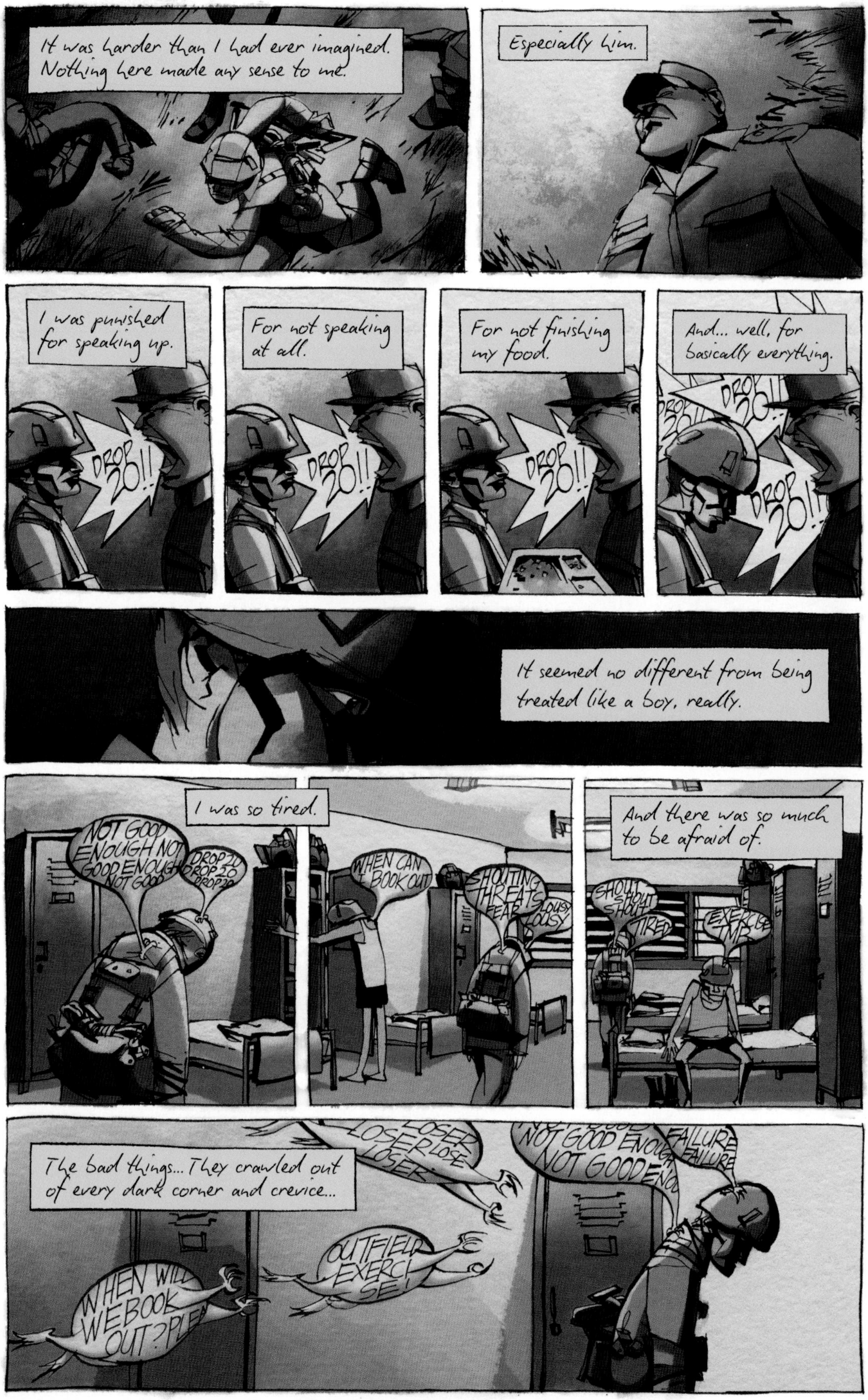
It was harder than I had ever imagined. Nothing here made any sense to me.
Especially him.
I was punished for speaking up.
DROP 20!!
For not speaking at all.
DROP 20!!
For not finishing my food.
DROP 20!!
And... well, for basically everything.
DROP 20!!
DROP 20!!
DROP 20!!
It seemed no different from being treated like a boy, really.
I was so tired.
NOT GOOD ENOUGH NOT GOOD ENOUGH NOT GOOD
DROP 20 DROP 20 DROP 20
WHEN CAN I BOOK OUT
SHOUTING THREATS FEAR
LOUSY LOUSY
And there was so much to be afraid of.
SHOUT SHOUT SHOUT
TIRED
EXERCISE TMR
The bad things... They crawled out of every dark corner and crevice...
LOSER LOSER LOSE LOSER
NOT GOOD ENOUGH NOT GOOD
FAILURE FAILURE
OUTFIELD EXERCISE!
WHEN WILL WE BOOK OUT? PLE

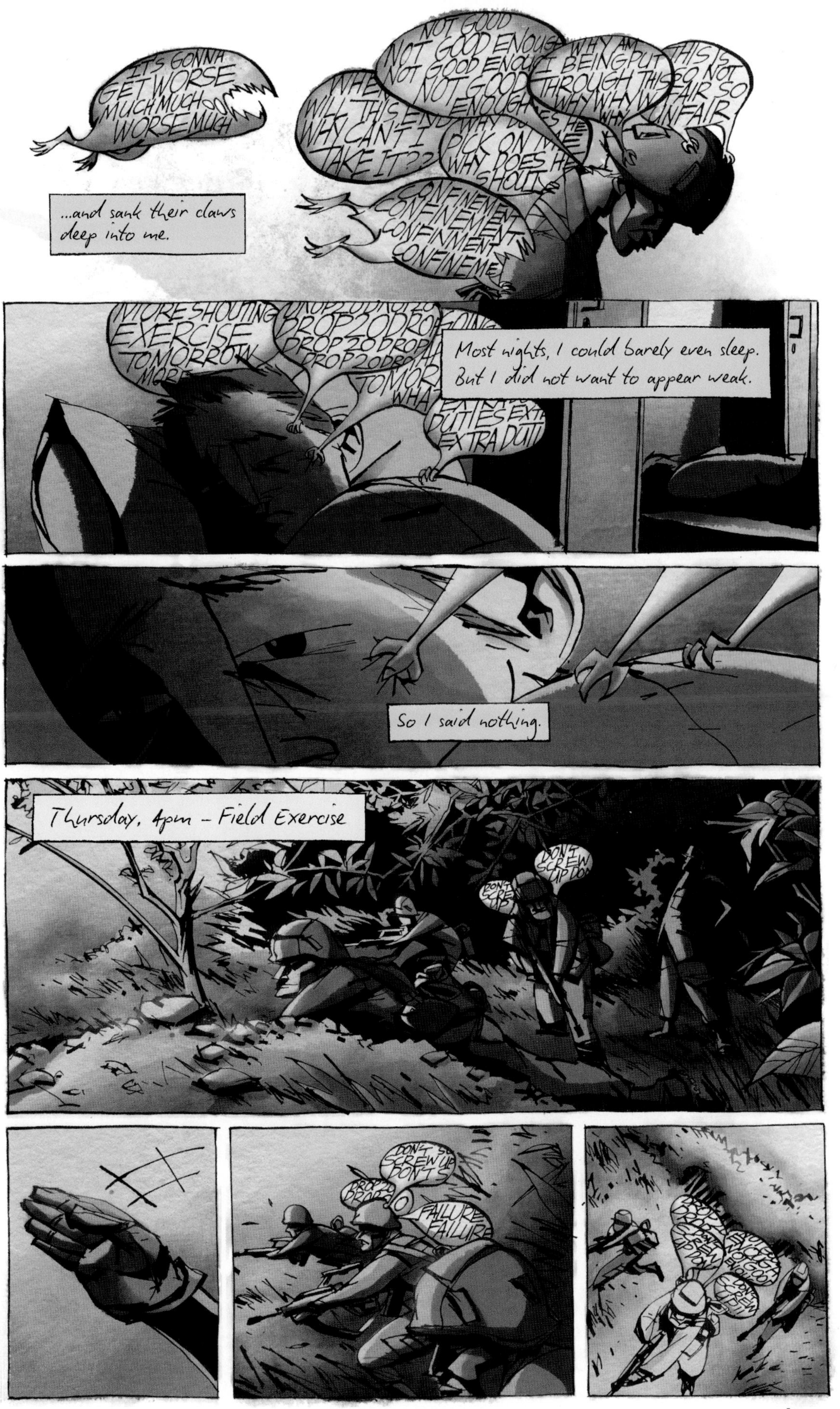
IT'S GONNA GET WORSE MUCH MUCH WORSE MUCH
NOT GOOD NOT GOOD ENOUGH NOT GOOD ENOUGH NOT GOOD ENOUGH
WHY AM I BEING PUT THROUGH THIS WHY WHY
THIS IS SO NOT FAIR SO UNFAIR
WILL THIS END WHY CAN'T I TAKE IT??
PICK ON ME WHY DOES HE
CONFINEMENT CONFINEMENT CONFINEMENT CONFINEMENT
...and sank their claws deep into me.
MORE SHOUTING EXERCISE TOMORROW
DROP 20 DROP 20 DROP 20
Most nights, I could barely even sleep. But I did not want to appear weak.
DUTIES EXTRA DUTIES
So I said nothing.
Thursday, 4pm – Field Exercise
DON'T SCREW UP
DON'T SCREW UP DON'T
FAILURE FAILURE

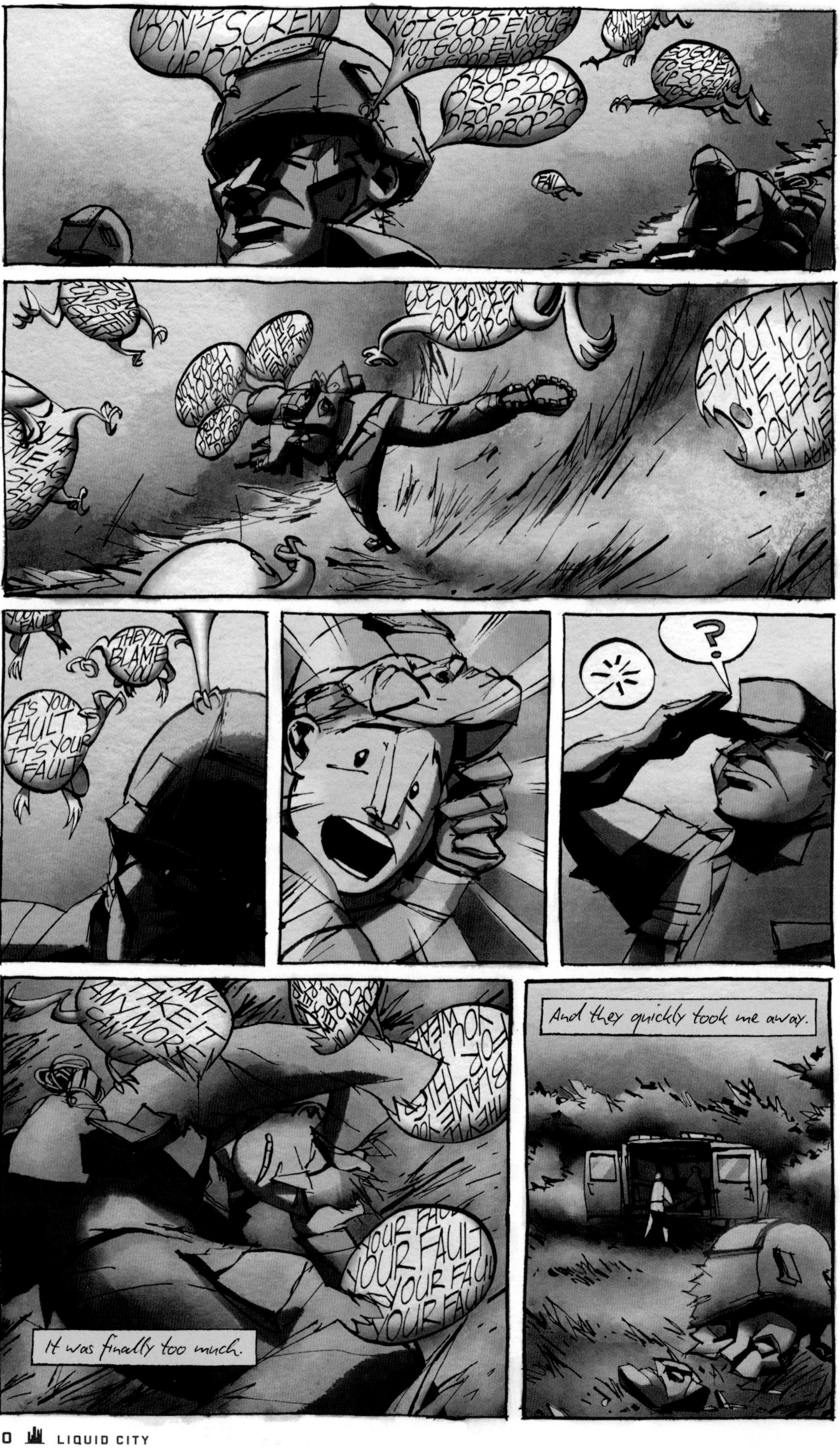
DON'T SCREW
NOT GOOD ENOUGH NOT GOOD ENOUGH
SO GOING TO SCREW UP SO GOING TO SCREW
FAIL
WILL THIS NEVER END
THEY'LL BLAME YOU
IT'S YOUR FAULT IT'S YOUR FAULT
?
It was finally too much.
YOUR FAULT YOUR FAULT
And they quickly took me away.

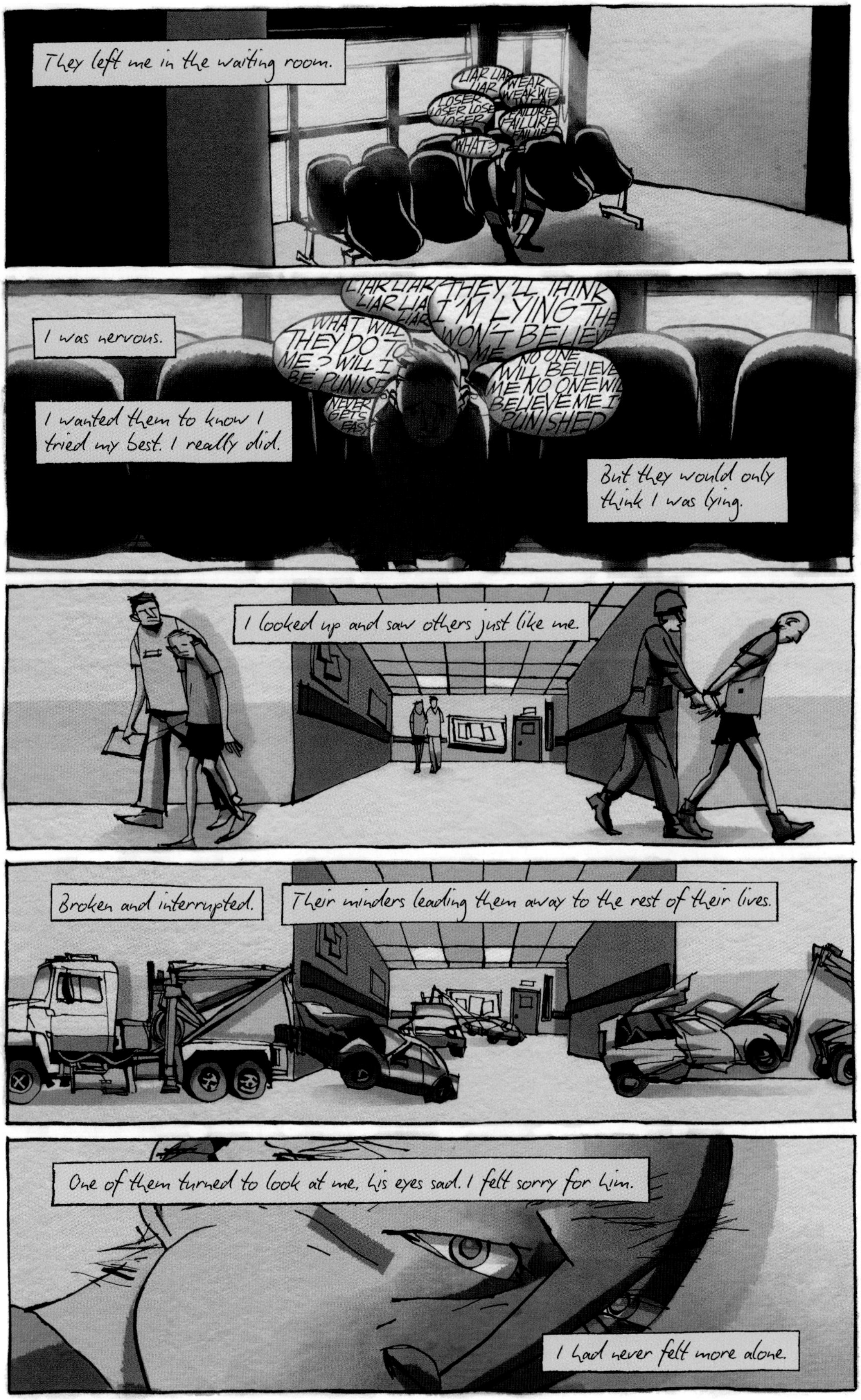
They left me in the waiting room.
LIAR LIAR
LOSER
WHAT?
I was nervous.
WHAT WILL THEY DO TO ME? WILL I BE PUNISHE
LIAR LIAR LIAR
THEY'LL THINK I'M LYING THE WON'T BELIEVE ME
NO ONE WILL BELIEVE ME NO ONE WIL BELIEVE ME I PUNISHED
NEVER GETS EASY
I wanted them to know I tried my best. I really did.
But they would only think I was lying.
I looked up and saw others just like me.
Broken and interrupted.
Their minders leading them away to the rest of their lives.
One of them turned to look at me, his eyes sad. I felt sorry for him.
I had never felt more alone.

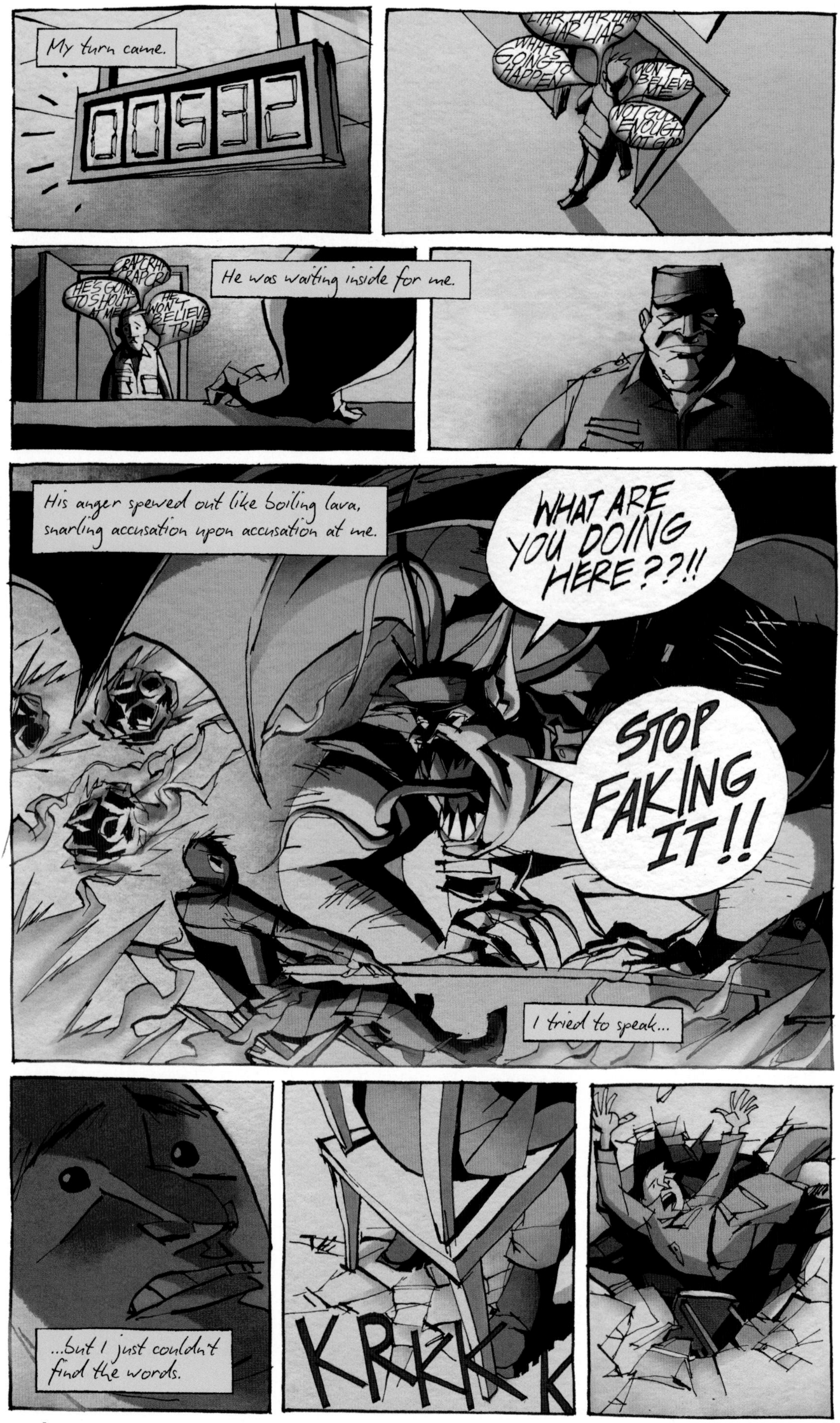
My turn came.
00532
LIAR LIAR LIAR LIAR LIAR
WHATS GOING TO HAPPEN
WON'T BELIEVE ME
ENOUGH
HE'S GOING TO SHOUT AT ME
HE WON'T BELIEVE
He was waiting inside for me.
His anger spewed out like boiling lava, snarling accusation upon accusation at me.
WHAT ARE YOU DOING HERE??!!
STOP FAKING IT!!
I tried to speak...
...but I just couldn't find the words.
KRKKK

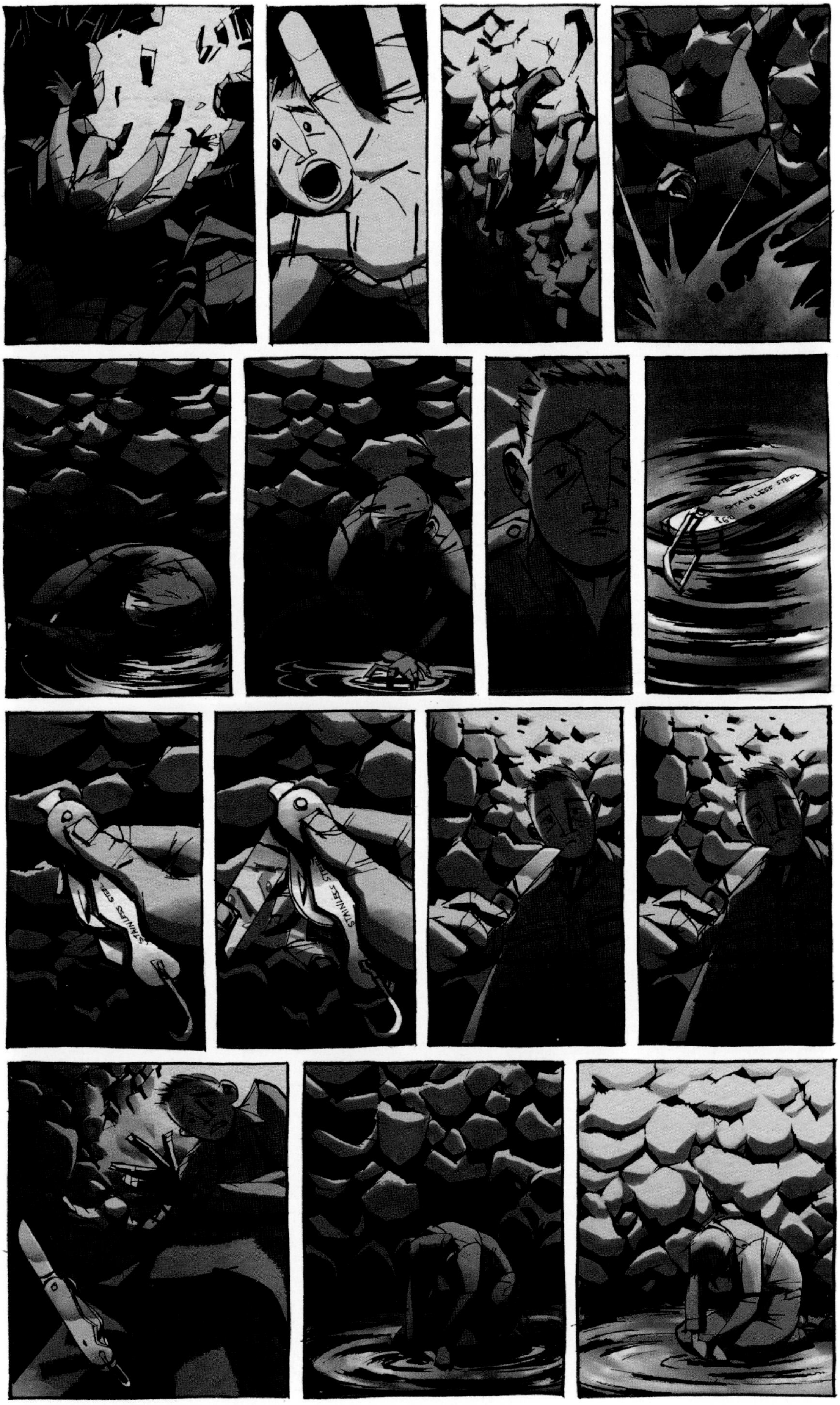
STAINLESS STEEL

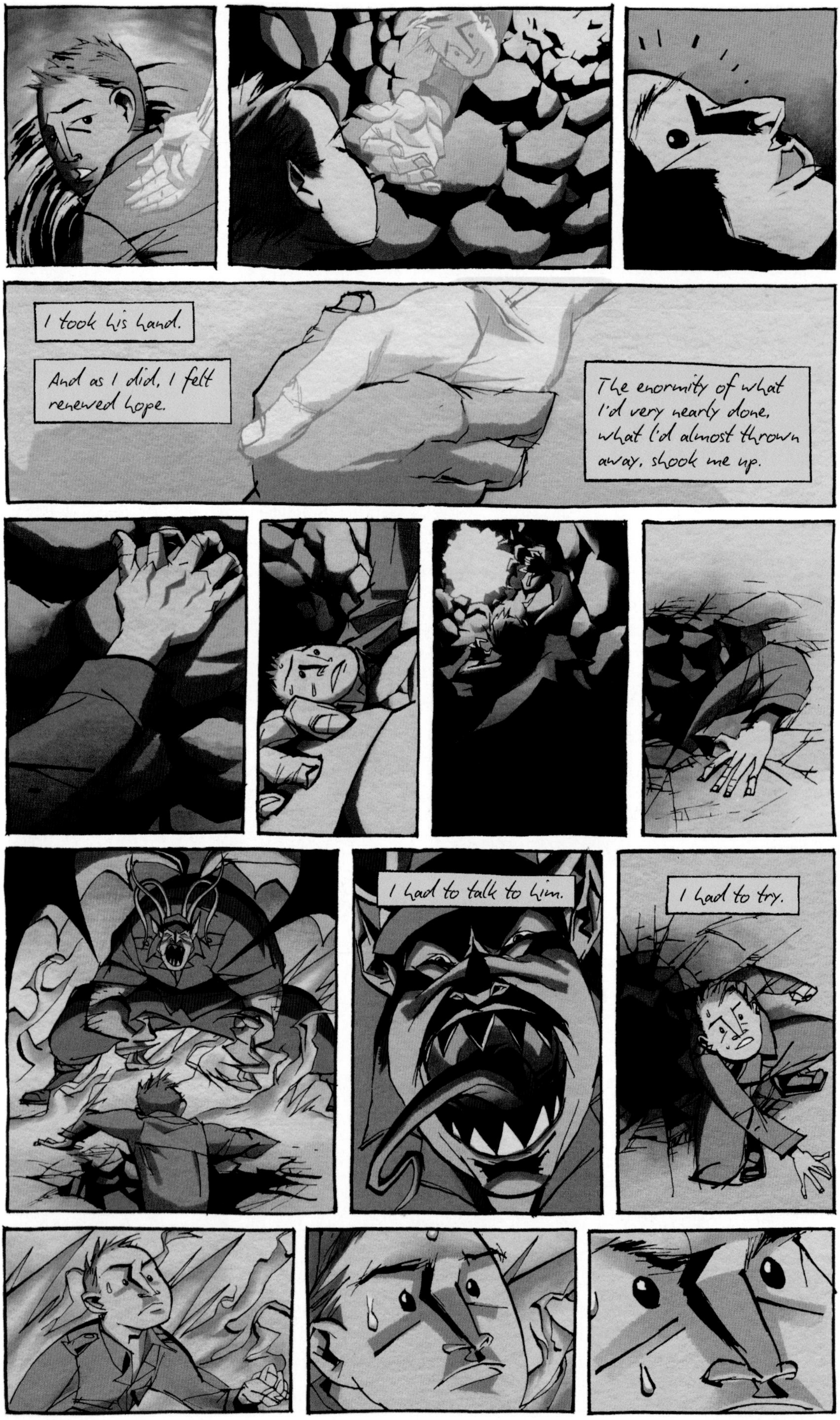
I took his hand.
And as I did, I felt renewed hope.
The enormity of what I'd very nearly done, what I'd almost thrown away, shook me up.
I had to talk to him.
I had to try.

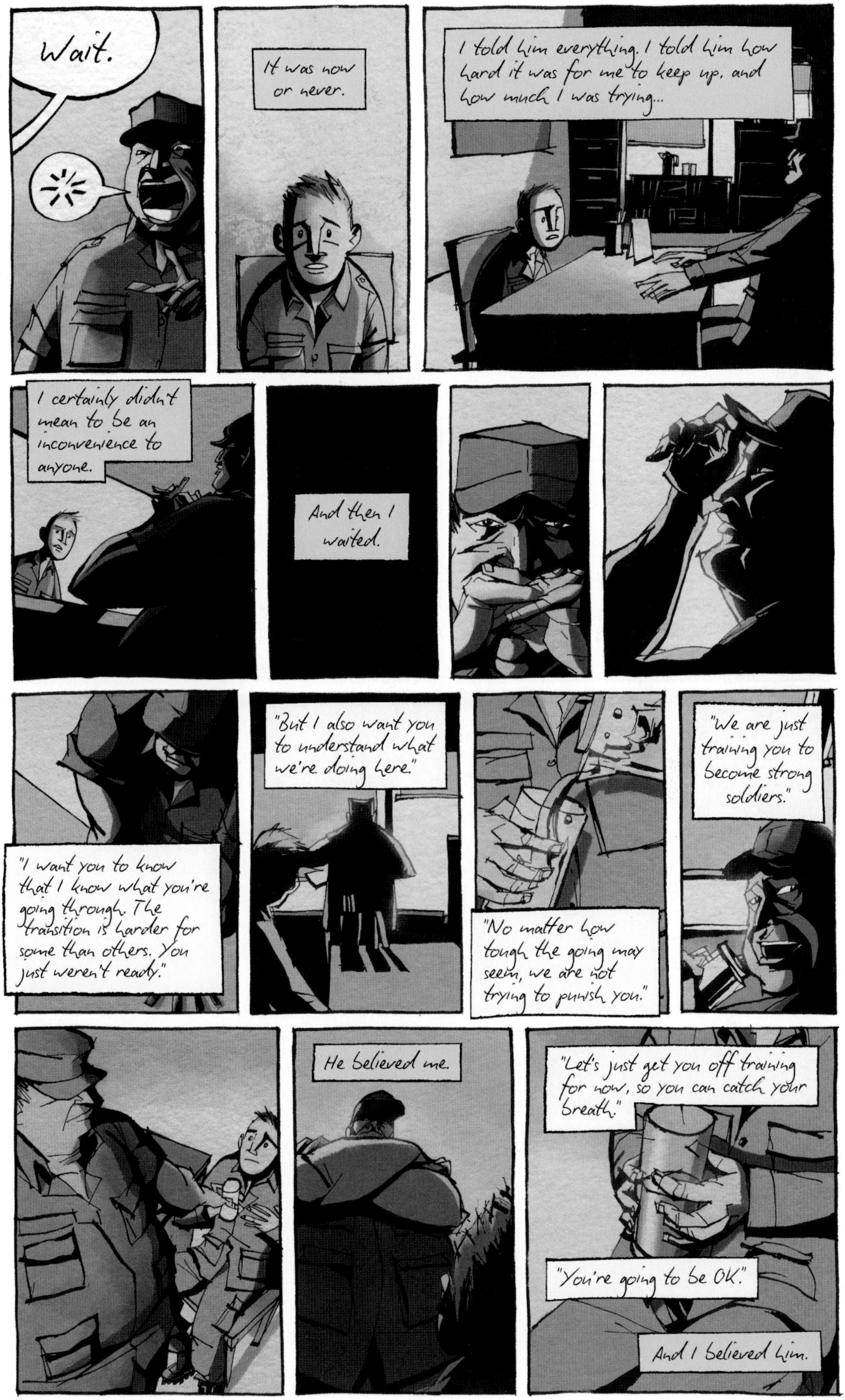
Wait.
It was now or never.
I told him everything. I told him how hard it was for me to keep up, and how much I was trying...
I certainly didn't mean to be an inconvenience to anyone.
And then I waited.
"I want you to know that I know what you're going through. The transition is harder for some than others. You just weren't ready."
"But I also want you to understand what we're doing here."
"No matter how tough the going may seem, we are not trying to punish you."
"We are just training you to become strong soldiers."
He believed me.
"Let's just get you off training for now, so you can catch your breath."
"You're going to be OK."
And I believed him.

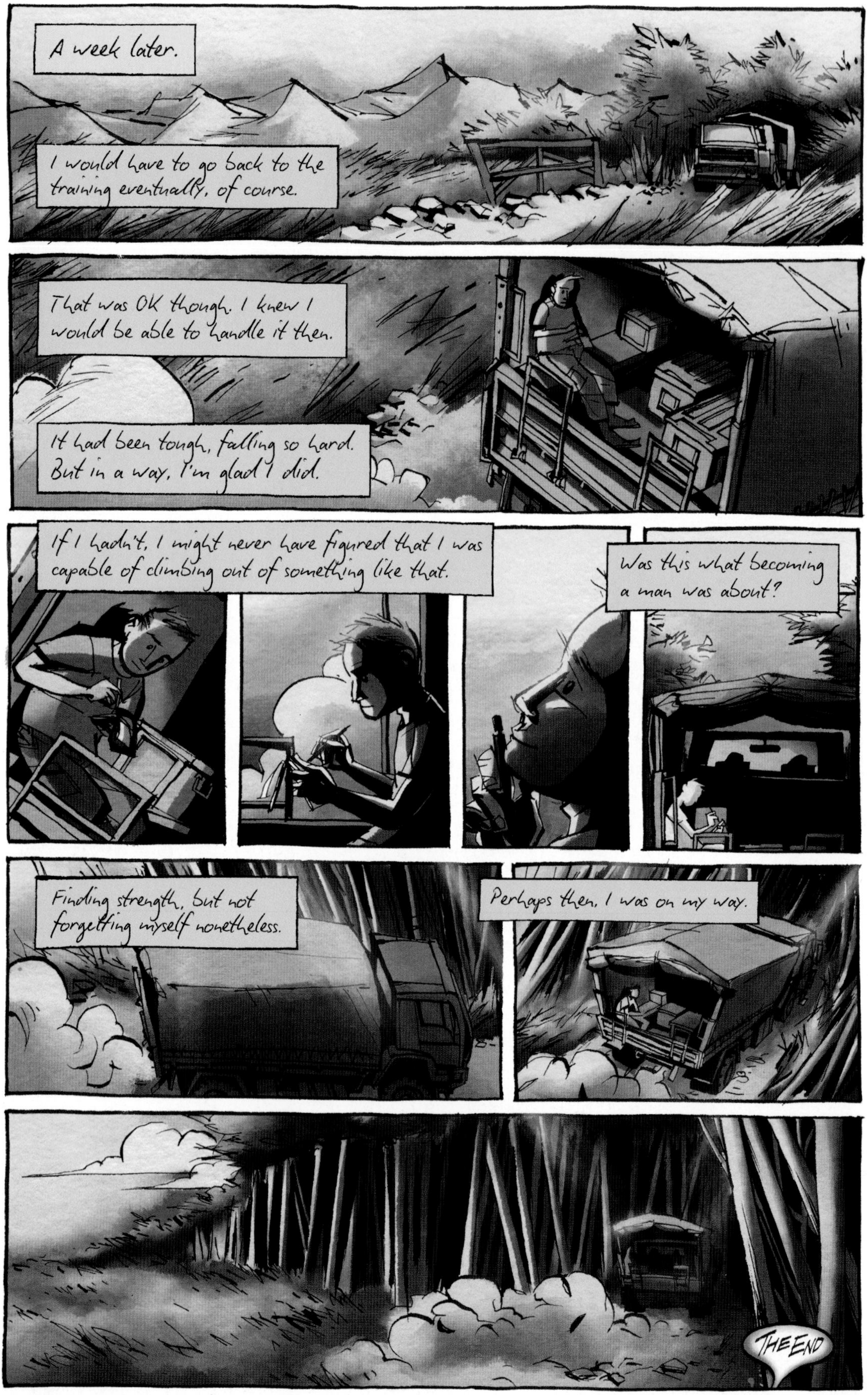
A week later.
I would have to go back to the training eventually, of course.
That was OK though. I knew I would be able to handle it then.
It had been tough, falling so hard. But in a way, I'm glad I did.
If I hadn't, I might never have figured that I was capable of climbing out of something like that.
Was this what becoming a man was about?
Finding strength, but not forgetting myself nonetheless.
Perhaps then, I was on my way.
THE END

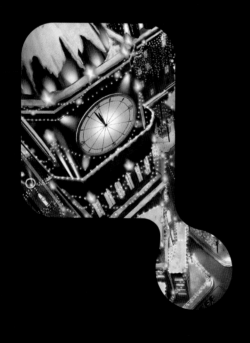

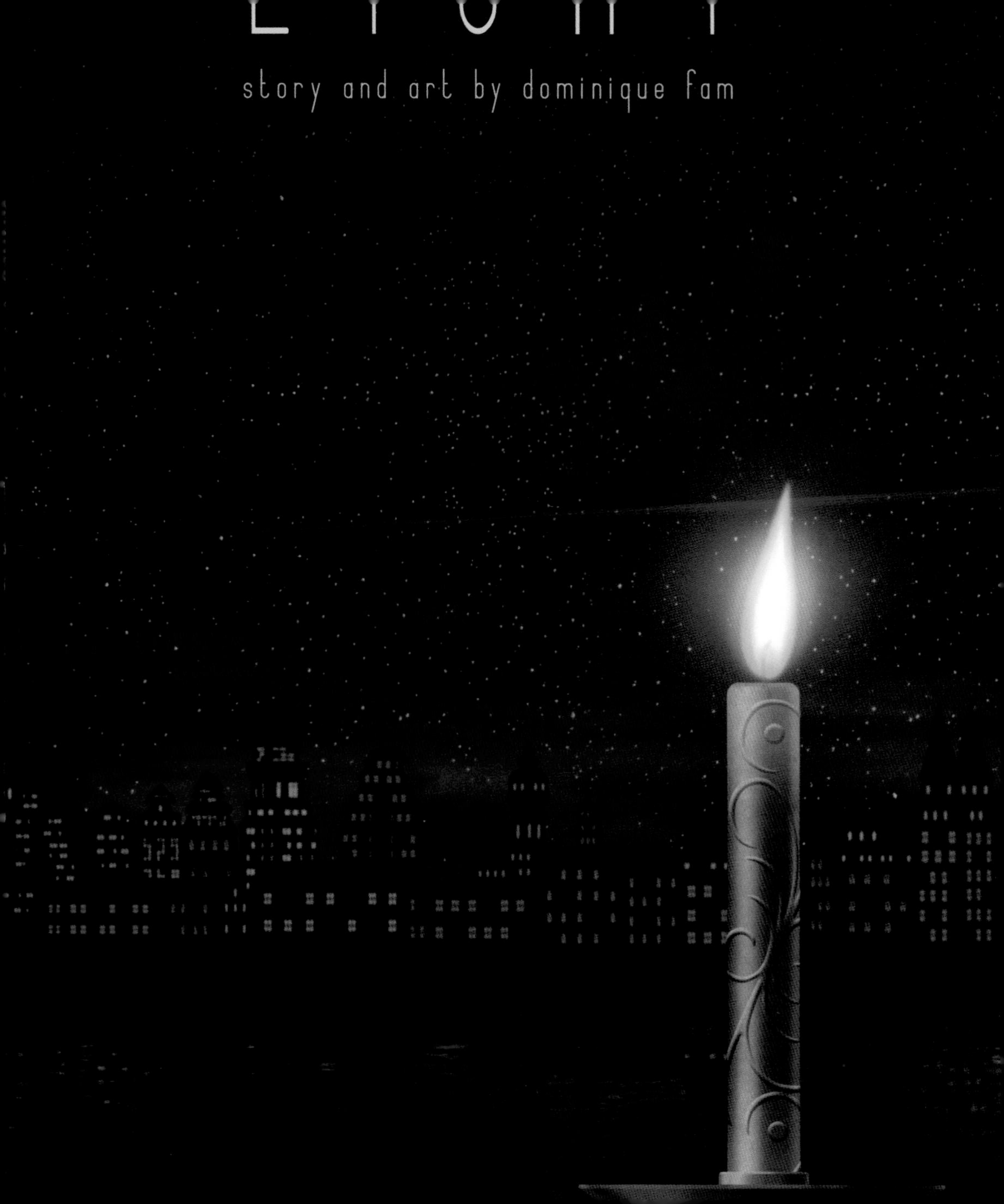
story and art by dominique fam

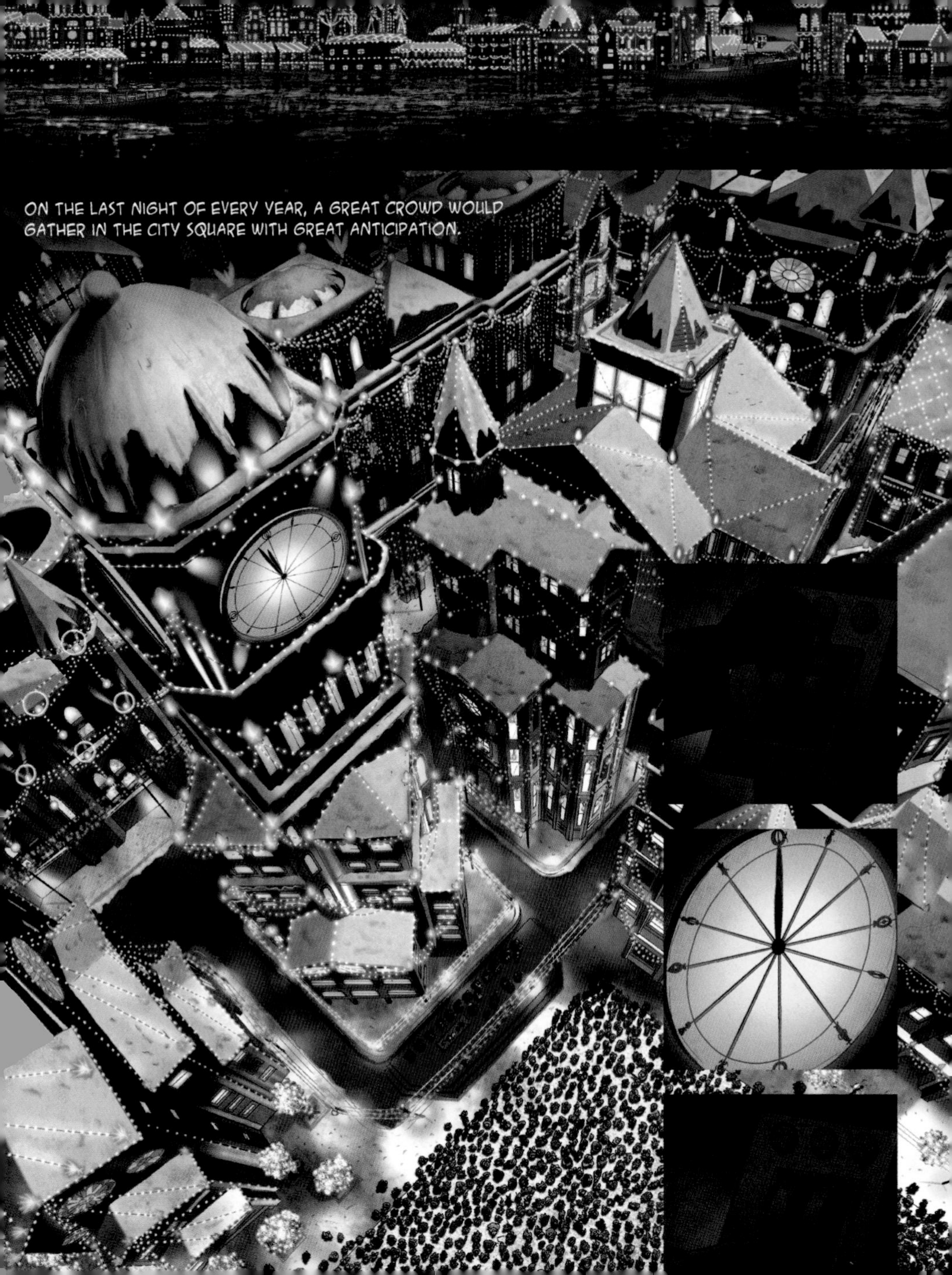
ON THE LAST NIGHT OF EVERY YEAR, A GREAT CROWD WOULD GATHER IN THE CITY SQUARE WITH GREAT ANTICIPATION.

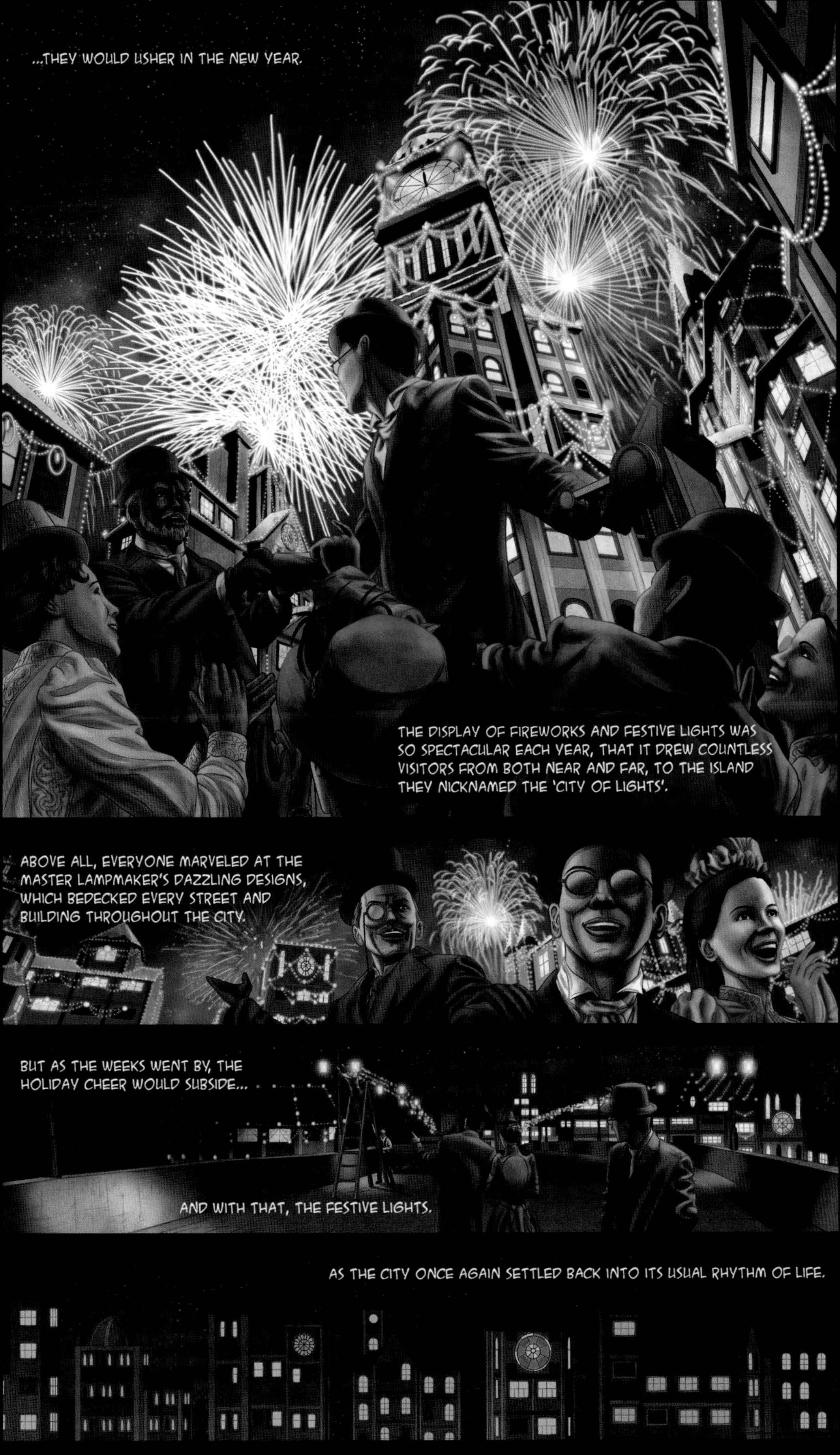
...THEY WOULD USHER IN THE NEW YEAR.
THE DISPLAY OF FIREWORKS AND FESTIVE LIGHTS WAS SO SPECTACULAR EACH YEAR, THAT IT DREW COUNTLESS VISITORS FROM BOTH NEAR AND FAR, TO THE ISLAND THEY NICKNAMED THE 'CITY OF LIGHTS'.
ABOVE ALL, EVERYONE MARVELED AT THE MASTER LAMPMAKER'S DAZZLING DESIGNS, WHICH BEDECKED EVERY STREET AND BUILDING THROUGHOUT THE CITY.
BUT AS THE WEEKS WENT BY, THE HOLIDAY CHEER WOULD SUBSIDE...
AND WITH THAT, THE FESTIVE LIGHTS.
AS THE CITY ONCE AGAIN SETTLED BACK INTO ITS USUAL RHYTHM OF LIFE.

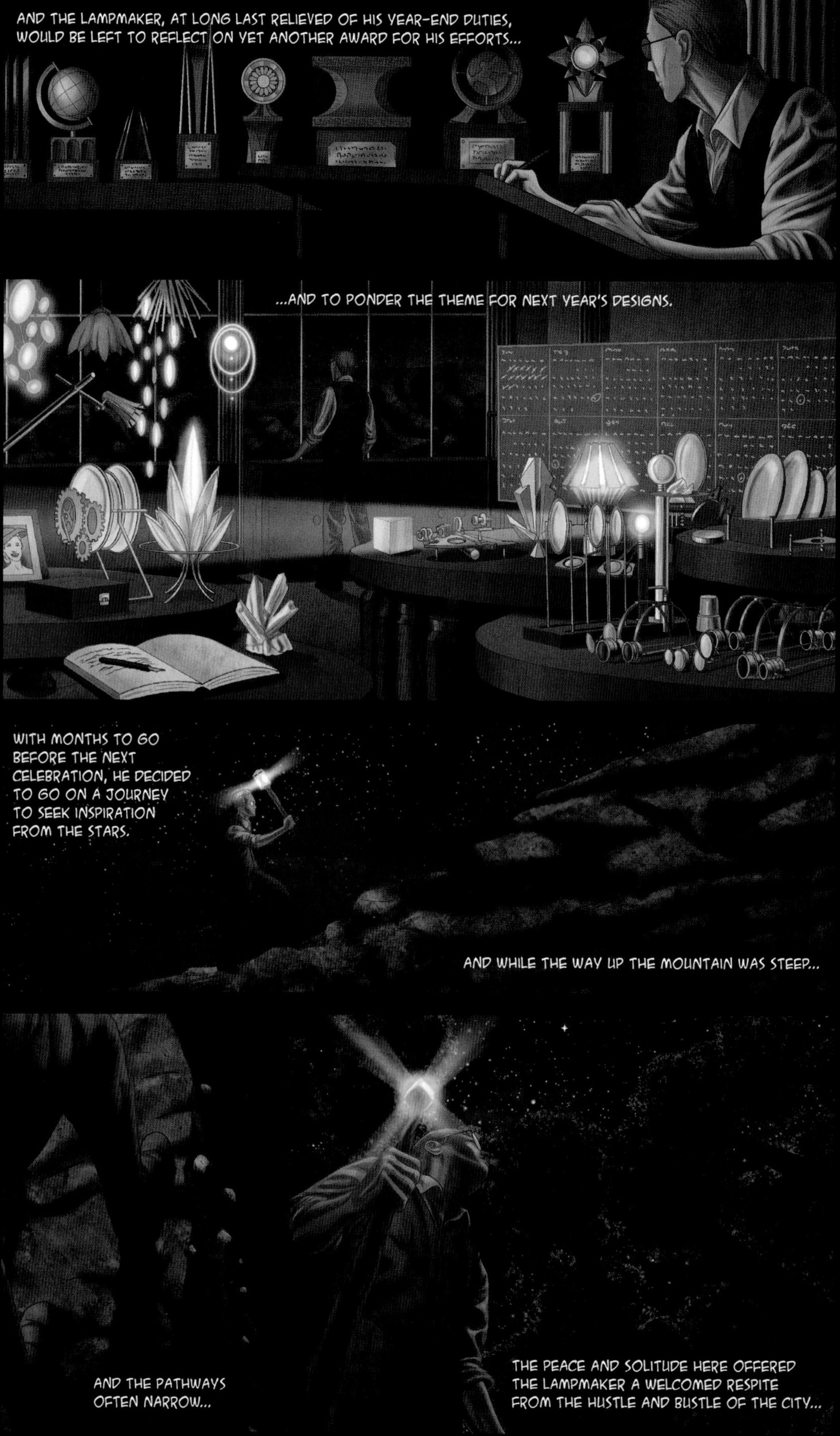
AND THE LAMPMAKER, AT LONG LAST RELIEVED OF HIS YEAR-END DUTIES, WOULD BE LEFT TO REFLECT ON YET ANOTHER AWARD FOR HIS EFFORTS...
...AND TO PONDER THE THEME FOR NEXT YEAR'S DESIGNS.
WITH MONTHS TO GO BEFORE THE NEXT CELEBRATION, HE DECIDED TO GO ON A JOURNEY TO SEEK INSPIRATION FROM THE STARS.
AND WHILE THE WAY UP THE MOUNTAIN WAS STEEP...
AND THE PATHWAYS OFTEN NARROW...
THE PEACE AND SOLITUDE HERE OFFERED THE LAMPMAKER A WELCOMED RESPITE FROM THE HUSTLE AND BUSTLE OF THE CITY...

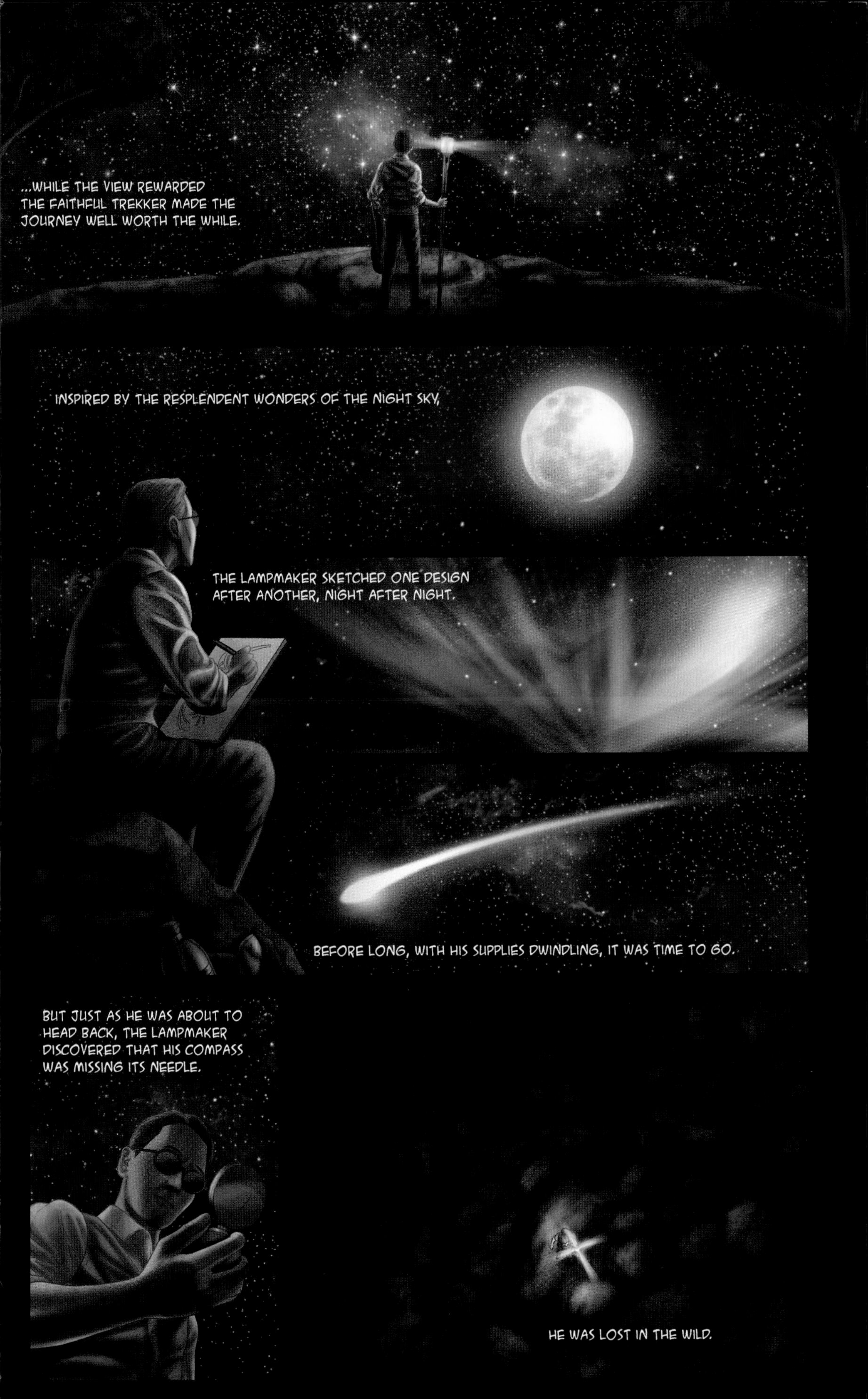
...WHILE THE VIEW REWARDED THE FAITHFUL TREKKER MADE THE JOURNEY WELL WORTH THE WHILE.
INSPIRED BY THE RESPLENDENT WONDERS OF THE NIGHT SKY,
THE LAMPMAKER SKETCHED ONE DESIGN AFTER ANOTHER, NIGHT AFTER NIGHT.
BEFORE LONG, WITH HIS SUPPLIES DWINDLING, IT WAS TIME TO GO.
BUT JUST AS HE WAS ABOUT TO HEAD BACK, THE LAMPMAKER DISCOVERED THAT HIS COMPASS WAS MISSING ITS NEEDLE.
HE WAS LOST IN THE WILD.

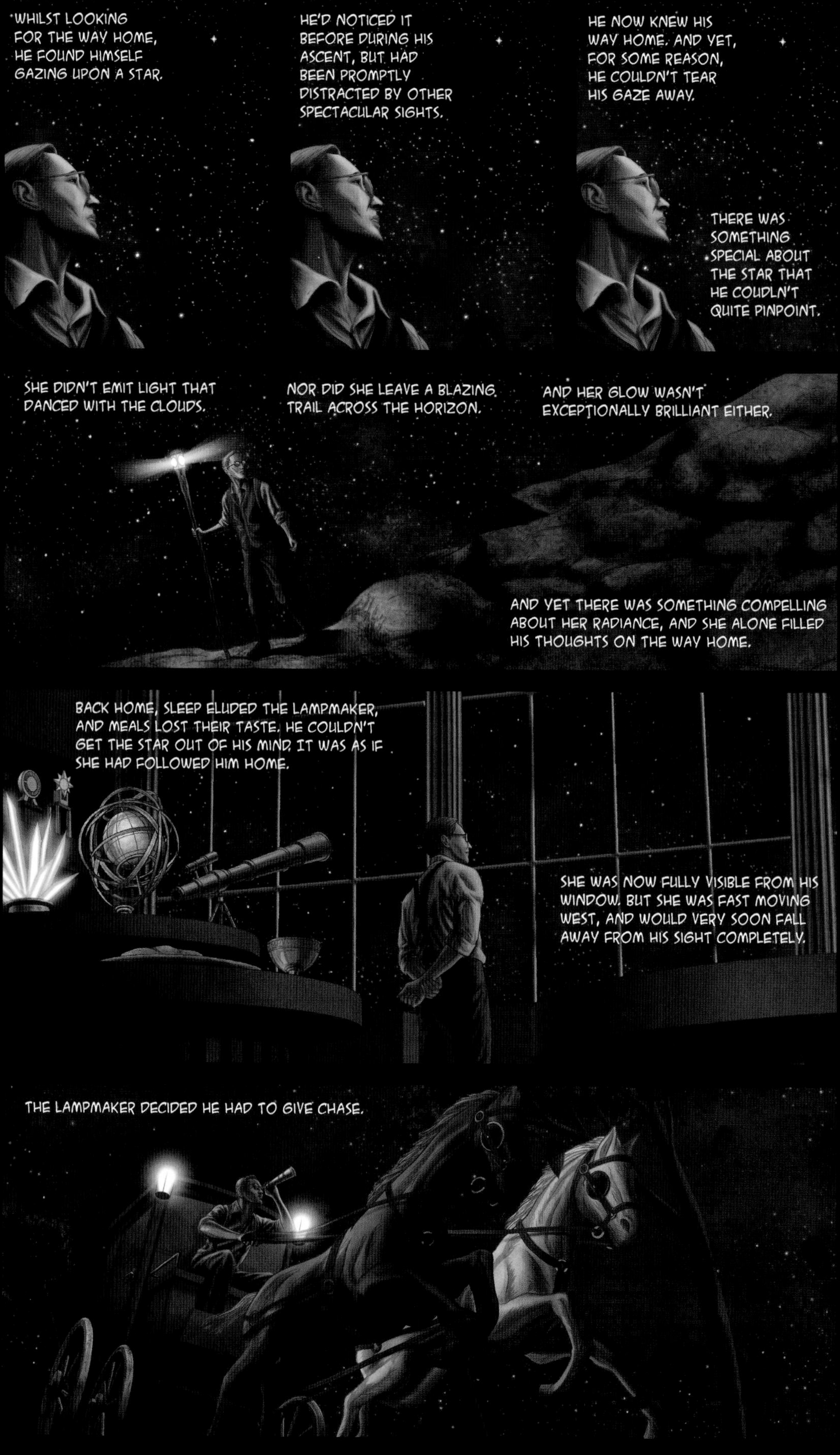
WHILST LOOKING FOR THE WAY HOME, HE FOUND HIMSELF GAZING UPON A STAR.
HE'D NOTICED IT BEFORE DURING HIS ASCENT, BUT HAD BEEN PROMPTLY DISTRACTED BY OTHER SPECTACULAR SIGHTS.
HE NOW KNEW HIS WAY HOME. AND YET, FOR SOME REASON, HE COULDN'T TEAR HIS GAZE AWAY.
THERE WAS SOMETHING SPECIAL ABOUT THE STAR THAT HE COUDLN'T QUITE PINPOINT.
SHE DIDN'T EMIT LIGHT THAT DANCED WITH THE CLOUDS.
NOR DID SHE LEAVE A BLAZING TRAIL ACROSS THE HORIZON.
AND HER GLOW WASN'T EXCEPTIONALLY BRILLIANT EITHER.
AND YET THERE WAS SOMETHING COMPELLING ABOUT HER RADIANCE, AND SHE ALONE FILLED HIS THOUGHTS ON THE WAY HOME.
BACK HOME, SLEEP ELUDED THE LAMPMAKER, AND MEALS LOST THEIR TASTE. HE COULDN'T GET THE STAR OUT OF HIS MIND. IT WAS AS IF SHE HAD FOLLOWED HIM HOME.
SHE WAS NOW FULLY VISIBLE FROM HIS WINDOW. BUT SHE WAS FAST MOVING WEST, AND WOULD VERY SOON FALL AWAY FROM HIS SIGHT COMPLETELY.
THE LAMPMAKER DECIDED HE HAD TO GIVE CHASE.

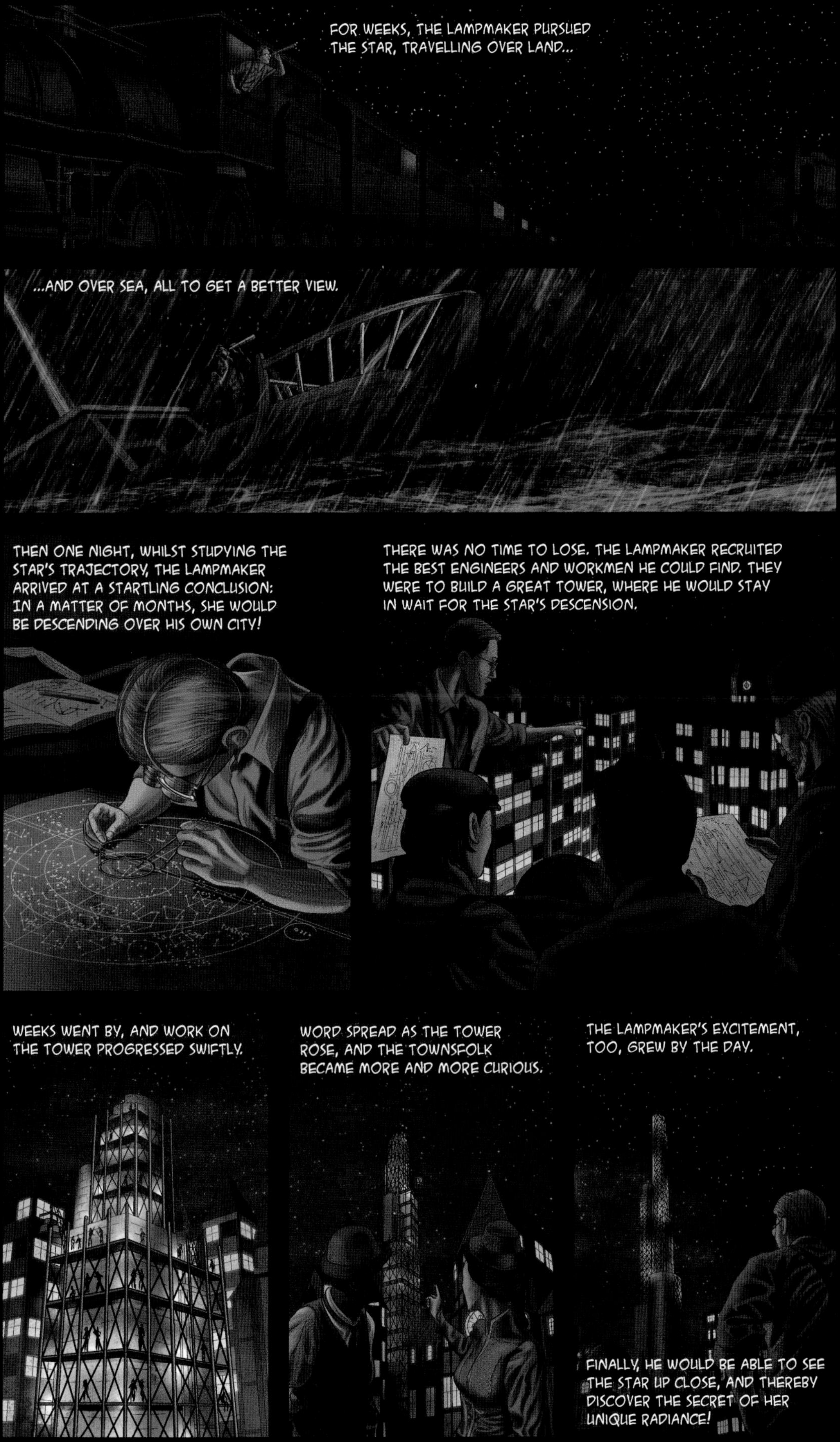
FOR WEEKS, THE LAMPMAKER PURSUED THE STAR, TRAVELLING OVER LAND...
...AND OVER SEA, ALL TO GET A BETTER VIEW.
THEN ONE NIGHT, WHILST STUDYING THE STAR'S TRAJECTORY, THE LAMPMAKER ARRIVED AT A STARTLING CONCLUSION: IN A MATTER OF MONTHS, SHE WOULD BE DESCENDING OVER HIS OWN CITY!
THERE WAS NO TIME TO LOSE. THE LAMPMAKER RECRUITED THE BEST ENGINEERS AND WORKMEN HE COULD FIND. THEY WERE TO BUILD A GREAT TOWER, WHERE HE WOULD STAY IN WAIT FOR THE STAR'S DESCENSION.
WEEKS WENT BY, AND WORK ON THE TOWER PROGRESSED SWIFTLY.
WORD SPREAD AS THE TOWER ROSE, AND THE TOWNSFOLK BECAME MORE AND MORE CURIOUS.
THE LAMPMAKER'S EXCITEMENT, TOO, GREW BY THE DAY.
FINALLY, HE WOULD BE ABLE TO SEE THE STAR UP CLOSE, AND THEREBY DISCOVER THE SECRET OF HER UNIQUE RADIANCE!

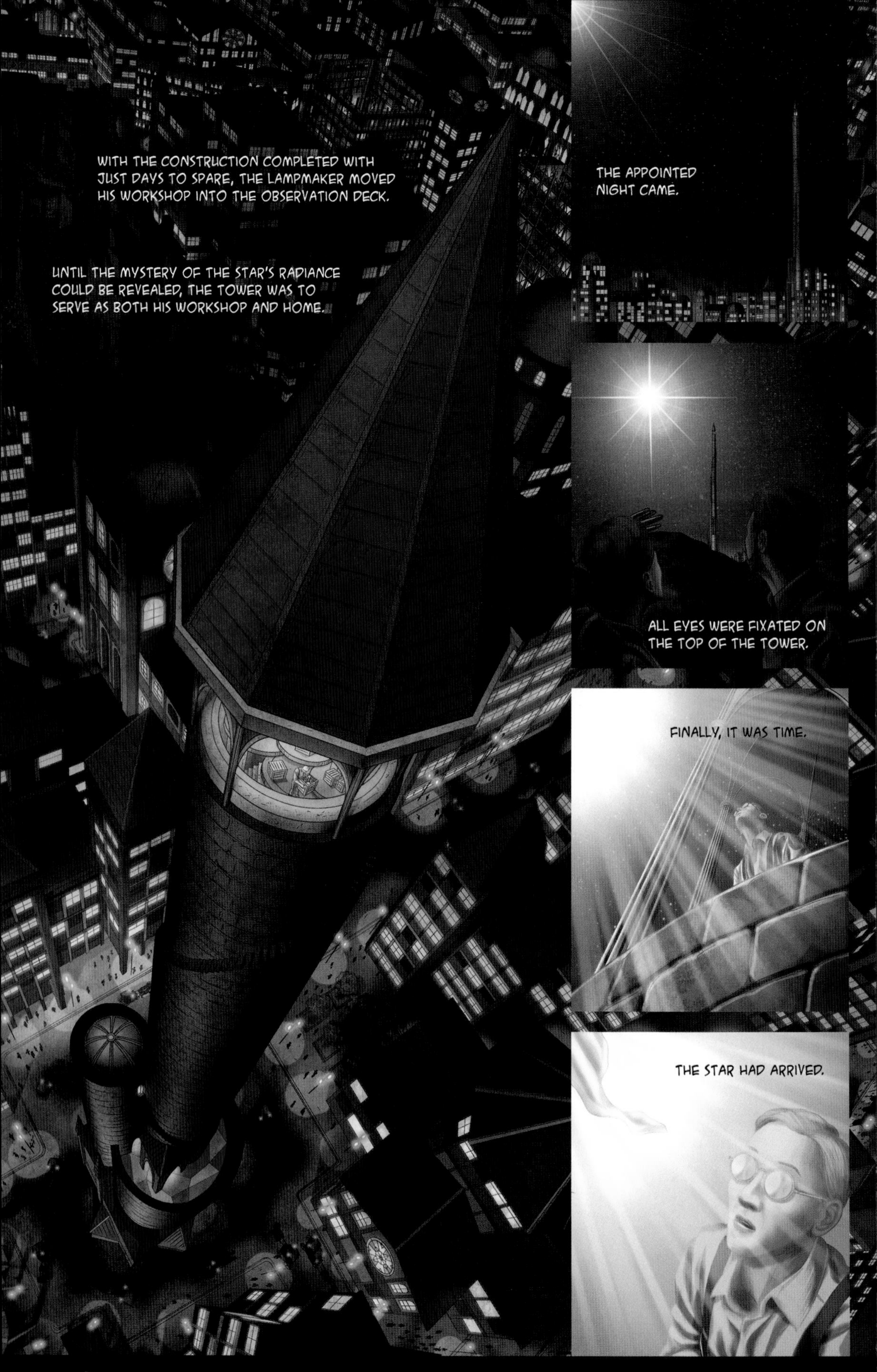
WITH THE CONSTRUCTION COMPLETED WITH JUST DAYS TO SPARE, THE LAMPMAKER MOVED HIS WORKSHOP INTO THE OBSERVATION DECK.
UNTIL THE MYSTERY OF THE STAR'S RADIANCE COULD BE REVEALED, THE TOWER WAS TO SERVE AS BOTH HIS WORKSHOP AND HOME.
THE APPOINTED NIGHT CAME.
ALL EYES WERE FIXATED ON THE TOP OF THE TOWER.
FINALLY, IT WAS TIME.
THE STAR HAD ARRIVED.

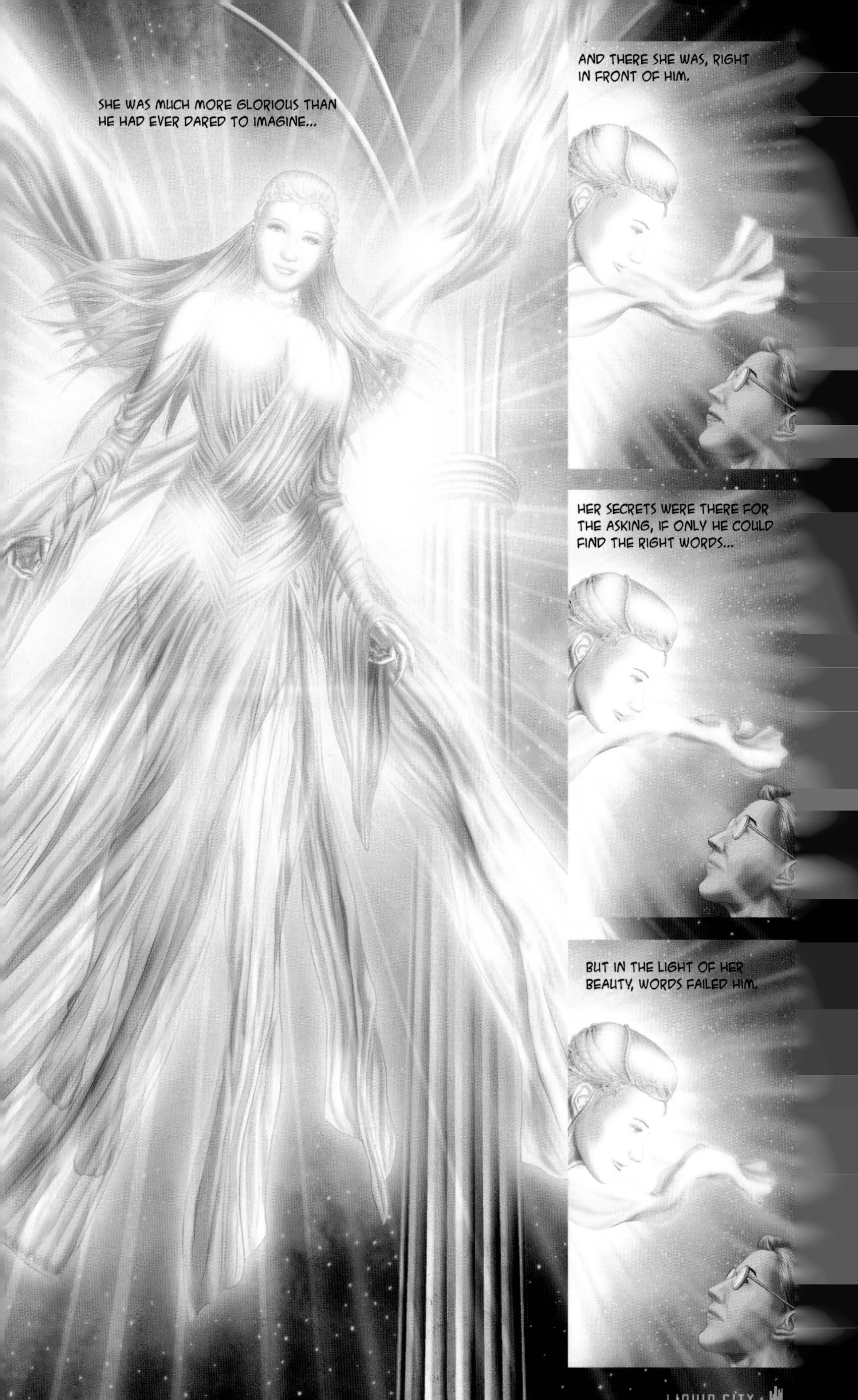
SHE WAS MUCH MORE GLORIOUS THAN HE HAD EVER DARED TO IMAGINE...
AND THERE SHE WAS, RIGHT IN FRONT OF HIM.
HER SECRETS WERE THERE FOR THE ASKING, IF ONLY HE COULD FIND THE RIGHT WORDS...
BUT IN THE LIGHT OF HER BEAUTY, WORDS FAILED HIM.

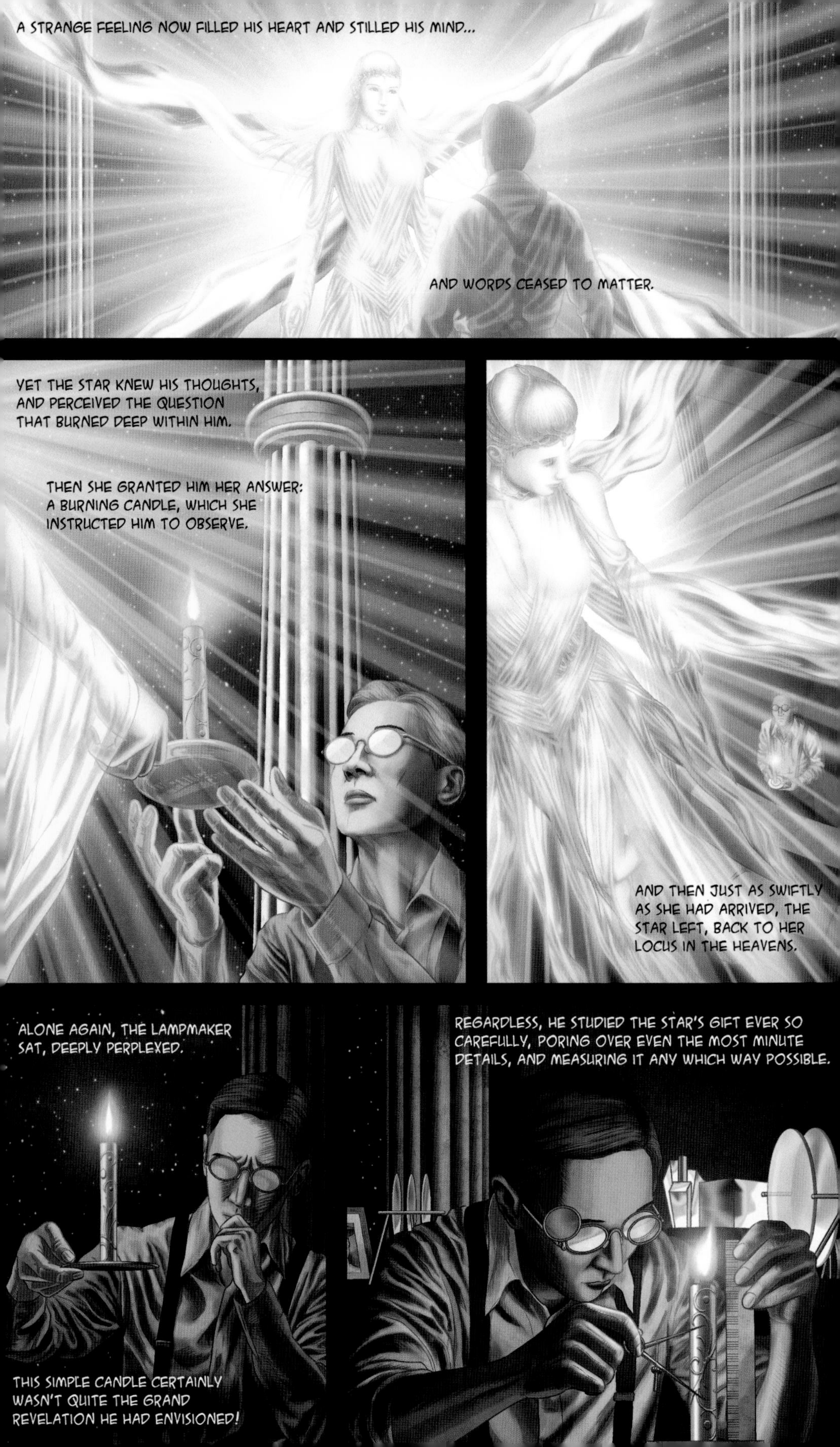
A STRANGE FEELING NOW FILLED HIS HEART AND STILLED HIS MIND...
AND WORDS CEASED TO MATTER.
YET THE STAR KNEW HIS THOUGHTS, AND PERCEIVED THE QUESTION THAT BURNED DEEP WITHIN HIM.
THEN SHE GRANTED HIM HER ANSWER: A BURNING CANDLE, WHICH SHE INSTRUCTED HIM TO OBSERVE.
AND THEN JUST AS SWIFTLY AS SHE HAD ARRIVED, THE STAR LEFT, BACK TO HER LOCUS IN THE HEAVENS.
ALONE AGAIN, THE LAMPMAKER SAT, DEEPLY PERPLEXED.
THIS SIMPLE CANDLE CERTAINLY WASN'T QUITE THE GRAND REVELATION HE HAD ENVISIONED!
REGARDLESS, HE STUDIED THE STAR'S GIFT EVER SO CAREFULLY, PORING OVER EVEN THE MOST MINUTE DETAILS, AND MEASURING IT ANY WHICH WAY POSSIBLE.

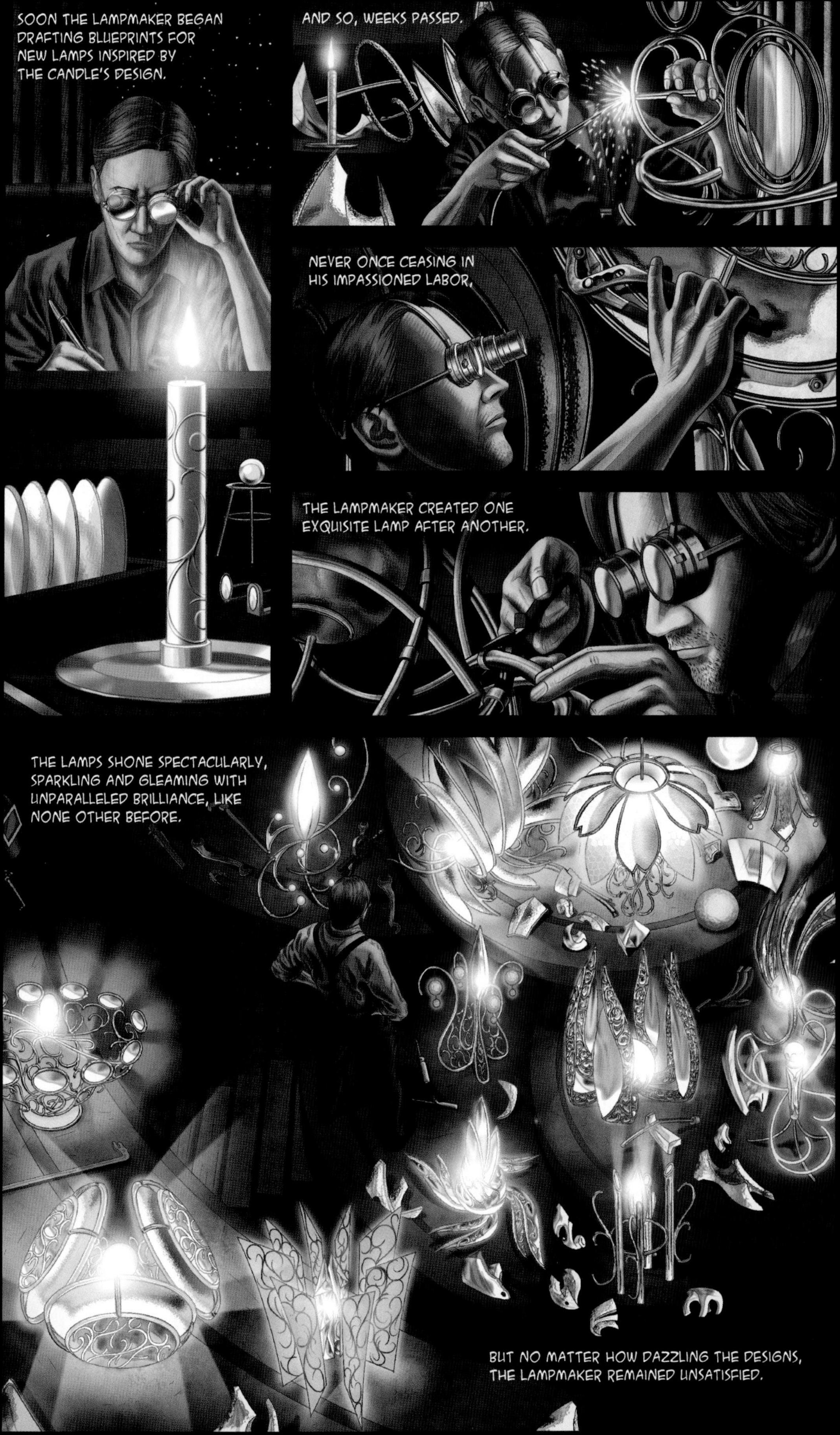
SOON THE LAMPMAKER BEGAN DRAFTING BLUEPRINTS FOR NEW LAMPS INSPIRED BY THE CANDLE'S DESIGN.
AND SO, WEEKS PASSED.
NEVER ONCE CEASING IN HIS IMPASSIONED LABOR,
THE LAMPMAKER CREATED ONE EXQUISITE LAMP AFTER ANOTHER.
THE LAMPS SHONE SPECTACULARLY, SPARKLING AND GLEAMING WITH UNPARALLELED BRILLIANCE, LIKE NONE OTHER BEFORE.
BUT NO MATTER HOW DAZZLING THE DESIGNS, THE LAMPMAKER REMAINED UNSATISFIED.

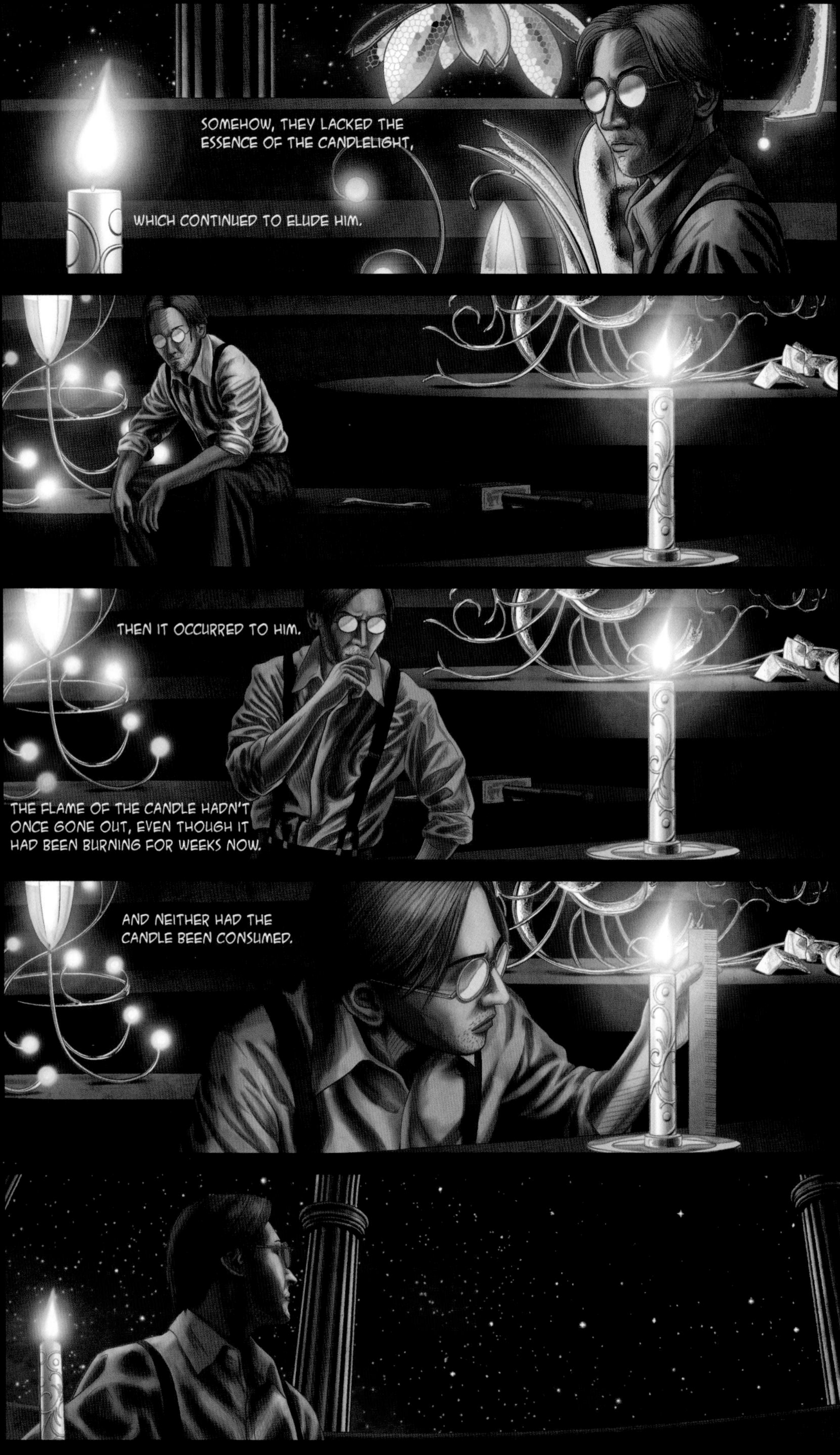
SOMEHOW, THEY LACKED THE ESSENCE OF THE CANDLELIGHT,
WHICH CONTINUED TO ELUDE HIM.
THEN IT OCCURRED TO HIM.
THE FLAME OF THE CANDLE HADN'T ONCE GONE OUT, EVEN THOUGH IT HAD BEEN BURNING FOR WEEKS NOW.
AND NEITHER HAD THE CANDLE BEEN CONSUMED.

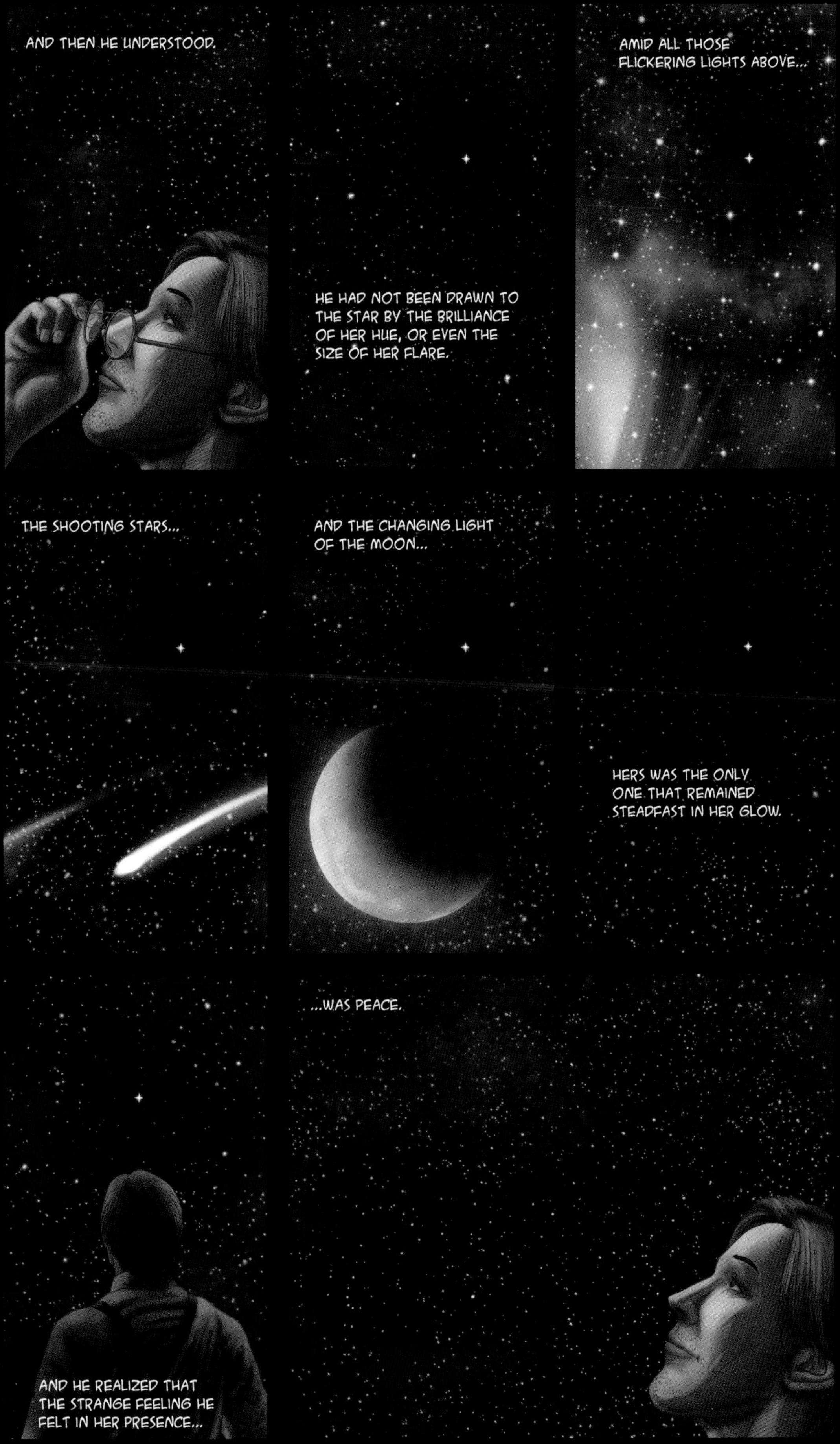
AND THEN HE UNDERSTOOD.
HE HAD NOT BEEN DRAWN TO THE STAR BY THE BRILLIANCE OF HER HUE, OR EVEN THE SIZE OF HER FLARE.
AMID ALL THOSE FLICKERING LIGHTS ABOVE...
THE SHOOTING STARS...
AND THE CHANGING LIGHT OF THE MOON...
HERS WAS THE ONLY ONE THAT REMAINED STEADFAST IN HER GLOW.
AND HE REALIZED THAT THE STRANGE FEELING HE FELT IN HER PRESENCE...
...WAS PEACE.

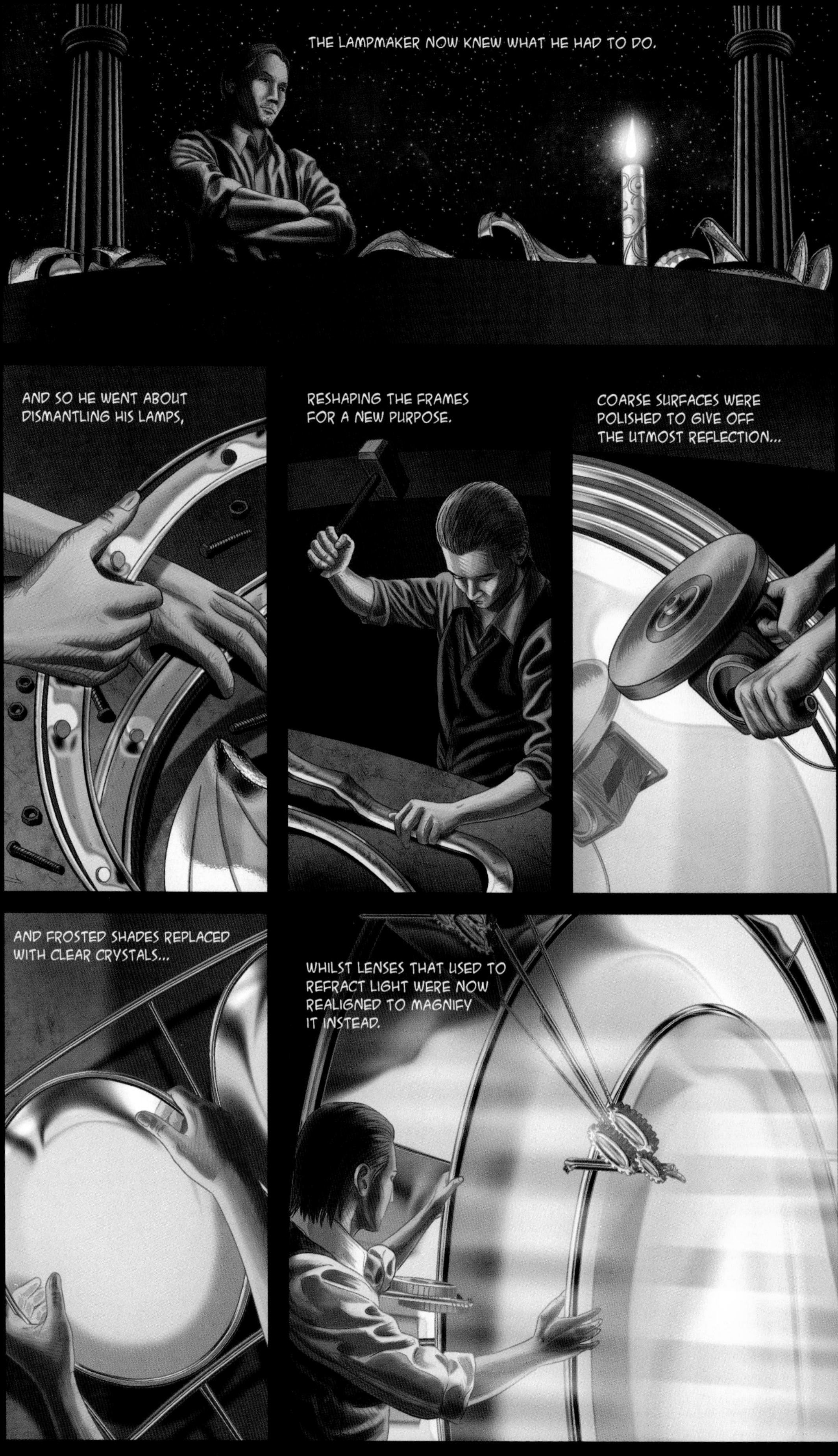
THE LAMPMAKER NOW KNEW WHAT HE HAD TO DO.
AND SO HE WENT ABOUT DISMANTLING HIS LAMPS,
RESHAPING THE FRAMES FOR A NEW PURPOSE.
COARSE SURFACES WERE POLISHED TO GIVE OFF THE UTMOST REFLECTION...
AND FROSTED SHADES REPLACED WITH CLEAR CRYSTALS...
WHILST LENSES THAT USED TO REFRACT LIGHT WERE NOW REALIGNED TO MAGNIFY IT INSTEAD.

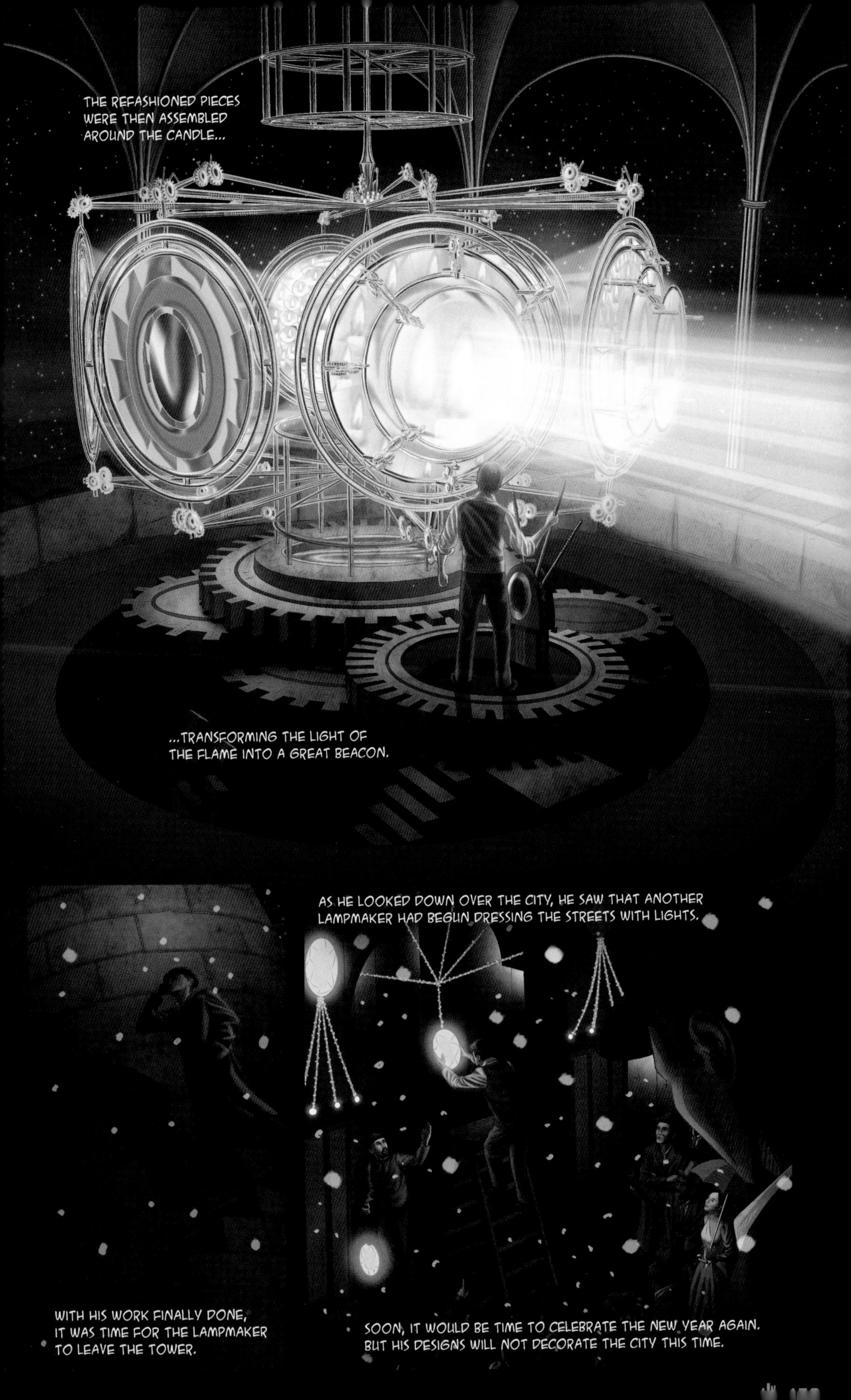
THE REFASHIONED PIECES WERE THEN ASSEMBLED AROUND THE CANDLE...
...TRANSFORMING THE LIGHT OF THE FLAME INTO A GREAT BEACON.
WITH HIS WORK FINALLY DONE, IT WAS TIME FOR THE LAMPMAKER TO LEAVE THE TOWER.
AS HE LOOKED DOWN OVER THE CITY, HE SAW THAT ANOTHER LAMPMAKER HAD BEGUN DRESSING THE STREETS WITH LIGHTS.
SOON, IT WOULD BE TIME TO CELEBRATE THE NEW YEAR AGAIN. BUT HIS DESIGNS WILL NOT DECORATE THE CITY THIS TIME.

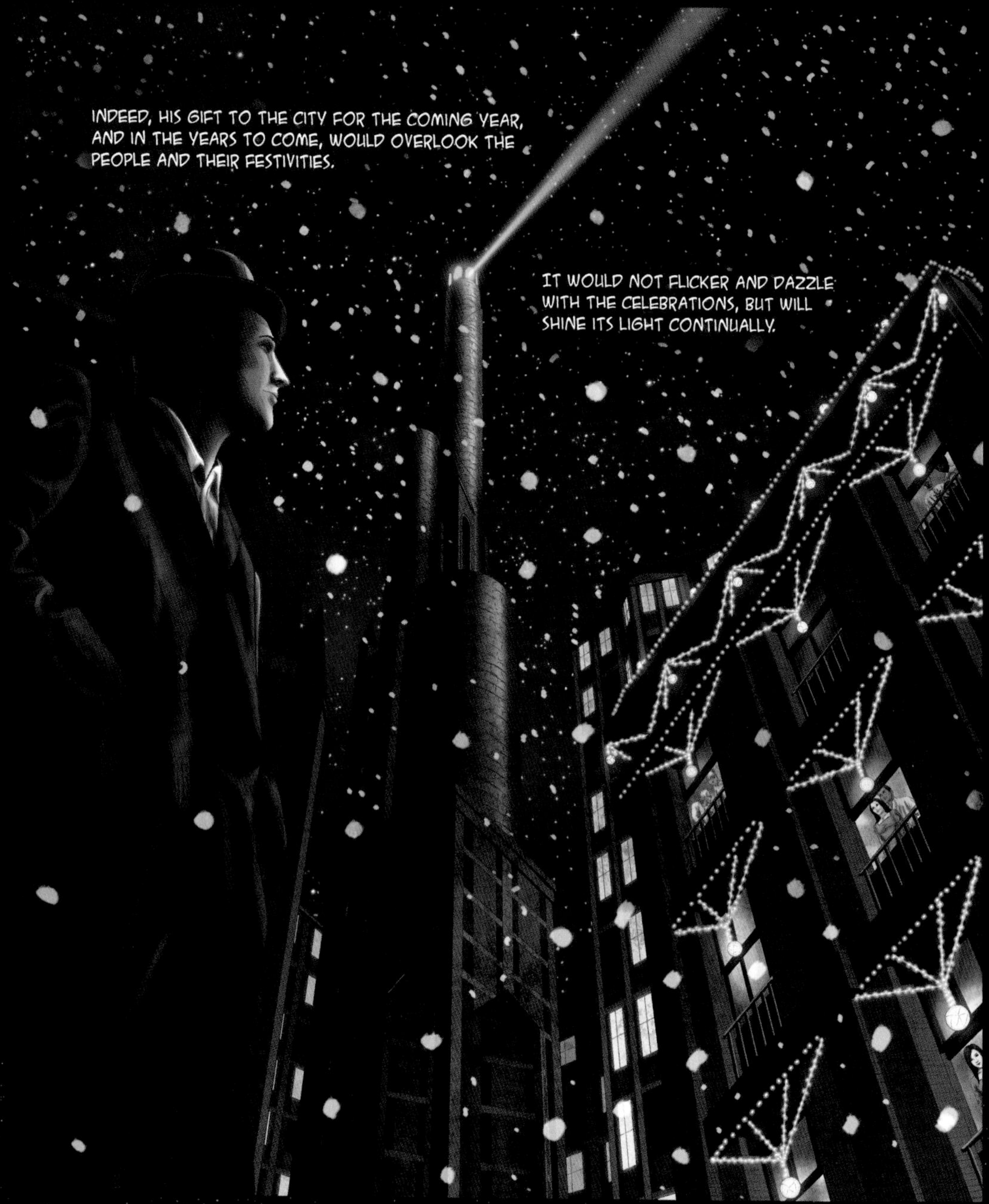
INDEED, HIS GIFT TO THE CITY FOR THE COMING YEAR, AND IN THE YEARS TO COME, WOULD OVERLOOK THE PEOPLE AND THEIR FESTIVITIES.
IT WOULD NOT FLICKER AND DAZZLE WITH THE CELEBRATIONS, BUT WILL SHINE ITS LIGHT CONTINUALLY.

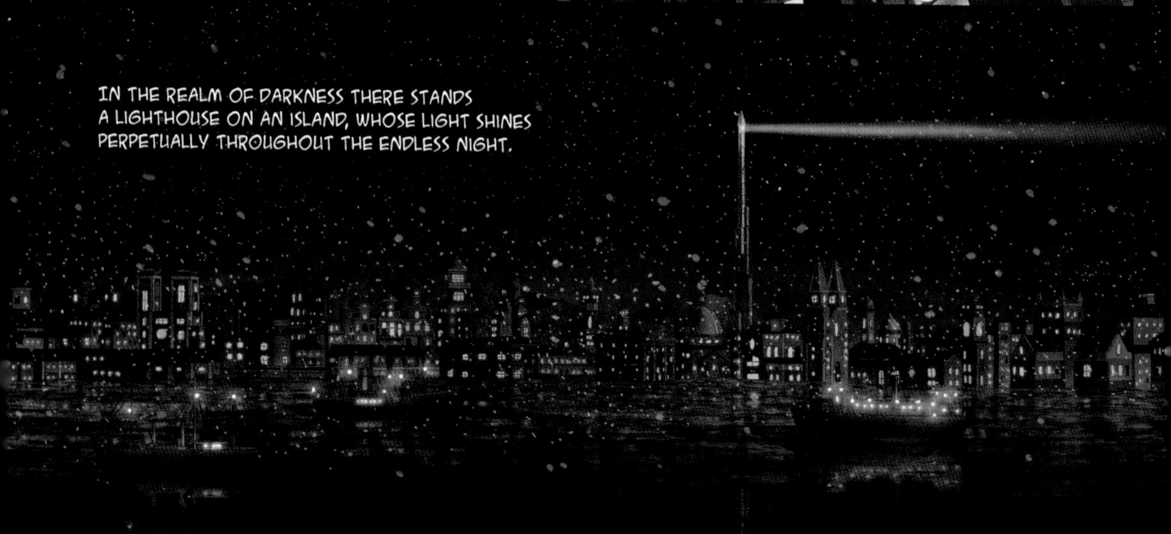
IN THE REALM OF DARKNESS THERE STANDS A LIGHTHOUSE ON AN ISLAND, WHOSE LIGHT SHINES PERPETUALLY THROUGHOUT THE ENDLESS NIGHT.

LET ME SEE THE GIANT FALL

BY BENJAMIN CHEE

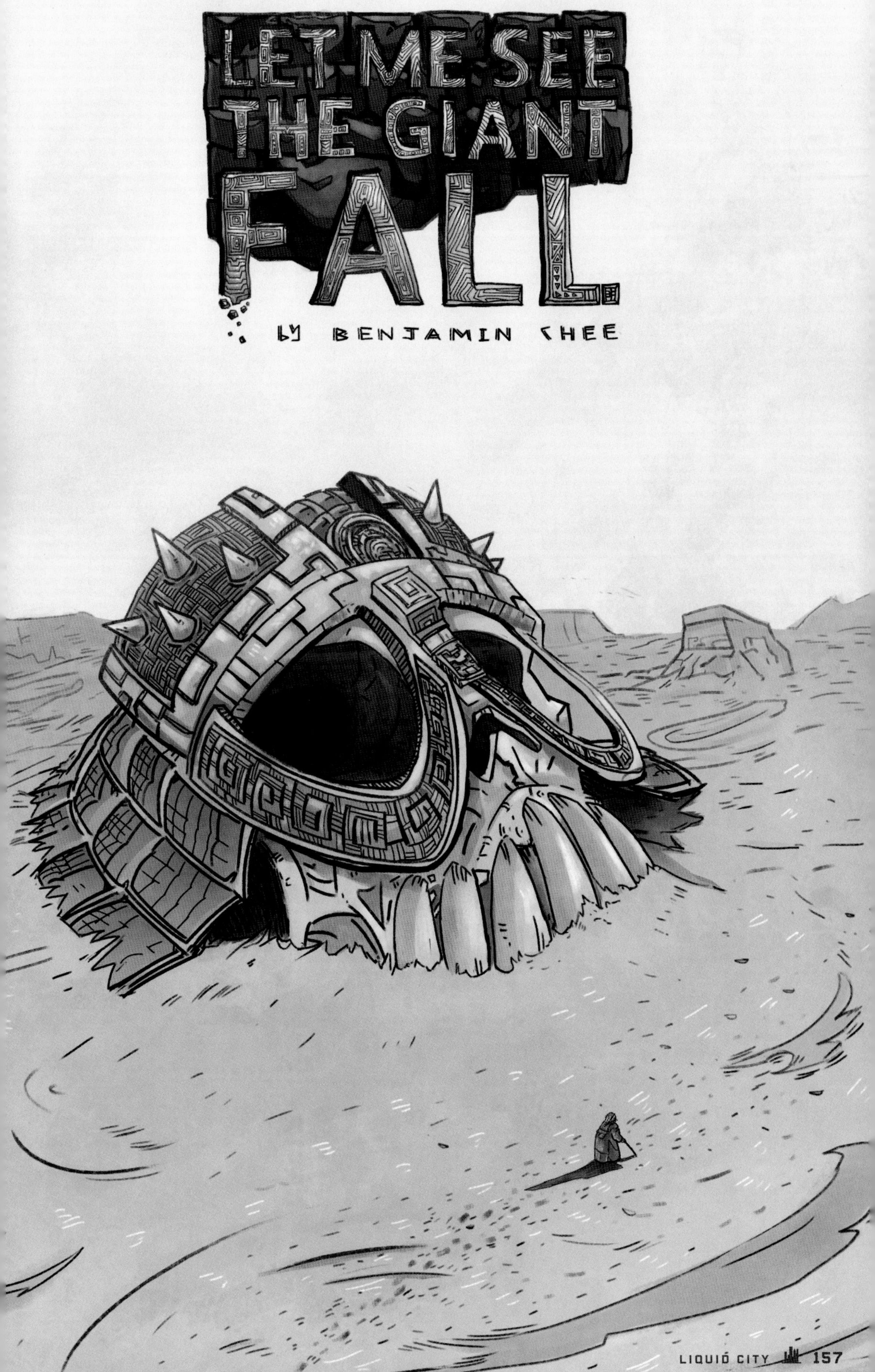

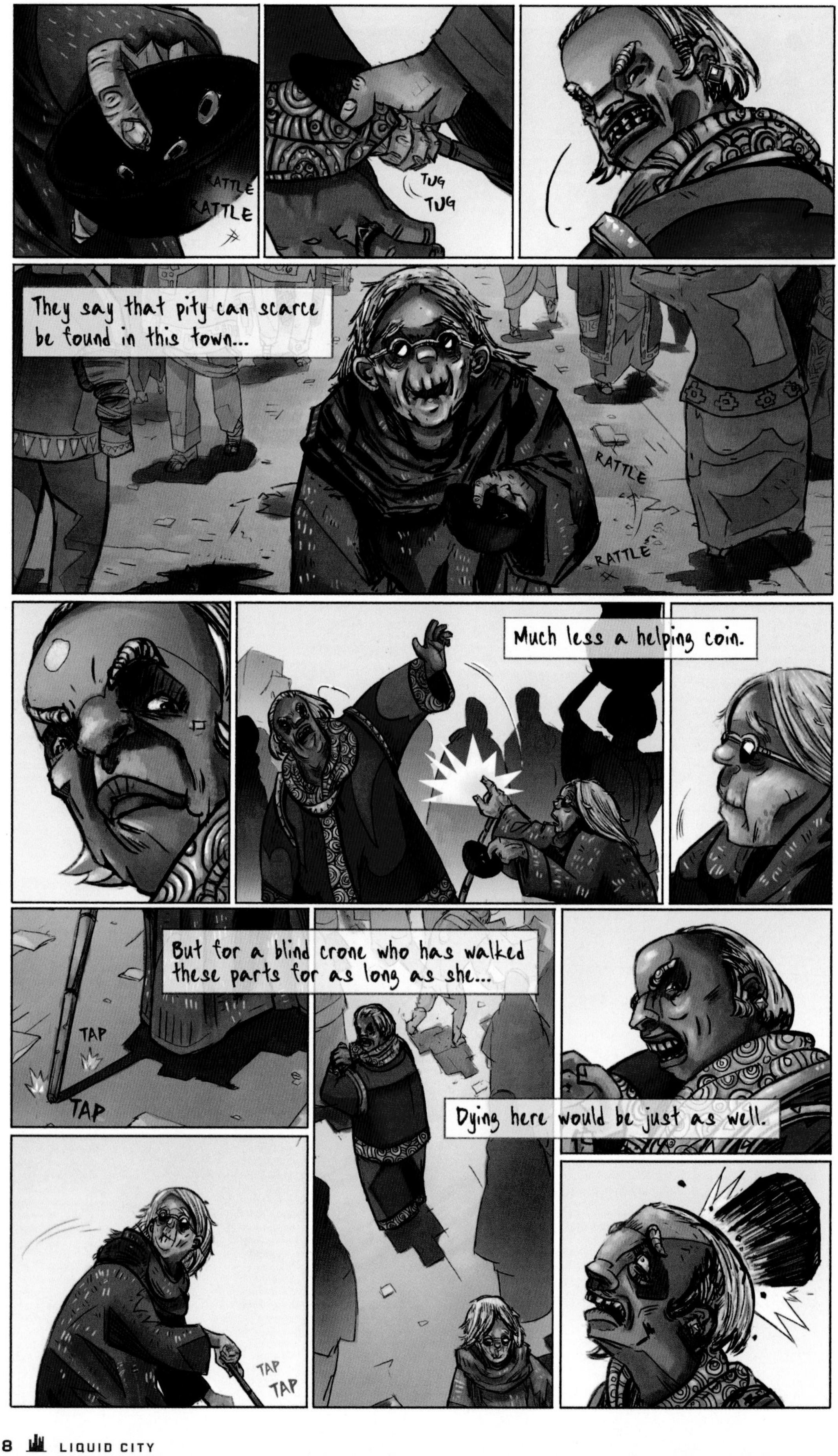
RATTLE
RATTLE
TUG
TUG
They say that pity can scarce be found in this town...
RATTLE
RATTLE
Much less a helping coin.
But for a blind crone who has walked these parts for as long as she...
TAP
TAP
Dying here would be just as well.
TAP
TAP

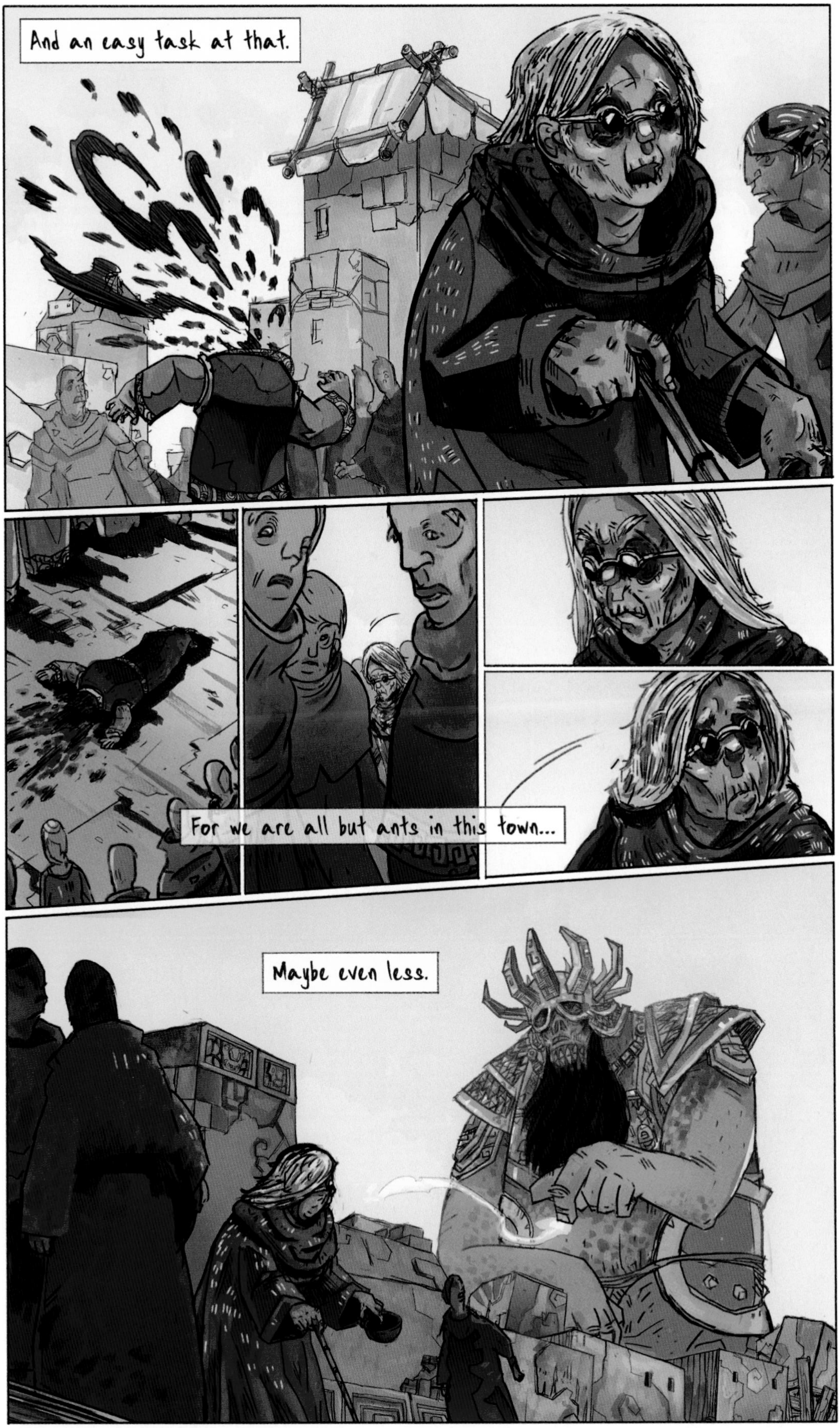
And an easy task at that.
For we are all but ants in this town...
Maybe even less.

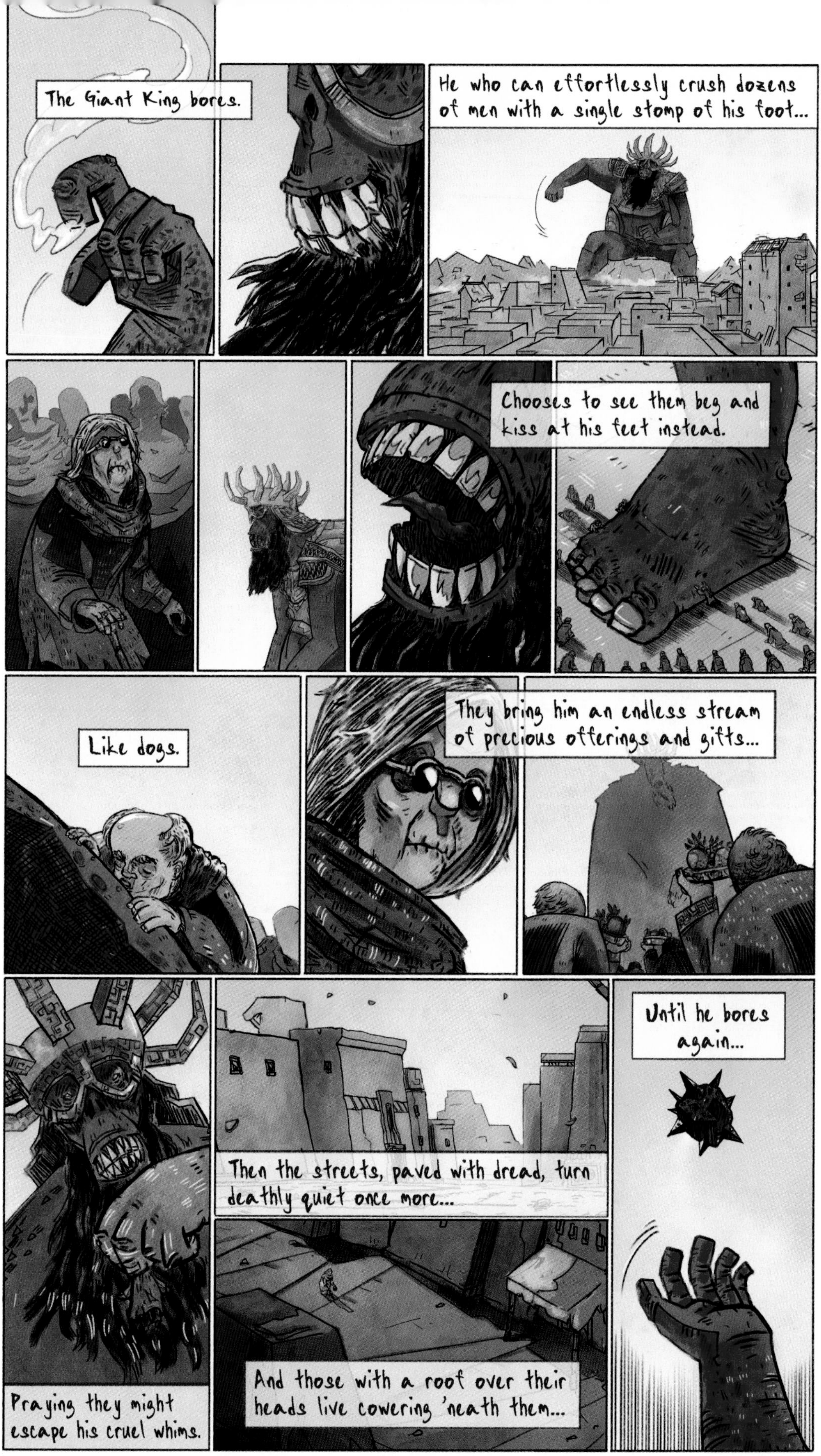
The Giant King bores.
He who can effortlessly crush dozens of men with a single stomp of his foot...
Chooses to see them beg and kiss at his feet instead.
Like dogs.
They bring him an endless stream of precious offerings and gifts...
Praying they might escape his cruel whims.
Then the streets, paved with dread, turn deathly quiet once more...
And those with a roof over their heads live cowering 'neath them...
Until he bores again...

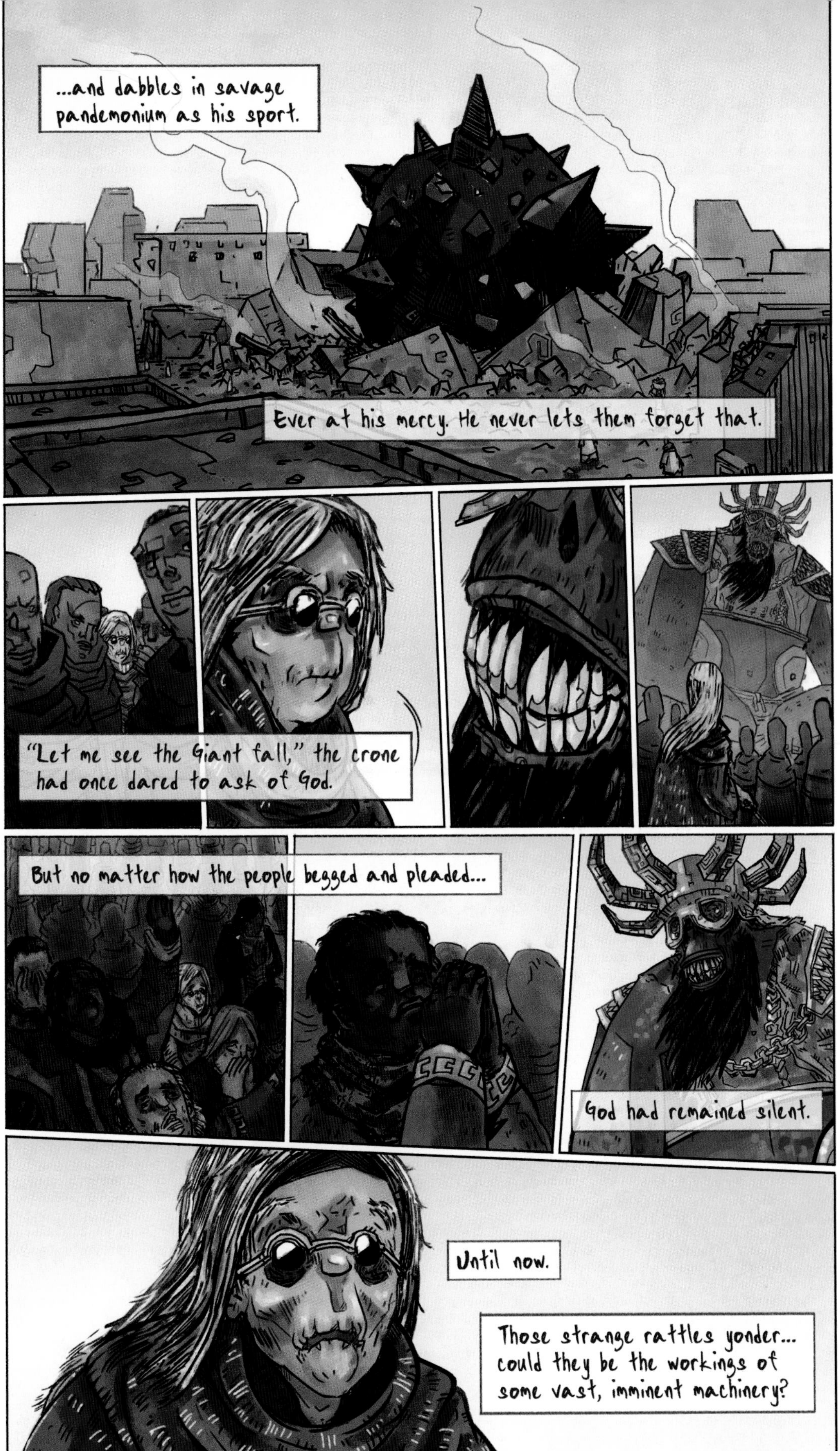
...and dabbles in savage pandemonium as his sport.
Ever at his mercy. He never lets them forget that.
"Let me see the Giant fall," the crone had once dared to ask of God.
But no matter how the people begged and pleaded...
God had remained silent.
Until now.
Those strange rattles yonder... could they be the workings of some vast, imminent machinery?

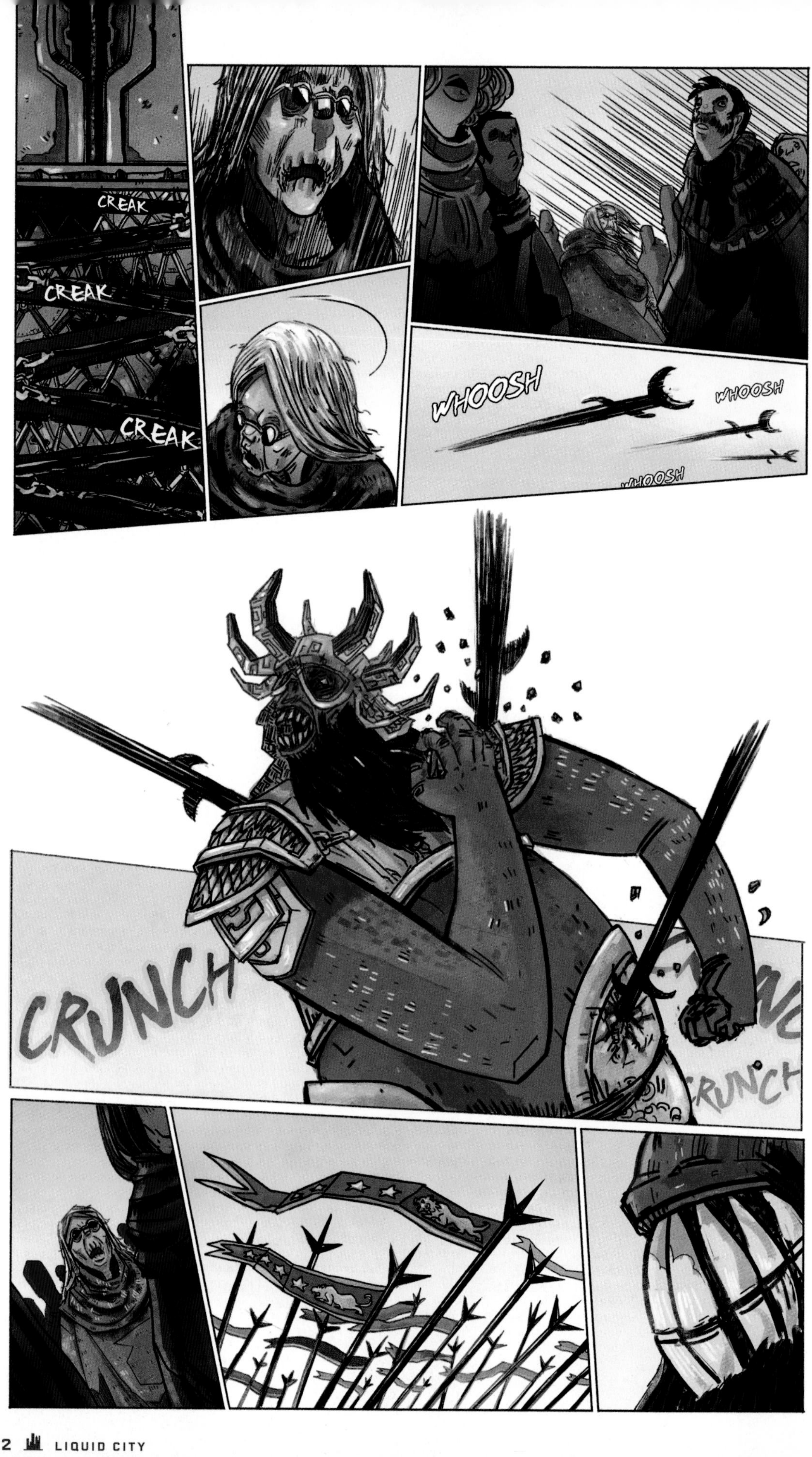
CREAK
CREAK
CREAK
WHOOSH
WHOOSH
WHOOSH
CRUNCH
CRUNCH

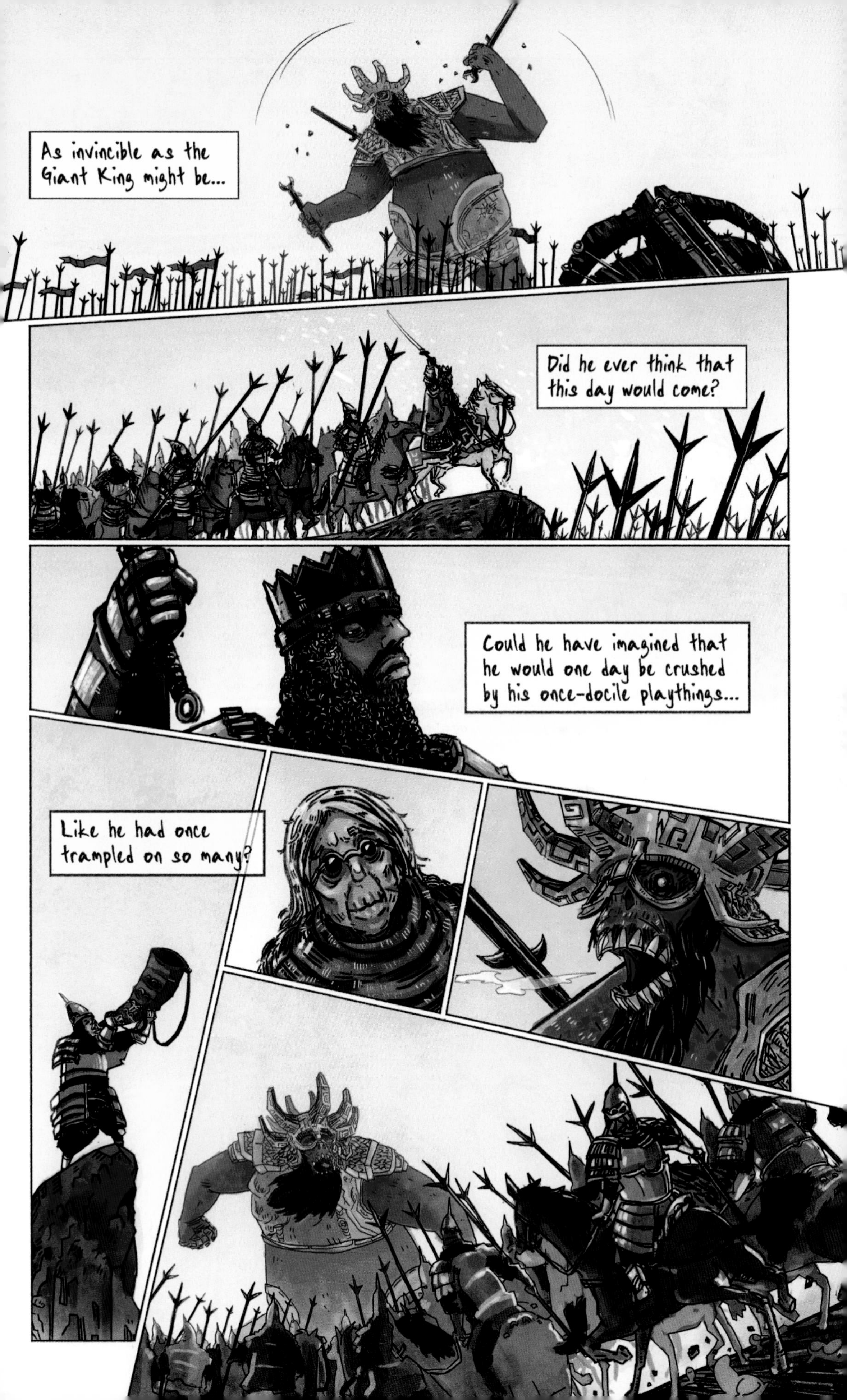

As invincible as the Giant King might be...
Did he ever think that this day would come?
Could he have imagined that he would one day be crushed by his once-docile playthings...
Like he had once trampled on so many?

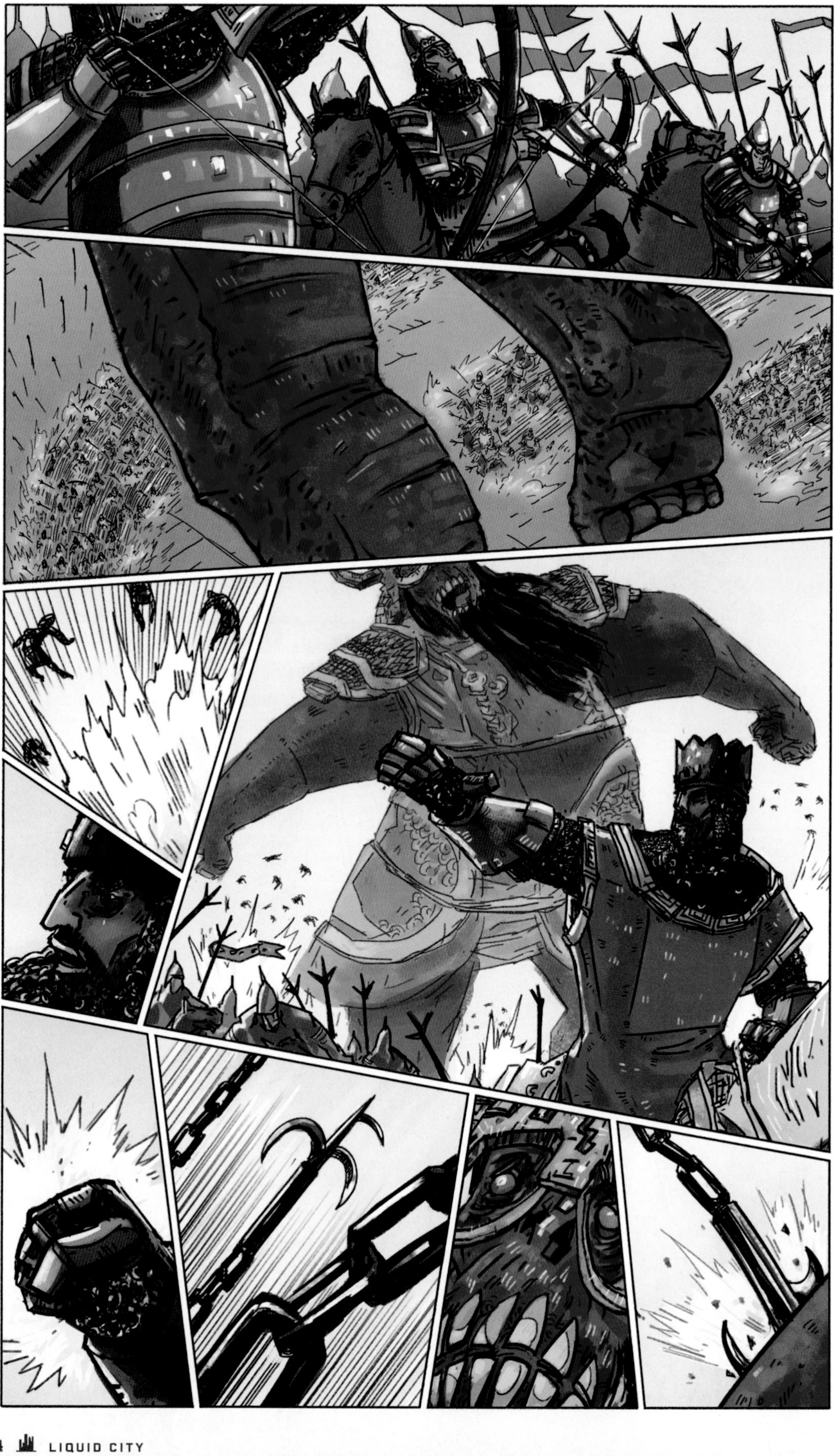

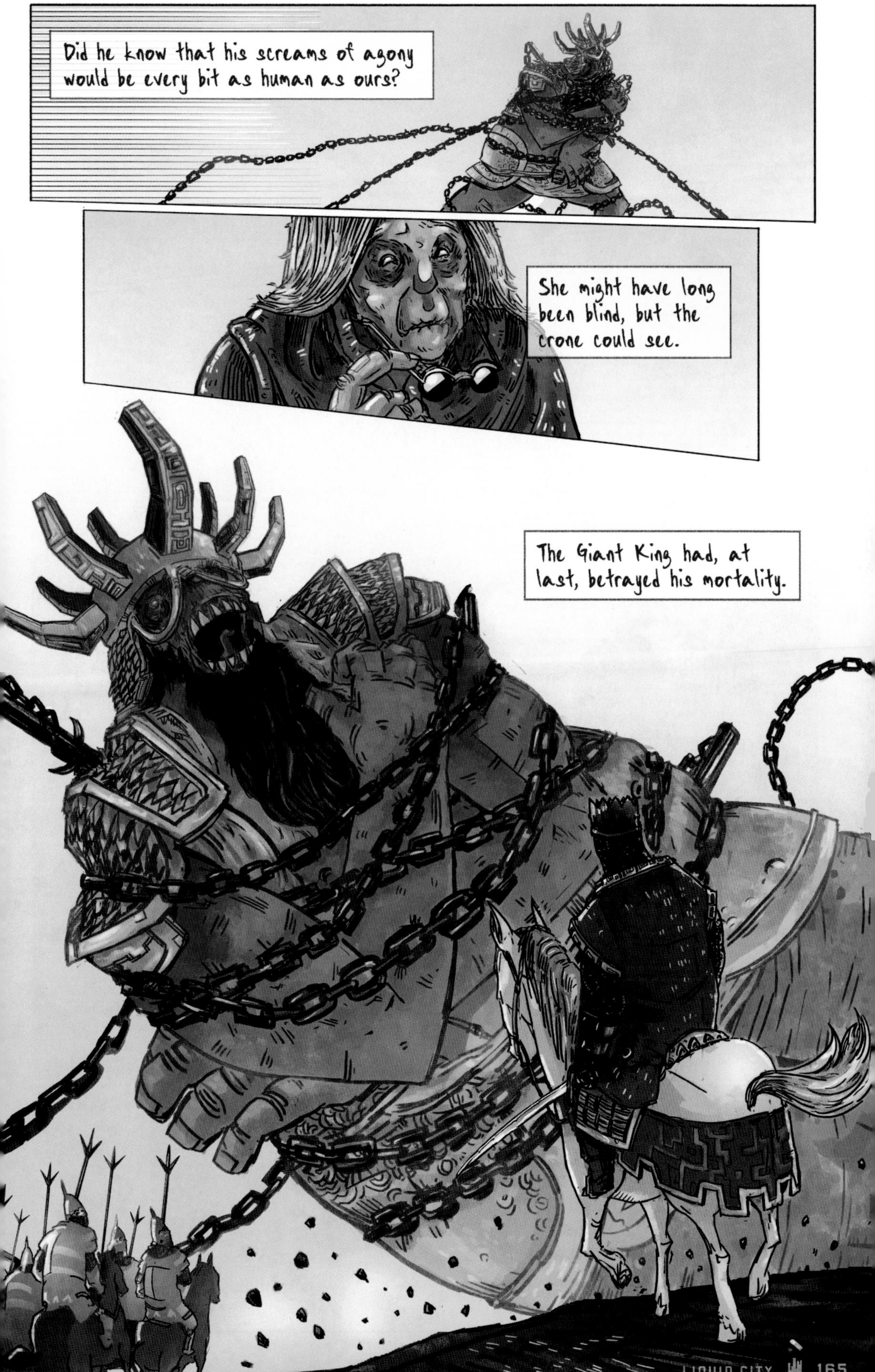

Did he know that his screams of agony would be every bit as human as ours?
She might have long been blind, but the crone could see.
The Giant King had, at last, betrayed his mortality.

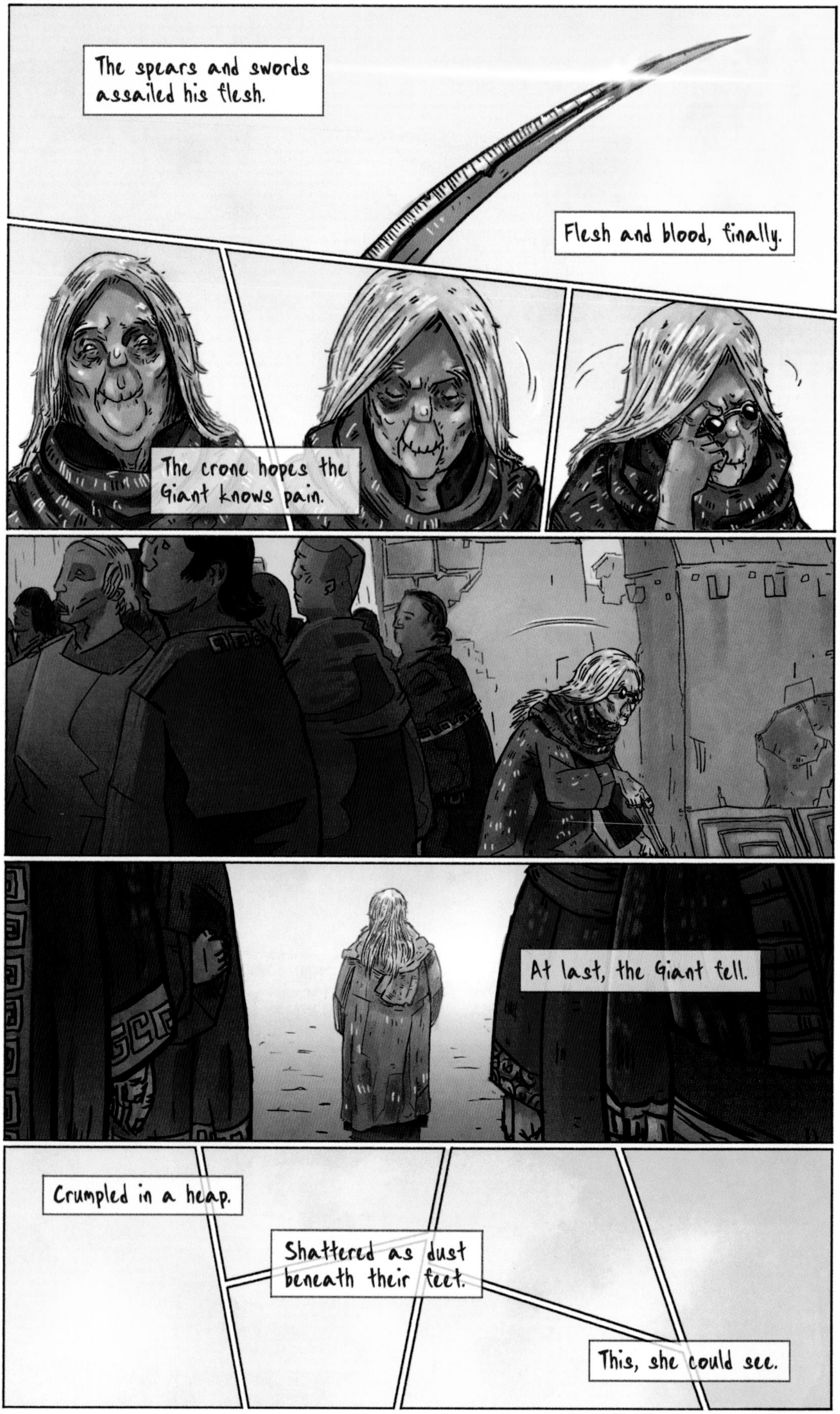
The spears and swords assailed his flesh.
Flesh and blood, finally.
The crone hopes the Giant knows pain.
At last, the Giant fell.
Crumpled in a heap.
Shattered as dust beneath their feet.
This, she could see.

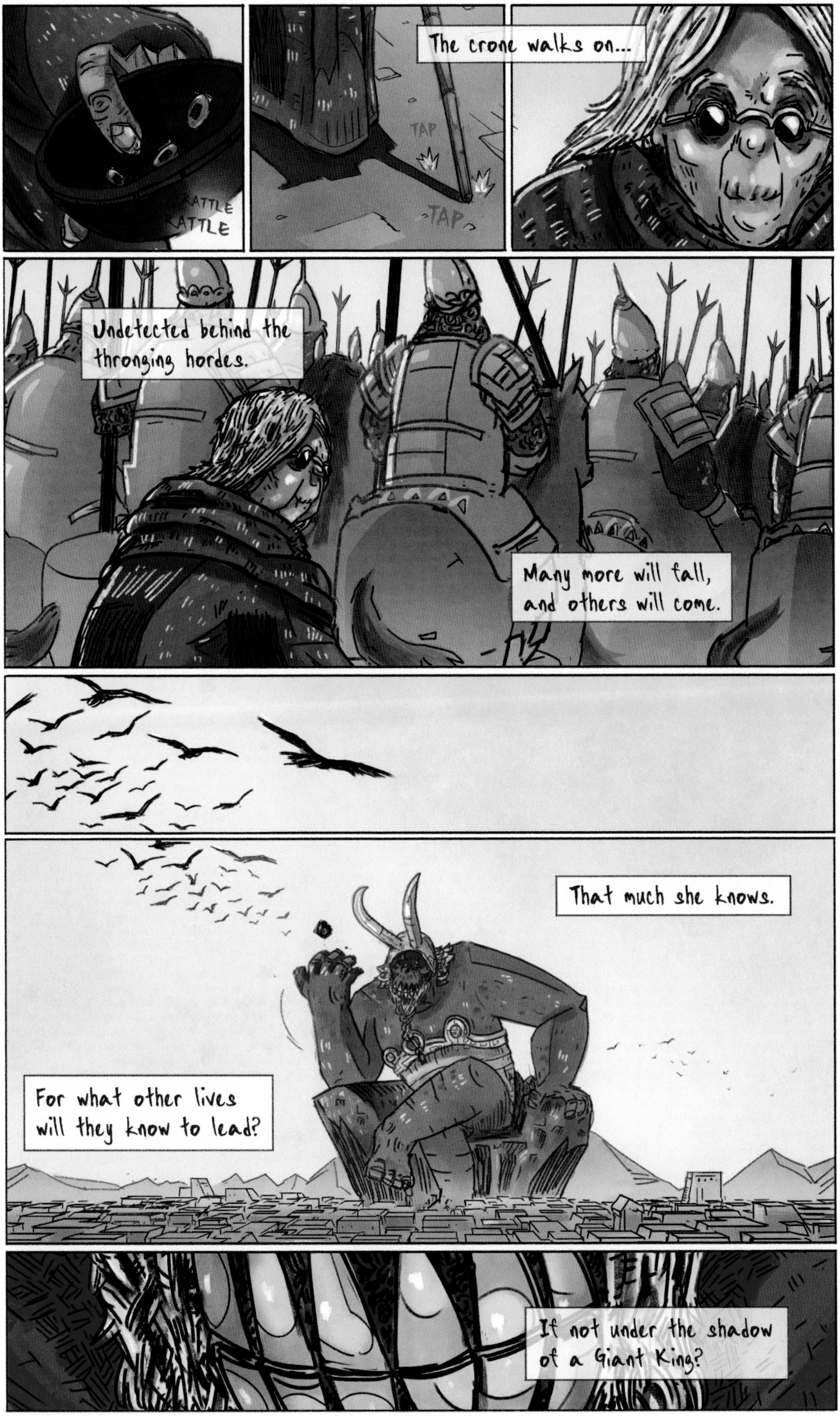
RATTLE
RATTLE
The crone walks on...
TAP
TAP
Undetected behind the thronging hordes.
Many more will fall, and others will come.
That much she knows.
For what other lives will they know to lead?
If not under the shadow of a Giant King?

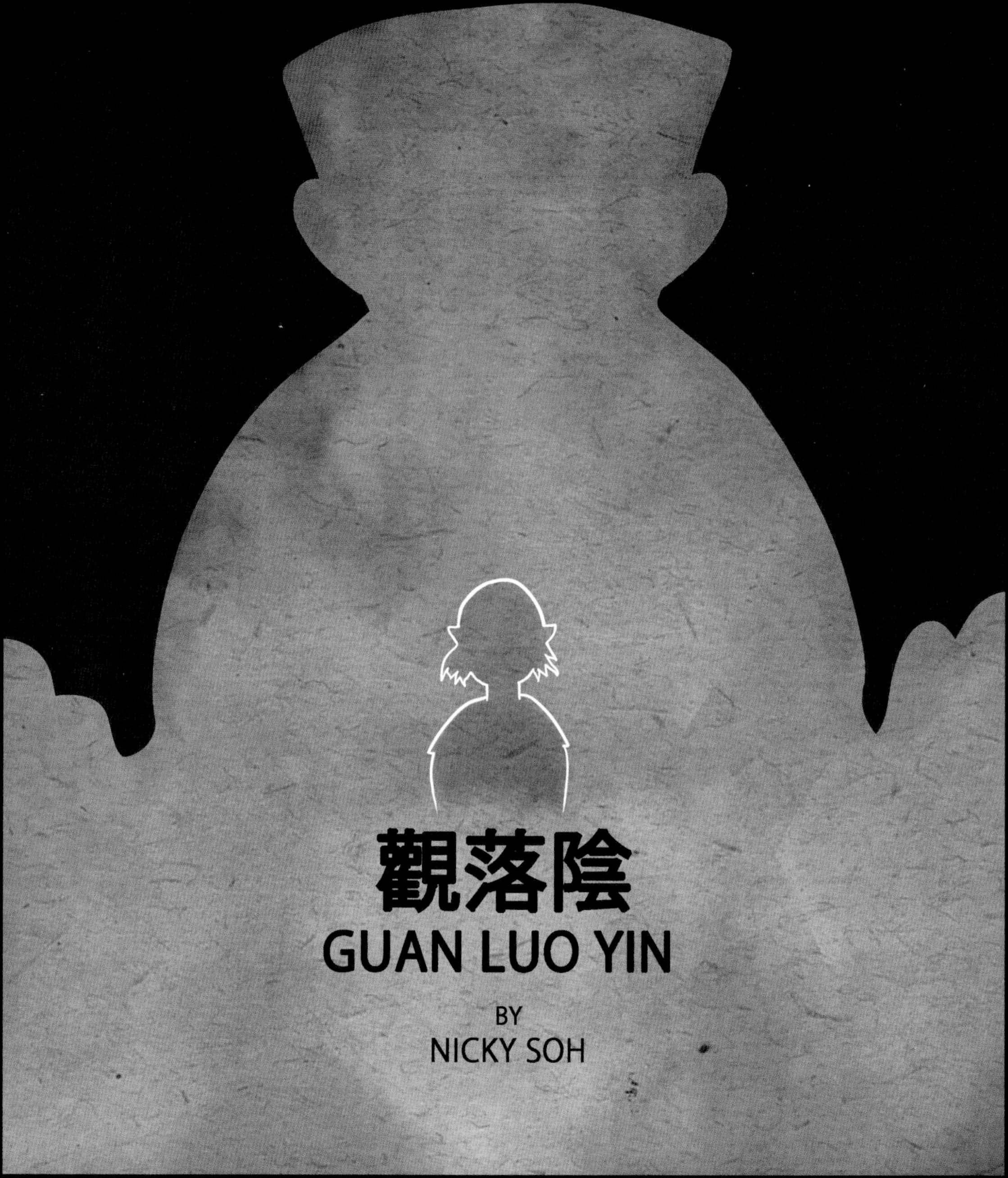

觀落陰
GUAN LUO YIN

BY
NICKY SOH

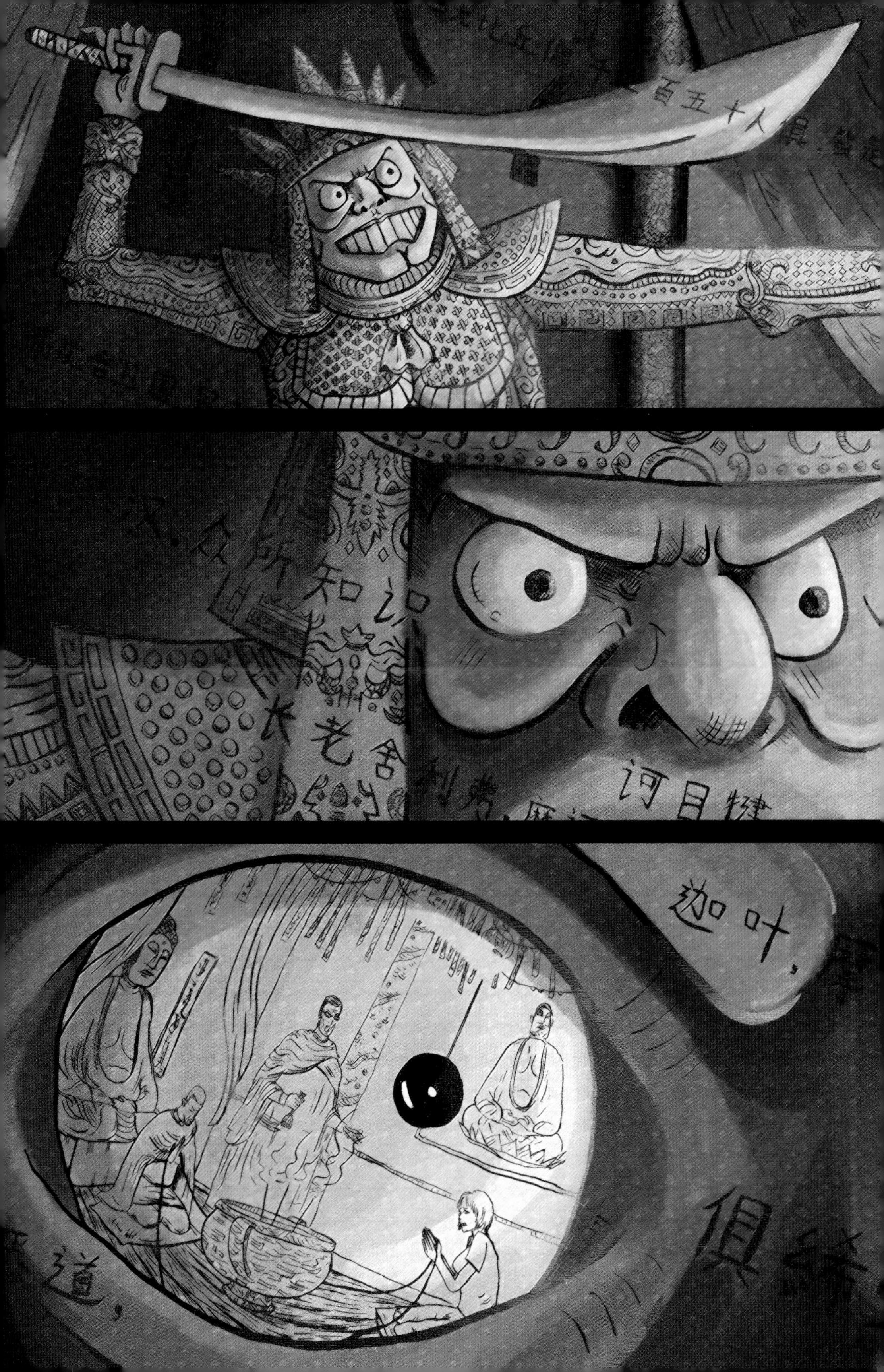
百五十人俱
知识
老舍
诃目犍
迦叶，
道，
俱

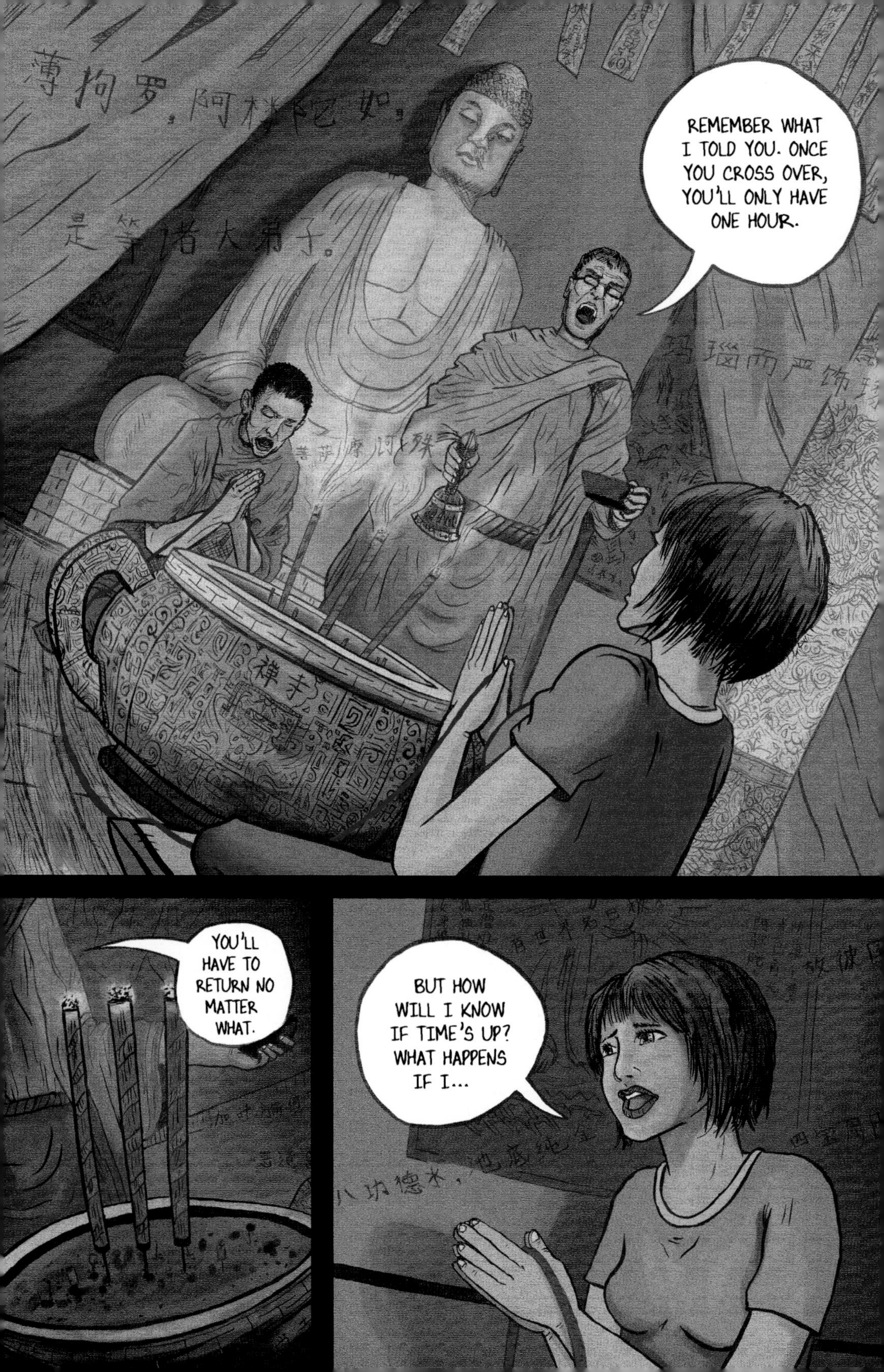
REMEMBER WHAT I TOLD YOU. ONCE YOU CROSS OVER, YOU'LL ONLY HAVE ONE HOUR.
YOU'LL HAVE TO RETURN NO MATTER WHAT.
BUT HOW WILL I KNOW IF TIME'S UP? WHAT HAPPENS IF I...

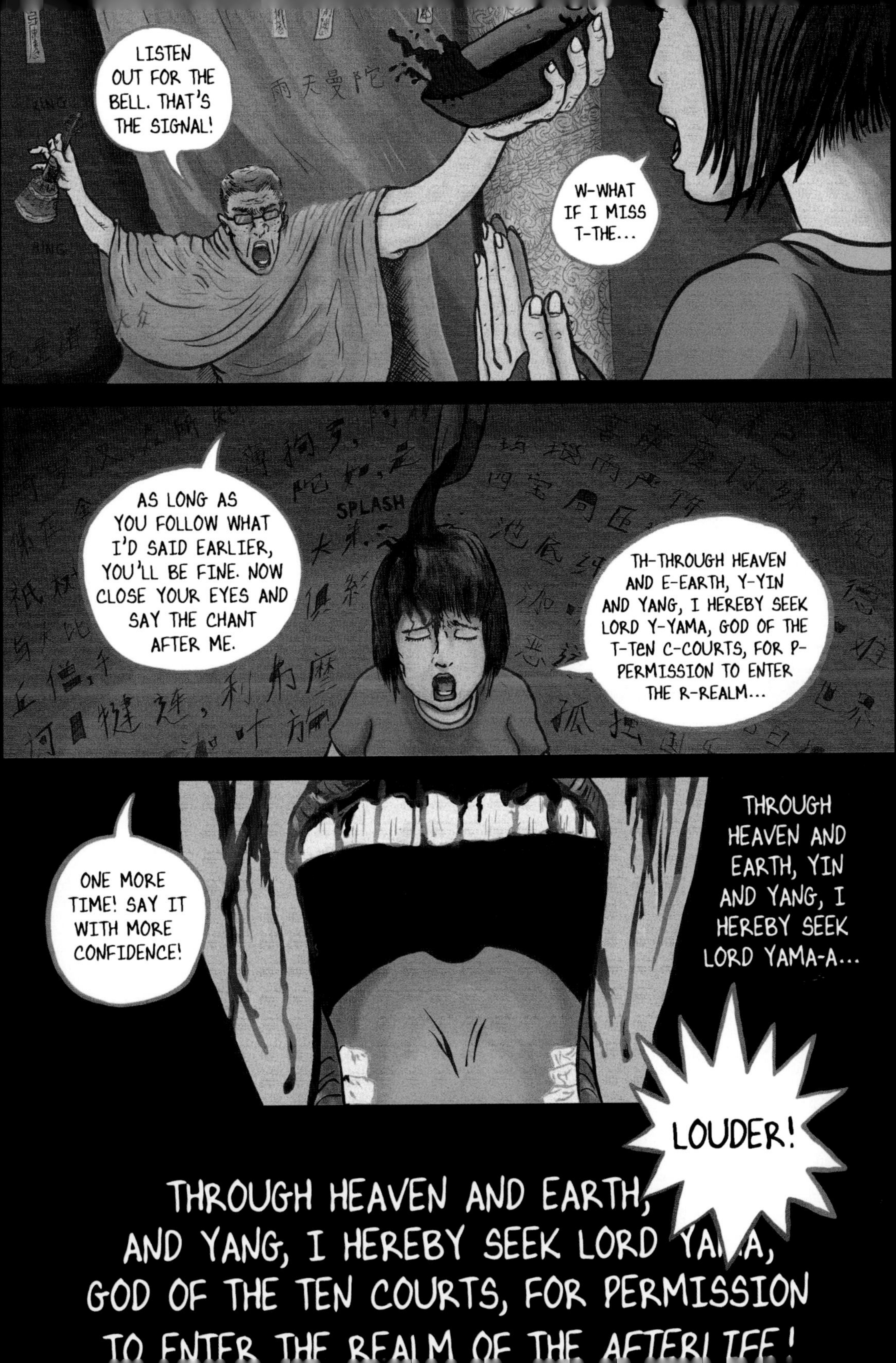

RING
LISTEN OUT FOR THE BELL. THAT'S THE SIGNAL!
RING
W-WHAT IF I MISS T-THE...
SPLASH
AS LONG AS YOU FOLLOW WHAT I'D SAID EARLIER, YOU'LL BE FINE. NOW CLOSE YOUR EYES AND SAY THE CHANT AFTER ME.
TH-THROUGH HEAVEN AND E-EARTH, Y-YIN AND YANG, I HEREBY SEEK LORD Y-YAMA, GOD OF THE T-TEN C-COURTS, FOR P-PERMISSION TO ENTER THE R-REALM...
ONE MORE TIME! SAY IT WITH MORE CONFIDENCE!
THROUGH HEAVEN AND EARTH, YIN AND YANG, I HEREBY SEEK LORD YAMA-A...
LOUDER!
THROUGH HEAVEN AND EARTH,
AND YANG, I HEREBY SEEK LORD YA A,
GOD OF THE TEN COURTS, FOR PERMISSION
TO ENTER THE REALM OF THE AFTERLIFE!

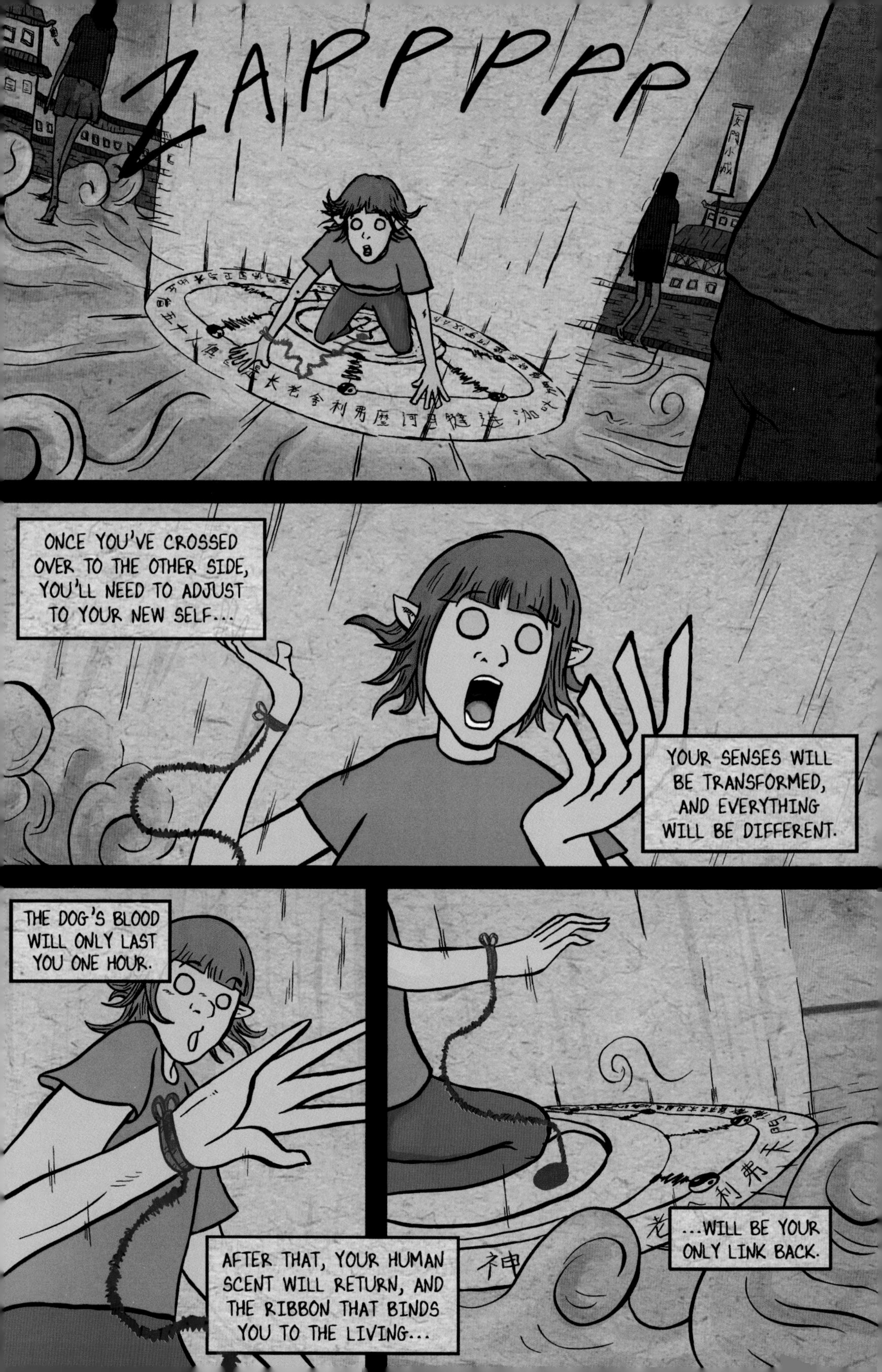
ZAPPPPPP
ONCE YOU'VE CROSSED OVER TO THE OTHER SIDE, YOU'LL NEED TO ADJUST TO YOUR NEW SELF...
YOUR SENSES WILL BE TRANSFORMED, AND EVERYTHING WILL BE DIFFERENT.
THE DOG'S BLOOD WILL ONLY LAST YOU ONE HOUR.
AFTER THAT, YOUR HUMAN SCENT WILL RETURN, AND THE RIBBON THAT BINDS YOU TO THE LIVING...
...WILL BE YOUR ONLY LINK BACK.

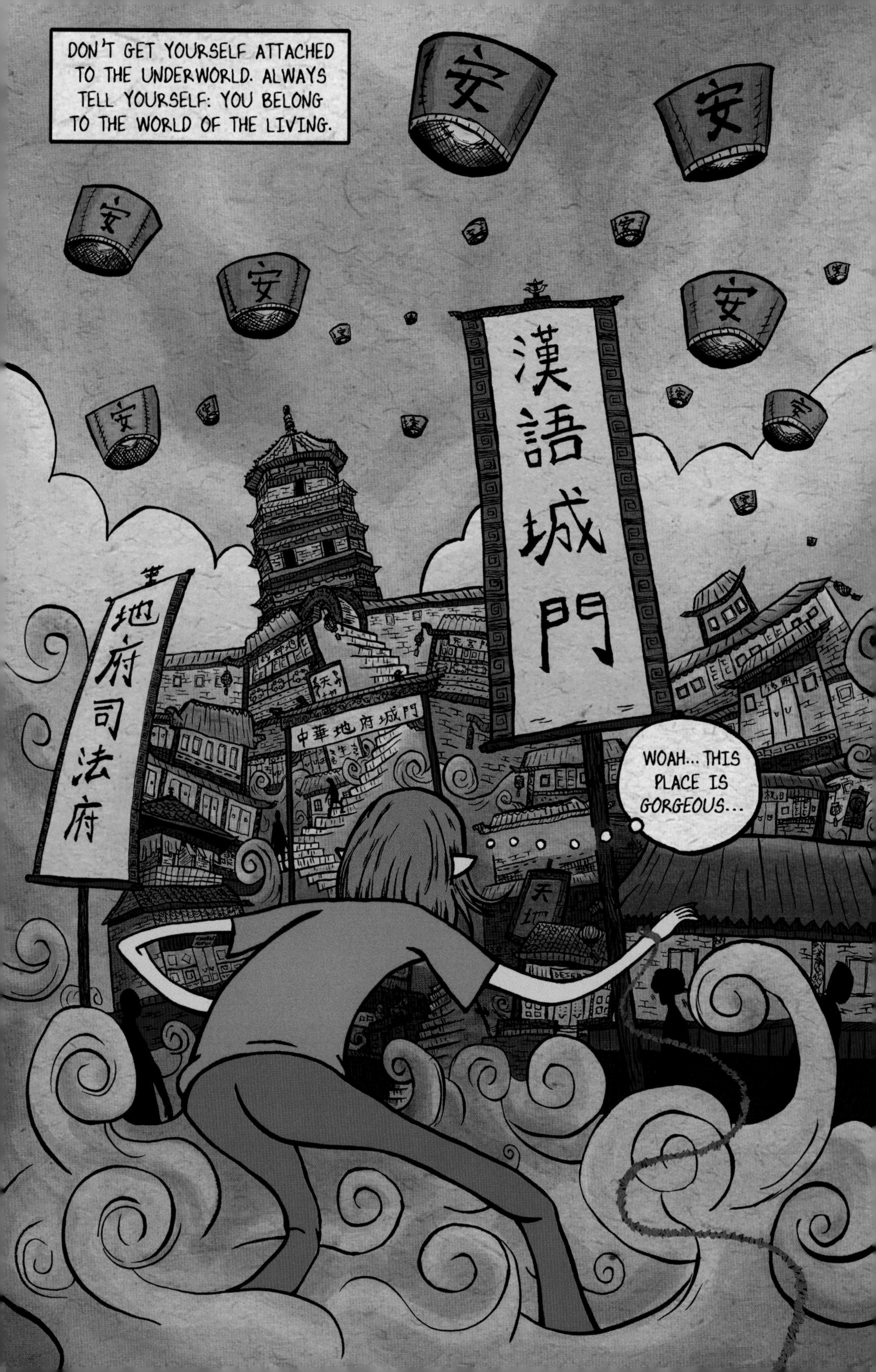
DON'T GET YOURSELF ATTACHED TO THE UNDERWORLD. ALWAYS TELL YOURSELF: YOU BELONG TO THE WORLD OF THE LIVING.
安
漢語城門
地府司法府
中華地府城門
WOAH... THIS PLACE IS GORGEOUS...

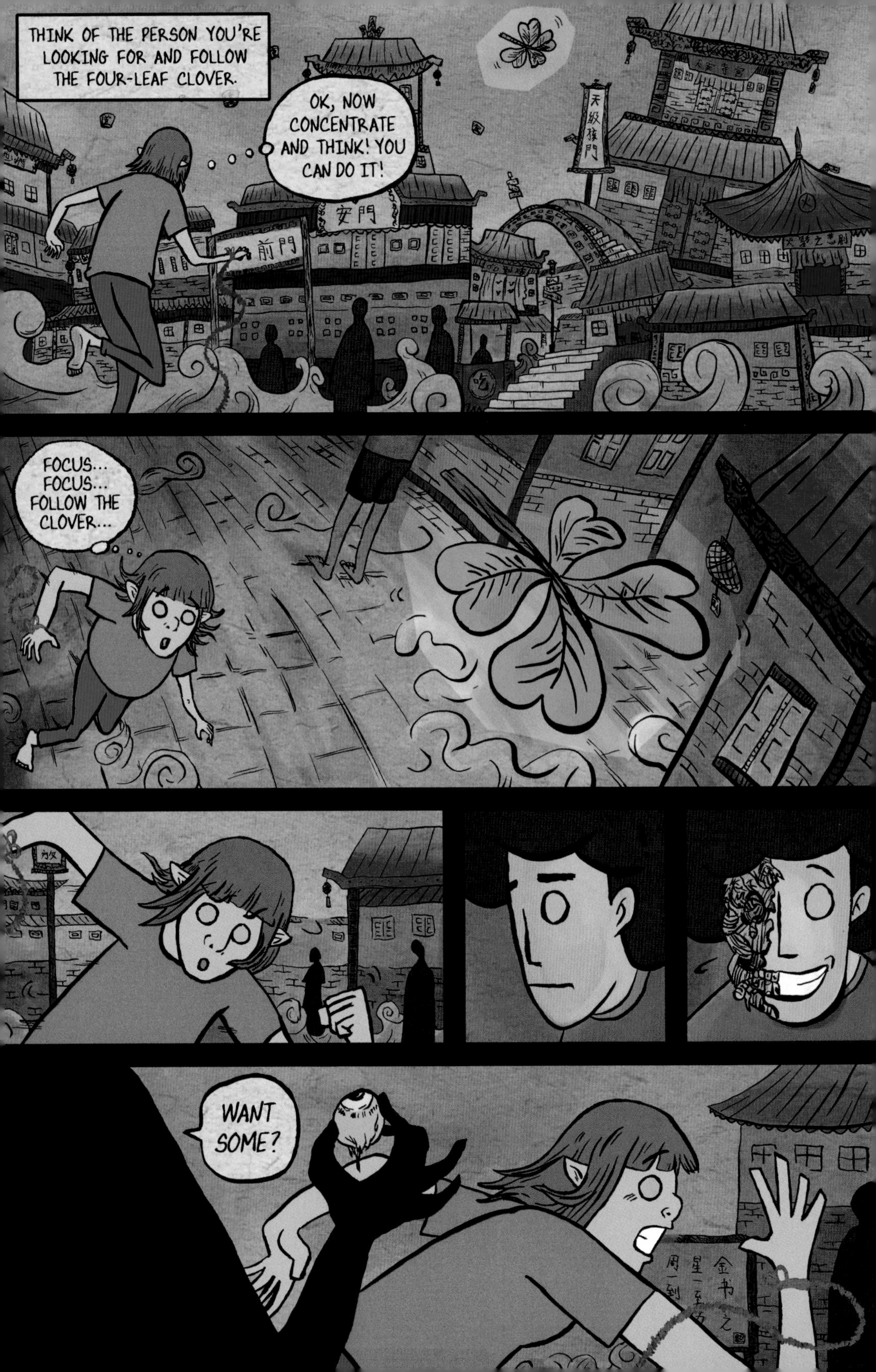
THINK OF THE PERSON YOU'RE LOOKING FOR AND FOLLOW THE FOUR-LEAF CLOVER.
OK, NOW CONCENTRATE AND THINK! YOU CAN DO IT!
安門
前門
天級猿門
FOCUS... FOCUS... FOLLOW THE CLOVER...
WANT SOME?

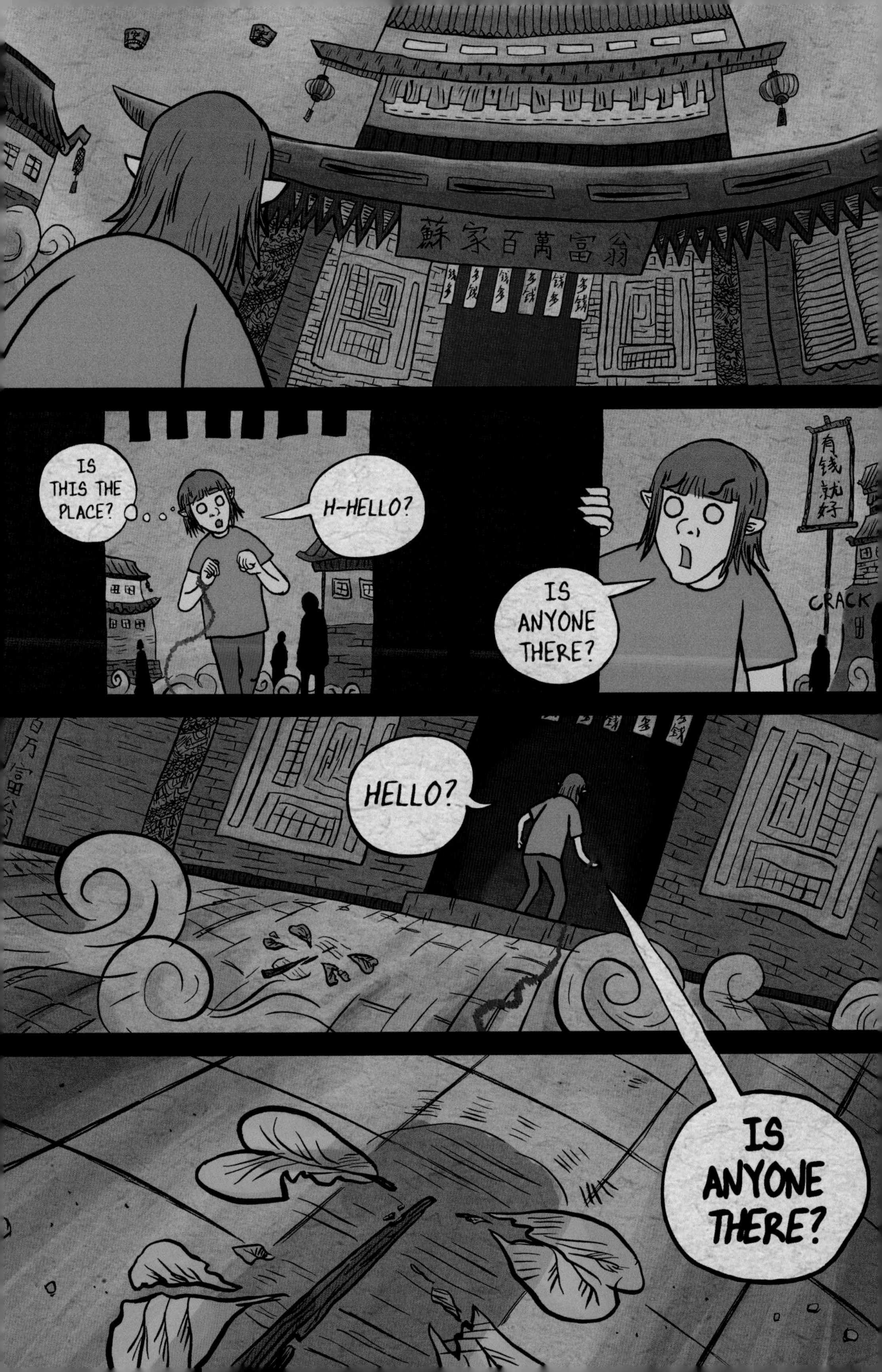

蘇家百萬富翁
IS THIS THE PLACE?
H-HELLO?
有钱就好
IS ANYONE THERE?
CRACK
HELLO?
IS ANYONE THERE?

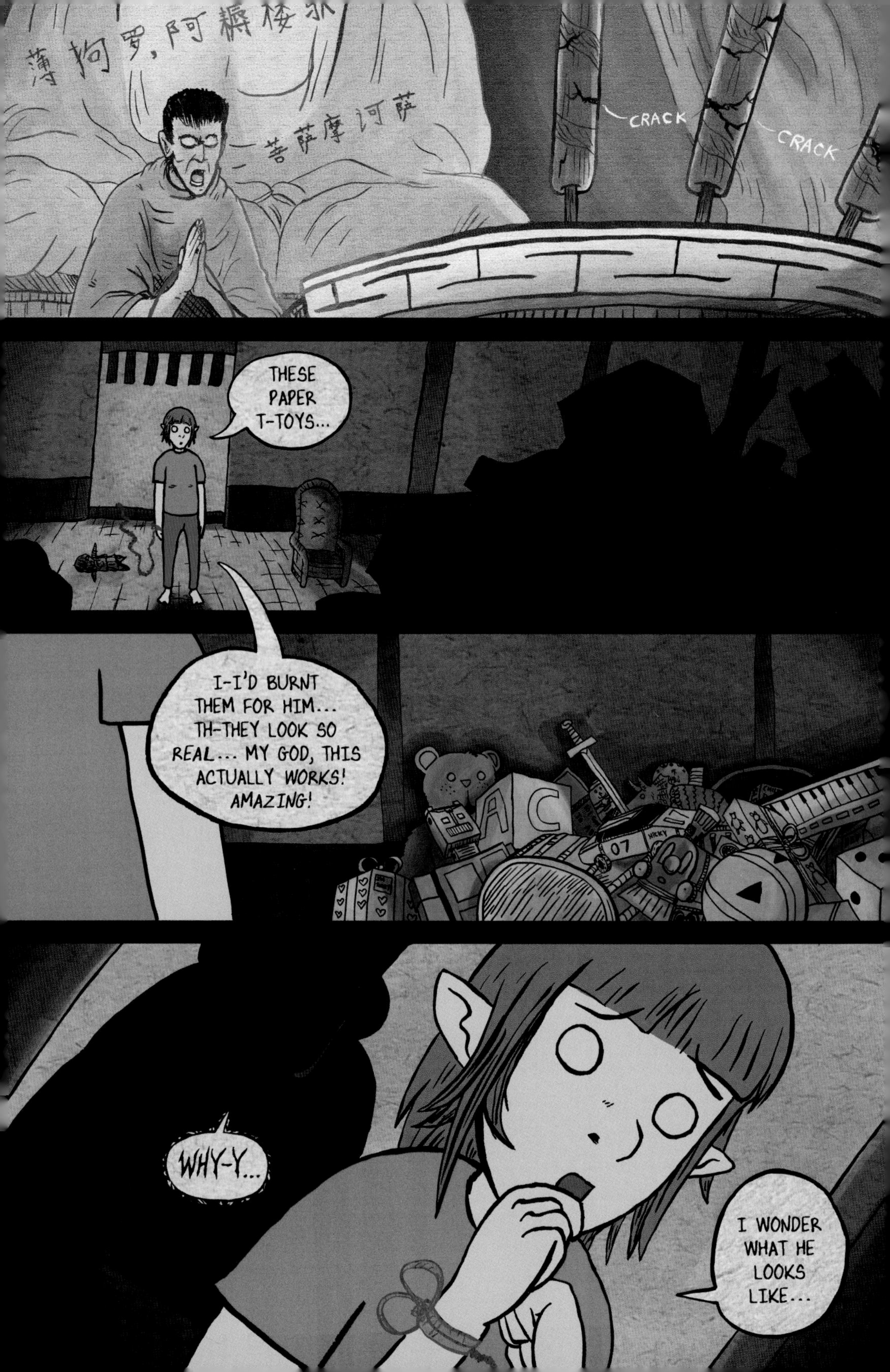

薄拘罗,阿耨楼驮
菩萨摩诃萨
CRACK
CRACK
THESE PAPER T-TOYS...
I-I'D BURNT THEM FOR HIM... TH-THEY LOOK SO REAL... MY GOD, THIS ACTUALLY WORKS! AMAZING!
WHY-Y...
I WONDER WHAT HE LOOKS LIKE...

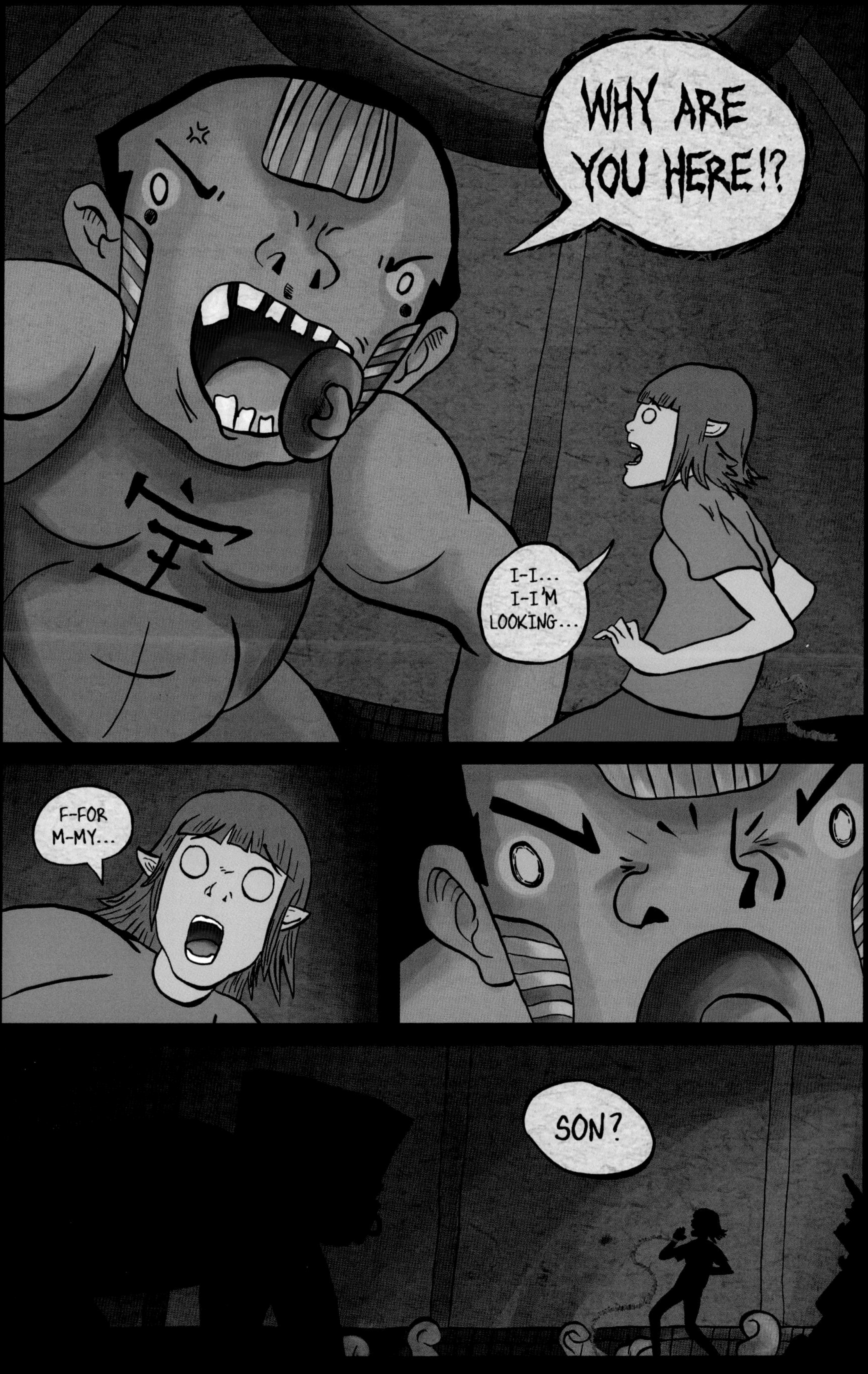
WHY ARE YOU HERE!?
I-I... I-I'M LOOKING...
F-FOR M-MY...
SON?

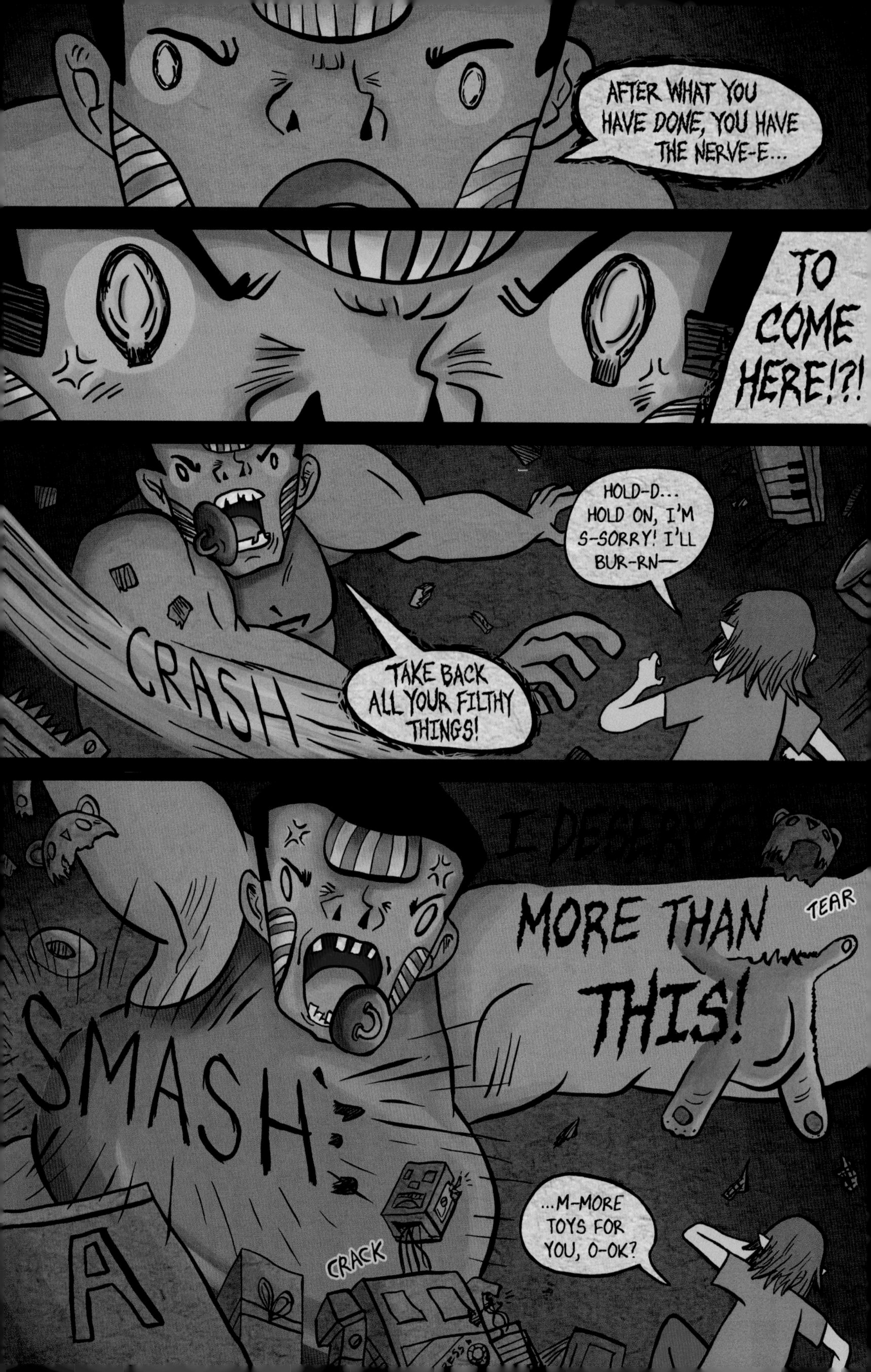
AFTER WHAT YOU HAVE DONE, YOU HAVE THE NERVE-E...
TO COME HERE!?!
HOLD-D... HOLD ON, I'M S-SORRY! I'LL BUR-RN—
CRASH
TAKE BACK ALL YOUR FILTHY THINGS!
MORE THAN
TEAR
THIS!
SMASH
CRACK
...M-MORE TOYS FOR YOU, O-OK?

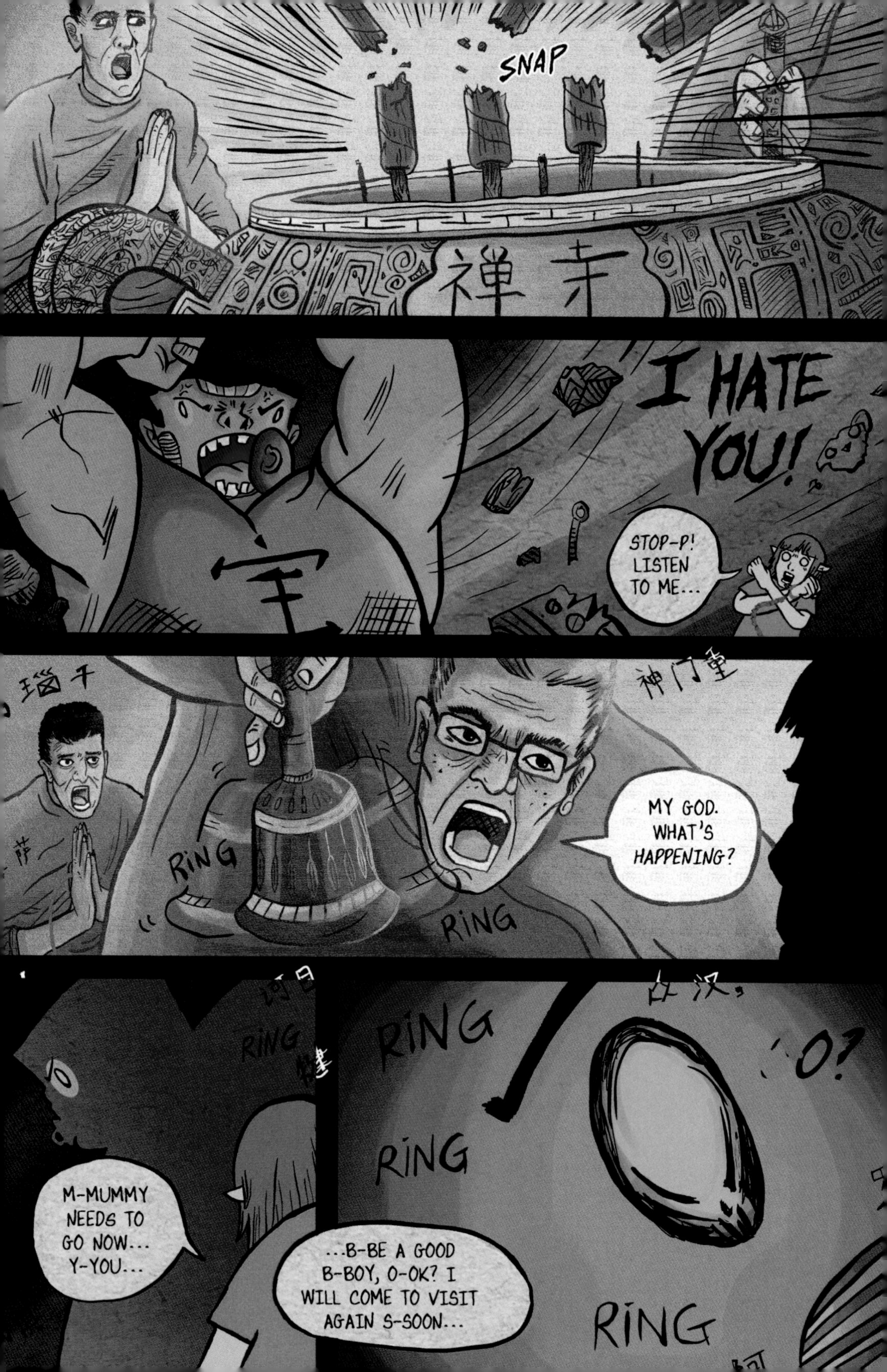
SNAP
禅寺
I HATE YOU!
STOP-P! LISTEN TO ME...
RING
RING
MY GOD. WHAT'S HAPPENING?
RING
M-MUMMY NEEDS TO GO NOW... Y-YOU...
RING
RING
...B-BE A GOOD B-BOY, O-OK? I WILL COME TO VISIT AGAIN S-SOON...
..O?
RING

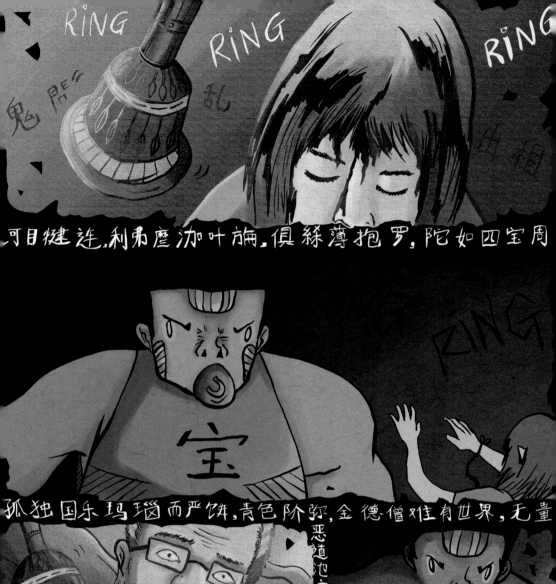

RING
RING
RING
鬼門
乱
可目犍连，利弗摩沏叶旃，俱絺薄抱罗，陀如四宝周
RING
宝
孤独国乐玛瑙而严饰，青色阶弥，金德僧难有世界，无量
恶道池广
佛
RING
长老舍利诃目犍连，阿罗汉天門之神，与大比丘僧，千二百皆是众

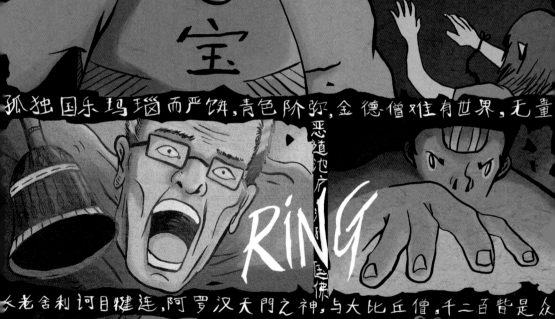

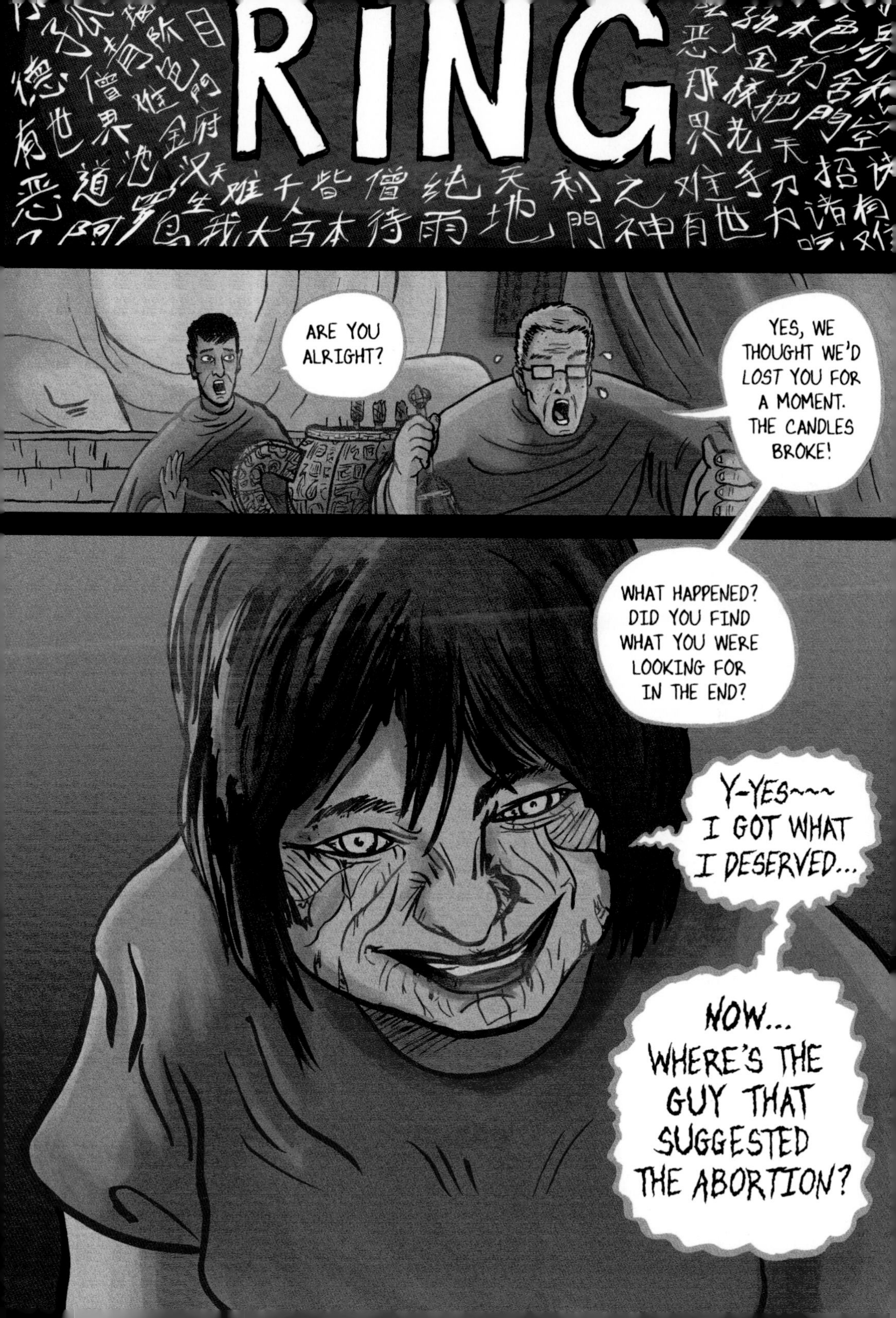
RING
ARE YOU ALRIGHT?
YES, WE THOUGHT WE'D LOST YOU FOR A MOMENT. THE CANDLES BROKE!
WHAT HAPPENED? DID YOU FIND WHAT YOU WERE LOOKING FOR IN THE END?
Y-YES~~~ I GOT WHAT I DESERVED...
NOW... WHERE'S THE GUY THAT SUGGESTED THE ABORTION?

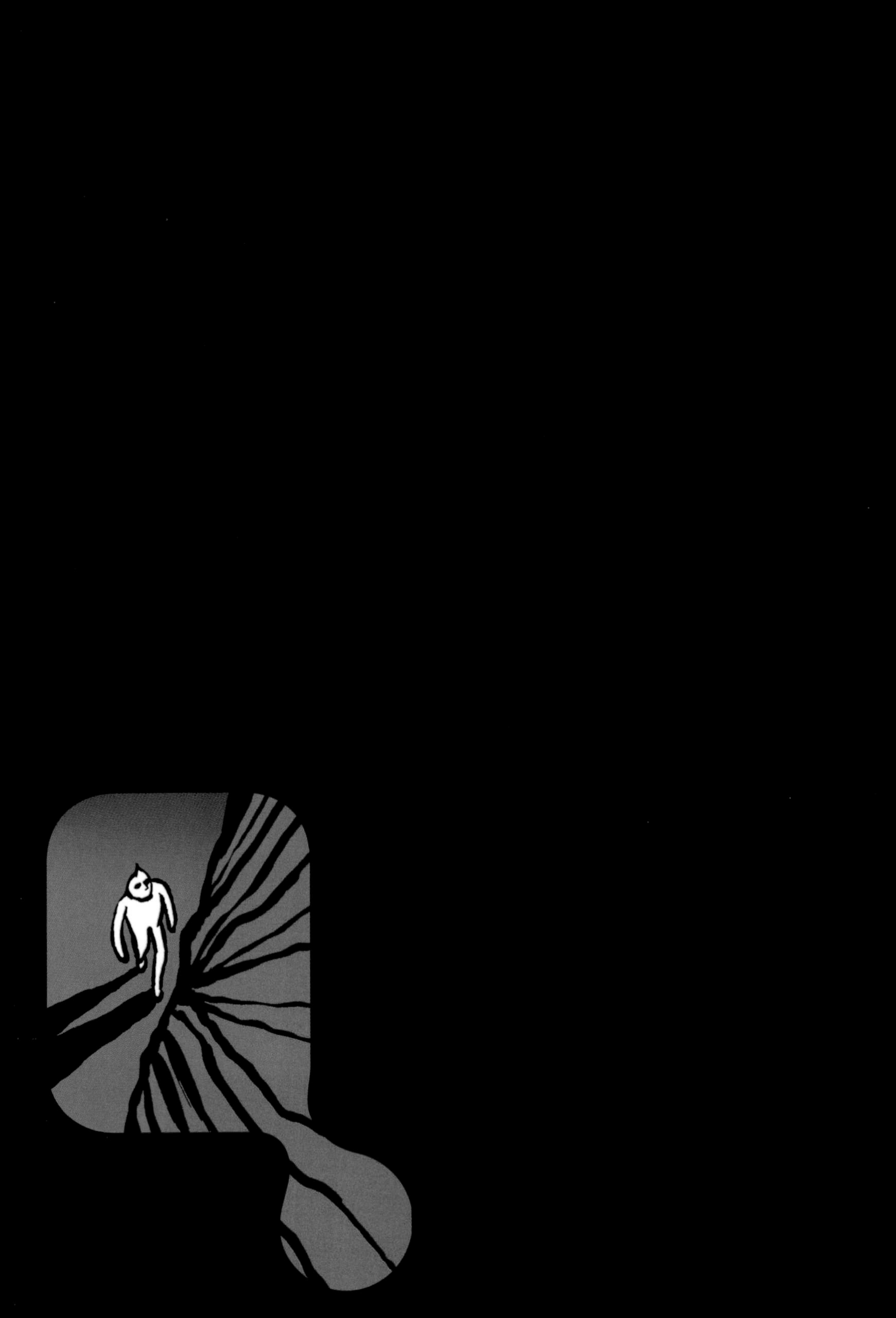

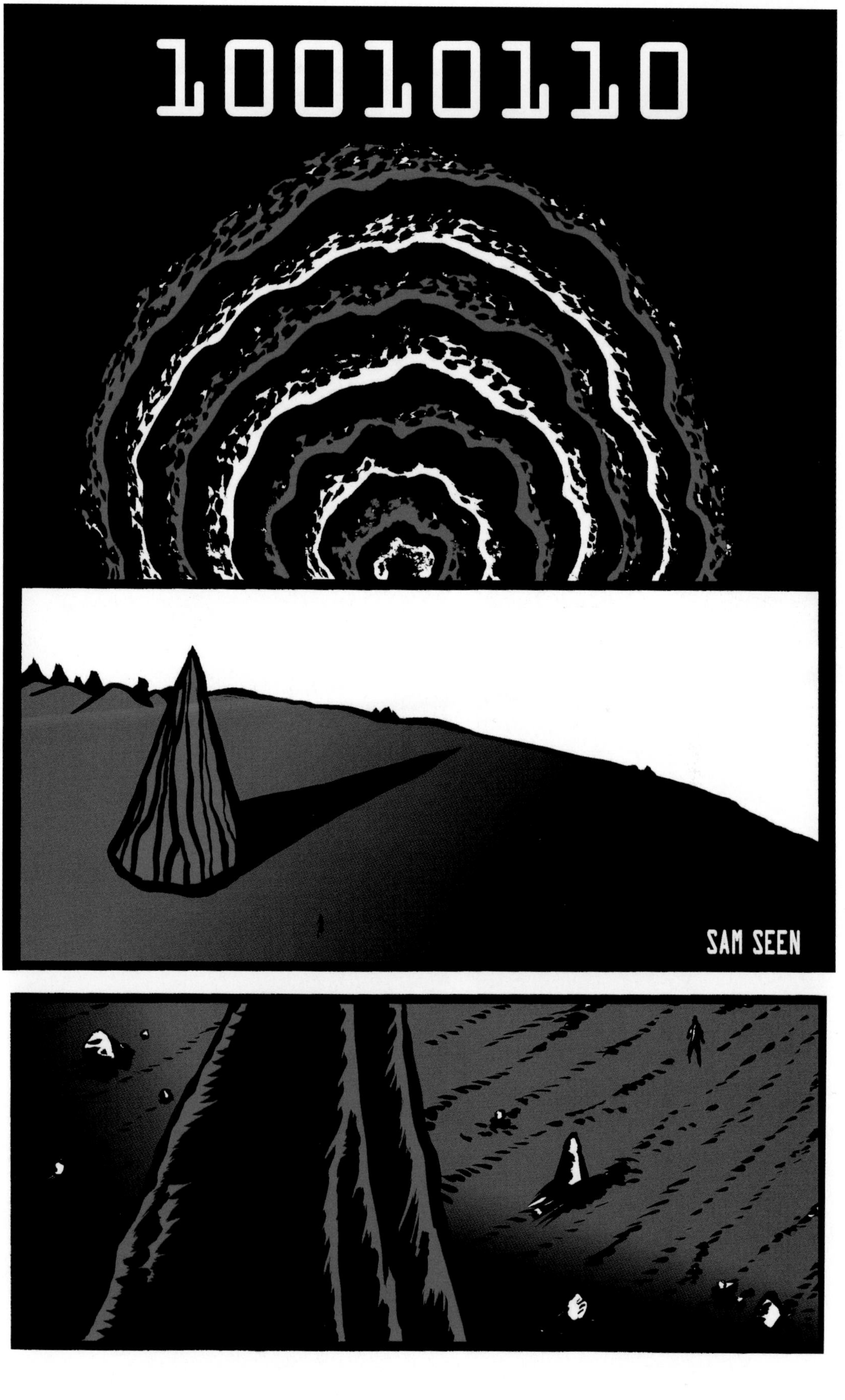
10010110
SAM SEEN

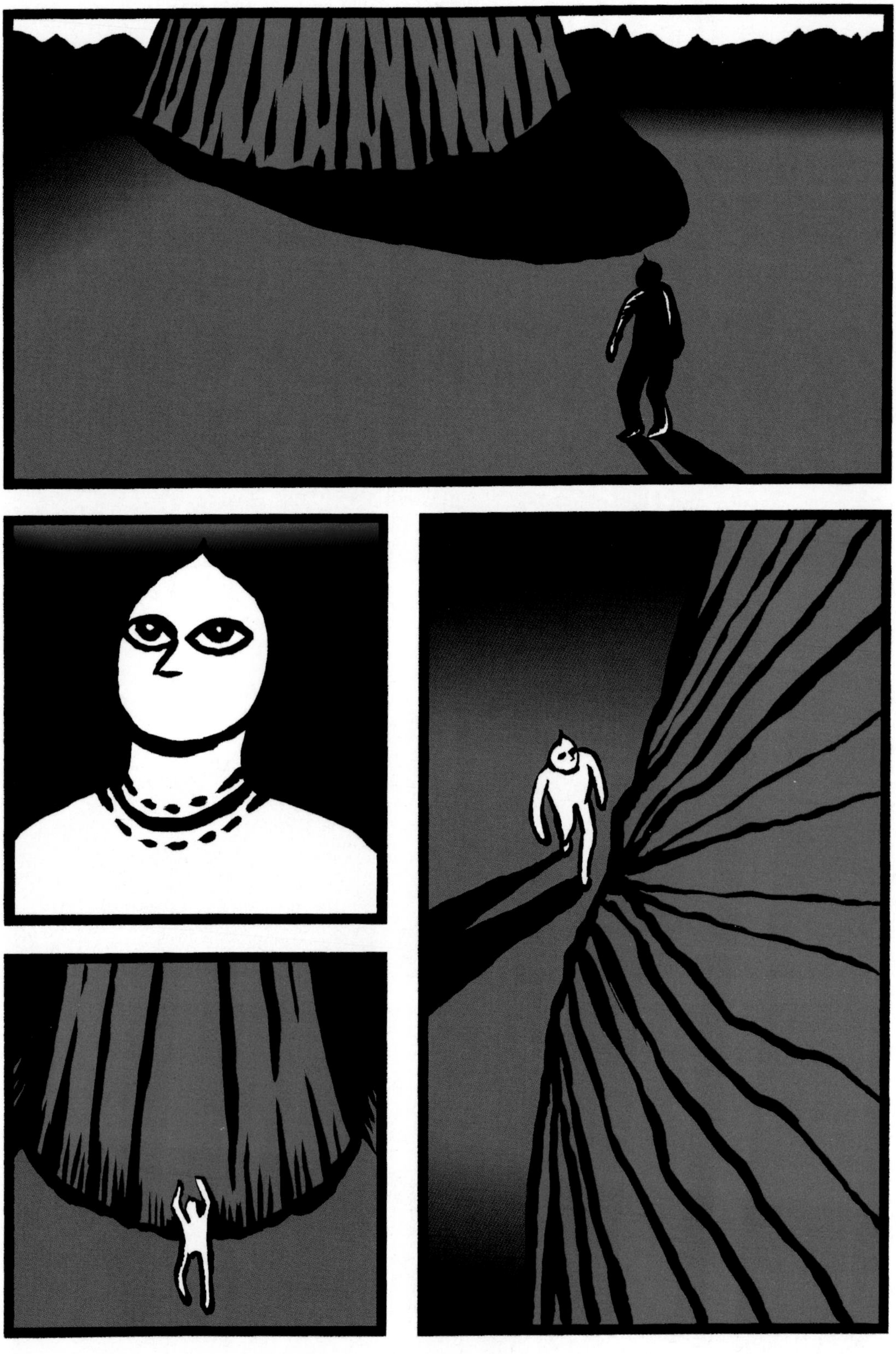

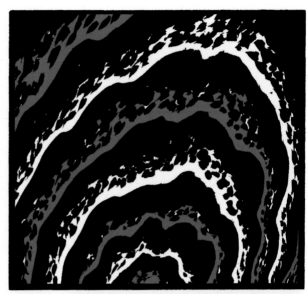

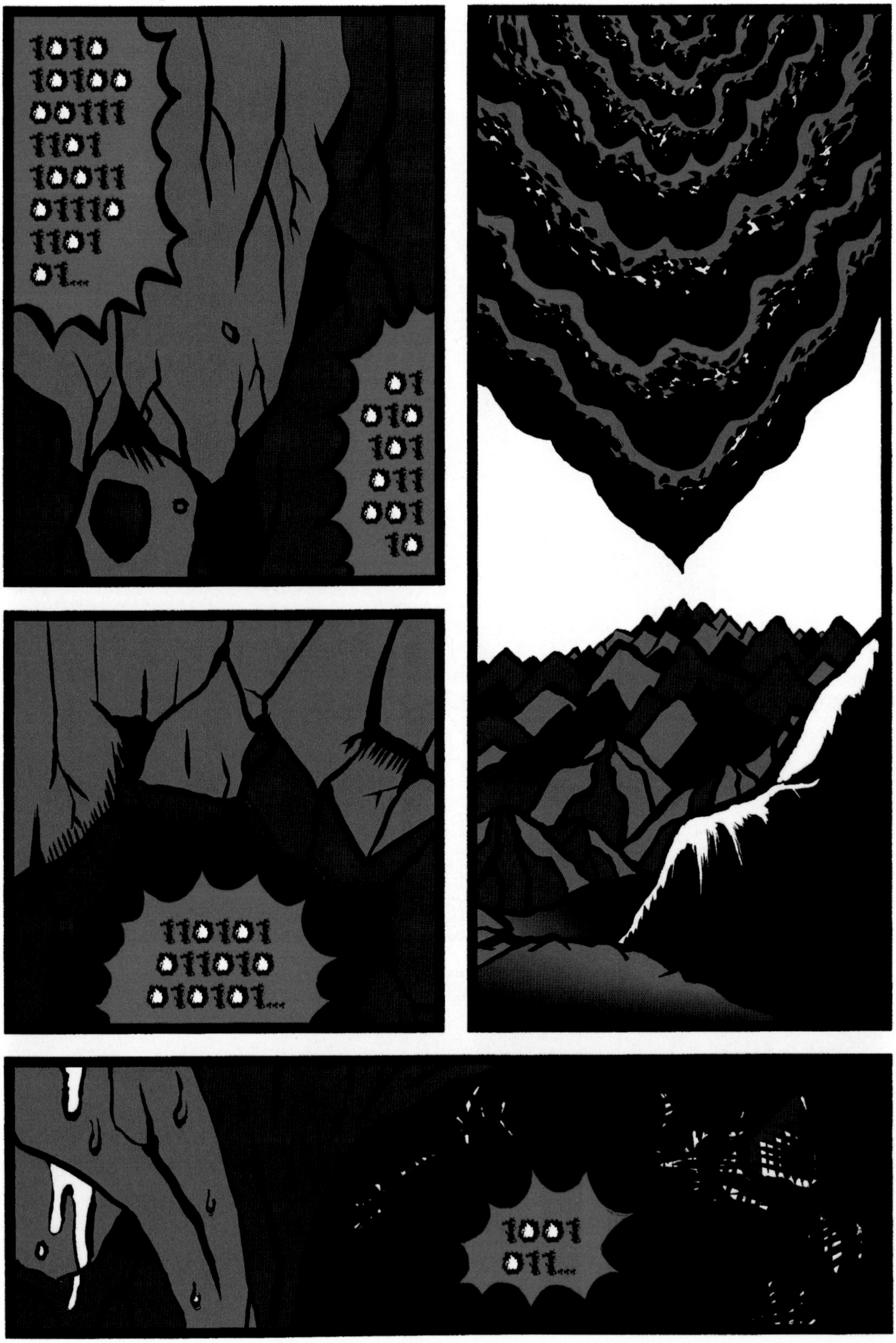
1010
10100
00111
1101
10011
01110
1101
01...
01
010
101
011
001
10
110101
011010
010101...
1001
011...

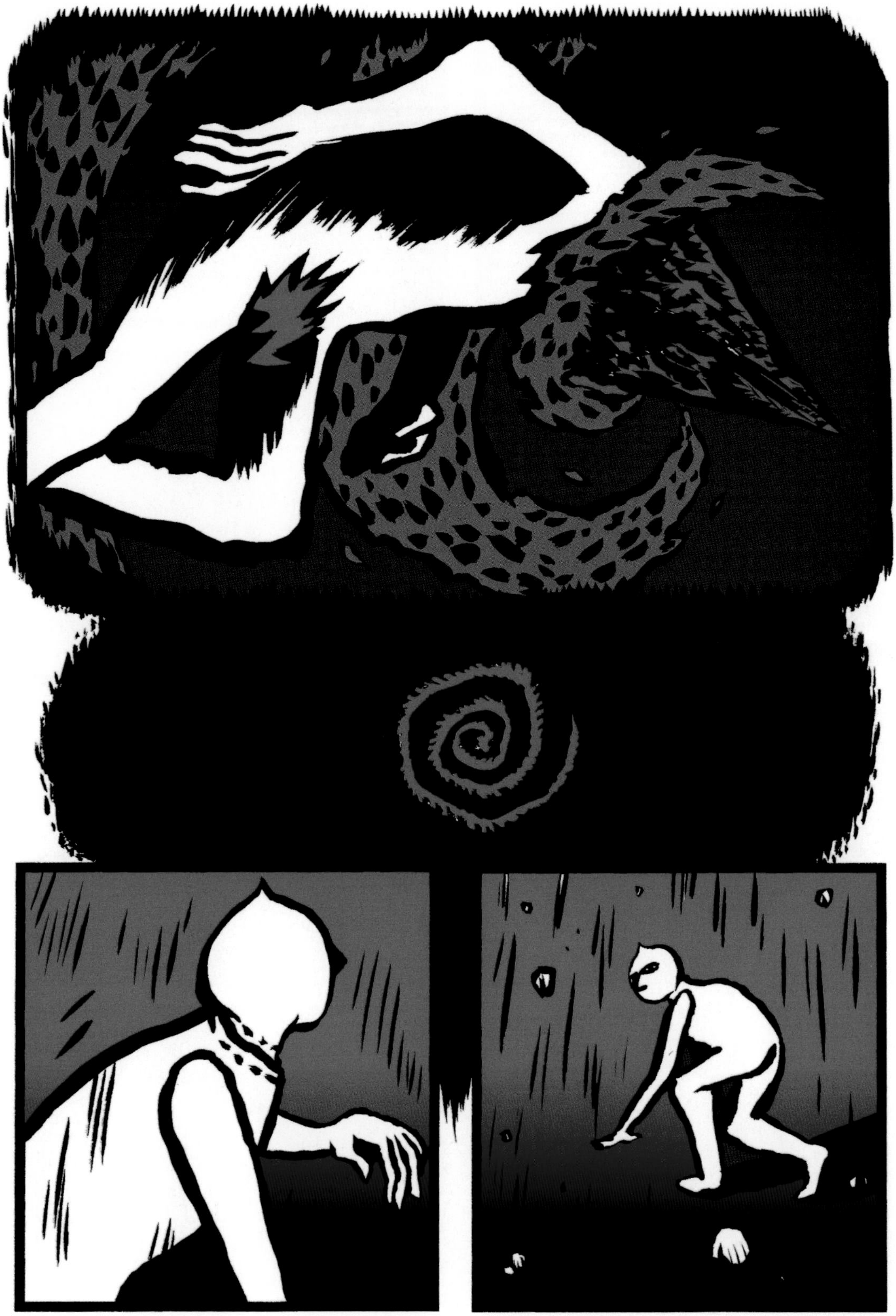

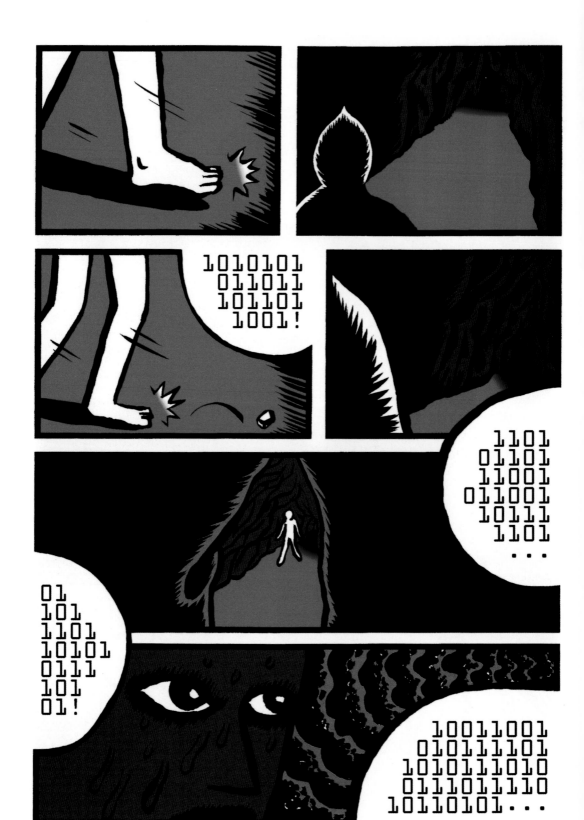

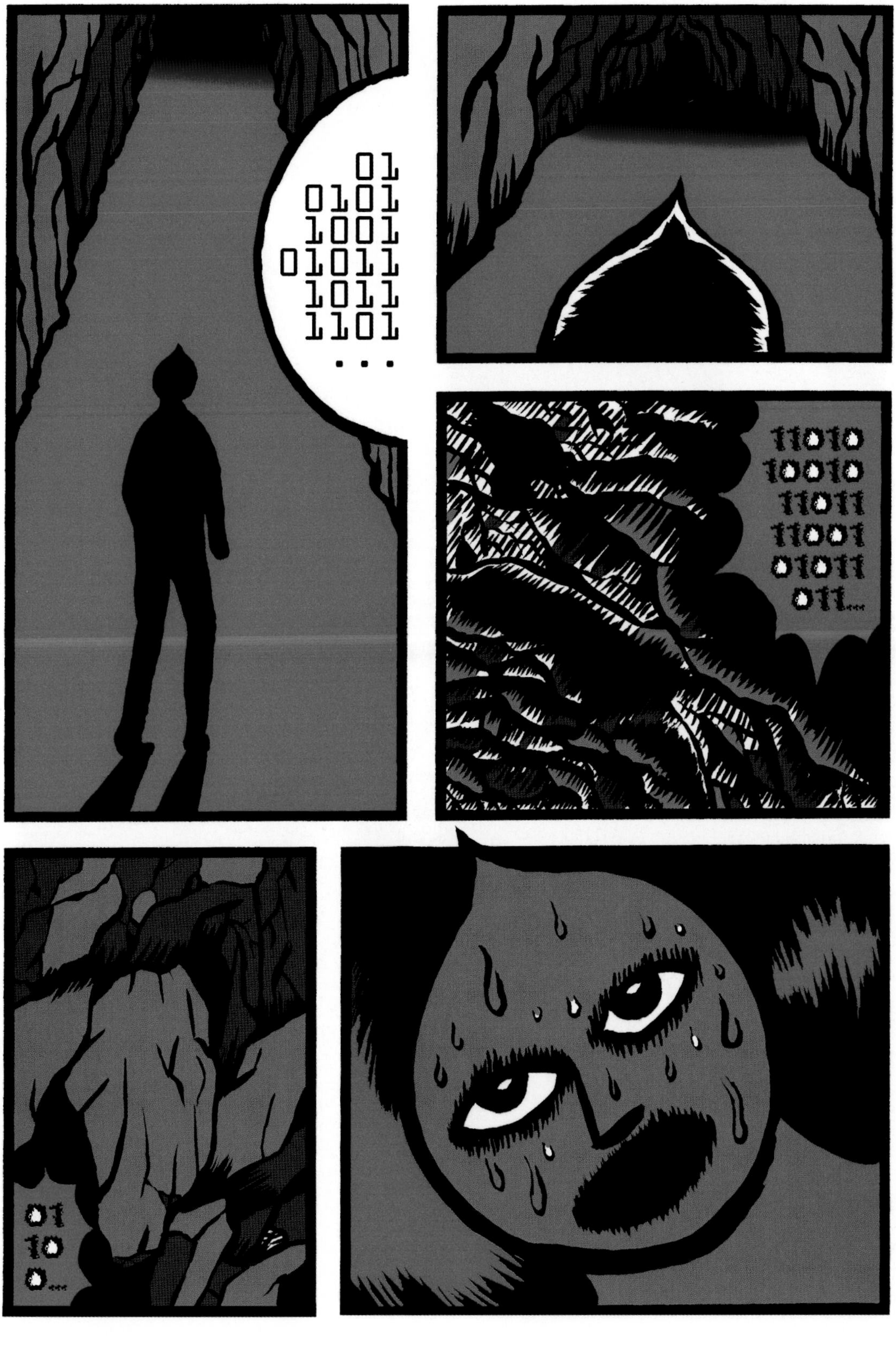
01
0101
1001
01011
1011
1101
...
11010
10010
11011
11001
01011
011...
01
10
0...

1011101 0
0101110
1011001
1101011
11010
0110
10...

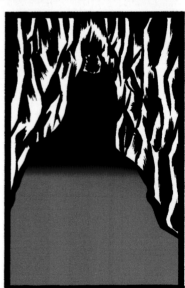

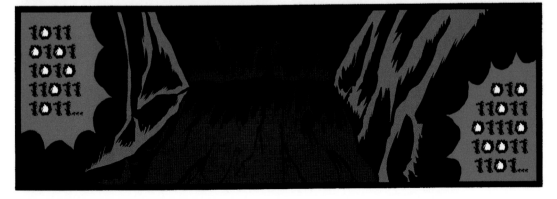

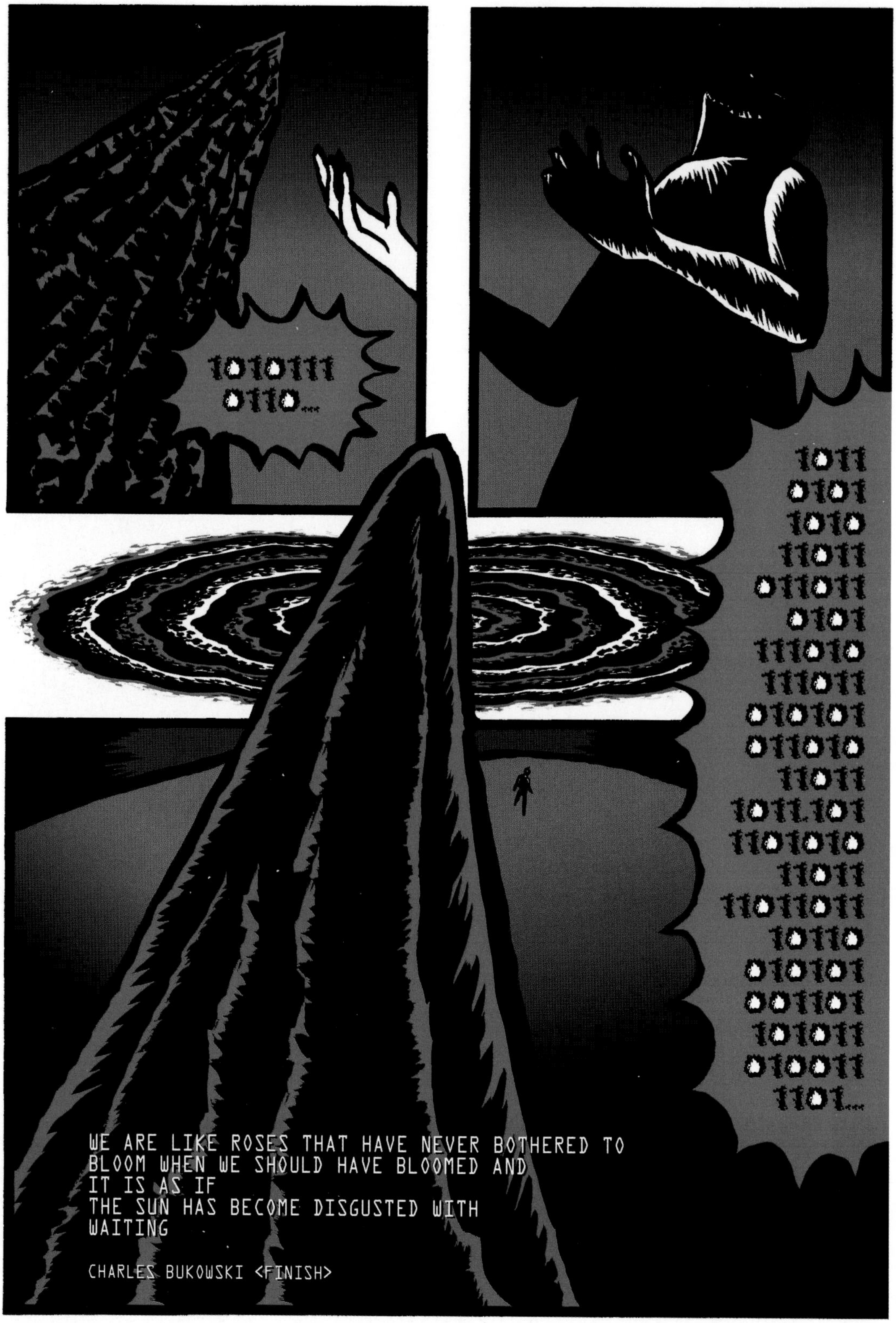

1010111
0110...
1011
0101
1010
11011
011011
0101
111010
111011
010101
011010
11011
1011.101
1101010
11011
11011011
10110
010101
001101
101011
010011
1101...
WE ARE LIKE ROSES THAT HAVE NEVER BOTHERED TO
BLOOM WHEN WE SHOULD HAVE BLOOMED AND
IT IS AS IF
THE SUN HAS BECOME DISGUSTED WITH
WAITING
CHARLES BUKOWSKI <FINISH>

Ghost Kid

BILLY TAN & THE ONE ACADEMY PENANG

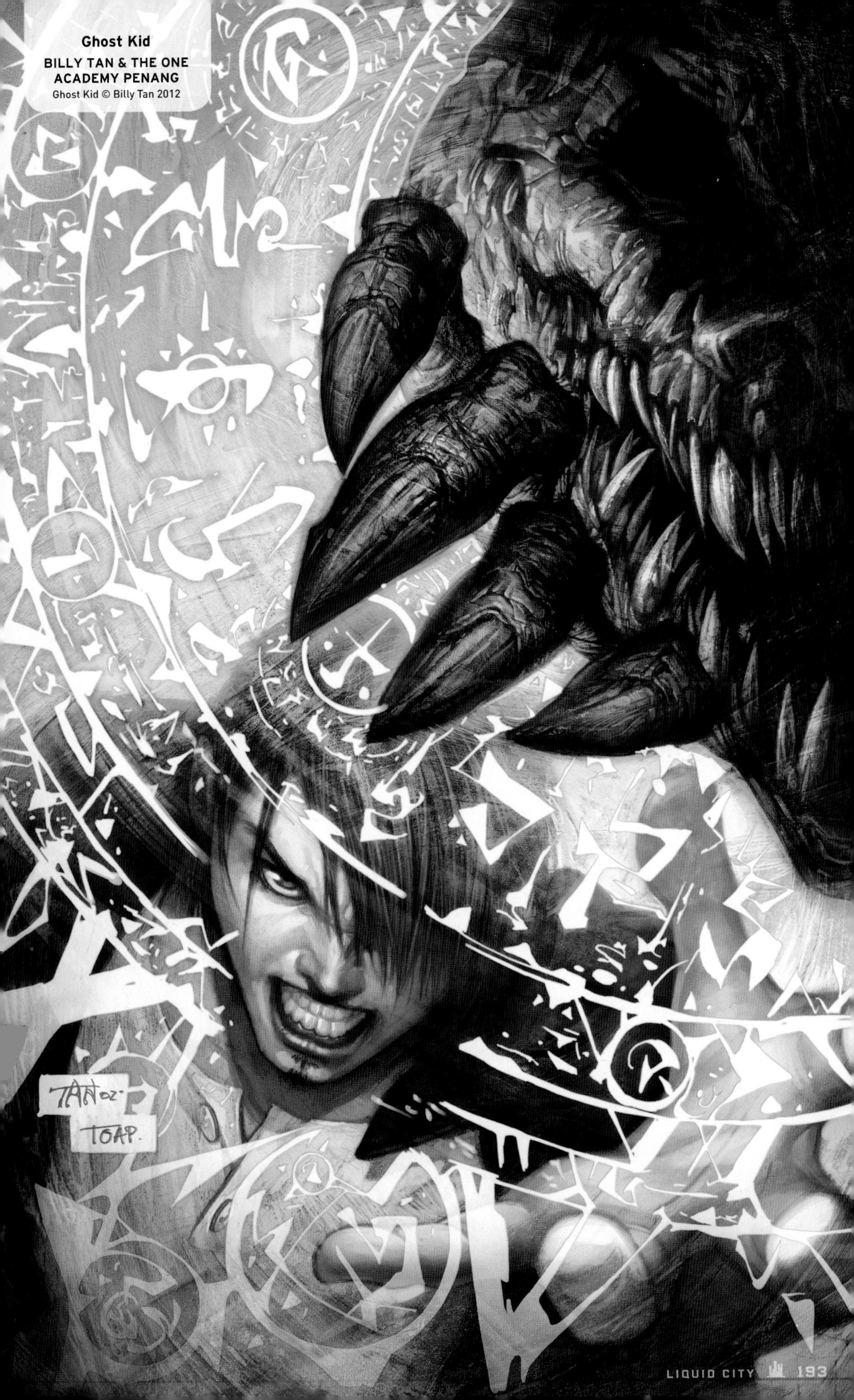
TAN 02
TOAP.

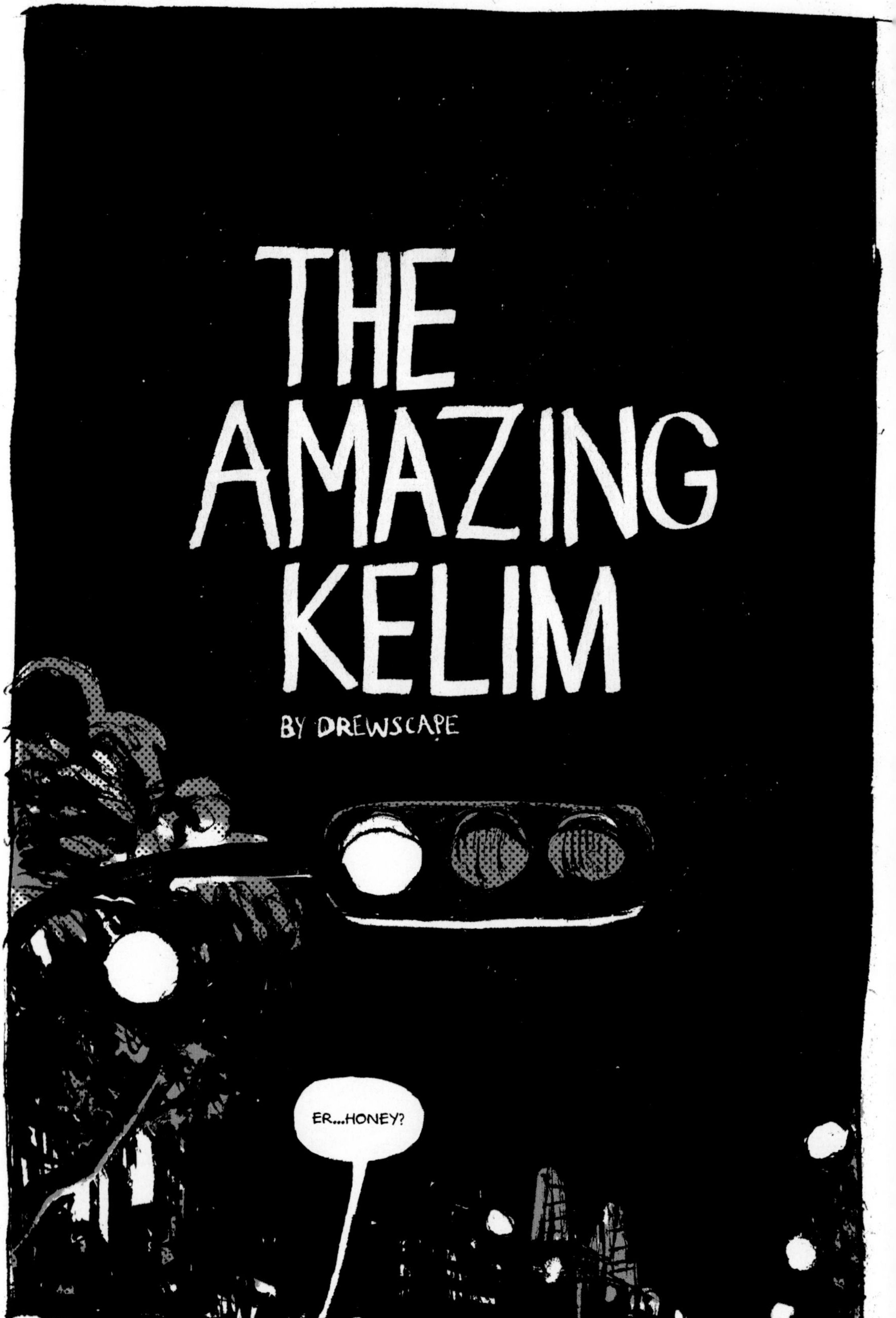
THE AMAZING KELIM
BY DREWSCAPE
ER...HONEY?

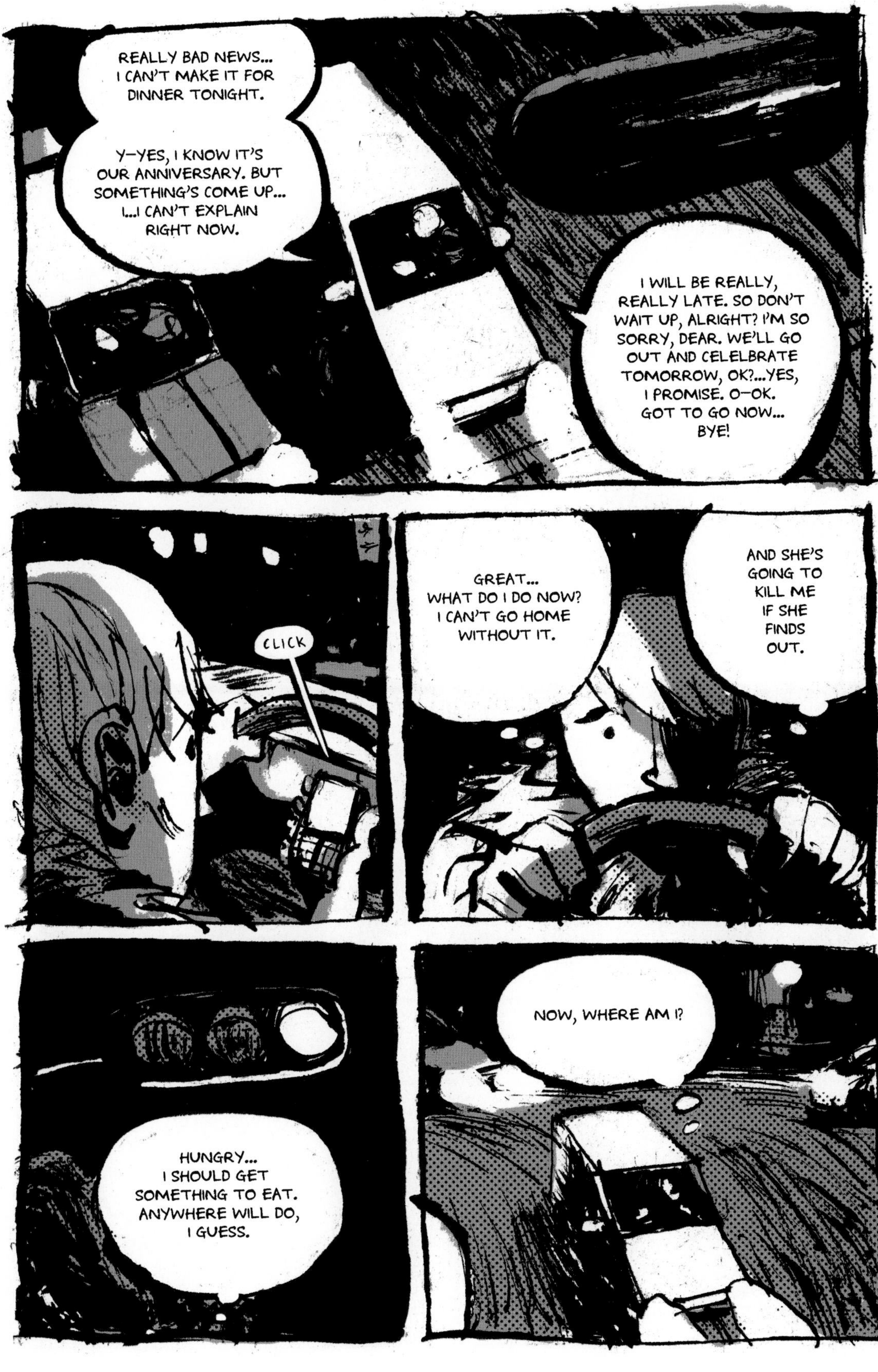
REALLY BAD NEWS... I CAN'T MAKE IT FOR DINNER TONIGHT.
Y-YES, I KNOW IT'S OUR ANNIVERSARY. BUT SOMETHING'S COME UP... I...I CAN'T EXPLAIN RIGHT NOW.
I WILL BE REALLY, REALLY LATE. SO DON'T WAIT UP, ALRIGHT? I'M SO SORRY, DEAR. WE'LL GO OUT AND CELELBRATE TOMORROW, OK?...YES, I PROMISE. O-OK. GOT TO GO NOW... BYE!
CLICK
GREAT... WHAT DO I DO NOW? I CAN'T GO HOME WITHOUT IT.
AND SHE'S GOING TO KILL ME IF SHE FINDS OUT.
HUNGRY... I SHOULD GET SOMETHING TO EAT. ANYWHERE WILL DO, I GUESS.
NOW, WHERE AM I?

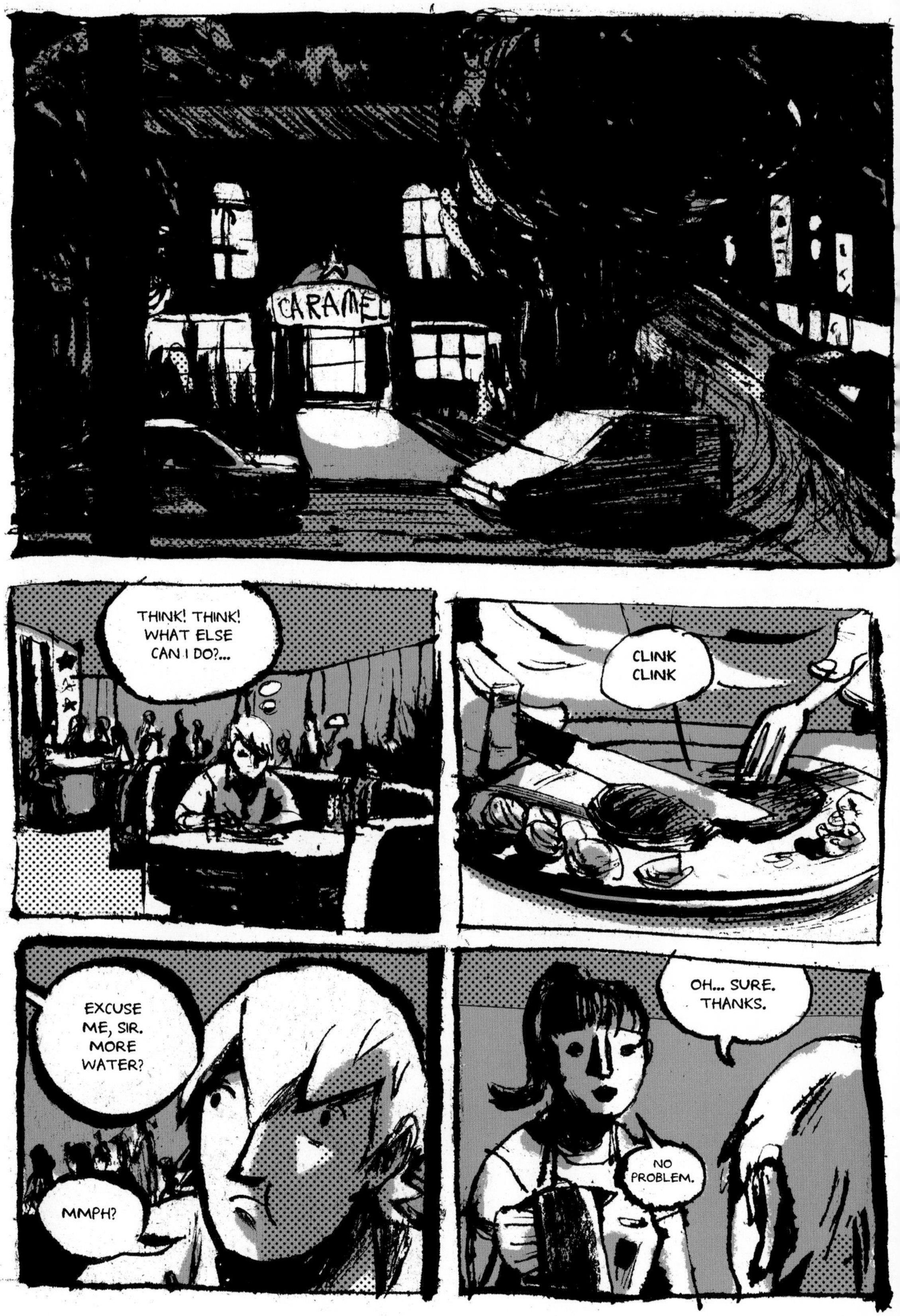
CARAMEL
THINK! THINK! WHAT ELSE CAN I DO?...
CLINK CLINK
EXCUSE ME, SIR. MORE WATER?
MMPH?
OH... SURE. THANKS.
NO PROBLEM.

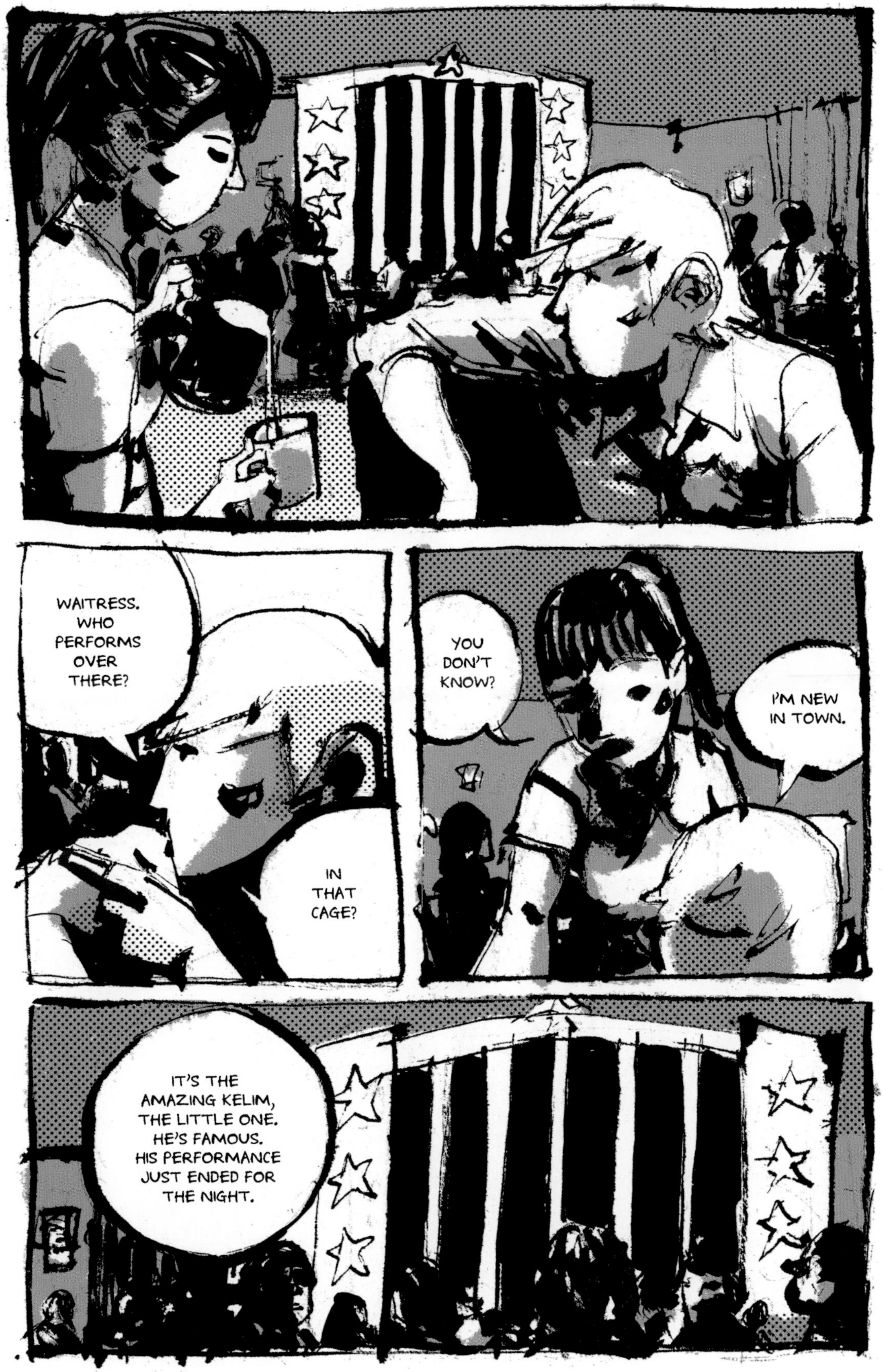
WAITRESS. WHO PERFORMS OVER THERE?
IN THAT CAGE?
YOU DON'T KNOW?
I'M NEW IN TOWN.
IT'S THE AMAZING KELIM, THE LITTLE ONE. HE'S FAMOUS. HIS PERFORMANCE JUST ENDED FOR THE NIGHT.

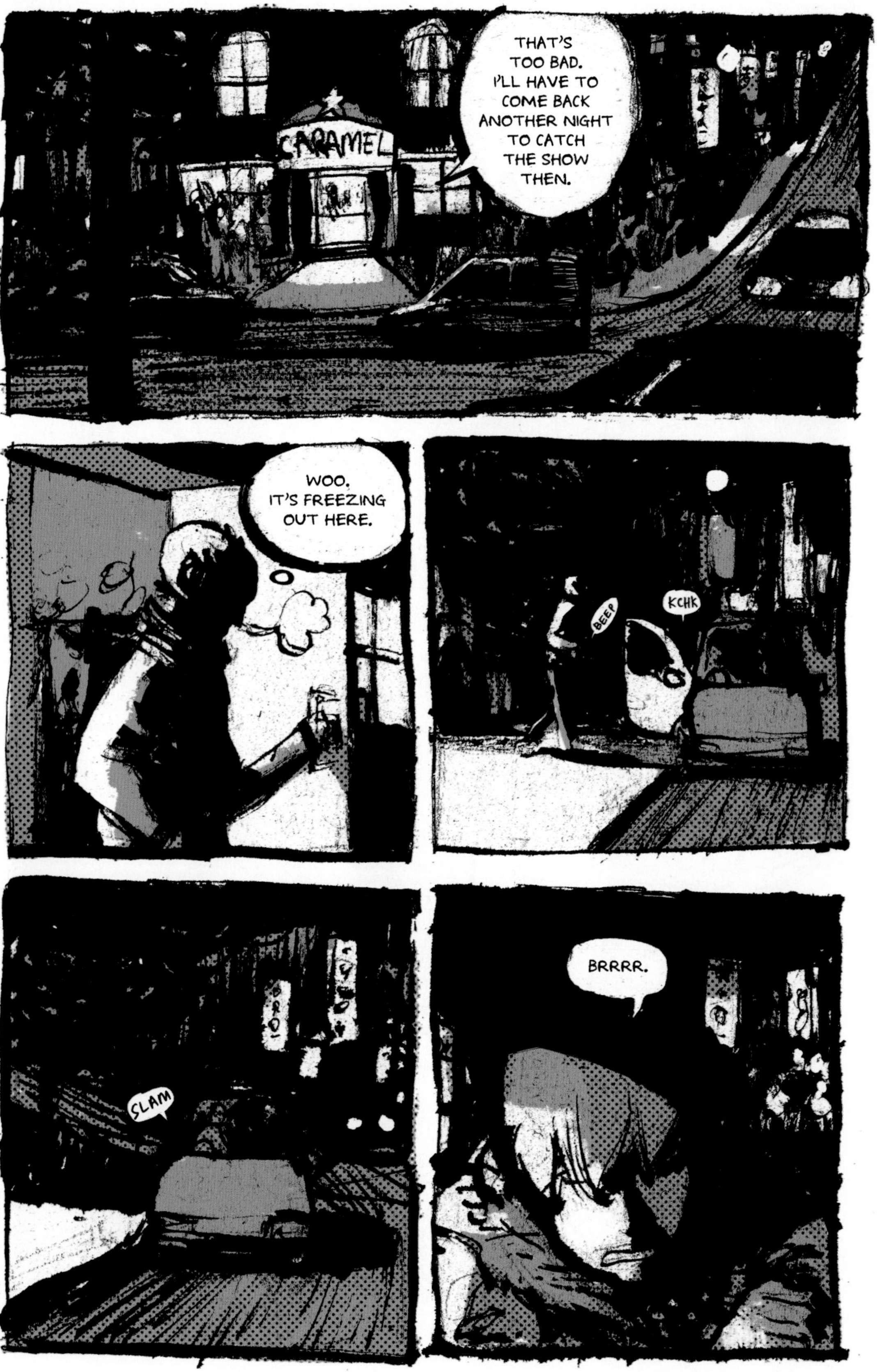

CARAMEL
THAT'S TOO BAD. I'LL HAVE TO COME BACK ANOTHER NIGHT TO CATCH THE SHOW THEN.
WOO. IT'S FREEZING OUT HERE.
BEEP
KCHK
SLAM
BRRRR.

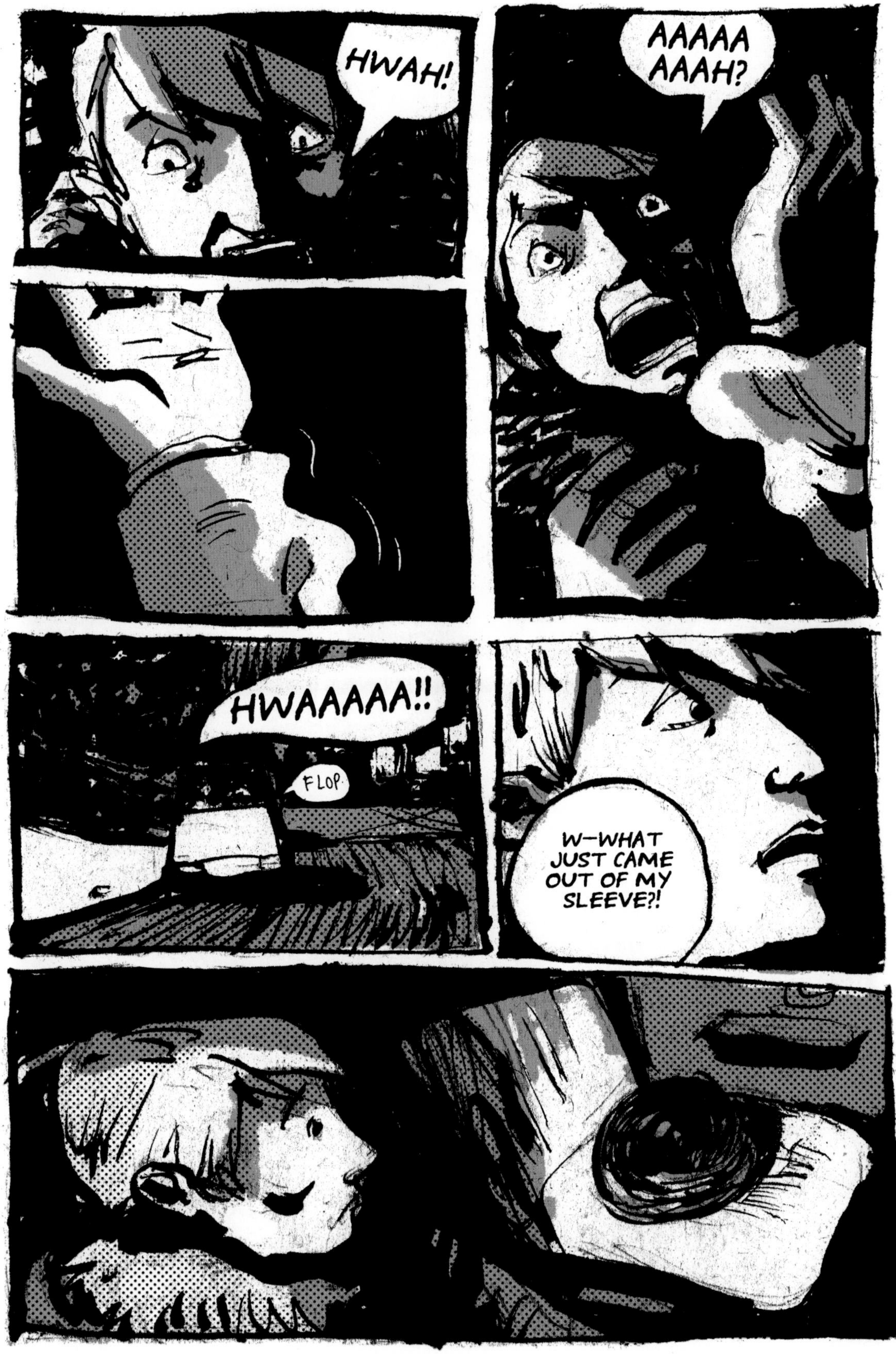
HWAH!
AAAAA AAAH?
HWAAAAA!!
FLOP.
W-WHAT JUST CAME OUT OF MY SLEEVE?!

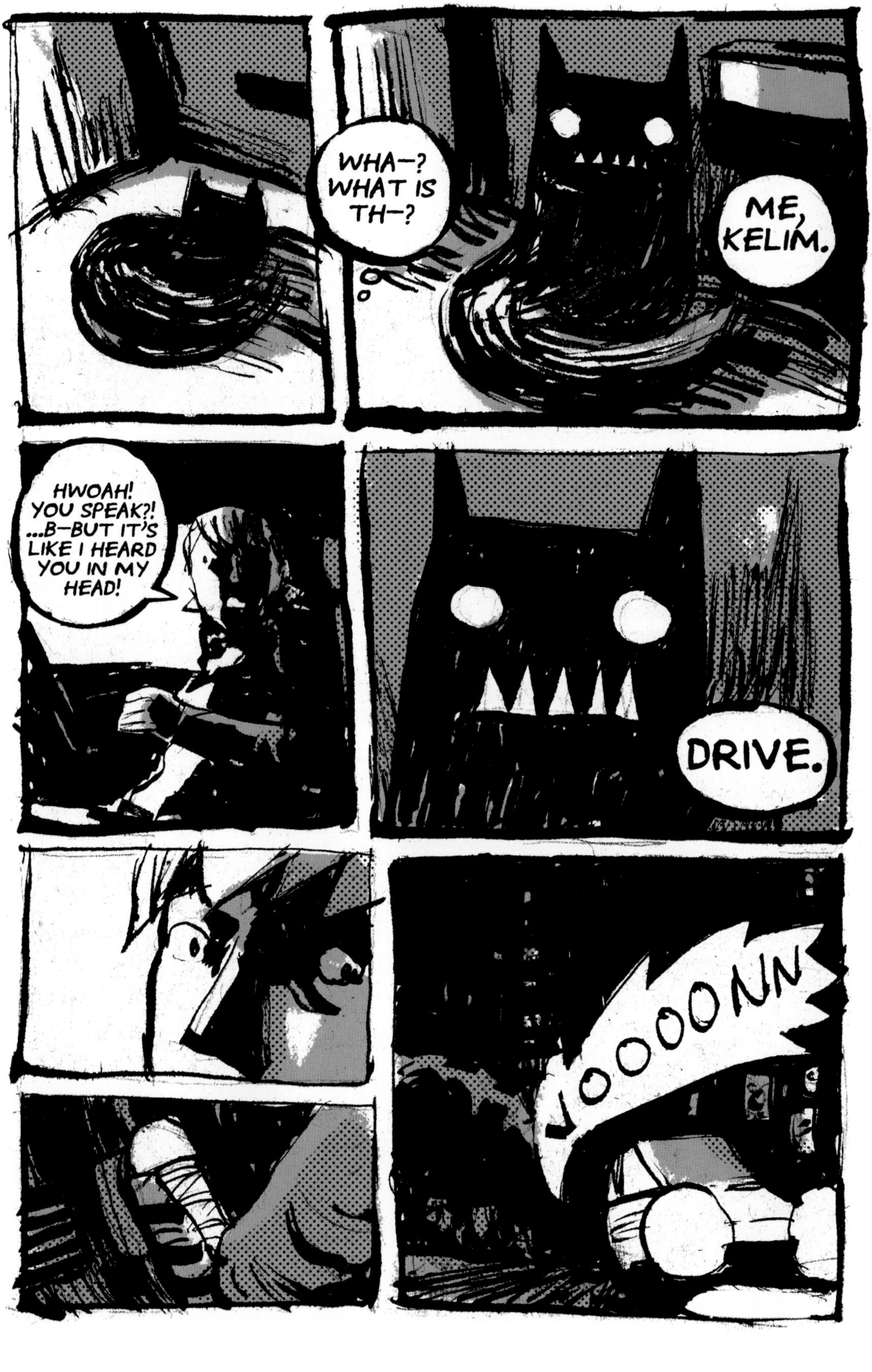
WHA–? WHAT IS TH–?
ME, KELIM.
HWOAH! YOU SPEAK?! ...B–BUT IT'S LIKE I HEARD YOU IN MY HEAD!
DRIVE.
VOOOONN

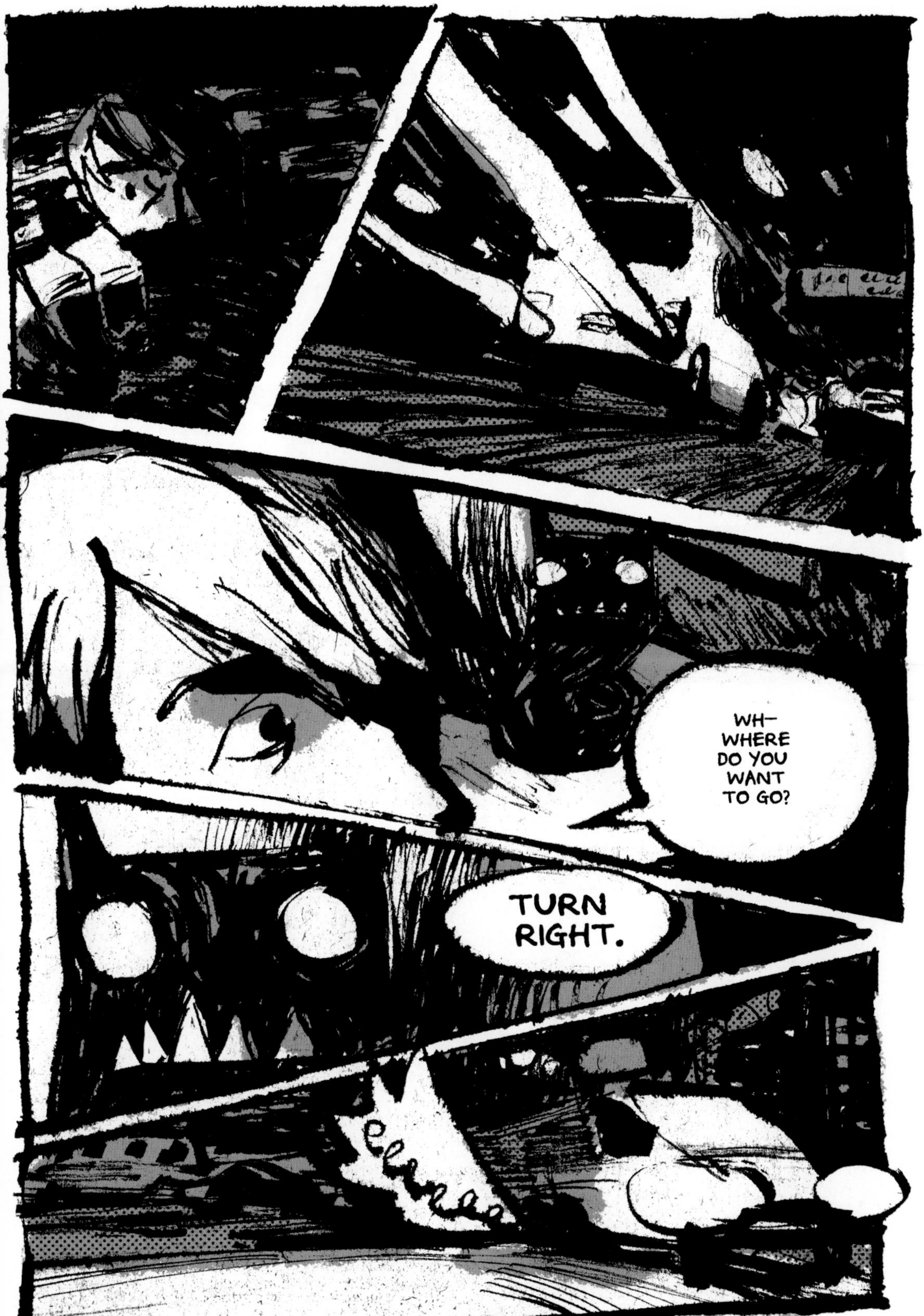
WH— WHERE DO YOU WANT TO GO?
TURN RIGHT.

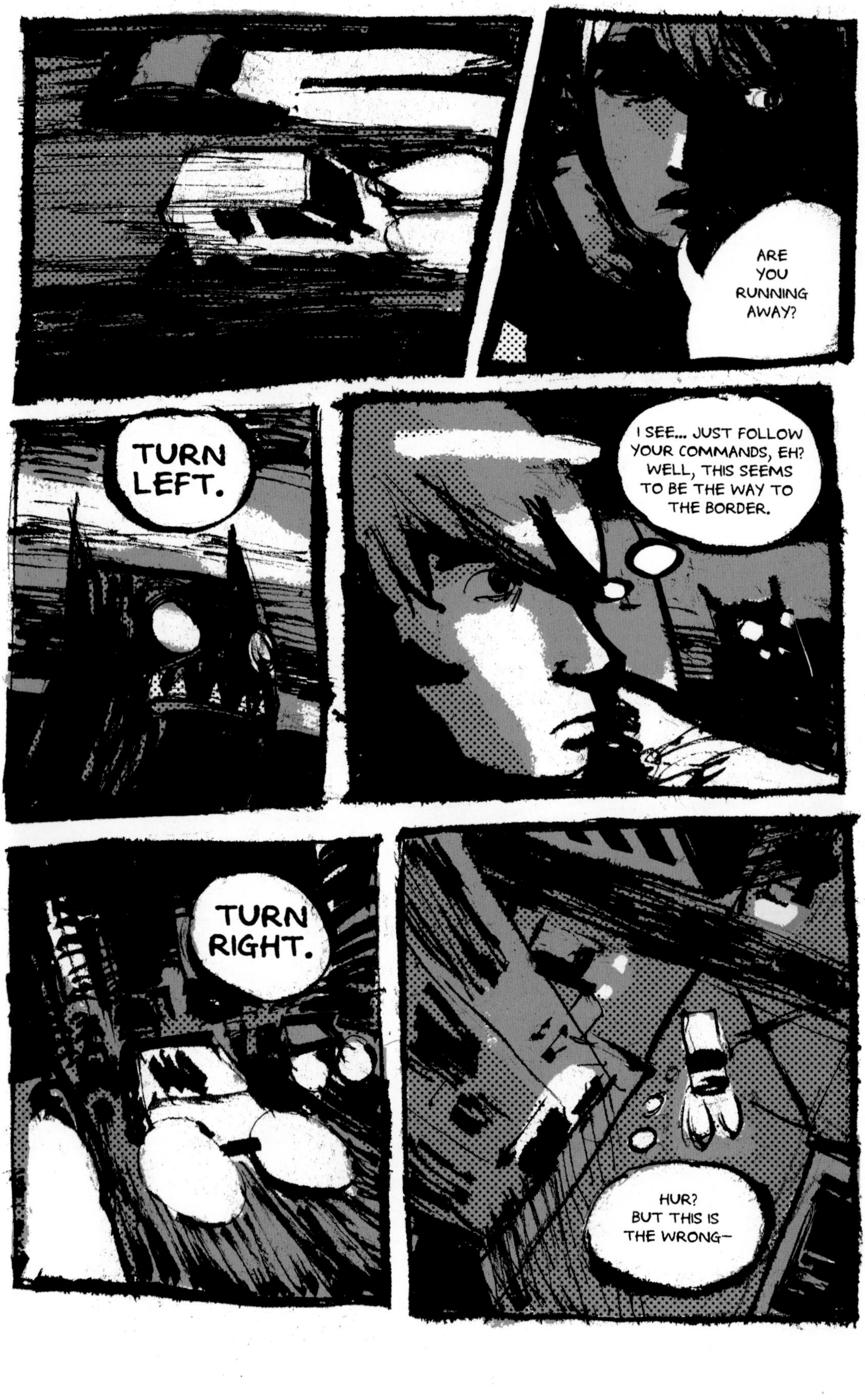
ARE YOU RUNNING AWAY?
TURN LEFT.
I SEE... JUST FOLLOW YOUR COMMANDS, EH? WELL, THIS SEEMS TO BE THE WAY TO THE BORDER.
TURN RIGHT.
HUR? BUT THIS IS THE WRONG—

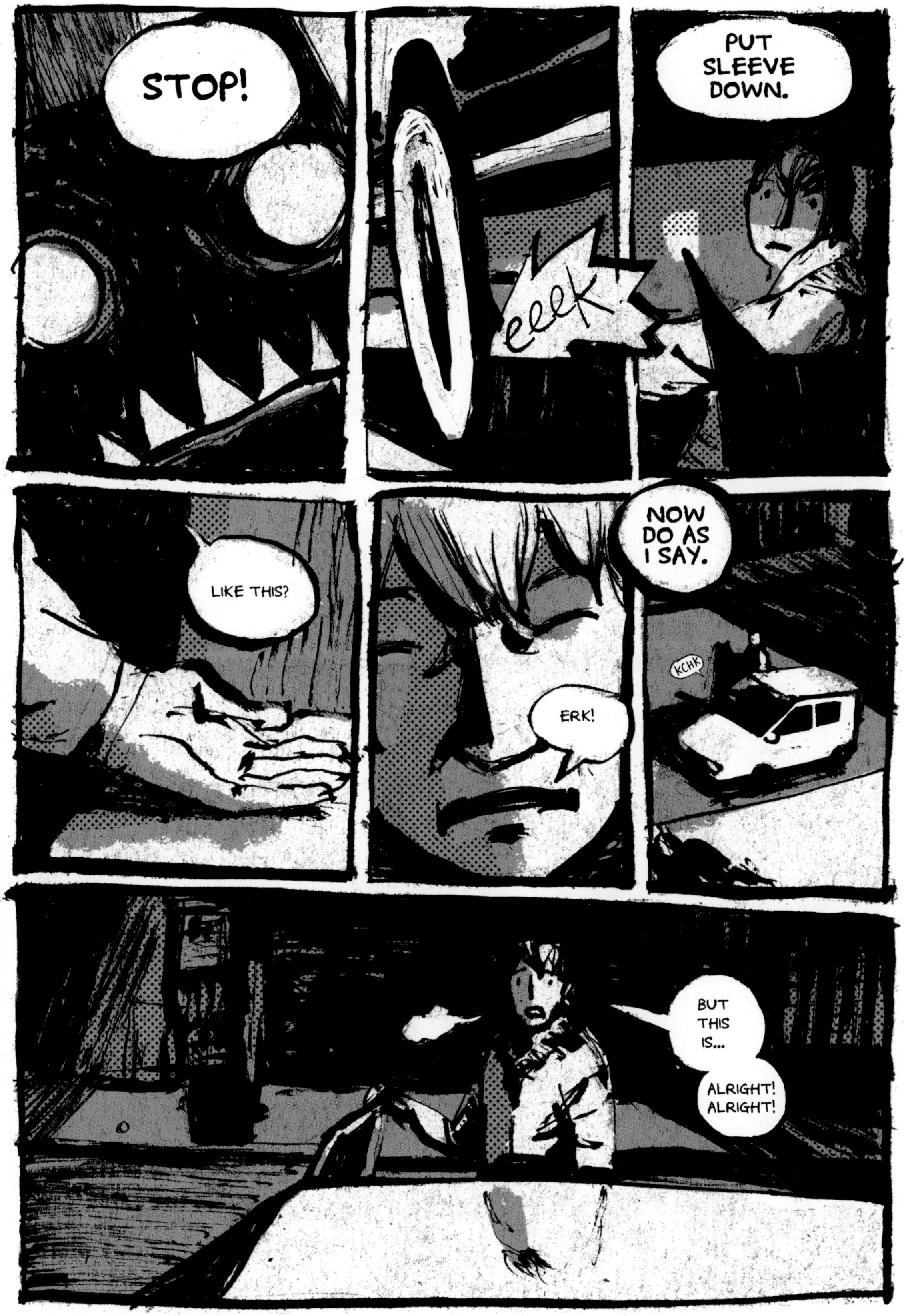
STOP!
eeek!
PUT SLEEVE DOWN.
LIKE THIS?
ERK!
NOW DO AS I SAY.
KCHK
BUT THIS IS...
ALRIGHT! ALRIGHT!

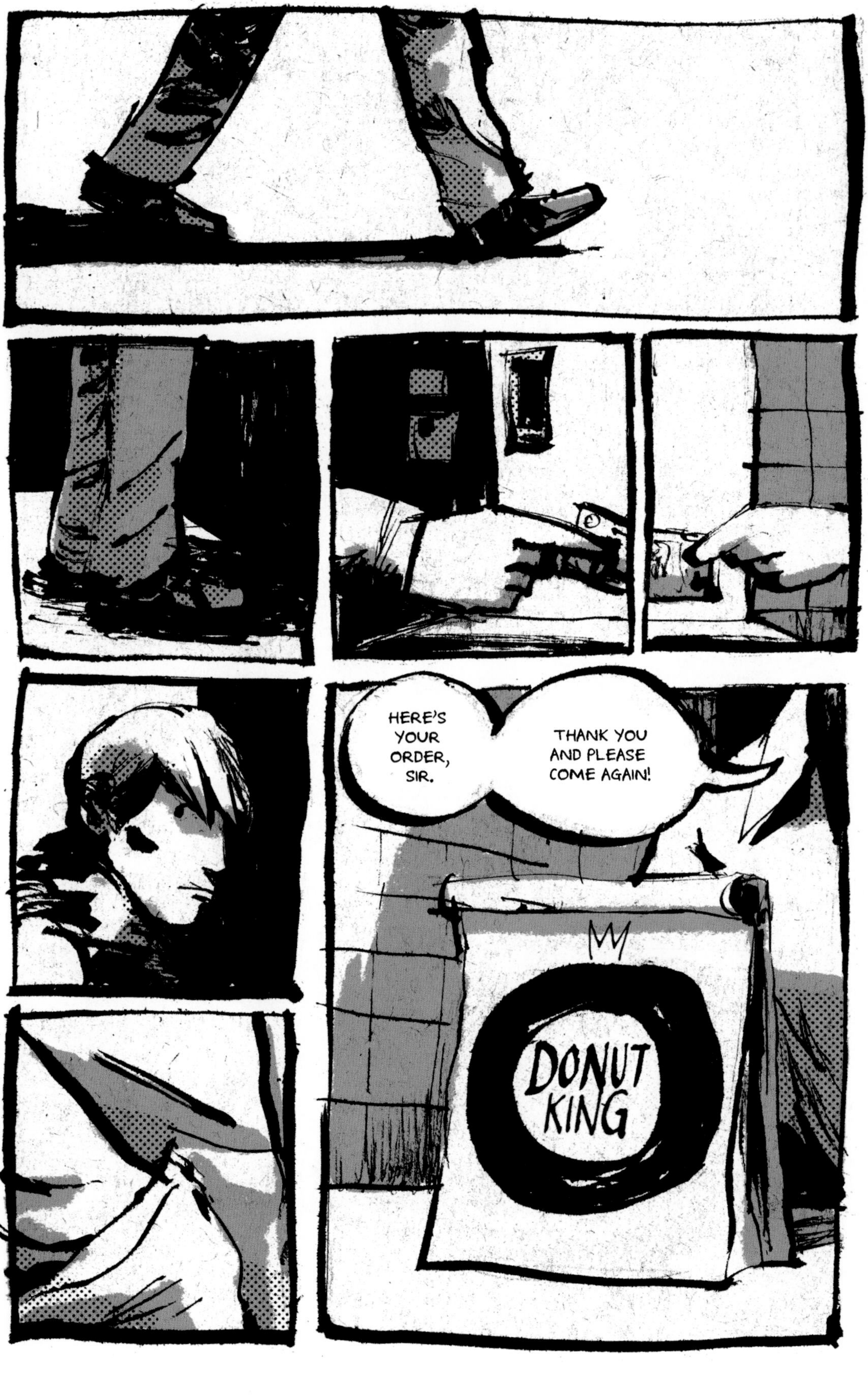
HERE'S YOUR ORDER, SIR.
THANK YOU AND PLEASE COME AGAIN!
DONUT KING

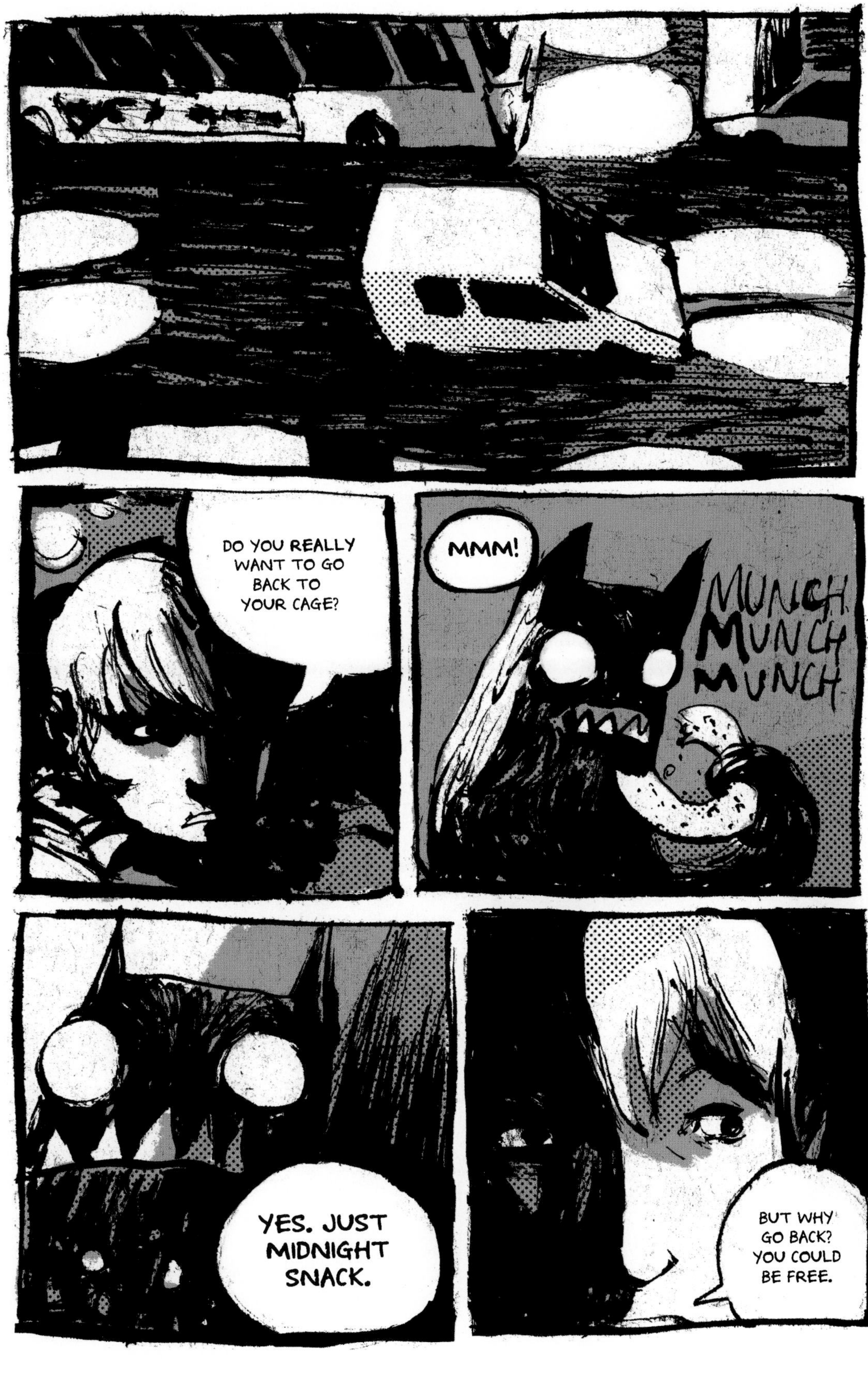
DO YOU REALLY WANT TO GO BACK TO YOUR CAGE?
MMM!
MUNCH MUNCH MUNCH
YES. JUST MIDNIGHT SNACK.
BUT WHY GO BACK? YOU COULD BE FREE.

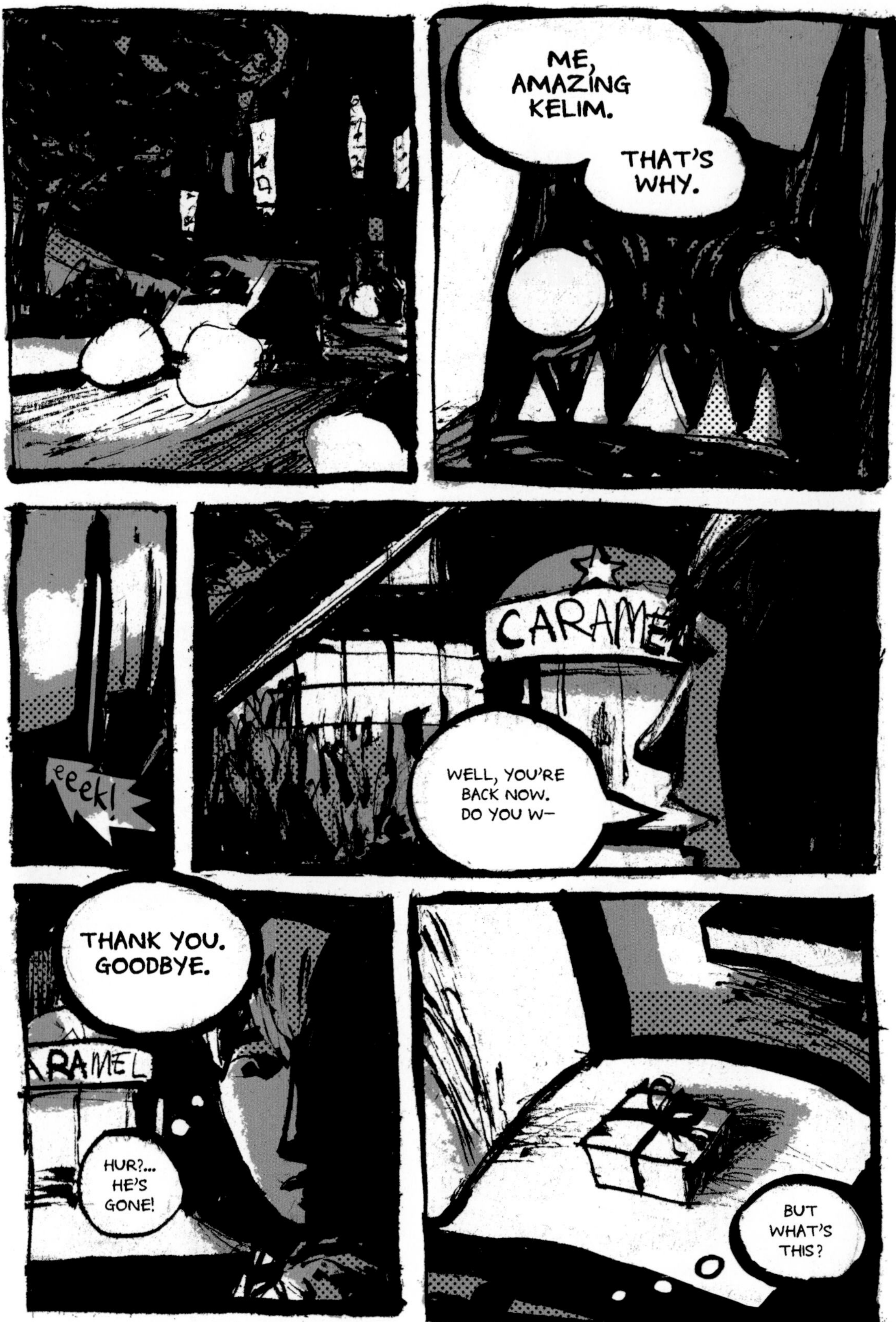
ME, AMAZING KELIM.
THAT'S WHY.
eeek!
CARAMEL
WELL, YOU'RE BACK NOW. DO YOU W–
THANK YOU. GOODBYE.
ARAMEL
HUR?... HE'S GONE!
BUT WHAT'S THIS?

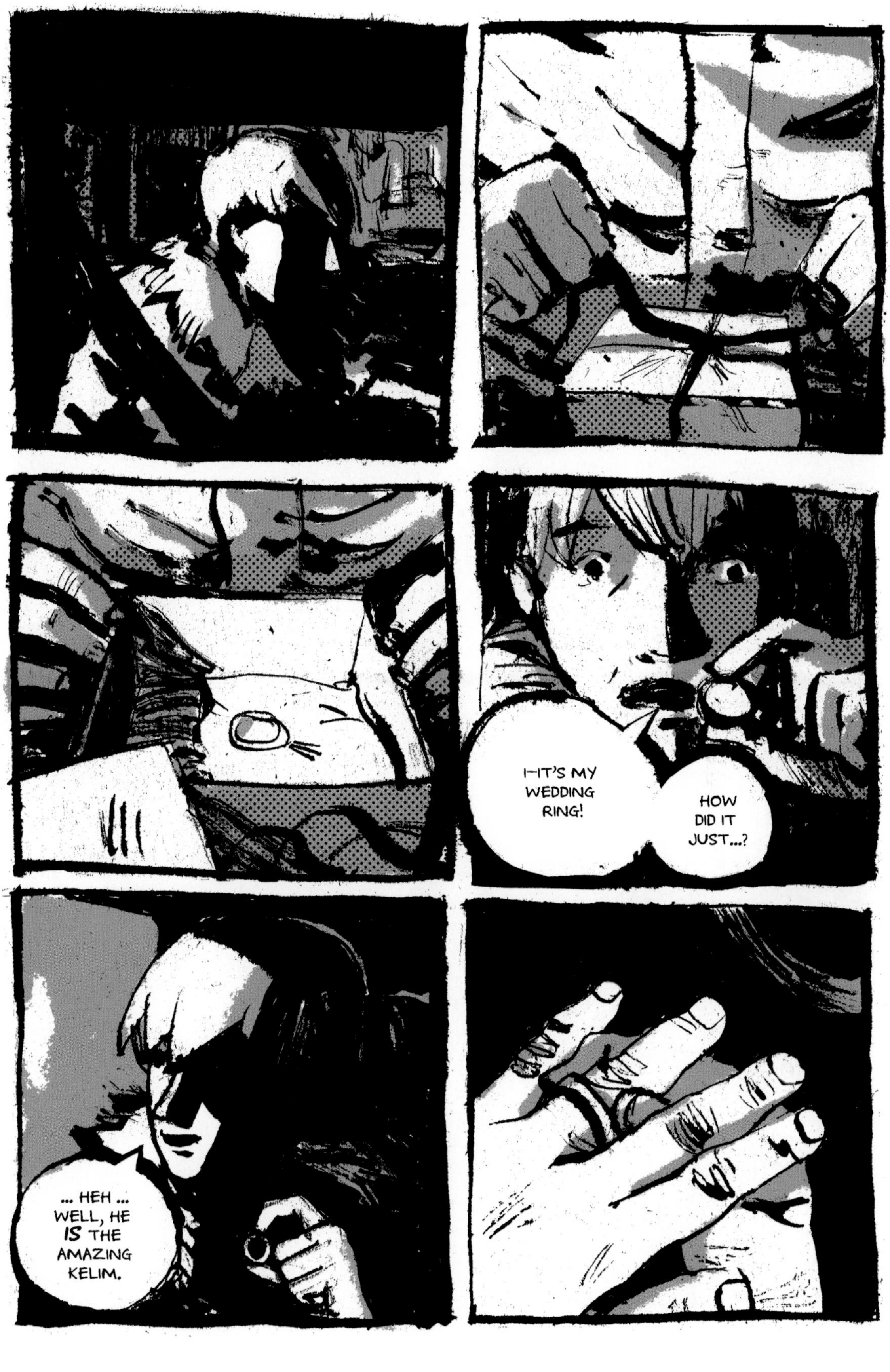
I-IT'S MY WEDDING RING!
HOW DID IT JUST...?
... HEH ... WELL, HE IS THE AMAZING KELIM.

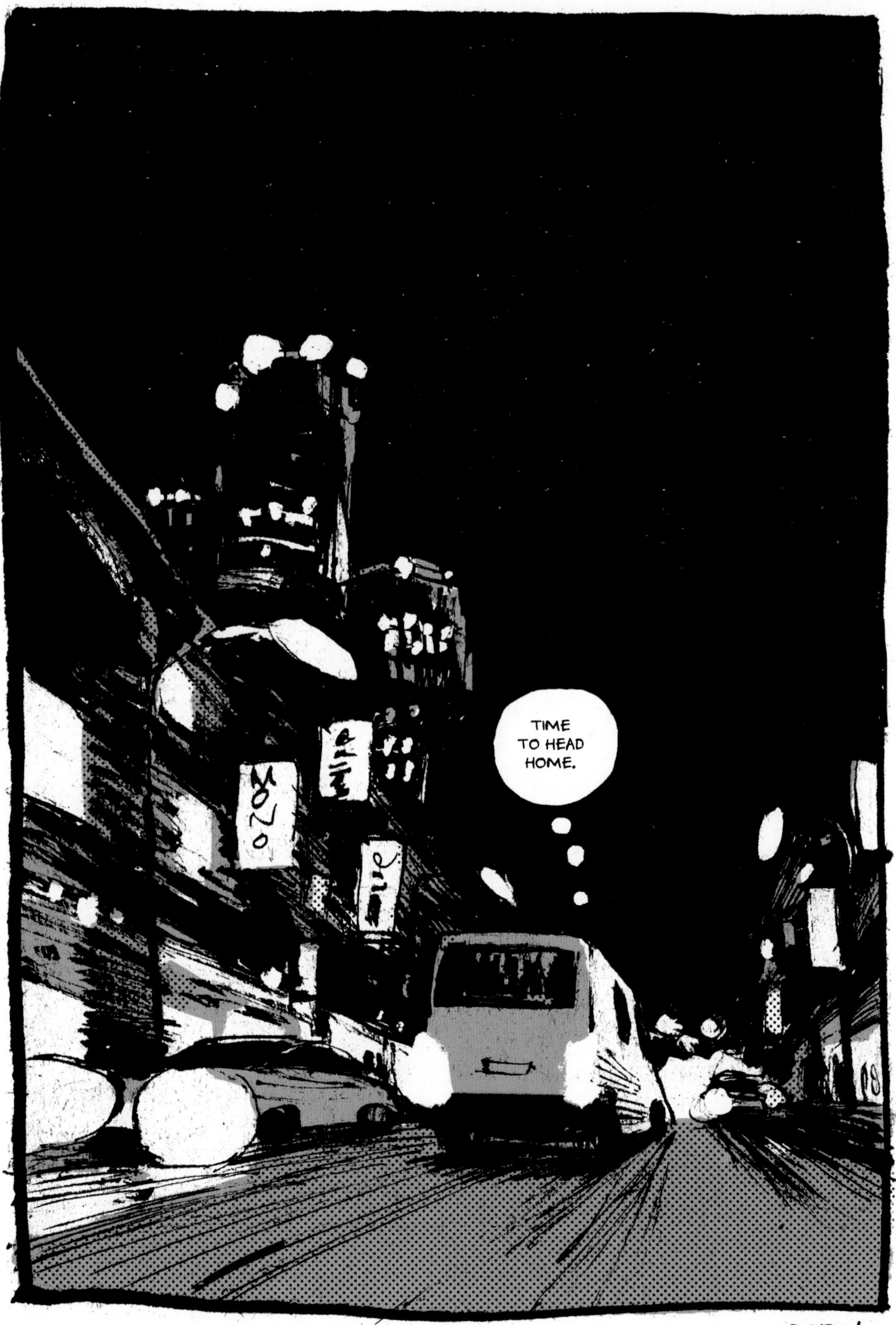
TIME
TO HEAD
HOME.
DREW 12

Zero Hero
TAN ENG HUAT

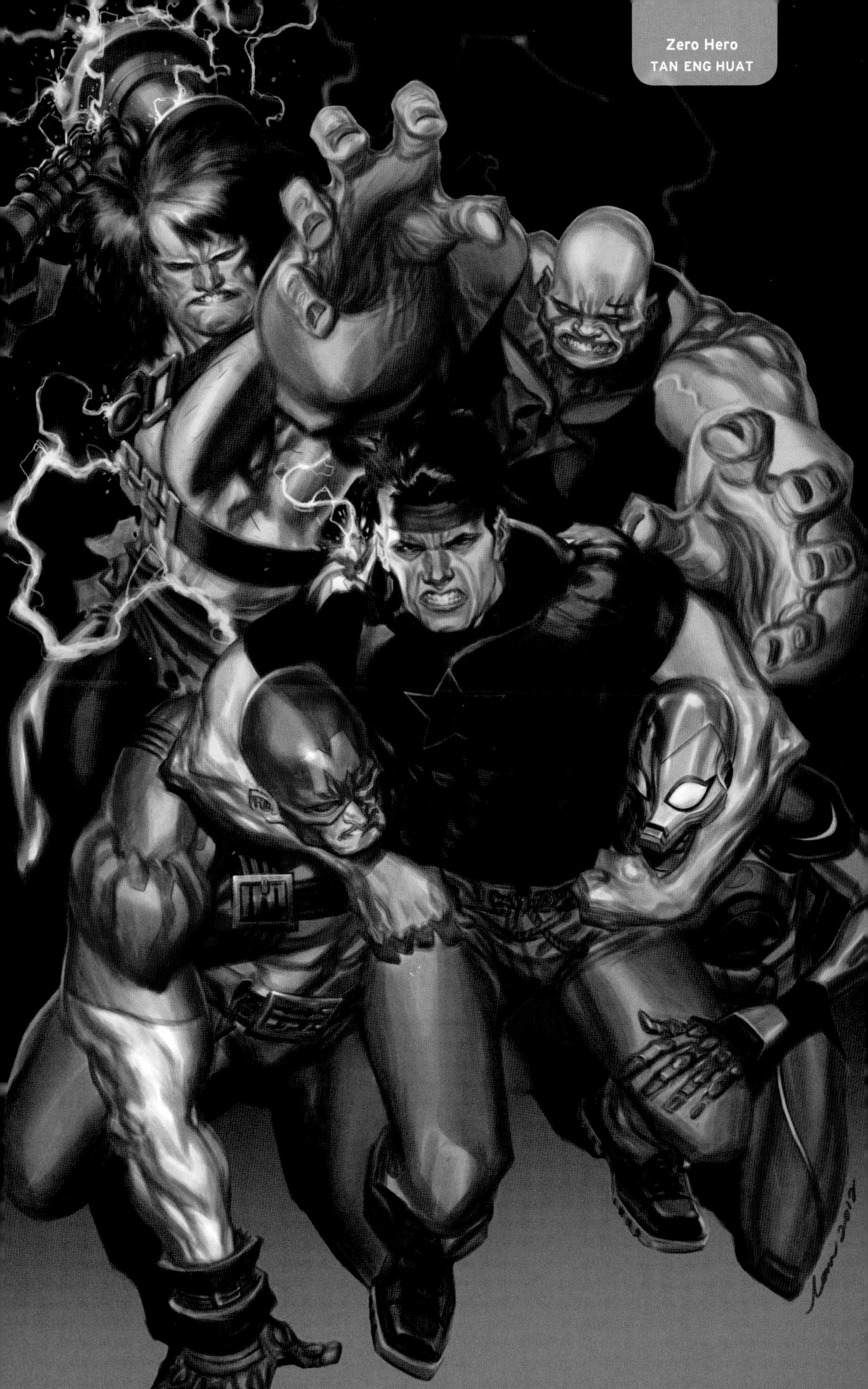

CrystalMire

JINGXUAN HU

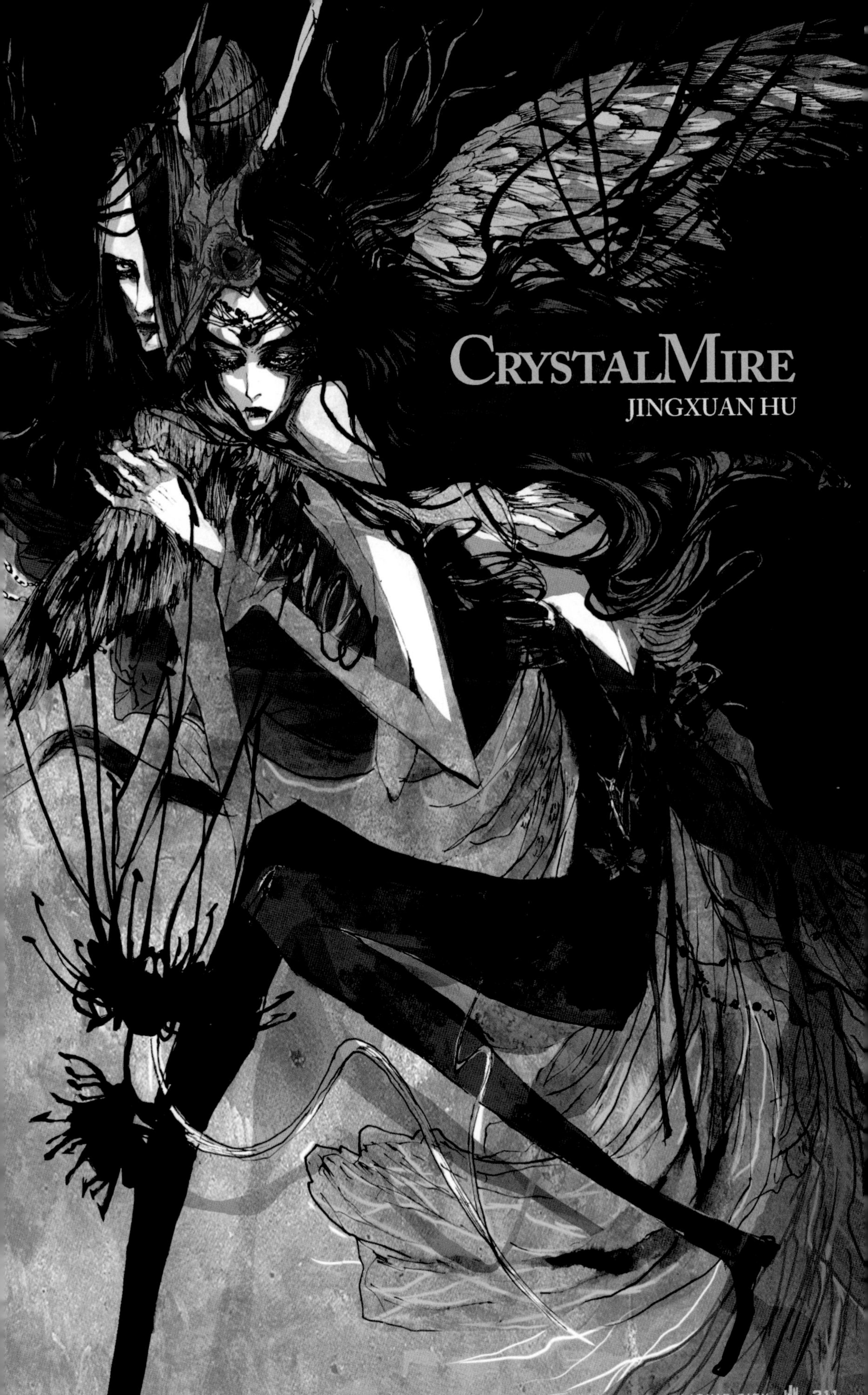

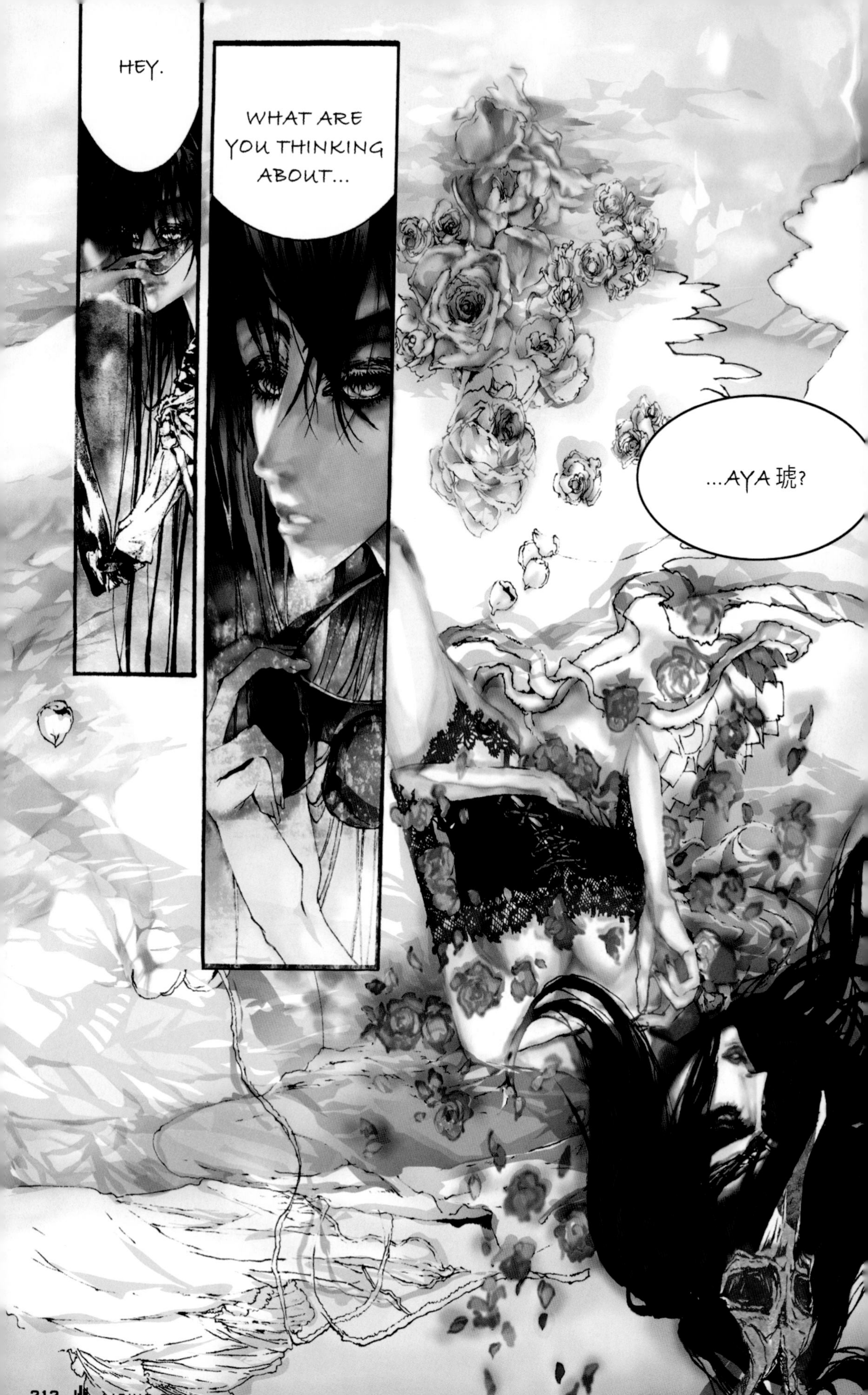
HEY.
WHAT ARE YOU THINKING ABOUT...
...AYA 琥?

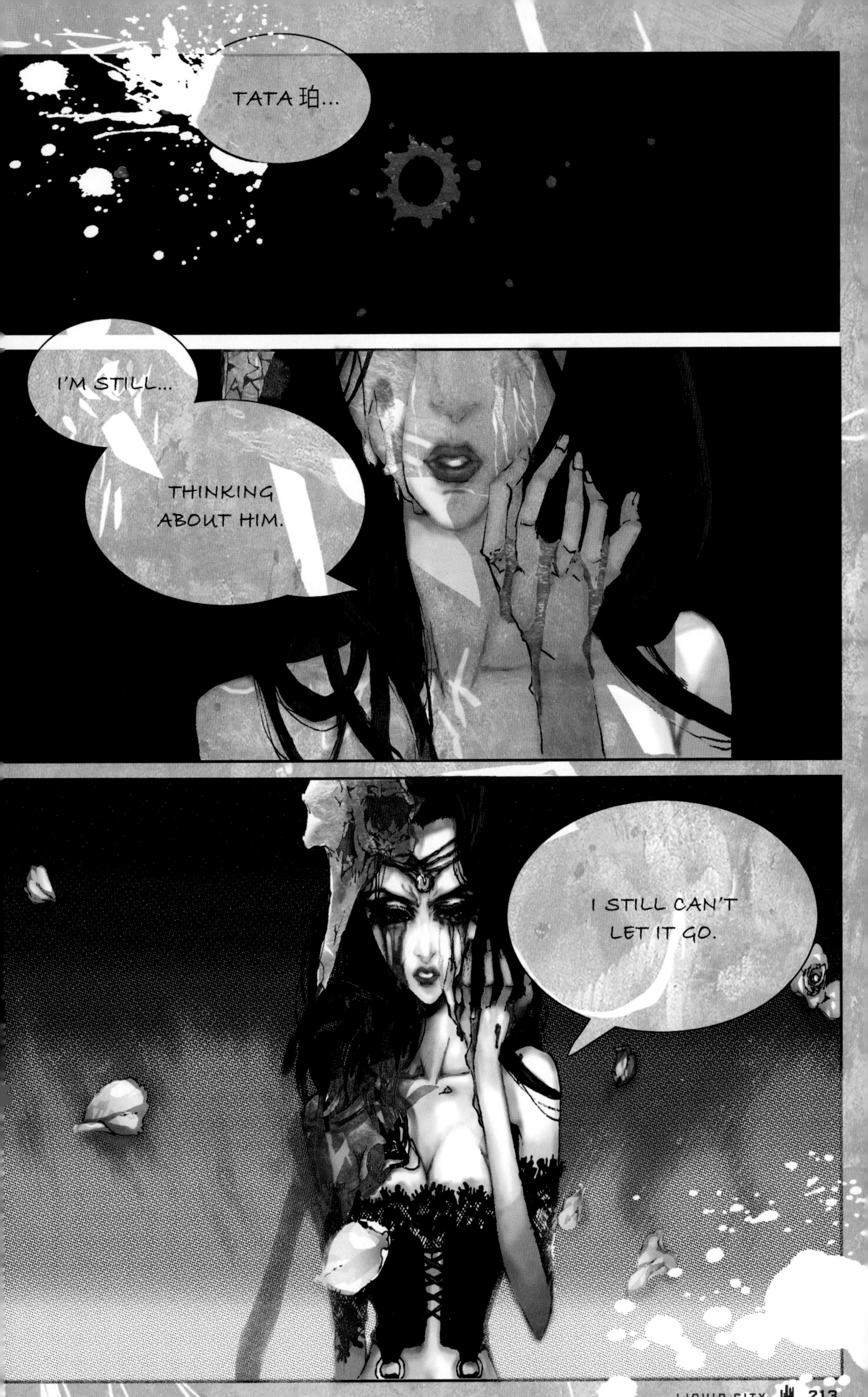
TATA 珀...
I'M STILL...
THINKING ABOUT HIM.
I STILL CAN'T LET IT GO.

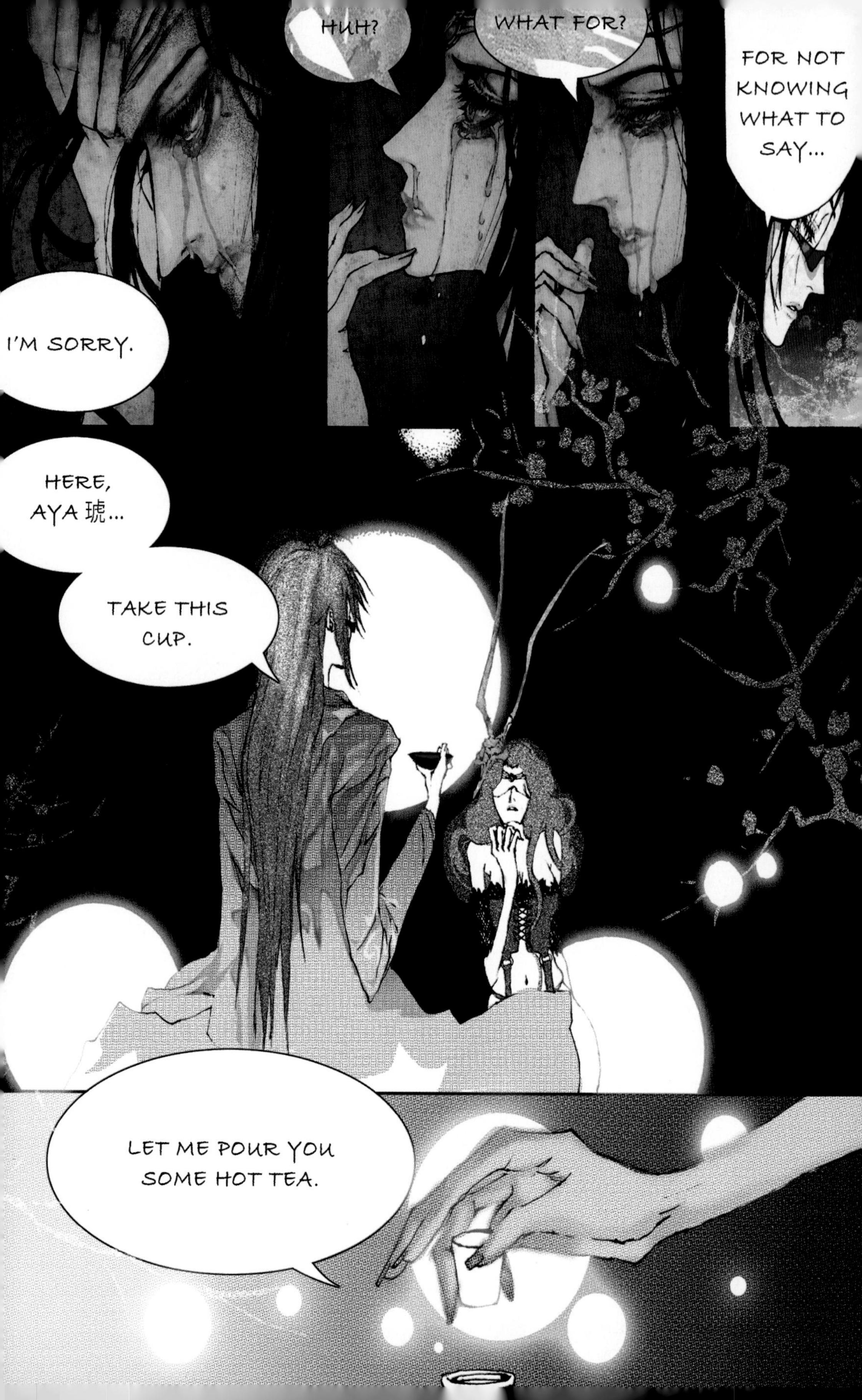
I'M SORRY.
HUH?
WHAT FOR?
FOR NOT KNOWING WHAT TO SAY...
HERE, AYA 琥...
TAKE THIS CUP.
LET ME POUR YOU SOME HOT TEA.

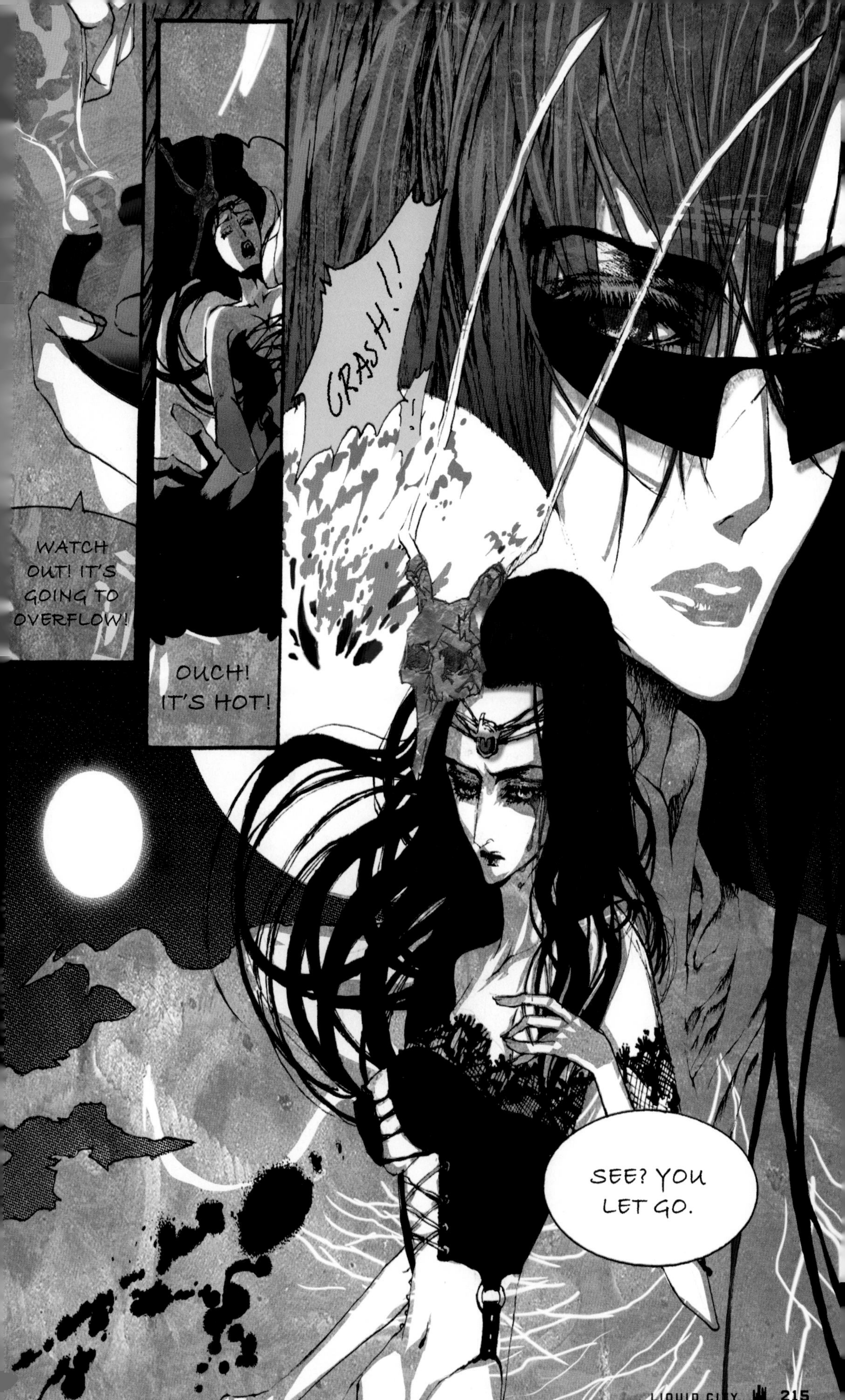
OUCH! IT'S HOT!
WATCH OUT! IT'S GOING TO OVERFLOW!
CRASH!!
SEE? YOU LET GO.

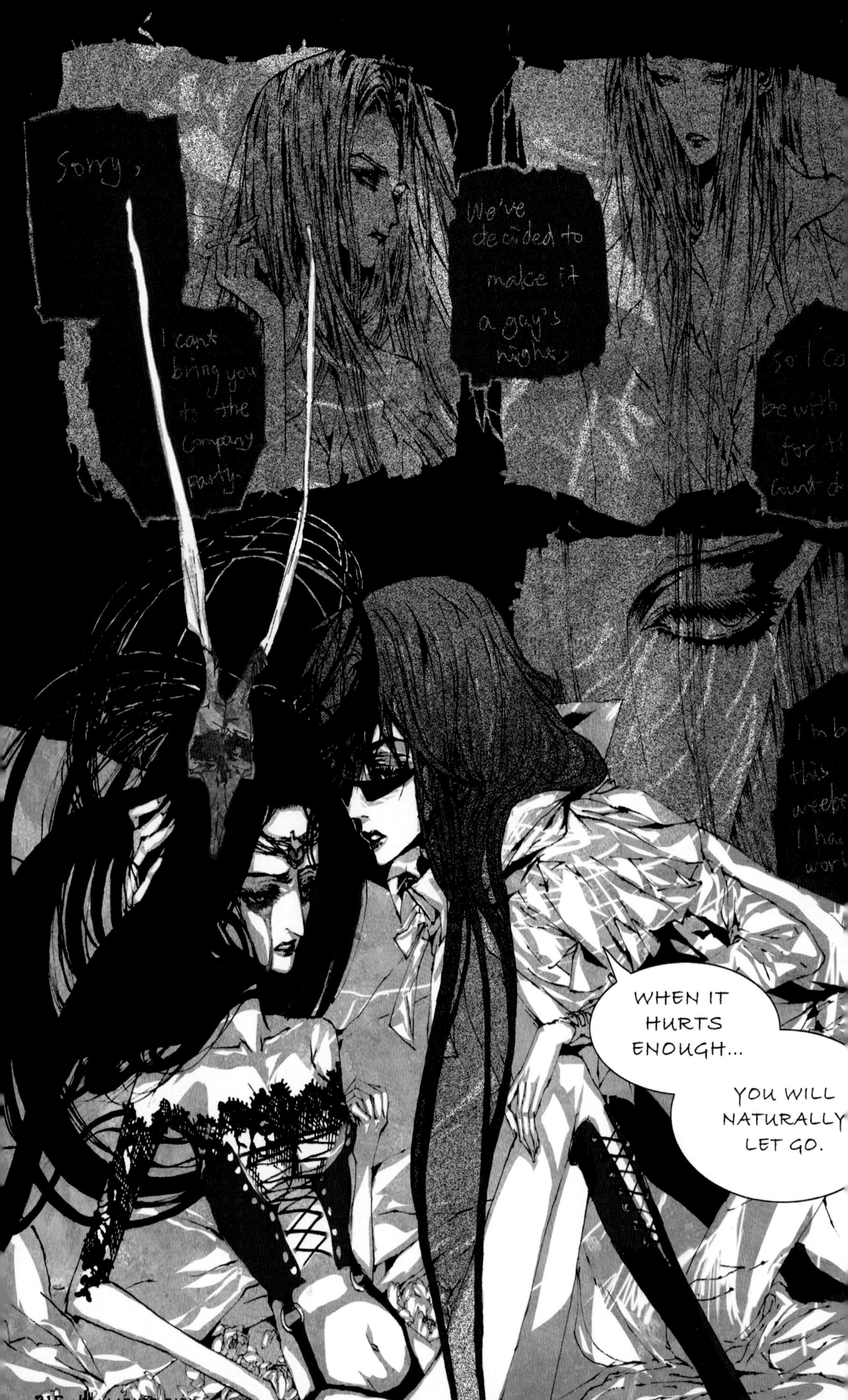
Sorry,
I can't bring you to the company party.
We've decided to make it a guy's night,
WHEN IT HURTS ENOUGH...
YOU WILL NATURALLY LET GO.

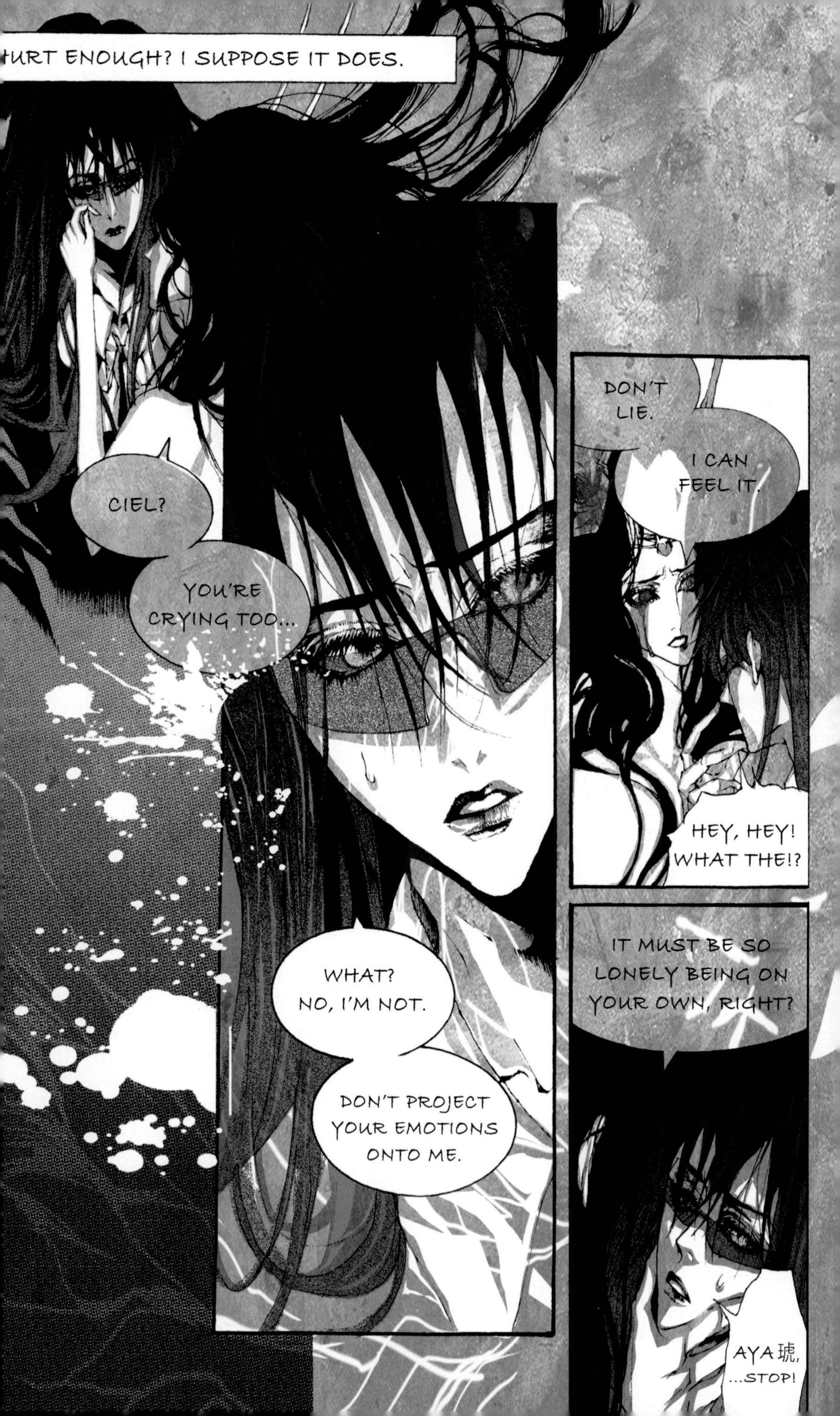
HURT ENOUGH? I SUPPOSE IT DOES.
CIEL?
YOU'RE CRYING TOO...
WHAT? NO, I'M NOT.
DON'T PROJECT YOUR EMOTIONS ONTO ME.
DON'T LIE.
I CAN FEEL IT.
HEY, HEY! WHAT THE!?
IT MUST BE SO LONELY BEING ON YOUR OWN, RIGHT?
AYA琥, ...STOP!

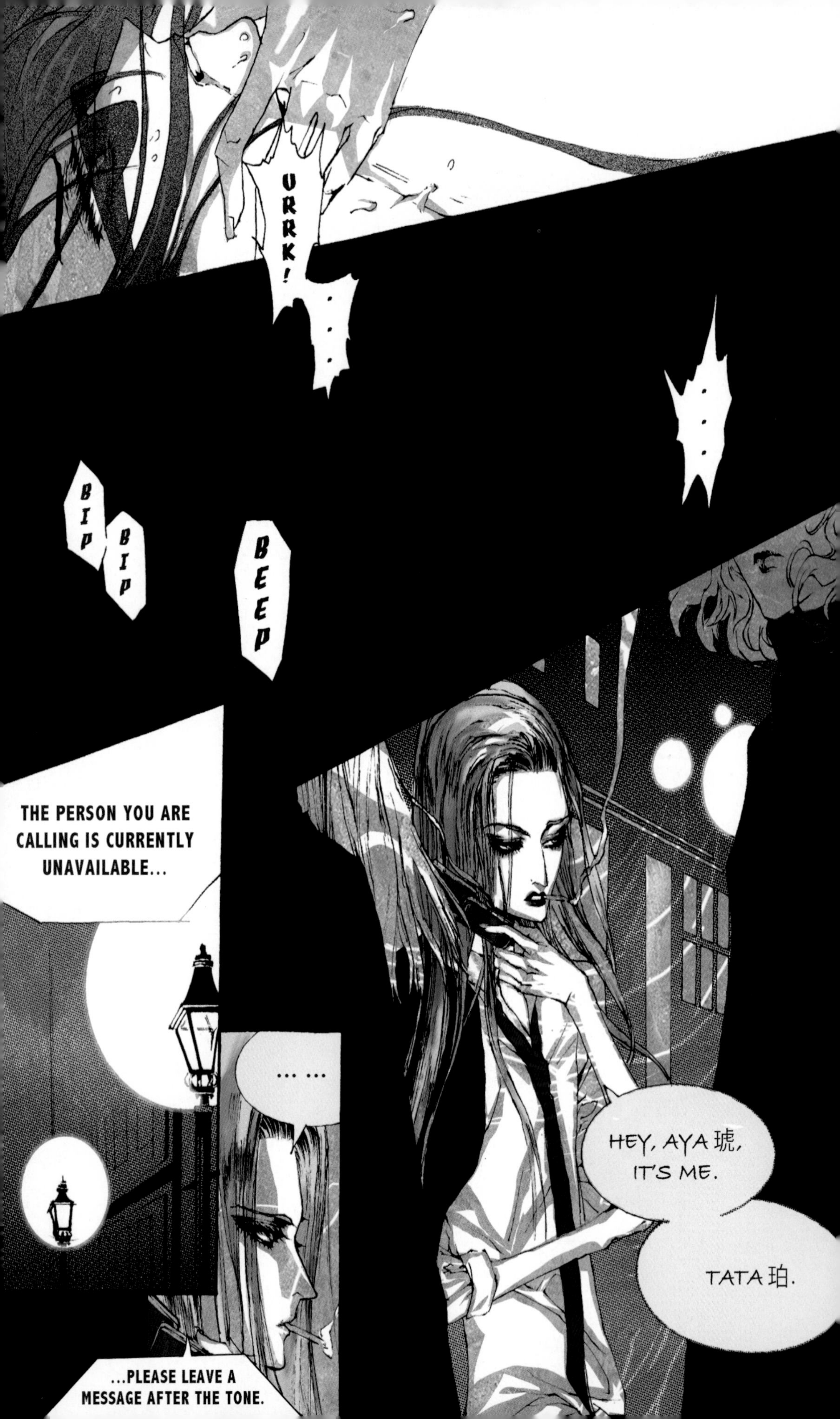
URRK!
...
...
BIP
BIP
BEEP
THE PERSON YOU ARE CALLING IS CURRENTLY UNAVAILABLE...
...PLEASE LEAVE A MESSAGE AFTER THE TONE.
... ...
HEY, AYA 琥, IT'S ME.
TATA 珀.

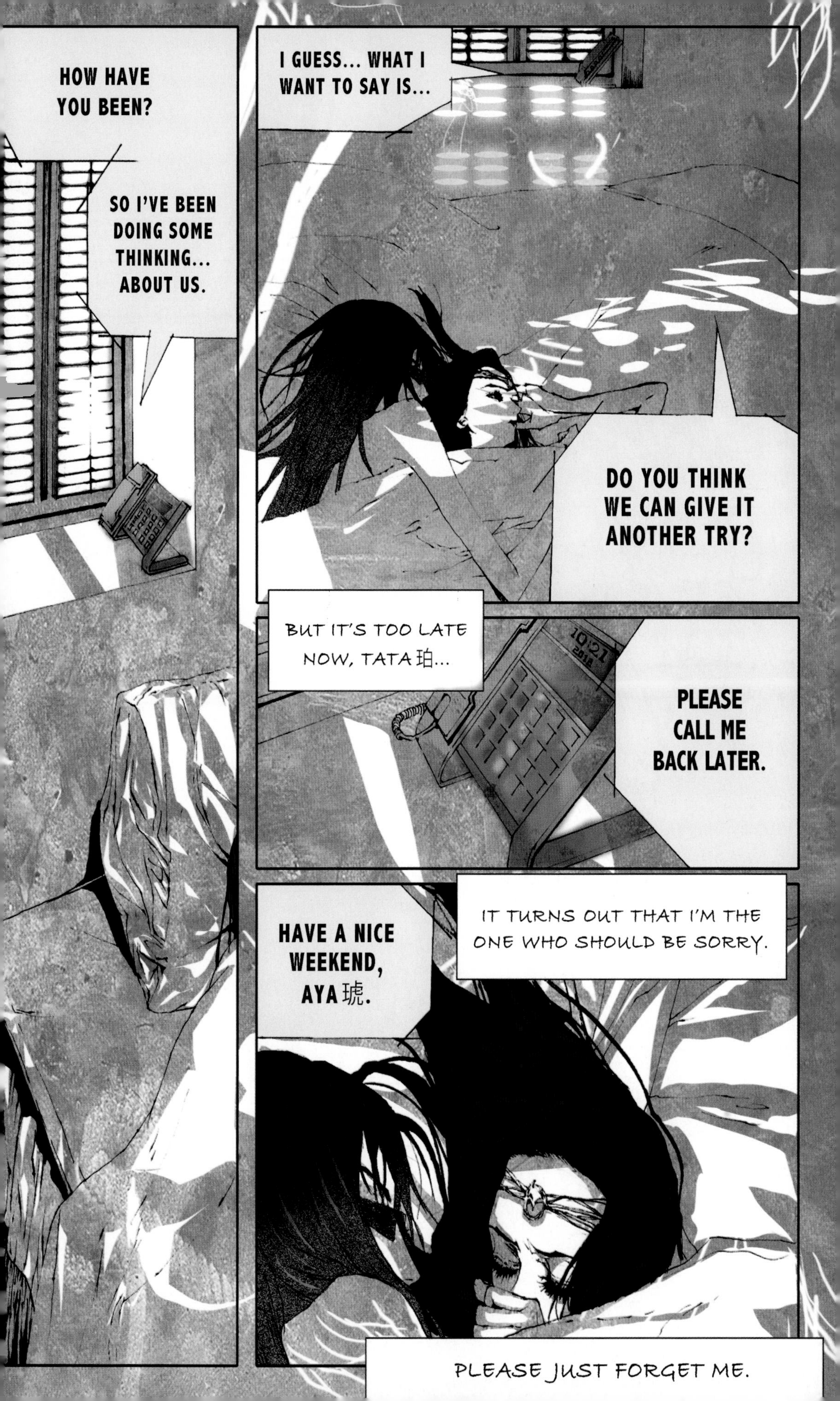
HOW HAVE YOU BEEN?
SO I'VE BEEN DOING SOME THINKING... ABOUT US.
I GUESS... WHAT I WANT TO SAY IS...
DO YOU THINK WE CAN GIVE IT ANOTHER TRY?
BUT IT'S TOO LATE NOW, TATA珀...
10:21
PLEASE CALL ME BACK LATER.
HAVE A NICE WEEKEND, AYA琥.
IT TURNS OUT THAT I'M THE ONE WHO SHOULD BE SORRY.
PLEASE JUST FORGET ME.

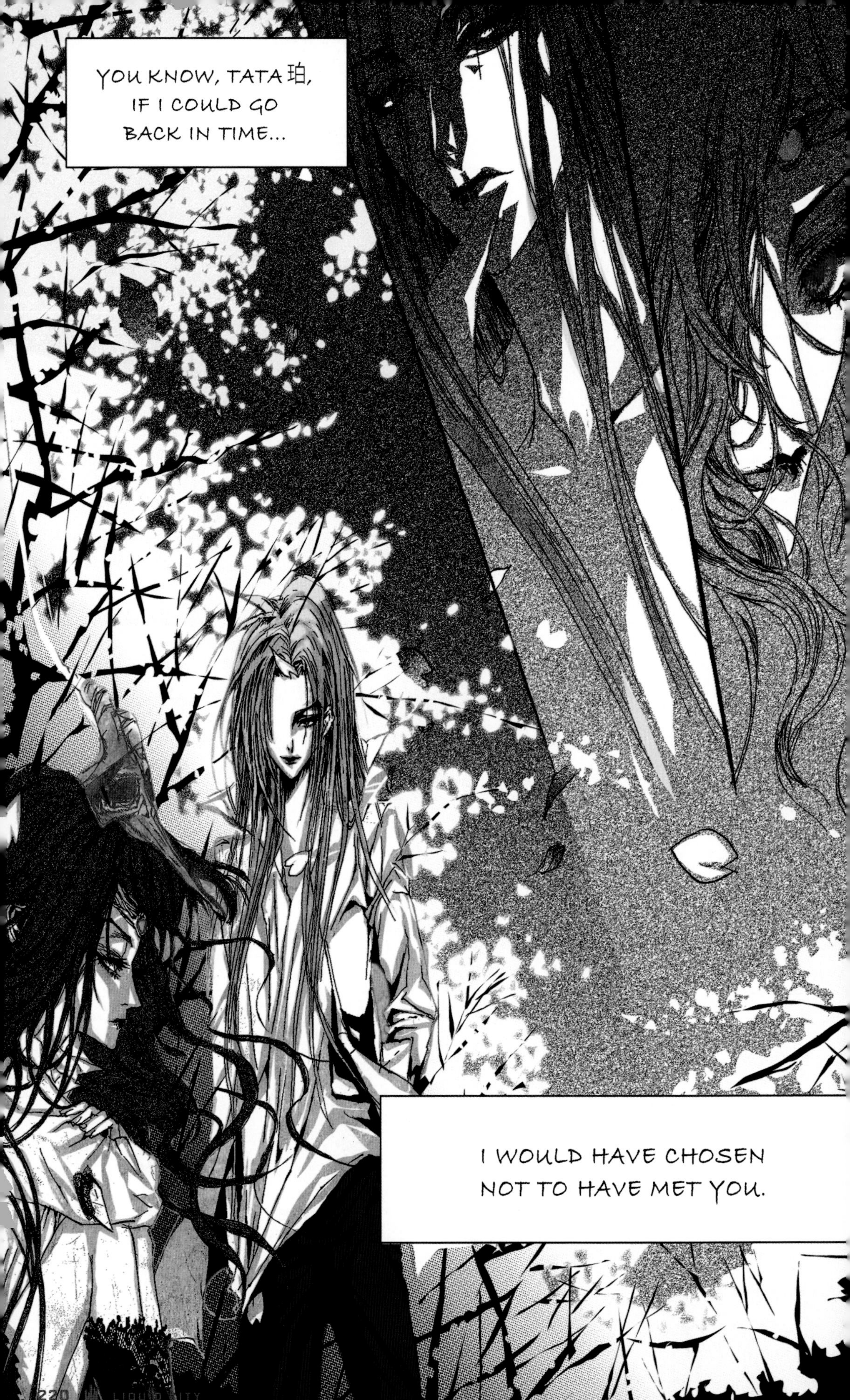
YOU KNOW, TATA珀,
IF I COULD GO
BACK IN TIME...
I WOULD HAVE CHOSEN
NOT TO HAVE MET YOU.

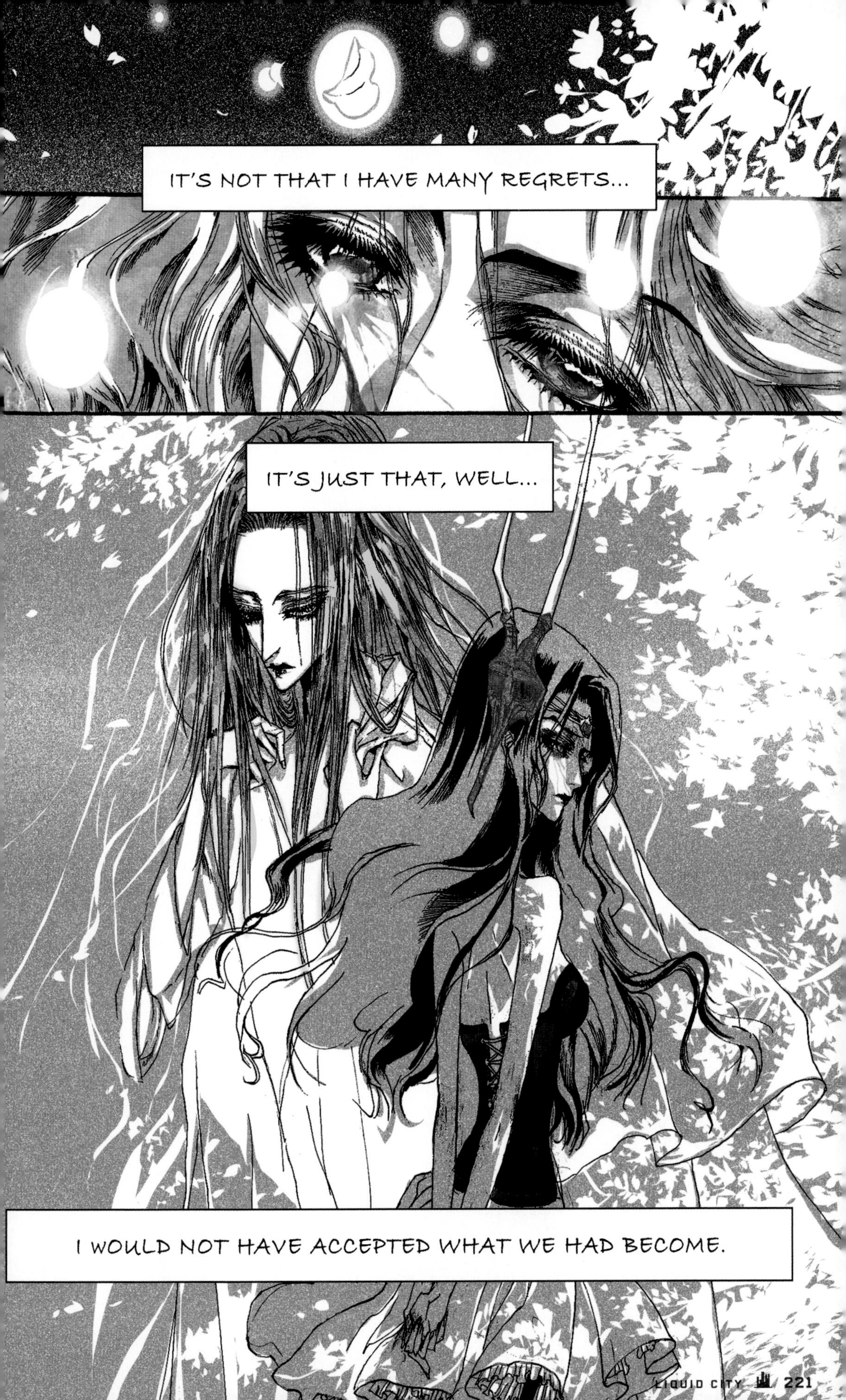
IT'S NOT THAT I HAVE MANY REGRETS...
IT'S JUST THAT, WELL...
I WOULD NOT HAVE ACCEPTED WHAT WE HAD BECOME.

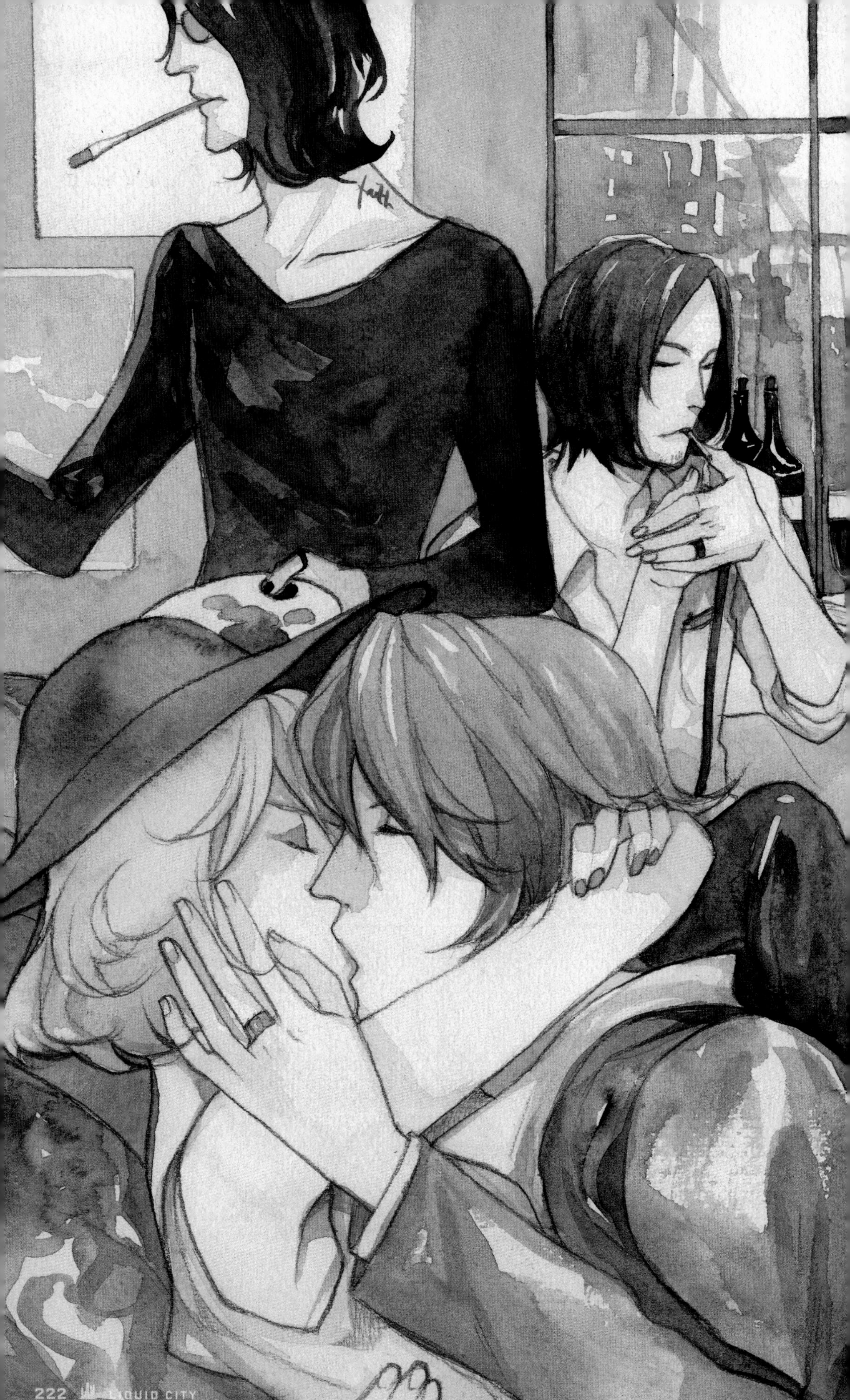

Let's Do the Things We Normally Do

VIC-MON

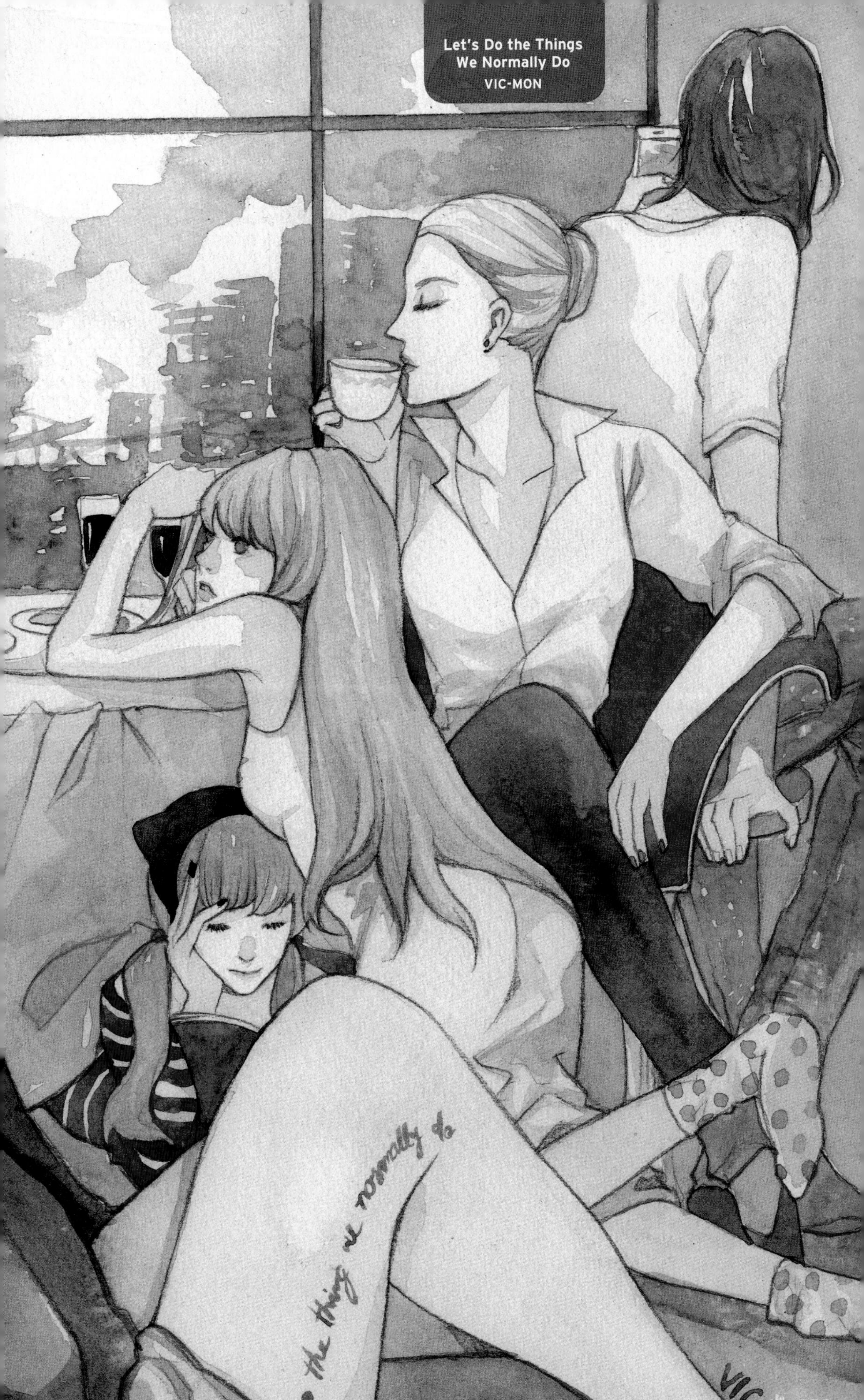
Do the thing we normally do
VIC

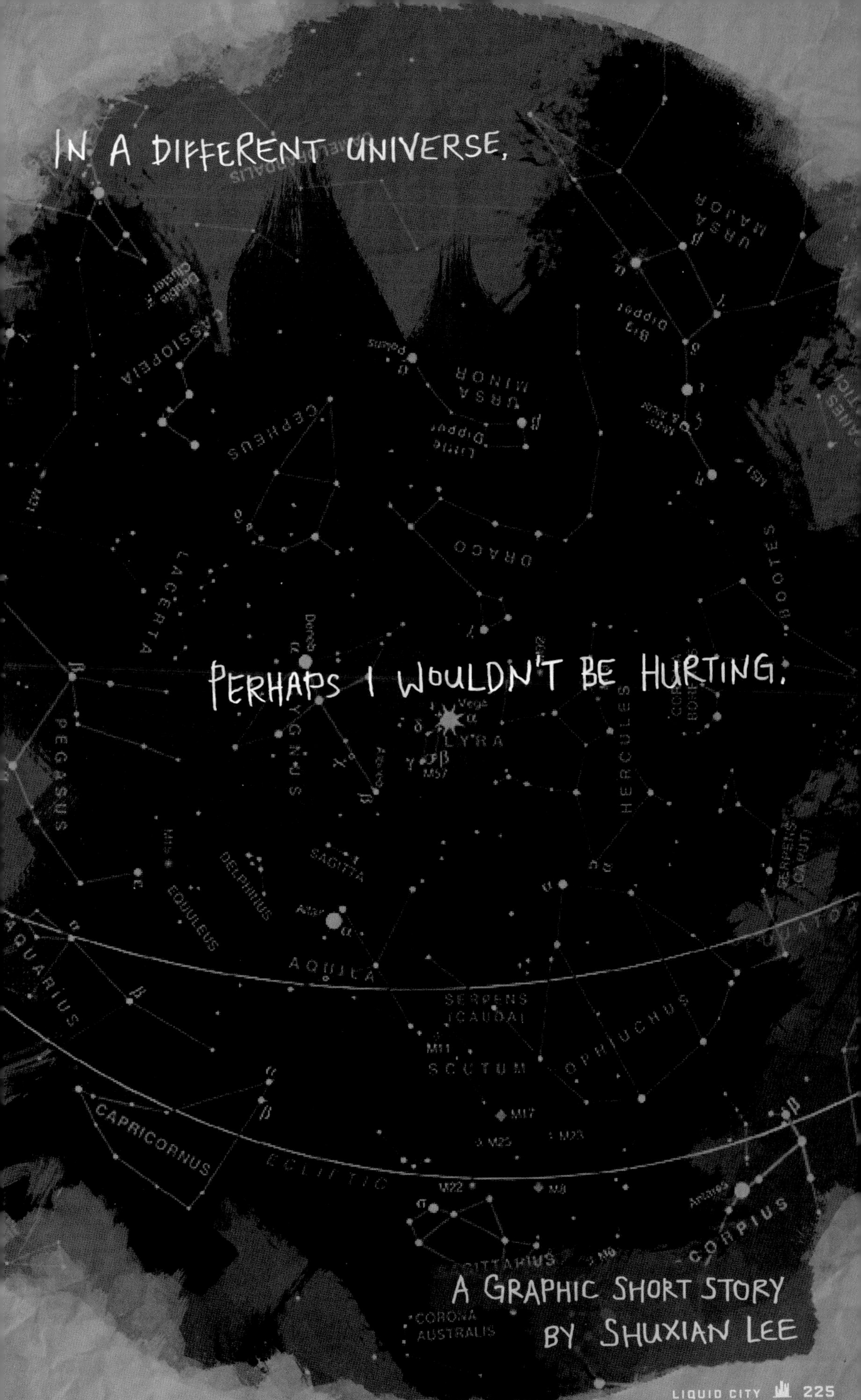
IN A DIFFERENT UNIVERSE,
PERHAPS I WOULDN'T BE HURTING.
A GRAPHIC SHORT STORY
BY SHUXIAN LEE
URSA MAJOR
Big Dipper
URSA MINOR
Little Dipper
Polaris
CASSIOPEIA
Double Cluster
CEPHEUS
DRACO
LACERTA
BOOTES
Vega
LYRA
M57
CYGNUS
HERCULES
PEGASUS
SAGITTA
DELPHINUS
EQUULEUS
Altair
AQUILA
AQUARIUS
SERPENS CAUDA
M11
SCUTUM
OPHIUCHUS
M17
M25
M23
CAPRICORNUS
ECLIPTIC
M22
M8
Antares
SCORPIUS
SAGITTARIUS
CORONA AUSTRALIS

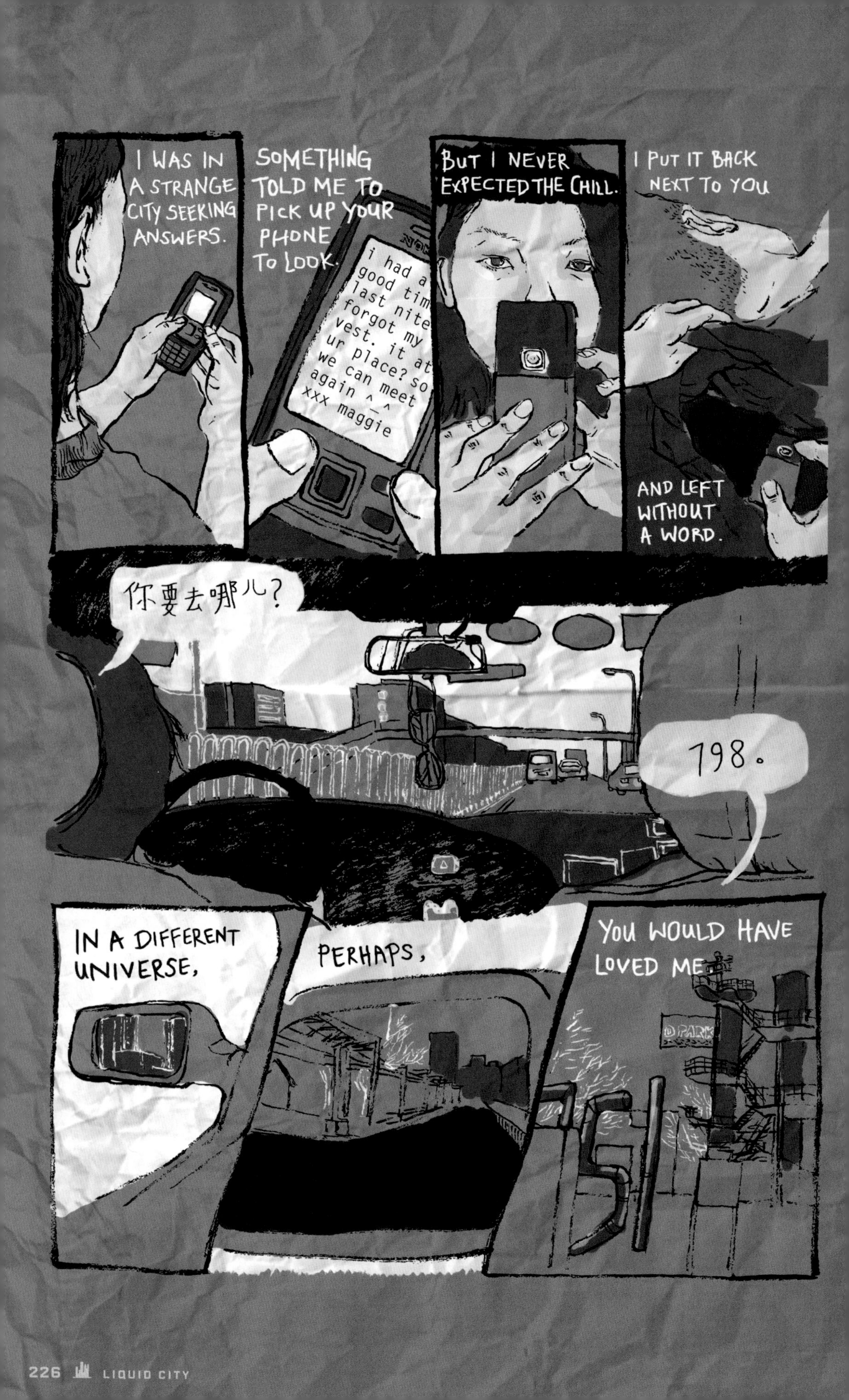
I WAS IN A STRANGE CITY SEEKING ANSWERS.
SOMETHING TOLD ME TO PICK UP YOUR PHONE TO LOOK.
i had a good tim last nite forgot my vest. it at ur place? so we can meet again ^_^ xxx maggie
BUT I NEVER EXPECTED THE CHILL.
I PUT IT BACK NEXT TO YOU
AND LEFT WITHOUT A WORD.
你要去哪儿？
798。
IN A DIFFERENT UNIVERSE,
PERHAPS,
YOU WOULD HAVE LOVED ME.

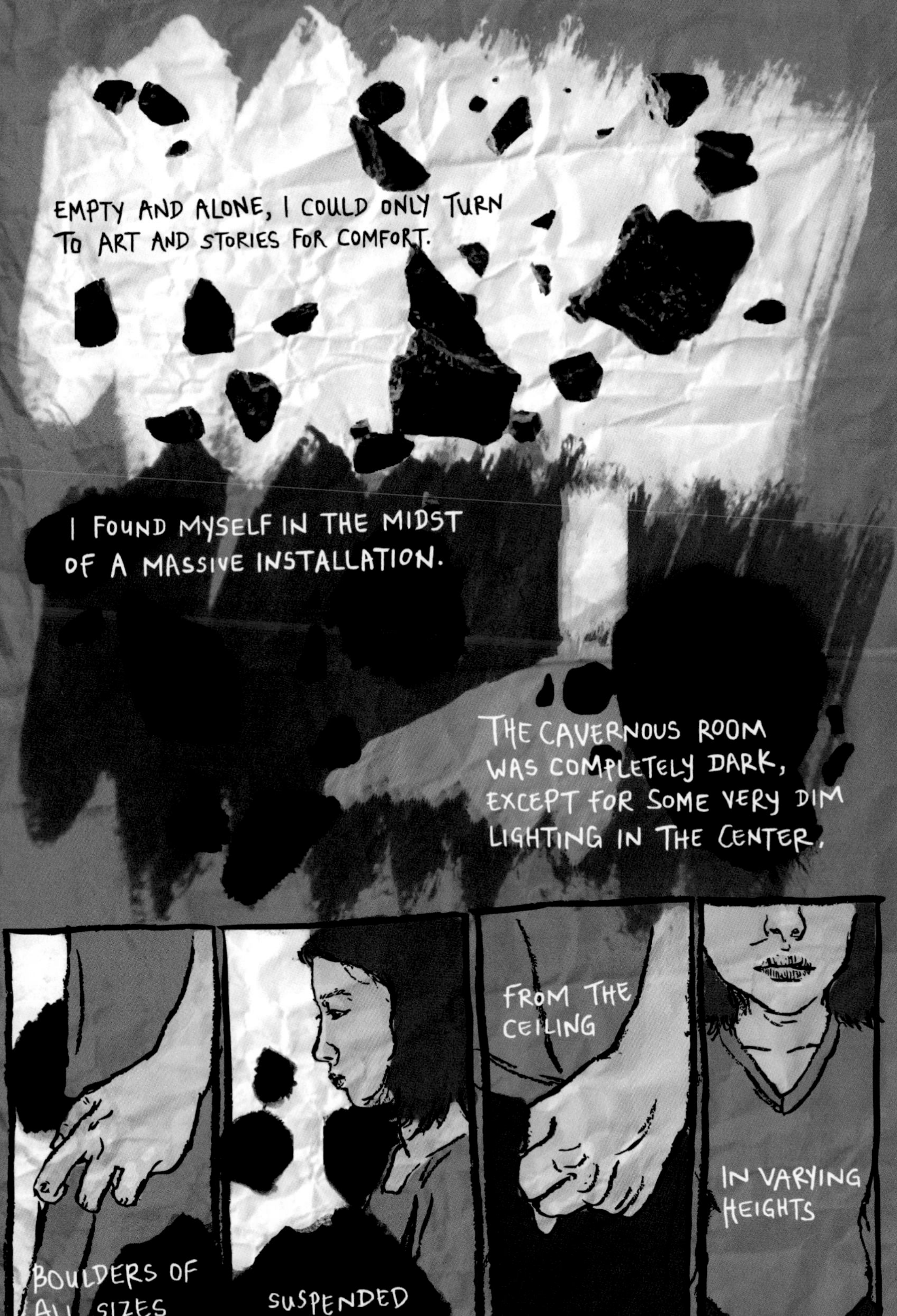
EMPTY AND ALONE, I COULD ONLY TURN TO ART AND STORIES FOR COMFORT.
I FOUND MYSELF IN THE MIDST OF A MASSIVE INSTALLATION.
THE CAVERNOUS ROOM WAS COMPLETELY DARK, EXCEPT FOR SOME VERY DIM LIGHTING IN THE CENTER.
BOULDERS OF ALL SIZES
SUSPENDED
FROM THE CEILING
IN VARYING HEIGHTS

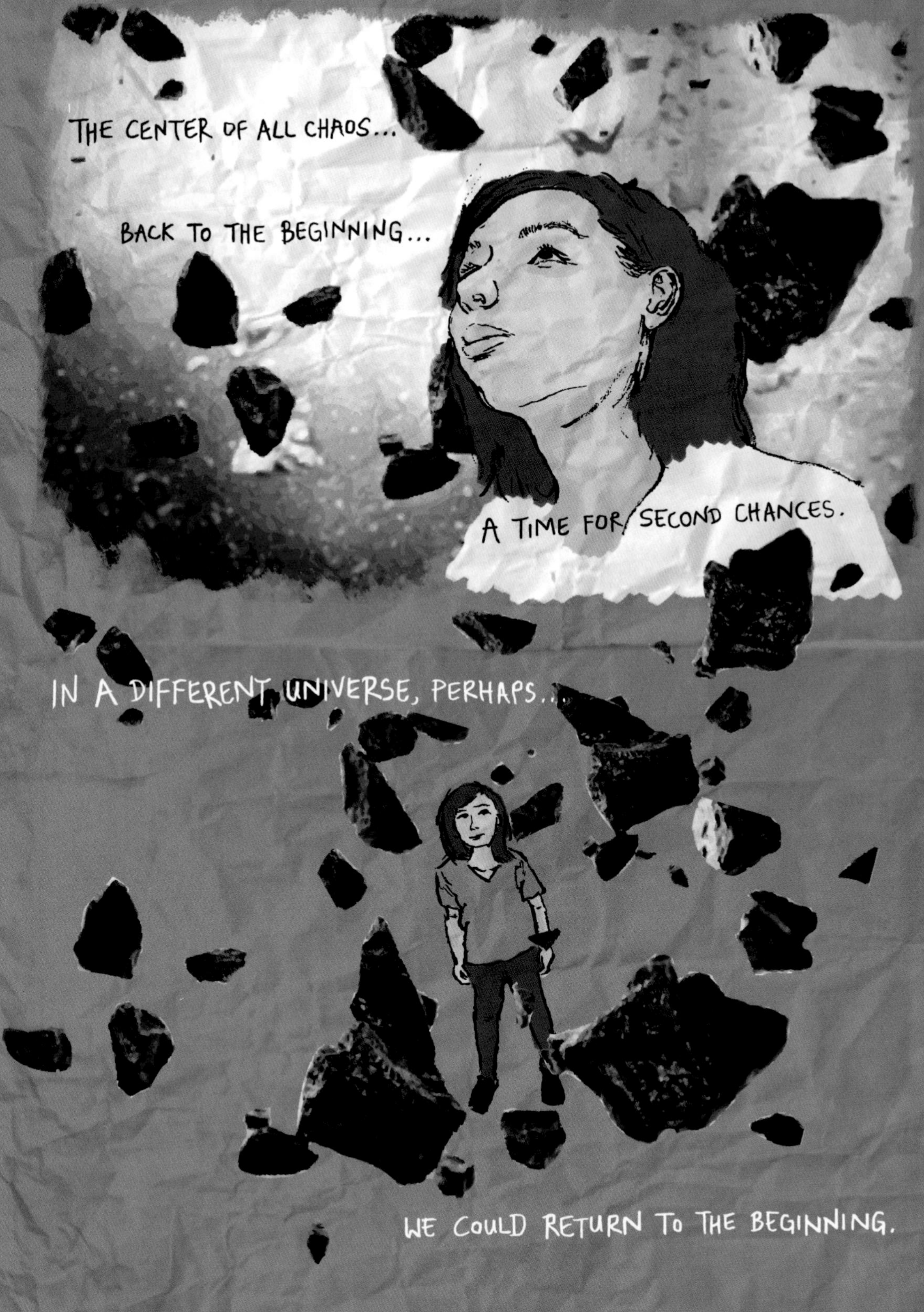
THE CENTER OF ALL CHAOS...
BACK TO THE BEGINNING...
A TIME FOR SECOND CHANCES.
IN A DIFFERENT UNIVERSE, PERHAPS...
WE COULD RETURN TO THE BEGINNING.

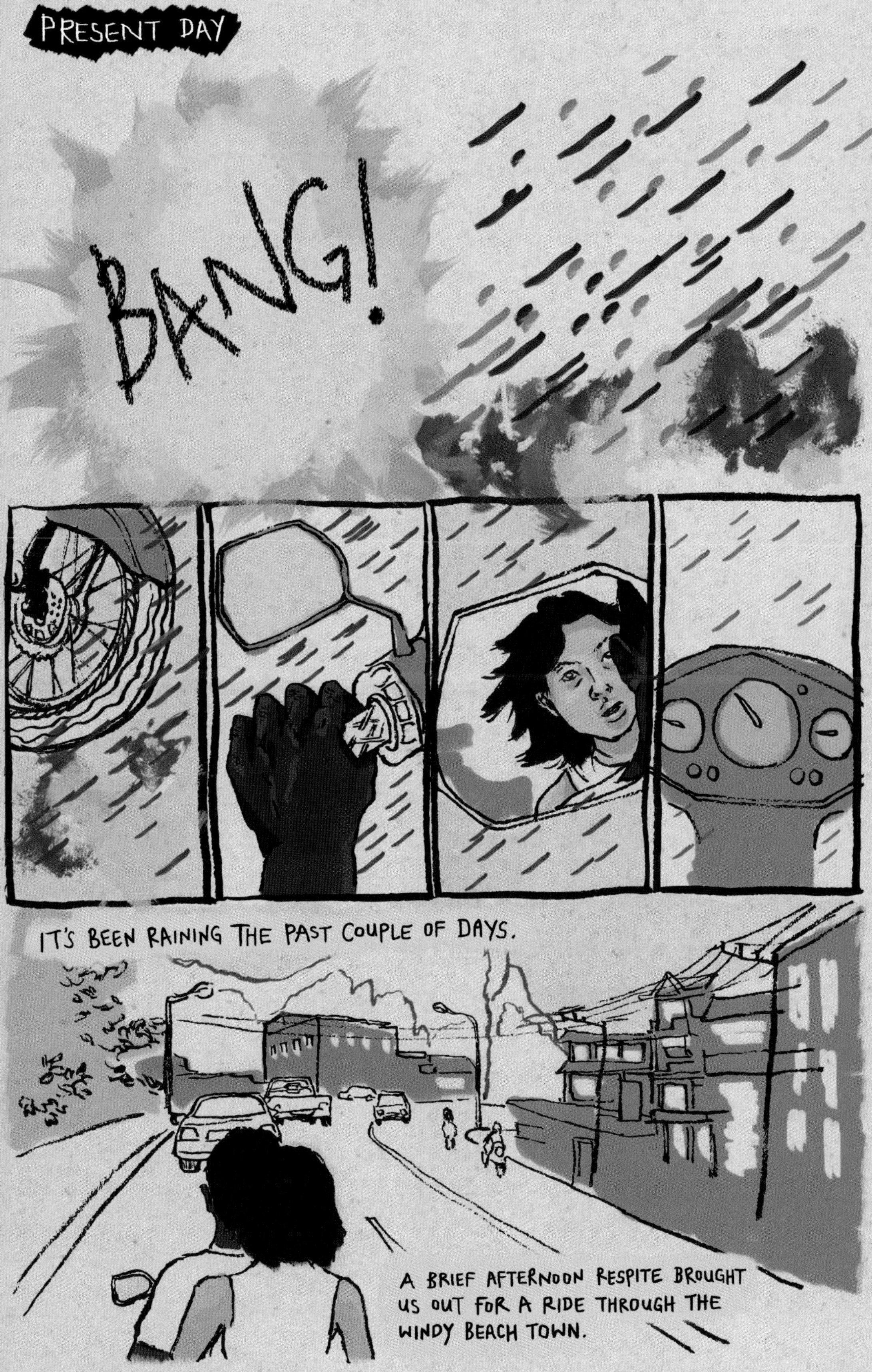
PRESENT DAY
BANG!
IT'S BEEN RAINING THE PAST COUPLE OF DAYS.
A BRIEF AFTERNOON RESPITE BROUGHT US OUT FOR A RIDE THROUGH THE WINDY BEACH TOWN.

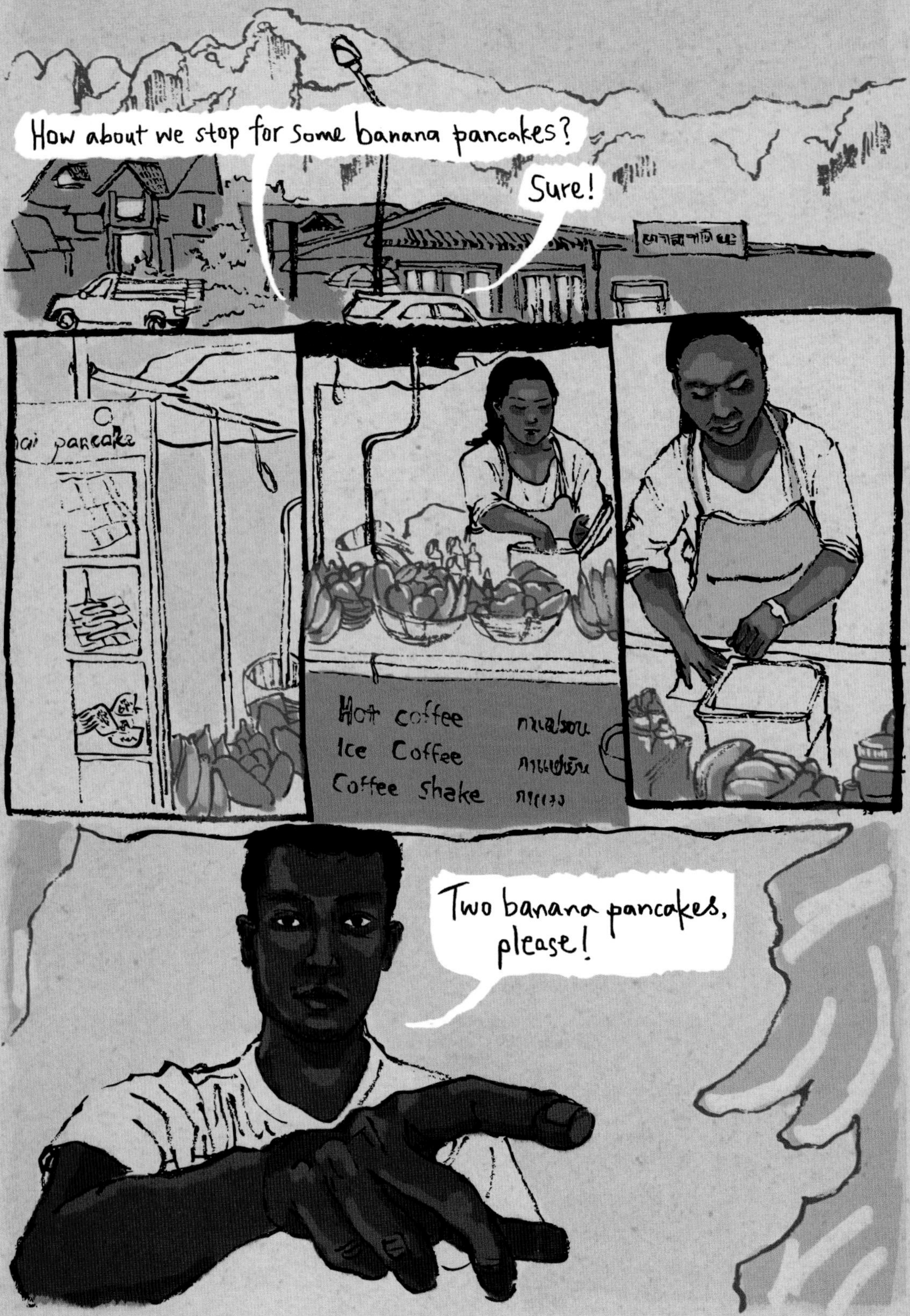

How about we stop for some banana pancakes?
Sure!
Hot coffee
Ice Coffee
Coffee shake
Two banana pancakes, please!

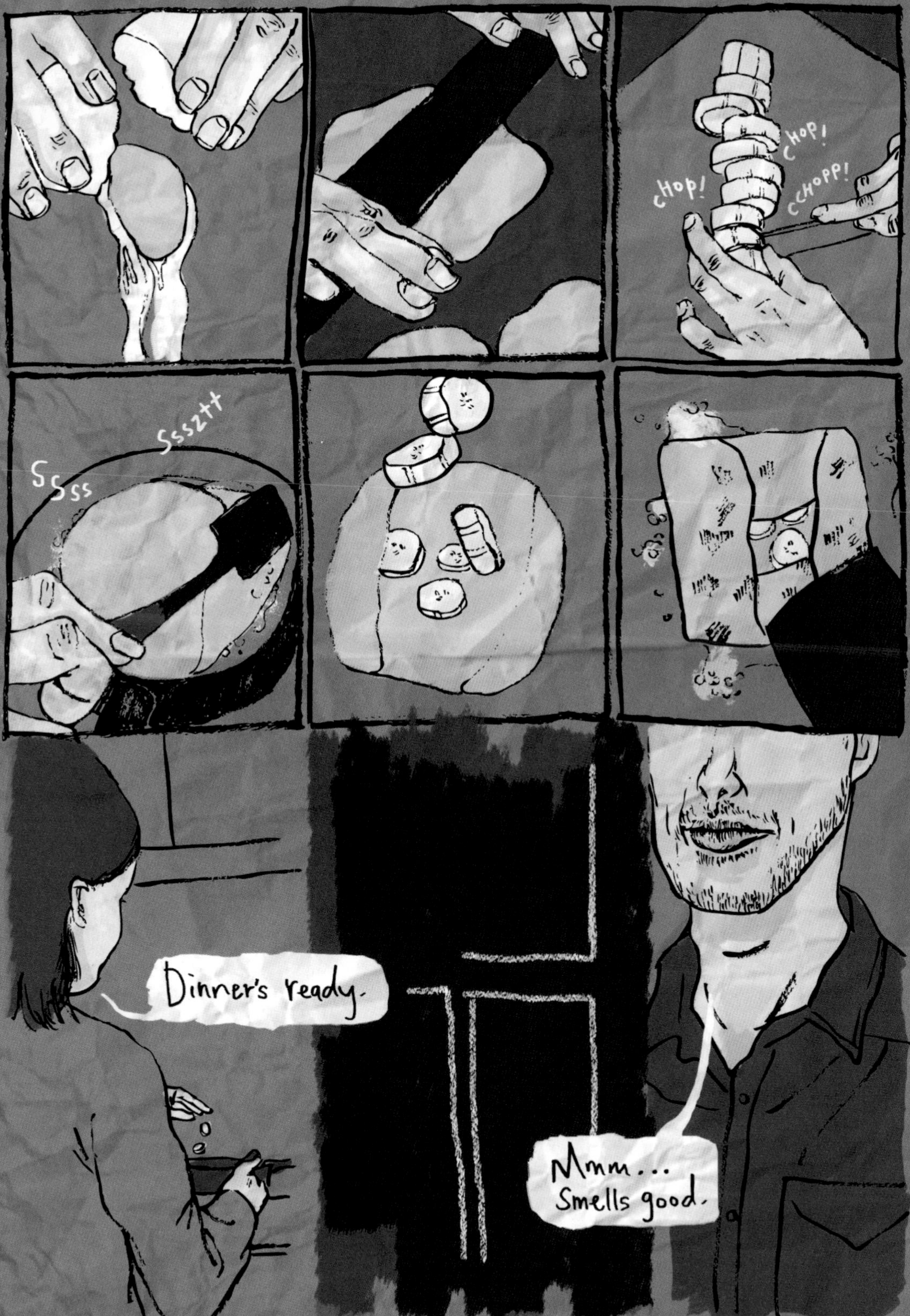
CHOP!
CHOP!
CCHOPP!
SSss
Sssztt
Dinner's ready.
Mmm...
Smells good.

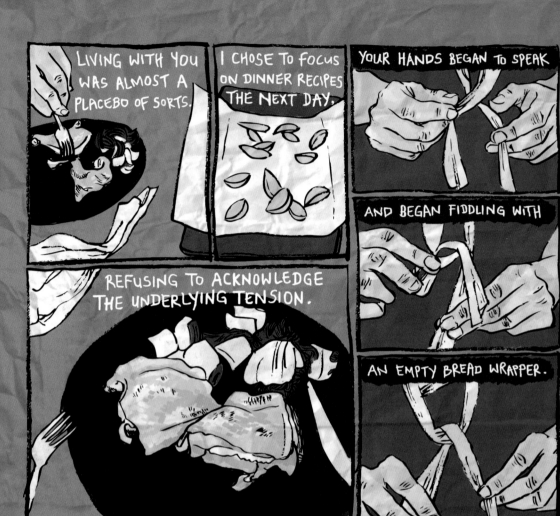

LIVING WITH YOU WAS ALMOST A PLACEBO OF SORTS.

I CHOSE TO FOCUS ON DINNER RECIPES THE NEXT DAY.

YOUR HANDS BEGAN TO SPEAK

AND BEGAN FIDDLING WITH

REFUSING TO ACKNOWLEDGE THE UNDERLYING TENSION.

AN EMPTY BREAD WRAPPER.

Would you like this ring?

I WAS SILENT.

YOU NEVER BELIEVED IN SECOND CHANCES.

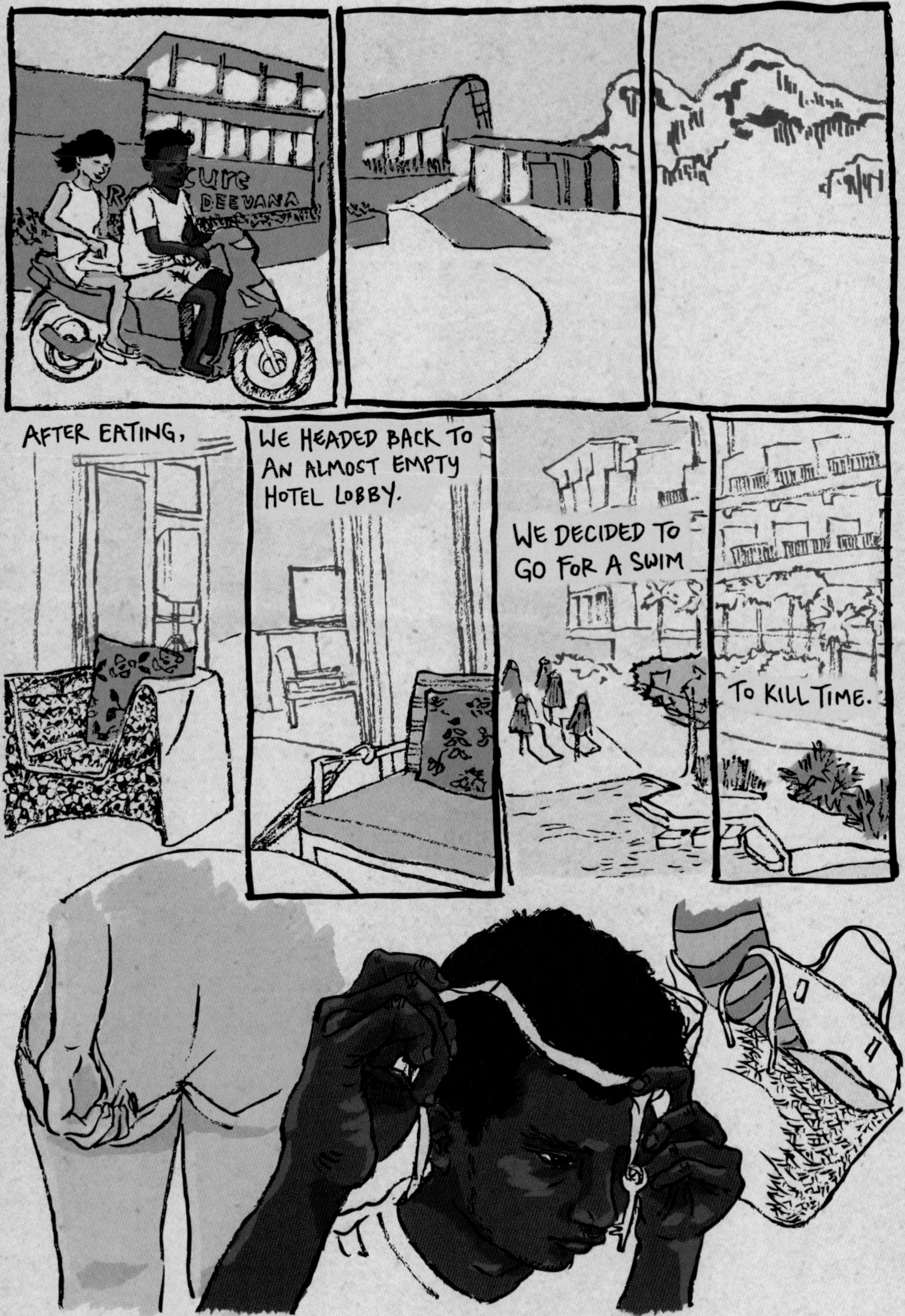
DEEVANA
AFTER EATING,
WE HEADED BACK TO AN ALMOST EMPTY HOTEL LOBBY.
WE DECIDED TO GO FOR A SWIM
TO KILL TIME.

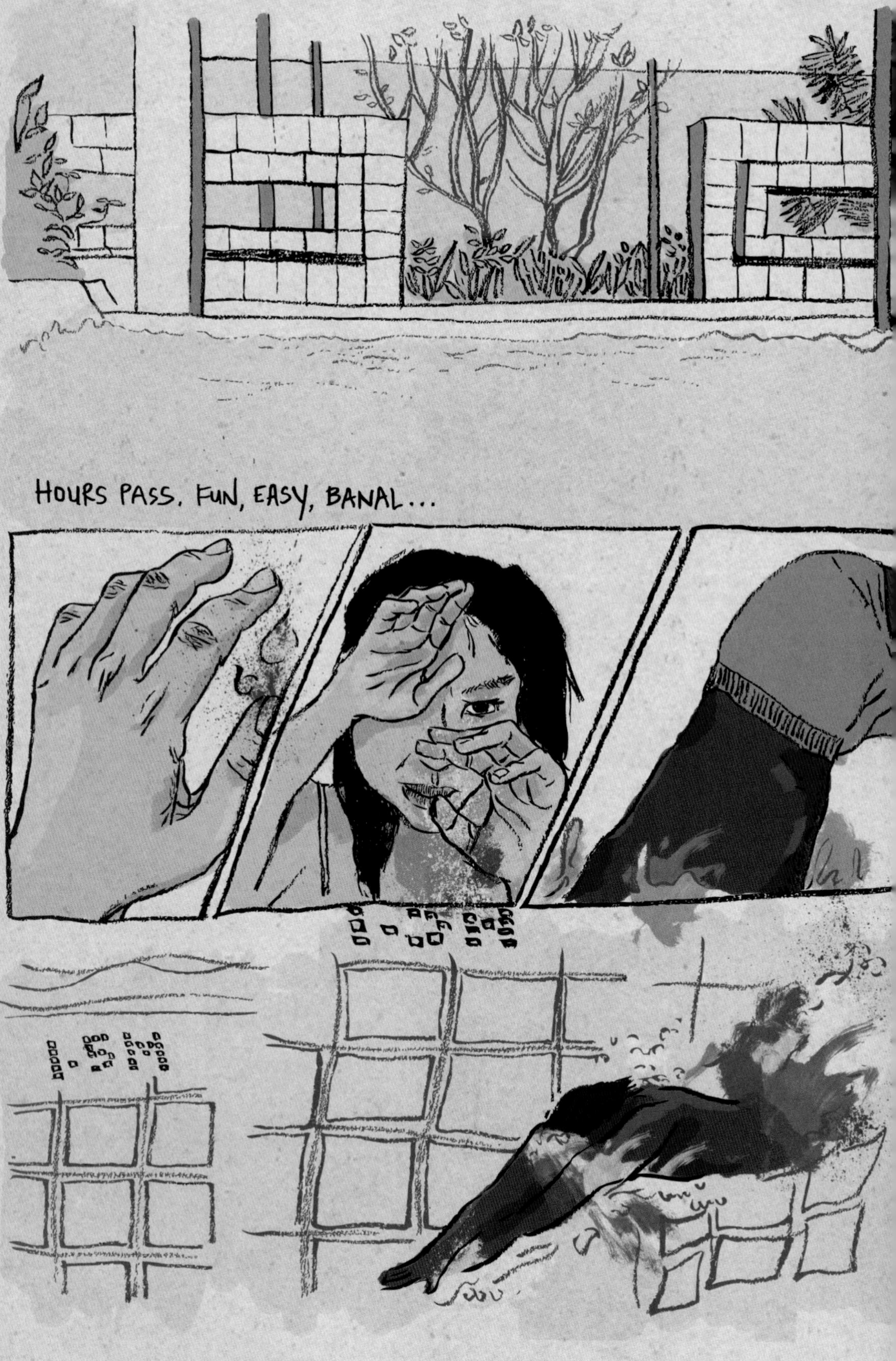
HOURS PASS. FUN, EASY, BANAL...

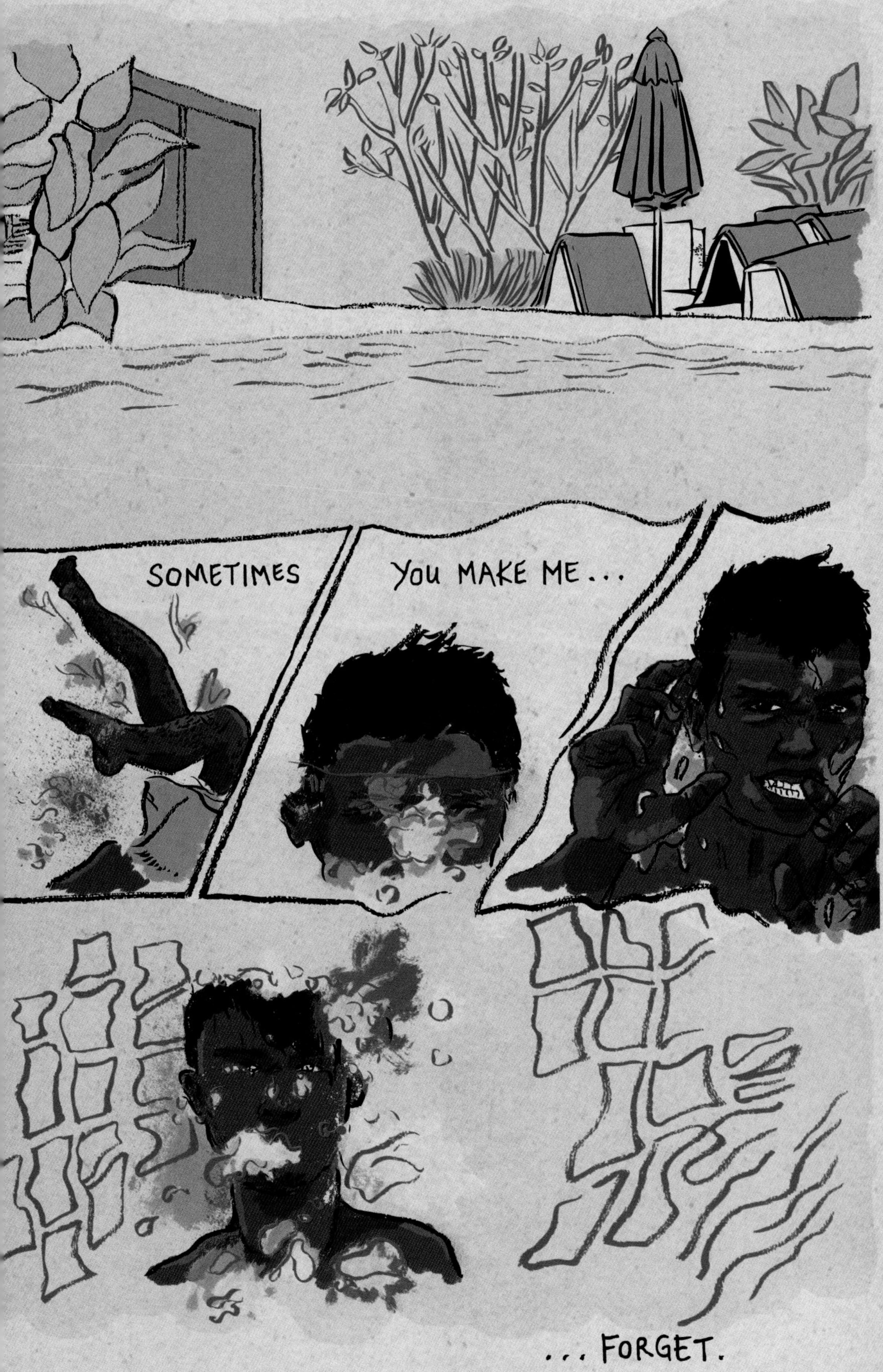
SOMETIMES
YOU MAKE ME...
...FORGET.

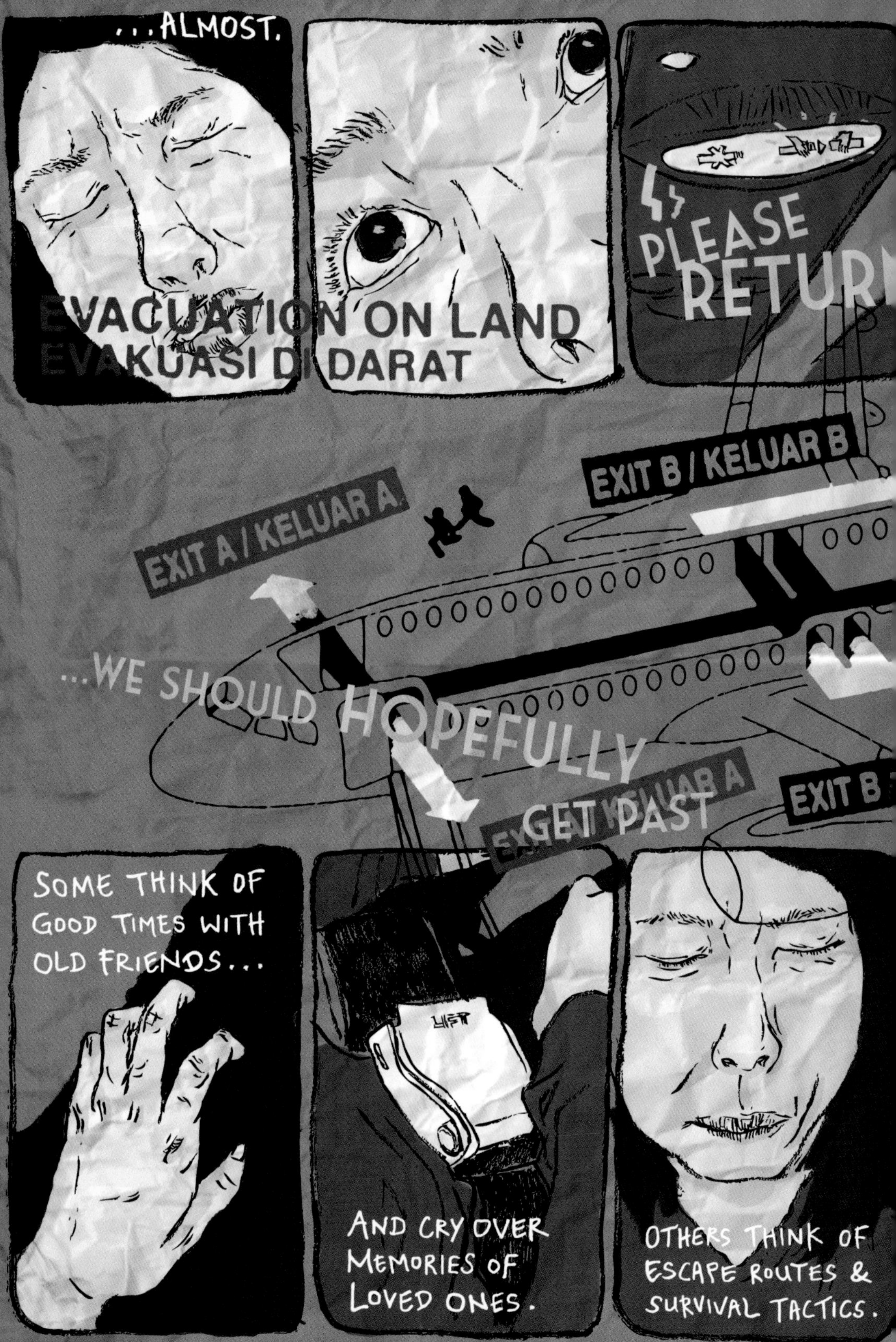
...ALMOST.
EVACUATION ON LAND
EVAKUASI DI DARAT
PLEASE RETURN
EXIT B / KELUAR B
EXIT A / KELUAR A.
...WE SHOULD HOPEFULLY
GET PAST
EXIT B
SOME THINK OF GOOD TIMES WITH OLD FRIENDS...
AND CRY OVER MEMORIES OF LOVED ONES.
OTHERS THINK OF ESCAPE ROUTES & SURVIVAL TACTICS.

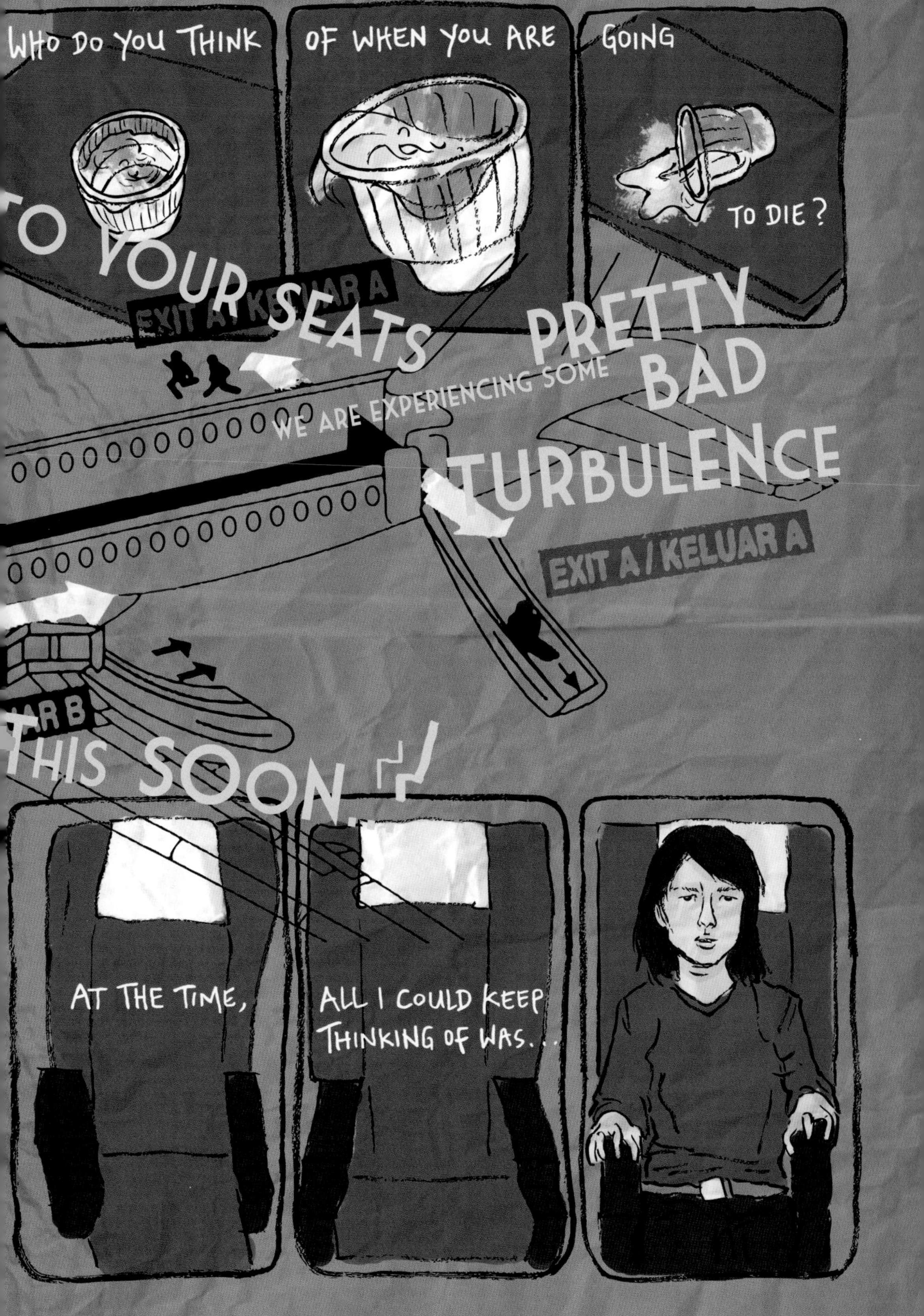
WHO DO YOU THINK
OF WHEN YOU ARE
GOING
TO DIE?
TO YOUR SEATS
EXIT A / KELUAR A
PRETTY
WE ARE EXPERIENCING SOME
BAD
TURBULENCE
EXIT A / KELUAR A
THIS SOON.
AT THE TIME,
ALL I COULD KEEP THINKING OF WAS...

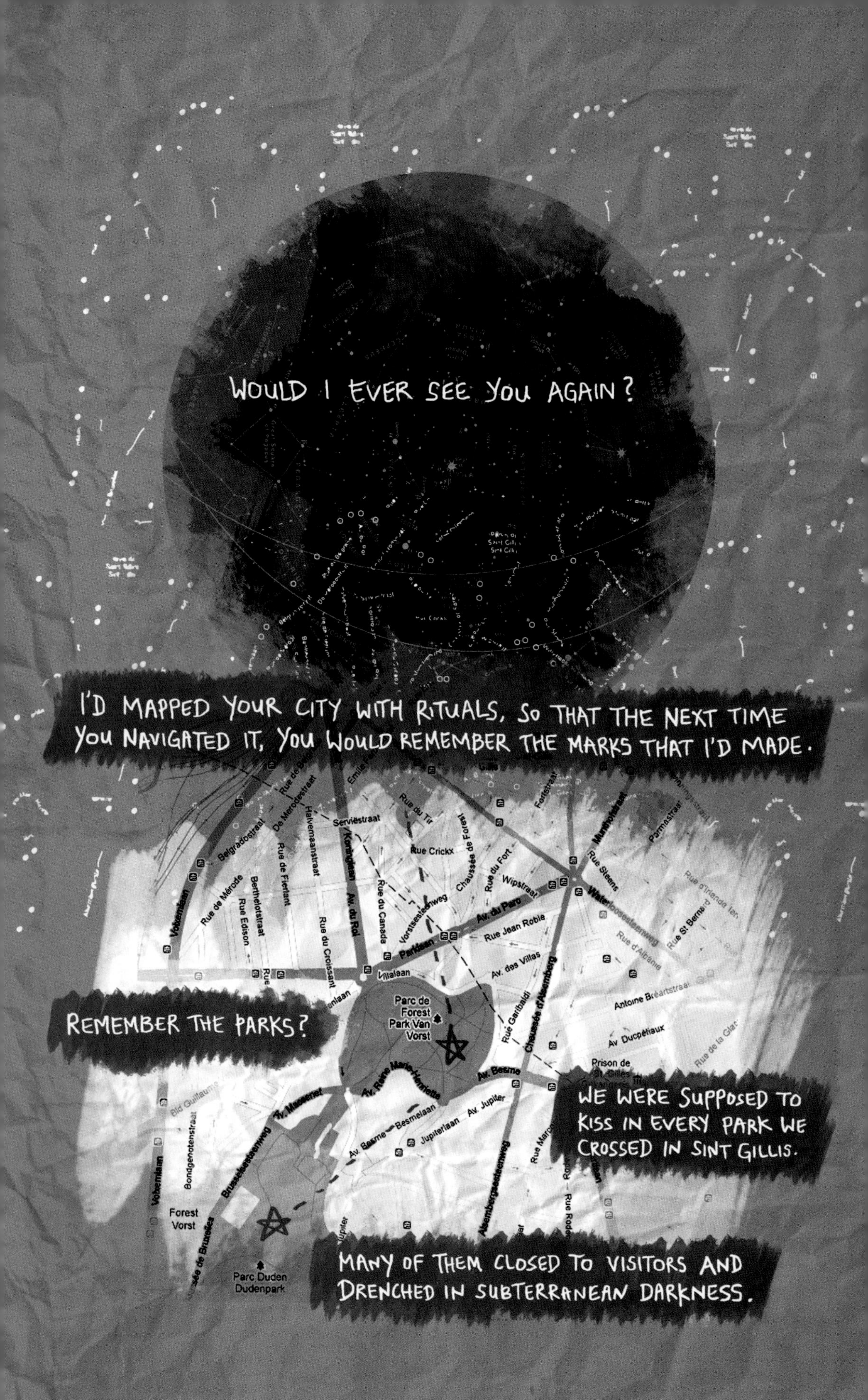
WOULD I EVER SEE YOU AGAIN?
I'D MAPPED YOUR CITY WITH RITUALS, SO THAT THE NEXT TIME YOU NAVIGATED IT, YOU WOULD REMEMBER THE MARKS THAT I'D MADE.
REMEMBER THE PARKS?
WE WERE SUPPOSED TO KISS IN EVERY PARK WE CROSSED IN SINT GILLIS.
MANY OF THEM CLOSED TO VISITORS AND DRENCHED IN SUBTERRANEAN DARKNESS.
Parc de Forest Park Van Vorst
Forest Vorst
Parc Duden Dudenpark
Av. du Roi
Av. du Parc
Av. Besme
Av. Jupiter
Rue du Canada
Rue du Croissant
Rue Crickx
Chaussée de Forest
Rue Jean Robie
Av. des Villas
Antoine Bréartstraat
Av. Ducpétiaux
Belgradostraat
Rue de Mérode
Rue Edison
Wipstraat
Rue Steens
Serviëstraat

WE FOUND A PEAK

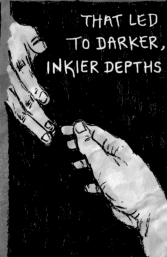

THAT LED TO DARKER, INKIER DEPTHS

BENEATH FAINT TREETOPS & CITY LIGHTS

WE KISSED

AND HELD HANDS

AND NOW THE CITY RAVAGES ME WITH A MAZE OF RITUALS

THAT COULD NEVER BE COMPLETED...

...WITHOUT YOU.

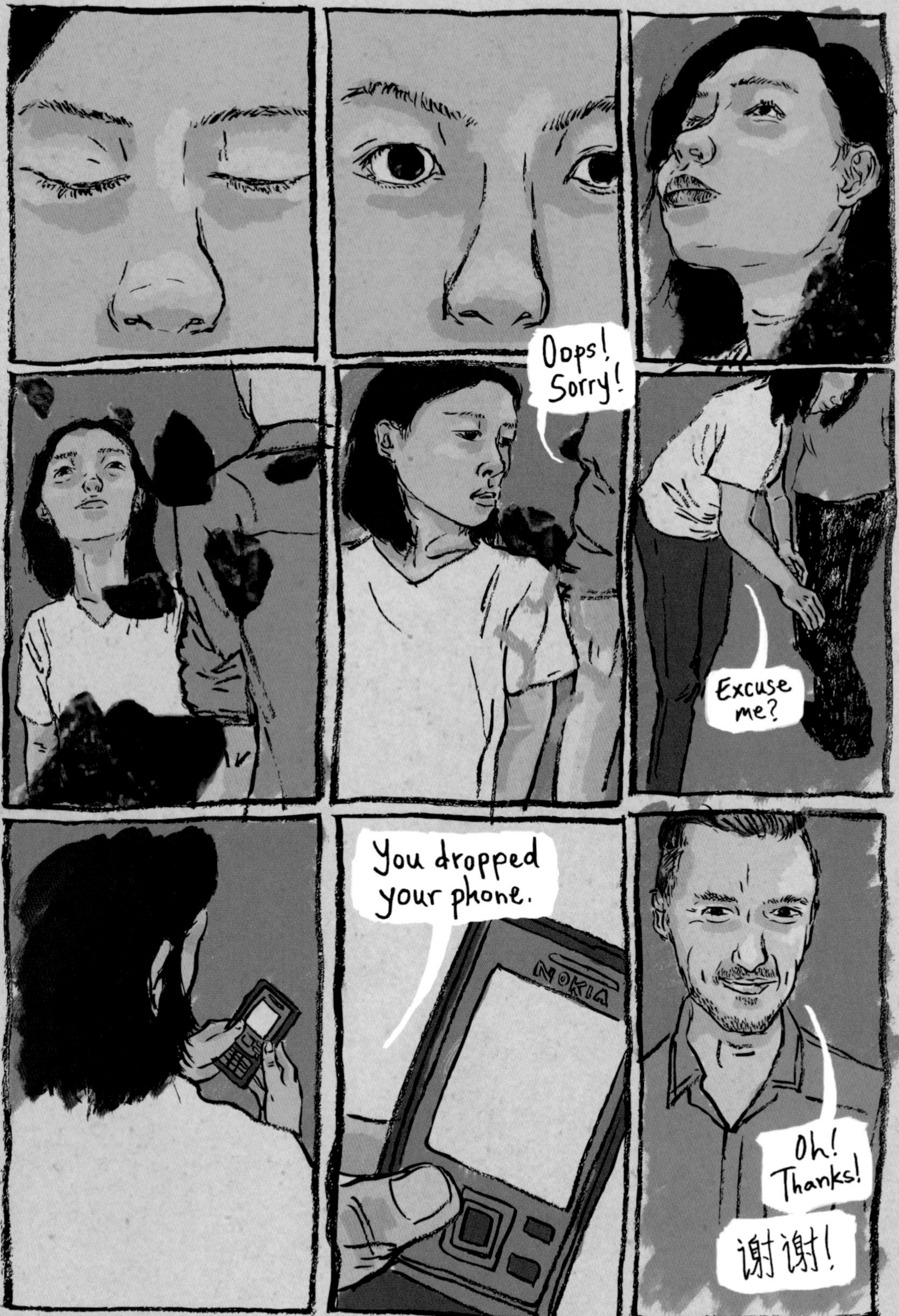
Oops! Sorry!
Excuse me?
You dropped your phone.
NOKIA
Oh! Thanks!
谢谢!

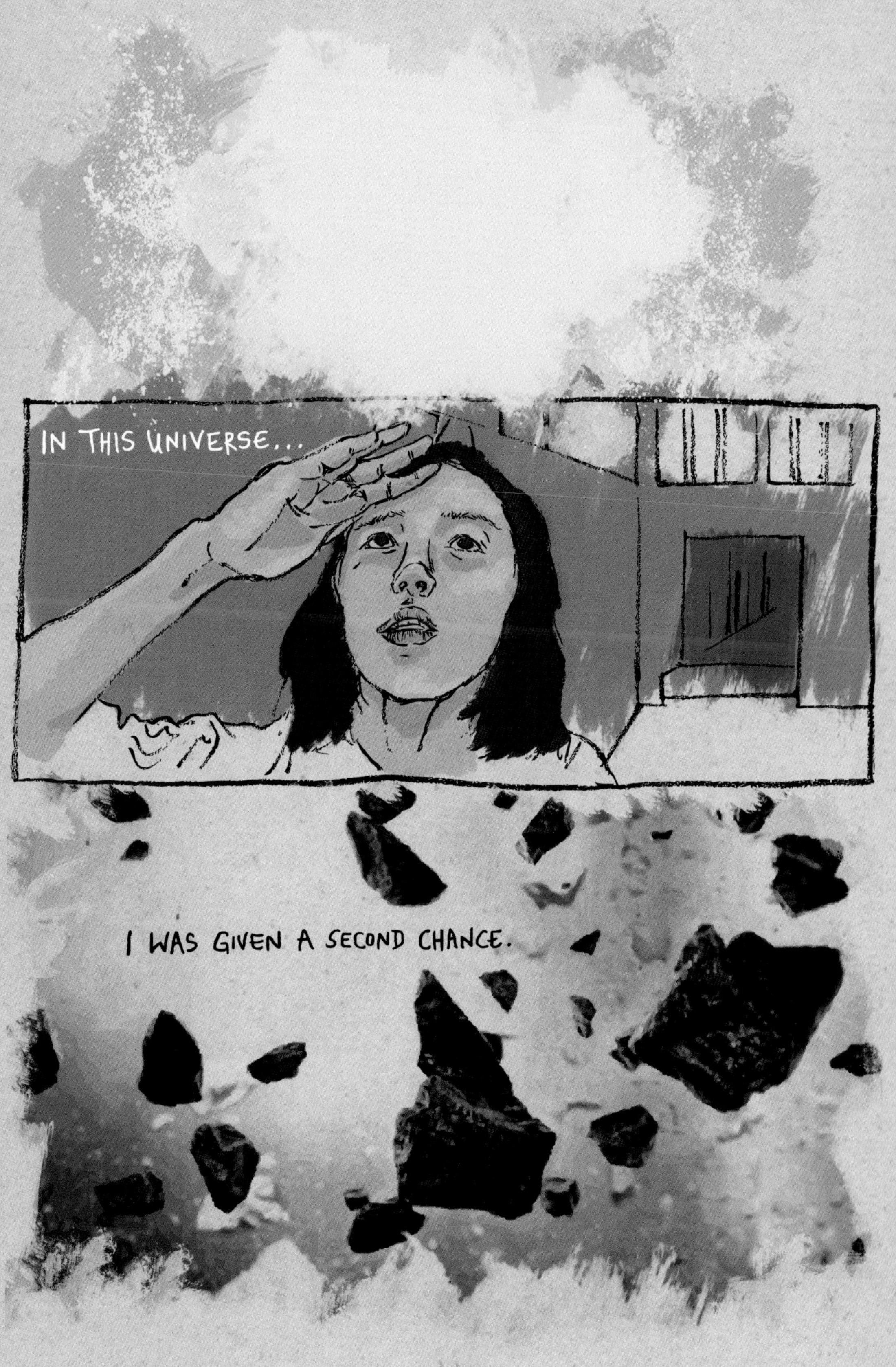
IN THIS UNIVERSE...
I WAS GIVEN A SECOND CHANCE.

nothing to lose

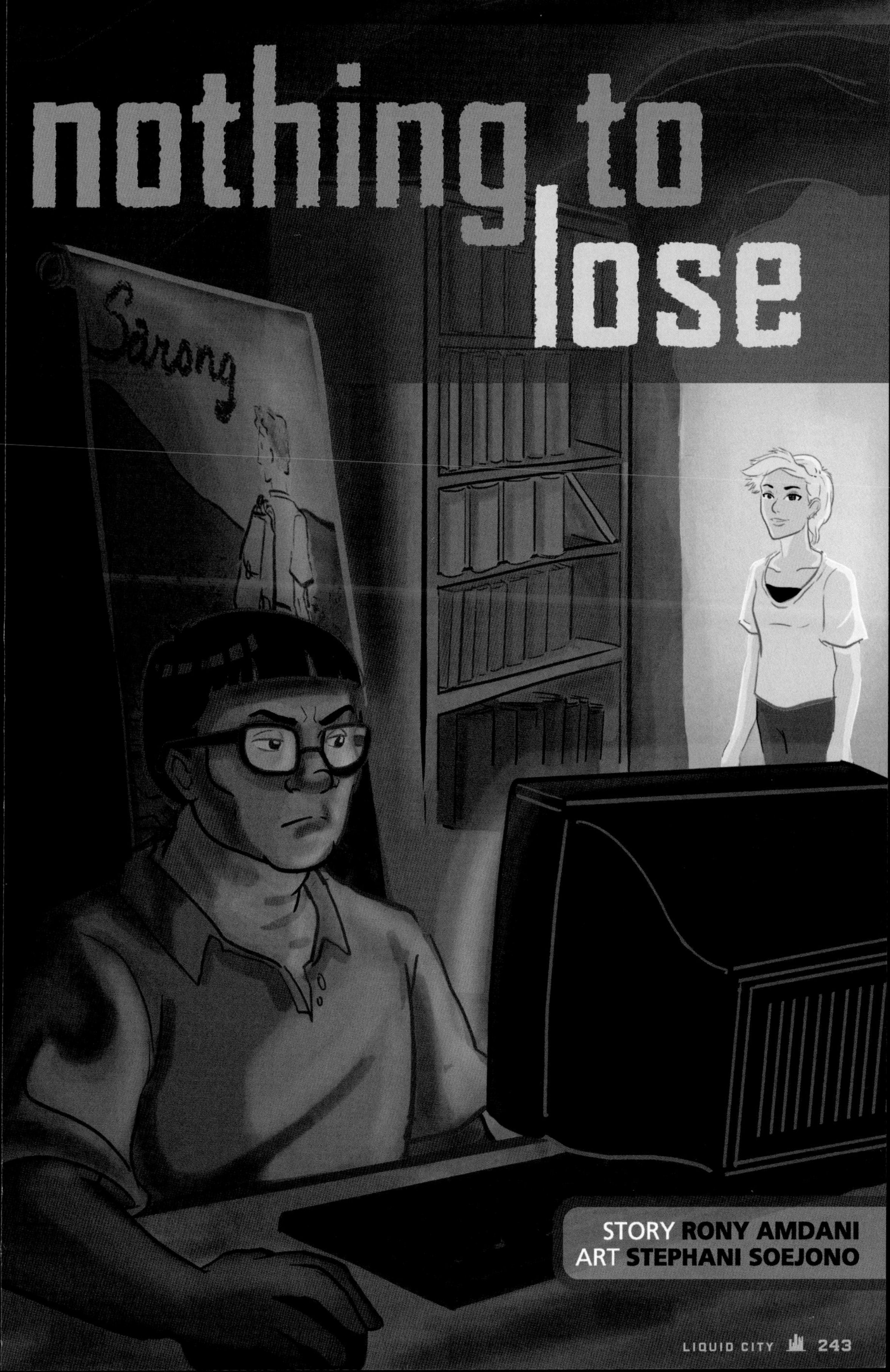
Sarong

STORY **RONY AMDANI**
ART **STEPHANI SOEJONO**

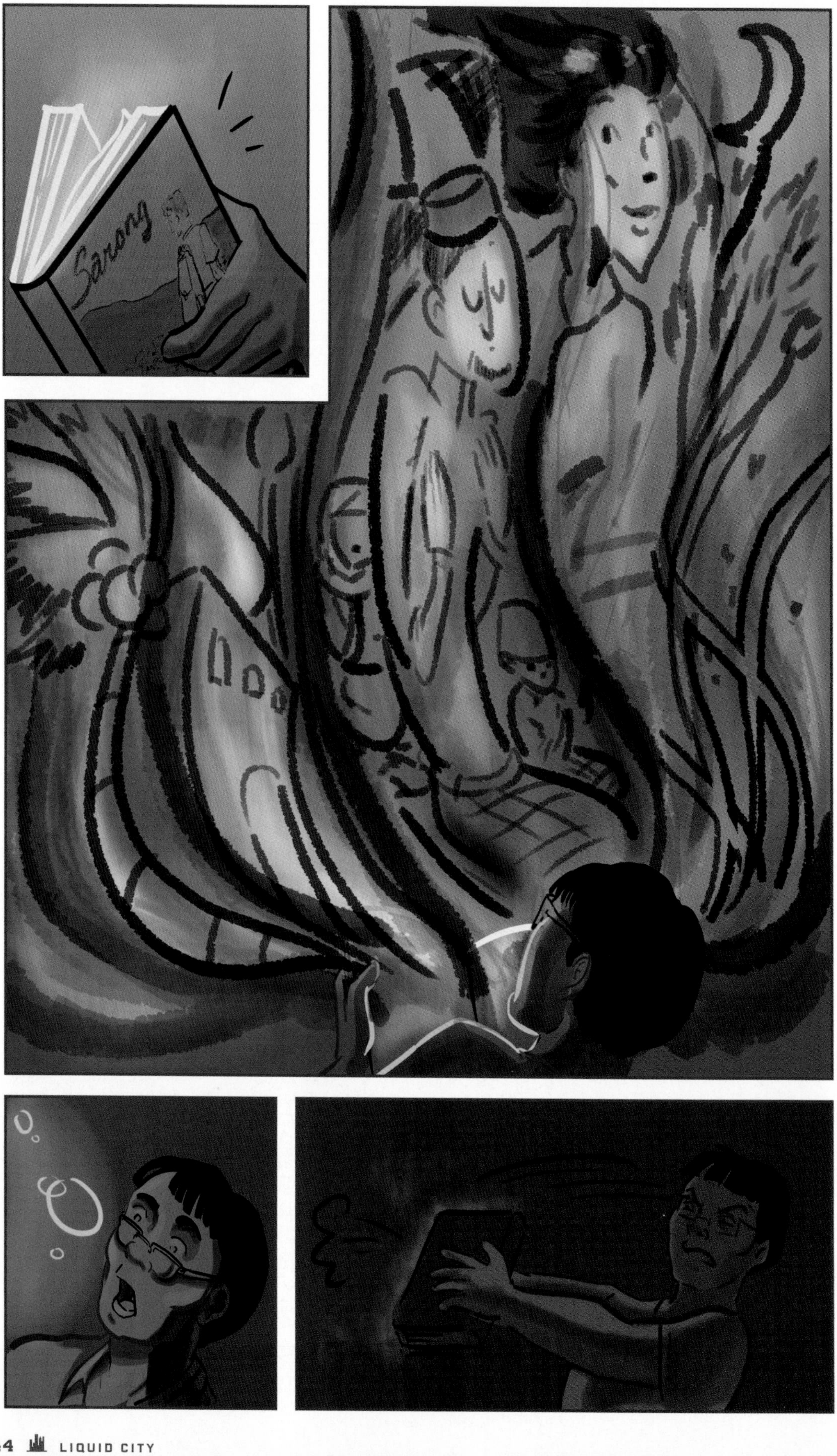
Sarong

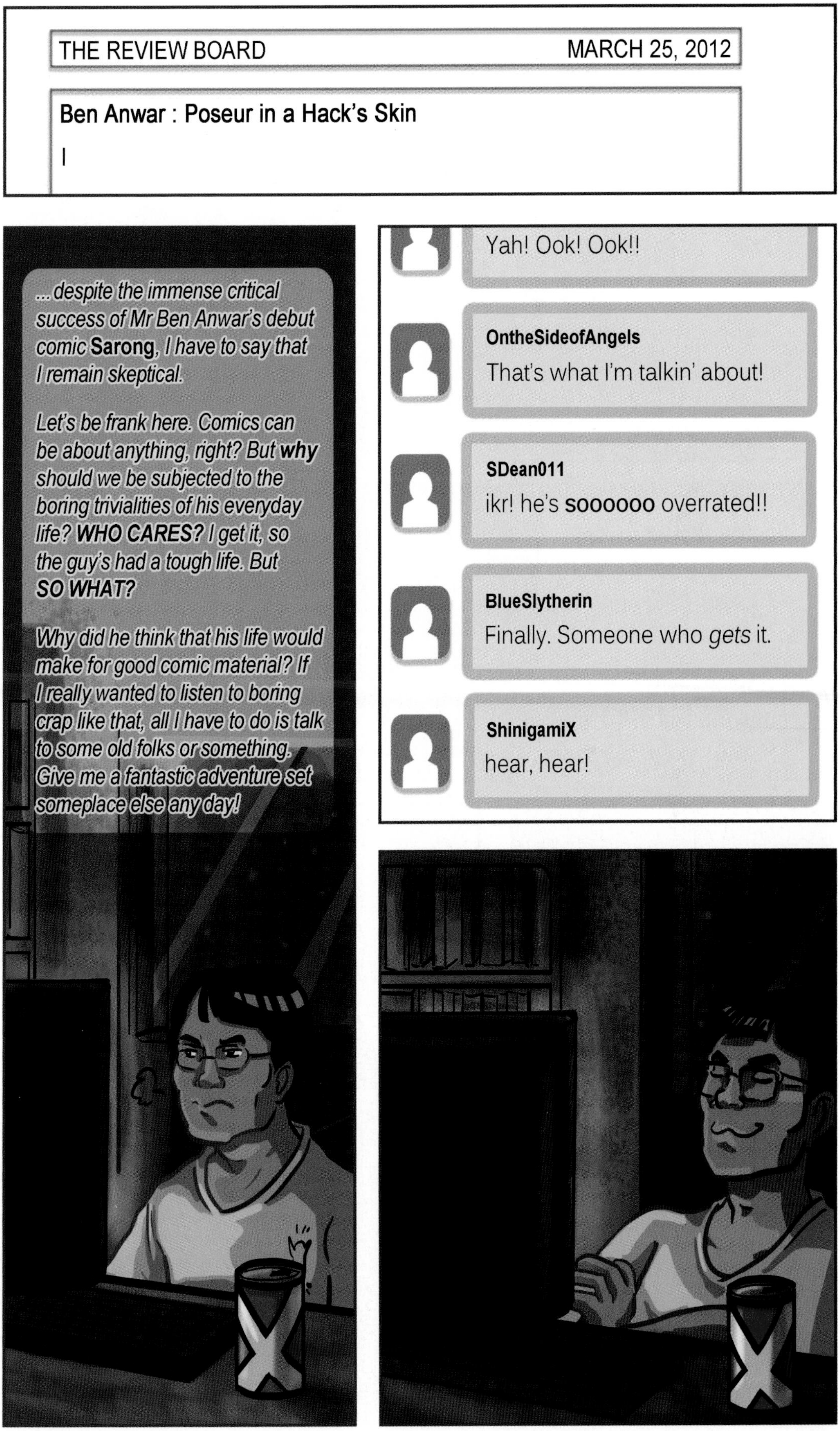

Ben Anwar : Poseur in a Hack's Skin

I

... despite the immense critical success of Mr Ben Anwar's debut comic **Sarong***, I have to say that I remain skeptical.*

Let's be frank here. Comics can be about anything, right? But **why** *should we be subjected to the boring trivialities of his everyday life?* **WHO CARES?** *I get it, so the guy's had a tough life. But* **SO WHAT?**

Why did he think that his life would make for good comic material? If I really wanted to listen to boring crap like that, all I have to do is talk to some old folks or something. Give me a fantastic adventure set someplace else any day!

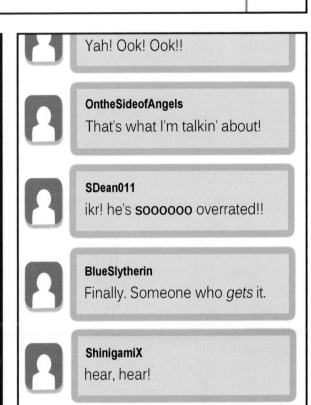

Yah! Ook! Ook!!

OntheSideofAngels
That's what I'm talkin' about!

SDean011
ikr! he's **soooooo** overrated!!

BlueSlytherin
Finally. Someone who *gets* it.

ShinigamiX
hear, hear!

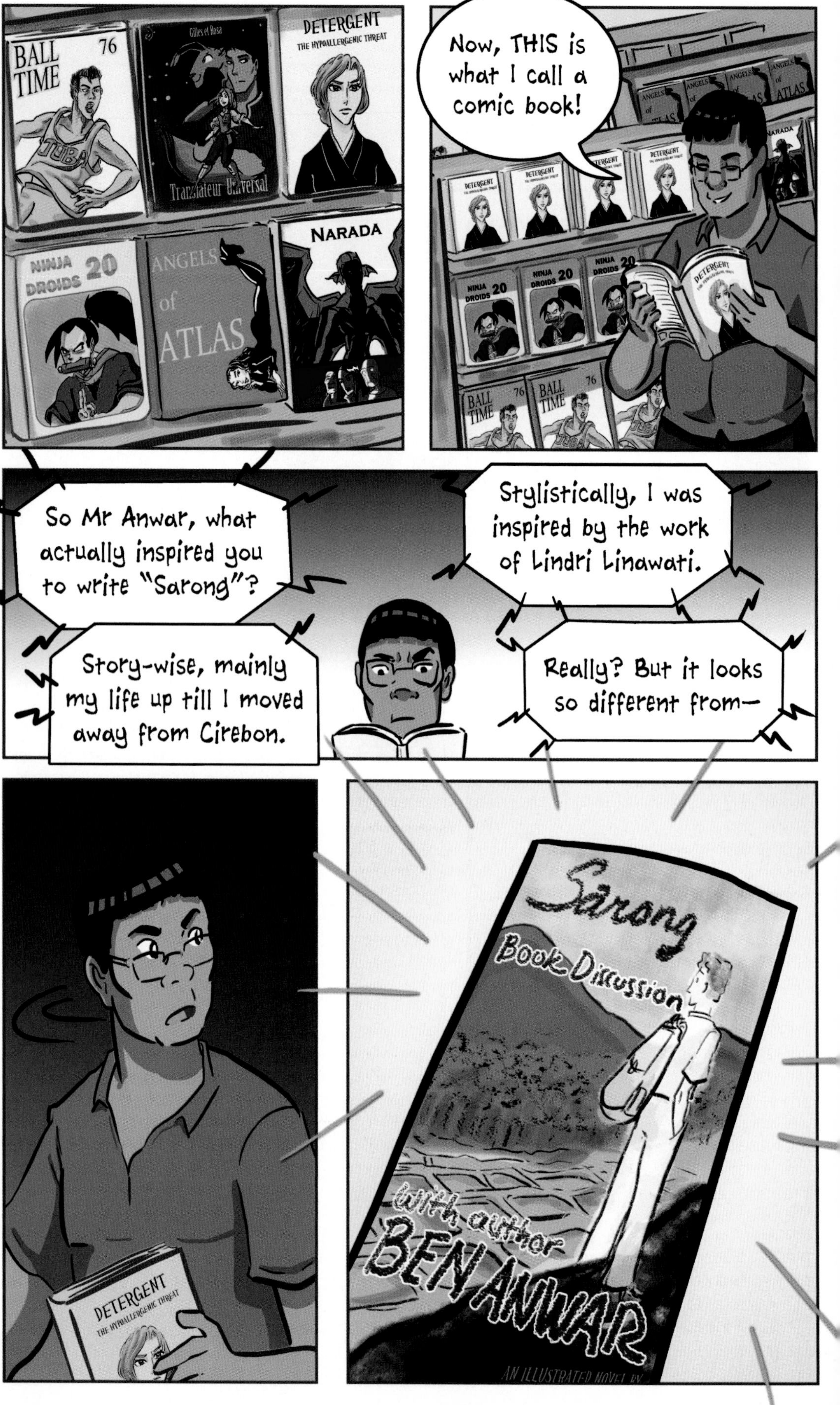
BALL TIME 76
Gilles et Rosa
Tranzlateur Universal
DETERGENT
THE HYPOALLERGENIC THREAT
NINJA DROIDS 20
ANGELS of ATLAS
NARADA
Now, THIS is what I call a comic book!
So Mr Anwar, what actually inspired you to write "Sarong"?
Story-wise, mainly my life up till I moved away from Cirebon.
Stylistically, I was inspired by the work of Lindri Linawati.
Really? But it looks so different from—
DETERGENT
THE HYPOALLERGENIC THREAT
Sarong
Book Discussion
with author
BEN ANWAR
AN ILLUSTRATED NOVEL BY

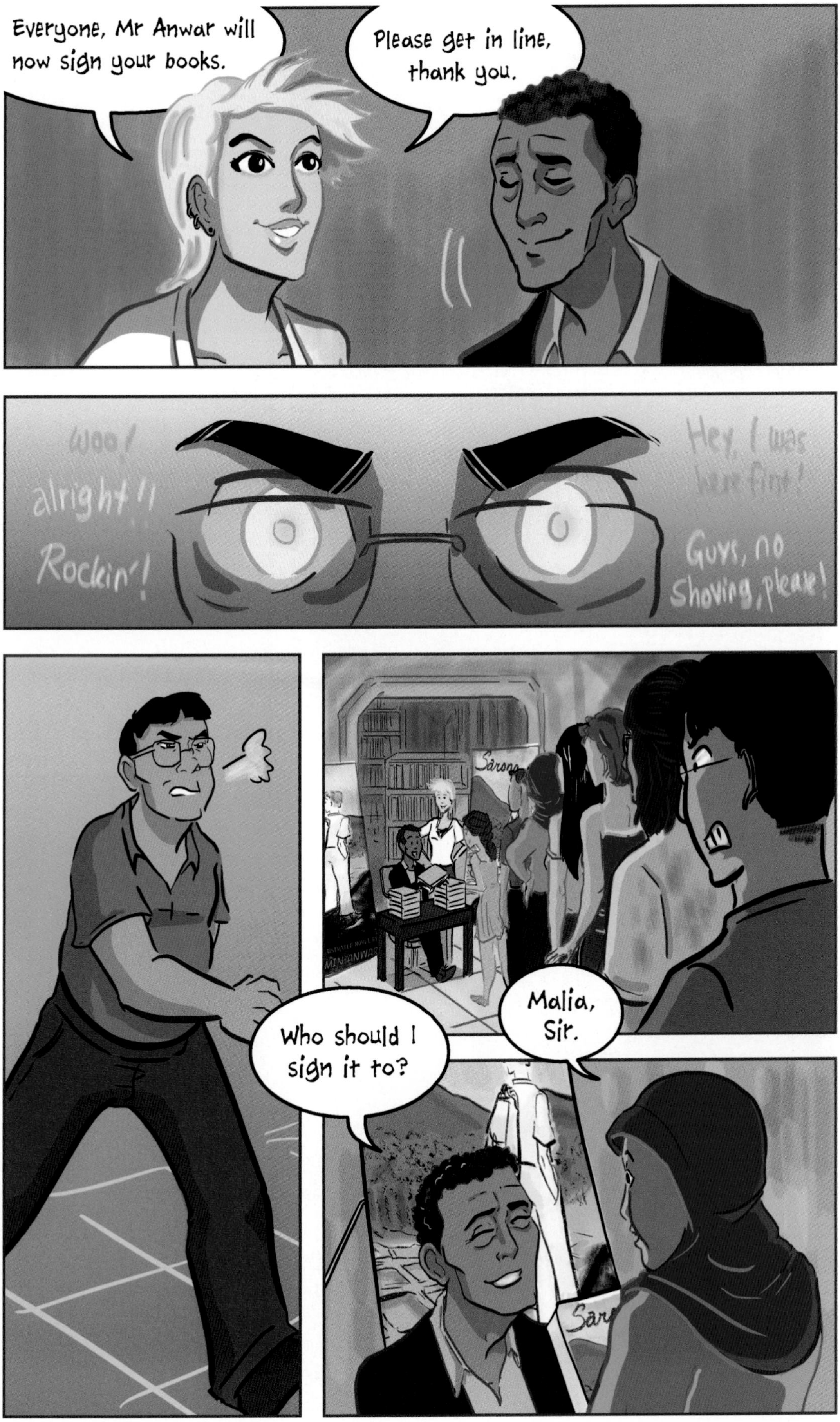
Everyone, Mr Anwar will now sign your books.
Please get in line, thank you.
woo!
alright!!
Rockin'!
Hey, I was here first!
Guys, no shoving, please!
Sarona
Who should I sign it to?
Malia, Sir.

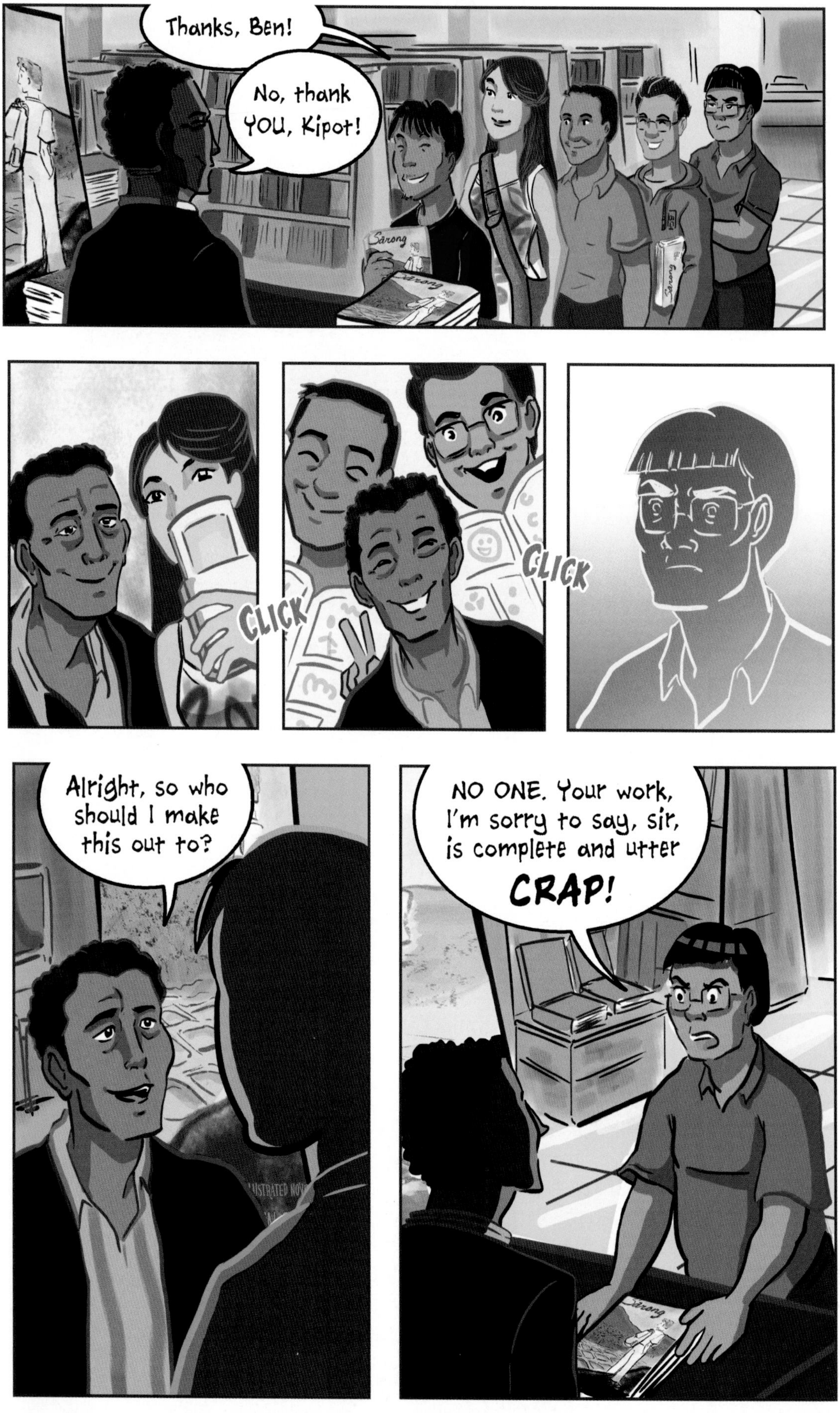

Thanks, Ben!
No, thank YOU, Kipot!
Sarong
CLICK
CLICK
Alright, so who should I make this out to?
NO ONE. Your work, I'm sorry to say, sir, is complete and utter CRAP!

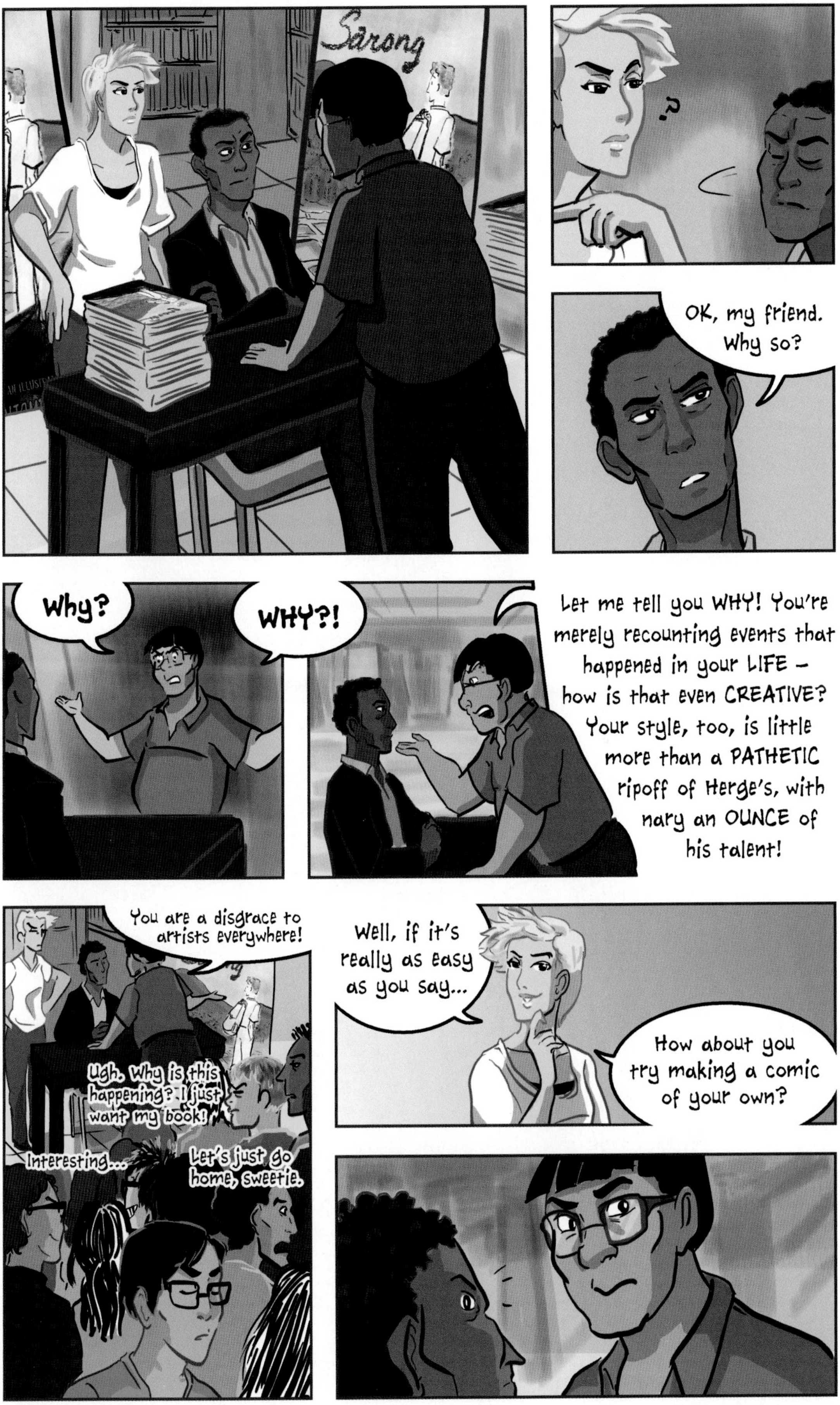
Sarong
OK, my friend.
Why so?
Why?
WHY?!
Let me tell you WHY! You're merely recounting events that happened in your LIFE – how is that even CREATIVE? Your style, too, is little more than a PATHETIC ripoff of Herge's, with nary an OUNCE of his talent!
You are a disgrace to artists everywhere!
Ugh. Why is this happening? I just want my book!
Interesting...
Let's just go home, sweetie.
Well, if it's really as easy as you say...
How about you try making a comic of your own?

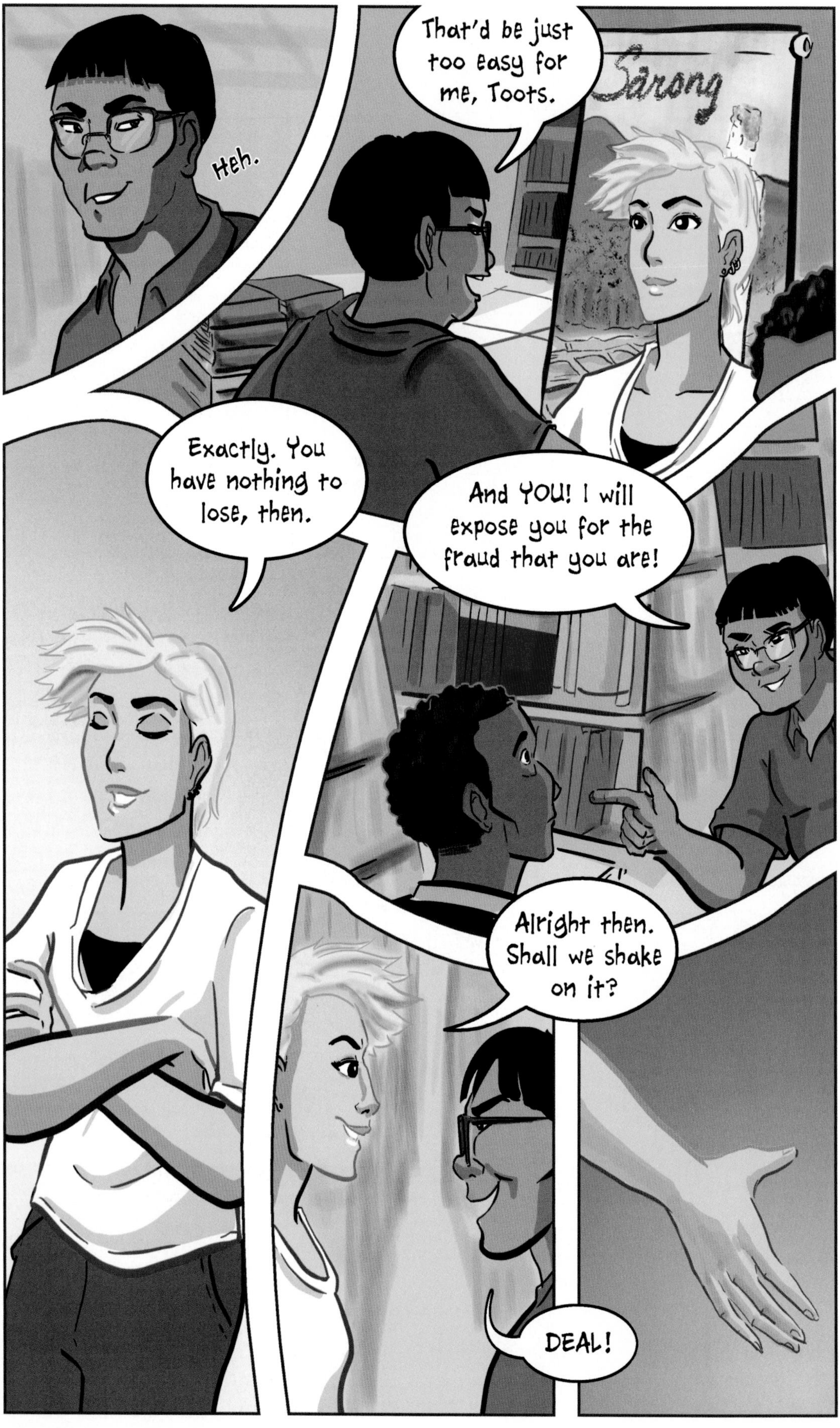
Heh.
That'd be just too easy for me, Toots.
Sarong
Exactly. You have nothing to lose, then.
And YOU! I will expose you for the fraud that you are!
Alright then. Shall we shake on it?
DEAL!

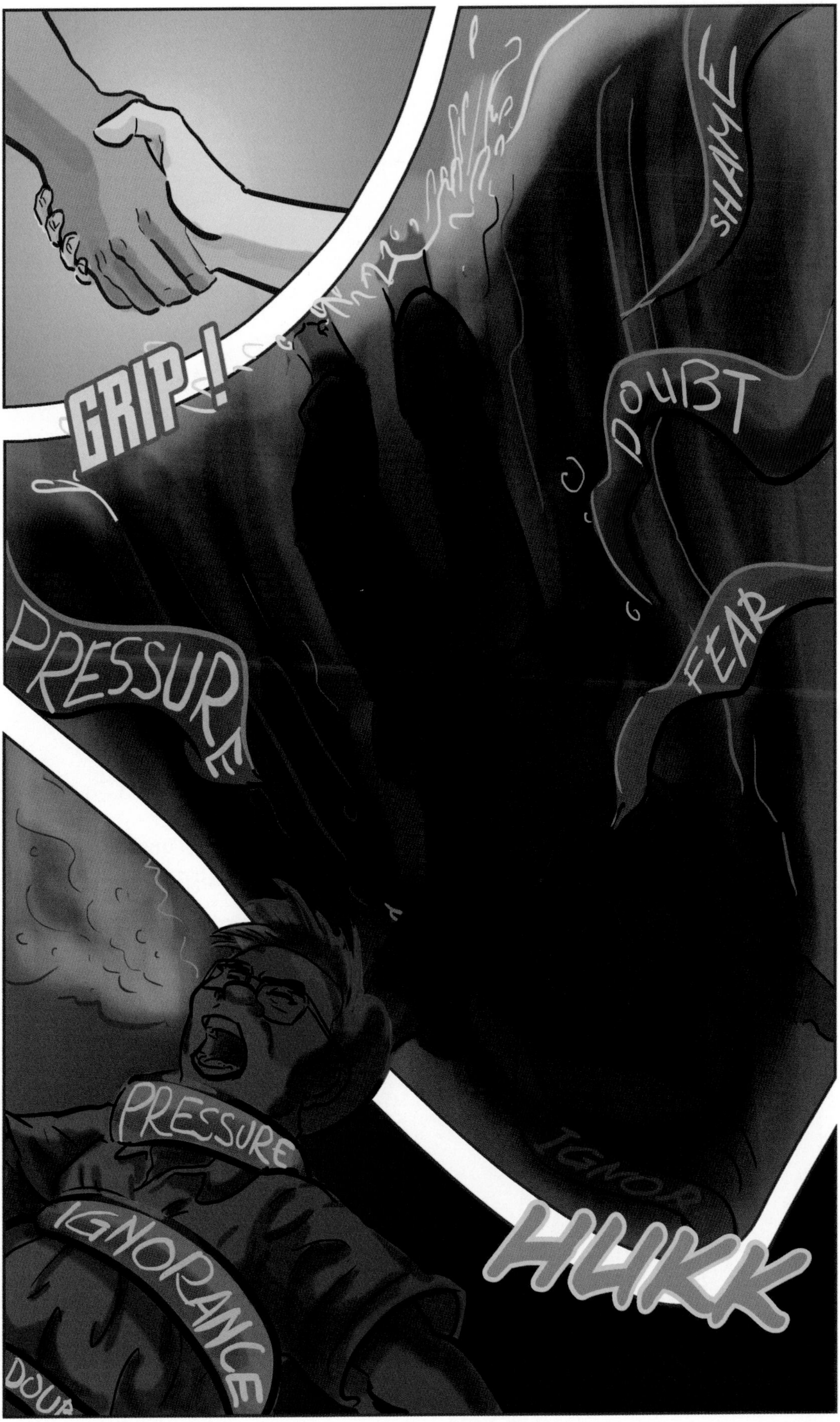
GRIP!
SHAME
DOUBT
PRESSURE
FEAR
PRESSURE
IGNORANCE
HUKK

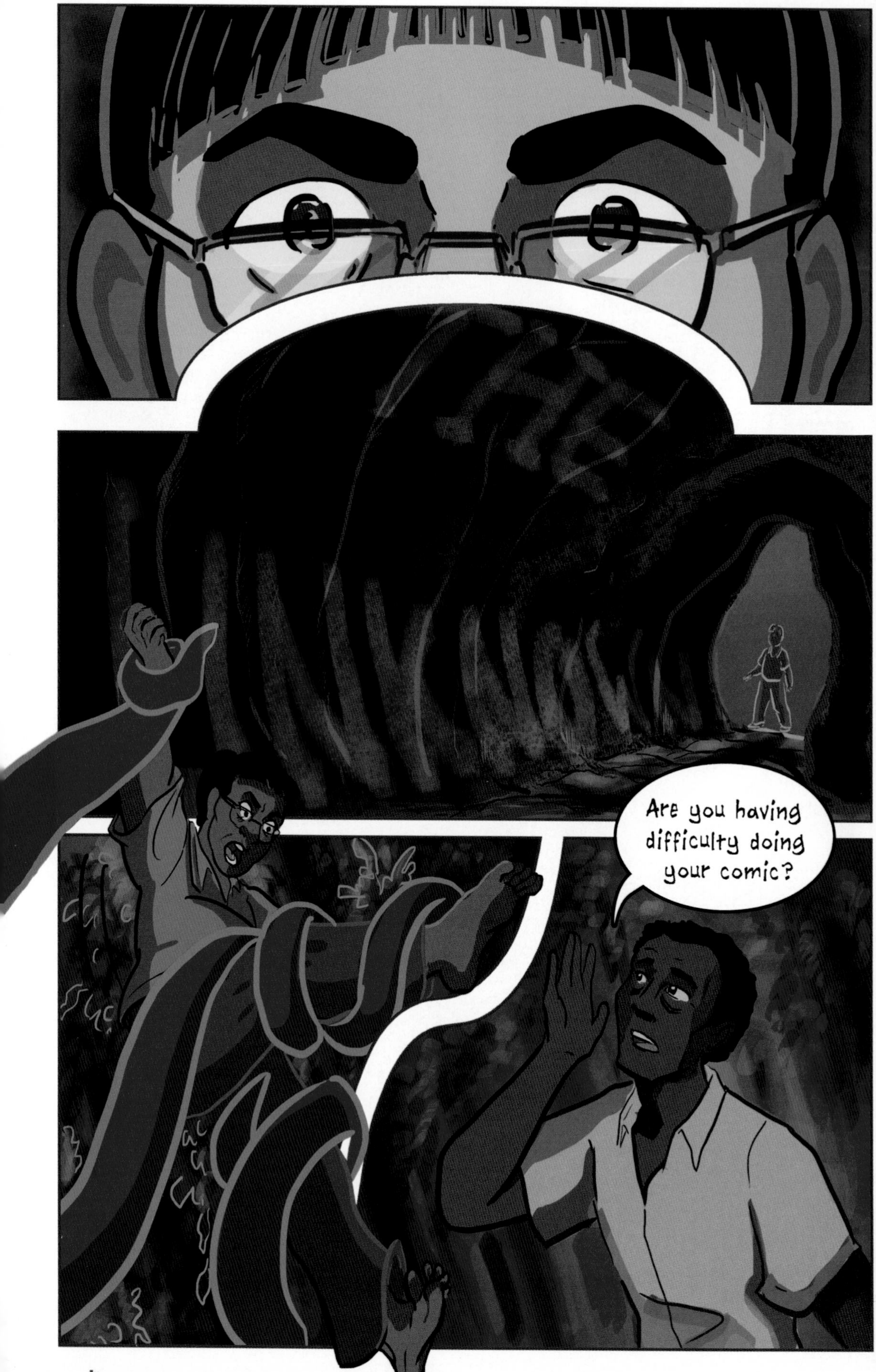
Are you having difficulty doing your comic?

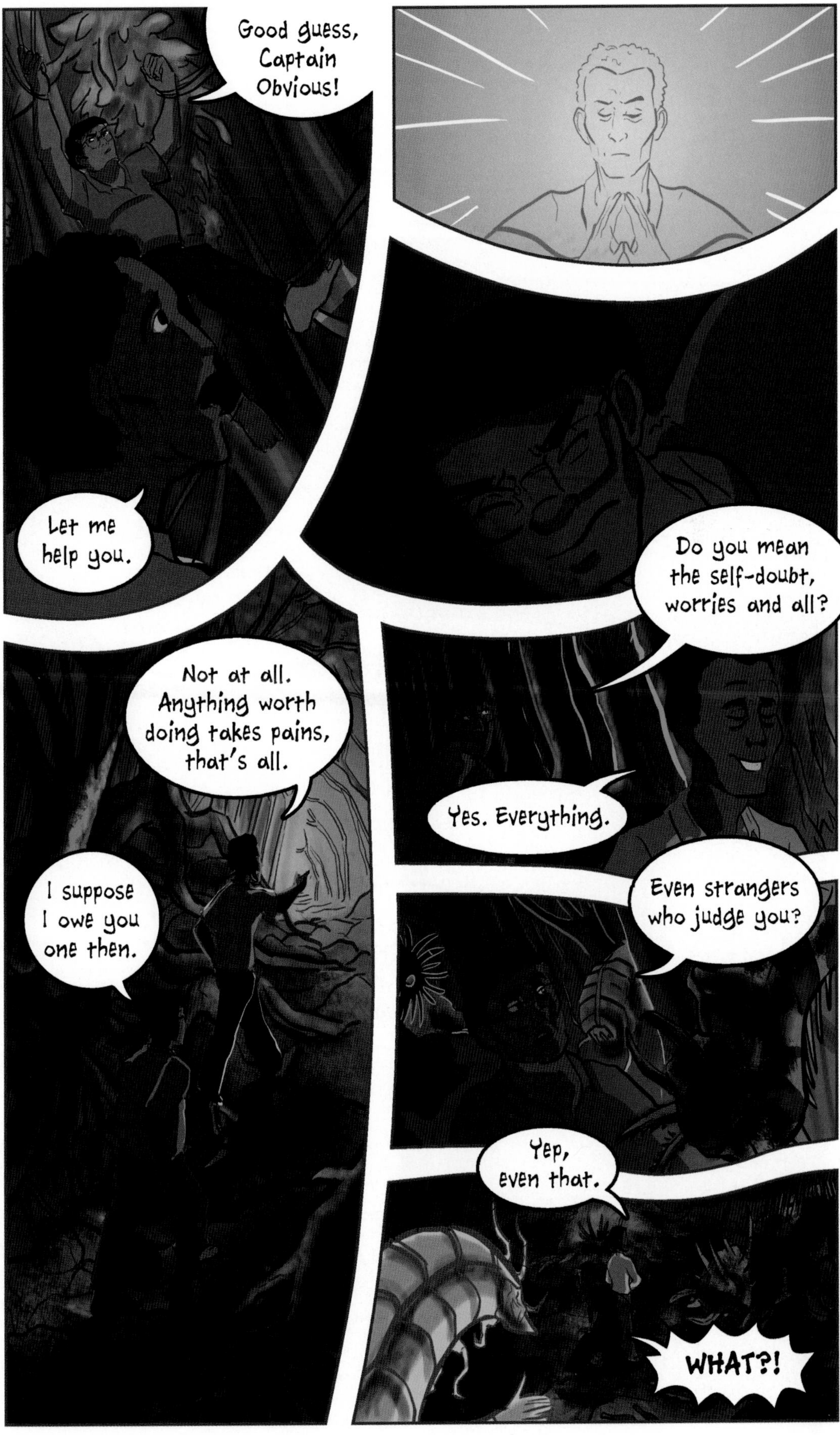
Good guess, Captain Obvious!
Let me help you.
Do you mean the self-doubt, worries and all?
Yes. Everything.
Not at all. Anything worth doing takes pains, that's all.
I suppose I owe you one then.
Even strangers who judge you?
Yep, even that.
WHAT?!

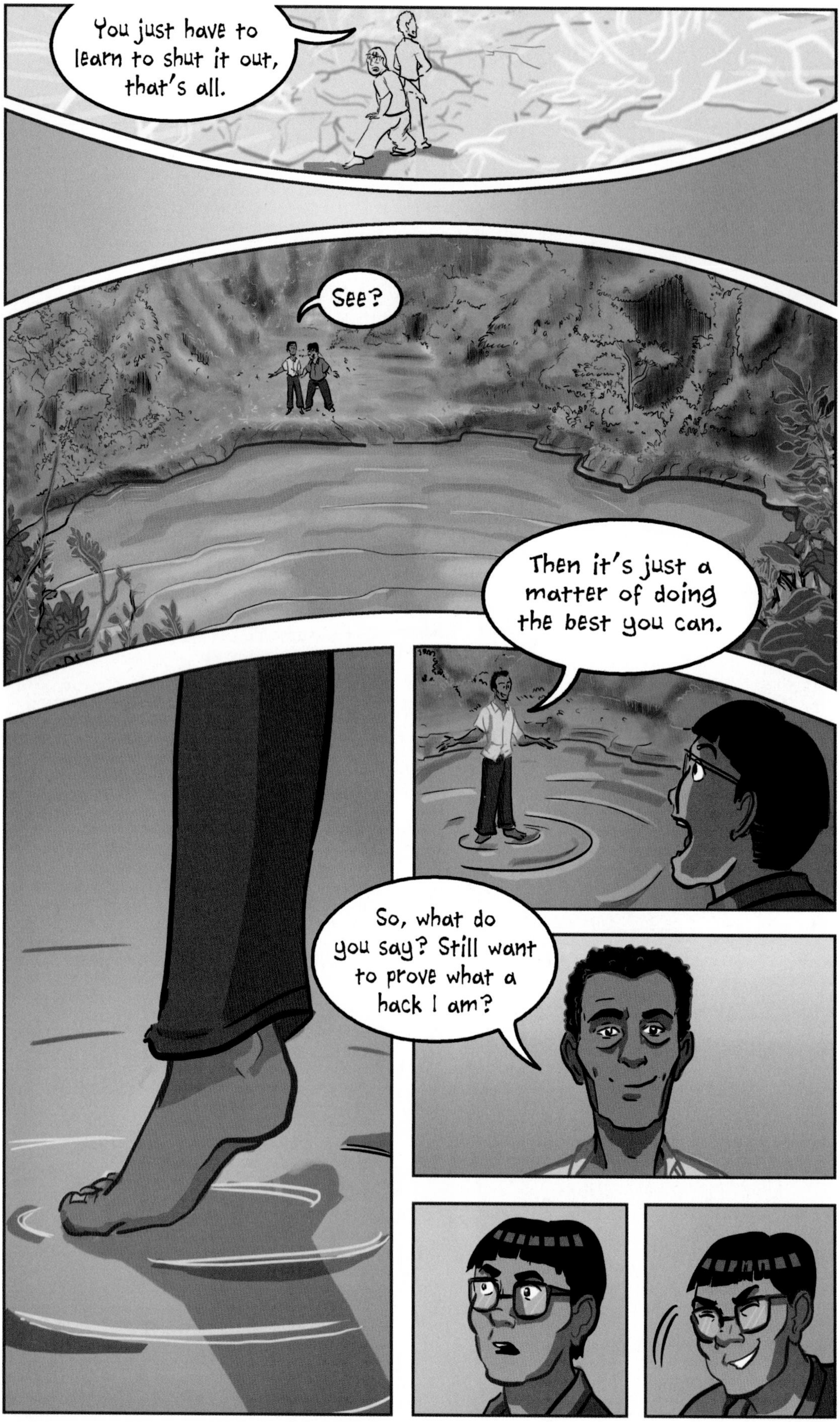
You just have to learn to shut it out, that's all.
See?
Then it's just a matter of doing the best you can.
So, what do you say? Still want to prove what a hack I am?

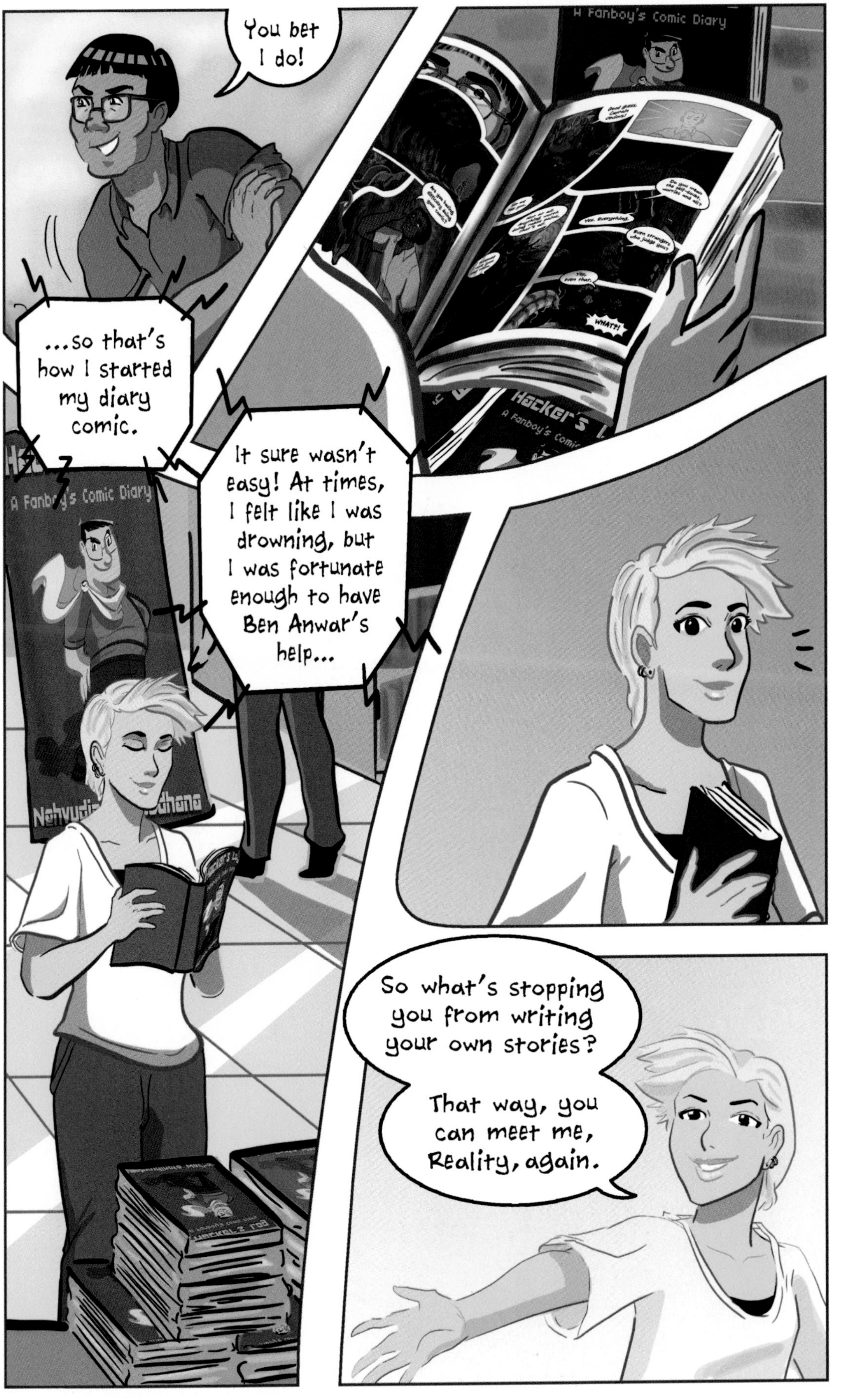
You bet I do!
A Fanboy's Comic Diary
...so that's how I started my diary comic.
It sure wasn't easy! At times, I felt like I was drowning, but I was fortunate enough to have Ben Anwar's help...
A Fanboy's Comic Diary
Hacker's Lab
A Fanboy's Comic Diary
So what's stopping you from writing your own stories?
That way, you can meet me, Reality, again.

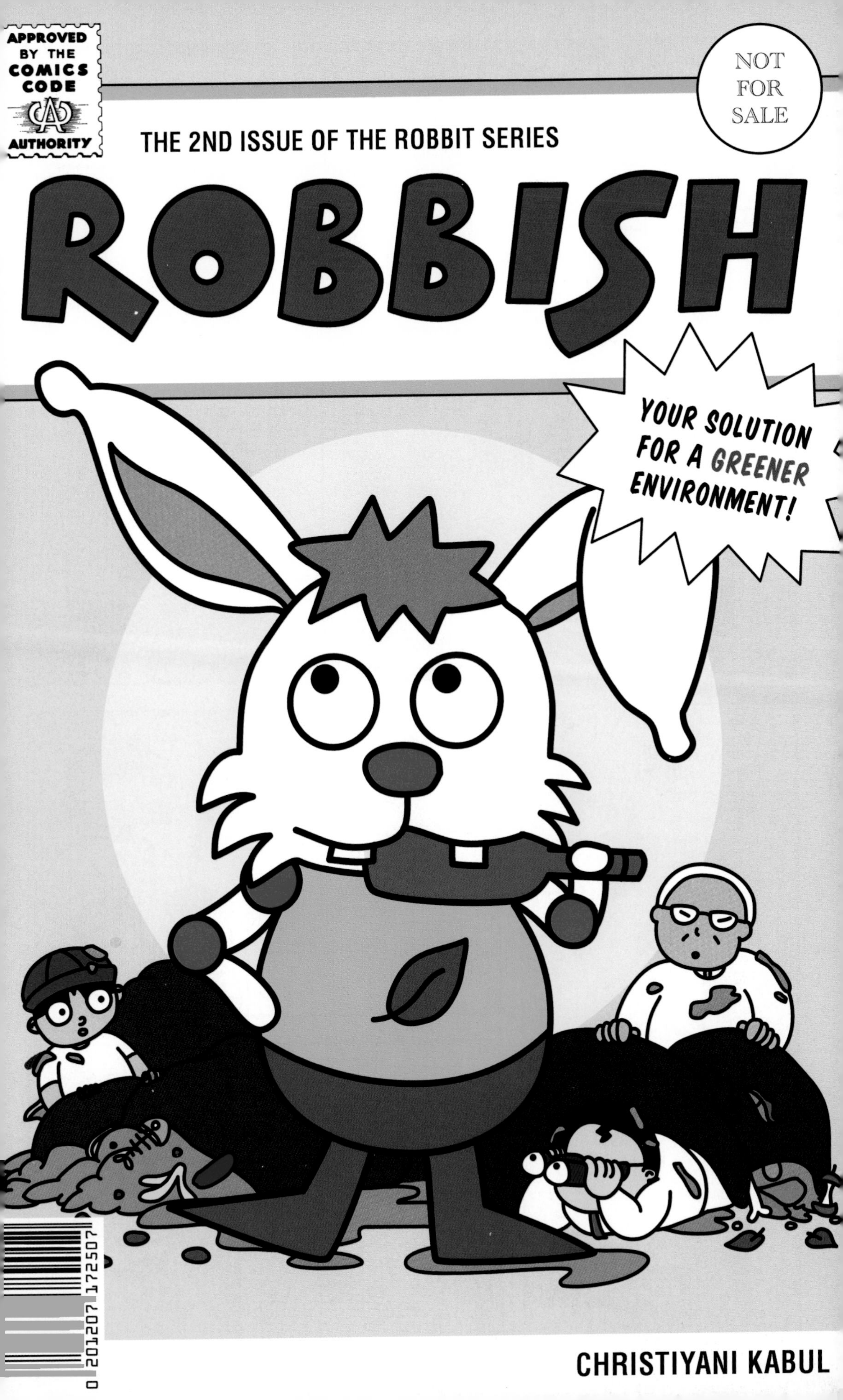
APPROVED BY THE COMICS CODE AUTHORITY
NOT FOR SALE
THE 2ND ISSUE OF THE ROBBIT SERIES
ROBBISH
YOUR SOLUTION FOR A GREENER ENVIRONMENT!
0 201207 172507
CHRISTIYANI KABUL

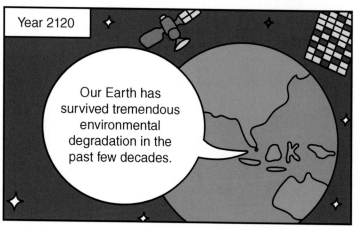

Year 2120

Our Earth has survived tremendous environmental degradation in the past few decades.

Our ever-robust and prosperous country, too...

Singapore

Semakau Island

...has managed to avert and overcome many a crisis and disaster over the years...

MUSEUM

I ♥ SG

And now here we stand, admiring the fruits of the labor of our industrious forefathers...

MUSEUM

KEEP QUIET

Joe Phua
Curator

Kindergarten

We have now come to the highlight of our tour today.

Joe Phua
Curator

Boys and girls, may I present the pride and joy of our great nation...

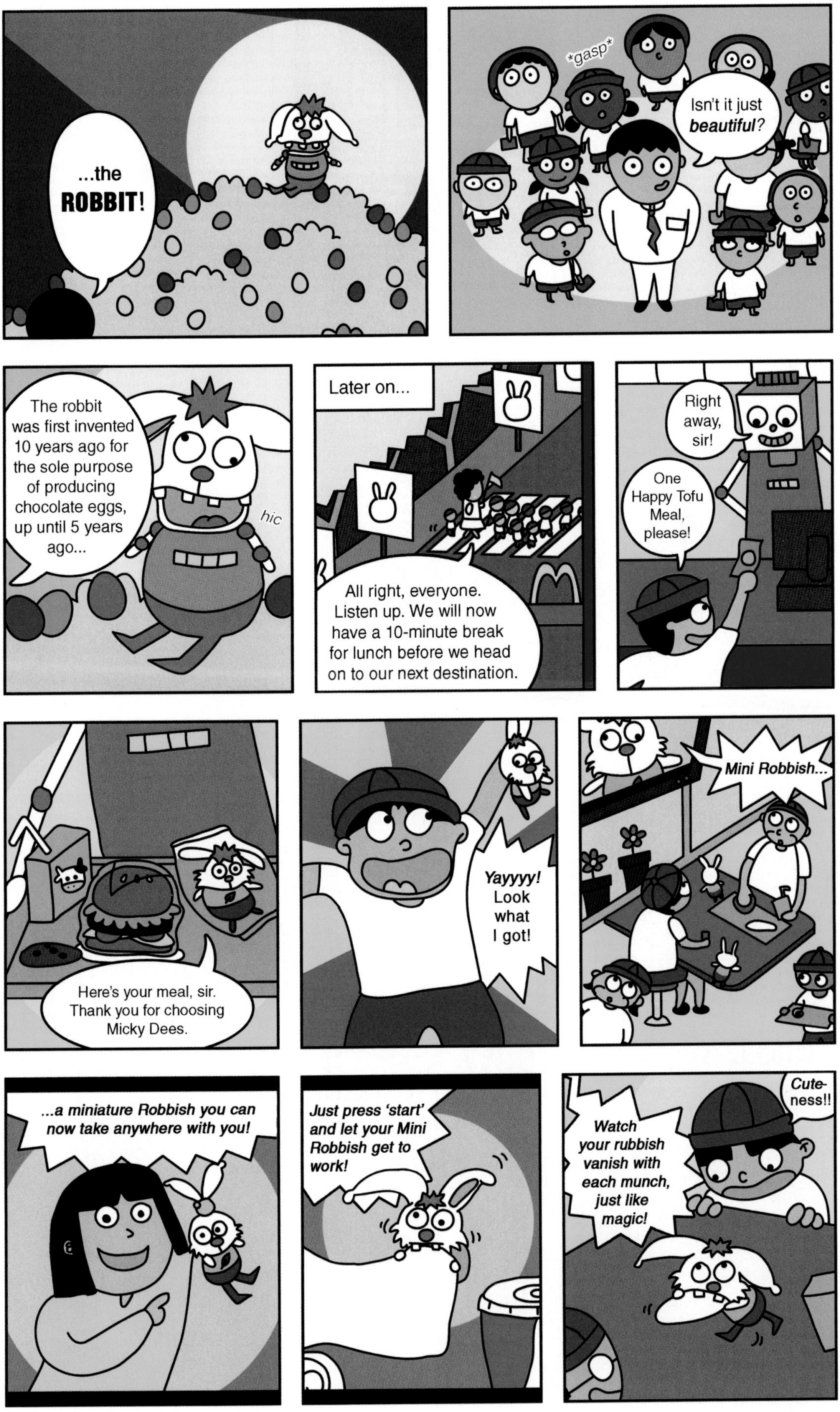
...the ROBBIT!
gasp
Isn't it just beautiful?
The robbit was first invented 10 years ago for the sole purpose of producing chocolate eggs, up until 5 years ago...
hic
Later on...
All right, everyone. Listen up. We will now have a 10-minute break for lunch before we head on to our next destination.
One Happy Tofu Meal, please!
Right away, sir!
Here's your meal, sir. Thank you for choosing Micky Dees.
Yayyyy! Look what I got!
Mini Robbish...
...a miniature Robbish you can now take anywhere with you!
Just press 'start' and let your Mini Robbish get to work!
Watch your rubbish vanish with each munch, just like magic!
Cute-ness!!

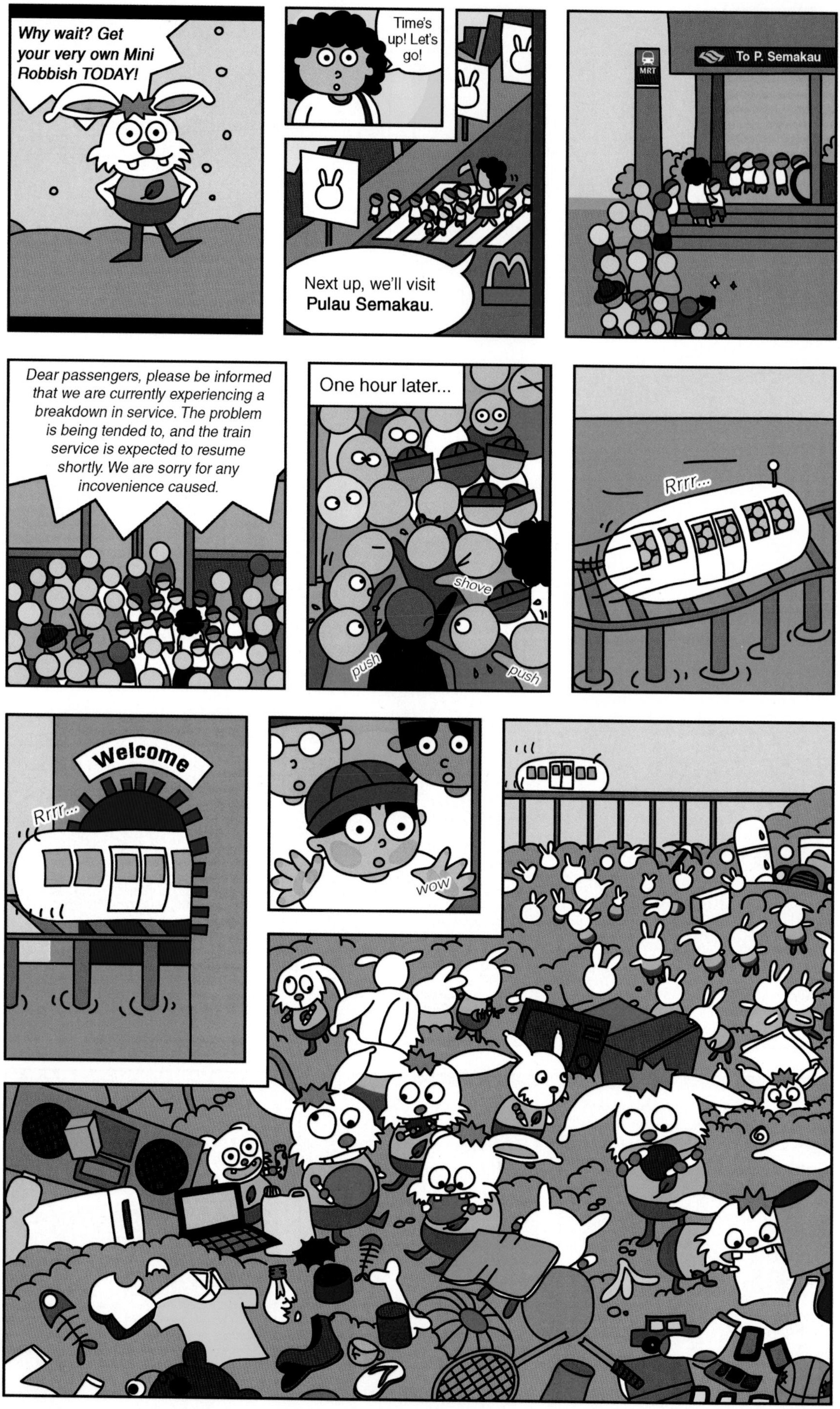
Why wait? Get your very own Mini Robbish TODAY!
Time's up! Let's go!
Next up, we'll visit Pulau Semakau.
MRT
To P. Semakau
Dear passengers, please be informed that we are currently experiencing a breakdown in service. The problem is being tended to, and the train service is expected to resume shortly. We are sorry for any incovenience caused.
One hour later...
shove
push
push
Rrrr...
Welcome
Rrrr...
wow

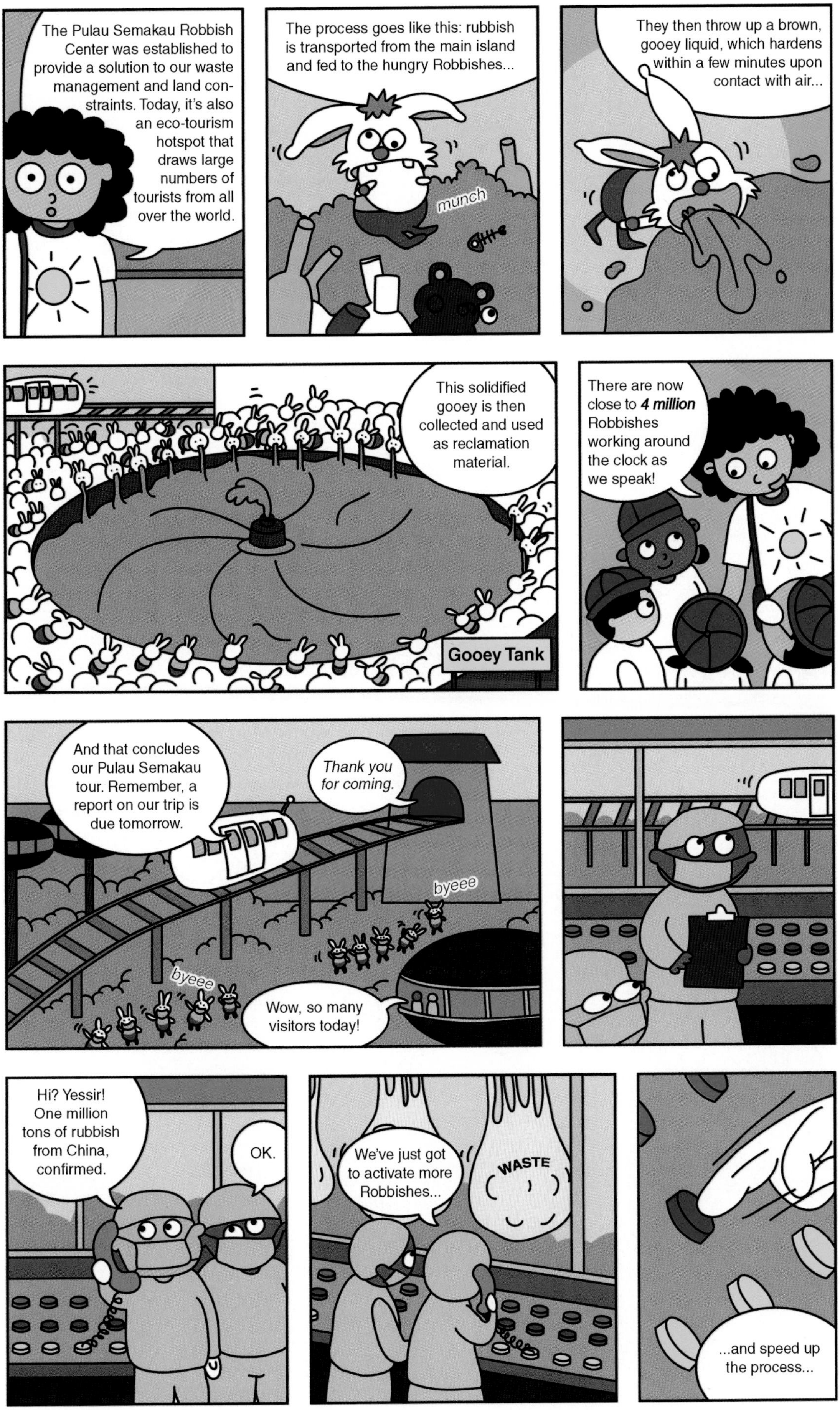
The Pulau Semakau Robbish Center was established to provide a solution to our waste management and land constraints. Today, it's also an eco-tourism hotspot that draws large numbers of tourists from all over the world.
The process goes like this: rubbish is transported from the main island and fed to the hungry Robbishes...
munch
They then throw up a brown, gooey liquid, which hardens within a few minutes upon contact with air...
This solidified gooey is then collected and used as reclamation material.
Gooey Tank
There are now close to 4 million Robbishes working around the clock as we speak!
And that concludes our Pulau Semakau tour. Remember, a report on our trip is due tomorrow.
Thank you for coming.
byeee
byeee
Wow, so many visitors today!
Hi? Yessir! One million tons of rubbish from China, confirmed.
OK.
We've just got to activate more Robbishes...
WASTE
...and speed up the process...

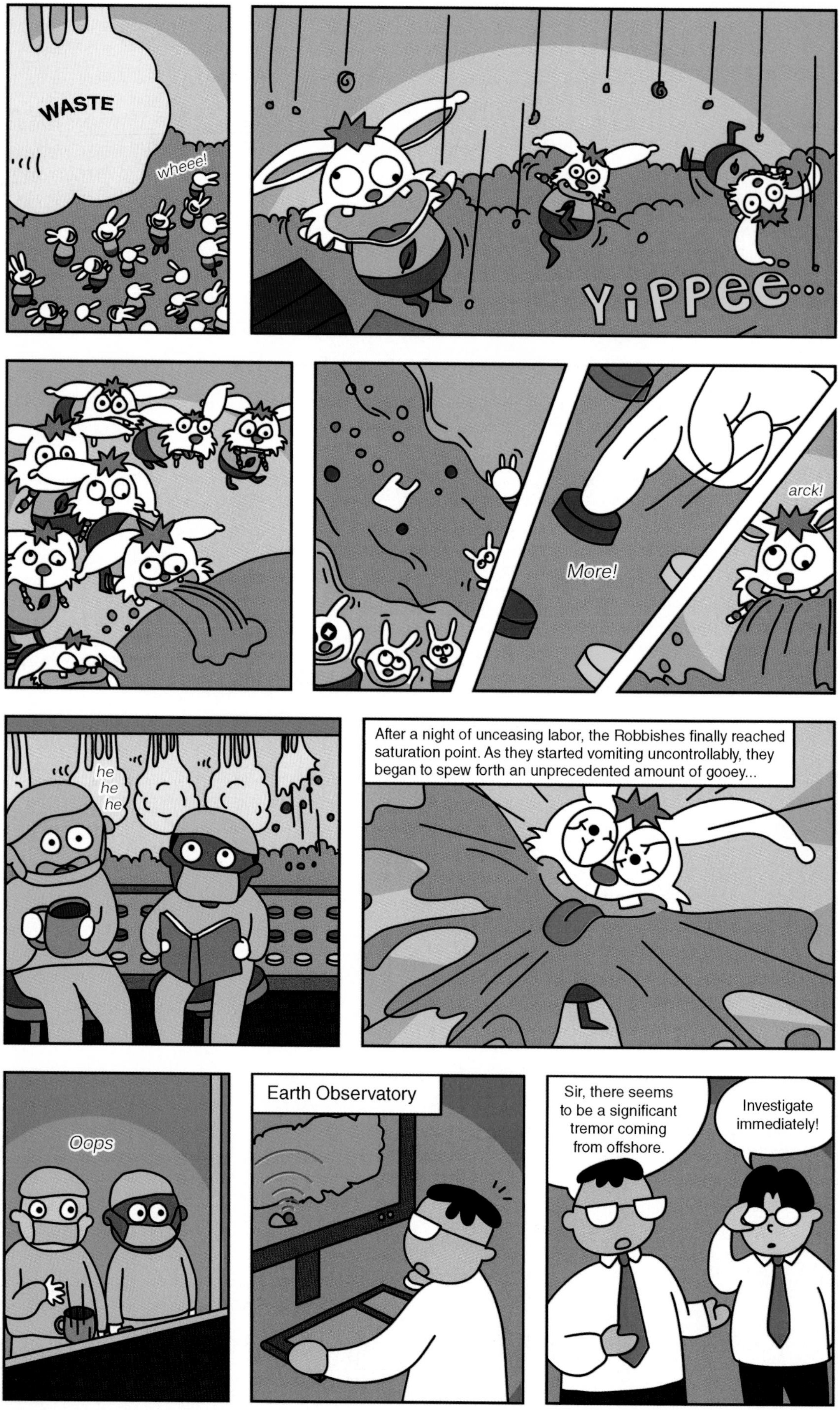
WASTE
wheee!
YiPPee...
More!
arck!
he
he
he
After a night of unceasing labor, the Robbishes finally reached saturation point. As they started vomiting uncontrollably, they began to spew forth an unprecedented amount of gooey...
Oops
Earth Observatory
Sir, there seems to be a significant tremor coming from offshore.
Investigate immediately!

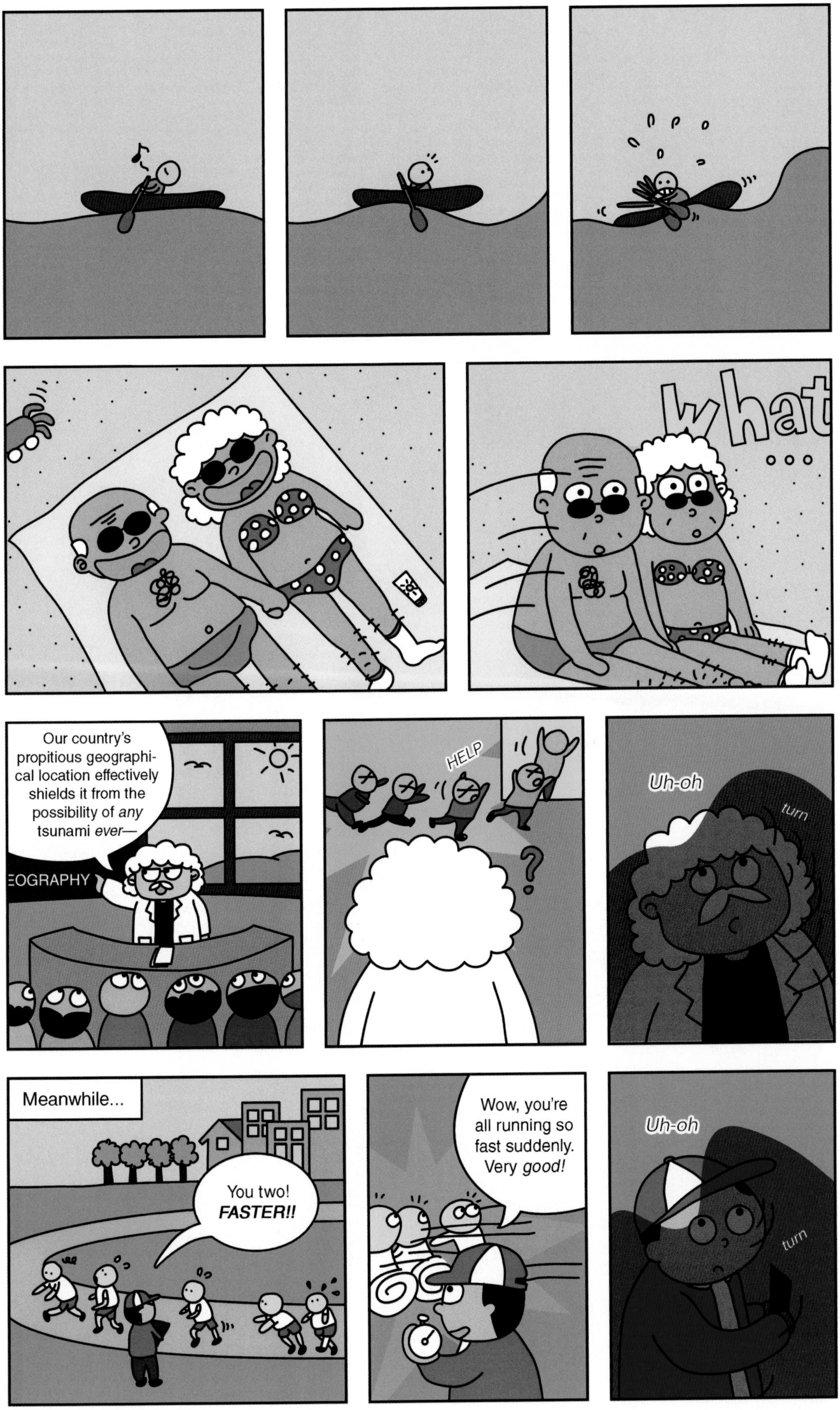
what
...
Our country's propitious geographical location effectively shields it from the possibility of *any* tsunami *ever*—
EOGRAPHY
HELP
?
Uh-oh
turn
Meanwhile...
You two! ***FASTER!!***
Wow, you're all running so fast suddenly. Very *good!*
Uh-oh
turn

Oh, my.
help
stiff

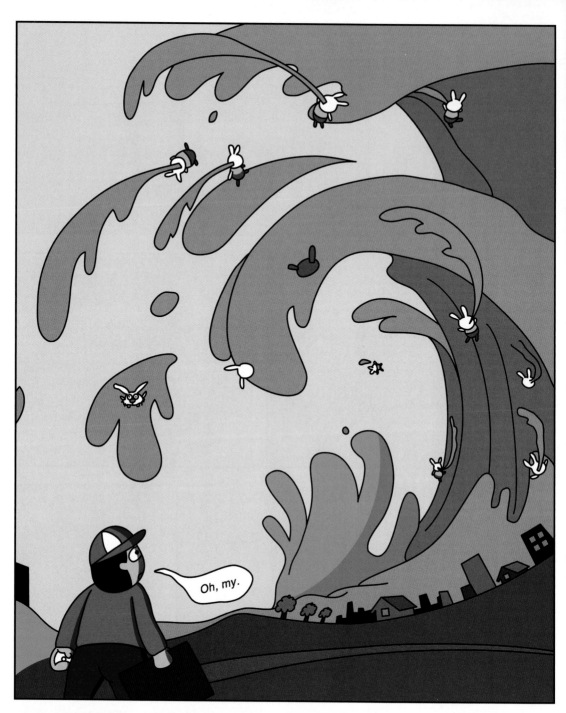

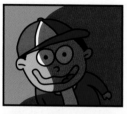

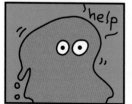

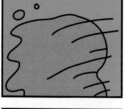

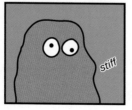

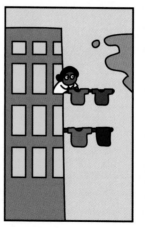

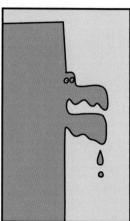

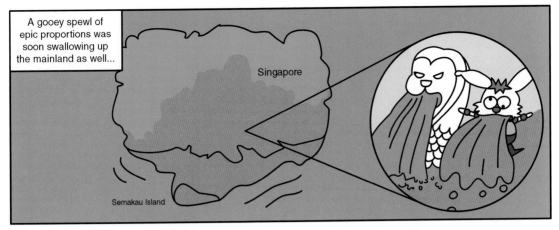

A gooey spewl of epic proportions was soon swallowing up the mainland as well...

Singapore

Semakau Island

Mr President, it's too late to shut down the center now.

The mainland backup system and all the staff there have all been buried too. Do you have any suggestions?

Yes. We are left with no choice but to execute Plan Z!

Bt. Timah

Any idea where we might be headed?

To be perfectly honest, sir, I never expected I'd live to see this day.

We have also evacuated some pairs of extinct animals.

EXIT

Now, sir, this way please.

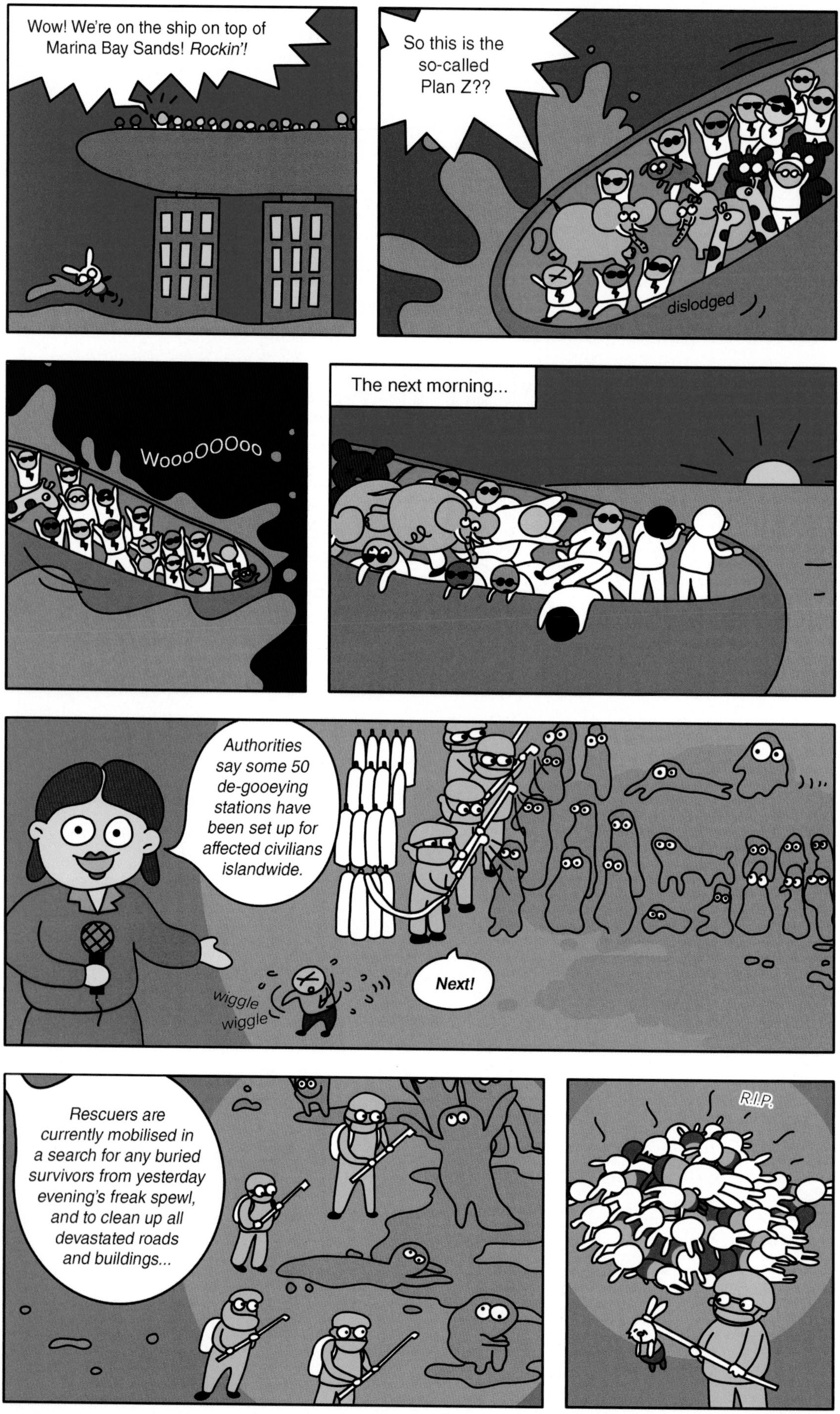
Wow! We're on the ship on top of Marina Bay Sands! Rockin'!
So this is the so-called Plan Z??
dislodged
WoooOOOoo
The next morning...
Authorities say some 50 de-gooeying stations have been set up for affected civilians islandwide.
wiggle wiggle
Next!
Rescuers are currently mobilised in a search for any buried survivors from yesterday evening's freak spewl, and to clean up all devastated roads and buildings...
R.I.P.

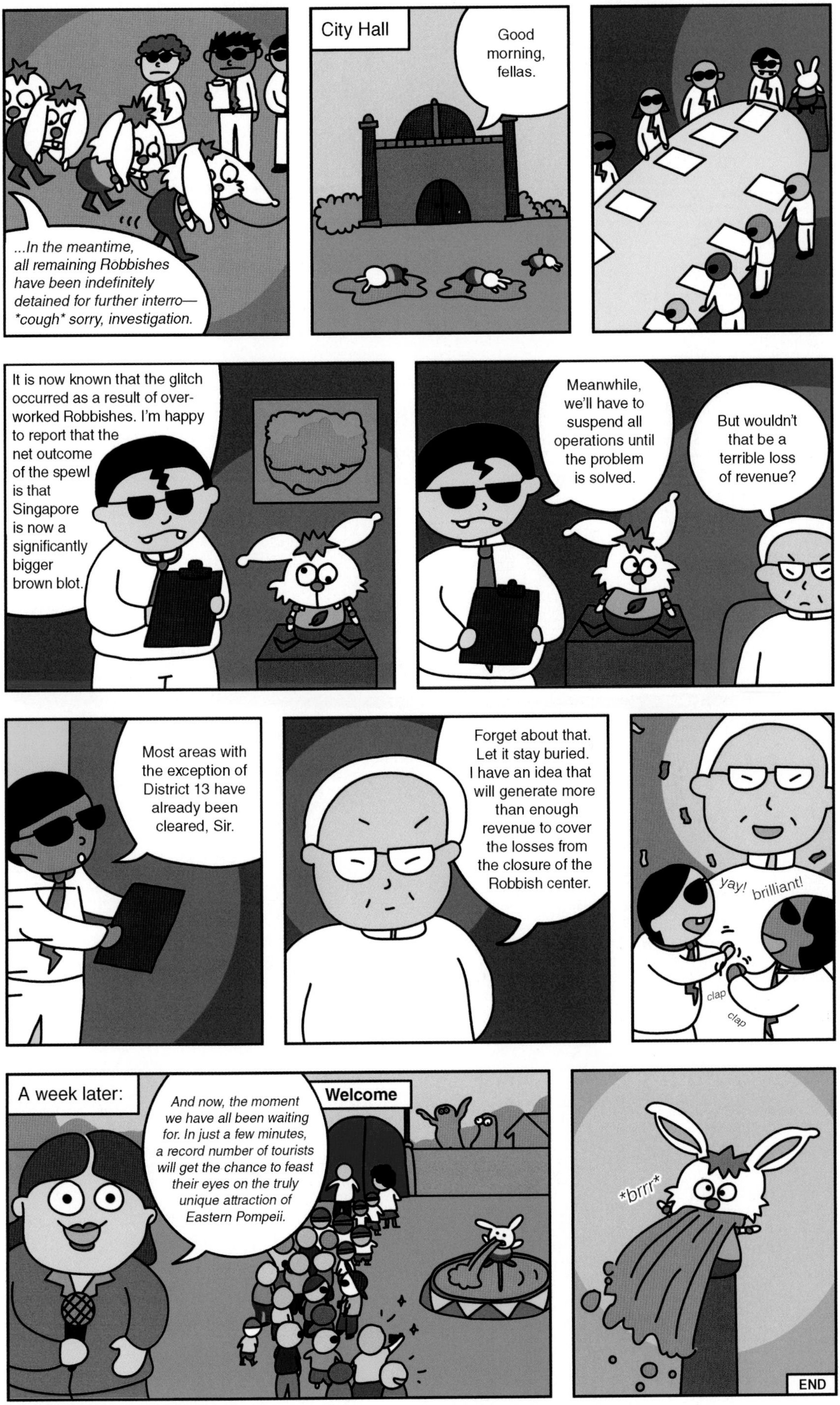
...In the meantime, all remaining Robbishes have been indefinitely detained for further interro— *cough* sorry, investigation.
City Hall
Good morning, fellas.
It is now known that the glitch occurred as a result of over-worked Robbishes. I'm happy to report that the net outcome of the spewl is that Singapore is now a significantly bigger brown blot.
Meanwhile, we'll have to suspend all operations until the problem is solved.
But wouldn't that be a terrible loss of revenue?
Most areas with the exception of District 13 have already been cleared, Sir.
Forget about that. Let it stay buried. I have an idea that will generate more than enough revenue to cover the losses from the closure of the Robbish center.
yay!
brilliant!
clap
clap
A week later:
And now, the moment we have all been waiting for. In just a few minutes, a record number of tourists will get the chance to feast their eyes on the truly unique attraction of Eastern Pompeii.
Welcome
brrr
END

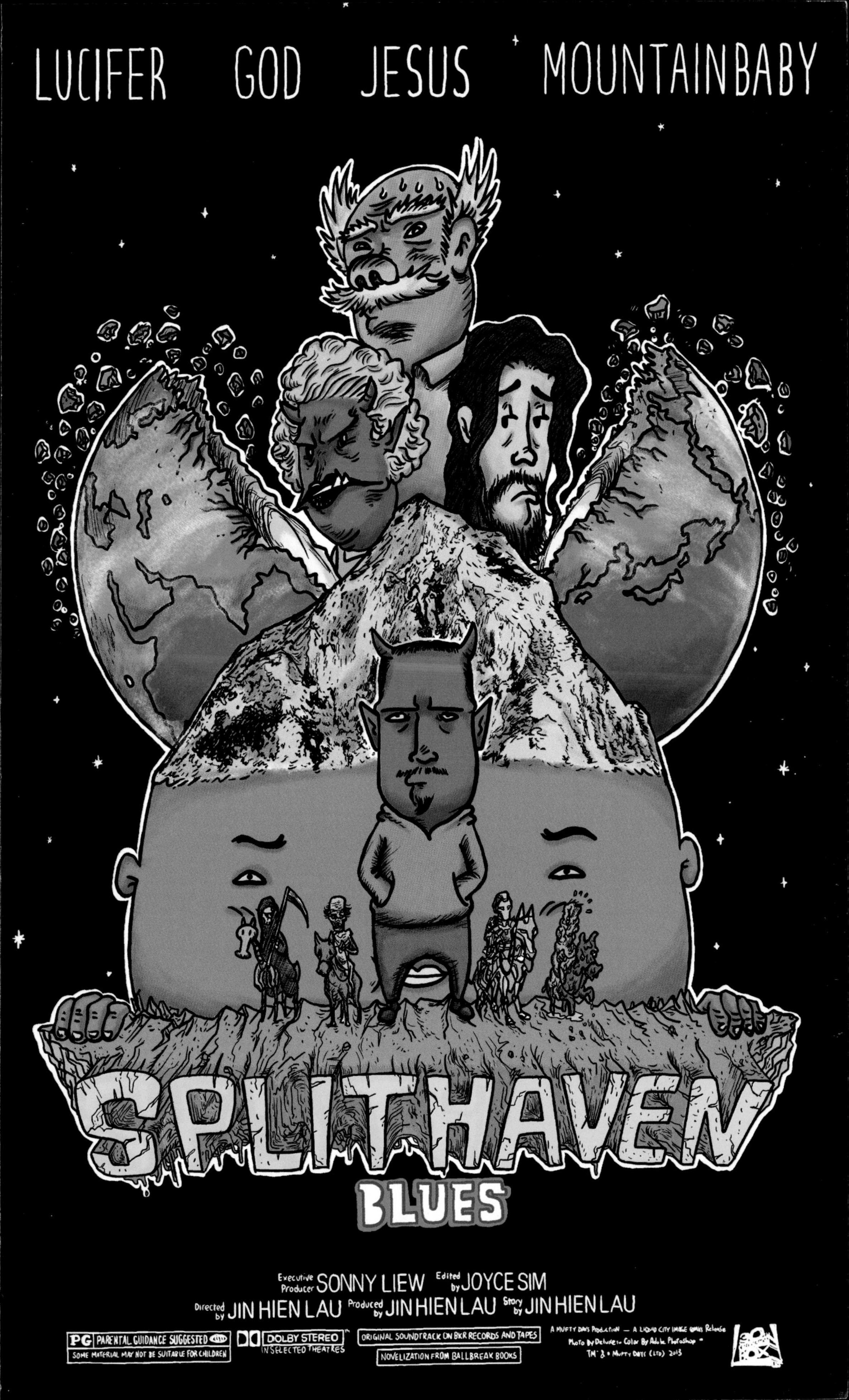
LUCIFER
GOD
JESUS
MOUNTAINBABY
SPLITHAVEN
BLUES
Executive Producer SONNY LIEW
Edited by JOYCE SIM
Directed by JIN HIEN LAU
Produced by JIN HIEN LAU
Story by JIN HIEN LAU
PG PARENTAL GUIDANCE SUGGESTED
SOME MATERIAL MAY NOT BE SUITABLE FOR CHILDREN
DOLBY STEREO
IN SELECTED THEATRES
ORIGINAL SOUNDTRACK ON BKR RECORDS AND TAPES
NOVELIZATION FROM BALLBREAK BOOKS
A MUFTY DAYS PRODUCTION — A LIQUID CITY IMAGE COMICS Release
Photo By Deluxe™ Color By Adobe Photoshop ®
TM & © MUFTY DAYS (LTD) 2013

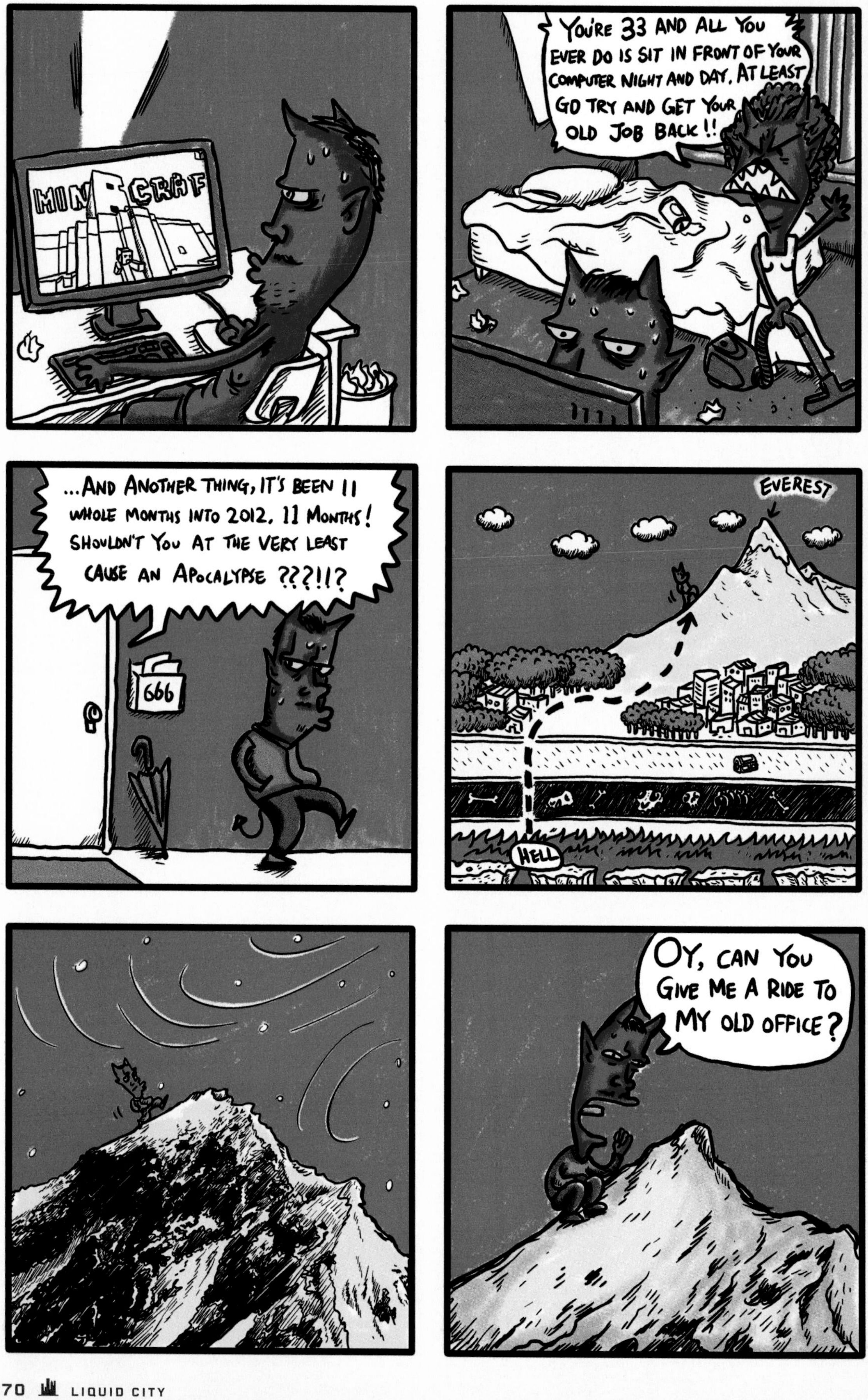
MIN CRAF
YOU'RE 33 AND ALL YOU EVER DO IS SIT IN FRONT OF YOUR COMPUTER NIGHT AND DAY. AT LEAST GO TRY AND GET YOUR OLD JOB BACK!!
...AND ANOTHER THING, IT'S BEEN 11 WHOLE MONTHS INTO 2012. 11 MONTHS! SHOULDN'T YOU AT THE VERY LEAST CAUSE AN APOCALYPSE ???!!?
666
EVEREST
HELL
OY, CAN YOU GIVE ME A RIDE TO MY OLD OFFICE?

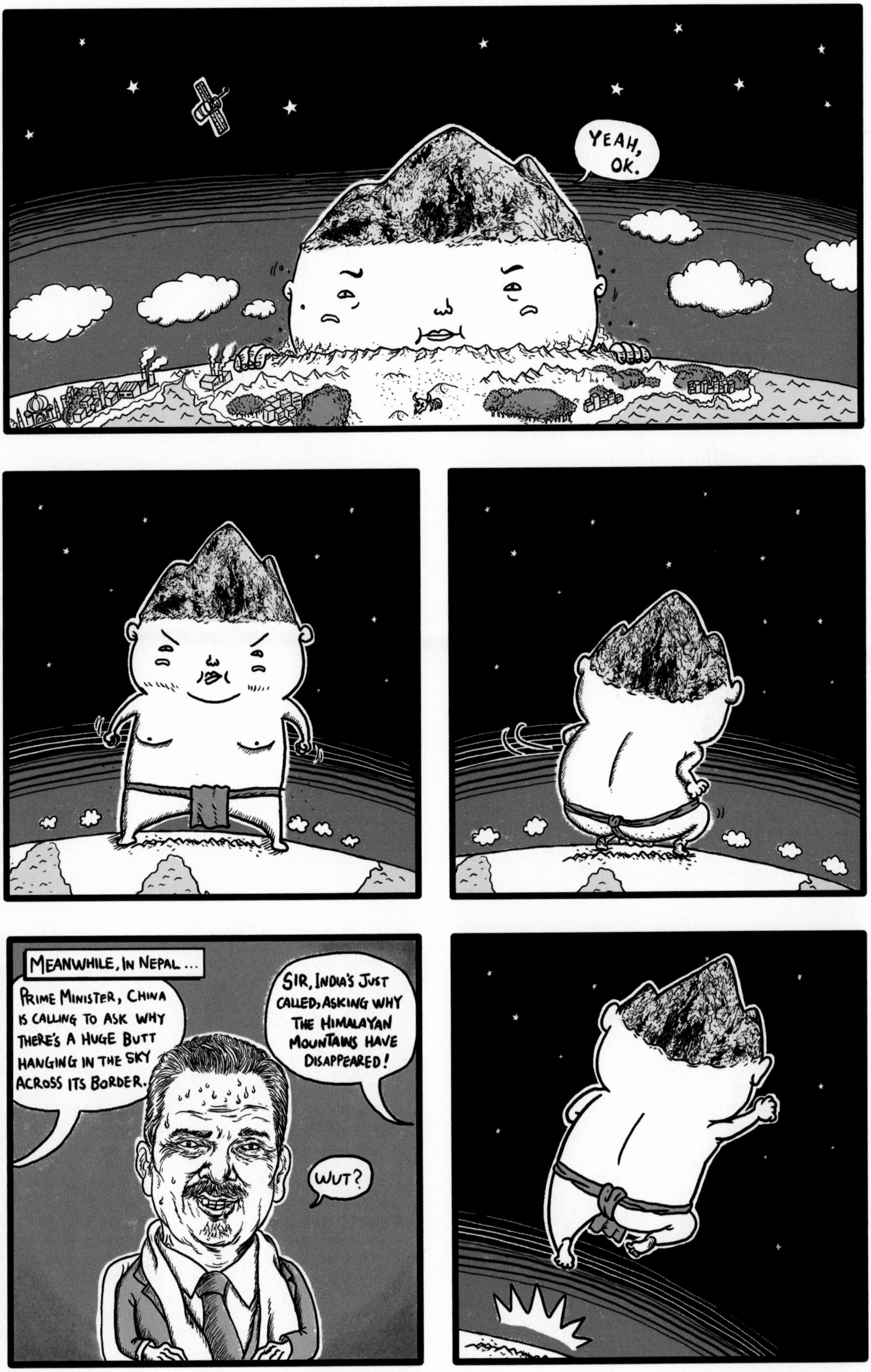
YEAH, OK.
MEANWHILE, IN NEPAL...
PRIME MINISTER, CHINA IS CALLING TO ASK WHY THERE'S A HUGE BUTT HANGING IN THE SKY ACROSS ITS BORDER.
SIR, INDIA'S JUST CALLED, ASKING WHY THE HIMALAYAN MOUNTAINS HAVE DISAPPEARED!
WUT?

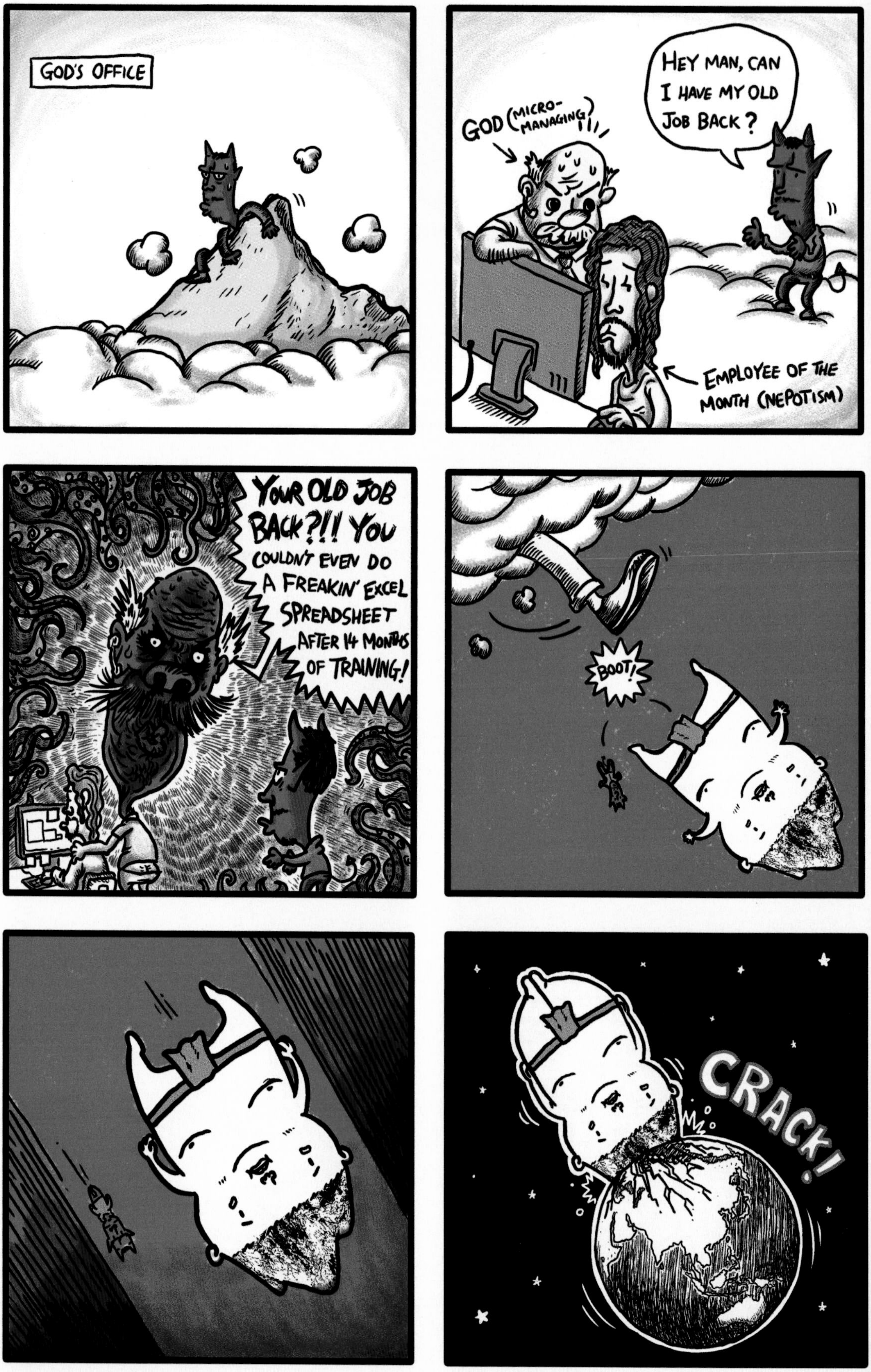
GOD'S OFFICE
GOD (MICRO-MANAGING)
HEY MAN, CAN I HAVE MY OLD JOB BACK?
EMPLOYEE OF THE MONTH (NEPOTISM)
YOUR OLD JOB BACK?!! YOU COULDN'T EVEN DO A FREAKIN' EXCEL SPREADSHEET AFTER 14 MONTHS OF TRAINING!
BOOT!
CRACK!

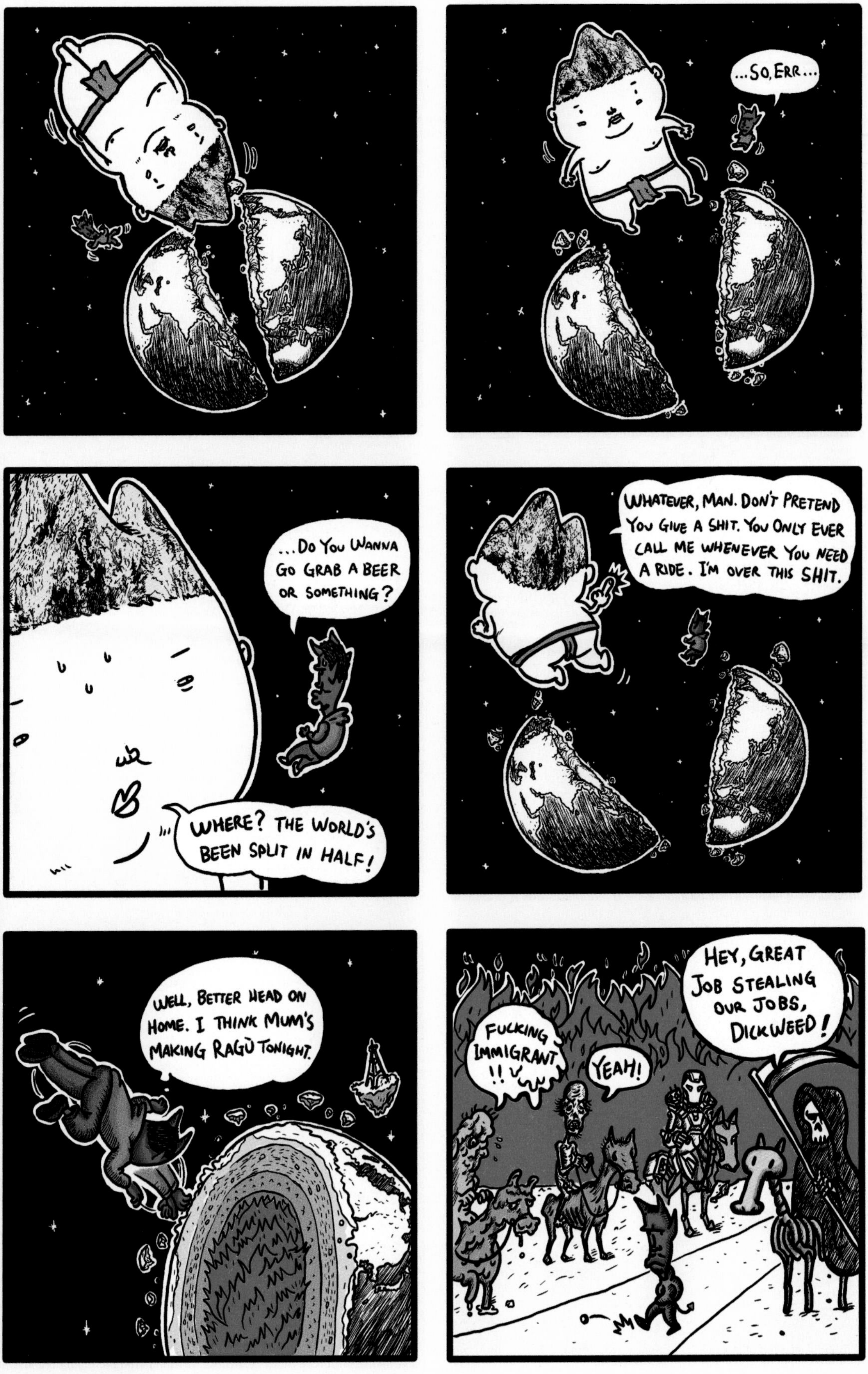
...SO, ERR...
...DO YOU WANNA GO GRAB A BEER OR SOMETHING?
WHERE? THE WORLD'S BEEN SPLIT IN HALF!
WHATEVER, MAN. DON'T PRETEND YOU GIVE A SHIT. YOU ONLY EVER CALL ME WHENEVER YOU NEED A RIDE. I'M OVER THIS SHIT.
WELL, BETTER HEAD ON HOME. I THINK MUM'S MAKING RAGÙ TONIGHT.
FUCKING IMMIGRANT!!
YEAH!
HEY, GREAT JOB STEALING OUR JOBS, DICKWEED!

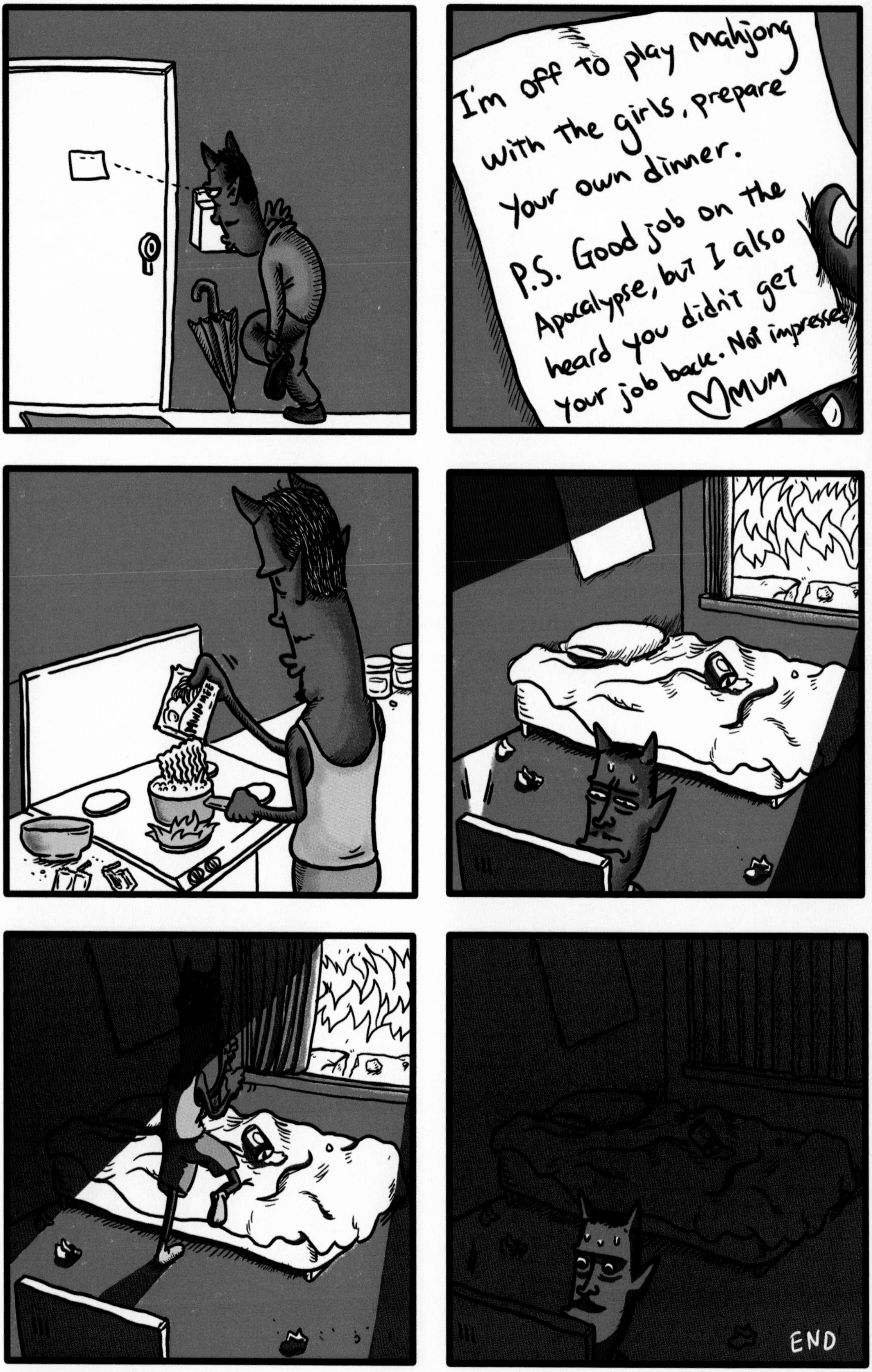
I'm off to play mahjong
with the girls, prepare
your own dinner.
P.S. Good job on the
Apocalypse, but I also
heard you didn't get
your job back. Not impressed
MUM
END

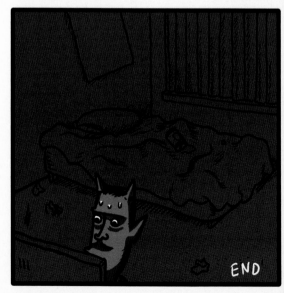

STORY STATEMENTS

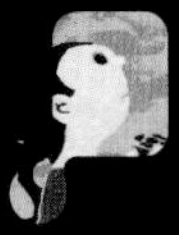

DISAPPEAR

AKS KWAN
MALAYSIA

If the world was going to end, what would be lost? The inspiration for my short story comes from a real experience from my childhood. Although not everyone might believe in the guardian spirits portrayed in the story, I feel fortunate that they will be able to know about the story through this comic, and be encouraged to look into the truth of everything.

aksfile.com
aksfile@gmail.com

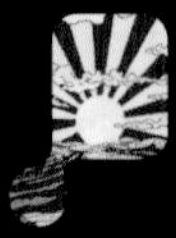

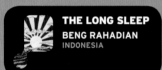

THE LONG SLEEP

BENG RAHADIAN
INDONESIA

In this story, the apocalypse happens on two scales: the collapse of a local environment, and the end of the wider world. In both instances, the same result ensues: loss. Here, a calamity falls upon humankind: in 2006, a catastrophic earthquake measuring 6.3 on the Richter scale struck Yogyakarta, Java. The devastation of the region can be seen to be a prototype for the eventual end of the world, a process that becomes cyclical. Let's just say that when the end finally comes, it will spell the genesis of a brand new generation of people in another universe.

facebook.com/beng.rahadian
bengrahadian29@gmail.com

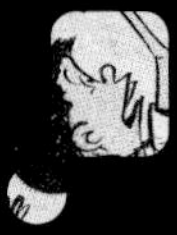

GEYLANG HILL

CHARLIE CHAN HOCK CHYE
SINGAPORE

This is a story about our memories of the past. Remembering is sometimes the only way to preserve the things that are gone, but it is almost always only a pale, fading copy of what was, and we find that we can never be quite sure of them. What's precious to any one of us may not count all that much in real terms, but they're significant to us nonetheless. I think that if the world were to end, many of us would make our last decisions based on such sentiments.

charliechanhc@gmail.com

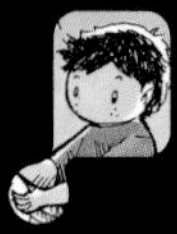

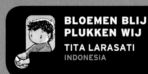

BLOEMEN BLIJ PLUKKEN WIJ

TITA LARASATI
INDONESIA

One's appearance can often conceal his or her ethnic origins, especially one that has been the target of negative sentiment for such a long time. For the better part of my life, I'd been in a sort of denial about my family's origins, and had always been reluctant to dig into its history. When my grandmother passed away, I felt the need to create some kind of commemoration for that part of her life and disclose this long-held family secret, knowing that this might be my last chance to unveil the truth before the world ends.

o2indonesia.wordpress.com
titalarasati@gmail.com

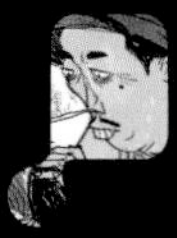

PIG WHEN SMALL COW WHEN BIG

NGUYEN THANH PHONG VIETNAM

Being faced with unsafe food is, unfortunately, rather commonplace, and truly one of the most serious problems we're facing nowadays in Vietnam. This is my attempt to offer a funny look at it.

behance.net/fong210
ronin_1986@yahoo.com

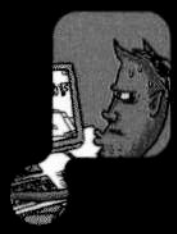

LIVING THE LAST DAY OF EVERYONE'S LIFE

JIN HIEN LAU
MALAYSIA/AUSTRALIA

I embarked on doing this trilogy of stories as a way to explore different facets of the idea of "the end": the end of childlike innocence, the end of youthful exuberance, and the end of motivation and purpose — although this probably makes it sound much more serious than it is!

jinhienlau.com
jinnaboy@gmail.com

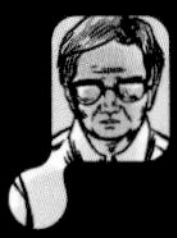

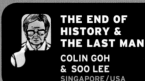

THE END OF HISTORY & THE LAST MAN

COLIN GOH & SOO LEE
SINGAPORE/USA

This story was done as a dig at those who believe in sacrificing homegrown culture in order to present a more international and 'professional' image to the rest of the world. It was inspired by the British comic *2000 AD*'s "Future Shocks" shorts, while its title references Francis

Fukuyama's influential book of the same name. Soo Lee's provocative artwork here is a departure from her gentler style in *Dim Sum Warriors*, a comic series on which we collaborate.

dimsumwarriors.com

colin@dimsumwarriors.com

soodlee.deviantart.com

sooleedraws@gmail.com

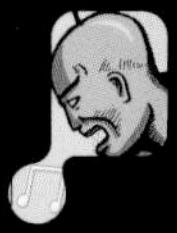

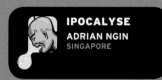

IPOCALYSE

ADRIAN NGIN

SINGAPORE

Instead of having yet another story with a superhero saving the world, I thought: why not shake the superhero archetype up a bit? What if the average person out there had unique abilities — say, if the retiree uncles and aunties frequenting your neighborhood coffeeshops had special powers? Wouldn't it be much more fun mashing up reality and fiction like this?

kontingency.tumblr.com

adrianngin@gmail.com

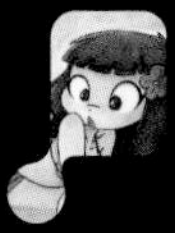

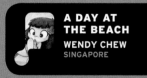

A DAY AT THE BEACH

WENDY CHEW

SINGAPORE

Being both an avid animal lover and an artist, I'd always hoped that I might someday be able to use my art to help animals in some way. Should this piece ever be sold, I'd like to donate some proceeds to the SPCA or any other animal welfare organizations that might benefit from it. Life is so unpredictable, so why not take this chance to do something worthwhile, before time runs out?

mashi.deviantart.com

ven_wen@yahoo.com

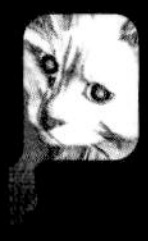

1 A.M.

TIDUS FAIR SUPERTRAMP

VIETNAM

I've always wondered why my cat would sleep for 12 hours a day. What's *that* for? And the first thing he'd do when he woke up was to run out of the house. Most people think that cats are usually out there looking for a mate, but I don't think so. I imagine it to be a rather different story.

be.net/Tidus902000

Tidus902000@gmail.com

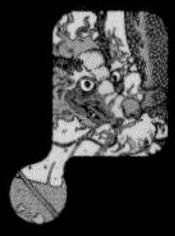

LIFE AFTER THE END OF THE WORLD AS WE KNOW IT

BABA CHUAH

MALAYSIA

Even if a worldwide disaster wipes out 99% of all of Earth's living species, new creatures will form to take its place, forging a new alien world. When that happens, I believe that humankind, being brainy, will somehow always find a way to survive just a little while longer.

tohbuku@yahoo.com

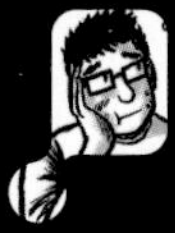

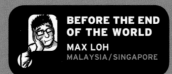

BEFORE THE END OF THE WORLD

MAX LOH

MALAYSIA/SINGAPORE

A bunch of friends end up traveling together to the Land of the Rising Sun before the prophesized end of the world in this condensed journal comic travelogue, based on a recent trip I took with some friends to Japan. Fun times filled with serendipitous discovery and wonder ensue, coupled with lots of tomfoolery to boot — because what's life without a few detours?

paperperil.tumblr.com

jlloh86@gmail.com

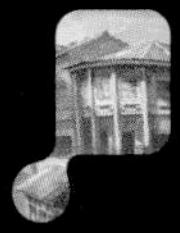

FANTASCENE

CHONG FEI GIAP

MALAYSIA

To me, the idea of *Liquid City* connotes a retro-futuristic city. This scene was created based on a childhood memory. It reminds me of how I used to see the world when I was young, when it was full of fantasy and imagination.

feigiap.deviantart.com

runningsnailstudio@gmail.com

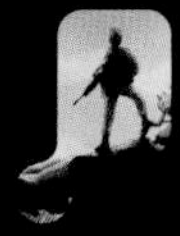

BOY

ELVIN CHING

SINGAPORE

Ironically (but perhaps rather fittingly as well), for a 'last story' to tell, this story is about finding strength, letting go of past burdens and facing new beginnings. There are some stories I've never really felt ready to let go of, only to find myself sitting on them for far too long. This story has been in my head for about 15 years now. One day I blinked, and "Boy" grew up.

theworkofzeropointfive.blogspot.sg

LIGHT
DOMINIQUE FAM
SINGAPORE

If the world was truly ending, the story I'd want to leave behind would be an epilogue about my brief time here. This is a fable about the things which, having emerged from our darkest times, turn out to be the anchors that we hold onto. Whilst these may be different for everyone, they are what truly matters, and what remains with us at the end.

⊕ dominiquefam.com
✉ info@dominiquefam.com

LET ME SEE THE GIANT FALL
BENJAMIN CHEE
SINGAPORE

An injustice is inflicted or a wrong is done, but in the face of our fears and insecurities, we are much too often rendered power-less. The giant is both the subject and symbol of these sources of anxiety. Made tangible, however, we see that what we live in fear of can be equally fallible, and far less powerful than we might think. When the giant is finally defeated, we are reminded that noth-ing is really too big to fail.

⊕ art-zhaomeng.blogspot.com
✉ benjamin.animate@gmail.com

NICKY SOH
SINGAPORE

I had the idea of creating a story that would showcase an aspect of Eastern culture,

whilst being on some level universal at the same time. As someone who's still relatively young in adult-hood, I wanted to focus on the consequences of rashness and karma, which sometimes end up altering our paths in life. At the end of the day, is it worth hating someone for what they've done, or would it be better to forgive and let go?

⊕ nickysoh.com
✉ nickysoh@gmail.com

10010110
SAM SEEN
MALAYSIA

This story explores the idea that, with the world on the way to its end, there might be some beings on this Earth, transformed from aliens a long time ago, who might not like return to their home planets, even as they are being recalled (using a binary language) by their leader. Is it possible to really know how they feel?

⊕ toonpool.com/artists/ sam seen_1169
✉ seensca@yahoo.com

GHOST KID
BILLY TAN
MALAYSIA / AUSTRALIA

Ghost Kid is a project that was co-created with my brother Mun Kao. I chose this piece because it shows just how badass the epony-mous hero, Jack, is. But that's not all. Jack's really a very kind-hearted and compassionate young man, who's always willing to put himself in jeopardy just so

he can help others, be they humans or beings in the supernatural world. This piece has gone from pencil straight to color, with the amazing color work done by the good people at the One Academy Penang.

⊕ billytanart.com
⊕ toa.edu.my/penang
✉ btan1234@yahoo.com

THE AMAZING KELIM
DREWSCAPE / ANDREW TAN
SINGAPORE

I was stressing myself out trying to come up with a meaningful and epic story to suit the theme of the book (the last story I'd write if it was the end of the world), with not much to show for it. Then I thought, why not just do an enjoyable story? At the very least, it would provide me with a good way to spend my last moments. This story sprang spontaneously out of all that, and was truly lots of fun to do.

⊕ drewscape.net
✉ andrew@drewscape.net

ZERO HERO
TAN ENG HUAT
MALAYSIA

When a group of super beings start to abuse the authority they had been given, the people have to rise up to put a stop to things. *Zero Hero* is a project by Gilamon Studio, an independent Malaysian comics studio focused on creator-owned projects.

⊕ gilamonstudio.daportfolio.com
✉ tannght8@gmail.com

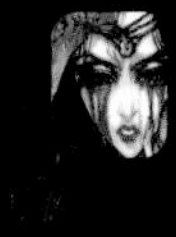

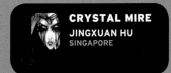

CRYSTAL MIRE
JINGXUAN HU
SINGAPORE

Lovers, friends, jobs and money... Certain elements may sporadically complement, conflict and integrate with, or stay alienated from one another, but the end result always tends towards a balanced and functional system, even if just barely. This is a story about the futility of our daily lives and our repeated attempts at making meaningful relationships despite the constant promise of anxiety, fear and regrets. There is perhaps no conclusion to be drawn. The only certainty is that, as days go by, nothing ever stays the same.

pinkjellyo.deviantart.com
jinghuart@gmail.com

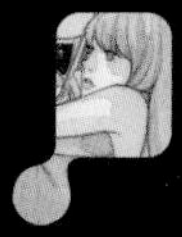

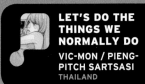

LET'S DO THE THINGS WE NORMALLY DO
VIC-MON / PIENG-PITCH SARTSASI
THAILAND

Let's pretend we'll be here tomorrow
Let's pretend this is just another day
It's hard to talk with people all around
We'll cry if we talk too much

If you love to kiss, just kiss
If you love to draw, just draw
It's too sad to leave this world
Without the things we love
So let's just do the things we normally do

vic-mon.deviantart.com
facebook.com/vicmonvicmon
vic970@hotmail.com

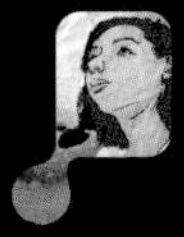

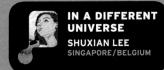

IN A DIFFERENT UNIVERSE
SHUXIAN LEE
SINGAPORE/BELGIUM

I've always wanted to tell the story of the hurt a certain ex-lover had put me through. The story concludes in a way that I wish it would — that I finally let go and he becomes just another stranger. I guess in reality, things never really turn out the way we want them to. He's become someone I don't recognize anymore. This story is for the memories.

cargocollective.com/shuxianlee
leeshuxian@gmail.com

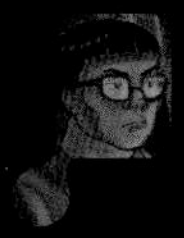

NOTHING TO LOSE
RONY AMDANI & STEPHANI SOEJONO
INDONESIA

Comics can be about anything. That's the mantra everyone keeps uttering nowadays, but it seems that where we come from, there are few who really believe in this. In our story, the 'fanboy' character represents the prevailing school of thought about comics here — that it should always be fantastical and action-packed. The author character, however, makes a daring proposition: a challenge to our protagonist to create and come face-to-face with reality.

buku-curhat.net
sstephani.blogspot.com

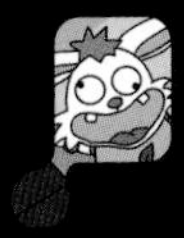

ROBBISH
CHRISTIYANI KABUL
INDONESIA/SINGAPORE

Singapore has always been shielded from all kinds of environmental disasters, so I thought it'd be comical to imagine a scenario in which something that has never been considered to be a source of threat goes unexpectedly wrong. Everyone keeps talking about the importance of recycling and being green nowadays, which is good, but is it all becoming a cliché? Can a man-made invention really solve the problems that we've started, or can we do what's needed to address the problem?

christykabul.wordpress.com
christykabul@gmail.com

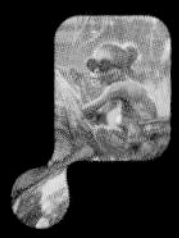

SEE YOU IF WE GET THERE
(COVER ART)
GARY CHOO
SINGAPORE

At world's end, I hope that we can each gain the wisdom to realise that all beings on Earth are created equal. But it would be a shame for us to achieve this hard-won harmony, only to meet our end. A great escape vessel would give us a second chance to find a new home, where we can work to preserve our newfound peace.

garychoo.cghub.com

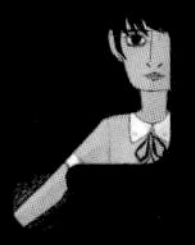

APOCALYPTIC
(CONTENTS PAGE)
REIMENA ASHEL YEE
MALAYSIA

This piece portrays the end of a personal world. The girl is floating in her own baggage, emotional or otherwise, that might have resulted from any series of events. When we think of an apocalypse, we think about falling buildings, destroyed landmarks and so on. But what about what happens to people within, and the potentially crushing effects on the human spirit?

artsyambitions.tumblr.com
callupish@gmail.com

ISBN: 978-1-63215-061-5

Liquid City, Vol 3.
First printing. June 2014.
www.liquidcitizen.net

Published by Image Comics, Inc.
Office of publication:
2001 Center Street, Sixth Floor
Berkeley, CA 94704
USA

For International Rights / Foreign Licensing,
contact: foreignlicensing@imagecomics.com

END